Guide to Higher Education in Africa

second edition

Association of African Universities
Association des Universités africaines

International Association of Universities
Association internationale des Universités

IAU/UNESCO INFORMATION CENTRE ON HIGHER EDUCATION
CENTRE AIU/UNESCO D'INFORMATION SUR L'ENSEIGNEMENT SUPERIEUR

palgrave

Prepared by the International Association of Universities,
IAU/UNESCO Information Centre on Higher Education
Director: Claudine Langlois

IAU ISBN 92–9002–168–3

This edition published 2002 by
PALGRAVE
Houndmills, Basingstoke, Hampshire RG21 6XS and
175 Fifth Avenue, New York, N. Y. 10010
Companies and representatives throughout the world

PALGRAVE is the new global academic imprint of
St. Martin's Press LLC Scholarly and Reference Division and
Palgrave Publishers Ltd (formerly Macmillan Press Ltd).

ISBN 0–333–99324–1

A catalogue record for this book is available from the British Library.

Library of Congress Cataloging-in-Publication Data
Guide to higher education in Africa / Association of African Universities,
International Association of Universities, IAU/UNESCO Information Centre on
Higher Education.--2nd ed.
        p. cm.
        Includes bibliographical references and index.
        ISBN 0–333–99324–1 (pbk.)
        1. Universities and colleges--Africa--Directories. 2. Education,
Higher-- Africa I. Association of African Universities. II. International
Association of Universities. III. IAU/UNESCO Information Centre on
Higher Education.

L970.G85 2002
378.6—dc21   2001057539

10   9   8   7   6   5   4   3   2   1
11   10   09   08   07   06   05   04   03   02

Printed and bound in Great Britain by Antony Rowe Ltd, Chippenham, Wiltshire

CONTENTS

FOREWORD

The current volume, the *Guide to Higher Education in Africa*, now in its Second Edition, is an expression of the continuing effort of the Association of African Universities (AAU), in collaboration with the International Association of Universities (IAU), to make reliable and updated information on higher education in Africa available and easily accessible. In doing so, it is hoped that it will further the objectives of promoting interchange, contact and cooperation among university institutions in Africa; of encouraging increased contacts between African higher education and the international academic world; and of disseminating information on higher education and research in Africa across and beyond the continent.

The First Edition, which was published in 1999, received positive comments together with suggestions for improvement, particularly from Member institutions, and additional information for re-entries.

Like the first volume, this *Guide* contains details on the educational systems of 46 African countries, their institutions of higher education and, for each country, the national bodies concerned with higher education. It is the result of a partnership and collaboration established between the Association of African Universities and the International Association of Universities to collect jointly and disseminate information on higher education on the continent.

The *Guide* has been produced from the computerized databases maintained at the AAU Secretariat in Accra and the IAU/UNESCO Information Centre on Higher Education in Paris. Institutional entries have been updated and revised by the AAU Information and Communication Section.

AAU and IAU are indebted to the many institutions, as well as to governmental agencies and academic bodies, which have provided material for this *Guide*. Where information was not available in time for inclusion, entries are based on those already existing in the database or on documentation available at the IAU/UNESCO Information Centre on Higher Education or at the AAU/Information and Communication Section.

It is our hope that the *Guide* will continue to meet the interest of our readers, particularly our Member Institutions, whose comments and suggestions have been invaluable as we strive to improve the quality and relevance of AAU and IAU publications.

We are indeed grateful to the International Development Research Centre (IDRC) for their financial contribution to the publication of the *Guide*, and for their interest in the promotion of higher education in Africa

October 2001

Prof. François Rajaoson
AAU Secretary-General,
Vice-President of IAU

Dr Franz Eberhard
IAU Secretary-General,
Executive Director, International Universities Bureau

GUIDE TO THE ENTRIES

This Second Edition of the *Guide to Higher Education in Africa* comprises entries for over 800 institutions of higher education, university and non-university level, in 46 African States, as well as background information on their educational system, qualifications and higher education agencies. Depending on the country, the information provided is generally based on the academic year 2000-2001.

COUNTRY PROFILES

The descriptions of education systems are based on entries in the current version of the *World Higher Education Database* CD-Rom. Each profile includes the following:
- description of primary and secondary education;
- description of higher education systems (vocational-technical studies and the different stages of university level studies);
- teacher education;
- non-formal higher education;
- main degrees awarded;
- grading system;
- admissions to higher education (including requirements for foreign students);
- recognition of studies and qualifications;
- student services, expenses and financial aid;
- international cooperation;
- national bodies and agencies dealing with higher education.

Information for this section has either been provided by the competent authorities in the country or has been compiled by the IAU/UNESCO Information Centre on Higher Education.

INSTITUTIONAL ENTRIES

Institutional entries in the *Guide* are of two types :
- Institutions of university level;
- Other institutions of higher education.

Institutions of university-level
For the first category, questionnaires have been sent by the Association of African Universities to those degree-granting institutions, which have been communicated by competent authorities in each country as being of "university level". The inclusion or omission of an institution, in consequence, does not imply any judgement by AAU or IAU as to the status of that institution. Similarly, the designations employed for countries and territories are those in use in the United Nations system and do not imply any expression of opinion with regard to their status or the delimitations of their frontiers.

Individual entries for university-level institutions are generally listed within Public and Private sections, where relevant, with postal address and telecommunication information. The name of each institution is systematically given first in English, followed by the name in the national language(s), where appropriate. Where available, the names and full communication details of the Academic Head, the Chief Administrative Officer, and the Director of International Relations are given.

The lists of faculties, colleges, departments, schools, institutes, etc. are intended primarily as a general guide to the academic structure of the institutions of which they form a part. Details including the names of heads, with full-time and part-time academic staff, and student figures at that level are provided where available. These are followed by brief descriptions of the history and structure of the institution and, where available, by information on cooperation arrangements with university institutions in other countries.

Admission requirements are usually listed for courses leading to a first degree or similar qualification. Special requirements for admission to studies leading to higher degrees and specialized diplomas are indicated where appropriate.

The names of degrees, diplomas and professional qualifications are generally given in the language of the country concerned. The duration of studies, indicated in years or semesters, is normally the minimum period required. Translations into English of fields of study are included where they are likely to be helpful.

Overall Academic Staff and Student Enrolment statistics complete the entry and include a breakdown of numbers for part-time and evening students and distance students.

Other institutions of higher education

Entries for the "other institutions of higher education" (institutions which have not been classified as "university-level" establishments by the competent national bodies) are usually less detailed. They include :

- Name in English and, where relevant, in the language of country;
- Postal and telecommunication details, with E-mail and Website addresses, where available;
- Names of the Academic Head, Administrative Officer and Director of International Relations and, where available, their telecommunication details;
- Listing of the Main Divisions of Study by Faculties, Colleges, Schools, Departments, Institutes, etc.; and
- Date(s) of foundation.

Institutions marked with a dot (•) are members of the Association of African Universities.

Institutions and agencies marked with an asterisk (*) are members of the International Association of Universities.

AAU - THE ASSOCIATION OF AFRICAN UNIVERSITIES

HISTORICAL BACKGROUND

The *Association of African Universities* (AAU) is an international non-governmental organization set up by the universities in Africa to promote cooperation among themselves, and between them and the international academic community.

AAU, whose headquarters is in Accra, Ghana, was formed in November 1967 at a founding conference in Rabat, Morocco, attended by representatives of 34 universities who adopted the Constitution of the Association. This followed earlier consultations among Executive Heads of African universities at a UNESCO Conference on Higher Education in Africa in Antananarivo, Madagascar (in 1962), and at a Conference of Heads of African Universities in 1963 in Khartoum, Sudan.

AAU is the apex organization and principal forum for consultation, exchange of information and cooperation among the universities and other higher education institutions in Africa, with a membership of 171 institutions from 43 African countries.

OBJECTIVES

The constitutional objectives of AAU are the following:
- to promote interchange, contact and cooperation among university institutions in Africa;
- to collect, classify and disseminate information on higher education and research, particularly in Africa.
- to promote cooperation among African Institutions in curriculum development, and in the determination of equivalence of degrees;
- to encourage increased contacts between its Members and the international academic world;
- to study and make known the educational and related needs of African university institutions and, as far as practicable, to coordinate the means whereby those needs may be met;
- to encourage the development and wider use of African languages;
- to organize, encourage and support seminars and conferences between African university teachers, administrators and others dealing with problems of higher education in Africa.

ORGANIZATIONAL STRUCTURE

AAU governing bodies are the General Conference, the Executive Board and the Conference of Rectors, Presidents and Vice-Chancellors (COREVIP), and the Secretariat.

The General Conference is an assembly of Vice-Chancellors, Presidents and Rectors of all Member Institutions or their representatives that meets every four years with the purpose of:
- assessing the activities implemented in the past four years against the background of a programme and a budget approved at the previous Conference;
- approving the core programme of activities and budget for the following four-year period;
- electing the governing bodies of the Association including election of one (1) President and three (3) Vice-Presidents from among the Vice-Chancellors, Presidents and Rectors of the Member Universities.

The Executive Board and its Standing Committees on Administration and Finances and on Membership and Programmes comprise 1 President, 3 Vice-Presidents and 11 Vice-Chancellors elected from among the African sub-regions. The Executive Board meets once a year and approves the annual programme and budget of AAU. It also appoints the Secretary-General and approves the appointment of other professional staff to a permanent Secretariat based in Accra, Ghana.

The Conference of Rectors, Vice-Chancellors and Presidents (COREVIP) is an assembly of the chief executive officers of Member Institutions or their representatives that meets every two years with the purpose of:
- examining collectively themes identified as common concerns and priorities for the development of higher education in Member Institutions;
- making recommendations primarily to Members, as well as to the Executive Board and to the Secretariat;
- acting as a Mid-term Conference and taking stock of the implementation of the decisions of the General Conference and recommending corrective measures.

The Secretariat, headed by the Secretary-General, currently comprises six senior, three junior professional staff and sixteen support staff. It is organized in an office of the Secretary-General with four sections, namely Administration and Finance, Communication Programmes and Cooperation, Information, and Research and one special project, the Database on African Theses and Dissertations (DATAD).

The current President of the Association elected at the 10th General Conference in February 2001 for a four-year term is Prof. George Eshiwani, Vice-Chancellor of the Kenyatta University, Kenya, and the current Secretary-General is Prof. François Rajaoson, former Rector of the University of Madagascar.

CORE PROGRAMME 2000-2004

For the more effective attainment of its objectives, the Association has, for some time now, directed its effort at formulating a coherent Core Programme of activities aimed at:
- contributing more effectively to capacity building in African Universities;
- creating a framework within which its partners can contribute more effectively to the funding of the Core Programme as a whole;
- ensuring better utilization of resources.

The first two Core Programmes (1993-1997 and 1997-2000) were approved at the 8th and 9th General Conferences of AAU respectively. As in the past, the Core Programme for 2001-2004 aims broadly at assisting African universities to respond effectively both to specific needs expressed by their communities, and to the rapidly changing national and global environment within which they operate. To address this general objective, AAU has prepared a programme under the general theme: *African Universities and the Challenge of Knowledge Creation and Application in the New Century.*

The Core Programme covers the following Sub-Themes:
- Leadership and Management;
- Quality of Training and Research;
- Information and Communication Technologies;
- Women in African Tertiary Institutions;
- Improving Management and Access to African Scholarly Work;
- Education for Peace and Conflict Avoidance;
- HIV/AIDS and the African University.

SPECIAL MEMBERSHIP SERVICE TO PROMOTE ACADEMIC MOBILITY AND QUALITY ENHANCEMENT

In addition to activities planned to fit within these sub-themes, AAU will continue to provide special Membership services aimed at promoting academic mobility and quality enhancement.

Currently these services cover:
- Staff Exchange: the Staff Exchange Scheme is to foster inter-university cooperation through exchange of external examiners, staff exchange for teaching, participation in seminars and conferences, and research cooperation;
- Fellowships and Scholarships: AAU makes available fellowships and scholarships on a competitive basis to citizenship or normal residence;
- Grants for thesis/dissertation writing: AAU makes available some small grants for graduate students to write their thesis or dissertation.

OTHER MEMBERSHIP SERVICES

On and off Campus Special Issues Workshops
Over the years, AAU has carried out a number of studies and conducted workshops and seminars on critical issues of higher education in Africa. In the process, considerable expertise on these issues has been accumulated both among the AAU Secretariat personnel and among resources persons in Member Universities. On the invitation of a Member University, AAU can arrange to send to the university campus, at AAU's expense, a resource person or a member of the Secretariat to conduct a seminar or workshop on an issue related to AAU programmes.

Information Exchange
AAU publishes a *Newsletter* three times each year in English and French. The *Newsletter* carries news about African universities and features articles on higher education in Africa. It is circulated widely to universities and university libraries throughout Africa. Member universities are encouraged to send information about their activities for inclusion in the *Newsletter*.

Guide to Higher Education in Africa
This is published every two years and contains:
- listing of Member Universities and other institutions of higher education in Africa;
- information about their executive officers;
- programmes offered in the institutions.

AAU Website

This represents the AAU's presence on the Internet. It provides information about AAU and Member Universities, and some useful Internet resources, as well as links to partner organizations.

Reports

Research reports and reports of workshops and seminars conducted by the Association are also published occasionally.

COOPERATION WITH OTHER ORGANIZATIONS

AAU collaborates with African Governments and national and international organizations. It is a Member of the International Association of Universities (IAU) and of the Permanent Council of International Congress of African Studies (ICAF), UNESCO and is accorded observer status by the Organization of African Unity. Collaborative linkages are maintained with: African and Malagasy Council for Higher Education (CAMES); United Nations University (UNU); Commonwealth Higher Education Support Scheme (CHESS); Commonwealth of Learning (COL); Commonwealth Secretariat (ComSec); African Virtual University, and United Nations Economic Commission for Africa (UNECA).

FINANCIAL RESOURCES

Funding of AAU programmes derives from the following sources:
- Membership subscriptions;
- Grants from developed countries, international and other donor agencies;
- Grants from OAU;
- Income from services provided and from publications;
- Capital investment fund.

AAU ONGOING PROGRAMMES 2001-2004

The following projects are being implemented:
- Study Programme on Higher Education Management in Africa;
- Academic Mobility (staff exchange, small grants, scholarships);
- Senior University Management Workshops;
- AAU/FAWE Gender Programme;
- Developing Quality Assurance Systems in African Universities;
- Graduate Programme for Humanitarian & Refugee Studies;
- Regional Cooperation in Graduate Training and Research;
- Use and application of ICTs in Higher Education in Africa;
- Database on African Thesis and Dissertation (DATAD);
- Ford Foundation International Fellowship Programme (IFP).

HEADQUARTERS

Association of African Universities
Aviation Road Extension, Airport Residential Area,
P. O. Box 5744, Accra-North, Ghana
Tel: +233-21-774495/761588
Fax: +233-21+774821
E-mails: Secretary-General: secgen@aau.org / info@aau.org
Website: http://www.aau.org

OFFICERS OF THE ASSOCIATION OF AFRICAN UNIVERSITIES (AAU)

Executive Board 2001-2004 (Elected at the 10th General Conference, February 2001, Nairobi, Kenya)

President

Prof. George Eshiwani   Vice-Chancellor, Kenyatta University, Kenya

Vice-Presidents

Dr. Dorothy L. Njeuma   Vice-Chancellor, University of Buea, Cameroon
Prof. Hamied Shalaby   President, Suez Canal University, Egypt
Prof. Julius Okojie   Vice-Chancellor, University of Agriculture, Ogun State, Nigeria

Members of the Executive Board

Prof. Peter Katjavivi   Vice-Chancellor, University of Namibia
Prof. John Melamu   Former Vice Chancellor, North-West University of Botswana
Dr. Thikhoi L. Jonathan   Deputy Vice-Chancellor, National University of Lesotho
Prof. Ndjabulo Ndebele   Vice-Chancellor, University of Cape Town, South Africa
Prof. Abdulkabir Saied Al- Fahry   President, Popular Committee University of Sebha, Libya
Prof. John Sefa K. Ayim   Vice-Chancellor, Kwame Nkrumah University of Science and Technology (KNUST), Ghana
Prof. Lamine Ahmadou Ndiaye   Recteur Fondateur, Université Gaston Berger, Sénégal
Prof. Moussa Ouattara   Recteur, Université polytechnique de Bobo-Dioulasso, Burkina Faso
Dr. Emile Rwamasirabo   Recteur, Université nationale du Rwanda
Prof. Matthew Luhanga   Vice-Chancellor, University of Dar-es-Salaam, Tanzania
Prof. Matthew A. Aduol   President, University of Bahr El Ghazal, Sudan

Alternate Members

Prof. Mutale Chanda, Vice-Chancellor, University of Zambia; Prof. Mazula Brazao, Rector, Eduardo Mondlane University, Mozambique; Prof. M. Ramashala, Vice-Chancellor, University of Durban Westville, South Africa; Dr. M. Takalo, Campus Principal, Vista University, South Africa; Prof. Amer Mohammed, President, Zagazig University, Egypt; Prof. Mohammed Alaoui, Rector, Mohammed V University, Morocco; Prof. Raymond Bening, Vice-Chancellor, University of Development Studies, Tamale, Ghana; Prof. Ginigeme Mbanefoh, Vice-Chancellor, University of Nigeria, Nsukka, Nigeria; Prof. Boubacar Cisse, Recteur, Université du Mali; Prof. Daouda Aidara, Président, Université d'Abobo-Adjamé, Côte d'Ivoire; Prof. Silas Lwakabamba, Rector, Kigali Institute of Science and Technology, Rwanda; Prof. Jean Tabi Manga, Recteur, Université de Yaoundé I, Cameroun; Prof. Ratemo Michieka, Vice-Chancellor, Jomo Kenyatta University of Agriculture and Technology, Kenya; Prof. Mogessie Ashenafi, President, Addis Ababa University, Ethiopia; Prof. A. B. Lwoga, Vice-Chancellor, Sokoine University of Agriculture, Tanzania

IAU - THE INTERNATIONAL ASSOCIATION OF UNIVERSITIES

The *International Association of Universities* (IAU), founded in 1950, is a worldwide organization with Member Institutions in some 140 countries which cooperates with a vast network of international, regional and national bodies. Its permanent Secretariat, the International Universities Bureau, is located at UNESCO, Paris, and provides a wide variety of services to Member Institutions and to the international higher education community at large.

MEETINGS

IAU provides a forum for higher education leaders to discuss major current trends and issues in higher education and higher education policy. Heads of all Member Institutions or their representatives are invited to the IAU quinquennial General Conferences (as from 2001, quadrennial), as well as to the Mid-Term Conferences and Regional Meetings. These Conferences, as well as different Seminars and Round Tables, are organized either by the Association itself or in cooperation with other academic bodies and provide unique opportunities for the exchange of experience and ideas on issues of international interest and importance. The Eleventh General Conference was held in Durban, South Africa, in August 2000, and discussed the theme "*Universities – Gateway to the Future*".

PUBLICATIONS

Services traditionally offered to Member Institutions include the right to receive, either on a complimentary basis or at considerably reduced rates, the Association's publications. These include two major reference works, prepared from IAU's institutional database (WHED), the *International Handbook of Universities* and the *World List of Universities and Other Institutions of Higher Education* (both published biennially), the *World Higher Education Database (WHED)* CD-Rom (annually), the quarterly journal *Higher Education Policy*, the bimonthly *IAU Newsletter* and a monograph series *Issues in Higher Education*. The two reference works are long-established, invaluable tools for all those concerned with international cooperation in higher education, providing detailed information on thousands of higher education institutions worldwide. The CD-Rom is a more recent addition which provides, apart from the information above, data on higher education systems and credentials and many search facilities. In addition, a series of regional guides has been launched with the *Guide to Higher Education in Africa*. *Higher Education Policy* and *Issues in Higher Education* focus on policy issues and the role of higher education in society today, offering a platform for the exchange and sharing of information and debate within the world community of higher education. (See list of IAU Publications p. xv - xvi).

INFORMATION SERVICES

Also available to Member Universities is the vast body of information housed in the specialized IAU/UNESCO Information Centre on Higher Education. The Centre, managed by IAU, contains over 50,000 volumes on higher education worldwide and operates two major databases (WHED, mentioned above, and HEDBIB, the Higher Education Bibliographical Database) from which directories and CD-Roms are produced, but different types of information services (topical bibliographies, institutional and statistical data, credential evaluation and advice, and address labels) are also provided. The IAU website (http://www.unesco.org/iau) is another new important source of information and links.

COOPERATION

IAU, through its unique network and linkage system, provides an important clearing-house function to Members for academic exchange and cooperation, implying active involvement and participation of Member universities in the important mission of bringing a real international perspective to the life of universities. Among the major areas retained for cooperation are concerns related to Academic Freedom and University Autonomy, Higher Education and Sustainable Human Development, Universities and Information Technologies and Internationalization of Higher Education.

Headquarters
International Association of Universities
Unesco House, 1 rue Miollis, F-75732 Paris Cedex 15, France
Telephone: +33(1) 4568 2545 Telefax: +33(1) 4734 7605 E-mail: iau@unesco.org
Website: http://www.unesco.org/iau
IAU/UNESCO Information Centre on Higher Education
Director: Claudine Langlois, centre.iau@unesco.org

OFFICERS OF THE INTERNATIONAL ASSOCIATION OF UNIVERSITIES

Administrative Board 2000-2004

President

Hans Van Ginkel — Rector, United Nations University, Tokyo, Japan - Former Rector, University of Utrecht, Netherlands

Vice-Presidents

Flavio Fava de Moraes — Former Rector, University of São Paulo, Brazil

Hanna Nasir — President, Birzeit University, Palestine

François Rajaoson — Secretary-General, Association of African Universities

Luc Weber — Ancien Recteur, Université de Genève, Switzerland

Honorary Presidents

Walter Kamba — President 1990-1995, Former Vice-Chancellor, University of Zimbabwe

Martin Meyerson — Acting President 1983 & 1985, President Emeritus, University of Pennsylvania, U.S.A.

Wataru Mori — President 1995-2000, Former President, University of Tokyo, Japan

Blagovest Sendov — Acting President 1984, Former Rector, University of Sofia, Bulgaria

Guillermo Soberón — President 1980-1985, Former Rector, UNAM, Mexico

Justin Thorens — President 1985-1990, Ancien Recteur, Université de Genève

Board Members

Saiyid Nazir Ahmad — Vice-Chancellor, Sir Syed University of Engineering & Technology, Pakistan

Abdulla Al-Khulaifi — President, University of Qatar

Paolo Blasi — Former Rector, University of Florence, Italy

Juan Ramón de la Fuente — Rector, National Autonomous University of Mexico

Edgard Elbaz — Vice-Président, Université Lyon 1, France

Brenda Gourley — Vice-Chancellor, Open University, United Kingdom

Zixin Hou — President, Nankai University, China

A.J. Jassbi — President, Islamic Azad University, Iran

Henrik Toft Jensen — Rector, Roskilde University, Denmark

Triloki Kapoor — Former Vice-Chancellor, Panjab University, India

Goolam Mohamedbhai — Vice-Chancellor, University of Mauritius

Wataru Mori — Past IAU President, Former President, University of Tokyo, Japan (Ex-Officio Member)

David K. Scott — Former Chancellor, University of Massachusetts at Amherst, U.S.A.

Tatchai Sumitra — President, Chulalongkorn University, Thailand

Julio Terán Dutari — Former President, International Federation of Catholic Universities

Ludmila Verbitskaja — Rector, St Petersburg University, Russian Federation

Ivan Wilhelm — Rector, Charles University Prague, Czech Republic

Deputy Board Members

Mostafa Abdel Motaal, Former President, Menoufia University, Egypt; Ofelia M. Carague, President, Polytechnic University of the Philippines; Osmar Correal Cabral, Rector, University of Boyaca, Colombia; Saeed A. Fakhri, Professor, Tabriz University, Iran; Madeleine Green, Vice-President, American Council on Education; Fayez Khasawneh, President, Yarmouk University, Jordan; Kestutis Krisciunas, Former Rector, Kaunas University of Technology, Lithuania; Henning Lehmann, Rector, University of Aarhus, Denmark; Gamal Mokhtar, President, Arab Academy for Science & Technology, Egypt ; Ian Newbould, President, North Carolina Wesleyan College, USA; Takayasa Okushimo, President, Waseda University, Japan; Izzeldin Osman, Vice-Chancellor, Sudan University of Science & Technology; Moussa Ouattara, Rector, Université Polytechnique de Bobo-Dioulasso, Burkina Faso; Slawomir Owczarski, President, Higher School of Trade, Lódz, Poland; Khetsuriani Ramaz, Rector, Tbilisi State Medical University, Georgia; Sharon Siverts, Vice-Chancellor, University of Botswana; Istvan Teplan, Vice-President, Central European University, Hungary; Juan Alesandro Tobias, Rector, Universidad del Salvador, Argentina; Brigitte Winklehner, Vice-Rector, University of Salzburg, Austria

Secretary-General

Eva EGRON-POLAK — Executive Director, International Universities Bureau (as from 1 January 2002)

MAIN AAU PUBLICATIONS 1993-2001

- Cost-effectiveness and Efficiency in African Universities: case study - University of Zambia, 1993.
- Cost-effectiveness and Efficiency in African Universities: case study - University of Ghana,1993.
- Cost-effectiveness and Efficiency in African Universities: case study - Obafemi Awolowo University, 1993.
- Cost-effectiveness and Efficiency in African Universities: case study - Université de Cocody, 1993.
- Cost-effectiveness and Efficiency in African Universities: case study - University of Gezira, Sudan,1993.
- Consultative Meeting on Professional Development for Academic Staff of African Universities, 1994.
- Report of the Round Table Conference with Vice-Chancellors of South Africa and other African Universities, 1994.
- Report of the AAU/UNESCO/CHEMS Workshop on Strategic Planning in African Universities, 1995.
- The African Experience with Higher Education, 1996.
- Revitalizing Universities in Africa: Strategy and Guidelines (in collaboration with the World Bank), 1997.
- Report of the 9th General Conference, 1998.
- Strategic Planning at Selected African Universities, 1996.
- Demand, Access and Equity Issues in Africa Higher Education: Past Policies, Current Practices, and Readiness for the 21st Century, 1995.
- Enhancing Linkages between African Universities, the Wider Society, the Business Community and Governments, 1995.
- Governance Issues in African Universities: Improving Management and Governance to make African Universities viable in the 1990s and beyond, 1995.
- Universities in Africa: Challenges and Opportunities of International Cooperation, 1995.
- Adequate and Sustainable Funding of African Universities, 1995.
- Quality and Relevance: African Universities in the 21st Century, 1995.
- The Emerging Role of African Universities in the Development of Science and Technology,1995.
- The Future Missions and Roles of the African Universities, 1995.
- Evaluation of the Status of Teaching and Use of African Languages in Higher Education,1998.
- University Libraries in Africa: Workshop on Funder-Recipient Relationships, 1998.
- Report of the Meeting on Collection and Dissemination of Science and Technology Results from African Tertiary Institutions, 1998.
- Strengthening University Linkages with the Productive Sector, 1999.
- The Political Economy of Development, an African Perspective, 2 Volumes, 1999.
- Higher Education Leadership in Africa: A Casebook, 1999.
- Senior University Management Workshop: Course Director's Reports, 1999.
- Towards the Introduction and Application of Information and Communication Technologies in African Universities, 2001.
- COREVIP'99: Revitalizing Universities in Africa: Strategies for the 21st Century, (English & French), 1999.
- Guide to Higer Education in Africa, first edition 1999.
- A Study on Private Universities in Africa, 2000.
- AAU Annual Report (yearly).
- Newsletter in English & French (3 times a year).
- Information Brochure.
- Membership List.

OCCASIONAL PAPERS

- Women in Higher Education and Research in Africa,1999.
- North-South Cooperation to Strengthen Universities in Africa, 1999.
- The Role of University Libraries in African Universities, (English & French), 1999.
- Post-Genocide Restructuring of Higher Education in Rwanda, an Overview, 2000.

RESEARCH PAPERS

- Statistical Data: The Underestimated Tool for Higher Education Management. The Case of Makerere University, 1998.
- Revitalizing Financing of Higher Education in Kenya: Resource Allocation in Public Universities, 1998.
- The Social Background of Makerere University Students and the Potential for Cost Sharing, 1998.
- Modeling for Resource Allocation to Departments and Faculties in African Universities, 1998.
- An Innovative Approach to Undergraduate Education in Nigeria, 2000.
- The Stories We Tell and the Way We Tell Them: An Investigation into the Institutional Culture of the University of the North, South Africa, 2000.
- Etude sur le Suivi des Diplômés de l'Universite Cheikh Anta Diop de Dakar (UCAD-Sénégal) dans le Milieu du Travail, 2001.
- Knowledge and Skills of BCom Graduates of the Faculty of Commerce and Management, University of Dar-Es-Salaam in the Job Market, 2001.

MAIN IAU PUBLICATIONS 1993-2002

For a worldwide Association, sharing information, expertise and experience amongst leaders and decision-makers on the central issues facing higher education is key. IAU has made - and continues to make - a very substantial input to informed debate on public policy. It maintains databases and produces reference works on higher education systems, institutions and credentials and brings out state of the art research on vital issues that concern higher education. By doing so, it serves the academic community and its leadership, stimulating discussion and advancing action. Major publications resulting from this commitment are:

REFERENCE WORKS

- **International Handbook of Universities**. Sixteenth Edition, 2001, Palgrave, ISBN: 0-333-94513-1; ISBN: 92-9002-167-5 (IAU).

- **World List of Universities and Other Institutions of Higher Education**. Twenty-third Edition, 2002, Palgrave, ISBN: 0-333-67152-X; 92-9002-169-1 (IAU).

- **Guide to Higher Education in Africa**. Second Edition, 2002, Palgrave, ISBN: 0-333-99324-1; 92-9002-168-3 (IAU).

- **World Higher Education Database 2001-2002 CD-Rom**, combines information from the latest editions of the *International Handbook of Universities* and the *World List of Universities* (16,000 institutions) and offers descriptions of the higher education systems and qualifications in over 180 countries. Palgrave. ISBN: 0-333-96259-1.

PUBLISHED BY: Palgrave, Houndmills, Basingstoke, Hampshire RG21 6XS and 175 Fifth Avenue, New York, N.Y. 10010. www.palgrave.com

ISSUES IN HIGHER EDUCATION SERIES (IHES)

Higher Education and the Nation State: the International Dimension of Higher Education. Edited by Jeroen Huisman, Peter Maassen and Guy Neave (Centre for Higher Education Policy Studies, University of Twente, Enschede, The Netherlands). Oxford, Pergamon/IAU Press, 2001. 237pp. ISBN: 0080427901

Access to Knowledge: New Information Technologies and the Emergence of the Virtual University. Edited by F. T. Tschang (United Nations University, Institute of Advanced Studies, Tokyo, Japan) & T. Della Senta (United Nations University, Institute of Advanced Studies, Tokyo, Japan). Oxford, Pergamon Press/IAU Press, 2001. 411pp. ISBN: 0-08-043670-6

Abiding Issues, Changing Perspectives: Visions of the University Across a Half-Century. Edited by Guy Neave (International Association of Universities, Paris). IAU Press, 2000. 320 pp. ISBN: 92-9002-166-7

The Universities' Responsibilities to Society: International Perspectives. Edited by Guy Neave (International Association of Universities, Paris). Oxford, Pergamon Press/IAU Press, 2000. 289pp. ISBN: 0-08-043569-6 (Report of IAU Fourth Mid-Term Conference, Bangkok, 1997).

Local Knowledge and Wisdom in Higher Education. Edited by G. R. (Bob) Teasdale (Flinders University Institute of International Education, Adelaide, Australia) and Zane Ma Rhea (National Centre for Gender and Cultural Diversity, Swinburne University of Technology, Melbourne, Australia). Oxford, Pergamon/IAU Press, 2000. 264pp. ISBN: 0-08-043453-3

Higher Education Research: Its Relationship to Policy and Practice. Edited by Ulrich Teichler (Centre for Research on Higher Education and Work, University of Kassel, Germany) and Jan Sadlak (UNESCO). Oxford, Pergamon/IAU Press, 2000. 192pp. ISBN: 0-08-043452-5

Challenges Facing Higher Education at the Millennium. Edited by Werner Z. Hirsch and Luc E. Weber – Oxford, Pergamon Press/IAU Press, 1999. 199pp. ISBN: 0-08-0428177

Distance and Campus Universities: Tensions and Interactions. A Comparative Study of Five Countries. Edited by S. Guri-Rosenblit (The Open University of Israel, Israel). Oxford, Pergamon Press/IAU Press, 1999. 290pp. ISBN: 0-08-043066-X

Creating Entrepreneurial Universities: Organizational Pathways of Transformation. Edited by Burton R. Clark (University of California, Los Angeles, USA). Oxford, Pergamon Press/IAU Press, 1998, 160pp. ISBN: 0-08-043342-1

Organising Innovative Research: The Inner Life of University Departments. Edited by Li Bennich-Björkman (Uppsala University, Sweden). Oxford, Pergamon Press/IAU Press, 1997. 250pp. ISBN: 0-08-043072-4

The Mockers and Mocked: Comparative Perspectives on Differentiation, Convergence and Diversity in Higher Education. Edited by V. Lynn Meek (University of New England, Australia), L. Goedegebuure (Centre for Higher Education Policy Studies (CHEPS), University of Twente, The Netherlands), O. Kivinen and R. Rinne (University of Turku, Finland). Oxford, Pergamon Press/IAU Press, 1996. 236pp. ISBN: 0-08-042563-1

Emerging Patterns of Social Demand and University Reform: Through a Glass Darkly. Edited by David D. Dill (University of North Carolina, USA) and Barbara Sporn (Vienna University of Economics and Business Administration, Austria). Oxford, Pergamon/IAU Press, 1995. 244pp. ISBN: 0-08-042564-x

East Asian Higher Education: Traditions and Transformations. By Albert H. Yee (Division of Academic Affairs, Florida International University, Miami, USA). Oxford, Pergamon/IAU Press, 1995. 213pp. ISBN: 0-08-042385X

Revitalizing Higher Education. Edited by Jamil Salmi and Adriaan Verspoor (The World Bank, Washington DC, USA). Oxford, Pergamon/IAU Press, 1994. 419pp. ISBN: 0-08-041948-8

Government and Higher Education Relationships Across Three Continents: the Winds of Change. Edited by Guy Neave (International Association of Universities, Paris, France) and Frans van Vught (Centre for Higher Education Policy Studies (CHEPS), University of Twente, The Netherlands). Oxford, Pergamon/IAU Press, 1994. 322pp. Incl. bibl. ISBN: 0-08-042391-4

Higher Education Policy: an International Comparative Perspective. Edited by Leo Goedegebuure, Frans Kaiser, Peter Maassen, Lynn Meek, Frans van Vught and Egbert de Weert (Centre for Higher Education Policy Studies (CHEPS), University of Twente, The Netherlands). Oxford; New York; Pergamon/IAU Press, 1993. 362pp. Incl. bibl. ISBN: 0-08-0423930

PUBLISHED BY: Pergamon Press; Elsevier Service Ltd., The Boulevard, Langford Lane, Kidlington, Oxford 0X5 1GB, England (see availability below).

HIGHER EDUCATION POLICY

The Quarterly Journal of the International Association of Universities
Editor: Guy Neave, International Association of Universities

Recent issues have focused on the following themes:

• **Policy Making: Perspectives from Eastern Europe**	Vol. 14, no. 3, 2001
• **Out of Africa: Planning Change and Reform**	Vol. 14, no. 2, 2001
• **The Changing Frontiers of Autonomy and Accountability**	Vol. 14, no. 1, 2001
• **Organising for Leadership**	Vol. 13, no. 4, 2000
• **Higher Education and European Integration**	Vol. 13, no. 3, 2000
• **The Pace of Change**	Vol. 13, no. 2, 2000
• **Diversity, Differentiation and Markets**	Vol. 13, no. 1, 2000
• **Change and Outcomes**	Vol. 12, no. 4, 1999
• **Standards in Higher Education**	Vol. 12, no. 3, 1999
• **Key Issues**	Vol. 12, no. 2, 1999
• **Institutional Behaviour**	Vol. 12, no. 1, 1999

AVAILABLE FROM:

Both *Issues in Higher Education* and *Higher Education Policy* are available from Elsevier Science.
Contact the Customer Support Department at the Regional Sales Office nearest you:
New York: Elsevier Science, PO Box 945, New York, NY 10159-0945, USA; phone: +1(212) 633 3730 [(toll free number for North American customers: 1-888-4ES-INFO (437-4636)]; fax: +1(212) 633 3680; e-mail: usinfo-f@elsevier.com
Amsterdam: Elsevier Science, PO Box 211, 1000 AE Amsterdam, The Netherlands; phone: +31(20) 4853757; fax: +31(20) 4853432; e-mail: nlinfo-f@elsevier.nl
Tokyo: Elsevier Science, 9-15 Higashi-Azabu 1-chome, Minato-ku, Tokyo 106-0044, Japan; phone: +81(3) 5561 5033; fax: +81(3) 5561 5047; e-mail: info@elsevier.co.jp
Singapore: Elsevier Science, No. 1 Temasek Avenue, #17-01 Millenia Tower, Singapore 039192; phone: +65 434 3727; fax: +65 337 2230; e-mail: asiainfo@elsevier.com.sg
Rio de Janeiro: Elsevier Science, Rua Sete de Setembro 111/16 Andar, 20050-002 Centro, Rio de Janeiro – RJ, Brazil; phone: +55(21) 509 5340; fax +55(21) 507 1991; e-mail elsevier@campus.com.br [Note (Latin America): for orders, claims and help desk information, please contact the Regional Sales Office in New York as listed above].

IAU NEWSLETTER / NOUVELLES DE L'AIU

The bimonthly Newsletter of the International Association of Universities in English and French.

AVAILABLE FROM:
International Association of Universities
UNESCO House
1, rue Miollis, 75732 Paris Cedex 15, France
Tel: +33-1-45 68 25 45 - Fax: +33-1-47 34 76 05 - E-mail: iau@unesco.org
Website: http://www.unesco.org/iau

Country Entries

Algeria

INSTITUTION TYPES AND CREDENTIALS

Types of higher education institutions:

Université (University)
Centre universitaire (University Centre)
Ecole nationale (National School)
Institut national (National Institute)
Ecole normale supérieure (Higher Teacher Training College)

School leaving and higher education credentials:

Baccalauréat de l'Enseignement secondaire
Certificat de Capacité en Droit
Diplôme de Technicien supérieur
Diplôme d'Etudes universitaires appliquées (DEUA)
Diplôme
Diplôme d'Etudes supérieures (DES)
Diplôme d'Ingénieur
Licence
Diplôme de Docteur
Magister
Doctorat d'Etat

STRUCTURE OF EDUCATION SYSTEM

Pre-higher education:

Duration of compulsory education:

    Age of entry: 6
    Age of exit: 15

Structure of school system:

    Basic
    Type of school providing this education: Ecole fondamentale
    Length of programme in years: 9
    Age level from: 6 to: 15
    Certificate/diploma awarded: Brevet d'Enseignement fondamental

Secondary
Type of school providing this education: Ecole secondaire, Technicum
Length of programme in years: 3
Age level from: 15 to: 18
Certificate/diploma awarded: Baccalauréat de l'Enseignement secondaire

Vocational Secondary
Type of school providing this education: Centre de formation professionnellle
Length of programme in years: 3
Certificate/diploma awarded: Certificat d'aptitude professionnelle etc..

School education:

Primary education lasts for nine years (Ecole fondamentale). Secondary education is compulsory and consists of a three-year cycle of study provided in secondary schools and technicums. There are three branches of secondary education: general, specialized and technical/vocational. Students in general secondary and specialized secondary education study for three years and sit for the Baccalauréat examination. Successful students are awarded the Baccalauréat de l'Enseignement secondaire in one of the various streams offered. The Baccalauréat gives access to higher education but some institutions require it to be of a certain type (science, arts, etc.). The objective of technical and vocational secondary education is to prepare students for active life and industry (technicians and qualified workers). Studies last between one and four years, according to the type of training undertaken and can also lead to higher education.

Higher education:

Higher education is provided by universities, specialized institutes, national institutes of higher education, and teacher training institutes, which fall under the responsibility of the Ministry of Higher Education and Scientific Research, as well as by institutes run by other ministries. The specific degrees awarded are determined by the field of study, not the institution. The Ministry of Higher Education approves the curriculum, which is standardized for each field of study. Algerian institutions also award graduate degrees (Diplômes de Postgraduation) in most fields in which a Licence or DES is awarded.

Main laws/decrees governing higher education:

Decree: Loi n°99-05 d'Orientation sur l'Enseignement supérieur   Year: 1999
Concerns: Higher Education

Decree: Décret exécutif n° 98-253   Year: 1998
Concerns: Status of Universities

Decree: Décret exécutif n° 98-254   Year: 1998
Concerns: Doctorate, postgraduation and habilitation

Academic year:

Classes from: September *to:* June
Long vacation from: 1 July *to:* 31 August

Languages of instruction:

Arabic, French

Stages of studies:

Non-university level post-secondary studies (technical/vocational type):

The Technological Institutes are national Institutes under the responsibility of one of the main ministries. They offer a variety of courses at the higher and graduate levels and students are trained in specific skills. Recruitment is at Baccalauréat level, and studies lead to a Diplôme d'Ingénieur after a five-year course, which is considered of university level. At the lower level, students who have reached Baccalauréat level but not passed the examination may follow a two-and-a-half-year course leading to the Diplôme de Technicien supérieur. This Diplôme is not recognized as a qualification for university entrance. However, a Technicien supérieur with five years' experience may continue to study for the Diplôme d'Ingénieur.

University level studies:

University level first stage:

At undergraduate level, higher education is divided into a short (three-year) cycle, leading to a Diplôme d'Etudes universitaires appliquées (DEUA), and a long (four to six-year) cycle, leading to the Licence or the Diplôme d'Etudes supérieures in Science or, in technological institutions, to the Diplôme d'Ingénieur. In most cases, the two cycles are parallel rather than consecutive programmes. Courses for the Diplôme in Engineering, Dental Surgery, Pharmacy, Architecture and Veterinary Medicine last for five years while the title of Doctor in Medicine is awarded after seven years' study.

University level second stage: *Postgraduation*:

After the main stage, the best students undertake postgraduate studies (Diplôme de Postgraduation). Studying for the Magister requires a minimum of four semesters after the DES or Licence and the defence of a thesis. The Magister is conferred by the major universities and replaces the Doctorat de 3ème cycle.

University level third stage: *Doctorat d'Etat*:

The last stage leads to the Doctorat d'Etat. Usually lasting three to five years, studies involve individual research work and submission of a substantial thesis.

Teacher education:

Training of pre-primary and primary/basic school teachers

Primary school teachers are trained at Ecoles normales supérieures. They obtain the Diplôme de Maître d'Enseignement fondamental (1st and 2nd stage) after three years and the Diplôme de Professeur de l'Enseignement fondamental after four years.

Training of secondary school teachers

Secondary school teachers are trained at the Ecoles normales supérieures where they obtain the Diplôme de Professeur de l'Enseignement secondaire after five years.

Training of higher education teachers

Teaching at the university level requires at least a Magister. Technological institutes outside the purview of the Ministère de l'Enseignement supérieur recruit teachers who hold the Ingéniorat d'Etat,

5

Licence or Diplôme d'Etudes supérieures, depending on the specialization and the function the teacher is to serve. Experience in the relevant field of study is also taken into consideration.

Non-traditional studies:

Lifelong higher education
L'Université de la Formation Continue (UFC) opened in 1989. UFC is a network composed of ten regional institutes which is open to workers having at least five years' professional experience and who successfully completed the final secondary year but failed the Baccalauréat exam. Study consists of a preparatory year to enable a transition to "university" studies in Natural Science, Maths, Letters and Law, followed by three years' (short cycle) or four years' (long cycle) study. In 1990, the Université du Soir was created for people who do not hold the Baccalauréat or want to resume their studies after several years of professional life.

NATIONAL BODIES

Responsible authorities:

Ministry of Higher Education and Scientific Research (Ministère de l'Enseignement supérieur et de la Recherche scientifique)

Minister: Amar Fakhri
11 Chemin Doudou Mokhtar
Ben-Aknoun
Alger
Tel: +213(2) 91-18-86 +213(2) 91-47-96
Fax: +213(2) 91-18-23 +213(2) 91-21-41
EMail: mesrs@ist.cerist.dz
WWW: http://www.mesrs.edu.dz/english

Role of governing body: Coordinates higher education.

ADMISSIONS TO HIGHER EDUCATION

Admission to non university higher education studies

Name of secondary school credential required: Baccalauréat de l'Enseignement secondaire

Alternatives to credentials: At the lower level of the technological institutes, students who have reached Baccalauréat level but not passed the examination may follow a two-and-a-half-year course leading to the Diplôme de Technicien supérieur. This diploma, added to five years' experience, allows them to study for the Diplôme d'Ingénieur.

Admission to university-level studies

Name of secondary school credential required: Baccalauréat de l'Enseignement secondaire

Alternatives to credentials: Specific competitive examinations give access to certain streams (filières) to candidates having attended third-year classes without obtaining the Baccalauréat. Postsecondary programmes in sports, fine arts, music and youth affairs admit students on the basis of an aptitude test rather than Baccalauréat results.

Foreign students admission

Admission requirements: Students must hold the Baccalauréat or an equivalent diploma.

Entry regulations: Foreign students must hold a visa or copy of agreement between their country and Algeria (e.g. proof of an equivalence agreement).

Language requirements: Students must have good knowledge of Arabic. Arabic language courses are compulsory for specialized studies

Recognition of studies and qualifications:

Studies pursued in foreign countries (bodies dealing with recognition of foreign credentials):
Commission nationale d'Equivalences, Ministère de l'Enseignement supérieur et de la Recherche scientifique

11 Chemin Doudou Mokhtar
Ben Aknoun
Alger
Tel: +213(2) 91-17-96
Fax: +213(2) 91-46-01
Telex: 61381/67446DZ
EMail: mesrs@ist.cerist.dz; allia@wissal.dz
WWW: http://www.mesrs.edu.dz/english

Deals with credential recognition for entry to: University and Profession

Special provisions for recognition:

For access to university level studies: All necessary prerequisites and documents required are listed in the Ministry of Higher Education Website with forms to be downloaded.

Multilateral agreements concerning recognition of foreign studies

Name(s) of agreement(s): Convention on the Recognition of Studies, Certificates, Diplomas, Degrees and Other Academic Qualifications in Higher Education in the African States
Year of signature: 1981

Convention on the Recognition of Studies, Diplomas and Degrees in Higher Education in the Arab States
Year of signature: 1978

International Convention on the Recognition of Studies, Certificates, Diplomas and Degrees in Higher Education in the Arab and European States Bordering on the Mediterranean.
Year of signature: 1976

References to further information on foreign student admissions and recognition of studies

Title: Guide de l'Étudiant étranger en Algérie

STUDENT LIFE

Main student services at national level
Office national des Oeuvres universitaires
  Route de Dely-Brahim
  Wilaya d'Alger

Student expenses and financial aid
Bodies providing information on student financial aid:

Ministère de l'Enseignement supérieur et de la Recherche scientifique
  11 Chemin Doudou Mokthar, Ben-Aknoun
  Alger
  Tel: +213(2) 91-18-86
  Fax: +213(2) 91-18-23
  WWW: http://www.mesrs.edu.dz

  Deals with: Grants
  Category of students: Students from all countries with Baccalauréat & knowledge of Arabic & French.

Publications on student services and financial aid:

  Title: Study Abroad 2000-2001
  Publisher: UNESCO/IBE
  Year of publication: 1999

GRADING SYSTEM

Usual grading system in secondary school
Full Description: 0-20: 16-20 très bien; 14-15 bien; 12-13 assez bien; 10-11 passable; 0-9 insuffisant
Highest on scale: 16-20 Très-Bien (Excellent)
Pass/fail level: 10-11 pass
Lowest on scale: 0-9 poor

Main grading system used by higher education institutions
Full Description: 0-20: 15-20 très bien; 13-14 bien; 12 assez bien; 11 passable; 10 sans mention
Highest on scale: 15-20 very good
Pass/fail level: 11-Pass
Lowest on scale: 0-10

NOTES ON HIGHER EDUCATION SYSTEM

Data for academic year: 2000-2001
Source: International Association of Universities (IAU), updated from Algerian Ministry of Higher Education website, 2001

INSTITUTIONS OF HIGHER EDUCATION

UNIVERSITIES

• UNIVERSITY OF ALGIERS
Université d'Alger
2, rue Diddouche Mourad, Alger 16000
Tel: +213(21) 64-69-70
Fax: +213(21) 63-53-03
Telex: 66529 unial dz
Website: http://www.univ-alger.dz

Recteur: Tahar Hadjar

Faculties
Economics and Management (Business and Commerce; Economics; Management)
Humanities (Archaeology; Arts and Humanities; History; International Relations; Library Science; Political Science)
Islamic Studies (Arabic; Islamic Law; Islamic Studies; Law; Religious Studies)
Law (Law; Private Law; Public Law)
Letters and Languages (Arabic; Communication Studies; English; French; German; Information Sciences; Italian; Linguistics; Literature; Oriental Languages; Slavic Languages; Spanish; Translation and Interpretation)
Medical Sciences (Dentistry; Medicine; Pharmacy)
Social Sciences (Educational Sciences; Philosophy; Physical Education; Psychology; Social Sciences; Sociology)

History: Founded 1859 as a School of Medicine and Pharmacy, followed in 1879 by schools of law, science, and letters. Formally established as University 1909.

Academic Year: October to June (October-December; January-April; April-June)

Admission Requirements: Secondary school certificate (baccalauréat) or recognized equivalent or entrance examination

Main Language(s) of Instruction: Arabic, French

Accrediting Agencies: Ministry of Higher Education and Scientific Research

Degrees and Diplomas: *Certificat de Capacité en Droit*: 2 yrs; *Diplôme*: Midwifery (Professional Qualification), 3 yrs; Dentistry, 4 yrs; Pharmacy, 5 yrs; Medicine, 6 yrs; *Licence*: 4 yrs; *Magister*: 2 yrs following Licence; *Doctorat d'Etat*: by thesis

Student Residential Facilities: Yes

Special Facilities: Musée du Bardo; Musée national des Beaux-Arts; Musée Savorgnan de Brazza; Musée Stéphane Csell; Musée Franchet d'Esperey

Publications: Majalatou Koulyat el Adab; Revue africaine; Errihla el Maghribia; Revue Lybica; Sciences médicales de Constantine; Bulletin d'Information historique

Student Numbers *1999:* Total: c. 32,000

• UNIVERSITY OF SCIENCE AND TECHNOLOGY 'HOUARI BOUMEDIÈNE' ALGIERS
Université des Sciences et de la Technologie 'Houari Boumediène' (USTHB)
B.P.32 USTHB, Bab-Ezzouar, Alger 16123
Tel: +213(21) 24-79-50
Fax: +213(21) 24-79-92
Telex: 64343 dz usta
EMail: webmaster@usthb.dz
Website: http://www.usthb.dz

Recteur: Benali Benzagliou
Secrétaire général: Reda Djellid
International Relations: Mehrez Drir

Faculties
Biological Sciences (Biological and Life Sciences)
Chemistry
Civil Engineering
Earth Sciences, Geography and Regional Planning (Earth Sciences; Geography; Geology; Geophysics; Regional Planning) *Dean:* H. Benhallou
Electronic and Computer Engineering (Computer Engineering; Electronic Engineering) *Dean:* A. Aissani
Mechanical and Process Engineering (Mechanical Engineering; Systems Analysis)
Physics
Science (Science Education)

History: Founded 1974.

Governing Bodies: Scientific Council

Academic Year: September to June (September-December; January-April; April-June)

Admission Requirements: Secondary school certificate (baccalauréat)

Main Language(s) of Instruction: Arabic, French

Accrediting Agencies: Ministry of Higher Education and Scientific Research

Degrees and Diplomas: *Diplôme d'Etudes supérieures (DES)*: 3-4 yrs; *Diplôme d'Ingénieur*: 5 yrs; *Magister*; *Doctorat d'Etat*

Student Services: Academic Counselling, Social Counselling, Employment Services, Cultural Centre, Sports Facilities, Health Services, Canteen

Special Facilities: Earth Sciences Museum. Biological Garden. Experimental Station (In Sahara, Beni Abbes)

Libraries: Central Library, c. 30,000 vols; libraries of the institutes

Academic Staff *1999:* Total: c. 1,365

Student Numbers *1999:* Total: c. 19,340

• UNIVERSITY 'BADJI MOKHTAR'-ANNABA
Université 'Badji Mokhtar'-Annaba
B.P. 12, Route El Hadjar, Annaba 23000
Tel: +213(8) 87-24-10   +213(8) 83-34-29
Fax: +213(8) 87-24-36
Telex: 81847 uarto dz
EMail: rectorat@univ-annaba.net
Website: http://www.univ-annaba.net

Recteur: Mourad Barkat Tel: +213(8) 87-24-10

Secrétaire général: Kamel Ghilassi Tel: +213(8) 87-15-19
Fax: +213(8) 87-15-19

Faculties
Earth Sciences and Agronomy *(El Tarf)* (Agronomy; Earth Sciences; Geology; Hydraulic Engineering; Mining Engineering; Regional Planning) *Dean:* Rachid Ouzrout
Economics and Management *(Sidi Achour)* (Communication Studies; Economics; Finance; Management) *Dean:* Mahfoud Benosmane
Engineering *(Sidi Amar)* (Architecture; Civil Engineering; Electronic Engineering; Materials Engineering; Mechanical Engineering; Production Engineering) *Dean:* Nasr-Eddine Debbache
Law *(Annaba)* (Political Science; Private Law; Public Law) *Dean:* Lakhdar Boukhil
Letters, Humanities and Social Sciences *(Annaba)* (Arabic; Arts and Humanities; Modern Languages; Psychology; Sociology; Translation and Interpretation) *Dean:* Mohamed Aïlane
Medicine *(Annaba)* (Medicine; Pharmacy; Stomatology) *Dean:* Abdesslem Kaïdi
Science *(Sidi Amar)* (Biochemistry; Biology; Chemistry; Computer Science; Marine Science and Oceanography; Mathematics; Physics) *Dean:* Fatma-Zohra Nouri

Research Centres
Entrepreneurial Training (Management)
Environment and Pollution (Environmental Studies)
Industrial Health
Materials Science (Materials Engineering)

History: Founded 1971 as Institute of Mining and Metallurgy, acquired present status 1998.
Governing Bodies: Conseil d'Université; Conseil scientifique
Academic Year: September to July (September-February; March-July)
Admission Requirements: Secondary school certificate (baccalauréat) or foreign equivalent
Fees: (Dinars): c. 65 per annum
Main Language(s) of Instruction: Arabic, French
International Co-operation: University of Nouakchott; Université de Lausanne; Ain Shams University; Université du Droit et de la Santé (Lille II); University of Siegen
Accrediting Agencies: Ministry of Higher Education and Scientific Research
Degrees and Diplomas: *Diplôme de Technicien supérieur:* 2-5 yrs; *Diplôme d'Etudes universitaires appliquées (DEUA):* 3 yrs; *Diplôme d'Etudes supérieures (DES):* 4 yrs; *Diplôme d'Ingénieur:* 5 yrs; *Licence:* 4 yrs; *Magister:* a further 2 yrs; *Doctorat d'Etat:* a further 4 yrs

Student Services: Cultural Centre, Sports Facilities, Handicapped Facilities, Health Services, Canteen
Student Residential Facilities: Yes
Libraries: Central Library, c. 200,000 vols; libraries of the Institutes
Publications: El Tawassol (biannually); Synthèse
Academic Staff *1999:* Full-Time: c. 1,230 Part-Time: c. 330 Total: c. 1,560
Staff with Doctorate: Total: c. 360
Student Numbers *1999:* All (Foreign Included): c. 22,870 Foreign Only: c. 130

UNIVERSITY OF BATNA
Université de Batna
1, avenue Chahid Boukhlouf Med El Hadi, Batna 05000
Tel: +213(33) 81-47-07
Fax: +213(33) 81-24-80
EMail: webmaster@univ-batna.dz
Website: http://www.univ-batna.dz

Recteur: Mohamed Laabassi

Secrétaire général: Rachid Marazguia

International Relations: Rachid Marazguia
Fax: +213(4) 86-00-39

Faculties
Economics and Management (Economics; Management)
Engineering
Law
Letters and Humanities (Arts and Humanities)
Medicine (Health Sciences; Medicine)
Science (Mathematics; Natural Sciences; Physics)
Social Sciences and Islamic Sciences (Islamic Studies; Social Sciences)

History: Founded 1989. Acquired present status and title 1990.
Degrees and Diplomas: *Diplôme d'Etudes universitaires appliquées (DEUA); Diplôme d'Ingénieur, Licence; Diplôme de Docteur:* Veterinary Medicine, 5 yrs; Medicine, 6 yrs; *Magister*
Libraries: Central University Library
Press or Publishing House: University of Batna Press
Student Numbers *1999:* Total: c. 13,350

UNIVERSITY OF BÉJAÏA
Université de Béjaïa
Route de Targua Ouzemour, Béjaïa 06000
Tel: +213(34) 21-43-33
Fax: +213(34) 21-43-32
EMail: infobei@univbei.dz
Website: http://www.univbej.dz

Recteur: Djoudi Merabet

Secrétaire général: Brahim Mira

Faculties
Law and Economics (Business and Commerce; Economics; Law; Management) *Dean:* Hamid Kherbachi

Letters and Humanities (Arabic; Arts and Humanities; English; French; Literature; Modern Languages; Oriental Languages) *Dean*: Farida Boualit

Science and Engineering (Biological and Life Sciences; Biology; Chemistry; Civil Engineering; Computer Science; Demography and Population; Electronic Engineering; Food Science; Hydraulic Engineering; Mathematics; Mechanical Engineering; Operations Research; Physics; Production Engineering) *Dean*: Boualem Saidani

History: Founded 1983 as Centre universitaire de Béjaia. Acquired present status 1998.

Student Numbers *1999:* Total: c. 3,900

UNIVERSITY OF BISKRA 'MOHAMED KHIDER'
Université de Biskra 'Mohamed Khider'
B.P. 145, Biskra
Tel: +213(33) 74-83-68
Fax: +213(33) 74-07-30
Telex: 88094
EMail: noureddine@ist.cerist.dz

Institutes
Architecture
Development of Saharan Agronomy (Agronomy)
Electronics (Electronic Engineering)
Hydraulics (Hydraulic Engineering)

UNIVERSITY OF BLIDA
Université de Blida
B.P. 270, Route de Soumaa, Blida
Tel: +213(25) 41-10-00
Fax: +213(25) 41-78-13
Telex: 72970
Website: http://www.univ-blida.edu.dz
Recteur: Zineddine Youbi **EMail:** zyoubi@wissal.dz

Faculties
Agro-Veterinary Science (Agronomy; Biology; Veterinary Science)
Economics
Engineering (Aeronautical and Aerospace Engineering; Architecture; Civil Engineering; Electronic Engineering; Engineering; Industrial Chemistry; Mechanical Engineering)
Exact Sciences (Chemistry; Computer Science; Mathematics; Physics)
Law
Medicine (Medicine; Stomatology)
Sociology and Modern Languages (Arabic; English; French; Italian; Modern Languages; Sociology)

History: Founded 1981.
Publications: Revue de l'Université
Academic Staff *1999:* Total: c. 650
Student Numbers *1999:* Total: c. 8,000

UNIVERSITY M'HAMMED BOUGUERRA OF BOUMERDÈS
Université M'hamed Bouguerra de Boumerdès
Avenue de l'Indépendance, Boumerdès 35000
Tel: +213(24) 81-69-01
Fax: +213(24) 81-69-01
Website: http://www.univ-boumerdes-dz.net

Faculties
Engineering
Hydrocarburates and Chemistry (Automation and Control Engineering; Chemical Engineering; Geophysics; Industrial Management; Mining Engineering; Petroleum and Gas Engineering)
Science (Biology; Chemistry; Computer Science; English; Finance; Management; Mathematics; Physics; Private Law; Public Law; Science Education)

History: Founded 1981.

• MENTOURI UNIVERSITY OF CONSTANTINE
Université Mentouri Constantine
BP 325, Route Aïn-El-Bey, Constantine 25000
Tel: +213(31) 61-43-48
Fax: +213(31) 61-43-49
Telex: 92436 unczl dz
EMail: univ-constantine@fr.fm
Website: http://www.univ-constantine.dz
Recteur: Mourad Bensari (1992-)
EMail: constantine@ist.cerist.dz
Secrétaire général: Fodil Belaouira Tel: +213(4) 92-57-79
International Relations: Fouzia Bensouiki
Tel: +213(4) 92-61-81 Fax: +213(4) 92-52-57

Faculties
Earth Sciences, Geography and Regional Planning (Architecture; Earth Sciences; Geography; Regional Planning; Town Planning)
Economics and Management (Economics; Management)
Engineering (Civil Engineering; Computer Engineering; Electronic Engineering; Industrial Chemistry; Mechanical Engineering; Meteorology)
Humanities and Social Sciences (Arts and Humanities; History; Library Science; Philosophy; Physical Education; Psychology; Social Sciences; Sociology)
Languages and Literature (Arabic; Literature; Modern Languages; Translation and Interpretation)
Law (Law; Private Law; Public Law)
Medicine (Medicine; Pharmacy; Stomatology)
Science (Chemistry; Mathematics; Natural Sciences; Nutrition; Physics; Veterinary Science)

Further Information: Also Audiovisual Centre

History: Founded 1961 as Centre universitaire attached to the University of Algiers, acquired present status 1969.

Governing Bodies: Conseil universitaire

Academic Year: September to June (September-January; February-June)

Admission Requirements: Secondary school certificate (baccalauréat)

Main Language(s) of Instruction: Arabic, French, English

Accrediting Agencies: Ministry of Higher Education and Scientific Research

Degrees and Diplomas: *Diplôme d'Etudes universitaires appliquées (DEUA):* 3 yrs; *Diplôme d'Etudes supérieures (DES):* 4 yrs; *Diplôme d'Ingénieur:* Architecture; *Licence; Magister:* a further 2 yrs; *Doctorat d'Etat:* 4 yrs; *Médecine vétérinaire,* veterinary medicine, 5 yrs

Student Residential Facilities: Yes

Libraries: Central Library, 260,000 vols

Academic Staff *1999:* Total: c. 1,510

Student Numbers *1999:* Total: c. 27,480

• UNIVERSITY FOR ISLAMIC SCIENCES 'EMIR ABDELKADER' CONSTANTINE

Université des Sciences Islamiques 'Emir Abdelkader'
B.P.137, Constantine 25000
Tel: +213(31) 93-92-92
Fax: +213(31) 93-80-73
EMail: usieak1@ist.cerist.dz

Recteur: A. Boukhelkhal (1998-)

Secrétaire général: A. Krada

Institutes
Daawa and Oussoul Eddine
Islamic Civilization (Islamic Studies)
Islamic Law
Islamic Sciences

History: Founded 1984.

Academic Year: September to June (September-February; February-June)

Admission Requirements: Secondary school certificate (baccalauréat)

Fees: None

Main Language(s) of Instruction: Arabic

Degrees and Diplomas: *Licence:* 4 yrs; *Magister:* a further 2 yrs; *Doctorat d'Etat:* a further 2 yrs

Student Residential Facilities: Yes

Libraries: University library, c. 10 000 vols

Publications: Revue de l'Université (biannually)

Press or Publishing House: University Emir Abdelkader Press

Academic Staff *1999:* Total: c. 80

Student Numbers *1999:* All (Foreign Included): c. 1,970 Foreign Only: c. 10

12

UNIVERSITY OF GUELMA (8 MAY 1945)

Université de Guelma (8 Mai 1945)
Guelma
Tel: +213(37) 20-72-68
Fax: +213(37) 20-87-58
Telex: 85912 INES.G

Institutes
Civil Engineering
Industrial Chemistry
Mechanical Engineering

UNIVERSITY CENTRE OF JIJEL 'ABDELHAK BENHAMMOUDA'

Centre Universitaire de Jijel 'Abdelhak Benhammouda'
B.P. 98 Ouled Aissa, Jijel
Tel: +213(5) 49-80-16
Fax: +213(5) 49-55-78
Website: http://www.univ-jijel.dz/

Departments
Economics (Economics; International Business; Management; Production Engineering)
Law (Administration; Law)

Institutes
Biology (Agronomy; Biochemistry; Biology; Microbiology)
Computer Science
Exact Sciences (Chemistry; Mathematics; Physics)
Technology (Automation and Control Engineering; Civil Engineering; Electrical Engineering; Electronic Engineering; Geological Engineering; Industrial Chemistry; Machine Building)

UNIVERSITY CENTRE OF LAGHOUAT 'AMAR TELIDJI'

Centre Universitaire 'Amar Telidji' (CUAT)
Laghouat
Website: http://www.lagh-univ.dz

Directeur: Ahmed Aouissi

Departments
Arab Literature (Arabic; Literature)
Biology
Computer Science
Industrial Chemistry
Law
Psychology

Institutes
Civil Engineering
Economics
Electrical Engineering
Mechanical Engineering

UNIVERSITY OF MOSTAGANEM
Université de Mostaganem
B.P. 227, Mostaganem
Tel: +213(45) 26-46-60
Fax: +213(45) 26-46-62
EMail: cumosta@elbahia.cerist.dz
Website: http://www.univ-mosta.dz

Faculties
Arts and Letters (Arabic; Arts and Humanities; English; French; Literature)
Law and Commerce (Administration; Business and Commerce; Law)
Science (Agriculture; Biology; Building Technologies; Chemistry; Civil Engineering; Computer Science; Electronic Engineering; Mathematics; Mechanical Engineering; Natural Sciences; Physics; Technology)
Social Sciences and Physical Training (Physical Education; Social Sciences)

Schools
Public Works

History: Founded 1977.

UNIVERSITY CENTRE OF M'SILA 'MOHAMED BOUDIAF'
Centre Universitaire de M'sila 'Mohamed Boudiaf'
B.P. 166 Draa El Hadjar, M'sila
Tel: +231(5) 54-04-04
Fax: +231(5) 55-04-11
Telex: 92807
EMail: cubmsila@ist.cerist.dz

Institutes
Civil Engineering
Management of Urban Techniques (Town Planning; Urban Studies)
Mechanical Engineering

• UNIVERSITY OF ORAN ES-SENIA
Université d'Oran Es-Senia
B.P. 1524, Oran El-Manaouer 31000
Tel: +213(41) 41-96-51
Fax: +213(41) 33-72-16   +213(41) 38-86-72
Telex: 22993 unirex dz
Website: http://www.univ-oran.dz

Recteur: Abdelkader Derbal
Secrétaire général: Abdelkader Bekada
International Relations: Abdelbaki Benziane

Faculties
Earth Sciences, Geography and Regional Planning (Earth Sciences; Geography; Regional Planning)
Economics, Management and Commerce (Business and Commerce; Economics; Management) *students:* 5,178

Humanities and Islamic Civilization (Arts and Humanities; History; Islamic Studies; Library Science) *students:* 2,235
Law (Law; Political Science; Private Law; Public Law)
Letters, Languages and Arts (Arabic; Arts and Humanities; Literature; Modern Languages) *students:* 7,079
Medicine (Medicine; Pharmacy; Stomatology)
Science (Chemistry; Computer Science; Industrial Maintenance; Maintenance Technology; Mathematics; Natural Sciences; Physics) *students:* 1,543
Social Sciences (Demography and Population; Philosophy; Psychology; Social Sciences; Sociology) *students:* 2,135

History: Founded 1961 as Centre universitaire d'Oran attached to the University of Algiers. Acquired present status and title 1966.
Academic Year: October to July (October-February; March-July)
Admission Requirements: Secondary school certificate (baccalauréat)
Main Language(s) of Instruction: Arabic, French
Degrees and Diplomas: *Certificat de Capacité en Droit*: 2 yrs; *Diplôme*: Pharmacy, 5 yrs; Medicine, 6 yrs; *Licence*: 4 yrs
Academic Staff *1999:* Total: c. 1,000
Student Numbers *1999:* Total: c. 22,000

• UNIVERSITY OF SCIENCE AND TECHNOLOGY OF ORAN
Université des Sciences et de la Technologie d'Oran
B.P.1505, El M'Naouer, Oran 31000
Tel: +213(41) 35-58-72
Fax: +213(41) 45-15-81
Telex: 22701
Website: http://www.univ-usto.dz

Recteur: Mohamed Mebarki
Secrétaire général: Ahmed S. Benziane

Institutes
Applied Biology (Biology)
Applied Geology (Geology)
Architecture
Civil Engineering
Computer Science
Electronics (Electronic Engineering)
Electrotechnology (Electronic Engineering)
Hydraulics (Hydraulic Engineering)
Industrial Chemistry
Marine Engineering
Mechanical Engineering
Metallurgy (Metallurgical Engineering)
Technology

History: Founded 1975.
Academic Year: September to June
Admission Requirements: Secondary school certificate (baccalauréat) or equivalent
Main Language(s) of Instruction: French

13

Accrediting Agencies: Ministry of Higher Education and Scientific Research

Degrees and Diplomas: *Diplôme d'Etudes universitaires appliquées (DEUA)*; *Diplôme d'Ingénieur*; *Magister*

Student Residential Facilities: Yes

Student Numbers *1999:* Total: c. 10,000

UNIVERSITY CENTRE OF OUARGLA

Centre Universitaire de Ouargla (CUO)
Route de Ghardaia, Ouargla
Tel: +213(29) 71-24-68
Fax: +213(29) 71-51-61
Website: http://www.ouargla-univ.dz

Directeur: Mohamed El-Khames Tidjani

Institutes

Economics and Management (Economics; Management) *Director*: Mohammed Djemoi Korichi

Exact Sciences (Computer Science; Mathematics; Physics; Science Education) *Director*: B. Dadamoussa

Hydraulics (Hydraulic Engineering) *Director*: Abdelwahed Kriker

Industrial Chemistry *Director*: Mohamed Ridha Ouahrani

Letters and Languages (Literature; Modern Languages) *Director*: Salah Khennour

Saharan Agronomy (Agronomy) *Director*: Mohammed Tahar Halilat

Social Sciences and Humanities (Arts and Humanities; Social Sciences) *Director*: Nasreddine Semar

UNIVERSITY CENTRE OF OUM EL BOUAGHI

Centre Universitaire d'Oum El Bouaghi
B.P. 358, Oum El Bouaghi 04000
Tel: +213(4) 42-10-51
Fax: +213(4) 48-52-50
Telex: 94149 DZ

Directeur général: Ali Khelil

Secrétaire général: Mostepha Amokrane

Colleges
Teacher Training

Institutes
Agronomy
Analytical Chemistry (Analytical Chemistry; Chemistry)
Electrotechnology (Electronic Engineering)
Mechanical Engineering

History: Founded 1983.

Student Numbers *1999:* Total: c. 3,200

UNIVERSITY FERHAT ABBAS, SÉTIF

Université Ferhat Abbas, Sétif
Cité Mabouda, Sétif 19000
Tel: +213(36) 90-88-93
Fax: +213(36) 90-38-79
Telex: 86077 unset dz

Recteur: Djafer Benachour (1993-)

Secrétaire général: Nadjib Bouguessa

Faculties

Economics and Management (Business and Commerce; Economics; Management)

Engineering (Architecture; Civil Engineering; Computer Science; Electronic Engineering; Engineering; Industrial Chemistry; Measurement and Precision Engineering)

Law (Law; Private Law; Public Law)

Medical Sciences (Medicine; Pharmacy)

Sciences (Biology; Chemistry; Mathematics; Physics)

Social Sciences and Letters (Arabic; Arts and Humanities; Modern Languages; Psychology; Social Sciences; Sociology)

History: Founded 1978 as Centre Universitaire, acquired present status and title 1985. The institutes are financially autonomous but maintain a joint structure presided over by a Conseil de Coordination.

Academic Year: September to June (September-January; March-June)

Admission Requirements: Secondary school certificate (baccalauréat)

Main Language(s) of Instruction: Arabic, French

Accrediting Agencies: Ministry of Higher Education and Scientific Research

Degrees and Diplomas: *Diplôme d'Etudes supérieures (DES)*: 4 yrs; *Diplôme d'Ingénieur*: 5 yrs; *Licence*: 4 yrs; *Magister*: 2 yrs after Licence

Student Residential Facilities: Yes

Libraries: c. 100,000 vols

Academic Staff *1999:* Total: c. 800

Student Numbers *1999:* Total: c. 18,500

UNIVERSITY OF SIDI-BEL-ABBÈS

Université de Sidi-Bel-Abbès
Sidi-Bel-Abbès
Website: http://www.univ-sba.dz

Faculties
Economics
Engineering (Civil Engineering; Engineering)
Law
Letters and Humanities (Arts and Humanities; Literature)
Medicine
Science (Biology; Chemistry; Mathematics; Natural Sciences; Physics) *Directeur*: A. Berlabi

Institutes
Mechanical Engineering

UNIVERSITY OF SKIKDA

Université de Skikda
Porte des Aurès, Skikda
Tel: +213(8) 95-94-05
Fax: +213(8) 75-51-78

UNIVERSITY CENTRE OF TEBESSA 'LARBI TEBESSI'

Centre Universitaire de Tebessa 'Larbi Tebessi'
B.P. 289 Route de Constantine, Tebessa
Tel: +213(37) 48-44-38
Fax: +231(37) 48-44-56
Telex: 95133
EMail: cutebessa@ist.cerist.dz

Institutes
Civil Engineering
Earth Sciences
Mining Engineering

Research Centres
Minerals *(URMFB)* (Mineralogy)

UNIVERSITY CENTRE OF TIARET

Centre Universitaire de Tiaret
B.P. 78, Tiaret 14000
Tel: +213(7) 42-42-13
Fax: +213(7) 42-41-47
EMail: cut@ist.cerist.dz
Website: http://www.wtiaret.gov.dz/univ.htm
Directeur général: Nassredine Hadj Zoubir

Departments
Accountancy and Taxation (Accountancy; Taxation)
Agricultural Engineering
Arabic Language and Literature (Arabic)
Commerce and Economics (Business and Commerce; Economics)
Computer Science
Hydrology (Water Science)
Juridical Sciences and Administration (Administration; Law)
Natural and Life Sciences (Biological and Life Sciences; Natural Sciences)
Physics
Production Management (Industrial and Production Economics)

Institutes
Agronomy (Agronomy; Biology)
Civil Engineering
Electrotechnology (Electronic Engineering)
Veterinary Science

History: Founded 1980 as Institut national d'Enseignement supérieur de Tiaret, acquired present status and title 1992.
Main Language(s) of Instruction: Arabic, French
Accrediting Agencies: Ministry of Higher Education and Scientific Research

Degrees and Diplomas: *Diplôme d'Etudes universitaires appliquées (DEUA)*: 3 yrs; *Diplôme d'Etudes supérieures (DES)*: 4 yrs; *Diplôme d'Ingénieur*: 5 yrs; *Licence*: 4 yrs; *Magister*

UNIVERSITY 'MOULOUD MAMMERI' TIZI-OUZOU

Université 'Mouloud Mammeri' Tizi-Ouzou (UMMTO)
Hasnaoua, Tizi-Ouzou
Tel: +213(26) 40-56-51
Fax: +213(26) 21-29-68
Telex: 76079 unive dz
Recteur: Rabah Kahlouche
Vice-Recteur: Idir Ahmed Zaid

Faculties
Arts and Humanities *Dean*: Rabah Kalouche
Economics and Management (Economics; Management) *Dean*: Chaabane Bya
Engineering *Dean*: Soltane Ameur
Law *Dean*: Mohand Said Djaafour
Medicine *Dean*: Hocine Ait Ali
Sciences (Mathematics; Natural Sciences) *Dean*: Omar Lamrous

History: Founded 1977 as University Centre of Tizi-Ouzou, acquired present status and title 1989.
Academic Year: September to June (September-January; February-June)
Admission Requirements: Secondary school certificate (baccalauréat) and entrance examination
Main Language(s) of Instruction: Arabic, French
Accrediting Agencies: Ministry of Higher Education and Scientific Research
Degrees and Diplomas: *Diplôme d'Etudes supérieures (DES)*; *Diplôme d'Ingénieur*; *Licence*; *Magister*; *Doctorat d'Etat*: Medicine (University of Algiers)
Libraries: Central Library; libraries of the institutes
Academic Staff *1999:* Total: c. 470
Student Numbers *1999:* Total: c. 4,700

UNIVERSITY 'ABOU BEKR BELKAID' TLEMCEN

Université 'Abou Bekr Belkaid' Tlemcen
B.P. 119, 22 rue Abi Ayed Abdelkrim, Faubourg Pasteur, Tlemcen 13000
Tel: +213(7) 20-23-36
Fax: +213(7) 27-15-03
Telex: uv.tlm/ 18971
Website: http://www.univ-tlemcen.dz
Recteur: Zoubir Chaouche-Ramdane (1990-)
Secrétaire général: Abdeldjellil Sari-Ali
Tel: +213(7) 20-64-32 Fax: +213(7) 20-64-32
International Relations: Sidi-Mohamed Bouchnak Kheladi
Tel: +213(7) 20-16-31 Fax: +213(7) 20-16-31

Faculties
Arabic Language and Literature (Arabic; Literature)
Economics and Management (Economics; Management)
Engineering
Law
Medical Sciences (Medicine)

Departments
Earth Sciences
Technology

History: Founded as Centre universitaire de Tlemcen 1974, acquired present status 1989 and title 1998.

Governing Bodies: Scientific Council

Academic Year: September to July (September-December; January-March; April-July)

Admission Requirements: Secondary school certificate (baccalauréat) or equivalent

Fees: (Dinars): 50 per annum

Main Language(s) of Instruction: Arabic, French

International Co-operation: University of Alexandria; Yarmouk University; University of Irak; University Mohamed I, Oujda; University of Mosul; University of Fès; University of Marrakech; University of Sfax; University of Tunis; University of Lyon I; University of Aix-Marseilles II; University of Rennes; University of Strasbourg I; University of Paris VII; University of Paris X; University of Trieste; University of Mansourah

Accrediting Agencies: Ministry of Higher Education and Scientific Research

Degrees and Diplomas: *Diplôme d'Etudes universitaires appliquées (DEUA)*: 3 yrs; *Diplôme d'Etudes supérieures (DES)*: 4 yrs; *Diplôme d'Ingénieur*: 5 yrs; *Licence*: 4 yrs; *Diplôme de Docteur*. Medicine, 6 yrs; *Magister*: 2-3 yrs and thesis; *Doctorat d'Etat*: by thesis

Student Services: Sports Facilities, Health Services, Canteen

Student Residential Facilities: For c. 5 300 students

Libraries: Libraries of the Institutes

Publications: Arabic Literature Magazine (biannually); Popular Culture Magazine

Academic Staff *1999:* Total: c. 630

Student Numbers *1999:* All (Foreign Included): c. 11,370 Foreign Only: c. 100

MUSTAPHA STOMBOULI UNIVERSITY CENTRE WILAYA DE MASCARA
Centre Universitaire Mustapha Stombouli
B.P. 763, Wilaya de Mascara 29000
Tel: +231(6) 80-41-68
Fax: +231(6) 80-41-64
Website: http://www.cuniv-mascara.edu.dz

Institutes
Agronomy
Biology
Biology *(short cycle)*
Computer Science
History
Hydraulics (Hydraulic Engineering)

Law and Administration (Administration; Law)
Management
Management Informatics (Computer Science; Management)
Mechanical Engineering

OTHER INSTITUTIONS

ECOLE NATIONALE D'ADMINISTRATION (ENA)
Alger
EMail: ena@wissel.dz
Website: http://www.cerist.dz/ena

Programmes
Economics and Finance (Economics; Finance)
International Institutions (International Relations)
Law (Private Law; Public Law)
Public Administration

ECOLE NATIONALE POLYTECHNIQUE
10, Avenue Hassen Badi El Harrach, Alger
Tel: +213(21) 52-14-94
Fax: +213(21) 52-29-73
EMail: ENP@ist.cerist.dz
Website: http://www.enp.edu.dz

Departments
Basic Science (Science Education) *Head*: M. Ouadjaout
Chemical Engineering *Head*: Toudert Ahmed Zaïd
Civil Engineering *Head*: Saadi Lakhal
Electrical Engineering *Head*: Abdelouahab Mekhaldi
Electronics (Electronic Engineering; Information Management; Microwaves; Telecommunications Engineering) *Head*: Mohamed Trabelsi
Environmental Engineering *Head*: Djazia Arar
Hydraulics (Hydraulic Engineering) *Head*: Saadia Benmamar
Industrial Engineering *Head*: Nacéra Aboun
Languages (English; Modern Languages) *Head*: C. Larbes
Mechanical Engineering
Metallurgical Engineering *Head*: Med Lamine Djeghlal
Mining Engineering *Head*: Salima Chabou

ECOLE NATIONALE SUPÉRIEURE DE L'HYDRAULIQUE (ENSH)
B.P. 31, Blida 09000
Tel: +213(25) 39-94-47
Fax: +213(25) 43-80-44
EMail: miah@ensh.edu.dz
Website: http://www.ensh.edu.dz
Directeur: M.S. Benhafid

Programmes
Hydraulic Engineering and Environment (Environmental Engineering; Hydraulic Engineering)
Irrigation and Draining (Irrigation)
Non-conventional Water Re-use (Water Management; Water Science)

Urban Hydraulics (Hydraulic Engineering)
Urban Techniques (Urban Studies)

ECOLE NATIONALE DES TRAVAUX PUBLICS (ENTP)
1, rue Sidi Garidi, Vieux Kouba, Alger 16051
Tel: +213(21) 28-68-38
Fax: +213(21) 28-87-61
Website: http://www.entp.edu.dz

Programmes
Computer Science
Economics and Management (Economics; Management)
Hydraulics (Hydraulic Engineering)
Public Works (Civil Engineering)
Transport (Transport and Communications)

ECOLE NATIONALE VÉTÉRINAIRE
BP 161, Avenue Pasteur , El-Harrach, Alger
Tel: +213(21) 76-67-81
Fax: +213(21) 52-59-04
Veterinary Science

History: Founded 1974.

ECOLE NORMALE SUPÉRIEURE
Kouba, Alger
Education; Teacher Training

ECOLE NORMALE SUPÉRIEURE D'ENSEIGNEMENT TECHNIQUE (ENSET)
B.P. 1523 El-M'naouer, Oran
Tel: +213(41) 41-97-19
Fax: +213(41) 41-64-30
Website: http://www.enset-oran.dz
Directeur: Abdelbaki Benziane

Departments
Civil Engineering
Electrical Engineering
Exact Sciences (Mathematics; Physics)
Mechanical Engineering

History: Founded 1970 as Ecole Normale Supérieure d'Enseignement polytechnique, became Ecole Normale Supérieure de l'Enseignement technique in 1984.

ECOLE POLYTECHNIQUE D'ARCHITECTURE ET D'URBANISME
B.P. 2, El-Harrach, Alger
Architecture; Town Planning

History: Founded 1970 attached to the Université d'Alger.

ECOLE SUPÉRIEURE DE BANQUE (ESB)
B.P. 156, Route de Baïnem Bouzaréah, Alger
Tel: +213(21) 90-29-29
Fax: +213(21) 90-43-16
Website: http://www.esb.edu.dz

Programmes
Banking

INSTITUT NATIONAL AGRONOMIQUE
1, avenue Pasteur, El-Harrach, Alger
Tel: +213(21) 76-19-87
Telex: 54802 ina dz
Agronomy

History: Founded 1905, acquired present title 1966.

INSTITUT NATIONAL D'INFORMATIQUE (INI)
B.P. 68M Oued Smar El Harrach, Alger
Tel: +213(21) 51-60-77
Fax: +213(21) 51-61-56
Website: http://www.ini.dz
Directeur: Abderrazak Henni **EMail:** henni@ini.dz
Secrétaire générale: Hassina Brahimi
EMail: h_brahimi@ini.dz

Programmes
Computer Science

INSTITUT NATIONAL DE LA MAGISTRATURE (INM)
Boulevard du 11 Décembre 1960 El Biar, Alger
Tel: +213(21) 91-51-92
Fax: +213(21) 91-52-01
EMail: inm@inm-dz.org
Website: http://www.inm-dz.org

Programmes
Law (Administrative Law; Commercial Law; Law)

INSTITUT DE TÉLÉCOMMUNICATIONS D'ORAN
Es-Senia, Oran
Telecommunications Engineering

History: Founded 1971.

Angola

INSTITUTION TYPES AND CREDENTIALS

Types of higher education institutions:

Universidade (University)
Instituto (Institute)

School leaving and higher education credentials:

Habilitações Literárias
Bacharel
Licenciado

STRUCTURE OF EDUCATION SYSTEM

Pre-higher education:

Duration of compulsory education:

Age of entry: 6
Age of exit: 10

Structure of school system:

Basic
Type of school providing this education: Ensino de Base
Length of programme in years: 8
Age level from: 6 to: 14

General Secondary
Type of school providing this education: Ensino medio
Length of programme in years: 3
Age level from: 14 to: 17
Certificate/diploma awarded: Habilitações Literarias (Secondary School Leaving Certificate)

Vocational Secondary
Type of school providing this education: Ensino Medio
Length of programme in years: 4
Age level from: 14 to: 18
Certificate/diploma awarded: Habilitações Literarias (Secondary School Leaving Certificate)

Pre-university
Type of school providing this education: Specialized Schools

Length of programme in years: 3
Age level from: 15 to: 18

School education:

Basic education lasts for eight years. Secondary education or Ensino Medio is either a three year general course or a four-year technical/vocational course culminating in the Habilitaçãos Literárias. There are also two- to three-year specialized pre-university courses running parallely. A reform to be established between 1995 and 2005 foresees a primary education of six years followed by a secondary education of six to seven years, divided into two cycles of three years each for the general course and three and four years for the technical/vocational course.

Higher education:

There is one State university, the Universidade Agostinho Neto. Founded in 1962 as Estudios Gerais Universitarios. It became the University of Luanda in 1968, the University of Angola in 1976, and acquired its present title 1985. It is closely ruled by the government. The Rector is appointed by the President of the Republic and the directors of faculties and schools are appointed by the Minister of Education on the Rector's recommendation. The University is financially supported by public funds and its management follows the public administration pattern. It is autonomous and is responsible to the Ministry of Education. Its governing body is the University Council. Recently, a private institution, the Universidade Católica de Angola, has been established. There are also teacher training institutes.

Main laws/decrees governing higher education:

Decree: No. 3/92   Year: 1991
Concerns: Management of higher education institutions

Academic year:

Classes from: October *to:* July

Languages of instruction:

Portuguese

Stages of studies:

University level studies:

University level first stage: Bacharel:
The title of Bacharel is obtained after three years' study. It is a terminal degree which may be followed by two years' study leading to the Licenciatura.

University level second stage:
The title of Licenciado is obtained after five years' study, or two years after the Bacharel. In Medicine, it is conferred after six years. The proposed reform foresees a two-cycle programme leading to a Bacharelato after three years and to the title of Licenciado after two more years, as well as a further stage leading to a Mestre and a Doctorate

University level third stage: Postgraduate:
A proposed reform foresees a postgraduate stage leading to a Mestre and a Doctorate

Teacher education:

Training of pre-primary and primary/basic school teachers
Primary school teachers are trained in two years in primary teacher training centres for first level primary teachers and in Institutos Medios Normales (IMN) where studies last for four years.

Training of secondary school teachers
Teachers for the first cycle of secondary education are trained in teacher training schools. They receive the title of Magistério Primário. There are also physical education schools.
Second cycle secondary school teachers are trained at the Instituto Superior de Ciências de Educação (ISCED) of the University. Courses last for five years, the last (estagio) being spent in classroom practice and writing a dissertation. Secondary school teachers must hold a Bachalerato or Licenciatura.

Training of higher education teachers
Higher education teachers are trained at the University. Studies last for five years and lead to the Licenciatura.

Non-traditional studies:

Distance higher education
There are distance education programmes to upgrade unqualified teachers offered by the Instituto Superior de Ciências de Educação. Students sit for examinations at the University.
Teachers can also follow distance education courses to upgrade their professional training.

NATIONAL BODIES

Responsible authorities:

Ministry of Education and Culture
    Minister: Antonio Burity Da Silva Neto
    Caixa postal 1451 Rua Comandante Gika
    Luanda
    Tel: +211(2) 32-33-26
    Fax: +244(2) 32-15-92 +244(2) 32-11-18

ADMISSIONS TO HIGHER EDUCATION

Admission to university-level studies

Name of secondary school credential required: Habilitações Literárias

Entrance exams required: Entrance examination

Other admission requirements: Period of State employment or pre-university education

Foreign students admission

Admission requirements: Secondary-school-leaving certificate equivalent to the Habilitações Literárias and success in the entrance examination

Language requirements: Good knowledge of Portuguese

GRADING SYSTEM

Usual grading system in secondary school

Full Description: 0-20
Highest on scale: 20
Pass/fail level: 10
Lowest on scale: 0

NOTES ON HIGHER EDUCATION SYSTEM

Data for academic year: 2000-2001
Source: International Association of Universities (IAU), updated from IBE website, 2001

INSTITUTIONS OF HIGHER EDUCATION

UNIVERSITIES

CATHOLIC UNIVERSITY OF ANGOLA, LUANDA
Universidade Católica de Angola (UCAN)
Rua N. Sra da Maxima 29, Luanda
Tel: +244(2) 331-973
Fax: +244(2) 398-759
EMail: info@ucan.edu
Website: http://www.ucan.edu
Reitor: Joao Sebastiao Teta
Vice-Reitor: Filomeno Vieira Dias

Faculties
Computer Science
Economics
Law
Management

• UNIVERSITY AGOSTINHO NETO
Universidade Agostinho Neto
Caixa postal 815-C, Avenida 4 de Fevereiro 7, Luanda
Tel: +244(2) 332-089
Fax: +244(2) 330-520
Telex: (0991) 3076 univela an
Website: http://www.uan.ao
Reitor: José Luis Guerra Marques
Vice-Reitor: Kianvo Tamo

Faculties
Agrarian Sciences *(Huambo)* (Agriculture)
Economy (Accountancy; Economics; Finance)

Engineering (Architecture; Chemical Engineering; Civil Engineering; Electronic Engineering; Engineering; Mining Engineering)
Jurisprudence (Law)
Medicine
Sciences (Biology; Chemistry; Engineering; Geophysics; Mathematics; Physics)

Higher Institutes
Educational Sciences *(Benguela)*
Educational Sciences *(Luanda)*
Educational Sciences *(Lubango)* (Biology; Chemistry; Educational Sciences; English; French; Geography; Mathematics Education; Modern Languages; Pedagogy; Philosophy; Physics; Portuguese; Psychology)

Centres
National Scientific Investigation

History: Founded 1963 as Estudos Gerais Universitários, became University of Luanda 1968, University of Angola 1976 and acquired present title 1985. An autonomous State institution.
Governing Bodies: Conselho Universitário
Academic Year: October to June (October-February; March-June)
Admission Requirements: Secondary school certificate and entrance examination
Main Language(s) of Instruction: Portuguese
Degrees and Diplomas: *Bacharel*: 3 yrs; *Licenciado*: 5 yrs; Medicine, 6 yrs
Student Residential Facilities: Yes
Special Facilities: Geology Museum; Archaeology Museum
Libraries: Central Library, 8000 vols; libraries of the faculty
Academic Staff *1999:* Total: c. 715
Student Numbers *1999:* Total: c. 6,820

Benin

INSTITUTION TYPES AND CREDENTIALS

Types of higher education institutions:

Université (University)
Ecole (School)
Institut (Institute)

School leaving and higher education credentials:

Baccalauréat
Baccalauréat technique
Certificat d'Aptitude au Professorat de l'Enseignement secondaire
Diplôme d'Etudes techniques supérieures
Brevet d'Aptitude au Professorat de l'Enseignement moyen
Diplôme d'Etudes universitaires générales (DEUG)
Diplôme universitaire d'Etudes littéraires (DUEL)
Diplôme universitaire d'Etudes scientifiques (DUES)
Licence
Diplôme
Diplôme d'Ingénieur agronome
Ingénieur
Maîtrise
Doctorat en Médecine
Diplôme d'Etudes approfondies (DEA)
Diplôme d'Etudes supérieures spécialisées (DESS)

STRUCTURE OF EDUCATION SYSTEM

Pre-higher education:

Duration of compulsory education:

   Age of entry: 6
   Age of exit: 12

Structure of school system:

   Primary
   Type of school providing this education: Primary School
   Length of programme in years: 6

Age level from: 6 to: 12

Certificate/diploma awarded: Certificat d'Etudes Primaires

First Cycle Secondary

Type of school providing this education: Etablissement d'Enseignement secondaire général

Length of programme in years: 4

Age level from: 12 to: 16

Certificate/diploma awarded: Brevet d'Etudes du premier Cycle (BEPC)

Technical Secondary

Type of school providing this education: Ecole technique (Premier cycle)

Length of programme in years: 4

Age level from: 12 to: 16

Certificate/diploma awarded: Certificat d'Aptitude professionnelle

Second Cycle Secondary

Type of school providing this education: Lycée

Length of programme in years: 3

Age level from: 16 to: 19

Certificate/diploma awarded: Baccalauréat

Technical

Type of school providing this education: Lycée technique

Length of programme in years: 3

Age level from: 16 to: 19

Certificate/diploma awarded: Baccalauréat technique; Diplôme de Technicien industriel (DTI)

School education:

Primary education lasts for six years leading to the Certificat d'Etudes primaires. Secondary education lasts for seven years, divided into two cycles: Niveau I, which lasts four years and leads to the Brevet d'Etudes du Premier Cycle and Niveau II, which lasts three years. At the end of the second cycle, pupils obtain the Baccalauréat. In technical secondary education, the first cycle leads to the Certificat d'Aptitude professionnelle (CAP) and the second cycle to the Baccalauréat technique or Diplôme de Technicien industriel. Agricultural education leads to the Brevet d'Etudes agricoles tropicales at the end of the second cycle.

Higher education:

Higher education is provided by two State universities -including one created in 2001- which group all the institutions of higher education. The universities are responsible to the Ministry of Education and Scientific Research. Institutions of higher education are autonomous as far as management is concerned. The contents of the curricula are prepared by the administrative heads and teaching staff of the institutions.

Main laws/decrees governing higher education:

Decree: Education Act   Year: 1975

Academic year:

Classes from: October *to:* July

Languages of instruction:

French

Stages of studies:

University level studies:

University level first stage: Premier Cycle:
The first phase of studies lasts for two years and leads to the Diplôme universitaire d'Etudes littéraires (DUEL), the Diplôme universitaire d'études scientifiques (DUES) and the Diplôme universitaire d'Etudes générales (DEUG) in Law and Economics. The DUEL comprises specialized work in Foreign Languages, Philosophy, Modern Languages, Linguistics, History and/or Geography. The first year of the DUES offers two main options: Pure Science and Biological Science and Geology. The second year is more specialized. In Agronomy, the Diplôme d'Ingénieur agronome is awarded after six years' study. The Diplôme d'Etudes techniques supérieures is conferred by the Collège Polytechnique Universitaire at the end of a three-year course. The qualification Ingénieur de Conception is awarded four or five years after the Baccalauréat.

University level second stage: Deuxième Cycle:
Students who hold the DUES, DUEL or DEUG may continue their studies for a further one year to obtain the Licence or two years to obtain the Maîtrise.

University level third stage: Troisième Cycle:
A year beyond the Maîtrise leads to the DEA in Management and Arts and Humanities or to the DESS in Demography and Natural Resources. In Medicine, the Doctorat de Médecine is awarded after seven years of university study.

Teacher education:

Training of pre-primary and primary/basic school teachers
Primary school teachers must hold the Brevet d'Etudes du premier Cycle and sit for an entrance examination. They train at one of the Ecoles normales intégrées (ENI). The course lasts for three years and leads to the award of the Certificat élémentaire d'Aptitude professionnelle/Certificat d'Aptitude pédagogique (CEAP/CAP).

Training of secondary school teachers
First cycle secondary school teachers are also trained at the Ecoles normales intégrées (ENI). They follow a three-year course leading to the Certificat élémentaire d'Aptitude professionnelle/Certificat d'Aptitude pédagogique (CEAP/CAP). Those who train as second-cycle teachers follow a three-year course at the Ecole normale supérieure (ENS) in Porto Novo. The first two years are spent at university where students complete the DUEL or the DUES. First-cycle secondary school teachers follow a three-year course on their return to the ENS leading to the Brevet d'Aptitude au Professorat de l'Enseignement moyen (BAPEM) and are called Professeurs adjoints. Second cycle secondary school teachers returning to the ENS complete a three-year course leading to the award of the Certificat d'Aptitude au Professorat de l'Enseignement secondaire (CAPES) and are called

Professeurs certifiés. The Institut national pour la Formation et la Recherche en Education (INFRE) offers distance courses for teachers wanting to obtain credentials in primary education such as the Certificat d'Aptitude pédagogique.

NATIONAL BODIES

Responsible authorities:

Ministry of Education and Scientific Research (Ministère de l'Education nationale et de la Recherche scientifique)

    Minister: Damien Zinsou Modéran Alahassa
    PO Box 520
    Cotonou
    Tel: +229 30-19-91
    Fax: +229 30-18-48
    WWW: http://www.un.org/french/Depts/dpi/Abidjan99/edu_benin

ADMISSIONS TO HIGHER EDUCATION

Admission to non university higher education studies

Name of secondary school credential required: Baccalauréat technique

Alternatives to credentials: Diplôme de Technicien industriel

Other admission requirements: In professional schools, portfolio and recruitment test in addition to the Baccalauréat.

Admission to university-level studies

Name of secondary school credential required: Baccalauréat

Entrance exams required: Competitive examination in some cases (professional schools)

Other admission requirements: In professional schools, portfolio.

Foreign students admission

Admission requirements: Students should hold a Secondary School Leaving Certificate (Baccalauréat) or its equivalent. For vocational education, the students' files are studied. They may have to sit for an examination.

Language requirements: Good knowledge of French is indispensable.

Application procedures:

Apply to individual institution for entry to: university

Apply to: Direction des Affaires académiques, Rectorat de l'Université nationale du Bénin
    BP 526
    Cotonou

Tel: +229 36-00-74
Fax: +229 36-00-28

Recognition of studies and qualifications:

Studies pursued in foreign countries (bodies dealing with recognition of foreign credentials):
Commission universitaire d'Orientation / Commission nationale d'Etude des Equivalences de Diplômes
PO Box 348
Cotonou
Tel: +229 30-19-91
Fax: +229 30-18-48

Multilateral agreements concerning recognition of foreign studies

Name(s) of agreement(s): Convention on the Recognition of Studies, Certificates, Diplomas, Degrees and Other Academic Qualifications in Higher Education in the African States
Year of signature: 1981

References to further information on foreign student admissions and recognition of studies

Title: Guide d'information et d'orientation pour s'inscrire à l'université nationale du Bénin
Publisher: Université nationale du Bénin

Title: Study Abroad 2000-2001
Publisher: UNESCO/IBE
Year of publication: 1999

STUDENT LIFE

Main student services at national level

Centre national des Oeuvres universitaires (CENOU)
B.P. 526
Cotonou
Tel: +229 36-00-74
Fax: +229 30-00-28

Category of services provided: Social and welfare services

Service des Etudes et de l'Orientation universitaire (SEOU)
B.P. 526
Campus universitaire d'Abomey-Calavi
Cotonou
Tel: +229 36-00-74
Fax: +229 36-00-28   +229 30-00-96

Category of services provided: Academic and career counselling services

Student expenses and financial aid

Student costs:

Home students tuition fees: Minimum: 6,500 (CFA Franc-O)

GRADING SYSTEM

Usual grading system in secondary school

Full Description: 14-20; 12-13; 10-11; 9; 0-8.
For the Baccalauréat: passable, assez bien, bien, très bien

Main grading system used by higher education institutions

Full Description: 0-20
Highest on scale: 20
Pass/fail level: 10/12
Lowest on scale: 0

NOTES ON HIGHER EDUCATION SYSTEM

Data for academic year: 2000-2001
Source: International Association of Universities (IAU), updated from IBE website, 2001

INSTITUTIONS OF HIGHER EDUCATION

UNIVERSITIES

PUBLIC INSTITUTIONS

*• ABOMEY-CALAVI UNIVERSITY

Université d'Abomey-Calavi (UAC)

BP 526, Abomey-Calavi University Campus, Abomey-Calavi
Tel: +229 36-00-74   +229 36-01-26   +229 36-01-05
Fax: +229 30-00-28   +229 30-16-38   +229 30-09-38
Telex: 5010 unb
EMail: bolory@syfed.bj.refer.org

Rector: Issifou Takpara (2001-) Tel: +229 36-00-28
Secretary-General: Sumanou Seibou Toleba
Tel: +229 36-00-53

International Relations: Bienvenu Olory Tel: +229 36-00-27
Fax: +229 30-55-50 EMail: bolory@intnet.bj

Faculties
Agronomy and Animal Husbandry (Agronomy; Animal Husbandry; Economics; Environmental Management; Food Technology; Nutrition; Rural Studies; Vegetable Production) *Dean:* Mathurin Nago, *full-time staff: 50, part-time staff: 30, students: 233*
Health Sciences *Dean:* Nazaire Padonou, *full-time staff: 84, students: 542*
Law, Economics and Political Science (Economics; Finance; Law; Management; Political Science) *Dean:* Géro Fulbert Amoussouga, *full-time staff: 70, students: 7,772*
Letters, Arts and Human Sciences (Archaeology; Arts and Humanities; Communication Studies; English; French; Geography; German; History; Linguistics; Philosophy; Sociology; Spanish) *Dean:* Ascension Boghiaho, *full-time staff: 105, part-time staff: 35, students: 5,393*
Science and Technology (Biochemistry; Biology; Chemistry; Ecology; Geology; Mathematics; Natural Sciences; Physics; Technology) *Dean:* Cyprien Gnanvo, *full-time staff: 83, part-time staff: 18, students: 2,195*

Colleges
Polytechnic (Animal Husbandry; Electronic Engineering; Energy Engineering; Mechanical Engineering; Radiology) *Director:* Paulin Yovo, *full-time staff: 94, students: 855*

Schools
Administration (Administration; Communication Studies; Finance; Management; Secretarial Studies) *Director:* Lydia Pognon, *full-time staff: 66, part-time staff: 76, students: 521*
Social Workers *(Cotonou)* (Social Work) *students: 87*
Teacher Training (ENS) *(Porto Novo)* (Teacher Training)

Institutes
Arabic Language and Islamic Culture (Arabic; Islamic Studies) *Director:* Taofiki Aminou, *students: 46*
Economics *(National, Cotonou)* (Accountancy; Banking; Business Administration; Business and Commerce; Computer Science; Demography and Population; Economics; Statistics) *Director:* Siméon Fagnisse, *full-time staff: 40, students: 549*
Mathematics and Physics *(Porto-Novo)* (Mathematics; Physics) *Director:* Jean-Pierre Ezin, *full-time staff: 6, students: 20*
Public Health *(Cotonou) Director:* Ayite Manko D'almeida, *students: 35*
Sports and Physical Education *(Porto-Novo)* (Physical Education; Sports) *Director:* Souaïbou Gouda, *full-time staff: 35, students: 285*

History: Founded 1970 as Université du Dahomey incorporating departments of former Institut d'Enseignement supérieur du Bénin, established 1962. Acquired present status 1976 and present title 2000. A State Institution responsible to the Ministry of Higher Education and Scientific Research.

Governing Bodies: Conseil scientifique; Comité de Direction

Academic Year: October to July (October-January; January-March; April-July)

Admission Requirements: Secondary school certificate (baccalauréat) or equivalent

Fees: (Francs CFA): 6,500

Main Language(s) of Instruction: French

Accrediting Agencies: African and Malagasy Council for Higher Education (CAMES)

Degrees and Diplomas: *Certificat d'Aptitude au Professorat de l'Enseignement secondaire:* Teaching Qualification, secondary level (CAP), 2-4 yrs; *Diplôme d'Etudes techniques supérieures:* (DETS); *Diplôme d'Etudes universitaires générales (DEUG):* Law, Economics, 2 yrs; *Diplôme universitaire d'Etudes littéraires (DUEL):* Arts, Humanities, 2 yrs; *Diplôme universitaire d'Etudes scientifiques (DUES):* 2 yrs; *Licence:* Law, Economics, Arts and Humanities, Science and Technology, 1 further yr following DEUG, DUEL, DUES; *Diplôme:* Administration, 5 yrs; *Ingénieur:* Polytechnics, Agronomy, 5 yrs; *Maîtrise:* Law, Economics, Arts and Humanities, Science and Technology, 1 further yr following Licence; *Doctorat en Médecine:* Health Sciences, 7 yrs; *Diplôme d'Etudes approfondies (DEA):* Law, Economics, Arts and Humanities, Science and Technology, 1 further yr following Licence; *Diplôme d'Etudes supérieures spécialisées (DESS):* Demography and Population, Natural Resources Management, 1 further yr following Maitrise

Student Services: Academic Counselling, Sports Facilities, Health Services, Canteen

Student Residential Facilities: For 1000 students

Libraries: Central Library, c. 40,000 vols; Agriculture, c. 10,000; Medicine, c. 7000; Education, c. 5000

Publications: Revue générale des Sciences juridiques économiques et politiques (quarterly); Annales de la Faculté des Lettres (annually)

Press or Publishing House: Service des Publications universitaires

Academic Staff 2000	MEN	WOMEN	TOTAL
FULL-TIME	427	57	484
PART-TIME	–	–	166
TOTAL	–	–	**650**

Staff with doctorate: Total: **472**

Student Numbers 2000	MEN	WOMEN	TOTAL
All (Foreign Included)	14,866	3,667	**18,533**
FOREIGN ONLY	–	–	693

PARAKOU UNIVERSITY
Université de Parakou (UP)
BP 123, Parakou
Tel: 229 61-07-12
Fax: 229 61-07-12
EMail: mboko@syfed.bj.refer.org

Recteur: Michel Boko

Botswana

INSTITUTION TYPES AND CREDENTIALS

Types of higher education institutions:

University
Vocational and Technical Institution

School leaving and higher education credentials:

Botswana General Certificate of Secondary Education
Certificate
Diploma
Bachelor's Degree
Post-Graduate Diploma
Master's Degree
PhD

STRUCTURE OF EDUCATION SYSTEM

Pre-higher education:

Duration of compulsory education:

Age of entry: 7
Age of exit: 15

Structure of school system:

Basic First Stage
Type of school providing this education: Primary School
Length of programme in years: 7
Age level from: 7 to: 14
Certificate/diploma awarded: Standard 7 Certificate

Junior Secondary
Type of school providing this education: Junior Secondary School
Length of programme in years: 3
Age level from: 14 to: 17
Certificate/diploma awarded: Junior Certificate

Senior Secondary
Type of school providing this education: Senior Secondary School
Length of programme in years: 2

Age level from: 17 to: 19

Certificate/diploma awarded: Botswana General Certificate of Secondary Education

School education:

Primary education lasts for seven years leading to the Standard 7 Certificate. Secondary education begins at fourteen. It covers five years and is divided into two cycles: Junior Secondary education which leads to the Junior Certificate and Senior Secondary education which leads to the Botswana General Certificate of Secondary Education, which is a prerequisite for admission to the university. The Cambridge Overseas School Certificate has been phased out. Vocational education is provided through Brigades Centres and Vocational Training Centres and prepares skilled manpower.

Higher education:

Higher Education refers to all education that stipulates a minimum entry requirement of successful completion of senior secondary school. This refers to Diploma or Degree programmes and other advanced professional courses. Higher Education is provided by the University of Botswana. The governing body of the University is the University Council consisting of 21 members. The Senate formulates and carries out the academic policy, regulates courses and examinations, admits students and supervises research.

Main laws/decrees governing higher education:

Decree: The University of Botswana Act   Year: 1982

Academic year:

Classes from: August *to:* May

Languages of instruction:

English

Stages of studies:

Non-university level post-secondary studies (technical/vocational type):

Three-year Diploma programmes are offered in different broad areas, professional studies, technical, engineering and business studies. The entry requirement is the Botswana General Certificate of Secondary Education with a minimum of a C grade pass. One-year certificates are also offered in broad areas. Entry requirements for these programmes are a minimum of a pass in Junior Certificate plus a working experience in the area to be studied. Botswana Polytechnic used to offer Certificate, Diploma and Degree courses in engineering. It has been incorporated in the University of Botswana as the Faculty of Engineering.

University level studies:

University level first stage: First Degree:

First degree programmes are carried out over a period of four to five years. First degrees offered are Bachelor of Arts (in Humanities or Social Sciences); Bachelor of Accounting/Business Administration; Bachelor of Education; Bachelor of Science (Agriculture); Bachelor of Science (Computing Science); Bachelor of Science (Urban and Regional Planning); Bachelor of Social Work; Bachelor of Library and Information Studies. They all take four years, except the Bachelor of Laws, which takes five years.

University level second stage: *Postgraduate Level*:

At postgraduate level, there are one-year postgraduate programmes and one-and-a-half to two-and-a-half years Master programmes. Postgraduate Diplomas are awarded in Secondary Education; Library and Information Studies; and Counselling Education. The two-year master programmes is offered in Arts (in Humanities or Social Sciences); Education; Business Administration; Public Administration; and Science. Entry requirements for postgraduate studies is a first degree pass with a minimum overall average of 65% in the relevant field. Ph.D. programmes are under review.

Teacher education:

Training of pre-primary and primary/basic school teachers

Primary school teachers are trained in primary teacher training colleges. Programmes last for three years. After completion, students are awarded a Diploma in Primary Education. Entry requirement for this course is the Botswana General Certificate of Secondary Education third class.

Training of secondary school teachers

A two-year Diploma in Secondary Education course is open to those who are training to teach in junior secondary schools. They must hold the Botswana General Certificate of Secondary Education. Senior secondary teachers are trained in four years at the University of Botswana where they obtain a Bachelor of Education or in three years for a Diploma in Education.

Training of higher education teachers

MEd and PhD programmes in Education are available.

Non-traditional studies:

Distance higher education

Distance education is currently being developed at Diploma and first degree level.

NATIONAL BODIES

Responsible authorities:

Ministry of Education
    Minister: Pontashego Kedikilwe
    Deputy Secretary-General: Violet Essilfe
    Private Bag 005
    Gaborone
    Tel: +267(31) 365-5471
    Fax: +267(31) 365-5458
    EMail: vessilfie@gov.bw
    WWW: http://www.gov.bw/moe/ministry_of_education.html

ADMISSIONS TO HIGHER EDUCATION

Admission to university-level studies

Name of secondary school credential required: Botswana General Certificate of Secondary Education
Minimum score/requirement: Grade B
For entry to: BA (Humanities or Social Sciences)/BSc/BEd/BNS, etc

Alternatives to credentials: Mature entry : students should be 25 years old or more (with an entrance examination).

Foreign students admission

Definition of foreign student: All students who are not Botswana nationals.

Quotas: At University level all foreign students are free to apply.

Admission requirements: Candidates must be holders of a senior Secondary School Certificate or a General Certificate of Education (GCE), Ordinary ('O') level.

Entry regulations: Visas are required for some countries.

Language requirements: Students must be proficient in English.

Application procedures:

Apply to individual institution for entry to: University (colleges of education admit locals only).

Application closing dates:

   For university level studies: 30 December
   For advanced/doctoral studies: 30 December

References to further information on foreign student admissions and recognition of studies

Title: Study Abroad 2000-2001
Publisher: UNESCO/IBE
Year of publication: 1999

Title: University of Botswana Calendar
Publisher: University of Botswana

STUDENT LIFE

National student associations and unions

Student Representative Council (SRC)
   Private Bag 0022
   Gaborone

Health/social provisions

Social security for home students: No

Special student travel fares:

By road: No
By rail: No
By air: No
Available to foreign students: No

Student expenses and financial aid

Student costs:

Home students tuition fees: Minimum: 4,000 (Pula)
Maximum: 7,500 (Pula)
Foreign students tuition fees: Minimum: 8,000 (Pula)
Maximum: 15,000 (Pula)

INTERNATIONAL COOPERATION AND EXCHANGES

Principal national bodies responsible for dealing with international cooperation and exchanges in higher education:

Ministry of Education
Private Bag 005
Gaborone
Tel: +267(31) 365-5471
Fax: +267(31) 365-5458
Telex: 2944 THUTO BD
WWW: http://www.gov.bw/moe/ministry_of_education.html

GRADING SYSTEM

Usual grading system in secondary school

Full Description: The Botswana General Certificate of Secondary Education is marked on an A-G grade scale with A as the highest grade.
Highest on scale: A
Lowest on scale: G

Main grading system used by higher education institutions

Full Description: 1st class A average; 2nd class 1st division B average; 2nd class 2nd division C average; pass D average; fail E or F average
Highest on scale: A
Pass/fail level: D
Lowest on scale: E-F

NOTES ON HIGHER EDUCATION SYSTEM

Data for academic year: 2001-2002
Source: University of Botswana, Gaborone, 2001

INSTITUTIONS OF HIGHER EDUCATION

UNIVERSITIES

*• UNIVERSITY OF BOTSWANA

Private Bag 0022, Gaborone
Tel: +267(31) 355-0000
Fax: +267(31) 356-591
EMail: webadmin@mopipi.ub.bw
Website: http://www.ub.bw

Vice-Chancellor: Sharon A. Siverts (1998-2003)
Tel: +267(31) 352-252 Fax: +267(31) 584-747
EMail: sivertss@mopipi.ub.bw

Deputy Vice-Chancellor (Finance and Administration):
Shabani Ndzinge EMail: ndzinges@mopipi.ub.bw

International Relations: Brian Mokopakgosi, Deputy
Vice-Chancellor (Academic Affairs)
EMail: mokopakgosib@mopipi.ub.bw

Faculties
Business (Accountancy; Business Administration; Business
and Commerce; Management) *Dean (Acting)*: S. Chinyoka,
full-time staff: 42, *students:* 685
Education (Adult Education; Education; Educational Sciences;
Home Economics; Nursing; Physical Education; Primary Edu-
cation; Science Education) *Dean*: L. Nyati-Ramahobo, *full-time
staff:* 130, *students:* 1,879
Engineering and Technology (Civil Engineering; Electrical
Engineering; Engineering; Mechanical Engineering; Technol-
ogy) *Head*: T. Oladiran, *full-time staff:* 70, *students:* 998
Humanities (African Languages; Arts and Humanities; English;
French; History; Library Science; Religious Studies; Theology)
Head: J. Tsonope, *full-time staff:* 98, *students:* 1,629
Science (Biology; Chemistry; Computer Science; Environmen-
tal Studies; Geology; Mathematics; Natural Sciences; Physics)
Dean: S. Mpuchane, *full-time staff:* 169, *students:* 1,354
Social Sciences (Demography and Population; Economics;
Law; Political Science; Public Administration; Social Sciences;
Social Work; Sociology; Statistics) *Dean*: B. Otloghile, *full-time
staff:* 109, *students:* 1,237

Schools
Graduate Studies *V*: S. Weeks, *full-time staff:* 1, *students:* 419

Centres
Academic Development *Director*: A. Morisson
Continuing Education G. Adekanmbi, *students:* 1,966

Research Centres
Harry Oppenheimer Okavango *Director*: L. Ramberg
Research and Development *Director (Acting)*: I. Mazonde

Further Information: Also Legal Clinic and Business Clinic.

History: Founded 1964 as University of Basutoland,
Bechuanaland and Swaziland. Acquired present status and title
1982.

Governing Bodies: University Council

Academic Year: August to May (August-December;
January-May)

Admission Requirements: Cambridge Overseas School Certificate (COSC) or General Certificate of Education (GCE) or
recognized foreign equivalent. Direct entrance to second year
on completion of studies in another tertiary Institution

Fees: (Pula): 4000-7500 per annum; foreign students,
8000-15000

Main Language(s) of Instruction: English

International Co-operation: Stockholm Institute of Education;
University of Tromso; University of Oslo; South Bank University

Degrees and Diplomas: *Certificate*; *Diploma*; *Bachelor's De-
gree*: Education (BEd), 2 yrs following BA or BSc, or holders of
DipSecEd with credit, 2 yrs; Arts (BA); Commerce (BCom); Ed-
ucation (primary level) (BEd); Library and Information Sciences;
Science (BSc); Social Work (BSocWork), 4 yrs; Law (LLB), 5
yrs; Nursing (BSN), following SRN; *Master's Degree*: Arts (MA);
Education (MEd); Science (MSc), a further 1 1/2-2 1/2 yrs. Also
PhD programmes

Student Services: Academic Counselling, Social Counselling,
Employment Services, Sports Facilities, Handicapped Facilities, Health Services, Canteen

Student Residential Facilities: Yes

Libraries: Central Library, c. 290,000 vols

Publications: Calendar

Academic Staff *1999-2000:* Total: **566**

Student Numbers *1999-2000*	TOTAL
All (Foreign Included)	**10,161**
FOREIGN ONLY	927

BOTSWANA COLLEGE OF AGRICULTURE
PO Bag 0027, Gaborone
Tel: +267(31) 352-381
Fax: +267(31) 3314-253
Telex: 2429bd
Website: http://www.bca.bw

Principal: E.J. Kemsley (1991-)

Departments
Agricultural Economics Education and Extension (Agricul-
tural Economics)
Agricultural Education
Agricultural Engineering and Land Planning (Agricultural
Engineering; Regional Planning)
Animal Husbandry and Production (Animal Husbandry; Cat-
tle Breeding)
Basic Sciences (Natural Sciences)
Crop Science and Production (Crop Production)

Centres
In-service and Continuing Education

History: Founded 1991.

Burkina Faso

INSTITUTION TYPES AND CREDENTIALS

Types of higher education institutions:

Université (University)
Université polytechnique
Ecole (School)

School leaving and higher education credentials:

Baccalauréat
Baccalauréat technique
Brevet d'Etudes professionnelles
Brevet de Technicien supérieur
Diplôme
Diplôme d'Etudes universitaires générales (DEUG)
Diplôme universitaire de Technologie (DUT)
Certificat d'Aptitude au Professorat de l'Enseignement technique
Certificat d'Aptitude au Professorat des Collèges d'Enseignement général
Diplôme d'Ingénieur des Travaux
Licence
Certificat d'Aptitude au Professorat de l'Enseignement secondaire
Diplôme d'Ingénieur
Maîtrise
Diplôme d'Etudes approfondies (DEA)
Diplôme d'Etudes supérieures spécialisées (DESS)
Doctorat d'Etat en Médecine
Doctorat de troisième Cycle
Certificat d'Etudes spécialisées (CES)
Doctorat d'Etat

STRUCTURE OF EDUCATION SYSTEM

Pre-higher education:

Duration of compulsory education:

Age of entry: 6
Age of exit: 16

Structure of school system:

Primary
Type of school providing this education: Ecole primaire
Length of programme in years: 6
Age level from: 6 to: 12
Certificate/diploma awarded: Certificat d'Etudes primaires

Lower Secondary
Type of school providing this education: Collège d'Enseignement Général
Length of programme in years: 4
Age level from: 12 to: 16
Certificate/diploma awarded: Brevet d'Etudes du Premier Cycle (BEPC)

Technical Secondary
Type of school providing this education: Collège d'Enseignement Technique
Length of programme in years: 3
Age level from: 12 to: 15
Certificate/diploma awarded: Certificat d'Aptitude Professionnelle (CAP)

Upper Secondary
Type of school providing this education: Lycée
Length of programme in years: 3
Age level from: 16 to: 19
Certificate/diploma awarded: Baccalauréat

Technical
Type of school providing this education: Lycée Technique
Length of programme in years: 2
Age level from: 16 to: 18
Certificate/diploma awarded: Brevet d'Etudes Professionnelles

Technical
Type of school providing this education: Lycée Technique
Length of programme in years: 3
Age level from: 16 to: 19
Certificate/diploma awarded: Baccalauréat Technique

School education:

Primary education lasts for six years leading to the Certificat d'Etudes primaires. Secondary education lasts for seven years and is divided into four-year lower secondary education followed at a Collège d'Enseignement général or a Lycée. It culminates in the Brevet d'Etudes du Premier Cycle (BEPC). The upper cycle lasts for three years and may only be taken at a Lycée. It leads to the Baccalauréat. Short technical secondary education leads to the Certificat d'Aptitude professionnelle in Collèges d'Enseignement technique after three years. Completion of the upper cycle in a technical specialization leads to the Baccalauréat technique after three years. On completion of two years of upper cycle in a technical specialization, candidates sit for the Brevet d'Etudes professionnelles (BEP).

Higher education:

Higher education is provided by two universities and several institutions of higher education. The universities are autonomous institutions under the jurisdiction of the Ministère des Enseignements secondaire, supérieur et de la Recherche scientifique. In 1995-96, the Institut universitaire de Technologie, the Institut de Développement rural and the Ecole supérieure d'Informatique were transferred to Bobo-Dioulasso to constitute the Centre universitaire Polytechnique de Bobo-Dioulasso which is now the Université Polytechnique de Bobo-Dioulasso. In 1996-97, the Institut des Sciences de l'Education was transferred to Koudougou and is now called the Ecole Normale supérieure de Koudougou. The Grand Séminaire de Koumi and the Grand Séminaire Saint Jean de Wayalgé train future priests.

Main laws/decrees governing higher education:

Decree: Loi d'Orientation de l'Education   Year: 1996

Decree: Décret n°91-0346   Year: 1991
Concerns: Université de Ouagadougou

Decree: Décret n°AN/VIII-184   Year: 1991
Concerns: Private education

Academic year:

Classes from: October *to:* June

Languages of instruction:

French

Stages of studies:

Non-university level post-secondary studies (technical/vocational type):

Higher technical and vocational education is offered at the Ecole Inter-Etats des Techniciens supérieurs de l'Hydraulique et de l'Equipement rural, which awards the title of Technicien supérieur after two years' study. Several private higher technical institutions have been founded: the Centre d'Etudes et de la Formation en Informatique de Gestion, which confers a Brevet de Technicien supérieur en Informatique de Gestion after two years; the Ecole supérieure des Sciences appliquées; the Ecole des Sciences et Techniques informatiques du FASO which trains for the Diplôme de Technicien supérieur en Informatique.

University level studies:

University level first stage: *Premier Cycle*:
The first stage of university studies leads to the Diplôme d'Etudes universitaires générales after two years. In Health Sciences, the first stage leads to the Premier Cycle d'Etudes médicales (PCEM) and in the Institut universitaire de Technologie it leads to the Diplôme universitaire de Technologie (DUT).

University level second stage: *Deuxième Cycle*:
The second stage leads after one year to the Licence. One year after the Licence, the Maîtrise may be obtained in some fields. In Medicine, the second stage lasts for four years. In Engineering, it leads

after three years' further study to the Diplôme d'Ingénieur. The Ecole Inter-Etats d'Ingénieurs de l'Equipement rural awards a Diplôme d'Ingénieur after three years.

University level third stage: Troisième Cycle:
A third stage is offered in Economics, Law, Chemistry, Mathematics, Biology and Linguistics. It leads after one year to the Diplôme d'Etudes supérieures spécialisées (DESS) and to the Diplôme d'Etudes approfondies (DEA), and after two years following the DEA, to the Doctorat de troisième Cycle. After three to five years following the DEA, the Doctorat or the Doctorat d'Etat is conferred in some fields of study. In Medicine, after one further year following the four-year second cycle, the Doctorat d'Etat en Médecine is awarded.

Teacher education:

Training of pre-primary and primary/basic school teachers
Primary school teachers are trained at the Ecole nationale des Enseignants du Primaire (ENEP). Access to the ENEP is by entrance examination open to candidates holding the BEPC. Studies last for two years and lead to the Certificat de Fin d'Etudes des ENEP. Primary school teachers are recruited following a competitive examination.

Training of secondary school teachers
General and technical secondary school teachers are trained in the appropriate university department or institute for three years following the Baccalauréat. They either hold a Licence, a Maîtrise or a Doctorat de Troisième cycle, a DEUG or the CAPES. English teachers are trained in the Département de Langues Vivantes by means of a teacher training option in the third year. The Ecole normale supérieure de Koudougou offers secondary teacher training courses preparing for the CAPCEG (Certificat d'Aptitude au Professorat des Collèges de l'Enseignement général), for the CAPES (Certificat d'Aptitude au Professorat de l'Enseignement secondaire) and for the CAPET (Certificat d'Aptitude au Professorat de l'Enseignement technique).

Training of higher education teachers
Higher education teachers must hold a Doctorat.

Non-traditional studies:

Other forms of non-formal higher education
Non-formal studies are provided by the Université populaire africaine. Evening courses are also offered.

NATIONAL BODIES

Responsible authorities:
Ministry of Secondary and Higher Education and Scientific Research (Ministère des Enseignements secondaire, supérieur et de la Recherche scientifique)
    Minister: Laya Sawadogo
    Secretary-General: Bila Dipama
    BP 7047
    Ouagadougou 03

Tel: +226 31-09-68
Fax: +226 31-09-68

National Centre for Science and Technology Research (Centre National de la Recherche Scientifique et Technologique) (CNRST)

Délégué général: Michel P. Sedogo
Administrative Officer: Jean Marc Palm
BP 7047
Ougadougou 03
Tel: +226 32-46-48   +226 32-45-04
Fax: +226 31-50-03
EMail: dg.cnrst@fasonet.bf

ADMISSIONS TO HIGHER EDUCATION

Admission to non university higher education studies

Name of secondary school credential required: Baccalauréat technique

Admission to university-level studies

Name of secondary school credential required: Baccalauréat

Foreign students admission

Admission requirements: Foreign students must hold the Baccalauréat or its equivalent or sit for a special entrance examination. Applications should be sent to the rector of the Université de Ouagadougou between 15 August and 30 October. Foreign students enjoy the same facilities as nationals with regard to social and welfare services, counselling and scholarships. They may also work on campus.

Entry regulations: Conditions vary according to relations with the country of origin.

Language requirements: Students must have a good command of French.

Recognition of studies and qualifications:

Studies pursued in foreign countries (bodies dealing with recognition of foreign credentials):
Commission nationale d'Equivalence des Titres et Diplômes (National Commission for the Equivalence of Diplomas)

Permanent Secretary: Dafrassi Jean-François Sanou
B.P. 1990
Ouagadougou
Tel: +226 33-34-62

Multilateral agreements concerning recognition of foreign studies

Name(s) of agreement(s): Convention on the Recognition of Studies, Certificates, Diplomas, Degrees and Other Academic Qualifications in Higher Education in the African States
Year of signature: 1981

References to further information on foreign student admissions and recognition of studies

Title: Présentation de l'Université de Ouagadougou
Publisher: Université de Ouagadougou

STUDENT LIFE

Main student services at national level

Centre national des oeuvres universitaires
B.P. 1926
Ouagadougou

Category of services provided: Social and welfare services

Student expenses and financial aid

Bodies providing information on student financial aid:

Direction de l'orientation et des bourses
B.P. 3419
Ouagadougou

Publications on student services and financial aid:

Title: Study Abroad 2000-2001
Publisher: UNESCO/IBE
Year of publication: 1999

GRADING SYSTEM

Usual grading system in secondary school

Full Description: 0-20
Highest on scale: 20
Pass/fail level: 10
Lowest on scale: 0

Main grading system used by higher education institutions

Full Description: 0-20. 16-20 très bien; 14-15 bien; 12-13 assez bien; 10-11 passable
Highest on scale: 20
Pass/fail level: 10-11
Lowest on scale: 0

NOTES ON HIGHER EDUCATION SYSTEM

Data for academic year: 2000-2001
Source: International Association of Universities (IAU), updated from IBE website, 2001

INSTITUTIONS OF HIGHER EDUCATION

UNIVERSITIES AND UNIVERSITY LEVEL INSTITUTIONS

*• POLYTECHNIC UNIVERSITY OF BOBO-DIOULASSO

Université Polytechnique de Bobo-Dioulasso (UPB)
B.P. 1091, Bobo-Dioulasso 01
Tel: +226 98-06-35
Fax: +226 97-25-77
EMail: recteur@esi.univ.ouaga.bf

Recteur: Akri Coulibaly (2002-) Tel: +226 97-27-58
Fax: +226 98-25-77 EMail: ouattara@esi.univ-ouaga.bf

Secrétaire général: Lazare Ouedrago

International Relations: Chantal Zoungrana
EMail: chantal@esi.univ-ouaga.bf

Schools
Informatics (Computer Science; Mathematics; Statistics) *Director.* Théodore Tapsoba, *full-time staff:* 8, *part-time staff:* 38, *students:* 120

Institutes
Rural Development (Agricultural Economics; Agriculture; Cattle Breeding; Forestry; Rural Studies) *Director.* Chantal Yvette Zoungrana-Kaboré, *full-time staff:* 21, *part-time staff:* 18, *students:* 118
Technology *(IUT)* (Electrical Engineering; Management; Mechanical Engineering; Mechanical Equipment and Maintenance; Secretarial Studies; Technology) *Director.* Ousmane Kaboré, *full-time staff:* 22, *part-time staff:* 22, *students:* 214

History: Founded 1997.

Degrees and Diplomas: *Brevet de Technicien supérieur.* Technology, 2 yrs; *Diplôme:* Diplôme Universitaire de Technologie en Finance et Comptabilité: Finance and Accountancy, 2 yrs; *Diplôme universitaire de Technologie (DUT):* Business and Commerce, 2 yrs; *Diplôme d'Ingénieur des Travaux:* Civil Engineering, 3 yrs; *Diplôme d'Ingénieur.* Développement Rural - Option Agronomie: Rural Planning-Agronomy; Développement Rural - Option Eaux et Forêts: Rural Planning-Forestry; Développement Rural - Option Elevage: Rural Planning-Animal Husbandry; Développement Rural - Option Sociologie et Economie: Rural Planning-Socio-Economics; Informatique: Computer Engineering, 5 yrs; *Doctorat de troisième Cycle:* Sciences Agronomiques: Agronomy, 8 yrs

Student Services: Sports Facilities, Health Services, Canteen

Student Residential Facilities: Yes

Academic Staff *1999-2000*	MEN	WOMEN	TOTAL
FULL-TIME	47	4	51
PART-TIME	78	5	83
TOTAL	**125**	**9**	**134**

STAFF WITH DOCTORATE			
FULL-TIME	26	2	28
PART-TIME	45	4	49
TOTAL	**71**	**6**	**77**

Student Numbers *1999-2000*	MEN	WOMEN	TOTAL
All (Foreign Included)	326	126	**452**
FOREIGN ONLY	28	8	36

INTER-STATES SCHOOL OF RURAL ENGINEERING OF OUAGADOUGOU

Ecole inter-Etats d'Ingénieurs de l'Equipement rural
B.P. 7023, Ouagadougou 03
Tel: +226 30-20-53
Fax: +226 31-27-24
Telex: EIER (978) 5266 BF
EMail: eier@eier.org
Website: http://www.eier.org

Directeur: Philippe Mangé
Directeur, Administration et Finances: Roger Esculier

Programmes
Agricultural Engineering
Civil Engineering
Computer Engineering
Energy Engineering
Industrial Engineering
Mathematics
Water Management

History: Founded 1968.

Degrees and Diplomas: *Diplôme d'Ingénieur des Travaux:* Rural Equipment, 3 yrs; *Diplôme d'Ingénieur.* Engineering, 5 yrs

• UNIVERSITY OF OUAGADOUGOU

Université de Ouagadougou
B.P. 7021, Ouagadougou 03
Tel: +226 30-70-64
Fax: +226 30-72-42
Telex: uniouga (978) 5270 bf
EMail: info@univ-ouaga.bf
Website: http://www.univ-ouaga.bf

Président: Alfred Traoré Tel: +226 30-38-71
Secrétaire général: O. Sidiki Traoré
International Relations: Norbert Nikiema
Fax: +226 31-40-30

Faculties
Economics and Management Science (Accountancy; Economics; Finance; Management)
Health Sciences (Gynaecology and Obstetrics; Health Sciences; Medicine; Pharmacy)

Languages, Letters, Arts, Human and Social Sciences (Archaeology; Arts and Humanities; Communication Studies; Geography; Linguistics; Modern Languages; Philosophy; Psychology; Social Sciences; Sociology)
Law and Political Science (Law; Political Science)
Science and Technology (Biochemistry; Biology; Chemistry; Geology; Mathematics; Natural Sciences; Physics; Technology)

History: Founded 1965 as Ecole normale supérieure, became Centre d'Enseignement supérieur 1969. Acquired present title and status 1974. Reorganized 1985, 1991 and 1997. An autonomous institution under the jurisdiction of the Ministry of Education and Culture.

Governing Bodies: Conseil d'Administration; Assemblée; Conseil de l'Université

Academic Year: September to June (September-December; January-March; April-June)

Admission Requirements: Secondary school certificate (baccalauréat) or recognized equivalent and entrance examination

Main Language(s) of Instruction: French

International Co-operation: University of Paris VII; University of Paris XII; University of Amiens; University of Bordeaux II; University of Tours; University of Groningen; University of Heidelberg; University of Namur; University of Côte d'Ivoire; University of Niamey; University of Ghana; Ecole normale supérieure de Fontenay-aux-Roses; University of Delft

Degrees and Diplomas: *Diplôme d'Etudes universitaires générales (DEUG)*: 2 yrs; *Diplôme universitaire de Technologie (DUT)*: 2 yrs; *Certificat d'Aptitude au Professorat de l'Enseignement technique*: 3 yrs; *Certificat d'Aptitude au Professorat des Collèges d'Enseignement général*: 3 yrs; *Licence*: 1 yr after DEUG; *Certificat d'Aptitude au Professorat de l'Enseignement secondaire*: 5 yrs; *Maîtrise*: 1 yr after Licence; *Diplôme d'Etudes approfondies (DEA)*: 1 yr after Maîtrise; *Diplôme d'Etudes supérieures spécialisées (DESS)*: 1 yr after Maîtrise; *Doctorat d'Etat en Médecine*: Medicine, 6 yrs; *Doctorat de troisième Cycle*: Chemistry; Linguistics; Mathematics; Economics, 5 yrs after DEA; *Certificat d'Etudes spécialisées (CES)*: Surgery, 3 yrs following Doctorat d'Etat en Médecine; *Doctorat d'Etat*. Also teaching qualifications, secondary level, 2 yrs

Student Services: Social Counselling, Cultural Centre, Health Services, Canteen

Special Facilities: Experimental Fields at Gampela and Leo

Libraries: Central Library, c. 75,000 vols; libraries of the Faculties, c. 25,250 vols

Publications: Journal de l'Université Campus Echos; Bulletin du Laboratoire universitaire pour la Tradition orale (quarterly); Revue Burkinabe de Droit (biannually); Annales de l'Université (Série A: Sciences humaines et sociales, Série B: Sciences exactes); Annales de l'Ecole supérieure des Lettres et des Sciences humaines (annually); la Revue du CEDRES

Press or Publishing House: Direction des Presses Universitaires (DPU)

Academic Staff *1999*: Full-Time: c. 270 Part-Time: c. 270 Total: c. 540

Student Numbers *1999*: All (Foreign Included): c. 7,800 Foreign Only: c. 650

OTHER INSTITUTIONS

ECOLE INTER-ETATS DES TECHNICIENS SUPÉRIEURS DE L'HYDRAULIQUE ET DE L'EQUIPEMENT RURAL (ETSHER)
BP 594, Ouagadougou 01
Tel: +226 31-92-03
Fax: +226 31-92-34 +226 31-74-24
EMail: etsher@etsher.org
Website: http://www.eier.org/etsher/index.htm

Directeur général: Philippe Mange EMail: dir@etsher.org

Directeur des Études et de la Recherche: Jérôme Makin Djegui Tel: 226 31-92-18 Fax: 226 31-92-03

Departments
3D Graphics (Computer Graphics)
Advanced Systems Engineering (Computer Engineering)
Agrarian Sciences (Agriculture)
Agricultural Equipment (Agricultural Equipment; Agriculture)
Concrete Technology (Building Technologies)
Construction Engineering (Building Technologies; Construction Engineering)
Foundation Engineering (Construction Engineering)
Hydrodynamics (Mechanics)
Irrigation
Irrigation Engineering (Irrigation)
Road Engineering (Civil Engineering)
Topography (Surveying and Mapping)

Degrees and Diplomas: *Brevet de Technicien supérieur*: Hydrologie, Equipement Rural: Hydraulics, Rural Equipment, 2 yrs

Student Residential Facilities: Yes

Libraries: Library

Publications: Sud Sciences et Technologies (2 per annum)

Academic Staff *1999-2000*	MEN	WOMEN	TOTAL
FULL-TIME	90	10	**100**

ECOLE NATIONALE D'ADMINISTRATION ET DE MAGISTRATURE
BP 7013, Charles de Gaulle, Ouagadougou
Tel: +226 30-66-09
Fax: +226 30-66-11
Administration; Justice Administration

History: Founded 1959.

ECOLE NORMALE SUPÉRIEURE DE KOUDOUGOU
Koudougou

Teacher Training

History: Founded 1997.

INSTITUT NATIONAL DES SPORTS
BP 7035, Ouagadougou

Physical Education; Sports

PEDAGOGICAL INSTITUTE OF BURKINA
Institut pédagogique du Burkina (IPB)
B.P. 7043, Ouagadougou
Tel: +226 32-47-09
Fax: +226 32-47-10
EMail: ipb@liptinfor.bf

Directeur général: Ouri Sanou (1998-) Tel: +226 32-47-10
EMail: sanououri@liptinfor.bf

Teacher Training

History: Founded 1965.

Burundi

INSTITUTION TYPES AND CREDENTIALS

Types of higher education institutions:

Université (University)

Institut supérieur (Higher Institute)

School leaving and higher education credentials:

Diplôme d'Etat

Technicien

Candidature

Diplôme

Ingénieur technicien

Diplôme d'Ingénieur

Licence

Doctorat en Médecine

Diplôme d'Etudes approfondies (DEA)

Diplôme de Spécialité

Doctorat de Spécialité (3e Cycle)

STRUCTURE OF EDUCATION SYSTEM

Pre-higher education:

Duration of compulsory education:

    Age of entry: 6

    Age of exit: 12

Structure of school system:

    Primary

    Type of school providing this education: Ecole primaire

    Length of programme in years: 6

    Age level from: 6 to: 12

    Certificate/diploma awarded: Certificat de Fin d'Etudes primaires (Primary School Leaving Certificate)

    Lower Secondary

    Type of school providing this education: Collège

    Length of programme in years: 4

Age level from: 12 to: 16
Certificate/diploma awarded: Certificat du Tronc commun (Lower Secondary Level Certificate)

Technical Secondary
Type of school providing this education: Technical Secondary School (Lower Level)
Length of programme in years: 5
Age level from: 12 to: 17
Certificate/diploma awarded: Technicien (Technician Diploma A3 For Lower Level)

Technical Secondary
Type of school providing this education: Technical Secondary School (Upper Level)
Length of programme in years: 7
Age level from: 12 to: 19
Certificate/diploma awarded: Technicien (Diploma A2 For Upper Level)

Upper Secondary
Type of school providing this education: Lycée
Length of programme in years: 3
Age level from: 16 to: 19
Certificate/diploma awarded: Diplôme d'Etat

School education:

Primary education lasts for six years leading to the Certificat d'Etudes primaires. Secondary education is divided into lower and upper secondary education. Lower secondary education is available to those who pass the National Entrance Examination and lasts four years. A national test is imposed on all those who complete lower secondary education. Their records are submitted to a National Orientation Commission. Schooling at upper secondary level lasts three years and leads to the Diplôme d'Etat, which gives access to higher education. Technical secondary education lasts seven years. A Diplôme A2 sanctions success in technical studies and a Diplôme A3 is conferred after a cycle of studies lasting five years following upon primary education.

Higher education:

Higher education is mainly provided by the Université du Burundi. It is largely financed by the State and enjoys administrative and management autonomy. It is administered by a rector appointed by the President of the Republic for four years. Policy-making is the responsibility of a Governing Board appointed by the President of the Republic and representing the major spheres of activity with connections to higher education development. Four private universities have been created recently.

Main laws/decrees governing higher education:

Decree: Décret-loi n°1/025   Year: 1989
Concerns: reorganization of educational system

Decree: Décret n° 100/181   Year: 1988
Concerns: Ministry of Education

Academic year:

Classes from: October *to:* June

Long vacation from: 1 July *to:* 1 October

Languages of instruction:

French

Stages of studies:

Non-university level post-secondary studies (technical/vocational type):

Several Ministries organise higher level courses.

University level studies:

University level first stage: Candidature:
The first stage of study in preparation for the Licence lasts for two years and leads to the Candidature.

University level second stage: Licence:
A further two years' study beyond the Candidature leads to the Licence. In Medicine, the professional title of Docteur en Médecine is awarded after a further four years of study following the Candidature. In Civil and Agronomic Engineering, courses last for five years and lead to the award of the professional title of Ingénieur. The Diplôme d'Ingénieur Technicien is conferred after three or four years' training in the technical institutes.

University level third stage: Diplôme d'Etudes approfondies (DEA), Doctorat de 3ème Cycle:
A Diplôme d'Etudes approfondies is conferred in subjects such as Computing, Physics and Agricultural Planning following the Licence or the Diplôme d'Ingénieur. In Medicine, there are two stages which lead to a professional Doctorat in Medicine after six years and a Special Doctorat after five more years of study and the presentation of a major thesis in Clinical Biology, Paediatrics, Surgery, Gynaecology and Internal Medicine. The University also awards a Doctorat de 3ème Cycle.

Teacher education:

Training of pre-primary and primary/basic school teachers
Primary school teachers are trained in lycées pédagogiques which offer studies divided into two cycles of two years each. In-service training of primary teachers is a regular activity of the Office for Rural Education (BER), a curriculum development agency.

Training of secondary school teachers
Secondary school teachers are trained at the University of Burundi from which they graduate after four years in the various specialities. Some teachers, specifically trained for secondary education, are also trained at the Pedagogical Institute for three to five years. They may also be trained in Ecoles normales supérieures.

Non-traditional studies:

Other forms of non-formal higher education
Non-formal studies consist of in-service courses offered by the Institut supérieur de Gestion d'Entreprise for management professionals. There are two levels of training: short cycle training for holders of the Diplôme d'Etat and long cycle training for holders of degrees in economics or their equivalent. Evening courses are also organized in computer sciences.

NATIONAL BODIES

Responsible authorities:

Ministry of National Education (Ministère de l'Education nationale)
    Minister: Prosper Mpawenayo
    PO Box 1990
    Bujumbura
    Tel: +257(22) 5112 +257(22) 5514
    Fax: +257(22) 68-39

Role of governing body: Central administration and coordination body.

ADMISSIONS TO HIGHER EDUCATION

Admission to non university higher education studies

Name of secondary school credential required: Diplôme d'Etat
Minimum score/requirement: Varies according to year

Alternatives to credentials: State examination

Admission to university-level studies

Name of secondary school credential required: Diplôme d'Etat
Minimum score/requirement: Varies according to year

Alternatives to credentials: An Examen d'Etat is required for the Higher Technical Institute.

Foreign students admission

Admission requirements: Foreign students must have followed seven years' general education or hold a technician's diploma.

Entry regulations: They must hold a visa and a residence permit.

Language requirements: Good knowledge of French

Application procedures:

Apply to national body for entry to: University

Apply to: Commission nationale d'Orientation à l'Enseignement supérieur
    PO Box 1990
    Bujumbura
    Tel: +257(22) 44-07
    Fax: +257(22) 84-77

Recognition of studies and qualifications:

Studies pursued in foreign countries (bodies dealing with recognition of foreign credentials):
Commission Nationale d'Equivalence des Diplômes, Titres Scolaires et Universitaires
    Head: Aaron Barutwanayo

PO Box 1990
Bujumbura
Tel: +257(22) 5112 +257(22) 5514

Special provisions for recognition:

For access to university level studies: The holder of a foreign credential must submit to the "Commission d'Equivalence des Titres et Diplômes universitaires" the following data: curriculum vitae specifying the duration of the training abroad; total number of hours of all the training modules; contents of training programmes; methods of assessment, and certified copy of the original credential.

For access to advanced studies and research: Same as above.

Multilateral agreements concerning recognition of foreign studies

Name(s) of agreement(s): Convention on the Recognition of Studies, Certificates, Diplomas, Degrees and Other Academic Qualifications in the African States
Year of signature: 1981

References to further information on foreign student admissions and recognition of studies

Title: Vademecum de l'Etudiant
Publisher: Université du Burundi

STUDENT LIFE

Main student services at national level

Régie des Oeuvres universitaires (ROU)
   PO Box 1644
   Bujumbura

   Category of services provided: Social and welfare services

Secrétariat du Service académique de l'Université du Burundi
   PO Box 1550
   Bujumbura
   Tel: +257(22) 20-59   +257(22) 34-68
   Fax: +257(22) 32-88

   Category of services provided: Academic and career counselling services

National student associations and unions

Association des Etudiants RUMURI (ASSER)
   PO Box 1644
   Bujumbura

Special student travel fares:

By air: Yes

Student expenses and financial aid

Bodies providing information on student financial aid:

Bureau des Bourses d'Etudes et de Stages (BBES)
   PO Box 1990
   Bujumbura
   Tel: +257(22) 51-12 +257(22) 55-14
   Fax: +257(22) 68-39

GRADING SYSTEM

Usual grading system in secondary school

Full Description: 0-100%: 90-100% excellent; 80-89% la plus grande distinction; 70-79% grande distinction; 60-69% distinction; 50-59% satisfaction; below 50% fail
Highest on scale: 100%
Pass/fail level: 50%
Lowest on scale: 0%

Main grading system used by higher education institutions

Full Description: 0%-100% 90-100% excellent; 80-89% la plus grande distinction; 70-79% grande distinction; 60-69% distinction; 50-59% satisfaction; below 50% fail
Highest on scale: 100%
Pass/fail level: 50%
Lowest on scale: 0%

NOTES ON HIGHER EDUCATION SYSTEM

Data for academic year: 2000-2001
Source: Ministère de l'Education nationale, Département de l'Enseignement supérieur, Bujumbura, 2001

INSTITUTIONS OF HIGHER EDUCATION

UNIVERSITIES

PUBLIC INSTITUTIONS

*• UNIVERSITY OF BURUNDI
Université du Burundi
B.P. 1550, Bujumbura
Tel: +257(22) 2059 +257(22) 3468
Fax: +257(22) 3288
Telex: (903) 5161 iniv bdi
EMail: rectorat@biblio.ub.edu.bi
Website: http://www.ub.edu.bi

Recteur: Théodore Niyongabo (1999-) Tel: +257(21) 9838
EMail: tniyong@cabinet.ub.edu.bi

Directeur Administratif et Financier: Oda Sindayizeruka
Tel: +257(22) 9209 Fax: +257(22) 7534
EMail: ondayi@cabinet.ub.edu.bi

International Relations: Firmard Nsabimana
Tel: +257(22) 2852

Faculties
Agronomy
Applied Sciences (Applied Chemistry; Applied Mathematics; Applied Physics; Natural Sciences)
Economics and Administrative Sciences (Administration; Economics)
Law
Letters and Human Sciences (Arts and Humanities)
Medicine
Psychology and Education (Education; Psychology)
Sciences (Mathematics and Computer Science; Natural Sciences)

Institutes
Pedagogy
Physical Education and Sports (Physical Education; Sports)

Higher Institutes
Agriculture *(Gitega)*
Commerce (Business and Commerce)
Technical Studies (Technology)

History: Founded 1960, incorporating the Institut agronomique du Ruanda-Urundi, previously Faculty of Agriculture of the Université officielle du Congo Belge founded 1958 and the Centre universitaire Rumuri founded 1960. Title of Université officielle de Bujumbura adopted 1964, acquired present title 1977. Largely financed by the State.

Governing Bodies: Conseil d'Administration comprising 15 members, appointed by the President of the Republic

Academic Year: October to July (October-December; January-April; April-July)

Admission Requirements: Secondary school certificate (Certificat d'Humanités complètes) or foreign equivalent

Main Language(s) of Instruction: French

Degrees and Diplomas: *Candidature*: Agriculture; Economics and Social Sciences; Education and Psychology; Law; Letters and Human Sciences; Medical Sciences; Physical Education; Pure and Applied Sciences, 2 yrs; Civil Engineering, 3 yrs; *Diplôme*: Commerce; Journalism; Teacher Training, 2 yrs; *Ingénieur technicien*: Agriculture, 3-4 yrs; *Diplôme d'Ingénieur*: Agronomy; Civil Engineering, 5 yrs; *Licence*: Administration; Economics; Education; Law; Letters and Human Sciences; Mathematics and Physics; Physical Education; Psychology; Pure and Applied Sciences, 2 yrs following Candidature; *Doctorat en Médecine*: Medicine, 6 yrs; *Diplôme d'Etudes approfondies (DEA)*: Agricultural Planning; Management Systems; Mathematics; Physics; *Diplôme de Spécialité*: Medicine; *Doctorat de Spécialité (3e Cycle)*

Student Residential Facilities: Yes

Libraries: c. 100,000 vols

Publications: Revue de l'Université (Séries: Sciences humaines; Sciences exactes, naturelles, et médicales)

Academic Staff *1999*: Full-Time: c. 170 Part-Time: c. 45 Total: c. 215

Student Numbers *1999:* Total: c. 4,200

PRIVATE INSTITUTIONS

UNIVERSITY OF THE GREAT LAKES
Université des Grands Lacs (UGL)
B.P. 2310, Bujumbura
Tel: +257(24) 3554
Telex: +257(27) 2020

Recteur: Sylvère Suguru
International Relations: Nicodème Niyongabo

Faculties
Administration and Business Management (Administration; Business Administration)
Education

UNIVERSITY OF LAKE TANGANYIKA
Université du Lac Tanganyika (ULT)
B.P. 5403, Bujumbura
Tel: +257(24) 3645

Recteur: Evariste Ngayimpenda

Faculties
Applied Economics (Economics)
Political and Administrative Studies (Administration; Political Science)
Social Sciences

UNIVERSITY 'LUMIÈRE' OF BUJUMBURA
Université Lumière de Bujumbura (ULBu)
B.P. 1368, Bujumbura
Tel: +257(23) 5549
Fax: +257(22) 9275
EMail: ulbu@cbinf.com
Website: http://www.ulbu.org

Recteur: Grégoire Njejimana

Directeur administratif: Parfait Mboninyibuka

Faculties
Communication Sciences (Communication Studies)
Management and Administration (Administration; Management)
Theology

UNIVERSITY OF NGOZI
Université de Ngozi
B.P. 137, Ngozi
Tel: +257(30) 2171
Fax: +257(30) 2259
EMail: Ungozi@cbinf.com

Recteur: Théophile Ndikumana

Directeur administratif: Erasme Nzeyimana

Faculties
Arts and Humanities
Higher Education
Paramedical Studies (Paramedical Sciences)
Political Science, Economics and Administration (Administration; Economics; Political Science)

OTHER INSTITUTIONS

PUBLIC INSTITUTIONS

ECOLE NATIONALE DE POLICE (ENAPO)
Bujumbura
Police Studies

ECOLE NORMALE SUPÉRIEURE (ENS)
B.P. 6983, Bujumbura
Tel: +257(24) 2799
Fax: +257(24) 3356
EMail: ENS@cbinf.com

Directeur: Charles Nditije

Chef du Service administratif: Gaspard Habarugira

Arts and Humanities; Modern Languages; Natural Sciences; Science Education; Teacher Training

INSTITUT SUPÉRIEUR DE GESTION DES ENTREPRISES (ISGE)
B.P. 2450, Bujumbura
Tel: +257(22) 4698 +257(21) 4875
Fax: +257(22) 1785
EMail: isge@cbinf.com

Directeur général: Damien Karerwa

Business Administration

PRIVATE INSTITUTIONS

COLLÈGE UNIVERSITAIRE DE BUJUMBURA (CUB)
B.P. 2393, Bujumbura
Tel: +257(24) 3944 +257(9) 20308
Fax: +257(22) 9656
EMail: cub@hotmail.com

Représentant légal: Laurent Tugizimana

Directeur administratif: Gérard Muringa

Administration; Business Administration

INSTITUT SUPÉRIEUR DE CONTRÔLE DE GESTION (ISCG)
B.P. 439, Bujumbura
Tel: +257(22) 4418
Fax: +257(24) 2186

Directeur général: André Nkundikije

Directeur administratif: Frédéric Hatungimana

Management

INSTITUT SUPÉRIEUR DES TECHNOLOGIES (IST)
B.P. 6960, Bujumbura
Tel: +257(21) 6662
EMail: istkana@yahoo.fr

Directeur: Emmanuel Kana

Computer Science; Electronic Engineering; Telecommunications Engineering

Cameroon

INSTITUTION TYPES AND CREDENTIALS

Types of higher education institutions:

Université (University)
Institut (Institute)
Grande Ecole (Higher School)

School leaving and higher education credentials:

Baccalauréat
City and Guilds Part III
General Certificate of Education Advanced Level
Brevet de Technicien
Certificat d'Aptitude de Maître d'Enseignement
Diplôme de Technicien supérieur
Diplôme d'Etudes universitaires en Sciences sociales (DEUSS)
Diplôme d'Etudes universitaires générales (DEUG)
Diplôme en Soins infirmiers
Diplôme universitaire de Technologie (DUT)
Bachelor's degree
Diplôme d'Ingénieur des Travaux
Diplôme de Professeur des Collèges d'Enseignement général
Diplôme de Professeur des Collèges d'Enseignement technique
Licence
Bachelor's Degree (Honours)
Diplôme
Diplôme d'Ingénieur
Diplôme de Professeur des Lycées d'Enseignement général
Diplôme de Professeur des Lycées d'Enseignement technique
Diplôme d'Etudes supérieures spécialisées (DESS)
Doctorat en Médecine
Diplôme d'Etudes approfondies (DEA.)
Maîtrise
Master's Degree
Postgraduate Diploma
Doctorat de troisième Cycle
Doctorat/Doctorate

STRUCTURE OF EDUCATION SYSTEM

Pre-higher education:

Duration of compulsory education:

Age of entry: 6
Age of exit: 12

Structure of school system:

Primary
Type of school providing this education: Ecole primaire (Francophone system)
Length of programme in years: 6
Age level from: 6 to: 12
Certificate/diploma awarded: Certificat d'Etudes primaires élémentaires (CEPE)

Primary
Type of school providing this education: Primary School (Anglophone system)
Length of programme in years: 7
Age level from: 5 to: 12
Certificate/diploma awarded: First School Leaving Certificate

Lower Secondary
Type of school providing this education: Lower Secondary School (Anglophone system)
Length of programme in years: 5
Age level from: 12 to: 17
Certificate/diploma awarded: Cameroon GCE "O' Level

General Secondary
Type of school providing this education: Collège d'Enseignement général, Collège d'Enseignement secondaire (Francophone system)
Length of programme in years: 4
Age level from: 12 to: 16
Certificate/diploma awarded: Brevet d'Etudes du premier Cycle du second Degré

Upper Secondary
Type of school providing this education: Lycée (Francophone system)
Length of programme in years: 3
Age level from: 16 to: 19
Certificate/diploma awarded: Baccalauréat

Upper Secondary
Type of school providing this education: Upper Secondary School (Anglophone system)
Length of programme in years: 2
Age level from: 17 to: 19
Certificate/diploma awarded: GCE' A' Level

Technical
Type of school providing this education: Lycée technique (Francophone system)
Length of programme in years: 7
Age level from: 12 to: 19
Certificate/diploma awarded: Brevet de Technicien, Baccalauréat

Technical
Type of school providing this education: Technical Secondary School (Anglophone system)
Length of programme in years: 7
Age level from: 12 to: 19
Certificate/diploma awarded: City and Guilds Part III

School education:

Primary education lasts for seven years in the Anglophone system, leading to the First School Leaving Certificate, and six years in the Francophone system, leading to the Certificat d'Etudes primaires élémentaires (CEPE). In the Anglophone system, the first cycle of secondary education lasts for five years and leads to the Cameroon GCE Ordinary level. Higher schools offer two-year courses leading to the GCE Advanced level. In the Francophone system, the first four years lead to the Brevet d'Etudes du premier Cycle du second Degré. At the Lycées (upper secondary), three years' study lead to the Baccalauréat. Technical secondary education leads to the City and Guilds Part III and to the Baccalauréat or the Brevet de Technicien respectively.

Higher education:

Higher education is mainly provided by universities, specialized institutions and schools. The Minister in charge of higher education takes final policy decisions regarding universities, although each university has a governing council. Councils have responsibility for personnel recruitment. The creation of new departments, degrees, courses and changes in regulations must receive ministerial consent. Each university receives a budget from the State. The University of Buéa is headed by a Vice-Chancellor who is nominated by the government and who in turn is chair of the Administrative Council. Other public universities are headed by a Rector. A Catholic University Institute was established in 1990. Several higher education institutions do not fall directly under the Ministry of Higher Education, but the Minister must ascertain that they meet academic standards. Some are directly run by other ministries and offer specialized training in such fields as agriculture, health, post and telecommunications, forestry and public works.

Main laws/decrees governing higher education:

Decree: Loi 005   Year: 2001
Concerns: Higher education

Decree: Decree 99/0055   Year: 1999
Concerns: Higher Education

Decree: Decree n°95/041   Year: 1995
Concerns: Ministry of Education

Decree: 93/026   Year: 1993
Concerns: universities

Academic year:

Classes from: October *to:* July

Long vacation from: 1 August *to:* 31 August

Languages of instruction:

English, French

Stages of studies:

Non-university level post-secondary studies (technical/vocational type):

Higher technical and vocational education is mainly provided by specialized schools and institutes in such fields as Administration, Technology, Social Work, and Public Works. They award diplomas generally recognized as equivalent to a first degree.

University level studies:

University level first stage: Premier Cycle, Bachelor's Degree:
In Economics and Management and in Law, the first stage leads to a Diplôme d'Etudes universitaires générales (DEUG) after two years. The Licence and Bachelor's degree are obtained after three years in the Humanities and in the Sciences. In Engineering, the Diplôme d'Ingénieur des Travaux and d'Ingénieur de Conception are conferred after three years' study (up to five years for Ingénieur de Conception). In Medical Sciences, the Diplôme de Technicien supérieur de la Santé is awarded after three years and the Diplôme en Soins infirmiers after two years. In Agronomy, a Diplôme d'Ingénieur agronome is conferred after four years' study at the Ecole nationale supérieure agronomique.

University level second stage: Deuxième Cycle:
In Law and Economics and Management, the Licence is conferred after a further year's study following the DEUG. The Maîtrise is conferred after a further two years' study after the Licence in Arts and Sciences. In Law it is conferred after a further year's study beyond the Licence. In Engineering a Diplôme d'Ingénieur is awarded after a total of five years' study. In Medicine, the Diplôme de Docteur en Médecine is conferred after six years. In Anglophone universities, Master's Degrees and Postgraduate Diplomas are conferred at least one year after the first terminal degree.

University level third stage: Troisième Cycle:
A Diplôme d'Etudes approfondies (DEA) and a Diplôme d'Etudes supérieures spécialisées (DESS) are conferred by the Francophone universities one year after the Maîtrise. A Doctorat de troisième Cycle is conferred after two to three years' further study. It is being replaced by the Doctorat unique, conferred four years after the Maîtrise. Anglophone universities award a Doctor's Degree.

Teacher education:

Training of pre-primary and primary/basic school teachers
Primary teachers are trained at the Ecoles normales d'Instituteurs (ENI). Holders of the BEPC are trained in two years and holders of the Baccalauréat are trained in three years. Holders of the Primary School Leaving Certificate are trained in three years. Holders of the GCE Ordinary level

examinations can complete the course in two years and holders of the GCE Advanced level examinations or those who have at least three years' teaching experience with the Grade II Certificate can complete the same course in one year.

Training of secondary school teachers

Secondary school teachers used to be trained in three years following secondary high school or two years following the first degree at the Ecoles normales supérieures for college teachers or at the Ecole normale supérieure d'Enseignement technique for technical education teachers. They obtained the Diplôme de Professeur des Collèges d'Enseignement secondaire général (three years), the Diplôme de Professeur des Lycées d'Enseignement général (five years), the Diplôme de Professeur des Collèges d'Enseignement technique or the Diplôme de Professeur des Lycées d'Enseignement technique. However, the Ecoles normales supérieures have stopped functioning since 1991.

Training of higher education teachers

Higher education teachers are recruited at the doctoral level.

NATIONAL BODIES

Responsible authorities:

Ministry of Higher Education (Ministère de l'Enseignement supérieur)
    Minister: Jean-Marie Antangana Mebara
    Secretary-General: Elie C. Ndjitoyap
    Director of Higher Education Development: F.-X. Etoa
    International Relations: Anaclet Fomethe
    PO Box 1457
    Yaoundé
    Tel: +237 (223) 3677
    Fax: +237 (223) 2282
    Telex: 8418 mesres ku
    WWW: http://www.minesup.gov.cm

ADMISSIONS TO HIGHER EDUCATION

Admission to non university higher education studies

Name of secondary school credential required: Baccalauréat

Name of secondary school credential required: General Certificate of Education Advanced Level

Admission to university-level studies

Name of secondary school credential required: Baccalauréat

Name of secondary school credential required: Brevet de Technicien
For entry to: Technical and Vocational School/Faculty

Name of secondary school credential required: General Certificate of Education Advanced Level

Entrance exams required: Entrance Examination

Foreign students admission

Definition of foreign student: Non-Cameroonian, non-member of CEMAC (Central African Economic Community)

Quotas: No.

Admission requirements: Foreign students must hold a Baccalauréat or its equivalent, a scientific Baccalauréat or a General Certificate of Education Advanced Level or the Higher School Certificate and have passed the competitive examination of one of the schools.

Entry regulations: Visa, residence permit

Health requirements: Medical assistance is offered free of charge at the university.

Language requirements: Good knowledge of French and English. Language and orientation courses are offered.

Recognition of studies and qualifications:

Studies pursued in foreign countries (bodies dealing with recognition of foreign credentials):
Division of Comparative University Systems and of Equivalences, Ministry of Higher Education
    Chief, Division of Comparative University Systems and Equivalences: Ebot Enaw
    Director, Student Assistance and Counselling: Eno Lafon
    PO Box 1457
    Yaoundé
    Tel: +237(223) 1407
    Telex: 8418 KN

    Services provided and students dealt with: Assistance to students of Cameroon nationality

References to further information on foreign student admissions and recognition of studies

Title: L'Annuaire de l'Université de Yaoundé
Publisher: Université de Yaoundé

Title: Livret de l'Etudiant (English and French editions)
Publisher: Université de Yaoundé

STUDENT LIFE

Main student services at national level

Service des oeuvres universitaires
    PO Box 337
    Yaoundé

National student associations and unions

MUSEC
 c/o University of Yaoundé
 Yaoundé

Health/social provisions

Social security for home students: Yes

Social security for foreign students: No

Student expenses and financial aid

Student costs:

 Home students tuition fees: Minimum: 50,000 (CFA Franc)
 Maximum: 825,000 (CFA Franc)
 Foreign students tuition fees: Minimum: 300,000 (CFA Franc)
 Maximum: 2,000,000 (CFA Franc)

Bodies providing information on student financial aid:

Direction de l'Assistance et de l'Orientation
 PO Box 1457
 Yaoundé

 Deals with: Grants and Loans
 Category of students: Scholarships for Cameroon students for Africa, Germany, Belgium, Brazil, Canada, China, Spain, United States, France, India, Italy, United Kingdom, Switzerland and Russia.

Publications on student services and financial aid:

 Title: Study Abroad 2000-2001
 Publisher: UNESCO/IBE
 Year of publication: 1999

INTERNATIONAL COOPERATION AND EXCHANGES

Principal national bodies responsible for dealing with international cooperation and exchanges in higher education:

Division de la Prospective, de la Recherche et de la Coopération, Ministère de l'Enseignement supérieur
 Chef: Anaclet Fomethe
 PO Box 1457
 Yaoundé
 Tel: +237 (223) 3677
 Fax: +237 (223) 2282
 WWW: http://www.minesup.gov.cm

GRADING SYSTEM

Usual grading system in secondary school

Full Description: 0-20 in the Francophone system. 0-9 fail; 10-11 passable; 12-13 assez bien; 14-15 bien; 16-20 très bien
Highest on scale: 20
Pass/fail level: 10
Lowest on scale: 0

Main grading system used by higher education institutions

Full Description: 0-20
Highest on scale: 20
Pass/fail level: 10
Lowest on scale: 0

Other main grading systems

In the Anglophone system grading follows the GCE Ordinary and Advanced level system.
Master's and Doctoral degrees can be awarded with the following classifications: très honorable avec félicitations du jury; très honorable; honorable. The University of Buea uses an A-F scale

NOTES ON HIGHER EDUCATION SYSTEM

Data for academic year: 2001-2002
Source: Ministry of Higher Education, Yaoundé, 2001

INSTITUTIONS OF HIGHER EDUCATION

UNIVERSITIES

PUBLIC INSTITUTIONS

• UNIVERSITY OF BUÉA
Université de Buéa
PO Box 63, Buéa, South West Province
Tel: +237(332) 2134
Fax: +237(343) 2508
Telex: 5155KN

Vice-Chancellor: Dorothy L. Njeuma (1993-)
Tel: +237(332) 2706

Registrar: Herbert N. Endeley Tel: +237(332) 2760

International Relations: Samson Abangma

Faculties
Agriculture and Veterinary Medicine (Agriculture; Veterinary Science)

Arts (Arts and Humanities; Curriculum; Educational Administration; English; French; History; Linguistics; Theatre) *Dean:* E. Gwan Achu

Engineering and Technology (Engineering; Technology)

Health Sciences *Dean:* Theodosia E. McMoli

Science (Biochemistry; Botany; Chemistry; Environmental Studies; Geology; Mathematics and Computer Science; Microbiology; Natural Sciences; Physics; Zoology) *Dean:* N.-M. Ntoko

Social and Management Sciences (Accountancy; Anthropology; Banking; Economics; Finance; Geography; Journalism; Law; Management; Mass Communication; Political Science; Social Sciences; Sociology; Women's Studies) *Dean:* Cornelius Lambi

Schools
Translation and Interpretation *(Advanced, ASTI) Director:* C. Nama

History: Founded 1977 as University Centre for postgraduate programme in translation and interpretation. Acquired present status and title 1992.

Governing Bodies: Conseil d'Administration, comprising 26 members; Senate

Academic Year: October to July (October-February; March-July)

Admission Requirements: Secondary school certificate and competitive entrance examination. Licence (Translation), or recognized equivalent for School of Translaltion and Interpretation

Fees: (Francs CFA): Foreign students, 300,000-1m. per annum

Main Language(s) of Instruction: French, English

International Co-operation: University College, London; Université René Descartes, Paris V; Leiden University; University of Strathclyde; University of Manchester; Université Stendhal, Grenoble III; Catholic University of Brussels; University of North Carolina; University of Wisconsin-Madison; University of South Carolina; Iowa State University of Science and Technology, Ames; South Bank University, London; University of Sussex, Brighton

Degrees and Diplomas: *Bachelor's degree*: Arts (BA); Law (LLB); Science (BSc), 3 yrs; *Bachelor's Degree (Honours)*: 4 yrs; *Master's Degree*: 1-2 yrs; *Postgraduate Diploma*: Education; Interpretation, 1 yr; *Doctorat/Doctorate*: 4 yrs

Student Services: Academic Counselling, Social Counselling, Foreign Student Adviser, Sports Facilities, Handicapped Facilities, Health Services, Canteen

Student Residential Facilities: Yes

Special Facilities: Language Laboratory; Interpretation Laboratory

Libraries: University of Buéa Library, c. 35,000 vols

Publications: Buéa University Newsletter, BUN (quarterly); UBDEF, University of Buéa Development Fund Newsletter; Epasa Moto, Bilingual Journal of Language, Letters and Culture (annually)

Academic Staff *1999:* Total: **255**

Student Numbers *1999*	MEN	WOMEN	TOTAL
All (Foreign Included)	2,585	1,962	**4,547**

UNIVERSITY OF DOUALA
Université de Douala
BP 2701, Douala
Tel: +237(340) 6415
Fax: +237(340) 4061

Recteur: Maurice Tchuente (2000-)

Secrétaire générale: Thérèse B. Wangue

International Relations: Nicole C. Ndoko

Faculties
Economics and Management (FSEGA) (Economics; Management; Marketing; Mathematics)

Law and Political Science (FSJP) (Law; Political Science; Private Law; Public Law)

Letters and Humanities (FLSH) (Arts and Humanities; Bilingual and Bicultural Education; Geography (Human); History; Literature)

Science (FS) (Biology; Chemistry; Computer Science; Mathematics; Natural Sciences; Physics)

Technical Studies (Technology)

Institutes
Economics and Commerce *(ESSEC)* (Business and Commerce; Economics)

Technical Studies *(ENSET)* (Management; Mathematics)
Technology *(IUT)* (Accountancy; Computer Science; Electrical and Electronic Engineering)

History: Founded 1977 as Centre Universitaire. Previously part of the University of Yaoundé. Acquired present status and title 1993.

Governing Bodies: Conseil d'Administration

Academic Year: October to July (October-December; January-March; April-July)

Admission Requirements: Competitive entrance examination following secondary school certificate (baccalauréat)

Main Language(s) of Instruction: French, English

International Co-operation: Ecole des hautes Etudes commerciales, Montréal; Ecole polytechnique, Montréal; Ecoles supérieures de Commerce Paris, Rouen; Ecoles normales supérieures de l'Enseignement technique, Cachan, Tunis

Degrees and Diplomas: *Diplôme de Technicien supérieur*: 3 yrs; *Diplôme de Professeur des Collèges d'Enseignement technique*: 3-5 yrs; *Licence*: 3 yrs; *Diplôme*: Commerce, 4 yrs; *Maîtrise*: 4 yrs. Also Brevet, 2 yrs

Student Services: Academic Counselling, Cultural Centre, Sports Facilities, Health Services, Canteen

Student Residential Facilities: Yes

Libraries: Central Library, c. 5570 vols; libraries of the schools, c. 3900

Academic Staff *1999:* Total: c. 100

Student Numbers *1999:* Total: c. 960

HIGHER SCHOOL OF ECONOMICS AND COMMERCE
ECOLE SUPÉRIEURE DES SCIENCES ÉCONOMIQUES ET COMMERCIALES
BP 1971, Douala
Tel: +237(342) 5298

Directeur: Emmanuel Kamdem

Departments
Economics, Business and Commerce (Business and Commerce; Economics)
Finance and Accountancy (Accountancy; Finance)
Human Relations Management (Behavioural Sciences)
Information Systems (Information Sciences)
International Management and Commerce (Business and Commerce; International Business)
Marketing

History: Founded 1979. Acquired present status and title 1993.

HIGHER SCHOOL OF TECHNICAL TEACHER TRAINING
ECOLE NORMALE SUPÉRIEURE DE L'ENSEIGNEMENT TECHNIQUE
BP 1872, Douala
Tel: +237(342) 6609

Directeur: John M. O. Ebanja

Education; Technology
Administration Techniques (Administration)

Chemistry
Civil Engineering
Economics
Mechanical Engineering

History: Founded 1979. Acquired present status and title 1993.

• UNIVERSITY OF DSCHANG
Université de Dschang
BP 96, Dschang
Tel: +237(345) 1381
Fax: +237(345) 1381
Telex: 970 7013 kn
EMail: udsrect@sdnemr.undp.org

Recteur: Remy S. Bouelet (2000-)

Secrétaire général: André Mvesso

Faculties
Economics and Management (FSEG) (Economics; Management) *Dean*: S. Ngogang
Law and Political Science (FSJP) (Law; Political Science) *Dean*: F. Anoukaha
Letters and Humanities (FALSH) (African Studies; Arts and Humanities; Philosophy; Psychology; Sociology) *Dean*: M. Kuete
Science (FS) (Natural Sciences) *Dean*: M. Mpoame
Science and Agriculture (FASA) (Animal Husbandry; Forestry; Rural Studies) *Dean*: A. Tchala

Institutes
Arts *(Foumban)* (Fine Arts)
Technology *(Bandjoun)*

Centres
Advanced Training
Audiovisual (Cinema and Television)
Computer (Computer Science)

History: Founded 1977 as Centre Universitaire. Previously part of the University of Yaoundé. Acquired present status and title 1993.

Academic Year: October to July (October-March; March-July)

Admission Requirements: Secondary school certificate (baccalauréat), or foreign equivalent at Advanced 'A' level

Fees: (Francs CFA): Foreign students, 500,000-1m. per annum

Main Language(s) of Instruction: French, English

Degrees and Diplomas: *Diplôme de Technicien supérieur*: Agriculture, 3 yrs; *Diplôme d'Etudes universitaires générales (DEUG)*: 2 yrs; *Licence*: 3 yrs; *Diplôme d'Ingénieur*: Agronomy, 5 yrs; *Maîtrise*: 4 yrs; *Master's Degree*: (MA), 5 yrs; *Doctorat/Doctorate*: Agronomy

Libraries: Central Library, c. 16,000 vols

Academic Staff *1999:* Total: **340**

Student Numbers *1999*	TOTAL
All (Foreign Included)	**8,156**
FOREIGN ONLY	18

*• UNIVERSITY OF NGAOUNDÉRÉ

Université de Ngaoundéré

BP 454, Ngaoundéré
Tel: +237(225) 2767 +237(225) 2765
Fax: +237(225) 2751
Telex: cundere 970 7645 kn

Recteur: Maurice Tchuente (2000-)

Secrétaire général: Hamadou Adama

International Relations: Joseph Kayem Guiffo

Faculties

Economics and Management (FSEG) (Economics; Management) *Dean*: L. Kombou
Education
Law and Political Science (FSJP) (Law; Political Science)
Letters and Human Sciences (FALSH) (Arts and Humanities) *Dean*: Jean-Louis Dongmo
Science (FS) (Mathematics and Computer Science; Natural Sciences) *Dean*: B. Oumarou

Schools

Agro-Industrial Sciences (ENSAI) (Agriculture; Industrial Engineering)
Chemical Engineering and Mineral Studies (Chemical Engineering; Mineralogy)
Geology and Mining Prospecting (Geology; Mining Engineering)
Science and Veterinary Medicine (Veterinary Science)

Institutes

Technology *(IUT) Director*: R. Parrot

History: Founded 1982 as Centre Universitaire, acquired present status and title 1993. A State institution.

Governing Bodies: Conseil d'Administration

Academic Year: October to July (October-February; March-July)

Admission Requirements: Secondary school certificate (baccalauréat), or foreign equivalent at Advanced ('A') level

Fees: (Francs CFA): Foreign students, undergraduate, 300,000-600,000 per annum; postgraduate, 3m.-5m

Main Language(s) of Instruction: French, English

International Co-operation: Institut national polytechnique de Lorraine; University Paris VI

Degrees and Diplomas: *Diplôme de Technicien supérieur*: Agroindustrial Sciences, 3 yrs; *Diplôme d'Etudes universitaires générales (DEUG)*: 2 yrs; *Diplôme d'Ingénieur des Travaux*: Agroindustrial Sciences; *Licence*: 3 yrs; *Diplôme d'Ingénieur*; *Diplôme d'Etudes approfondies (DEA.)*; *Doctorat/Doctorate*

Student Residential Facilities: Yes

Libraries: Total, c. 50,000 vols

Academic Staff *1999:* Total: **180**

Student Numbers *1999:* Total: **35**

HIGHER SCHOOL OF AGRO-FOOD INDUSTRIES OF CAMEROON
ECOLE NATIONALE SUPÉRIEURE DES AGRO-INDUSTRIES DU CAMEROUN
BP 455, Ngaoundéré
Tel: +237(225) 1313

Directeur: Carl M. Mbofung (2000-)

Schools

Agro-Food Technologies (Agricultural Engineering; Food Science)

History: Founded 1982.

• UNIVERSITY OF YAOUNDÉ I

Université de Yaoundé I (UY I)

BP 337, Yaoundé, Centre
Tel: +237(222) 0744
Fax: +237(222) 1320
EMail: uy.cdc@uninet.cm
Website: http://www.uninet.cm/uy1/uy1.html

Recteur: Jean Tabi Manga (2000-2003)

Secrétaire générale: Lisette Elomo Ntonba

International Relations: Edward Ako
EMail: tako@uycdc.uninet.cm

Faculties

Letters and Humanities (FALSH) (African Languages; African Studies; Anthropology; Archaeology; Arts and Humanities; English; Fine Arts; Foreign Languages Education; French; Geography; German; History; Philosophy; Psychology; Sociology; Spanish) *Dean*: André Marie Ntsobé, *full-time staff:* 178, *part-time staff:* 47, *students:* 6,429
Medicine and Biomedical Studies (FSMB) (Anaesthesiology; Anatomy; Behavioural Sciences; Biology; Biomedicine; Botany; Cardiology; Dentistry; Dermatology; Embryology and Reproduction Biology; Endocrinology; Environmental Studies; Epidemiology; Gastroenterology; Gynaecology and Obstetrics; Haematology; Health Education; Medical Technology; Medicine; Microbiology; Nephrology; Nutrition; Ophthalmology; Otorhinolaryngology; Paediatrics; Parasitology; Pathology; Pharmacology; Physiology; Pneumology; Psychiatry and Mental Health; Radiology; Surgery; Venereology; Virology) *Dean*: Peter Martins Ndumbe, *full-time staff:* 179, *part-time staff:* 6, *students:* 635
Science (FS) (Biochemistry; Biology; Computer Science; Earth Sciences; Inorganic Chemistry; Mathematics; Natural Sciences; Organic Chemistry; Physics; Physiology) *Dean*: Jean Wouafo Kamga, *full-time staff:* 232, *part-time staff:* 58, *students:* 8,126

Schools

Advanced Teacher Training College (ENS) (Biology; Chemistry; Education; Educational Sciences; English; Foreign Languages Education; French; Geography; History; Mathematics Education; Philosophy; Physics; Teacher Training) *Head*:

Mathieu-François Minyono Nkodo, *full-time staff:* 153, *part-time staff:* 33, *students:* 4,689

Polytechnic (ENSP) (Chemistry; Civil Engineering; Computer Engineering; Electrical Engineering; Engineering; Industrial Engineering; Mechanical Engineering; Physics; Technology; Urban Studies) *Head:* Gérard Michel, *full-time staff:* 86, *part-time staff:* 4, *students:* 464

History: Founded 1962, replacing the Institut national d'Etudes supérieures, founded 1961. Acquired present status and title 1993. A State Institution responsible to the Ministry of Education.

Governing Bodies: Conseil de l'Enseignement supérieur, presided over by the President of the Republic; Conseil d'Administration.

Academic Year: October to August (October-February; March-August)

Admission Requirements: Secondary school certificate (baccalauréat) or foreign equivalent, and entrance examination (for Medicine and Engineering)

Fees: (Francs CFA): 50,000 per annum; foreign students, 600,000-2m. per annum

Main Language(s) of Instruction: French, English

International Co-operation: University of Geneva; University François Rabelais of Tours. Participates in the Fulbright Grant programme

Degrees and Diplomas: *Diplôme de Professeur des Collèges d'Enseignement général:* Teaching Qualification, 2 yrs; *Licence:* Economics; Law; Letters; Science, 3 yrs; *Diplôme d'Ingénieur:* Engineering, 5 yrs; *Diplôme de Professeur des Lycées d'Enseignement général:* Teaching Qualification, 4 yrs; *Doctorat en Médecine:* Medicine, 6-7 yrs; *Maîtrise:* a further 1-2 yrs; *Doctorat de troisième Cycle:* 2-3 yrs

Student Residential Facilities: Yes

Libraries: Central Library, c. 90,000 vols

Publications: Annales des Facultés (annually); Revue Ecriture; Sosongo; Syllabus

Academic Staff *1999-2000*	TOTAL
FULL-TIME	781
PART-TIME	148
TOTAL	**929**

Student Numbers *1999-2000:* Total: **20,343**

UNIVERSITY OF YAOUNDÉ II

Université de Yaoundé II (UY II)
BP 1365, Yaoundé
Tel: +237(223) 6553
Fax: +237(223) 6554

Recteur: Bruno B. Ebe

Secrétaire général: Jean Ongla

International Relations: Georges E. Ekodeck

Faculties
Economics and Management (FSEG) (Economics; Management)
Law and Political Science (FSJP) (Law; Political Science)

Higher Schools
Information and Communication (ESSTIC) (Information Sciences; Journalism; Mass Communication; Radio and Television Broadcasting)

Institutes
International Relations (IRIC) (International Relations)
Training and Demographic Research (IFORD) (Demography and Population)

History: Founded 1993.

Academic Year: October to July (October-December; January-March; April-July)

Admission Requirements: Secondary school certificate (baccalauréat) or foreign equivalent, and entrance examination

Main Language(s) of Instruction: French, English

Degrees and Diplomas: *Brevet de Technicien:* Information, 2 yrs; *Licence:* Economics; Law, 3 yrs; *Diplôme:* Journalism, 3 yrs; *Maîtrise:* International Relations; Political Science, 5 yrs; Law, a further 2 yr; Economics, a further 2 yrs; *Doctorat/Doctorate:* Law; Science, 2-4 yrs following Maîtrise; International Relations, 4 yrs

Libraries: Bibliothèque de l'Université

PRIVATE INSTITUTIONS

CATHOLIC INSTITUTE OF YAOUNDÉ-CATHOLIC UNIVERSITY OF CENTRAL AFRICA
Institut catholique de Yaoundé-Université catholique d'Afrique centrale (ICY/UCAC)
Yaoundé, Centre 11628
Tel: +237(223) 7400
Fax: +237(223) 7402
EMail: ucac.icy-nk@camnet.cm

Recteur: Oscar Eone Eone (1999-2002)
Tel: +237(223) 7403 +237(223) 7400
EMail: ucac.icy-ek@camnet.cm

Faculties
Philosophy *Dean:* Gabriel Ndinga, *full-time staff:* 7, *part-time staff:* 21, *students:* 166
Social Sciences and Management (Accountancy; Computer Science; Economics; Law; Management; Political Science; Social Sciences) *Dean:* Louis De Vaocelles, *full-time staff:* 13, *part-time staff:* 64, *students:* 728
Theology *Dean:* Antoine Babe, *full-time staff:* 10, *part-time staff:* 23, *students:* 193

Board of Studies
Accountancy-Finance (Accountancy; Finance)
Human Rights Research *(GRDH)* (Human Rights) *Director:* Denis Maugenest
Interdisciplinary Studies on African Theology (African Studies; Theology) *Director:* Antoine Babé
Promotion of Human Dignity in Africa (Ethics) *Director:* Jean Didier Boukongou

Socio-Anthropology *(IRSA)* (Anthropology; Sociology) *Director*: Séverin Cécile Abega

Departments
Canon Law *Director*: Alfred Nothum, *full-time staff:* 4, *part-time staff:* 18, *students:* 20
Nursing *Director*: Renée Geoffray, *full-time staff:* 23, *part-time staff:* 50, *students:* 131

Research Groups
Artificial Intelligence and Management Sciences (GRIAGE) (Artificial Intelligence; Management) *Director*: Philippe Dubin
Business and Culture (GREC) (Business Administration; Cultural Studies) *Director*: Philippe Dubin

History: Founded 1989, opened 1991

Governing Bodies: Administrative Council; Private Council; Permanent Council; Academic Council

Academic Year: October to June (October-February; March-June)

Admission Requirements: Secondary school certificate (baccalauréat), or foreign equivalent

Fees: (Francs CFA): 363,000-825,000 per annum

Main Language(s) of Instruction: French

International Co-operation: Université catholique de Paris; Université catholique de Lille; Université catholique de Toulouse; Université catholique de Lyon; Université catholique de Strasbourg; Université de Paris Sud; Université Montesquieu Bordeaux IV; Salesian Pontifical University, Rome; Université du Québec, Chicoutimi; Université de Libreville

Degrees and Diplomas: *Diplôme d'Etudes universitaires en Sciences sociales (DEUSS)* : Social Sciences, 2 yrs; *Diplôme d'Etudes universitaires générales (DEUG)*: General Studies, 2 yrs; *Diplôme universitaire de Technologie (DUT)*: Gestion: Management, 2 yrs; *Licence*: 3 yrs; *Diplôme d'Etudes supérieures spécialisées (DESS)*: Management des Projets en Afrique: African Projects Management, 5 yrs; *Diplôme d'Etudes approfondies (DEA.)*: 6 yrs; *Maîtrise*: 3-5 yrs; Sciences et Techniques Comptables et Financières: Finance and Accountancy (MSTCF), 4 yrs

Student Services: Academic Counselling, Social Counselling, Employment Services, Foreign Student Adviser, Nursery Care, Cultural Centre, Sports Facilities, Health Services, Canteen

Student Residential Facilities: For 215 students

Libraries: 34,250 vols

Publications: Cahiers de l'UCAC (annually)

Press or Publishing House: Presses de l'USAC

Academic Staff *1999-2000*	MEN	WOMEN	TOTAL
FULL-TIME	30	9	39
PART-TIME	141	64	205
TOTAL	**171**	**73**	**244**
STAFF WITH DOCTORATE			
FULL-TIME	24	4	28
PART-TIME	80	16	96
TOTAL	**104**	**20**	**124**

Student Numbers *1999-2000*		TOTAL
All (Foreign Included)		**1,107**
FOREIGN ONLY		169

Evening Students, 54

OTHER INSTITUTIONS

PUBLIC INSTITUTIONS

HIGHER SCHOOL OF POST AND TELECOMMUNICATIONS
Ecole supérieure des Postes et Télécommunications
BP 1186, Yaoundé
Tel: +237(222) 3700
Post and Telecommunications (Postal Services; Telecommunications Services)

INSTITUTE OF ADMINISTRATION AND FINANCE
Institut des Techniques administratives et financières
BP 23-11-40, Yaoundé
Tel: +237(223) 2013
Administration; Finance

INSTITUTE OF STATISTICS AND ECONOMICS
Institut sous-régional de Statistiques et d'Economie appliquée
Yaoundé
Applied Statistics and Economics (Economics; Statistics)

History: Founded 1961

INSTITUTE OF TRAINING AND RESEARCH IN DEMOGRAPHY
Institut de Formation et de Recherche démographiques
BP 1556, Yaoundé
Tel: +237(222) 2471
Demography Research (Demography and Population)

History: Founded 1972

INTERNATIONAL INSTITUTE OF INSURANCE
Institut International des Assurances (IIA)
BP 1575, Yaoundé, Centre 1575
Tel: +237(220) 7152
Fax: +237(220) 7151
EMail: iia@syfed.cm.refer.org
Website: http://www.cm.refer.org

67

Directeur général: Jean Gratien Zanouvi (1996-)
EMail: DG-iia@syfed.cm.org

Directeur Administratif et Financier: Albert Mboko
Mondombélé EMail: DAF-iia@syfed.cm.refer.org

International Relations: Momath Ndao
EMail: DE-iia@syfed.cm.refer.org

Insurance Management and Studies (Insurance)

History: Founded 1972. Acquired present status 1992.

Governing Bodies: Conseil des Ministres; Conseil d'Administration

Academic Year: December to November

Admission Requirements: DEUG for cycle II, MSTA; Master for cycle III, DESSA

Fees: None for national students and students of member countries. Foreign students, US$ 7500

Main Language(s) of Instruction: French

International Co-operation: Ecole Nationale des Assurances (Paris). CAMES; AUPELF-UREF; Association des Etablissements Francophones de Formation à l'Assurance (AIEFFA)

Degrees and Diplomas: *Diplôme*: Technicien, 2 yrs; *Diplôme d'Etudes supérieures spécialisées (DESS)*: Insurance, Management, 2 yrs

Student Services: Foreign Student Adviser, Cultural Centre, Sports Facilities, Health Services, Canteen

Student Residential Facilities: Yes

Libraries: Main Library

Publications: Afrique Assurance, Research in the field of Insurance (biannually); 'Assur Echo', Student magazine (annually)

Academic Staff *1999-2000:* Total: **4**

Staff with doctorate: Total: **1**

Student Numbers 1999-2000	MEN	WOMEN	TOTAL
All (Foreign Included)	50	5	**55**

NATIONAL HIGHER SCHOOL OF PUBLIC WORKS

Ecole nationale supérieure des Travaux publics (ENSTP)
BP 510, Yaoundé, Centre
Tel: +237(222) 0406 +237(223) 0944
Fax: +237(223) 0944
EMail: enstp@iccnet.cm

Directeur: George Elambo Nkeng Fax: +237(223) 0499
EMail: gnkeng@yahoo.com

Departments
Civil Engineering (Civil Engineering; Town Planning) *Head*: Emmanuel Etonde Sosso, *full-time staff*: 28, *part-time staff*: 13, *students*: 293

Management (Engineering Management; Management) *Head*: Jean Tchami, *full-time staff*: 6, *part-time staff*: 35, *students*: 41
Rural Engineering (Agricultural Engineering; Surveying and Mapping) *Head*: André Talla, *full-time staff*: 41, *part-time staff*: 16, *students*: 162

History: Founded 1982.

Governing Bodies: Ministère des Travaux Publics

Academic Year: September to June

Admission Requirements: Secondary school certificate (GCE Advanced Level)

Fees: (Francs CFA): 185 000-315 000 per annum

Main Language(s) of Instruction: French, English

Degrees and Diplomas: *Diplôme de Technicien supérieur*: Civil Engineering, Rural Engineering, 2 yrs; *Diplôme d'Ingénieur des Travaux*: Civil Engineering, Rural Engineering, 3 yrs; *Master's Degree*: Engineering Management (MSc Engineering Mgt), 2 yrs

Student Services: Academic Counselling, Social Counselling, Sports Facilities, Language Programmes, Health Services

Student Residential Facilities: None

Libraries: Main Library

Academic Staff 1999-2000	MEN	WOMEN	TOTAL
FULL-TIME	58	2	60
PART-TIME	57	7	64
TOTAL	**115**	**9**	**124**
STAFF WITH DOCTORATE			
FULL-TIME	1	–	1
PART-TIME	24	3	27
TOTAL	**25**	**3**	**28**

Student Numbers 1999-2000	MEN	WOMEN	TOTAL
All (Foreign Included)	449	47	**496**
FOREIGN ONLY	2	1	3

NATIONAL CENTRE FOR ADMINISTRATION AND MAGISTRACY

Centre national d' Administration et de Magistrature
BP 128, Yaoundé
Tel: +237(222) 2431

Administration
Magistracy (Justice Administration)

NATIONAL HIGHER SCHOOL OF POLICE STUDIES

Ecole nationale supérieure de Police
BP 148, Yaoundé
Tel: +237(222) 4260

Police Studies

NATIONAL INSTITUTE OF YOUTH AND SPORT

Institut national de la Jeunesse et des Sports
BP 1016, Yaoundé

Physical Education

History: Founded 1961

NATIONAL SCHOOL FOR ADMINISTRATION AND MAGISTRACY

Ecole nationale d'Administration et de Magistrature (ENAM)
BP 7171, Yaoundé
Tel: +237(222) 3754
Fax: +237(223) 1308

Directeur général: Benjamin Amama Tel: +237(223) 1308

Directeur suppléant: André Abate Messanga
Tel: +237(223) 0931

International Relations: Constantin Abena

Divisions

Accountancy and Taxation (Accountancy; Taxation) *Head*:
Jacques Burnouf
Administration (Administration; Labour and Industrial Relations; Social Welfare) *Head*: Abdoulaye Nana
Justice Administration *Head*: Bruno Latastate, *full-time staff:* 4

Centres

Research and Documentation (Documentation Techniques)
Head: Constantin Abena, *full-time staff:* 7

History: Founded 1959. Acquired present status 1995.

Governing Bodies: Ministère de Tutelle; Conseil d'Administration

Admission Requirements: Secondary school certificate or equivalent and competitive entrance examination

Main Language(s) of Instruction: French, English

Degrees and Diplomas: *Diplôme*: Cycle A (ENAM); Cycle B (ENAM), 2 yrs

Student Services: Sports Facilities, Language Programmes

Libraries: Library and Documentation Office

Publications: Journal de l'ENAM (biannually)

Academic Staff *1999-2000*	TOTAL
FULL-TIME	63
PART-TIME	31
TOTAL	**94**

Staff with doctorate: Total: **6**

Student Numbers *1999-2000:* Total: **1,063**

NATIONAL SCHOOL OF SOCIAL WORKERS

Ecole nationale des Assistantes sociales
Yaoundé

Social Work

PANAFRICAN INSTITUTE FOR DEVELOPMENT IN CENTRAL AFRICA

Institut panafricain pour le Développement en Afrique Centrale (IPD-AC/PAID-CA)
BP 4078, Douala, Littoral
Tel: +237(340) 3770
Fax: +237(340) 3968
Telex: 6048 KN
EMail: ipdac@camnet.cm

Directeur: Ernest Zocli (1996-)

Directeur adjoint: Jacob Ngwa

International Relations: Faya Kondiano, Secrétaire général
Tel: +237(342) 1061 Fax: +237(342) 4335

Institutes

Panafrican Development (Adult Education; African Studies; Development Studies; Library Science; Natural Resources; Rural Studies) *Director*: Ernest Zocli, *full-time staff:* 13, *part-time staff:* 9, *students:* 128

History: Founded 1965, IPD-AC contributes to the development of regions through training, research and practical action, counselling, publication and institution development

Governing Bodies: Conseil d'Administration

Academic Year: October to September

Admission Requirements: Secondary school certificate or equivalent

Main Language(s) of Instruction: French

Degrees and Diplomas: *Diplôme de Technicien supérieur*:
Diplôme de Cadre Technique de Développement: Etude du Milieu, Projet de Développement, Gestion des Entreprises et Coopératives/Microfinance et Développement, Développement Local et Gestion des Ressources Naturelles: Development Studies and Management (DCTD), 2 yrs; *Diplôme d'Etudes supérieures spécialisées (DESS)*. Also Certificat de fin de Formation, 1-7 months

Student Services: Academic Counselling, Sports Facilities, Health Services, Canteen

Student Residential Facilities: None

Libraries: Main Library

Publications: Nouvelles de l'IPD-AC (biannually)

Academic Staff *1999-2000*	MEN	WOMEN	TOTAL
FULL-TIME	11	2	13
PART-TIME	5	4	9
TOTAL	**16**	**6**	**22**

Staff with doctorate: Total: **4**

Student Numbers *1999-2000*	MEN	WOMEN	TOTAL
All (Foreign Included)	76	52	**128**
FOREIGN ONLY	49	31	80

PRIVATE INSTITUTIONS

FACULTY OF PROTESTANT THEOLOGY
Faculté de Théologie protestante de Yaoundé
PO Box 4011, Yaoundé, Center Province
Tel: +237(221) 2690
Fax: +237(220) 5324
EMail: unipro@acamnet.cm

Dean: Maurice Kouam
Academic Secretary: Jean-Samuel Zoe-Obianga
International Relations: Friedegard Schneider Owono

Protestant Theology *Dean:* Maurice Kouam, *full-time staff:* 8, *part-time staff:* 8, *students:* 179

History: Founded 1962.
Admission Requirements: Baccalauréat; Licence
Fees: (Francs CFA) Maîtrise: 240,000 per annum; Doctorat: 440,000 per annum

Main Language(s) of Instruction: French

Degrees and Diplomas: *Maîtrise*: Theology, 2 yrs; *Doctorat/Doctorate*: Theology, 5 yrs

Student Services: Academic Counselling, Employment Services, Nursery Care, Sports Facilities, Health Services, Canteen

Publications: Marturia, Lettre de la Faculté

Press or Publishing House: Flambeau

Academic Staff 2000	MEN	WOMEN	TOTAL
FULL-TIME	8	–	8
PART-TIME	5	3	8
TOTAL	**13**	**3**	**16**
STAFF WITH DOCTORATE			
FULL-TIME			6
PART-TIME			3
TOTAL			**9**

Student Numbers 2000	MEN	WOMEN	TOTAL
All (Foreign Included)	160	13	**173**
FOREIGN ONLY	90	3	93

Central African Republic

INSTITUTION TYPES AND CREDENTIALS

Types of higher education institutions:

Université (University)
Institut (Institute)

School leaving and higher education credentials:

Baccalauréat
Capacité en Droit
Diplôme
Diplôme de Technicien supérieur de Santé
Diplôme d'Etudes économiques générales (DEEG)
Diplôme d'Etudes juridiques générales (DEJG)
Diplôme d'Etudes universitaires générales (DEUG)
Diplôme universitaire d'Etudes littéraires (DUEL)
Diplôme universitaire d'Etudes scientifiques (DUES)
Certificat d'Aptitude professionnelle à l'Enseignement dans les Collèges d'Enseignement général
Certificat d'Aptitude professionnelle du second Cycle dans les Lycées
Diplôme d'Ingénieur
Diplôme supérieur de Gestion (DSG)
Licence
Maîtrise
Doctorat en Médecine

STRUCTURE OF EDUCATION SYSTEM

Pre-higher education:

Duration of compulsory education:

    Age of entry: 6
    Age of exit: 14

Structure of school system:

    Basic First Stage
    Type of school providing this education: Ecole primaire
    Length of programme in years: 6

Age level from: 6 to: 12

Certificate/diploma awarded: Certificat d'Etudes fondamentales 1 (CEF)

Basic Second Stage

Type of school providing this education: College d'Enseignement secondaire

Length of programme in years: 4

Age level from: 12 to: 16

Certificate/diploma awarded: Brevet d'Etudes fondamentales 2 (BEF)(formerly Brevet d'Etudes du premier Cycle)

General Secondary

Type of school providing this education: Lycée

Length of programme in years: 3

Age level from: 16 to: 19

Certificate/diploma awarded: Baccalauréat

Technical Secondary

Type of school providing this education: Collège d'Enseignement technique

Length of programme in years: 3

Age level from: 15 to: 18

Certificate/diploma awarded: Certificat d'Aptitude professionnelle (CAP)

Technical

Type of school providing this education: Lycée technique

Length of programme in years: 3

Age level from: 16 to: 19

Certificate/diploma awarded: Baccalauréat de Technicien

School education:

Basic education lasts for ten years divided into six years' basic first stage (leading to the Certificat d'Etudes fondamentales 1) and four years' basic second stage (leading to the Brevet d'Etudes fondamentales 2). General secondary school lasts for three years and leads to the Baccalauréat which gives access to higher education.

Technical education at secondary level is offered at two levels: Form 4 school leavers may study for four years in a College d'Enseignement technique and obtain the Certificat d'Aptitude professionnelle (CAP); and Form 3 school leavers may study for three years at a lycée technique and obtain the Baccalauréat de Technicien.

Higher education:

Postsecondary education is offered at the Université de Bangui, which comprises faculties, institutes and a Higher Teacher Training College (Ecole normale supérieure). The Administrative Council, presided over by the Minister of national Education and Higher Education and composed of people nominated by the Minister of Finance, implements the University's development plan set out by the government. The University Council, presided over by the president of the university, approves proposed official documents to be submitted to higher authorities. It is consulted about the regulations, organization and programme of study.

Academic year:

Classes from: September *to:* June

Long vacation from: 30 June *to:* 1 September

Languages of instruction:

French

Stages of studies:

Non-university level post-secondary studies (technical/vocational type):

Technical and Engineering education are offered at the University of Bangui. Technical training in Agriculture is offered by the Institut d'Etudes Agronomiques d'Afrique Centrale M'Baiki which recently affiliated itself with the University of Bangui.

University level studies:

University level first stage: *Premier Cycle*:

The first cycle lasts two years. Admission is based on the Baccalauréat. It leads to a Degree which bears the name of the specialization in which it is awarded: Diplôme d'Etudes universitaires générales (DEUG), Diplôme universitaire d'Etudes littéraires (DUEL), Diplôme universitaire d'Etudes scientifiques (DUES), Diplôme universitaire d'Etudes juridiques (DUEJ), Diplôme d'Etudes économiques générales (DEEG).

University level second stage: *Deuxième Cycle*:

The second cycle lasts one year after the Diploma programme and leads to the Licence. In Engineering, the Diplôme d'Ingénieur is conferred after three years' study and a Diplôme d'Ingénieur d'Agriculture is awarded after four years. A further year leads to the Maîtrise (in the University). In Medicine, a Doctorate is awarded after six years. It is the only Doctorate awarded by the University.

Teacher education:

Training of pre-primary and primary/basic school teachers

Basic school teachers first stage are trained in two years after the Baccalauréat at the Ecole normale d'Instituteurs. The course leads to the Certificat d'Aptitude pédagogique.

Training of secondary school teachers

Basic school teachers second stage follow a three-year course after obtaining the Baccalauréat at the Université de Bangui or the Ecole normale Supérieure. They are awarded the Certificat d'Aptitude professionnelle au Professorat du premier Cycle (CAP/PC). Lycée teachers take a four-year course after obtaining the Baccalauréat at the Ecole normale Supérieure de Bangui. They are awarded the Certificat d'Aptitude pédagogique à l'Enseignement secondaire (CAPES).

NATIONAL BODIES

Responsible authorities:

Ministry of National Education and Higher Education (Ministère de l'Education nationale et de l'Enseignement supérieur (MENES))

Minister of Education: Timaléon Mbaikoua
Chief of Cabinet: François Bandio
International Relations: A. Clément Guyana-Massogo
PO Box 35
Bangui
Tel: +236(61) 72-19
Fax: +236(61) 72-19
Telex: mineduc5333rc bangui

ADMISSIONS TO HIGHER EDUCATION

Admission to non university higher education studies

Name of secondary school credential required: Baccalauréat

Alternatives to credentials: Baccalauréat de Technicien

Admission to university-level studies

Name of secondary school credential required: Baccalauréat

Alternatives to credentials: Completion of seven years study at secondary level is required for entrance to the following programmes: Diplôme d'Aide en Hygiène/Santé/Accoucheuse; Diplôme d'Agent de Développement communautaire.

GRADING SYSTEM

Usual grading system in secondary school

Full Description: 17-20=Très Bien; 14-16=Bien; 12-13=Assez Bien; 10-11=Passable; 0-9=Ajourné.
Highest on scale: 20
Pass/fail level: 10
Lowest on scale: 0

Main grading system used by higher education institutions

Full Description: 17-20=Très Bien; 14-16=Bien; 12-13=Assez Bien; 10-11=Passable; 0-9=Ajourné
Highest on scale: 20
Pass/fail level: 10
Lowest on scale: 0

NOTES ON HIGHER EDUCATION SYSTEM

Data for academic year: 2000-2001
Source: International Association of Universities (IAU), updated from IBE website, 2001

INSTITUTIONS OF HIGHER EDUCATION

UNIVERSITIES

PUBLIC INSTITUTIONS

• UNIVERSITY OF BANGUI
Université de Bangui
BP 1450, Avenue des Martyrs, Bangui
Tel: +236(61) 20-00
Fax: +236(61) 78-90
EMail: univ-bangui@yahoo.fr
Recteur: Luc Marboua-Bara Tel: +236(61) 17-67
Secrétaire général: Gabriel Ngouandji-Tanga
Tel: +236(61) 64-60
International Relations: Clément Anicet Guiyama-Massogo

Faculties
Health Sciences (Biomedicine; Community Health; Education; Health Sciences)
Law and Economics (Economics; Law)
Letters and Humanities (Arts and Humanities; English; History; Philosophy; Spanish)
Sciences (Building Technologies; Construction Engineering; Mathematics and Computer Science; Natural Sciences; Physics; Science Education; Technology)

Higher Schools
Teacher Training and Psycho-Pedagogy (Educational Psychology; Pedagogy; Teacher Training)

Institutes
Applied Linguistics

Business Management (Business Administration)
Rural Development (Cattle Breeding; Forestry; Rural Studies)
Technology
Further Information: Also 4 other Centres

History: Founded 1969. Formerly Institut d' Etudes juridiques of the Fondation de l' Enseignement supérieur en Afrique centrale. Acquired present status 1985.
Governing Bodies: Conseil d' Administration
Academic Year: September to June (September-December; January-March; April-June)
Admission Requirements: Secondary school certificate (Baccalauréat) or special entrance examination
Main Language(s) of Instruction: French
Degrees and Diplomas: *Capacité en Droit*: Law, 2 yrs; *Diplôme*: Midwifery; Nursing, 3 yrs; *Diplôme de Technicien supérieur de Santé*: 4 yrs; *Diplôme d'Etudes économiques générales (DEEG)*: Law and Economics, 2 yrs; *Diplôme d'Etudes juridiques générales (DEJG)*: Law and Economics, 2 yrs; *Diplôme d'Etudes universitaires générales (DEUG)*: 2 yrs; *Diplôme universitaire d'Etudes littéraires (DUEL)*: 2 yrs; *Diplôme universitaire d'Etudes scientifiques (DUES)*: Science, 2 yrs; *Diplôme d'Ingénieur*: 3-4 yrs; *Diplôme supérieur de Gestion (DSG)*: Management, 3 yrs; *Licence*: Arts and Humanities; Economics; Law; Mathematics; Natural Sciences; Physics, 3 yrs; *Maîtrise*: Economics; Law, 1 yr after Licence; Arts and Humanities, 1 yr following Licence; *Doctorat en Médecine*: Medicine, 7 yrs
Student Residential Facilities: Yes
Libraries: Central Library, c. 28,000 vols; Health Sciences, c. 3500
Academic Staff *1999:* Total: c. 140
Student Numbers *1999:* Total: c. 3,590

Chad

INSTITUTION TYPES AND CREDENTIALS

Types of higher education institutions:

Université (University)
Ecole nationale (National School)
Institut (Institute)

School leaving and higher education credentials:

Baccalauréat
Baccalauréat de Technicien
Diplôme d'Etudes universitaires générales (DEUG)
Diplôme universitaire d'Etudes scientifiques (DUES)
Licence
Diplôme d'Ingénieur
Maîtrise
Doctorat en Médecine

STRUCTURE OF EDUCATION SYSTEM

Pre-higher education:

Structure of school system:

Primary
Type of school providing this education: Ecole élémentaire
Length of programme in years: 6
Age level from: 6 to: 12
Certificate/diploma awarded: Certificat d'Etudes primaires (CEP)/Concours d'entrée en sixième

First Cycle Secondary
Type of school providing this education: Collège d'Enseignement général
Length of programme in years: 4
Age level from: 12 to: 16
Certificate/diploma awarded: Brevet d'Etudes du Premier Cycle (BEPC)

Technical Secondary
Type of school providing this education: Collège technique
Length of programme in years: 3

Age level from: 13 to: 16
Certificate/diploma awarded: Certificat d'Aptitude Professionnelle (CAP)

Second Cycle Secondary
Type of school providing this education: Lycée
Length of programme in years: 3
Age level from: 16 to: 19
Certificate/diploma awarded: Baccalauréat

Technical
Type of school providing this education: Lycée technique commercial/industriel
Length of programme in years: 3
Age level from: 16 to: 19
Certificate/diploma awarded: Baccalauréat de Technicien

School education:

Primary education lasts for six years and leads to the Certificat d'Etudes primaires (CEP). Secondary education consists of two cycles. The lower cycle, lasting four years, is offered at a Collège d'enseignement général (CEG) or a Lycée. Completion of the first cycle leads to the Brevet d'Etudes du Premier Cycle. The higher cycle of secondary education, offered by the Lycées, lasts three years and leads to the Baccalauréat, which is usually divided into one of four specializations: Physical or Natural Sciences, Philosophy and Literature, Mathematics, or Economics and Social Sciences. Technical Lycées offer three-year courses on completion of the BEPC that lead to the Baccalauréat de technicien. Technical vocational schools offer courses from the third year of lower secondary school lasting five years and leading to certificates of vocational aptitude.

Higher education:

Higher education in Chad is provided by the only university, the Université de N'Djaména (former Université du Tchad). It is divided into four faculties: Law, Economics, and Business Administration; Letters, Modern Languages, and Human Sciences; Exact and Applied Sciences; Medicine. There are also other institutions of higher education such as the Ecole nationale des Travaux publics and the Institut supérieur des Sciences de l'Education (formerly Ecole normale supérieure). As of 1994, some other institutions have also been conferring the Diplôme d'Etudes universitaires générales.

Main laws/decrees governing higher education:

Decree: Décret no 32/PR/MENCJS/94   Year: 1994
Concerns: Université de N'Djamena

Decree: Ordonnance no 26/PR/71   Year: 1971
Concerns: Université du Tchad

Academic year:

Classes from: October *to:* June
Long vacation from: 30 June *to:* 30 September

Languages of instruction:

Arabic, French

Stages of studies:

Non-university level post-secondary studies (technical/vocational type):

There are a number of professional training institutions at the tertiary level. Students need the Baccalauréat to enter them. In addition, most of these institutions impose a selective entrance examination. These professional training institutions award degrees that are equivalent to the first university cycle.

University level studies:

University level first stage: Premier Cycle:

The first cycle lasts for two years and leads to a Diplôme d'Etudes universitaires générales in Arts and Humanities, Law and Management, to a Diplôme universitaire d'Etudes scientifiques in Science.

University level second stage: Deuxième Cycle:

The second cycle of higher education leads to a Licence after one year's further study in Arts and Humanities, Law and Management, Science. The Maîtrise is conferred one or two years after the Licence. The University awards a Doctorate in Medicine after seven years of study.

Teacher education:

Training of pre-primary and primary/basic school teachers

Teachers are required to complete a three-year upper secondary course at an Ecole normale d'Instituteurs leading to the title of Instituteur. Those who leave on completion of the first two years obtain the title of Instituteur adjoint. The entry requirement to this course is the Brevet d'Etudes du premier Cycle (BEPC).

Training of secondary school teachers

Students who hold the Baccalauréat can sit for a competitive examination for entry to the Institut supérieur des Sciences de l'Education, N'Djaména, to follow a two-year course leading to the Certificat d'Aptitude professionnelle de l'Enseignement aux Collèges d'Enseignement général (CAPCEG). The CAPCEG entitles the holders to teach at the lower secondary cycle. Since 1989, teachers with the CAPCEG can follow a two-year course at the Institut supérieur des Sciences de l'Education leading to the Certificat d'Aptitude professionelle de l'Enseignement dans les Lycées (CAPEL). Holders of the Licence are required to follow a one-year course at the Institut supérieur des Sciences de l'Education which also leads to the CAPEL.

Training of higher education teachers

Same requirements as in other countries. In the Ecoles normales, teachers must hold a Licence en Sciences de l'Education or the CAPEL. For the Institut supérieur en Sciences de l'Education, teachers must hold the DEA, the Maitrîse en Sciences de l'Education, the DES or the Doctorat.

NATIONAL BODIES

Responsible authorities:

Ministry of Higher Education (Ministère de l'Enseignement supérieur)
   Minister: Laoukissam Nissala
   PO Box 731
   N'Djaména
   Tel: +235(51) 7624
   Fax: +235(51) 4017

ADMISSIONS TO HIGHER EDUCATION

Admission to non university higher education studies

Name of secondary school credential required: Baccalauréat de Technicien

Admission to university-level studies

Name of secondary school credential required: Baccalauréat

Foreign students admission

Admission requirements: Foreign students should hold the Baccalauréat or an equivalent qualification.

Entry regulations: Students should have a visa for entrance to Chad and a residence permit.

Health requirements: None

Language requirements: Good knowledge of French or Arabic is required.

Application procedures:

Application closing dates:

   For non-university level (technical/vocational type) studies: 30 September
   For university level studies: 30 September
   For advanced/doctoral studies: 30 September

Recognition of studies and qualifications:

Studies pursued in foreign countries (bodies dealing with recognition of foreign credentials):
Commission d'Admission de l'Université de N'Djaména
   PO Box 1117
   Avenue Mobutu
   N'Djaména
   Tel: +235(51) 5946   +235(51) 4444
   Fax: +235(51) 4033
   Telex: unitchad 5369 kd
   EMail: rectorat@intnet.td

References to further information on foreign student admissions and recognition of studies

Title: Annuaire de l'Université du Tchad
Publisher: Editions Université du Tchad

STUDENT LIFE

Student expenses and financial aid

Publications on student services and financial aid:

Title: Study Abroad 2000-2001
Publisher: UNESCO/IBE
Year of publication: 1999

INTERNATIONAL COOPERATION AND EXCHANGES

Principal national bodies responsible for dealing with international cooperation and exchanges in higher education:

Service des Affaires académiques et de la Coopération internationale, Université de N'Djaména
PO Box 1117
N'Djaména
Tel: +235(51) 5946
Fax: +235(51) 4033

GRADING SYSTEM

Usual grading system in secondary school
Full Description: 16-20=Très Bien; 14-15.9=Bien; 12-13.9=Assez Bien; 10-11.9=Passable.
Highest on scale: 20
Pass/fail level: 10
Lowest on scale: 0

Main grading system used by higher education institutions
Full Description: 16-20=Très Bien; 14-15.9=Bien; 12-13.9=Assez Bien; 10-11.9=Passable
Highest on scale: 20
Pass/fail level: 10
Lowest on scale: 0

NOTES ON HIGHER EDUCATION SYSTEM

Data for academic year: 2000-2001
Source: Commission nationale tchadienne pour l'UNESCO, N'Djamena, updated by the International Association of Universities (IAU) from IBE website, 2000

INSTITUTIONS OF HIGHER EDUCATION

UNIVERSITIES

*• UNIVERSITY OF N'DJAMÉNA
Université de N'Djaména
BP 1117, Avenue Mobutu, N'Djaména
Tel: +235(51) 5946 +253(51) 4444
Fax: +235(51) 4581
Telex: unitchad 53 69 kd
EMail: rectorat@intnet.td

Recteur: Yokabdjim Mandigui (1999-) Tel: +235(51) 4033
EMail: yok@intnet.td

Secrétaire général: Mahamat Barka EMail: syfed@intnet.td

International Relations: Gilbert Lawane

Faculties
Exact and Applied Sciences (Biology; Cattle Breeding; Chemistry; Computer Science; Geology; Mathematics; Physics; Technology) *Dean*: Tagui Guelbeye, *students:* 925

Law, Economics, and Business Administration (Business Administration; Economics; Law) *Dean*: Enoch Nodjigoto, *students:* 1,465

Letters, Modern Languages, and Human Sciences (Arabic; Arts and Humanities; English; Geography; History; Linguistics; Modern Languages; Philosophy; Social Sciences) *Dean*: Tchago Bouimon, *students:* 2,417

Medicine Joulsou Douniang, *students:* 225

Institutes
Human Sciences Research (Social Sciences) *Director*: Moukhtar Mahamat

History: Founded 1971, comprising Institutions formerly part of the Fondation de l' Enseignement supérieur en Afrique Centrale. Acquired present status and title 1994.

Governing Bodies: Conseil de l' Université, comprising Government representatives and members of the Academic staff and student body

Academic Year: October to June (October-February; March-June)

Admission Requirements: Secondary school certificate (baccalauréat)

Main Language(s) of Instruction: French, Arabic

Degrees and Diplomas: *Diplôme d'Etudes universitaires générales (DEUG)*: Arts and Humanities; Law; Management, 2 yrs; *Diplôme universitaire d'Etudes scientifiques (DUES)*: Science, 2 yrs; *Licence*: Arts and Humanities; Law; Management; Science, 3 yrs; *Diplôme d'Ingénieur*: Electromechanics; Stockraising, 4 yrs; *Maîtrise*: 4 yrs; *Doctorat en Médecine*: Médecine, 7 yrs. Also Certificates.

Student Services: Sports Facilities, Health Services

Libraries: University Documentation Centre, c. 30, 000 vols

Academic Staff *1999-2000*: Total: **181**

Staff with doctorate: Total: **101**

Student Numbers *1999-2000*	MEN	WOMEN	TOTAL
All (Foreign Included)	4,642	565	**5,207**

HIGHER INSTITUTE FOR EDUCATION
INSTITUT SUPÉRIEUR DES SCIENCES DE L'EDUCATION (ISSED)
BP 473, N'Djaména
Tel: +235(51) 4487
Fax: +235(51) 4550

Directeur: Mayore Karyo Tel: +235(51) 6175
EMail: issed@intnet.td

Departments
Education (Administration; Arabic; Biology; Chemistry; Curriculum; Education; Educational Technology; English; French; Geography; Geology; History; Mathematics; Physics; Secondary Education) *Head*: N. Natoyoun, *full-time staff:* 33, *part-time staff:* 4

Education (Education; Educational Administration; Educational Psychology; Primary Education) *Head*: Ganda Souleymane Malato, *full-time staff:* 10, *part-time staff:* 6, *students:* 50

Mathematics Education (Accountancy; Administration; Finance; Management; Mathematics Education) *Head*: M. Barounga, *full-time staff:* 2, *part-time staff:* 4, *students:* 15

History: Founded 1992.

Special Facilities: Workshop; Printing workshop. Computer centre

OTHER INSTITUTIONS

CENTRE NATIONAL D'APPUI À LA RECHERCHE
BP 1228, N'Djaména
Tel: +235(51) 2435
Fax: +235(51) 5884

Research

History: Founded 1988.

ECOLE NATIONALE D'ADMINISTRATION ET DE MAGISTRATURE
BP 758, N'Djaména
Tel: +235(51) 4097
Fax: +235(51) 4356
Administration; Finance; Law
Diplomacy Studies (International Relations)

Justice Administration
Technical Studies (Technology)

History: Founded 1963.

ECOLE NATIONALE DES TRAVAUX PUBLICS
N'Djaména
Tel: +235(52) 4971
Fax: +235(52) 3420
Telex: 5222 kd
Public Works (Civil Engineering)

History: Founded 1965.

INSTITUT DE RECHERCHE DU COTON ET DES TEXTILES
Route de Farcha, BP 764, N'Djaména
Tel: +235(51) 2751
Fax: +235(51) 3228
Textile Technology

History: Founded 1932.

Congo

INSTITUTION TYPES AND CREDENTIALS

Types of higher education institutions:

Université (University)
Institut (Institute)
Ecole (School)

School leaving and higher education credentials:

Baccalauréat
Certificat de Capacité en Droit
Certificat d'Aptitude au Professorat dans les Collèges d'Enseignement Géneral
Certificat d'Aptitude au Professorat de l'Enseignement Technique
Diplôme Universitaire d'Etudes Littéraires (DUEL)
Diplôme Universitaire d'Etudes Scientifiques (DUES)
Certificat d'Aptitude au Professorat d'Education Physique et Sportive
Certificat d'Aptitude au Professorat dans l'Enseignement secondaire
Licence
Diplôme d'Ingénieur
Maîtrise
Diplôme d'Etudes approfondies (DEA)
Diplôme d'Etudes supérieures (DES)
Doctorat en Médecine

STRUCTURE OF EDUCATION SYSTEM

Pre-higher education:

Duration of compulsory education:

Age of entry: 6
Age of exit: 11

Structure of school system:

Primary
Type of school providing this education: Ecole Primaire
Length of programme in years: 6
Age level from: 6 to: 12
Certificate/diploma awarded: Certificat d'Etudes primaires élémentaires (CEPE)

First Cycle Secondary
Type of school providing this education: College d'Enseignement General/Collège d'Enseignement Technique
Length of programme in years: 4
Age level from: 12 to: 16
Certificate/diploma awarded: Brevet d'Etudes du Premier Cycle (BEPC)

Technical Secondary
Length of programme in years: 3
Age level from: 16 to: 19
Certificate/diploma awarded: Brevet de Technicien

Second Cycle Secondary
Type of school providing this education: Lycée
Length of programme in years: 3
Age level from: 16 to: 19
Certificate/diploma awarded: Baccalauréat

Technical
Type of school providing this education: Lycée technique
Length of programme in years: 4
Age level from: 16 to: 20
Certificate/diploma awarded: Baccalauréat technique

School education:

Primary school education covers six years leading to the Certificat d'Etudes primaires élémentaires (CEPE). It is followed by seven years of secondary school which is divided into a four-year first cycle (6ème to 3ème) and a three-year second cycle (2nde to Terminale). During the second cycle, pupils may enter a general stream (Lycée d'Enseignement général) or a technical stream. On completion of this cycle, pupils take the examinations for the Baccalauréat. On completion of the first cycle of secondary education, pupils may take a 'short' technical secondary course (after passing an entrance examination in 5ème (Form 5)), leading to the qualification of Brevet de Technicien, or a "long" course leading to a Baccalauréat technique.

Higher education:

Higher education is provided by the Université Marien Ngouabi and its Instituts and Ecoles. The university is a public institution which is responsible to the Ministère de l'Enseignement primaire, secondaire et supérieur. Its resources come from a State subsidy as well as its own funds.

Main laws/decrees governing higher education:

Decree: Loi 25/95   Year: 1995
Concerns: Structure of educational system

Decree: Ordonnance No. 29/71   Year: 1971
Concerns: University

Academic year:

Classes from: October *to:* June

Long vacation from: 1 July *to:* 30 September

Languages of instruction:

French

Stages of studies:

University level studies:

University level first stage: *Premier Cycle*:
The first stage of studies leads, after two years, to the Diplôme universitaire d'Etudes littéraires (DUEL) in Arts and Humanities and the Diplôme universitaire d'Etudes scientifiques (DUES) in the Sciences.

University level second stage: *Deuxième Cycle*:
A further year's study after the DUEL or DUES leads to the Licence, and a further two years leads to the Diplôme d'Etudes supérieures (DES). The Institut de Développement Rural (IDR) provides training in Agricultural Science. At the Institut supérieur des Sciences de la Santé ((INSSA), three years' study is required to become a trained nurse (Licence en Sciences de la Santé pour les Infirmiers). INSSA also awards, after six years' study, the State degree of Doctorat en Médecine.

Teacher education:

Training of pre-primary and primary/basic school teachers
Primary school teachers are trained for three years in teacher training colleges (ENI) at secondary level. However, most of the ENIs have been closed.

Training of secondary school teachers
Secondary school teachers are trained at the Ecole normale supérieure for college and lycée teachers, at the Ecole Normale supérieure de l'Enseignement technique (ENSET) for technical education teachers, and at the Institut supérieur d'Education physique et sportive (ISEPS) for teachers of physical education and sports. A two-year course leads to the Certificat d'Aptitude au Professorat dans les Collèges d'Enseignement Général (CAP de CEG) and after a further year to the Certificat d'Aptitude au Professorat dans l'Enseignement Secondaire (CAPES). Technical teachers study for the Certificat d'Aptitude au Professorat de l'Enseignement Technique (CAPET). ISEPS offers both training and in-service training courses. A three-year course leads to the assistant teacher qualification and the Certificat d'Aptitude au Professorat d'Education Physique et Sportive (CAPEPS) is awarded on completion of a four-year course.

Training of higher education teachers
Higher education teachers must hold a Doctorat de 3ème cycle, a Doctorat or a Diplôme d'Ingénieur, generally obtained abroad.

NATIONAL BODIES

Responsible authorities:

Ministry of Primary, Secondary & Higher Education & Research (Ministère de l'Enseignement primaire, secondaire & supérieur chargé de la Recherche scientifique)
  Minister: Pierre Nzila
  Head of Cabinet: Prosper Mahoukou
  International Relations: Antoinette Mongo
  PO Box 14557/2078
  Brazzaville
  Tel: +242(81) 52-65
  Fax: +242(81) 52-65

  Role of governing body: Supervises the higher education system and the institutions.

ADMISSIONS TO HIGHER EDUCATION

Admission to university-level studies

Name of secondary school credential required: Baccalauréat

Other admission requirements: Competitive entrance examination for access to the university institutes and portfolio for access to the university faculties.

Foreign students admission

Quotas: 10% of study places are reserved for foreign students.

Application procedures:

Apply to: Division de la Scolarité et des Examens de l'Université Marien Ngouabi
  PO Box 69
  Brazzaville
  Tel: +242(81) 01-41   +242(81) 24-36
  Fax: +242(81) 01-41   +242(81) 42-07

INTERNATIONAL COOPERATION AND EXCHANGES

Principal national bodies responsible for dealing with international cooperation and exchanges in higher education:

Ministère de l'Enseignement primaire, secondaire et supérieur, chargé de la Recherche scientifique
  PO Box 14557/2078
  Brazzaville
  Tel: +242(81) 52-65
  Fax: +242(81) 52-65

GRADING SYSTEM

Usual grading system in secondary school

Full Description: Subjects are marked on a scale of 0-20 (maximum), with no official minimum pass mark. Overall grades in the Baccalauréat are: très bien (very good), bien (good), assez bien (quite good) passable (average).

Highest on scale: 20

Pass/fail level: 10

Lowest on scale: 0

Main grading system used by higher education institutions

Full Description: 0-20 (16-20 : TRES BIEN; 14-15 : BIEN; 12-13 : ASSEZ BIEN; 10-11 : PASSABLE)

Highest on scale: 20

Pass/fail level: 10

Lowest on scale: 0

NOTES ON HIGHER EDUCATION SYSTEM

Data for academic year: 2000-2001

Source: International Association of Universities (IAU), updated from IBE website, 2001

INSTITUTIONS OF HIGHER EDUCATION

UNIVERSITIES

*• UNIVERSITY MARIEN NGOUABI BRAZZAVILLE

Université Marien Ngouabi
BP 69, Brazzaville
Tel: +242(81) 42-07 +242(81) 24-36
Fax: +242(81) 42-07
Telex: 5331 kg

Recteur: Charles Gombe Mbalawa

Secrétaire général: Marie Alphonse Aya

Vice-Recteur: Laurent Tchissambou

Faculties

Economics (Economics; Finance) *Dean:* Hervé Diata, *full-time staff:* 37, *part-time staff:* 78, *students:* 4,437
Law (Law; Private Law; Public Law) *Dean:* Bernard Tchicaya, *full-time staff:* 33, *part-time staff:* 9, *students:* 1,549
Letters and Human Sciences (African Studies; Arts and Humanities; Communication Studies; English; Geography; History; Linguistics; Literature; Philosophy; Social Sciences; Sociology) *Dean:* Paul Nzete, *full-time staff:* 126, *part-time staff:* 82, *students:* 6,090
Sciences *(Dolisie)* (Biology; Chemistry; Earth Sciences; Mathematics; Natural Sciences; Physics) *Dean:* Jean Moali, *full-time staff:* 90, *part-time staff:* 31, *students:* 1,531

Schools

Administration and Training for the Magistrature (Administration; Commercial Law; Educational Sciences; Law; Management; Private Law; Psychology; Public Law) *Director:* Ayon Boue, *full-time staff:* 27, *part-time staff:* 104, *students:* 289
Teacher Training *Director:* Rosalie Kama Niamayoua, *full-time staff:* 78, *part-time staff:* 68, *students:* 659
Technical Education (Civil Engineering; Electrical Engineering; Food Technology; Technology Education) *Director:* Bernard Mabiala, *full-time staff:* 31, *part-time staff:* 79, *students:* 315

Institutes

Health Sciences (Embryology and Reproduction Biology; Haematology; Health Sciences; Histology; Medicine; Microbiology; Midwifery; Physiology; Surgery)

Management *Director:* François Sita, *full-time staff:* 22, *part-time staff:* 25, *students:* 266
Physical Education and Sport (Physical Education; Sports) *Director:* Bernard Packa Tchissambou, *full-time staff:* 30, *part-time staff:* 42, *students:* 233
Rural Development *(Ouesso)* (Agricultural Equipment; Botany; Forestry; Rural Studies; Zoology)

History: Founded 1959 as Centre d'Etudes administratives et techniques supérieures. Previously formed part of the Fondation de l'Enseignement supérieur en Afrique centrale. Became Université de Brazzaville 1971, acquired present title 1977.

Governing Bodies: Comité de Direction

Academic Year: October to June (October-December; January-March; April-June)

Admission Requirements: Secondary school certificate (baccalauréat) or equivalent

Main Language(s) of Instruction: French

International Co-operation: University Omar Bongo, Gabon; University of Kinshasa; University of Bangui; University of Burundi; University of Rwanda; University of Pennsylvania; Howard University; University of Louvain; University of Dijon; University of Montpellier; University of Strasbourg; University of Paris VII

Degrees and Diplomas: *Certificat de Capacité en Droit:* Law; *Certificat d'Aptitude au Professorat dans les Collèges d'Enseignement Géneral:* Education, 3 yrs; *Certificat d'Aptitude au Professorat d'Education Physique et Sportive:* Sports, 5 yrs; *Licence:* Fundamental Sciences, Letters and Human Sciences, Law, 3 yrs; *Diplôme d'Ingénieur:* Electrical Engineering, Food Technology, 2-5 yrs; *Maîtrise:* Economics; Fundamental Sciences, Arts and Humanities, Law; Geology, 1 yr following Licence; *Diplôme d'Etudes approfondies (DEA):* Botany, 1 year following Maîtrise; *Diplôme d'Etudes supérieures (DES):* Arts and Humanities, 2 yrs following licence; *Doctorat en Médecine:* Medicine. Also Teaching Qualifications

Student Services: Sports Facilities, Health Services

Libraries: Central Library, c.70,000 vols

Publications: Sango (Bulletin) (bimonthly); Mbongi (quarterly); Annales; Dimi; Mélanges; La Saison des Pluies (annually)

Academic Staff *1999:* Total: c. 600

Student Numbers *1999:* Total: c. 12,045

Congo (Democratic Republic)

INSTITUTION TYPES AND CREDENTIALS

Types of higher education institutions:

Université (University)

Institut supérieur (Higher Institute)

School leaving and higher education credentials:

Diplôme d'Etat d'Etudes secondaires du Cycle long

Graduat

Agrégation de l'Enseignement secondaire supérieur

Diplôme d'Ingénieur

Licence

Licence d'Enseignement

Docteur en Médecine

Docteur en Médecine Vétérinaire

Diplôme d'Etudes supérieures (DES)

Diplôme de Spécialiste

Agrégation de l'Enseignement supérieur en Médecine

Agrégation de l'Enseignement supérieur en Médecine vétérinaire

Doctorat

STRUCTURE OF EDUCATION SYSTEM

Pre-higher education:

Duration of compulsory education:

Age of entry: 6

Age of exit: 12

Structure of school system:

Primary

Type of school providing this education: Primary School

Length of programme in years: 6

Age level from: 6 to: 12

Certificate/diploma awarded: Certificat d'Etudes primaires

General Secondary

Type of school providing this education: Secondary school

Length of programme in years: 6
Age level from: 12 to: 18
Certificate/diploma awarded: Diplôme d'Etat d'Etudes secondaires du Cycle long

Technical Secondary
Length of programme in years: 6
Age level from: 12 to: 18
Certificate/diploma awarded: Diplôme d'Etat d'Etudes secondaires du Cycle long

Vocational
Type of school providing this education: Vocational school
Length of programme in years: 5
Age level from: 12 to: 17

School education:

Primary school lasts for six years leading to the Certificat d'Etudes primaires (CEP). Pupils then go on to secondary education (general or technical) which consists of one cycle lasting for six years after which they obtain the Diplôme d'Etat d'Etudes Secondaires du Cycle Long which gives access to higher education at university and technical institute levels. Pupils can also begin short technical courses in trade and crafts at age 12. Those who complete the long cycle in a technical field and pass the Examen d'Etat are eligible for admission to higher education. Vocational education is provided by vocational schools and courses last for four or five years. It does not give admission to higher education.

Higher education:

Higher education is mainly provided by universities, higher teacher training institutes, and higher technological institutes. Higher education comes under the authority of the Ministère de l'Education. Three Administrative Councils coordinate the activities of the universities with the teacher training institutes and with the technological institutes. They define overall policy and objectives, decide on new courses and the number of hours per subject. Each institution has a University or Institute Council, an Administrative Committee, faculties (or sections) and departments. The University or Institute Council is the highest authority. It is comprised of the Administration Committee, the deans, a faculty representative, a student representative, a representative of the administrative personnel and the head librarian. This body coordinates the academic and scientific policy of the institution. The Administration Committee is appointed by the central power. The Section or Faculty Council is exclusively concerned with the academic and scientific problems of that faculty or institute. It comprises full professors and department heads. The Department Council is the source of academic life in the universities. It comprises full professors who elect the department head. Several private institutions are also being established.

Main laws/decrees governing higher education:

Decree: Law n° 82-004 du 6 février 1982   Year: 1982
Concerns: Academic degrees in technical higher education institutions
Decree: Ordonnance-loi n°. 81-028 du 3 octobre 1981   Year: 1981
Concerns: higher education and universities

Academic year:

Classes from: October *to:* June

Languages of instruction:

French

Stages of studies:

Non-university level post-secondary studies (technical/vocational type):

Higher technical and vocational education is mainly provided in teacher-training and technological institutes. Studies generally last for three years and lead to the qualification of Gradué.

University level studies:

University level first stage: Premier Cycle:
The first stage of higher education lasts for three years and leads to the title of Gradué.

University level second stage: Deuxième Cycle:
The second cycle lasts for two years and grants the Licence, except in Medicine and Veterinary Medicine where this stage lasts for three years and leads to the title of Docteur en Médecine and Docteur en Médecine Vétérinaire.

University level third stage: Troisième Cycle:
The third cycle mainly consists in a programme of higher studies leading to the Diplôme d'Etudes supérieures (DES). This programme lasts for two years and includes a certain number of courses and seminars, as well as the presentation of a dissertation. After obtaining the DES, the candidate can register in a doctoral programme and prepare the thesis. The next stage leads to the Doctorate which is conferred after a further four to seven years' further study. At the Faculties of Medicine, doctors devote three or four years to a specialization in one of the medical fields, after which they obtain a Diplôme de Spécialiste. Most Spécialistes become practitioners. Those who prefer to teach prepare an Agrégation. Requirements are the possession of the Diplôme de Spécialiste with "distinction" plus three to five years' preparation. The degree is that of Agrégé de l'Enseignement supérieur en Médecine. In Veterinary Medicine, it leads to the Agrégation de l'Enseignement supérieur en Médecine vétérinaire.

Teacher education:

Training of pre-primary and primary/basic school teachers
Pre-primary and primary school teachers are trained in four to six years at secondary level in Ecoles normales or Ecoles pédagogiques. They obtain the Brevet d'Instituteur or a State Diploma in Pedagogy. Courses include general and educational studies and practical teaching experience.

Training of secondary school teachers
Secondary school teachers are trained at the Institut supérieur pédagogique (ISP), the Institut supérieur technique or education faculties. Candidates must hold the Diplôme d'Etat d'Etudes secondaires du Cycle long. Courses are offered in all subjects taught at secondary level. They last for five years which are divided into two cycles. The first cycle lasts for three years and leads to the qualification of Gradué en Enseignement. The second lasts for two years and culminates in a competitive examination. Successful students are awarded the Licence d'Enseignement. Holders of

the title of Gradué are qualified to teach the first four years of secondary school. Holders of the Licence d'Enseignement are qualified to teach the final two years of secondary school. Students who have completed a non-pedagogical first degree course and who wish to teach can qualify by completing a one-year course leading to the Agrégation de l'Enseignement secondaire supérieur.

Training of higher education teachers
There are five ranks of teachers in higher education: assistant, project head, associate professor, professor and full professor. An assistant must hold a Licence or its equivalent and is nominated for a two-year period, twice renewable. A project head needs four years as an assistant and two publications in a scientific journal. An associate professor must hold a first-level Doctorate. Promotion requires four years from the previous level, together with several publications. There is a Service de Pédagogie universitaire which organizes training sessions for higher education teachers.

Non-traditional studies:

Other forms of non-formal higher education
Non-formal studies are offered by the Centre interdisciplinaire pour l'Education permanente which trains adults for their vocational needs and updates their technical knowledge. It has several training centres.

NATIONAL BODIES

Responsible authorities:
Ministry of National Education (Ministère de l'Education nationale)
Minister: Kyota Kutumisa
PO Box 3162
Kinshasa/Gombe
Tel: +243(12) 88-02-133
EMail: iketebale@hotmail.com

Presidence of the Universities of the Democratic Republic of Congo (Présidence des Universités de la République démocratique du Congo)
President: Tshibangu Tshishiku Tharcisse
Permanent Secretary: Mwabila Malela Clement
International Relations: Matundu Lelo
PO Box 13399
Kinshasa 1
Tel: +243(99) 18198
Telex: 982-21 216 cau zr
EMail: caurdeg@hotmail.com

ADMISSIONS TO HIGHER EDUCATION

Admission to non university higher education studies

Name of secondary school credential required: Diplôme d'Etat d'Etudes secondaires du Cycle long

Admission to university-level studies

Name of secondary school credential required: Diplôme d'Etat d'Etudes secondaires du Cycle long

Entrance exams required: Entrance examination.

Foreign students admission

Admission requirements: Students must hold a diploma giving access to higher education in their country of origin.

Entry regulations: Students must ask for a visa at the Embassy of their country.

Language requirements: Students must have a good knowledge of French. Those who wish to improve their knowledge of French may follow courses in learning centres.

Recognition of studies and qualifications:

Studies pursued in foreign countries (bodies dealing with recognition of foreign credentials):
Commission permanente des Etudes, Ministère de l'Education
   PO Box 3162
   Kinshasa/Gombe XI
   Tel: +243(12) 88-02-133

STUDENT LIFE

Student expenses and financial aid

Student costs:
   Home students tuition fees: Maximum: 15,000 (CFA Franc)

GRADING SYSTEM

Usual grading system in secondary school

Full Description: 0-100%
Highest on scale: 100%
Pass/fail level: 50%
Lowest on scale: 0%

Main grading system used by higher education institutions

Full Description: 0%-100%; 90%-100% la plus grande distinction; 80%-89% grande distinction; 70%-79% distinction; 50%-69% satisfaction; 50%
Highest on scale: 100%

Pass/fail level: 50%
Lowest on scale: 0%

NOTES ON HIGHER EDUCATION SYSTEM

Data for academic year: 2000-2001
Source: International Association of Universities (IAU), updated from IBE website, 2001

INSTITUTIONS OF HIGHER EDUCATION

UNIVERSITIES

CATHOLIC FACULTIES OF KINSHASA

Facultés catholiques de Kinshasa
BP 1534, Avenue de l'Université 2, Limete, Kinshasa
Tel: +243(88) 46965
EMail: facakin@yahoo.fr

Recteur: Hippolyte Ngimbi Nseka (2001-)

Secrétaire général académique: René de Haes

Faculties
Philosophy
Sciences and Development Techniques (Development Studies; Mathematics and Computer Science; Natural Sciences)
Social Communication (Communication Studies; Journalism; Sociology)
Theology (Christian Religious Studies; Theology)

Centres
African Religions (African Studies; Religious Studies)
Ecclesiastical Archives (Religious Studies)

History: Founded 1957.

Admission Requirements: State Diploma (+60%), and recommendation by a member of the Clergy

Fees: (Francs CFA): 15,000

Degrees and Diplomas: *Licence*: Philosophy, Theology, Development Studies, Journalism, 5 yrs; *Doctorat*: Philosophy, Theology

Publications: Journal of African Theology; Journal of African Religions; Kinshasa Journal of Philosophy (quarterly)

Academic Staff 2000	TOTAL
FULL-TIME	41
PART-TIME	69
TOTAL	110

Student Numbers *2000:* Total: **1,038**

• CATHOLIC UNIVERSITY OF BUKAVU

Université catholique de Bukavu
BP 285, Bukavu
Tel: +243(88) 87762 +871(761) 470-721 +871(761) 470-722
Fax: +871(761) 470-723
Website: http://www.fiuc.org/ucb

Recteur: Déogratias Bisimwa Ruhamanyi (1996-)

International Relations: François-Xavier Migabo Mufungizi

Faculties
Agronomy
Economics

Law
Medicine

History: Founded 1989.

Governing Bodies: Conseil d'Administration, comprising 19 members; Conseil Académique et Scientifique, comprising 29 members; Comité de Direction, comprising 3 members

Academic Year: October to July (October-December; January-March; April-July)

Admission Requirements: Secondary school certificate and entrance examination

Main Language(s) of Instruction: French

International Co-operation: Catholic University of Louvain; National University of Bénin; University of Burundi

Degrees and Diplomas: *Graduat*: 3 yrs; *Licence*: Economics; Law; Medicine, a further 2-3 yrs; *Doctorat*: Medicine

Libraries: Central Library, c. 11,000 vols

Academic Staff *1999:* Full-Time: c. 30 Part-Time: c. 90 Total: c. 120

Staff with Doctorate: Total: c. 50

Student Numbers *1999:* Total: c. 1,210

CATHOLIC UNIVERSITY OF THE GRABEN

Université Catholique du Graben (UCG)
BP 29, Butembo, Nord-Kivu

Recteur: Apollinaire Malu Malu

Faculties
Agronomy
Economics
Human Medicine (Medicine)
Law
Social Sciences

FREE UNIVERSITY OF THE 'GREAT LAKES' REGION

Université libre des Pays des Grands Lacs
BP 368, Goma, Nord-Kivu
Tel: +243(88) 85608

Recteur: Léonard Masu-Ga-Rugamika

KONGO UNIVERSITY

Université Kongo
BP 8443, Kinshasa

Recteur: Jean Kanga Kalemba-Vita

History: Founded as Université du Bas-Zaïre.

UNIVERSITY CENTRE OF BUKAVU

Centre universitaire de Bukavu
BP 570, Bukavu

Recteur: Nyakabwa Mutabana

• UNIVERSITY OF KINSHASA

Université de Kinshasa
BP 127, Kinshasa XI
Tel: +243(12) 27793
Fax: +243(12) 21360
Telex: 982 23 068
EMail: unikin@kinpost.ccmail.compuserve.com

Recteur: Mpeye Nyango (2000-) Tel: +243(99) 15475
EMail: nyango.mpeye@caramail.com

Secrétaire général Administratif: Lushiku Kalenga
Tel: +243(99) 43825

International Relations: Moswa Lokonda
Tel: +243(99) 08388 EMail: josmoswa@yahoo.fr;
moswa@hotmail.com

Faculties
Economics
Law
Medicine (Dentistry; Medicine)
Pharmacy
Polytechnic (Civil Engineering; Engineering; Technology)
Science (Mathematics and Computer Science; Natural Sciences)

History: Founded 1949 as Université Lovanium, became a campus of the Université nationale du Zaïre 1971. Acquired present status and title 1981. A State institution.

Governing Bodies: Conseil d'Administration d'Université

Academic Year: October to June (October-February; February-June)

Admission Requirements: Secondary school certificate and entrance examination

Main Language(s) of Instruction: French

International Co-operation: University of Aix-Marseilles III; University Omar Bongo, Gabon; Laval University; Free University of Brussels; University of Siena; University Marien Ngouabi, Congo

Degrees and Diplomas: *Graduat*; *Diplôme d'Ingénieur*: Civil Engineering, 5 years; *Licence*: Economics, 4 yrs; Civil Engineering; Law; Science, 5 yrs; *Docteur en Médecine*: Medicine, 6 yrs; *Diplôme d'Etudes supérieures (DES)*: Law (DES); *Diplôme de Spécialiste*: Medicine; *Agrégation de l'Enseignement supérieur en Médecine*: Medicine; *Doctorat*: Economics; Pharmacy; Science

Special Facilities: Musée universitaire

Libraries: c. 300,000 vols

Publications: Bulletin d'Information (monthly); Cahiers économiques et sociaux des Religions africaines (quarterly); Annales of the Faculties of Science, Polytechnic and Pharmacy

Press or Publishing House: Presses universitaires de l'Université de Kinshasa

Academic Staff *1999:* Total: c. 970
Student Numbers *1999:* Total: c. 11,565

• UNIVERSITY OF KISANGANI

Université de Kisangani
BP 2012, Kisangani, Haut Zaïre
Tel: +243(21) 1335
Fax: +243(21) 1335
Telex: 21216 cau zr

Faculties
Education and Psychology (Education; Psychology)
Medicine (Dermatology; Gynaecology and Obstetrics; Medicine; Paediatrics; Stomatology)
Science (Biochemistry; Biology; Ecology; Natural Sciences)
Social Sciences, Administration, and Political Science (Administration; Political Science; Social Sciences; Sociology)

History: Founded 1963 as Université libre du Congo, became a campus of the Université nationale du Zaïre 1971. Acquired present status and title 1981. A State institution.

Governing Bodies: Conseil d'Administration

Academic Year: October to July (October-February; February-July)

Admission Requirements: Secondary school certificate and entrance examination

Main Language(s) of Instruction: French

International Co-operation: Free University of Brussels; Universities of Rwanda and Burundi

Degrees and Diplomas: *Graduat*; *Licence*: Administration; Sociology; Education, 4 yrs; Psychology; Science, 5 yrs; *Docteur en Médecine*: 6 yrs; *Diplôme d'Etudes supérieures (DES)*: Pedagogy; Psychology; Science; *Diplôme de Spécialiste*: Medicine; *Agrégation de l'Enseignement supérieur en Médecine*: Medicine; *Doctorat*: Pedagogy; Psychology; Sociology

Student Residential Facilities: Yes

Libraries: c. 46,000 vols

Publications: Bulletin d'Information (monthly); Annales de la Faculté des Sciences; Revue Zaïroise de Pédagogie et Psychologie. Kisangani Médical

Press or Publishing House: Presses universitaires de Kisangani

Academic Staff *1999*: Full-Time: c. 220 Part-Time: c. 40 Total: c. 260

Student Numbers *1999:* Total: c. 4,195

• UNIVERSITY OF LUBUMBASHI

Université de Lubumbashi
BP 1825, Lubumbashi, Shaba
Tel: +243(22) 5403
Fax: +243(22) 8099
Telex: 40179

Recteur: Kakoma Sakatolo Zambeze (1993-)
Secrétaire général: Thambu Masweka

Faculties

Economics

Law

Letters (Arts and Humanities; English; French; History; Literature; Philosophy)

Medicine

Science (Mathematics and Computer Science; Natural Sciences)

Social, Political, and Administrative Sciences (Administration; Political Science; Social Sciences)

Technology and Engineering (Applied Chemistry; Applied Mathematics; Applied Physics; Chemical Engineering; Civil Engineering; Engineering; Industrial Chemistry; Metallurgical Engineering; Natural Sciences; Technology)

Veterinary Medicine (Veterinary Science)

History: Founded 1955 as Université officielle du Congo, became a campus of the Université nationale du Zaïre 1971, and acquired present status and title 1981. A State institution.

Governing Bodies: Conseil d'administration d'Universités

Academic Year: October to June (October-February; February-June)

Admission Requirements: Secondary school certificate and entrance examination

Main Language(s) of Instruction: French

Degrees and Diplomas: *Graduat*; *Diplôme d'Ingénieur*: Civil Engineering, 5 yrs; *Licence*: Anthropology; International Relations; Political Science; Letters; Sociology, 4 yrs; Engineering; Science, 5 yrs; *Docteur en Médecine*: Medicine; *Docteur en Médecine Vétérinaire*: Veterinary Medicine, 6 yrs; *Diplôme de Spécialiste*: Medicine; *Agrégation de l'Enseignement supérieur en Médecine*: Medicine; *Doctorat*: Anthropology; International Relations; Letters; Political Science; Science; Sociology

Libraries: c. 92,230 vols

Academic Staff *1999:* Total: c. 400

Student Numbers *1999:* Total: c. 4,370

UNIVERSITY OF MBUJIMAYI

Université de Mbujimayi (UM)

BP 225, Avenue de l'Université, Campus de Tshikama, Dibindi, Mbujimayi

Tel: +243(88) 54890

Fax: +243(88) 54111

Recteur: Raphaël Mbowa Kalengayi

Secrétaire général: J. Ntumba Tshibambula

International Relations: P. Reyntjens

Faculties

Applied Science (Polytechnic) (Civil Engineering; Mechanical Engineering; Mining Engineering; Science Education)

Economics

Human Medicine (Biomedicine; Medicine)

Law (Law; Notary Studies; Private Law; Public Law)

History: Founded 1990.

Degrees and Diplomas: *Graduat*: 3 yrs; *Licence*: a further 2 yrs; *Doctorat*: Medicine, 4 yrs

Special Facilities: Research Laboratory

Libraries: 14,000 vols

Student Numbers *1999:* Total: c. 1,630

OTHER INSTITUTIONS

ACADÉMIE DES BEAUX-ARTS

BP 8249, Kinshasa

Tel: +243(12) 68476

Fine Arts

INSTITUT DE FORMATION DES CADRES DE L'ENSEIGNEMENT PRIMAIRE

BP 711, Kisangani

Primary Education; Teacher Training

History: Founded 1971. Acquired present status 1981.

INSTITUT DES BÂTIMENTS ET DES TRAVAUX PUBLICS

BP 4731, Kinshasa

Civil Engineering

History: Founded 1961. Acquired present status and title 1971.

INSTITUT FACULTAIRE DES SCIENCES DE L'INFORMATION ET DE LA COMMUNICATION

BP 14998, Kinshasa

Tel: +243(12) 25117

Recteur: Ya Mpiku Mbelolo

Directeur général: Melembe Tamandiak

Information Technology; Journalism; Library Science; Public Relations

History: Founded 1973 as Institut des Sciences et Techniques de l'Information. Acquired present status and title 1997.

INSTITUT NATIONAL DES ARTS

BP 8332, Kinshasa

Fine Arts

History: Founded 1971. Acquired present status and title 1981.

INSTITUT PÉDAGOGIQUE NATIONAL

BP 8815, Kinshasa-Binza

Teacher Training

History: Founded 1961. Acquired present status and title 1971.

INSTITUT SUPÉRIEUR D'ARTS ET MÉTIERS
BP 15198, Kinshasa-Gombe
Crafts and Trades; Fine Arts

History: Founded 1968. Acquired present status and title 1975.

INSTITUT SUPÉRIEUR DE COMMERCE
BP 16596, Kinshasa
Business and Commerce

History: Founded 1964. Acquired present status and title 1971.

INSTITUT SUPÉRIEUR DE COMMERCE
BP 2012, Kisangani
Business and Commerce

History: Founded 1971. Acquired present status and title 1981.

INSTITUT SUPÉRIEUR DE STATISTIQUE
BP 2471, Lubumbashi
Statistics

History: Founded 1967. Acquired present status and title 1971.

INSTITUT SUPÉRIEUR DES TECHNIQUES APPLIQUÉES
BP 6593, Kinshasa
Tel: +243(12) 23592
Technology

History: Founded 1971. Acquired present status and title 1981.

INSTITUT SUPÉRIEUR DES TECHNIQUES MÉDICALES
BP 774, Kinshasa
Medical Technology

History: Founded 1971. Acquired present status and title 1981.

INSTITUT SUPÉRIEUR D'ETUDES AGRONOMIQUES DE BENGAMISA
BP 202, Kisangani
Agronomy

History: Founded 1968. Acquired present status and title 1971.

INSTITUT SUPÉRIEUR D'ETUDES AGRONOMIQUES DE MONDONGO
BP 60, Lisala
Agronomy

History: Founded 1972. Acquired present status and title 1981.

INSTITUT SUPÉRIEUR D'ETUDES SOCIALES
BP 2849, Bukavu
Social Studies

History: Founded 1971. Acquired present status and title 1981.

INSTITUT SUPÉRIEUR D'ETUDES SOCIALES
BP 1575, Lubumbashi
Social Studies

History: Founded 1971. Acquired present status and title 1981.

INSTITUT SUPÉRIEUR PÉDAGOGIQUE
BP 854, Bukavu
Teacher Training

History: Founded 1964. Acquired present status and title 1971.

INSTITUT SUPÉRIEUR PÉDAGOGIQUE
BP 340, Bunia
Teacher Training

History: Founded 1968. Acquired present status and title 1971.

INSTITUT SUPÉRIEUR PÉDAGOGIQUE
BP 282, Kananga
Teacher Training

History: Founded 1966. Acquired present status and title 1971.

INSTITUT SUPÉRIEUR PÉDAGOGIQUE DE GOMBE (ISP-GOMBE)
BP 3580, Kinshasa-Gombe
Tel: +243(12) 34-092 +243(12) 34-094
Directeur général: Robert Mondo Kibwa Tuba (1997-)
Secrétaire général: Shadrack Nsimba-Lubaki

Departments
Biology and Chemistry (Biology; Chemistry; Teacher Training) *Head:* Ifuta Ndey Bibula, *full-time staff:* 16, *students:* 168
Commerce (Business Education) *Head:* Kabemba Assani, *full-time staff:* 5, *students:* 215
English and African Civilization (African Studies; English; Regional Studies; Teacher Training) *Head:* Katombe Mukengeshay, *full-time staff:* 13, *part-time staff:* 2, *students:* 248
French and African Linguistics (African Languages; French; Linguistics; Teacher Training) *Head:* Zandu dia Zulu M'Ndendi, *full-time staff:* 25, *part-time staff:* 5, *students:* 221
Geography and Natural Sciences (Geography; Natural Sciences; Teacher Training) *Head:* Bakunda Matezo, *full-time staff:* 13, *students:* 36

History and Social Sciences (History; Social Sciences; Teacher Training) *Head*: Kikokula Meno, *full-time staff:* 18, *part-time staff:* 1, *students:* 131
Hotel Management (Hotel Management; Teacher Training) *Head*: Zongwa Mbangilwa, *full-time staff:* 4, *students:* 75
Psychopedagogy (Educational Psychology; Teacher Training) *Head*: Manwana Mahinga, *full-time staff:* 11, *part-time staff:* 2
Teacher Training *Head*: Robert Mondo Kibwa Tuba, *full-time staff:* 119, *part-time staff:* 13, *students:* 1,094

History: Founded 1961 by Catholic Sisters to promote the study level of women. Acquired present status and title 1981.

Admission Requirements: Secondary school certificate

Fees: (Congolese Francs): c. 5000 per annum

Main Language(s) of Instruction: French

Degrees and Diplomas: *Graduat*: (G3); *Licence d'Enseignement*: Biology; English (L2); French; Geography; History

Student Services: Academic Counselling, Employment Services, Sports Facilities, Health Services

Student Residential Facilities: For 335 students

Libraries: Main Library

Publications: Les cahiers de l'ISP/Gombe, Pluridisciplinary review (2 per annum)

Academic Staff *1998-1999*	MEN	WOMEN	TOTAL
FULL-TIME	84	26	110
PART-TIME	11	2	13
TOTAL	**95**	**28**	**123**
STAFF WITH DOCTORATE			
FULL-TIME	20	5	25
PART-TIME	10	2	12
TOTAL	**30**	**7**	**37**
Student Numbers *1998-1999*	MEN	WOMEN	TOTAL
All (Foreign Included)	–	1,094	**1,094**

INSTITUT SUPÉRIEUR PÉDAGOGIQUE
BP 1514, Kisangani

Teacher Training

History: Founded 1967. Acquired present status and title 1971.

INSTITUT SUPÉRIEUR PÉDAGOGIQUE
BP 1796, Lubumbashi

Teacher Training

History: Founded 1959. Acquired present status and title 1971.

INSTITUT SUPÉRIEUR PÉDAGOGIQUE
BP 116, Mbandaka

Teacher Training

History: Founded 1971. Acquired present status and title 1981.

INSTITUT SUPÉRIEUR PÉDAGOGIQUE
BP 127, Mbanza-Ngungu

Teacher Training

History: Founded 1971. Acquired present status and title 1981.

INSTITUT SUPÉRIEUR PÉDAGOGIQUE
BP 682, Mbuji-Mayi

Teacher Training

History: Founded 1968. Acquired present status and title 1971.

INSTITUT SUPÉRIEUR PÉDAGOGIQUE TECHNIQUE
BP 3287, Kinshasa-Gombe

Technology Education

History: Founded 1976. Acquired present status and title 1981.

INSTITUT SUPÉRIEUR PÉDAGOGIQUE TECHNIQUE
BP 75, Likasi

Technology Education

History: Founded 1971. Acquired present status and title 1981.

Côte d'Ivoire

INSTITUTION TYPES AND CREDENTIALS

Types of higher education institutions:

Université (University)
Ecole nationale supérieure (National Higher School)
Centre universitaire (University Centre)
Institut supérieur (Higher Institute)
Ecole normale supérieure (Higher Teacher Training College)

School leaving and higher education credentials:

Baccalauréat
Brevet de Technicien Supérieur
Diplôme d'Infirmier d'Etat
Capacité en Droit
Diplôme d'Instituteur stagiaire
Diplôme universitaire
Certificat d'Aptitude au Professorat des Collèges d'Enseignement général
Diplôme en Pharmacie
Licence
Certificat d'Aptitude au Professorat de l'Enseignement secondaire
Diplôme d'Agronomie générale
Diplôme d'Ingénieur
Maîtrise
Docteur en Médecine
Diplôme d'Etudes approfondies (DEA)
Diplôme d'Etudes supérieures (DES)
Diplôme d'Etudes Supérieures Spécialisées (DESS)
Diplôme de Docteur Ingénieur
Doctorat

STRUCTURE OF EDUCATION SYSTEM

Pre-higher education:

Structure of school system:

Primary
Type of school providing this education: Ecole primaire

Length of programme in years: 6
Age level from: 6 to: 12
Certificate/diploma awarded: Certificat d'Etudes primaires élémentaires

First Cycle Secondary
Type of school providing this education: Collège d'Enseignement général
Length of programme in years: 4
Age level from: 12 to: 16
Certificate/diploma awarded: Brevet d'Etudes du Premier Cycle

Technical Secondary
Type of school providing this education: Centre de Formation Professionnelle
Length of programme in years: 4
Age level from: 12 to: 16
Certificate/diploma awarded: Brevet d'Etudes du Premier Cycle

Second Cycle Secondary
Type of school providing this education: Lycée
Length of programme in years: 3
Age level from: 16 to: 19
Certificate/diploma awarded: Baccalauréat/Diplôme de Bachelier de l'Enseignement du Second Degré

Technical
Type of school providing this education: Lycée technique/Lycée professionnel
Length of programme in years: 3
Age level from: 16 to: 19
Certificate/diploma awarded: Baccalauréat technique

School education:

Primary Education lasts for six years and leads to the Certificat d'Etudes primaires élémentaires (CEPE). Secondary schooling is divided into a four-year cycle culminating in the Brevet d'Etudes du Premier Cycle (BEPC), and a three-year cycle culminating in the Baccalauréat/Diplôme de Bachelier de l'Enseignement du Second Degré. Lower technical and vocational secondary education are available at the Centres de Formation professionnelle which offer four-year courses leading to the Brevet d'Etudes du Premier Cycle. After a three-year course at upper secondary level in a Lycée technique/professionnel, students are awarded the Baccalauréat technique.

Higher education:

Since 1996, higher education is offered at three separate universities (formerly the Université Nationale de Côte d'Ivoire), the Université de Cocody, the Université d'Abobo-Adjamé and the Université de Bouaké as well as at centres universitaires and at institutions providing higher professional training. The universities and the teacher college are under the auspices of the Ministère de l'Enseignement supérieur et de la Recherche scientifique. There are also some private institutions.

Academic year:

Classes from: October *to:* June

Long vacation from: 30 June *to:* 30 September

Languages of instruction:

French

Stages of studies:

Non-university level post-secondary studies (technical/vocational type):

Technical and professional education is offered at various institutes and higher schools. Courses usually last for two to three years and lead to such qualifications as the Brevet de Technicien supérieur and the Diplôme d'Infirmier d'Etat. An entrance examination is often required.

University level studies:

University level first stage: Premier Cycle:

Two years of university study lead to the Diplôme universitaire d'Etudes générales (DEUG). In medicine, the first cycle of studies is devoted to necessary grounding in the relevant sciences. A Capacité en Droit is conferred after two years' study to candidates who do not hold the Baccalauréat. A Diplôme universitaire de Technologie is awarded after three years' study by the Instituts universitaires de Technologie (IUT). A Diplôme en Pharmacie is conferred after three years. A Diplôme d'Agronomie générale is awarded after four years' study.

University level second stage: Deuxième Cycle:

A further year's study leads to the Licence. In engineering schools, studies last for five years and lead to the professional qualification of Ingénieur and the Diplôme d'Ingénieur des Travaux publics. In Agriculture, a Diplôme d'Agronomie générale is conferred after four years and a Diplôme d'Ingénieur agronome is awarded after five years' study with a further year's specialization. The Maîtrise in Arts and Science subjects takes one year after the Licence and includes a mini-thesis.

University level third stage: Troisième Cycle:

The Diplôme d'Etudes supérieures spécialisées (DESS) and the Diplôme d'Etudes approfondies (DEA) are conferred after one year's further study beyond the Licence or Maîtrise. After three more years candidates may be awarded the Doctorat. The qualification of Docteur-Ingénieur is conferred after three years' study and the submission of a thesis to holders of a diploma in Engineering. In Medicine, a professional Doctorate is awarded after seven years and in Dentistry and Pharmacy after five years.

Teacher education:

Training of pre-primary and primary/basic school teachers
Primary school teachers are trained at the Ecole normale Supérieure in a three-year post-Baccalauréat course which leads to the Certificat d'Aptitude pédagogique à l'Enseignement dans les Ecoles primaires (CAP/CEG).

Training of secondary school teachers
At lower secondary level, a three-year course leads to the Certificat d'Aptitude pédagogique pour les Collèges d'Enseignement général (CAP/CEG). Holders of CAP/CEG may go to university for a

further year to obtain the Licence. Upper secondary school teachers study for a Licence d'Enseignement or follow a one-year course and a one-year supervised and examined teaching practice if they have a degree. This leads to the Certificat d'Aptitude pédagogique pour l'Enseignement du Second Degré (CAPES).

For technical secondary education, students follow courses at the Institut Pédagogique National de l'Enseignement technique et professionnel where they obtain the title of Instructeur de Formation professionnelle after two years, of Professeur de Centre de Formation professionnelle after three years, of Professeur de Lycée professionnel after four years and of Professeur certifié de l'Enseignement technique et de la Formation professionnelle after five years.

Training of higher education teachers
University teachers must hold a Doctorat with a high pass mark.

Non-traditional studies:

Lifelong higher education
The Centre Africain et Mauricien de Perfectionnement des Cadres (CAMPC) awards the Diplôme de Direction du Personnel (five-week course), the Diplôme de Formation (six-week course), and the Diplôme de Gestion des Affaires (16-month programme). The Centre Ivoirien de Gestion des Entreprises provides short-term professional development courses for middle- and upper-level managers.

Other forms of non-formal higher education
The broadcast media offers two non-formal education opportunities, which include La Coupe Nationale du Progrès and the Télé Pour Tous. La Coupe Nationale du progrès is a 15-20 minute daily radio programme that provides agricultural information. The Télé Pour Tous offers televised lectures that are broadcast in French for 30 minutes each week and feature a variety of topics ranging from health care to agricultural practices. Télé Pour Tous is aimed at television classrooms run by lecturers who translate and explain the lectures.

NATIONAL BODIES

Responsible authorities:

Ministry of Higher Education and Scientific Research (Ministère de l'Enseignement supérieur et de la Recherche scientifique)
Minister: Zacharie Sery Bailly
BP V 151
Abidjan
Tel: +225(20) 21-33-16 +225(20) 21-57-73
Fax: +225(20) 21-49-87   +225(20) 21-22-25
Telex: 26138 rectu ci
WWW: http://www.pr.ci/gouvernement/ministeres/index.html

ADMISSIONS TO HIGHER EDUCATION

Admission to non university higher education studies

Name of secondary school credential required: Baccalauréat

Alternatives to credentials: Baccalauréat technique

Admission to university-level studies

Name of secondary school credential required: Baccalauréat

Foreign students admission

Admission requirements: Foreign students must hold a qualification that is equivalent to the Baccalauréat. Entrance to the Institut national polytechnique Félix Houphouët-Boigny is based on a competitive examination. For universities, students' files are examined.

Entry regulations: They must have a valid passport, a visa and scholarship from their government or an international organization.

Health requirements: Students must be vaccinated against yellow fever.

Language requirements: Knowledge of French necessary. The University organizes one- to three-year courses for students who are not proficient in French.

Recognition of studies and qualifications:

Studies pursued in foreign countries (bodies dealing with recognition of foreign credentials):
Université de Cocody
    BP V 34
    Abidjan 01
    Tel: +225(22) 44-90-00
    Fax: +225(22) 44-07-14
    Telex: 26138 rectu ci

Multilateral agreements concerning recognition of foreign studies

Name(s) of agreement(s): UNESCO Convention on the Recognition of Studies, Certificates, Diplomas, Degrees and Other Academic Qualifications in Higher Education in the African States
Year of signature: 1981

References to further information on foreign student admissions and recognition of studies

Title: Study Abroad 2000-2001
Publisher: UNESCO/IBE
Year of publication: 1999

STUDENT LIFE

Main student services at national level

Centre régional des Oeuvres universitaires d'Abidjan
   22 BP42
   Abidjan 22

   Category of services provided: Social and welfare services

Centre régional des Oeuvres universitaires de Bouaké
   01 BPV 18
   Bouaké 01

   Category of services provided: Social and welfare services

Centre régional des Oeuvres universitaires de Daloa
   BP 157
   Daloa

   Category of services provided: Social and welfare services

Student expenses and financial aid

Student costs:

   Home students tuition fees: Minimum: 6,000 (CFA Franc-O)
   Maximum: 25,000 (0)
   Foreign students tuition fees: Minimum: 200,000 (CFA Franc-O)
   Maximum: 500,000 (CFA Franc-O)

Bodies providing information on student financial aid:

Direction des Bourses et Aides, Ministère de l'Enseignement supérieur et de la Recherche scientifique
   Abidjan
   Tel: +225(20) 21-33-16
   Fax: +225(20) 21-49-87

INTERNATIONAL COOPERATION AND EXCHANGES

Principal national bodies responsible for dealing with international cooperation and exchanges in higher education:

Ministère de l'Enseignement supérieur et de la Recherche scientifique
   B.P. V 151
   Abidjan
   Tel: +225(20) 21-33-16 +225(20) 21-57-73
   Fax: +225(20) 21-49-87   +225(20) 21-22-25
   Telex: 26138 rectu ci
   WWW: http://www.pr.ci/gouvernement/ministeres/index.html

GRADING SYSTEM

Usual grading system in secondary school

Full Description: 16-20=Très Bien; 14-15=Bien; 12-13=Assez bien; 11=Passable; 0-9=Ajourné.
Highest on scale: 20
Pass/fail level: 10
Lowest on scale: 0

Main grading system used by higher education institutions

Full Description: 16-20=Très Bien; 14-15=Bien; 12-13=Assez Bien; 10-11=Passable; 8-9=Ajourné (Fail but allowed to retake exam); 0-7=Ajourné
Highest on scale: 20
Pass/fail level: 10
Lowest on scale: 0

NOTES ON HIGHER EDUCATION SYSTEM

Data for academic year: 2000-2001
Source: International Association of Universities (IAU)

INSTITUTIONS OF HIGHER EDUCATION

UNIVERSITIES

PUBLIC INSTITUTIONS

NATIONAL POLYTECHNIC INSTITUTE FÉLIX HOUPHOUËT-BOIGNY

Institut national polytechnique Félix Houphouët-Boigny
BP 1093, Yamoussoukro
Tel: +225(30) 64-05-41
Fax: +225(30) 64-04-06
Website: http://www.inphb.edu.ci

Directeur général: Ado Gossan Tel: +225(30) 64-03-63
Secrétaire général: Mamadou Mathias Zengbe
Tel: +225(30) 64-11-36

Schools
Agriculture (Agricultural Economics; Agriculture; Animal Husbandry; Development Studies; Food Technology; Rural Studies; Sociology)
Commerce and Business Administration (Business Administration; Business and Commerce)
Industrial Technology (Industrial Engineering)
Lifelong Education and Executive Proficiency
Mines and Geology (Geology; Mining Engineering)
Public Works (Civil Engineering)

History: Founded 1996, incorporating previously existing Institutions, including Ecole nationale supérieure Agronomique, Ecole nationale supérieure des Travaux Publics, and Institut national supérieur de l'Enseignement technique.

Degrees and Diplomas: *Brevet de Technicien Supérieur*; *Diplôme d'Agronomie générale*; *Diplôme d'Ingénieur*, *Diplôme d'Etudes approfondies (DEA)*

*• UNIVERSITY OF ABOBO-ADJAMÉ

Université d'Abobo-Adjamé
BP 801, Abidjan 02
Tel: +225 (20) 37-81-21
Fax: +225 (20) 37-81-18
EMail: abobo-adj@abobo.edu.ci-mes/rs-ci
Website: http://www.abobo.edu.ci

Président: Daouda Aïdara EMail: aidarad@hotmail.com
Secrétaire général: Woï Messe
International Relations: Pascal Houenou
EMail: phouenou@hotmail.com

Units
Basic Sciences (Natural Sciences)

Food Technology
Higher Education *(URES Daloa)*

Programmes
Natural Sciences (Mathematics and Computer Science; Natural Sciences)
Science and Environment Administration (Environmental Management; Natural Sciences)

Schools
Health Sciences

Institutes
Research

Centres
Advanced Training
Ecology Research (Ecology; Environmental Studies)

History: Founded 1995 as University Centre.

Degrees and Diplomas: *Diplôme universitaire*: Natural Sciences, 2 yrs; *Maîtrise*: 4 yrs; *Diplôme d'Etudes approfondies (DEA)*: a further 2 yrs

Academic Staff *1999:* Total: c. 50

Student Numbers *1999:* Total: c. 4,300

UNIVERSITY OF BOUAKÉ

Université de Bouaké
BP V 18, Bouaké 01
Tel: +225(31) 63-42-32
Fax: +225(31) 63-59-84
Website:
http://www.ci.refer.org/ivoir_ct/edu/sup/uni/bke/accueil.htm

Directeur: François Kouakou N'Guessan (1996-)
Tel: +225(31) 63-48-57
Secrétaire général: Jean Yao Sekou
Vice-président: Aka Landry Komenan

Units
Communication, Environment and Society (Communication Studies; Environmental Studies; Social Studies)
Economics and Development (Development Studies; Economics)
Higher Education *(URES, Korhogo)*
Law, Administration and Development (Administration; Development Studies; Law)
Medical Sciences (Health Sciences)

Centres
Development Research (Development Studies)
Lifelong Education

History: Founded 1994 as University Centre.

• UNIVERSITY OF COCODY
Université de Cocody
BP V34, Abidjan 01, Abidjan 01
Tel: +225(22) 44-50-00
Fax: +225(22) 44-07-14
Telex: 26138 rectu ci
Website:
http://www.refer.org/ivoir_ct/edu/sup/uni/abi/accueil.htm
Président: Asseypo Hauhouot (1996-)
Tel: +225(22) 44-08-95 EMail: hauhouot@minitel.refer.org
Secrétaire générale: Julienne Badia Tel: +225(22) 44-39-22
Fax: +225(22) 44-39-22
International Relations: Gérard Dago Lezou
Tel: +225(22) 44-87-51 Fax: +225(22) 44-87-51
EMail: lezoud.syfed@refer.org

Units
Bioscience (Biochemistry; Biomedicine; Biophysics) *Director:* Yao Tanoh, *full-time staff:* 86, *students:* 2,144
Criminology *Director:* Alain Sissoko, *full-time staff:* 5, *students:* 1,987
Earth Sciences and Mining Resources (Earth Sciences; Mineralogy) *Director:* Kouassi Aka, *full-time staff:* 19, *students:* 170
Economics and Management (Economics; Management) *Director:* Mbet Allechi, *full-time staff:* 91, *students:* 5,412
Information, Art and Communication (Communication Studies; Fine Arts; Information Sciences) *Director:* Yahaya Diaby, *full-time staff:* 12, *students:* 513
Languages, Literature and Civilizations (Cultural Studies; Literature; Modern Languages) *Director:* Bailly Sery, *full-time staff:* 118, *students:* 8,692
Law, Administration and Political Science (Administration; Law; Political Science) *Director:* Abou Ouraga, *full-time staff:* 89, *students:* 6,049
Mankind and Society (Geography; History; Sociology) *Director:* N'guessan Aloco, *full-time staff:* 105, *students:* 6,412
Mathematics and Computer Science (Computer Science; Mathematics) *Director:* Niango Niango, *full-time staff:* 40, *students:* 1,682
Medical Sciences (Health Sciences; Medicine) *Director:* Thérèse Ndri Yoman, *full-time staff:* 309, *students:* 3,679
Odonto-Stomatology (Dentistry; Stomatology) *Director:* Siaka Touré, *full-time staff:* 46
Pharmaceutical Sciences (Pharmacy) *Director:* Abbe Yapo, *full-time staff:* 59, *students:* 1,148
Structure of Matter and Technology (Physics; Technology) *Director:* Gokou Tea, *full-time staff:* 92, *students:* 2,556

Institutes
African History, Art and Archaeology (African Studies; Archaeology; Fine Arts; History) *Director:* Simon Pierre Mbra Ekanza
Applied Linguistics *Director:* Assi Adopo
Ethno-Sociology (Ethnology; Sociology) *Director:* Ismaila Touré
Mathematics *Director:* Etienne Desquith, *full-time staff:* 6

Centres
Communication Studies and Research (Communication Studies)

Economic and Social Research (Economics; Social Studies) *Director:* N'guessan Tchetche
Lifelong Education *Director:* Barthelemy Dembele, *full-time staff:* 4

History: Founded 1995 as University Centre. Acquired present status 1996

Admission Requirements: Baccalauréat or equivalent

Fees: (Francs CFA): Native students, 6000-25,000; foreign students, 200,000-500,000 (if agreements, foreign students may pay same fees as nationals)

Main Language(s) of Instruction: French

Degrees and Diplomas: *Licence:* 3 yrs; *Maîtrise:* 4 yrs; *Docteur en Médecine:* Medicine, 8 yrs; *Diplôme d'Etudes approfondies (DEA)*; *Diplôme d'Etudes Supérieures Spécialisées (DESS):* Pharmacy, Dentistry; *Doctorat:* 3 yrs following DEA

Student Services: Academic Counselling, Social Counselling, Nursery Care, Sports Facilities, Language Programmes, Handicapped Facilities, Health Services, Canteen

Libraries: Central Library and specialized Libraries per unit (13)

Publications: Revues médicales (quarterly); En-Quête, Letters; Revues sociales; Repères, Letters and Human Sciences (biannually)

Academic Staff *1999-2000:* Total: **1,081**

Staff with doctorate: Total: **1,005**

Student Numbers *1999-2000:* Total: **37,500**

Evening Students, 1,434

PRIVATE INSTITUTIONS

• INTER-AFRICAN ELECTRICAL ENGINEERING COLLEGE (IEEC)
Ecole supérieure Inter-Africaine de l'Electricité (ESIE)
BP 311, Bingerville
Tel: +225(22) 40-33-12
Fax: +225(22) 40-35-07
Directeur général: Mamadou Alioune N'diaye (1996-)
Tel: +225(22) 40-33-15
Directeur des Etudes et de la Recherche: Abou Badirou
Tel: +225(22) 40-33-04
International Relations: L.Y. Issiaka
Tel: +225(22) 40-33-03 +225(22) 40-33-14

Departments
Electrical Engineering (Electrical Engineering; Energy Engineering; Management)

History: Founded 1979.

Governing Bodies: Board of Directors

Admission Requirements: Baccalauréat C

Fees: (Francs CFA): On-Campus, 5m. per annum; off-Campus, 3m. per annum

Main Language(s) of Instruction: French, English

International Co-operation: Arrangements for co-operation with universities in Europe

Accrediting Agencies: Conseil Africain et Malgache de l' Enseignement Supérieur (CAMES)

Degrees and Diplomas: *Diplôme d'Ingénieur.* Electrical Engineering, 5 yrs

Student Services: Sports Facilities, Language Programmes, Health Services

Student Residential Facilities: Yes

Libraries: Central Library

OTHER INSTITUTIONS

PUBLIC INSTITUTIONS

CENTRE AFRICAIN DE MANAGEMENT ET DE PERFECTIONNEMENT DES CADRES (CAMPC)
BP 878, Abidjan 08
Tel: +225(22) 44-43-22
Fax: +225(22) 44-03-78
Telex: 26170 camp-ci

Directeur général: Palaki-Pawi Marcus Palouki Haredema (1995-) Tel: +225(22) 44-49-46

Management
Management Techniques (Management)

History: Founded 1970.

CENTRE D' ANIMATION ET DE FORMATION PÉDAGOGIQUE
BP 121, Abengourou
Tel: +225(35) 91-35-02

Directeur: Bi Bouyé Etienne Irié (1997-)
Tel: +225(35) 91-35-22

Primary Teacher Training (Primary Education)

History: Founded 1977.

CENTRE D' ANIMATION ET DE FORMATION PÉDAGOGIQUE
BP 351, Aboisso
Tel: +225(21) 30-40-52

Directeur: Gilbert Gbèlè Kone (1998-)
Tel: +225(21) 30-41-53

Primary Teacher Training (Primary Education)

History: Founded 1982.

CENTRE D' ANIMATION ET DE FORMATION PÉDAGOGIQUE
BP 125, Bouaké 1 01
Tel: +225(31) 63-35-21

Directeur: N'dri N'goran (1996-)

Primary Teacher Training (Primary Education)

History: Founded 1967.

CENTRE D' ANIMATION ET DE FORMATION PÉDAGOGIQUE
BP 125, Bouaké 2 01
Tel: +225(31) 63-03-33

Directeur: Mamadou Sanogo (1996-) Tel: +225(31) 63-34-71

Primary Teacher Training (Primary Education)

History: Founded 1969.

CENTRE D' ANIMATION ET DE FORMATION PÉDAGOGIQUE
BP 135, Dabou

Directeur: Vabélé Valentin Gnali (1997-)
Tel: +225(23) 57-22-12

Primary Teacher Training (Primary Education)

History: Founded 1966.

CENTRE D' ANIMATION ET DE FORMATION PÉDAGOGIQUE
BP 1410, Daloa

Directeur: Mamadou Koné (1994-) Tel: +225(32) 78-30-04

Primary Teacher Training (Primary Education)

History: Founded 1965.

CENTRE D' ANIMATION ET DE FORMATION PÉDAGOGIQUE
BP 583, Gagnoa
Tel: +225(32) 77-26-88

Directeur: Zogbo Pierre Bouabré (1997-)
Tel: +225(32) 77-26-99

Primary Teacher Training (Primary Education)

History: Founded 1977.

CENTRE D' ANIMATION ET DE FORMATION PÉDAGOGIQUE
BP 227, Grand-Bassam
Tel: +225(21) 30-12-31

Directeur: Yao Albert Kouakou (1996-)
Tel: +225(21) 30-14-43

Primary Teacher Training (Primary Education)

History: Founded 1969.

CENTRE D' ANIMATION ET DE FORMATION PÉDAGOGIQUE
BP 123, Katiola
Tel: +225(31) 66-04-88

Directeur: Gnoka François Tagro (1994-)
Tel: +225(31) 66-01-89

Primary Teacher Training (Primary Education)

History: Founded 1982.

CENTRE D' ANIMATION ET DE FORMATION PÉDAGOGIQUE
BP 77, Korhogo
Tel: +225(36) 86-06-02

Directeur: Kouakou N'zue (1997-) Tel: +225(36) 86-06-23

Primary Teacher Training (Primary Education)

History: Founded 1969.

CENTRE D' ANIMATION ET DE FORMATION PÉDAGOGIQUE
BP 493, Man
Tel: +225(33) 79-04-57
Fax: +225(33) 79-04-57

Directeur: Dounignan Ouattara (1998-)

Primary Teacher Training (Primary Education)

History: Founded 1975.

CENTRE D' ANIMATION ET DE FORMATION PÉDAGOGIQUE (CAFOP)
BP 612, Odienné
Tel: +225(33) 70-45-85

Directeur: Darius Anvire Oi Anvire (1997-)
Tel: +225 (33) 70-81-10 Fax: +255 (33) 70-81-10

Directeur des Etudes: Jean Kouame Kouassi

Centres
Primary Teacher Training (Educational Sciences; Primary Education) *Director*: Anvire Oi Anvire Darius, *full-time staff*: 14, *part-time staff*: 6, *students*: 158

History: Founded 1982.

Fees: (CFA Francs): 5000 per annum

Main Language(s) of Instruction: French

Degrees and Diplomas: *Diplôme d'Instituteur stagiaire*: Education and Teacher Training, 2 yrs

Student Services: Sports Facilities, Health Services

Student Residential Facilities: Yes

Libraries: Central Library

Academic Staff *1999-2000*	MEN	WOMEN	TOTAL
FULL-TIME	14	–	14
PART-TIME	5	1	6
TOTAL	**19**	**1**	**20**

Student Numbers *1999-2000*	MEN	WOMEN	TOTAL
All (Foreign Included)	134	24	**158**

CENTRE D' ANIMATION ET DE FORMATION PÉDAGOGIQUE
BP 224, Yamoussoukro
Tel: +225(30) 64-03-87

Directeur: Gilles Coupaye N'dri (1998-)
Tel: +225(30) 64-03-86

Primary Teacher Training (Primary Education)

History: Founded 1982.

ECOLE NATIONALE D'ADMINISTRATION (ENA)
BP V 20, Abidjan
Tel: +225(22) 41-40-33

Directeur: Djah Guillaume Kouacou (1996-)
Tel: +225(22) 44-52-25 Fax: +225(22) 41-49-63

Secrétaire général: Seydou Coulibaly
Tel: +225(22) 41-52-31

Schools
Administrative and Diplomatic Management (Administration; International Relations; Management Systems)
Economics and Financial Management (Economics; Finance; Management Systems)
Magisterial and Judicial Studies (Justice Administration)

Centres
Lifelong Education and Executive Retraining (Management)

History: Founded 1960.

ECOLE NATIONALE DE POLICE (ENP)
BP 855, Abidjan 08
Tel: +225(22) 44-02-82
Fax: +225(22) 44-62-43

Directeur: Edja Oi Edja (1998-) Tel: +225(22) 44-77-59

Police Studies

History: Founded 1967.

ECOLE NATIONALE SUPÉRIEURE DE STATISTIQUE ET D'ECONOMIE APPLIQUÉE (ENSEA)
BP 3, Abidjan 08
Tel: +225(22) 44-08-40
Fax: +225(22) 44-39-88

Directeur: Koffi N'guessan (1994-)

Statistics and Applied Economics (Economics; Statistics)

History: Founded 1961

ECOLE NORMALE SUPÉRIEURE (ENS)
BP 10, Abidjan 08
Tel: +225(22) 44-43-23
Fax: +225(22) 44-42-32
Website:
http://www.ci.refer.org/ivoir_ct/edu/sup/gec/ens/accueil.htm
Directeur: Goze Tape Tel: +225(22) 44-52-34

Departments
Arts and Humanities
Educational Sciences
History and Geography (Geography; History)
Languages (Modern Languages)
Science and Technology (Natural Sciences; Technology)
Teacher Training

History: Founded 1964

INSTITUT NATIONAL DE FORMATION DES AGENTS DE LA SANTÉ
BP 720, Abidjan 18
Tel: +225(21) 24-29-00
Fax: +225(21) 24-28-87
Directeur: Roger Charles Joseph Delafosse (1998-)
Tel: +225(21) 25-37-94

Schools
Specialization
Midwifery
Nursing
Technical Studies (Technology)

History: Founded 1992.

INSTITUT NATIONAL DE FORMATION DES AGENTS DE LA SANTÉ
BP V 20, Bouaké
Tel: +225(31) 63-10-26
Fax: +225(31) 63-10-28
Directeur: Renard Désiré Kei (1997-) Tel: +225(31) 63-10-28

Nursing

History: Founded 1988.

INSTITUT NATIONAL DE FORMATION DES AGENTS DE LA SANTÉ
BP 426, Korhogo
Tel: +225(36) 86-11-85
Fax: +225(36) 86-08-58
Directeur: Paul Séoué (1993-)

Midwifery
Nursing

History: Founded 1993.

INSTITUT NATIONAL DE FORMATION SOCIALE (INFS)
BP 2625, Abidjan 01
Tel: +225(22) 44-16-72
Fax: +225(22) 44-90-75
Directeur: Djénéba Coulibaly (1985-) Tel: +225(22) 44-16-75

Schools
Pre-School Teacher Training (Preschool Education)
Social Work
Specialized Teacher Training (Teacher Training)

History: Founded 1978.

INSTITUT NATIONAL DE LA JEUNESSE ET DES SPORTS (INJS)
BP V 54, Abidjan
Tel: +225(21) 35-70-60
Fax: +225(21) 25-76-60
Directeur: Alexis Aby Koffi (1991-) Tel: +225(21) 26-88-45

Lifelong Education
Sports
Youth Studies (Social Studies)

History: Founded 1961

INSTITUT NATIONAL SUPÉRIEUR DES ARTS ET DE L'ACTION CULTURELLE (INSAAC)
BP 49, Abidjan 08
Tel: +225(22) 44-20-31
Fax: +225(22) 44-26-73
Directeur: Climanlo Jérôme Coulibaly (1996-)
Secrétaire général: Jean-Pierre Adingra
Tel: +225(22) 44-03-05

Schools
Fine Arts
Music and Musicology (Music; Musicology)
Theatre and Dance (Dance; Theatre)
Training for Cultural Action (Art Education)

Centres
Pedagogy
Research

History: Founded 1991.

INSTITUT PÉDAGOGIQUE NATIONAL DE L'ENSEIGNEMENT TECHNIQUE ET PROFESSIONEL (IPNETP)
BP 2098, Abidjan
Tel: +225(22) 44-67-69
Fax: +225(22) 44-90-22

Directeur: Souleymane Bah (1976-)
Tel: +225(22) 44-90-22 +225(22) 44-58-37
International Relations: Mamadou Diomandé

Technology Education; Vocational Education

INSTITUT DES SCIENCES ET TECHNIQUES DE LA COMMUNICATION (ISTC)
BP V 205, Abidjan
Tel: +225(22) 44-88-38
Fax: +225(22) 44-84-33

Directeur: Joseph Koudougnon Balet (1991-)
Tel: +225(22) 44-88-58 +225(22) 44-86-66

Audiovisual (Multimedia)
Journalism
Media Studies
Production
Publishing (Publishing and Book Trade)

History: Founded 1992.

PRIVATE INSTITUTIONS

ACADÉMIE RÉGIONALE DES SCIENCES ET TECHNIQUES DE LA MER (ARSTM)
BP V 158, Locodjro
Tel: +225(23) 46-08-09

Schools
Navigation Studies (Nautical Science)

History: Founded 1987.

INSTITUT SUPÉRIEUR AFRICAIN DES POSTES ET TÉLÉCOMMUNICATIONS (ISAPT)
BP 1501, Abidjan 18
Tel: +225(21) 25-66-22
Fax: +225(21) 25-99-05

Directeur général: Gossan Biakou (1995-)
Tel: +225(20) 34-53-23

Directeur Administratif et Financier: Sam Kobina
Tel: +225(20) 34-53-37 Fax: +225(21) 25-26-94

Postal and Telecommunication Studies (Postal Services; Telecommunications Services)

History: Founded 1992.

Egypt

INSTITUTION TYPES AND CREDENTIALS

Types of higher education institutions:

University
Higher Institute
Higher Institute of Technology
Teacher Training Institute
Military Academy

School leaving and higher education credentials:

Technical Education School Certificate
Thanaweya Am'ma
Primary-School Teacher's Certificate
Technician's Diploma
Diploma
Baccalaureos
High Diploma
Magistr
Diplôme d'Etudes professionnelles approfondies
Doktora

STRUCTURE OF EDUCATION SYSTEM

Pre-higher education:

Duration of compulsory education:

   Age of entry: 6
   Age of exit: 14

Structure of school system:

   Primary
   Type of school providing this education: Primary School
   Length of programme in years: 5
   Age level from: 6 to: 11
   Certificate/diploma awarded: Primary School Certificate

   Preparatory
   Type of school providing this education: Preparatory School

Length of programme in years: 3
Age level from: 11 to: 14
Certificate/diploma awarded: Basic Education Completion Certificate

General Secondary
Type of school providing this education: General Secondary School
Length of programme in years: 3
Age level from: 14 to: 17
Certificate/diploma awarded: Thanaweya a' Amma (General Secondary Education Certificate (GSEC)

Technical Secondary
Type of school providing this education: Technical Secondary School (for technicians)
Length of programme in years: 3
Age level from: 14 to: 17
Certificate/diploma awarded: Technical Education Diploma

Technical
Type of school providing this education: Technical Secondary School (for high level technicians)
Length of programme in years: 5
Age level from: 14 to: 19
Certificate/diploma awarded: Advanced Technical Diploma

School education:

Compulsory education lasts for eight grades and is known as "basic education", split into two stages, primary school (Grades 1 - 5) and preparatory school (Grades 6 - 8). It leads to the award of the Basic Education Completion Certificate. Following the eight-year basic education, pupils have the choice of entering a general secondary school (academic option) or a technical option including three- and five-year technical schools as well as experimental schools teaching languages, education and physical education. Only general secondary school graduates (academic option) may be admitted to university after obtaining their General Secondary Education Certificate (GSEC) or an Advanced Technical Diploma with scores above 75%. However, since 1991, some graduates from technical schools have been allowed to enter higher education.

Higher education:

Higher education is provided by some 20 universities and by higher institutes of technical and professional training, both public and private. Responsibility for higher education lies mainly with the Ministry of Higher Education and Scientific Research. Organization and administration, as well as academic programmes, are determined by laws, decrees and government regulations. The State universities are under the authority of the Supreme Council of Universities. Universities have full academic and administrative autonomy. They also carry out scientific research. The higher institutes of professional and technical training award qualifications equivalent to the first qualification conferred by the universities. Open college education was introduced at the universities of Cairo, Alexandria and Assiut in 1991. Private universities are entitled to implement their own criteria of admission and to set fees without intervention from the Ministry.

Main laws/decrees governing higher education:

Decree: SCU Decree   Year: 1992
Concerns: Teacher Training Institutes

Decree: Law 49/1972   Year: 1972
Concerns: Universities

Academic year:

Classes from: October *to:* June

Long vacation from: 1 July *to:* 30 September

Languages of instruction:

Arabic, English, French

Stages of studies:

Non-university level post-secondary studies (technical/vocational type):

Non-university level post-secondary education is offered by industrial, commercial and technical institutes providing two-year courses leading to a Diploma in Accountancy, Secretarial Work, Insurance, Computer or Health Sciences and Electronics. Holders of a Technical Education Diploma in commercial, industrial and agricultural fields may be admitted to these technical institutes. Holders of an Advanced Technical Diploma, whose score is 75% and above may be admitted to Higher Institutes of similar specializations. Studies last for four to five years.

University level studies:

University level first stage:
The first stage of higher education consists of one or more years of multidisciplinary study in basic subjects, especially Science or Medicine. The main stage then normally lasts between three and five years. In scientific subjects, studies last four to five years. They lead to the award of the Baccalaureos degree.

University level second stage:
The second stage is more specialized and comprises two to three years of training in individual research work culminating in the submission of a thesis. The degree awarded is that of Magistr. In Medicine, studies last six years with one additional year of practical work.

University level third stage:
The third stage leads to the Doktora (PhD) after at least two years' study following the Magistr (Master's Degree). Students must have obtained the mark "good" in the Master's Degree. It is awarded for advanced research work culminating in a thesis. In Medicine, a Doktora in medical sciences may be prepared concurrently with the professional Doctor of Medicine Degree.

University level fourth stage:
In certain rare cases, after the Doktora, a degree of Doctor of Science is awarded. It is reserved for researchers who have undertaken a substantial body of research work.

Teacher education:

Training of pre-primary and primary/basic school teachers
Primary school teachers must hold a qualification from a University Faculty of Education. There is also a distance learning programme to upgrade, through the medium of Arabic, primary school teachers who do not hold a degree.The course leads to a BEd in Primary Education.

Training of secondary school teachers
Secondary school teachers are trained in the faculties of education of the universities in four years and in higher teacher-training colleges. Both preparatory and general secondary teachers follow the same course which leads to the Bachelor Degree. Graduates who hold a four-year university degree can also teach at secondary level after following a one-year postgraduate course at the Faculty of Education where they are awarded the General Diploma. Teachers of technical education are trained at special faculties.

Training of higher education teachers
Higher education teachers are required to hold at least a Magistr in the field of higher education.

Non-traditional studies:

Distance higher education
The Egyptian University for Distance Learning is being established.

Lifelong higher education
In some ministries full- or part-time in-service training is organized periodically. Non-formal studies are offered by universities in the form of refresher courses and evening or correspondence courses.

NATIONAL BODIES

Responsible authorities:

Ministry of Higher Education and Scientific Research
    Minister: Moufid Shehab
    First Under-Secretary: Safwat Salem
    101, Kasr Al-Aini Street
    Cairo
    Tel: +20(2) 795-2155
    Fax: +20(2) 794-2556
    Telex: 92312 frcu un
    EMail: mohe@frcu.eun.eg
    WWW: http://www.frcu.eun.eg

    Role of governing body: Coordinates and supervises post-secondary education

Supreme Council of Universities
    President: Moufid Shehab
    Secretary-General: Galal Abdellah
    Cairo University Buildings
    Giza

Cairo
Tel: +20(2) 573-2727 +20(2) 573-8583
Fax: +20(2) 582-8722
EMail: info@frcu.eun.eg
WWW: http://www.frcu.eun.eg/

Role of governing body: Determines the overall policy of higher education and scientific research in the universities and determines the number of students admitted in each faculty.

ADMISSIONS TO HIGHER EDUCATION

Admission to non university higher education studies

Name of secondary school credential required: Technical Education School Certificate
Minimum score/requirement: 70%
For entry to: Technical institutes

Admission to university-level studies

Name of secondary school credential required: Thanaweya Am'ma
Minimum score/requirement: 70% or above
For entry to: Universities and higher specialized institutes

Alternatives to credentials: Secondary school students holders of an Advanced Technical Education may enter university Higher Institutes in their speciality if they have obtained scores of at least 75%.

Numerus clausus/restrictions: The Supreme Council of Universities at the Ministry of Higher Education determines the number of students to be admitted by the faculties of each university.

Foreign students admission

Admission requirements: Foreign students should have qualifications equivalent to the Thanaweya A'amma or a university degree.

Entry regulations: Foreign students must obtain a student visa.

Language requirements: Knowledge of Arabic is essential for regular university studies. English is the language of instruction at the American University in Cairo, some faculties of Helwan University and at the Faculty of Agriculture of the University of Alexandria. French is the language of instruction at Senghor University.

Application procedures:

Apply to national body for entry to: Universities

Apply to: Supreme Council of Universities
Cairo University
Giza
Cairo
Tel: +20(2) 573-8583
Fax: +20(2) 582-8722

Telex: 92312 frcu un
EMail: info@frcu.eun.eg
WWW: http://www.frcu.eun.eg/supreme.html

Recognition of studies and qualifications:

Studies pursued in foreign countries (bodies dealing with recognition of foreign credentials):
Ministry of Higher Education and Scientific Research

101 Kasr Al-Aini Street
Cairo
Tel: +20(2) 795-2155
Fax: +20(2) 794-2556
Telex: 92312 frcu un
EMail: mohe@frcu.eun.eg
WWW: http://www.frcu.eun.eg

Services provided and students dealt with: Provides information on the admission of foreign students to universities and higher institutes.

Supreme Council of Universities

Secretary-General: Galal Abdellah
Cairo University
Giza
Cairo
Tel: +20(2) 573-8583
Fax: +20(2) 582-8722
Telex: 92312 frcu un
EMail: info@frcu.eun.eg
WWW: http://www.frcu.eun.eg

Services provided and students dealt with: Provides information on admission to universities.

Multilateral agreements concerning recognition of foreign studies

Name(s) of agreement(s): Convention on the Recognition of Studies, Certificates, Diplomas, Degrees and Other Academic Qualifications in Higher Education in the African States
Year of signature: 1981

Convention on the Recognition of Studies, Diplomas and Degrees in Higher Education in the Arab States
Year of signature: 1978

International Convention on the Recognition of Studies, Certificates, Diplomas and Degrees in Higher Education in the Arab and European States Bordering on the Mediterranean.
Year of signature: 1976

References to further information on foreign student admissions and recognition of studies

Title: A guide for the use of foreign students
Publisher: Students' Welfare Department

STUDENT LIFE

Student expenses and financial aid

Bodies providing information on student financial aid:
Supreme Council of Universities
    Cairo University
    Giza
    Cairo
    Tel: +20(2) 573-8583
    Fax: +20(2) 582-8722
    Telex: 92312 frcu un
    EMail: info@frcu.eun.eg
    WWW: http://www.frcu.eun.eg

    Category of students: African, Asian and Arab nationals.

Publications on student services and financial aid:
    Title: Study Abroad 2000-2001
    Publisher: UNESCO/IBE
    Year of publication: 1999

INTERNATIONAL COOPERATION AND EXCHANGES

Principal national bodies responsible for dealing with international cooperation and exchanges in higher education:
Ministry of Higher Education and Scientific Research
    101, Kasr Al-Aini Street
    Cairo
    Tel: +20(2) 794-2556
    Fax: +20(2) 796-3722
    Telex: 92312 frcu un
    EMail: mohe@frcu.eun.eg
    WWW: http://www.frcu.eun.eg

Participation of country in multilateral or bilateral higher education programmes
Name(s) of exchange programme(s): Agreement Concerning Scholarships For Studying German Language in Austria
Agreement Concerning Training of Language Teachers in Spain

GRADING SYSTEM

Usual grading system in secondary school

Full Description: 75-100: distinguished, excellent, very good; 65-74: good; 50-64: pass; 0-49: poor
Highest on scale: 75-100: distinguished
Pass/fail level: 50-64: pass
Lowest on scale: 0-49: poor

Main grading system used by higher education institutions

Full Description: 75-100: distinguished, excellent, very good; 65-74: good; 50-64: pass; 0-49: poor
Highest on scale: 75-100 Distinguished
Pass/fail level: 50-64 Pass (60 - 64 for medical sciences)
Lowest on scale: 0-49 Poor

NOTES ON HIGHER EDUCATION SYSTEM

Data for academic year: 2000-2001
Source: International Association of Universities (IAU), updated from IBE website, 2000

INSTITUTIONS OF HIGHER EDUCATION

UNIVERSITIES

PUBLIC INSTITUTIONS

*• AIN SHAMS UNIVERSITY

PO Box 11566, Kasr-el-Zaafaran, Abbassia, Cairo
Tel: +20(3) 284-7818 +20(3) 284-7823
Fax: +20(3) 282-6107 +20(3) 284-7824
Telex: 94070-u-shms-un
EMail: ain.shams@frcu.eun.eg
Website: http://asunet.shams.eun.eg

President: Mohamed Awad TagEldin (2002-)
Tel: +20(3) 283-1090 Fax: +20(3) 284-7827

Secretary-General: Sawsan Abdel-Hamid Boraay
Tel: +20(3) 284-7823 Fax: +20(3) 284-7824

International Relations: Mohamed Awad Afify Tag Al-den, Vice-President for Postgraduate Studies and Research

Faculties

Agriculture (Agriculture; Animal Husbandry) *Dean*: Hussein Mansour
Arts (Arts and Humanities) *Dean*: Raafat A. Mohamed
Commerce (Business and Commerce) *Dean*: Mohamed Abdel Mageed
Computer and Information Sciences (Computer Science; Information Technology) *Dean*: Mohamed F. Tolba
Dentistry *Dean*: Mokhtar Nagi Ibrahim
Education (Educational Sciences) *Dean*: Mohamed Amin El-Mofti
Engineering (Architecture; Engineering) *Dean*: Mohamed Sheirah
Languages (*Al-Alsun*) (Modern Languages) *Dean*: Saleh Hashem Mostafa
Law *Dean*: Hossam El-din Al-Ahwany
Medicine *Dean*: Hamed M.M. Shatla
Pharmacy *Dean*: Ahmed Shawky Geneidi
Science (Natural Sciences) *Dean*: Mohamed M. Abdel-Fattah
Special Education *Dean*: Salwa A. El-Moulla
Women for Arts, Science and Education (Women's Studies) *Dean*: Nefissa Eleishe

Institutes

Environmental Studies and Research (Environmental Studies) *Dean*: Abdel Azim M. El-Hammady
Nursing
Postgraduate Childhood Studies (Child Care and Development) *Director*: Faiza Y. Abdel Mageed

Centres

Childhood Studies (Child Care and Development)
Light and Energy (Electrical Engineering; Energy Engineering)

Middle East (Middle Eastern Studies) *Director*: Mohamed Reda El Adel
Papyrus Studies (Ancient Civilizations) *Director*: Alia Hanfy Hassanein
Psycho-Extension (Psychometrics)
Public Service and Development (Social and Community Services)
Science Education Development (Science Education)
Scientific Computing (Computer Science) *Director*: Mohamed F. Tolba
University Education Development (Higher Education)
Vectors and Diseases (Epidemiology)

Further Information: Also University Hospitals and specialized hospital

History: Founded 1950 as State university, incorporating Abbassia School of Medicine. Formerly known as Ibrahim Pasha University and also as University of Heliopolis. Faculties of Commerce, Education, Agriculture, and Veterinary Medicine at Zagazig detached 1973 to form new University.

Governing Bodies: University Council, composed of the President, three Vice-Presidents, deans of the faculties, a representative of the Ministry of Higher Education, the Secretary-General and three other members

Academic Year: September to May

Admission Requirements: Secondary school certificate or equivalent

Main Language(s) of Instruction: Arabic

Degrees and Diplomas: *Diploma*: Education and Psychology; Home Economics; Law; *Baccalaureos*: Agriculture; Arts; Arts and Education; Civil Engineering; Commerce; Electrical Engineering; Law; Mechanical Engineering; Science; Science and Education, 4-5 yrs; *Magistr.*: Agricultural Science; Agriculture; Arts; Arts in Commerce; Education; Engineering; Medicine; Psychology; Science, a further 2-3 yrs; *Doktora*: Architecture; Law; Letters; Medicine; Science, Agriculture, Education, Commerce

Student Residential Facilities: Yes

Libraries: Central Library, c. 90,000 vols; faculty libraries, c. 3300 vols

Publications: Annals of Agricultural Science; Bulletin of the Faculty of Engineering; Economics and Business Review; Al-Ulum Al-Kanounia wal Iktisadia (journal); Annals of the Faculty of Arts

Press or Publishing House: Ain Shams University Press

Academic Staff *1999:* Total: c. 6,400

Student Numbers *1999:* Total: c. 144,000

*• AL-AZHAR UNIVERSITY

PO Box 11751, Meddina Nasr, Cairo
Tel: +20(2) 262-3274   +20(2) 262-3278
Fax: +20(2) 261-1404
Telex: 21945 skircw
EMail: info@alazhar.org
Website: http://www.alazhar.org

Rector: Ahmed Omar Hashem (1995-) Tel: +20(2) 262-3282
Administrative Officer: Mohamed Mohy Al-Din Al-Sayed
Tel: +20(2) 261-1417
International Relations: Mamdoh Al-Serafy
Tel: +20(2) 262-3290

Faculties
Agriculture (Assiut)
Arabic (Assiut, Mansoura, Zagazig, Ital Al-Baroud, Shebin El-Kom)
Commerce (for Women) (Business and Commerce)
Commerce (Business and Commerce)
Dentistry
Education (Educational Sciences)
Engineering
Human Studies (for Women) (Social Sciences)
Islamic Call (Islamic Theology)
Islamic Fundamentals (Islamic Studies)
Islamic Fundamentals and Call (Assiut, Zagazig, Mansoura, Tanta, Shebin El-Kom) (Islamic Studies)
Islamic Jurisprudence and Law (Cairo, Assiut, Damanhour, Tafahna Al-Ashraf, Tanta)
Islamic Religion and Arabic Studies (Aswan, Cairo, Kena, Domietta) (Arabic; Islamic Theology)
Islamic Religion and Arabic Studies (for Women, Cairo, Alexandria, Mansoura, Sohag) (Arabic; Islamic Theology)
Koran Studies (Tanta) (Koran)
Languages and Translation (Modern Languages; Translation and Interpretation)
Medicine (Assiut)
Medicine (for Women)
Medicine
Pharmacy (Assiut)
Pharmacy
Science (Assiut) (Natural Sciences)
Science (for Women) (Natural Sciences)
Science (Natural Sciences)

Colleges
Islamic Studies (for Women)

Centres
Heart Diseases and Surgery

Research Centres
Childhood Disabilities (Child Care and Development)
Islamic Commercial Studies (Saleh Kamel) (Business and Commerce; Islamic Law)
Population Studies (The International Islamic Centre) (Demography and Population)

History: Founded 1970 as a school and developed 1961.
Governing Bodies: University Council

Academic Year: October to June
Admission Requirements: Secondary school certificate and entrance examination
Main Language(s) of Instruction: Arabic
Degrees and Diplomas: *Baccalaureos*: Arts; Science, 4-5 yrs; *Magistr*: Arts, 2-3 yrs; Science, 2-3 yrs following Baccalaureos; *Doktora*: Philosophy, 2-3 yrs following Magistr
Libraries: c. 80,000 vols
Academic Staff *1999:* Total: c. 6,000
Student Numbers *1999:* Total: c. 155,000

*• ALEXANDRIA UNIVERSITY

22 Al-Guish Avenue, Chatby, Alexandria
Tel: +20(3) 597-1675   +20(3) 596-2924
Fax: +20(3) 596-0720
Telex: 54467 univy un
EMail: alex@frcu.eun.eg
Website: http://www.frcu.eun.eg

President: Mohammed Nasr-Eldin Dameer (1999-)
Tel: +20(3) 596-1152
Vice-President for Education and Student Affairs: Saad El-Dakkak
International Relations: Mostapha Hassan Mostafa
Tel: +20(3) 596-5848

Faculties
Agriculture (Agriculture; Dairy; Entomology; Forestry; Genetics; Home Economics; Horticulture; Soil Science; Water Science; Wood Technology)
Agriculture (Saba Basha) (Agriculture; Fishery)
Arts (Arts and Humanities; Social Sciences) *Dean:* Mohamed Abdou Mahgoud
Commerce (Business and Commerce) *Dean:* Ahmed Mohamed Nour
Dentistry (Dentistry; Surgery) *Dean:* Abdel Rahman Wasfi
Education (Arabic; Biology; Chemistry; Curriculum; Education; Foreign Languages Education; Mathematics; Modern Languages; Physics; Psychology; Social Sciences; Teacher Trainers Education)
Education (Matrouh) (Educational Sciences)
Engineering (Architecture; Building Technologies; Chemical Engineering; Computer Engineering; Electrical Engineering; Engineering; Irrigation; Marine Engineering; Mathematics; Mechanical Engineering; Nuclear Engineering; Physics; Production Engineering; Sanitary Engineering; Textile Technology; Transport Engineering)
Fine Arts (Architecture; Fine Arts; Graphic Design; Painting and Drawing)
Law
Medicine (Dermatology; Gynaecology and Obstetrics; Health Sciences; Medicine; Neurological Therapy; Oncology; Ophthalmology; Paediatrics; Surgery; Tropical Medicine)
Nursing
Pharmacy *Dean:* Adel M. Metawe
Physical Education
Physical Education (For Women) (Physical Education; Sports)

123

Science (Biochemistry; Botany; Chemistry; Environmental Studies; Geology; Marine Science and Oceanography; Mathematics; Natural Sciences; Physics; Zoology)

Special Education

Tourism and Hotel Studies (Hotel Management; Tourism)

Veterinary Medicine (Veterinary Science)

Institutes

Graduate Studies and Research (Higher Education)

Medical Research (Medicine; Radiology)

Public Health (Behavioural Sciences; Public Health; Statistics; Tropical Medicine)

History: Founded 1942 as State university, incorporating former branches of the Faculties of Arts, Law, and Engineering of Fouad I University (Cairo), and known as Farouk I University until 1953. Faculty of Medicine and Colleges of Education at Tanta detached 1972 to form new University.

Governing Bodies: University Senate

Academic Year: October to June (October-February; March-June)

Admission Requirements: Secondary school certificate or equivalent

Main Language(s) of Instruction: Arabic, English

Degrees and Diplomas: *Baccalaureos*: Arts and Education; Science and Education, 4 yrs; Science in Anatomy; Science in Physiology, 5 yrs; *Magistr*: a further 1-3 yrs and thesis; *Doktora*: 2 yrs after Magistr and dissertation; Science, awarded after Doctorate for distinguished contributions to knowledge. Also postgraduate Diplomas

Student Residential Facilities: For c. 5 700 students

Special Facilities: Archaeology Museum. Forensic Medical Museum

Libraries: Central Library, c. 28,000 vols; also faculty and institute libraries, c. 40,000 vols

Publications: Bulletins

Academic Staff *1999-2000:* Total: **5,251**

Student Numbers *1999-2000:* Total: **75,577**

DAMANHOUR BRANCH
Damanhour

Vice-President: Ibrahim Abdel Salam Al Samra (1997-)

Faculties

Agriculture

Arts (Arts and Humanities)

Commerce

Education

History: Founded 1988.

124

*• ASSIUT UNIVERSITY
Assiut 71515
Tel: +20(88) 324-040   +20(88) 314-527
Fax: +20(88) 312-564   +20(88) 322-562
Telex: 92863 asunv-un
EMail: assiut@frcu.eun.eg
Website: http://www.aun.eun.eg

President: Mohamed Raafat Mahmoud (1996-)
Tel: +20(88) 314-527 EMail: rmahmoud@aun.eun.eg

Secretary-General: Nabila Mahmoud Abd El Maged
Tel: +20(88) 322-000

International Relations: Mohamed Ahmed Mohamed Shalaby Tel: +20(88) 324-033 Fax: +20(88) 313-970
EMail: shalaby@aun.eun.eg

Faculties

Agriculture *Dean*: Mohamed Atef Ahmed Sallam

Arts (Arabic; Archaeology; Arts and Humanities; English; French; Geography; History; Information Sciences; Library Science; Media Studies; Philosophy; Psychology; Sociology)

Commerce (Business and Commerce) *Dean*: Abd El-Hadi Saleh Swify

Education *Dean*: Abdel Tawab A. Abdel Tawab

Education *(New Valley)*

Engineering (Architecture; Civil Engineering; Engineering; Mechanical Engineering; Metallurgical Engineering; Mining Engineering) *Dean*: Ibrahiem Shafie Taha

Law (Islamic Law; Law) *Dean*: Gaber Ali Mahran

Medicine *Dean*: Mahmoud R. Kandil

Nursing *Dean*: Sana Soliman Kroosh

Pharmacy *Dean*: Samia M. El Sayyad

Physical Education *(for Men)*

Science (Botany; Chemistry; Entomology; Geology; Mathematics; Natural Sciences; Physics; Zoology) *Dean*: Mohamed Ebraheim Salem

Social Work *Dean*: Mohamed Talat Abdel Geliltohamy

Special Education *Dean*: Abbas Mohamed A. Hammam

Veterinary Medicine (Veterinary Science) *Dean*: Ahmed Abdelfatah Aamer

Institutes

Sugar Technology Research (Food Technology) *Dean*: Mohamed Ragab Bayouni

Centres

Future Studies (Futurology)

Scientific Computing (Computer Science)

Further Information: Also University Teaching Hospital

History: Founded 1949 by decree, opened 1957. A State institution enjoying administrative autonomy. Faculties of Agriculture, Arts and Education at Minya detached 1976 to form new University. Financed by the State. Branches in Sohag, Qena and Aswan merged 1995 to form South Valley University.

Governing Bodies: University Council, comprising the President as Chairman, four Vice-Presidents, the Deans, the Secretary-General, and 4 other members

Academic Year: September to May (September-December; January-May)

Admission Requirements: Secondary school certificate or equivalent

Fees: (Egyptian Pounds): undergraduate, 1000-1500; postgraduate, 1200-2500

Main Language(s) of Instruction: Arabic, English

Degrees and Diplomas: *Baccalaureos*: 4 yrs; Health Studies, 6 yrs; *Magistr*: All fields, a further 2-3 yrs and thesis; *Doktora*: by thesis. Also Diplomas of Specialization, 2 yrs following Baccalaureos

Student Residential Facilities: For 12,000 students

Special Facilities: Geological Museum

Libraries: Central Library and faculty libraries, c. 450,000 vols

Publications: Assiut Bulletin for Environmental Research; Faculty Bulletins

Press or Publishing House: Assiut University Publishing and Distributing House

Academic Staff *1999:* Total: c. 2,400

Staff with Doctorate: Total: c. 1,520

Student Numbers *1999:* All (Foreign Included): Men: c. 33,900 Women: c. 17,250 Total: c. 51,150

*• CAIRO UNIVERSITY

PO Box 12613, Nahdet Misr Street, Giza, Cairo
Tel: +20(2) 572-9584
Fax: +20(2) 568-8884
Telex: (091) 94372 uncai un
EMail: mailmaster@main-scc.cairo.eun.eg
Website: http://www.cairo.eun.eg

President: Nageeb E. Gohar (2001-) Tel: +20(2) 572-7066
Fax: +20(2) 572-8131 EMail: presidnt@main-scc.cairo.eun.eg

International Relations: Mohamed Hamdi Ibrahim

Faculties

Agriculture (Agricultural Economics; Agricultural Engineering; Agriculture; Animal Husbandry; Crop Production; Food Science; Genetics; Horticulture; Plant Pathology; Soil Science; Vegetable Production; Zoology)

Arabic and Islamic Studies *(Dar El-Eloum)* (Arabic; Islamic Law; Islamic Studies; Linguistics; Literature; Oriental Studies)

Archaeology (Archaeology; Restoration of Works of Art)

Arts (Arabic; Arts and Humanities; English; French; Geography; German; Greek (Classical); History; Japanese; Latin; Library Science; Philosophy; Psychology; Sociology; Spanish)

Commerce (Accountancy; Business Administration; Business and Commerce; Insurance; Mathematics)

Computer Science and Information (Computer Science; Information Sciences; Information Technology)

Dentistry (Dental Hygiene; Dentistry; Oral Pathology; Orthodontics)

Economics and Political Science (Economics; Political Science; Public Administration; Statistics)

Engineering (Air Transport; Architecture; Chemistry; Electrical Engineering; Engineering; Mechanical Engineering; Metallurgical Engineering; Mineralogy; Physics; Urban Studies)

Law (Civil Law; Commercial Law; Criminal Law; Finance; International Law; Islamic Law; Labour Law; Law; Public Law)

Mass Communication (Advertising and Publicity; Journalism; Mass Communication; Radio and Television Broadcasting)

Medicine (Anaesthesiology; Anatomy; Biochemistry; Cardiology; Dermatology; Forensic Medicine and Dentistry; Histology; Hygiene; Medicine; Neurology; Ophthalmology; Orthopedics; Paediatrics; Parasitology; Pathology; Physiology; Psychiatry and Mental Health; Radiology; Surgery; Urology; Venereology)

Pharmacy (Analytical Chemistry; Biochemistry; Microbiology; Organic Chemistry; Pharmacology; Pharmacy)

Physiotherapy (Physical Therapy)

Regional and Urban Planning (Engineering; Regional Planning; Urban Studies)

Science (Anatomy; Astronomy and Space Science; Biology; Chemistry; Computer Science; Entomology; Geology; Geophysics; Mathematics; Natural Sciences; Physics; Zoology)

Veterinary Medicine (Anatomy; Animal Husbandry; Biochemistry; Fishery; Forensic Medicine and Dentistry; Histology; Microbiology; Nutrition; Parasitology; Pharmacology; Physiology; Toxicology; Veterinary Science)

Institutes

African Studies and Research (African Languages; African Studies; Anthropology; Economics; Geography; History; Natural Resources; Political Science)

Cancer *(National)* (Oncology)

Educational Studies and Research (Curriculum; Educational Research; Educational Technology; Pedagogy)

Laser Science *(National)* (Laser Engineering)

Statistical Studies and Research (Statistics)

Higher Institutes
Nursing

Centres

Development and Technology Planning (Development Studies; Technology)

Environmental Studies and Research (Environmental Studies)

Future Studies and Research (Futurology)

Further Information: Also Qars El Ainy Hospital; Tumour Hospital and Infants Hospital

History: Founded 1908 as national university, became State university 1925. Known as Fouad I University between 1940 and 1953.

Governing Bodies: University Council, composed of the President, Deputies, Heads of the Faculties and Institutes, and four members dealing with university affairs (appointed for two years)

Academic Year: September to June (September-January; January-June)

Admission Requirements: Secondary school certificate or equivalent. University degree for Institutes of Statistical Studies and African Studies

Main Language(s) of Instruction: Arabic, English, French

International Co-operation: Tula State University; University of Victoria, Canada; Georgia State University; Georgia Institute of Technology; Sana'a University; Harkov State University; University of Damascus; Taškent University; Taškent State Technical University; Samarkand University

Degrees and Diplomas: *Diploma*: African Studies; Statistics, 2 yrs; *Baccalaureos*: Commerce; Journalism; Science in Economics; Science in Political Science; Science in Statistics, 4 yrs; Dental Surgery, 4 yrs following preparatory yr; Chemical Engineering; Civil Engineering; Electrical Engineering; Mechanical Engineering; Mining Engineering; Petroleum Engineering; Pharmaceutical Chemistry, 5 yrs; *Magistr*: Dental Surgery; Journalism; Surgery, a further 2 yrs; *Doktora*: Medical Science; Medicine; Pharmacy; Veterinary Medicine and Surgery, 2 yrs following Magistr; Dental Medicine, 2 yrs following Magistr

Student Services: Academic Counselling, Social Counselling, Employment Services, Foreign Student Adviser, Nursery Care, Cultural Centre, Sports Facilities, Handicapped Facilities, Health Services, Canteen

Student Residential Facilities: For c. 3130 men students, and c. 7650 women students

Special Facilities: Museum of Egyptology. Islamic Museum. Museum of Entomology. Collection of Papyrii and Ancient Coins

Libraries: Central Library, c. 950,000 vols. Fayoum Branch, c. 33,200 vols; Beni Sweif Branch, c. 37,000 vols

Publications: Publications of the faculties; Medical Journal of Cairo University; The Egyptian Statistical Magazine; Egyptian Journal of Generics and Psychology; Computer Magazine; Population and Family Planning Magazine

Press or Publishing House: Cairo University Press; Agriculture Faculty Press; Statistical Studies and Research Press; Law Faculty Press; Science Faculty Press

Academic Staff *2000-2001:* Total: **5,519**

Student Numbers *2000-2001:* Total: **155,000**

AL-FAYOUM BRANCH
Al-Fayoum
Tel: +20(2) 572-8779

Vice-President: Farghal Adbel-Hafez Zeid (1999-)

Faculties
Agriculture
Arabic and Islamic Studies (Arabic; Islamic Studies)
Archaeology
Education
Engineering
Medicine
Science (Natural Sciences)
Social Work (Social Welfare)
Special Education
Tourism and Hotel Management (Hotel Management; Tourism)

History: Founded 1988.

BENI-SWEIF BRANCH
Beni-Sweif
Tel: +20(2) 573-5334

Vice-President: Mohamed Anas Gha'far (1998-)

Faculties
Arts (Arts and Humanities)
Commerce (Business and Commerce)
Education

Law
Medicine
Pharmacy
Science
Veterinary Medicine (Veterinary Science)

History: Founded 1981.

KHARTOUM BRANCH
Khartoum

Faculties
Arts (Arts and Humanities)
Commerce (Business and Commerce)
Law
Science (Natural Sciences)

* HELWAN UNIVERSITY CAIRO
Ein Helwan, Cairo
Tel: +20(2) 344-6441
Fax: +20(2) 345-5461
Telex: 3455461
EMail: helwan@frcu.eun.eg
Website: http://www.halpha.hun.eun.eg

President: Hassan Mohamed Hosen Hosny (1997-)
Tel: +20(2) 555-5033 Fax: +20(2) 555-6048

Secretary-General: Ekram Mohamed Abdel Hamed

International Relations: Amr Azat Salama

Faculties
Applied Arts *(Giza)* (Fine Arts)
Art Education
Arts (Arts and Humanities)
Commerce and Business Administration (Business Administration; Business and Commerce)
Computer and Information Science (Computer Science; Information Sciences)
Education
Engineering
Engineering *(Mataria)* (Engineering; Technology)
Fine Arts
Home Economics
Law
Music Education
Pharmacy
Physical Education
Physical Education *(for Women)*
Science (Natural Sciences)
Social Work (Social and Community Services; Social Work)
Tourism and Hotel Management (Hotel Management; Tourism)

Centres
Foreign Trade Studies and Research (International Business)
Scientific Computing (Computer Science)
Scientific Instrument Maintenance (Instrument Making)
Small Projects Support
Social Service (Social and Community Services)

Technology Development Studies and Research (Technology)
University Education Development (Pedagogy)
Youth Studies and Research (Child Care and Development)

History: Founded 1975, incorporating previously existing faculties and institutes of higher education. A State institution under the supervision of the Ministry of Higher Education and financed by the State.

Governing Bodies: University Council, comprising twenty-five members

Academic Year: September to June

Admission Requirements: Secondary school certificate or equivalent

Main Language(s) of Instruction: Arabic, English

Degrees and Diplomas: *Diploma*; *Baccalaureos*: Arts (B.A.); Science (B.Sc.), 4-5 yrs; *Magistr*: Arts (M.A.); Science (M.Sc.), a further 2 yrs; *Doktora*: (PhD), 3 yrs following Magistr

Student Residential Facilities: Yes

Libraries: Central Library, c. 600,000 vols; faculty libraries, c. 320,000 vols

Academic Staff *1999:* Total: c. 1,200

Student Numbers *1999:* Total: c. 33,400

*• MANSOURA UNIVERSITY

60, El Gomhoria Street, Mansoura, Al-Dakahliya 35516
Tel: +20(50) 247-054
Telex: 23768 manu un
EMail: mua@mum.mans.eun.eg
Website: http://www.mans.eun.eg

President: Yehia Hussein Ebied (2001-)
Tel: +20(50) 247-800 Fax: +20(50) 247-900
EMail: yehiaebeid@mans.edu.eg

Secretary-General: Waar Al Said Shady
Tel: +20(50) 247-330 Fax: +20(50) 247-330

International Relations: Yehia Hussein Abeed
Tel: +20(50) 243-587 Fax: +20(50) 243-587

Faculties

Agriculture (Agricultural Economics; Agricultural Engineering; Agriculture; Agronomy; Animal Husbandry; Botany; Chemistry; Dairy; Floriculture; Food Science; Genetics; Microbiology; Plant Pathology; Soil Science; Vegetable Production; Zoology) *Dean*: Maher M. Ibrahim

Arts (Arabic; Archaeology; Arts and Humanities; Documentation Techniques; English Studies; French Studies; Geography; Greek; History; Journalism; Latin; Library Science; Oriental Languages; Philosophy; Psychology; Sociology) *Dean*: Mohamed Eisa Saber Al-Harery

Commerce (Accountancy; Business Administration; Business and Commerce; Economics; Insurance; Statistics) *Dean*: Ahmed Hamed Hagag

Computer and Information Science (Computer Science; Information Management; Information Sciences) *Dean*: Mostafa El Arabaty

Dentistry (Dentistry; Oral Pathology; Orthodontics) *Dean*: Ali Abdel-Mageed Sawan

Education (Arabic; Curriculum; Education; Educational Psychology; Educational Technology; Geography; History; Islamic Studies; Modern Languages) *Dean*: Zaki Mohamed Abd Allah

Education *(Damietta)* (Arabic; Biology; Curriculum; Education; Educational Psychology; Educational Technology; English; French; Geography; Geology; History; Islamic Studies; Modern Languages; Philosophy) *Dean*: Talaat Hasan Abdel-Raheem

Engineering (Architectural and Environmental Design; Computer Engineering; Construction Engineering; Engineering; Hydraulic Engineering; Industrial Engineering; Irrigation; Mathematics; Mechanical Engineering; Physics; Power Engineering; Textile Technology) *Dean*: Hamdi El-Mikati

Law (Civil Law; Commercial Law; Criminal Law; International Law; Islamic Law; Law; Private Law; Public Law) *Dean*: Ahmed Shawky Mohamed Abdel-Rahman

Medicine (Anaesthesiology; Anatomy; Biochemistry; Cardiology; Community Health; Dermatology; Forensic Medicine and Dentistry; Gynaecology and Obstetrics; Histology; Medicine; Microbiology; Neurology; Ophthalmology; Orthodontics; Orthopedics; Paediatrics; Parasitology; Pathology; Pharmacology; Physical Therapy; Physiology; Psychiatry and Mental Health; Radiology; Surgery; Urology) *Dean*: Aly Abd El-Lattif Hegazy

Nursing (Community Health; Gerontology; Gynaecology and Obstetrics; Hygiene; Nursing) *Dean*: Olfat Ferag Mohamed Ali

Pharmacy (Analytical Chemistry; Microbiology; Pharmacy) *Dean*: Ali Abdel-Rahman Al-Eman

Physical Education (Health Sciences; Physical Education; Sports; Sports Management) *Dean*: Mohamed El-Said Khalil, *full-time staff: 5, students: 384*

Science (Botany; Chemistry; Geology; Mathematics; Natural Sciences; Physics; Zoology) *Dean*: Fathy Abd El-Kader Amer

Science *(Damietta)* (Botany; Chemistry; Environmental Studies; Geology; Mathematics; Physics; Science Education; Zoology) *Dean*: Salah Kamel El-Labany

Veterinary Science (Anatomy; Animal Husbandry; Biochemistry; Embryology and Reproduction Biology; Food Science; Forensic Medicine and Dentistry; Histology; Hygiene; Immunology; Nutrition; Parasitology; Pathology; Pharmacology; Physiology; Surgery; Veterinary Science; Virology) *Dean*: El Said El Sherbini El-Said

Further Information: Also 2 Teaching Hospitals and 3 Laboratories

History: Founded 1972, incorporating faculties previously attached to the University of Cairo. Acquired present title 1973. A State institution under the authority of the Ministry of Higher Education.

Governing Bodies: Board; Boards of the Faculties

Academic Year: September to June (September-January; February-June)

Admission Requirements: Secondary school certificate or equivalent

Main Language(s) of Instruction: Arabic

International Co-operation: University Centre of Tlemcen; Catholic University of Louvain; University of Horticultural and Food Sciences; Technical University of Budapest; Gödöllö University of Agricultural Sciences; Omar-Al Mukhtar University; Hassan II University Ain Chock, Casablanca; Slovak Technical

University in Bratislava; United Arab Emirates University; Taškent University

Degrees and Diplomas: *Baccalaureos*: 4-6 yrs; *Magistr*: a further 2-3 yrs; *Doktora*: (Ph.D.), a further 2-4 yrs

Student Services: Academic Counselling, Social Counselling, Employment Services, Nursery Care, Cultural Centre, Sports Facilities, Health Services, Canteen

Student Residential Facilities: For c. 6000 students

Special Facilities: Midwifery Museum; Anatomy Museum; Forensic Medicine Museum; Pharmacology Museum; Zoology Museum; Botany Museum

Libraries: Central Library; faculty libraries, total, c. 425,000 vols

Publications: Scientific Journal; Periodicals of the Community and Environmental Council and the Cultural Affairs and Research Branch

Press or Publishing House: University Press

Academic Staff *1999*: Full-Time: c. 1,930 Part-Time: c. 20 Total: c. 1,950

Staff with Doctorate: Total: c. 1,950

Student Numbers *1999:* Total: c. 12,600

*• MENOUFIA UNIVERSITY

PO Box 32511, Gamal Abdel Nasser Street, Shebin Al-Kom, Menoufia
Tel: +20(48) 224-347
Fax: +20(21) 575-2777
Telex: (091) 23832 muske un

President: Maghawry Shehata Diab (2000-)
Tel: +20(21) 575-2777

Secretary-General: Mohamed F. Salah Tel: +20(48) 235-675

International Relations: Maghawrey Shehata IbrahimMaghawri Shehata Tel: +20(48) 235-678

Faculties
Agriculture
Arts (Arts and Humanities)
Commerce (Business and Commerce; Economics)
Education
Electronic Engineering *(Menouf)*
Engineering *(Shebin)*
Home Economics
Law
Medicine
Nursing
Physical Education
Science (Mathematics and Computer Science; Natural Sciences)
Special Education *(Ashmon)*
Tourism and Hotels *(Sadat City)* (Hotel and Restaurant; Hotel Management; Tourism)
Veterinary Medicine *(Sadat City)* (Veterinary Science)

Institutes
Desert Environment Research (Arid Land Studies)

Genetic Engineering and Biotechnology *(Sadat City)* (Biotechnology; Genetics)
Liver Studies and Research (Hepatology)

History: Founded 1976. A State institution under the authority of the Ministry of Higher Education.

Governing Bodies: University Council

Academic Year: October to May

Admission Requirements: Secondary school certificate or equivalent

Main Language(s) of Instruction: Arabic, English

Degrees and Diplomas: *Diploma*: Education; *Baccalaureos*: Arts in Education; Commerce; Science; Science in Agriculture; Science in Education, 4 yrs; Science in Engineering, 5 yrs; *Magistr*: a further 2 yrs; *Doktora*: (Ph.D.), 3 yrs following Magistr

Student Residential Facilities: Yes

Libraries: Central Library, c. 9000 vols; faculty libraries

Publications: Engineering Research Bulletin; Menoufia Journal of Agricultural Research; University Guide

Academic Staff *1999:* Total: c. 2,070

Student Numbers *1999:* Total: c. 60,000

*• MINIA UNIVERSITY

PO Box 61519, El-Minia
Tel: +20(86) 321-443
Fax: +20(86) 342-601
Telex: (091) 24000 minunv un
EMail: minia@frcu.eun.eg
Website: http://www.minia.eun.eg

President: Maher M. Kamel Tel: +20(86) 361-443

Secretary-General: Abdel Hakim Refaat
Tel: +20(86) 369-205

Faculties
Agriculture *Dean*: Elsayed Moftah
Arabic and Islamic Studies *(Dar El-Eloum)* (Arabic; Islamic Studies)
Arts (Arts and Humanities) *Dean*: Mohamed Naguib El-Tallawy
Dentistry *Dean*: Hany Ameen
Education *Dean*: Ahmed El-Sayed Moustafa
Engineering *Dean*: Mohamed Moness Bayoumi
Fine Arts *Dean*: Wafaa A. Musalam
Languages *(Al-Alsun)*
Medicine *Dean*: Hany El-Tonsy
Nursing *Dean*: Iglal A. Shawky
Pharmacy *Dean*: Mohamed Montaser Khalifa
Physical Education *Dean*: Bahaa Salama
Science (Natural Sciences) *Dean*: Mohamed Said Ali
Special Education *Dean*: Abdel-Azem A. El-Fergany
Tourism and Hotel Management (Hotel Management; Tourism) *Dean*: Abdel-Bary Dawood

Centres
Baking Research (Food Science)
Community Development (Urban Studies)
Furniture Manufacture Services (Furniture Design)
Scientific Computing (Computer Science)

History: Founded 1976, incorporating Faculties of Agriculture, Education, Humanities, Science, and Engineering, previously forming part of the University of Assiut. A State institution enjoying administrative autonomy. Financed by the government.

Governing Bodies: University Council; Council for Undergraduate Studies; Council for Graduate Studies and Research

Academic Year: October to May (October-January; February-May)

Admission Requirements: Secondary school certificate or equivalent

Main Language(s) of Instruction: Arabic, English

International Co-operation: University of Kassel; University of Debrecen; University of Glasgow; University of Newcastle; University of Gezira; University of Missouri-Rolla; University of Agriculture, Debrecen; North Dakota State University; Kazhak State University; International Studies University, Beijing; University of Hildesheim, Germany

Degrees and Diplomas: *Diploma*; *Baccalaureos*: Agriculture; Education; Physical Education; Science, 4 yrs; Engineering, 5 yrs; Surgery, 6 yrs; *Magistr*: Arts and Education, a further 2 yrs; *Doktora*: 2 yrs following Magistr, by thesis

Student Residential Facilities: For c. 3000 students

Special Facilities: Art Gallery

Libraries: Central Library, c. 7200 vols; libraries of the faculties, c. 130,000 vols

Publications: Technical Scientific Magazine; History and Future Magazine.; Physical Education Magazine; Minia Medical Magazine; Educational and Psychological Research Magazine; Journal of Agricultural Research; Bulletins

Press or Publishing House: University Press

Academic Staff *1999:* Total: c. 770

Student Numbers *1999:* Total: c. 16,120

• SOUTH VALLEY UNIVERSITY
Kena
Tel: +20(96) 211-277
Fax: +20(96) 211-279
EMail: sci@svalleyu-jwnet.eun.eg

President: Abd Al Matin Moussa Abd Al-Latif (1999-)

Secretary-General: Kamal Mohamed Moussa

Faculties
Arts (Arts and Humanities)
Education
Fine Arts *(Luxor)*
Science (Mathematics and Computer Science; Natural Sciences)
Special Education
Veterinary Medecine

History: Founded 1994.

ASWAN BRANCH
Aswan
Vice-President: Mohamed Hussein Mostafa (1996-)

Faculties
Education
Engineering and Technology (Engineering; Technology)
Science (Mathematics and Computer Science; Natural Sciences)
Social Services (Social and Community Services)

History: Founded 1979.

SOHAG BRANCH
Sohag

Faculties
Agriculture
Arts (Arts and Humanities)
Commerce (Business and Commerce)
Education
Medicine
Science (Mathematics and Computer Science; Natural Sciences)

History: Founded 1979.

• SUEZ CANAL UNIVERSITY
4,5 Km, New Building, Ismaelia
Tel: +20(64) 327-125
Fax: +20(64) 211-279
Cable: 63297 scu.fm.um
EMail: infor@suez.eun.eg
Website: http://www.suez.eun.eg

President: Abdel Hamid Shafik Shalaby (2000-)
EMail: shoukry@foci.suez.eun.eg

Secretary-General: Sayed Hassan Ali Al Nekely
Tel: +20(64) 324-820

International Relations: Ahmed Abd El Meneam Askar

Faculties
Agriculture
Commerce (Business and Commerce)
Computer and Information Science (Computer Science; Information Sciences)
Dentistry
Education *(Al Arish)*
Education *(Suez)*
Education
Engineering and Technology (Engineering; Technology)
Environmental and Agricultural Sciences *(Al-Arish)* (Agricultural Engineering; Environmental Studies)
Industrial Technical Education (Industrial Engineering; Technology Education)
Medicine
Petroleum and Mining Engineering *(Suez)* (Mining Engineering; Petroleum and Gas Engineering)
Pharmacy
Science (Mathematics and Computer Science; Natural Sciences)
Special Education
Tourism and Hotel Management (Hotel Management; Tourism)

Veterinary Medicine (Veterinary Science)

Research Institutes
Biotechnology

Further Information: Also Teaching Hospital

History: Founded 1976. A State institution under the supervision of the Ministry of Higher Education.

Governing Bodies: University Council

Academic Year: September to June (September-January; February-June)

Admission Requirements: Secondary school certificate or equivalent

Main Language(s) of Instruction: Arabic

International Co-operation: University of Boston; Iowa State University; Colorado State University; University of Maryland

Degrees and Diplomas: *Baccalaureos*: Arts in Education; Science; Science in Agriculture; Science in Education, 4 yrs; Commerce; Engineering; Science in Veterinary Science, 5 yrs; Medicine and Surgery, 6 yrs; *Magistr.* a further 1-5 yrs; *Doktora*: (PhD): Agriculture; Commerce; Education; Engineering; Science; Veterinary Science. Also postgraduate Diplomas

Student Residential Facilities: Yes

Libraries: Central Library, c. 6400 vols; faculty libraries, c. 186,500

Publications: Statistical Journal; Scientific Bulletins (Human Sciences, Basic Sciences, Applied Sciences)

Press or Publishing House: Suez Canal University Press

Academic Staff *1999:* Total: c. 700

Student Numbers *1999:* Total: c. 12,890

PORT-SAID BRANCH
Port-Said

Vice-President: Farouq Mahmoud Abdel Quader (1998-)

Faculties
Commerce (Business and Commerce)
Education
Nursing
Physical Education

Centres
Agriculture Services *(North Sinai)* (Agriculture)
Contagious Disease Research and Training (Epidemiology)
Ecological Research Studies of Sinai (Ecology; Regional Studies)
Environmental Research *(Saint Katherine)* (Environmental Studies)
Fish Research (Fishery)
Public Service (Public Administration; Social and Community Services)
Research and Development in Medical Education and Health Services (Medicine)
Scientific and Technical Information (Information Sciences; Information Technology)
Water Re-use Research and Training *(Abu-Attwa)* (Water Management; Water Science)

History: Founded 1989.

*• TANTA UNIVERSITY
PO Box 31512, El-Geish Street, Tanta, Al-Gharbia
Tel: +20(40) 317-929
Fax: +20(40) 331-800
Telex: 23605 un tha
EMail: tanta@frcu.eun.eg
Website: http://dec1.tanta.eun.eg/doc/home/logo.html
President: Fouad Khalifa Haras (2000-)
Tel: +20(40) 331-7928 Fax: +20(40) 302-785
EMail: fharras@dec1.tanta.eun.eg
Secretary-General: Rawia Soliman Gad
Tel: +20(40) 317-947 Fax: +20(40) 313-308
International Relations: Zacharia Mohamed Al Sadik Ismail
Tel: +20(64) 305-976

Faculties
Agriculture (Agricultural Equipment; Agriculture; Agronomy; Animal Husbandry; Botany; Dairy; Economics; Food Science; Food Technology; Genetics; Horticulture; Soil Science) *full-time staff:* 315, *students:* 1,000
Arts (Arabic; Arts and Humanities; French; Geography; History; Philosophy; Psychology; Sociology) *full-time staff:* 240, *students:* 14,965
Commerce (Accountancy; Business Administration; Business and Commerce; Economics; Finance; Insurance; Mathematics; Public Administration; Statistics; Taxation)
Dentistry
Education (Science Education)
Engineering (Architecture; Design; Electrical Engineering; Electronic Engineering; Engineering; Hydraulic Engineering; Irrigation; Mathematics; Mechanical Engineering; Physical Engineering; Production Engineering; Town Planning)
Law *full-time staff:* 45, *students:* 11,855
Medicine (Anaesthesiology; Gynaecology and Obstetrics; Medicine; Paediatrics) *full-time staff:* 695, *students:* 2,400
Pharmacy (Biochemistry; Microbiology; Pharmacy; Toxicology) *full-time staff:* 95, *students:* 895
Physical Education *full-time staff:* 95, *students:* 2,585
Science (Botany; Chemistry; Geology; Mathematics; Natural Sciences; Physics; Zoology) *full-time staff:* 380, *students:* 1,950
Veterinary Medicine (Veterinary Science) *full-time staff:* 50, *students:* 895

Higher Institutes
Nursing (Gynaecology and Obstetrics; Nursing; Paediatrics) *full-time staff:* 65, *students:* 1,255

Further Information: Also Teaching Hospital and Study Abroad Programmes

History: Founded 1972, incorporating faculties attached to the University of Alexandria. A State institution under the supervision of the Ministry of Higher Education.

Governing Bodies: University Council, comprising seventeen members

Academic Year: October to June

Admission Requirements: Secondary school certificate or equivalent

Fees: None

Main Language(s) of Instruction: Arabic, English

Degrees and Diplomas: *Diploma*: Commerce; Education; Law, 2 yrs; *Baccalaureos*: Agriculture; Arts; Arts in Education; Commerce; Law; Science; Science in Education, 4 yrs; Dentistry; Pharmacy, 5 yrs; Medicine and Surgery, 6 yrs; *Magistr*: a further 1-6 yrs; *Doktora*: Arts; Dentistry; Law; Medicine; Philosophy

Student Residential Facilities: Yes

Libraries: Faculty libraries: c. 135,000 vols in Arabic; c. 85,000 vols in other languages

Publications: Bulletin (monthly); Tanta University Mirror (quarterly); Commerce and Finance (biannually); Annual Report (annually)

Academic Staff *1999:* Total: c. 1,040

Student Numbers *1999:* Total: c. 36,510

KAFR EL-SHEIKH BRANCH
Kefr Al-Sheikh

Vice-President: Hassan Ibrahim Eid Ali (2000-)

Faculties
Agriculture
Education (Education; Special Education)
Veterinary Medicine (Veterinary Science)

History: Founded 1979.

*• ZAGAZIG UNIVERSITY
Zagazig, Sharkeya
Tel: +20(55) 324-577
Fax: +20(55) 345-452
Telex: 92860 zu un
EMail: zag@frcu.eun.eg
Website:
http://www.frcu.eun.eg/www/universities/html/zagzig.html

President: Amer Mohamed Tel: +20(55) 363-635
Fax: +20(55) 344-550

Secretary-General: Samir Abd El Azeim Rashwan

International Relations: Ahmed Hashim Basyuny
Tel: +20(55) 322-918

Faculties
Agriculture *Dean*: Ahmed Adel Ismail El-Badawy, *full-time staff:* 225, *students:* 1,950
Arts (Arts and Humanities) *Dean*: Ismail Hassan Abd El-Bary, *full-time staff:* 140, *students:* 16,170
Commerce (Business and Commerce) *Dean*: Mohamed Shawky Ahmed Shawky, *full-time staff:* 75, *students:* 17,595
Computer and Information Science (Computer Science; Information Sciences)
Education *Dean*: Mohamed Ahmed Mohamed Desouky, *full-time staff:* 120, *students:* 9,080
Engineering *full-time staff:* 165, *students:* 5,260
Law *Dean*: Kamal Mohamed Abo Seriea, *full-time staff:* 40, *students:* 10,850
Medicine *Dean*: Abd El-Zaher El-Said Tantawy, *full-time staff:* 870, *students:* 2,675
Nursing *Dean*: Leila Abd El-Mohsen Zaki, *full-time staff:* 5, *students:* 1,135

Pharmacy *Dean*: Maher Mohamed Ali El-Domiaty, *full-time staff:* 85, *students:* 2,960
Physical Education *Dean*: Mamoud Yehia Saad, *full-time staff:* 70, *students:* 2,430
Physical Education (for Women) *Dean*: Karima Abd El-Monem Serour, *full-time staff:* 30, *students:* 805
Science (Mathematics and Computer Science; Natural Sciences) *full-time staff:* 275, *students:* 2,625
Special Education

Higher Institutes
Ancient Near Eastern Studies (Middle Eastern Studies) *Dean*: Mohamed Mohamed Amen Amer, *full-time staff:* 8
Asian Studies and Research (Asian Studies)
Production Efficiency (Industrial and Production Economics) *Dean*: Abd El-Hamed Bahgat Fayed, *full-time staff:* 145, *students:* 10,305

History: Founded 1974.

Academic Year: October to May (October-January; January-May)

Admission Requirements: Secondary school certificate or equivalent

Fees: None

Main Language(s) of Instruction: Arabic, English, French

International Co-operation: Charles University, Prague; Virginia Polytechnic Institute; University College, Swansea, Wales; Uludag University, Bursa; Washington State University; Southampton University; Gödöllö University of Agricultural Sciences

Degrees and Diplomas: *Diploma*; *Baccalaureos*: Arts (B.A.); Science (B.Sc.), 4-6 yrs; *Magistr*: Arts (M.A.); Science (M.Sc.), a further 2-4 yrs; *Doktora*: (Ph.D.), 3 yrs following Magistr

Student Services: Social Counselling, Foreign Student Adviser, Nursery Care, Cultural Centre, Sports Facilities, Handicapped Facilities, Health Services, Canteen

Student Residential Facilities: Yes

Special Facilities: Tell Basta Museum (Arts)

Libraries: Central Library; libraries of the faculties

Publications: Scientific Journals

Academic Staff *1999:* Total: c. 3,000

Student Numbers *1999:* Total: c. 85,500
Note: Including c. 34,415 Women

BANHA BRANCH
Banha

Vice-President: Aziz Abd El-Aziz Kandeil (1997-)

Faculties
Agriculture *(Moshtohor)*
Arts (Arts and Humanities) *Dean*: Mostafa Yasein El-Said El-Saadany
Commerce (Business and Commerce) *Dean*: Hamid Tolba Mohamed Hayba
Education *Dean*: Hassan Hussein El-Bilawy
Engineering *(Shoubra) Dean*: Mostafa Zaki Zahran
Law
Medicine *Dean*: Hosny Ahamed El-Rahman

Nursing *Dean*: Samia Mostafa Mohamed Rashed
Physical Education
Science (Mathematics and Computer Science; Natural Sciences) *Dean*: Mahmoud Ahamed Mohamed Mousa
Specific Education (Special Education)
Veterinary Science *(Moshtohor) Dean*: Hussam El-Dein Mohamed Abd El-Aziz

History: Founded 1976.
Academic Staff *1999:* Total: **5,635**
Student Numbers *1999:* Total: **110,955**

PRIVATE INSTITUTIONS

• **THE AMERICAN UNIVERSITY IN CAIRO**
PO Box 2511, 113 Kasr El-Aini Street, Cairo 11511
Tel: +20(2) 794-2964 +1(212) 8381100 (New York Office)
Fax: +20(2) 795-7565 +1(212) 8381155 (New York Office)
Telex: 92224 aucai un
EMail: webley@aucegypt.edu
Website: http://www.aucegypt.edu

President: John D. Gerhart (1998-) Tel: +20(2) 797-5161
Fax: +20(2) 794-1830 EMail: jgerhart@aucegypt.edu

Vice-President, Finance and Administration: Andrew Snaith Tel: +20(2) 797-5200 EMail: snaith@aucegypt.edu

International Relations: John Swanson
Tel: +20(2) 797-5193 EMail: swanson@aucegypt.edu

Schools
Business, Economics and Communication (Business and Commerce; Communication Studies; Economics)
Humanities and Social Sciences (Arts and Humanities; Social Sciences)
Science and Engineering (Engineering; Mathematics and Computer Science; Natural Sciences)

Departments
Arabic
Computer Science
Engineering
English and Comparative Literature (English; English Studies; Literature)
Journalism and Mass Communication (Journalism; Mass Communication)
Management
Middle Eastern History (History; Middle Eastern Studies)
Performing and Visual Arts (Performing Arts; Visual Arts)
Political Science
Science (Mathematics and Computer Science; Natural Sciences)
Sociology, Anthropology and Psychology (Anthropology; Psychology; Sociology)

Centres
Adult and Continuing Education
Desert Development (Arid Land Studies; Development Studies)
Social Research (Social Studies)

Further Information: Through the Centre of Adult and Continuing Education's Outreach Services programme in English, Computer Education, Arabic and Translation, and/or Business Studies are offered in: The United Arab Emirates (Abu Dhabi and Dubai), Saudi Arabia (Jeddah and Riyadh), and in other cities in Egypt (Alexandria, Damanhour, Ismailia, El Minia, Esna, Heliopolis, Hurgada, Kafr El Shiekh, Mansoura, Tabbin, and Tanta)

History: Founded 1919. A private non-profit institution located on five campus/building sites in the heart and other parts of the Cairo metropolitan area. It operates as a private educational/cultural institute within the framework of the 1962 Egyptian-American Cultural Co-operation Agreement and in accordance with a protocol with the government of Egypt through which the University's degrees are recognized as those awarded by the Egyptian national universities. Accredited in the United States by the Commission on Higher Education through the Middle States Association of Colleges and Schools in Washington, D.C. and licensed to confer degrees by the Educational Institution Licensure Commission of the District of Columbia.

Governing Bodies: Board of Trustees, comprising primarily American educators and corporate administrators

Academic Year: September to July (September-January; February-June; June-July)

Admission Requirements: Secondary school certificate (Thanawiya 'Amma) or recognized equivalent

Main Language(s) of Instruction: English

International Co-operation: California State University at Long Beach; Northwestern University; University of Colorado; University of Nevada at Reno; University of Western Michigan. Brown University; Haverford College; United Nations University for Peace (Costa Rica); University of London's School of Oriental and African Studies

Degrees and Diplomas: *Baccalaureos:* Arts in Anthropology; Arts in Business Administration; Arts in Economics; Arts in Egyptology; Arts in Journalism and Mass Communication; Arts in Middle Eastern History; Arts in Political Science; Arts in Psychology; Arts in Sociology; Arts in Theatre, 4 yrs; Science in Chemistry; Science in Computer Science; Science in Construction Engineering; Science in Mathematics; Science in Mechanical Engineering; Science in Physics, 4-5 yrs; *Magistr:* Arts in Economics; Arts in Mass Communication; Arts in Political Science; Arts in Sociology-Anthropology; Arts in Teaching Arabic as a Foreign Language, Teaching English as a Foreign Language; Science in Business Administration; Science in Engineering; Science in Public Administration, a further 2 yrs. Also graduate Diplomas

Student Residential Facilities: Yes

Libraries: Central Library, c. 225,500 vols; Cresswell Collection of Islamic Art and Architecture, c. 10,000 vols

Publications: AUC News; Middle East Management Review; Cairo Papers in Social Science (quarterly); ALIF: Journal of Comparative Poetics (annually)

Press or Publishing House: American University Press in Cairo

Academic Staff *1999:* Total: c. **360**

Student Numbers *1999:* Total: c. 4,600

* ARAB ACADEMY FOR SCIENCE, TECHNOLOGY AND MARITIME TRANSPORT (AASTMT)

PO Box 1029, Gamal Abdel Nasser Avenue, Miami, Alexandria
Tel: +20(3) 560-1022
Fax: +20(3) 560-2144
Telex: 54160 acad un
Cable: arabcademy
EMail: webmaster@aast.edu
Website: http://www.aast.edu

President: Gamal Eldin A. Mokhtar (1972-)
Tel: +20(3) 548-7785 Fax: +20(3) 548-7786
EMail: mokhtar@intouch.com

Executive Vice-President: Mohamed Farghaly

International Relations: Mohamed El-Faham
Tel: +20(3) 561-4956 Fax: +20(3) 562-4027
EMail: mfaham@aast.edu

Colleges

Engineering and Technology (Engineering; Technology)
Management
Maritime Studies and Technology (Marine Science and Oceanography; Technology)

Institutes
Quality and Productivity

Centres
Research and Consultancy

History: Founded 1972. A specialized university in Maritime Transport. Buildings, land, majority of national staff members and personnel provided by the Egyptian government.

Governing Bodies: Board of Directors

Main Language(s) of Instruction: Arabic

International Co-operation: Old Dominion University; Coventry University; De Montfort University, Leicester; University of the West of England

Degrees and Diplomas: *Baccalaureos*: 4-5 yrs; *High Diploma*: 1 further yr; *Magistr*: Science in Computer Science from George Washington University: off campus degree); a further 2 yrs; *Doktora*: (Ph.D.), a further 3 yrs

Student Services: Academic Counselling, Social Counselling, Employment Services, Foreign Student Adviser, Cultural Centre, Sports Facilities, Health Services, Canteen

Libraries: AASTMT Library, c. 30,000 vols

Publications: Journal of Arab Maritime Academy (biannually); MRCC Research Magazine (annually); MRCC Bulletin; Bulletin of Arab Maritime Academy

Academic Staff *1999*: Full-Time: c. 230 Part-Time: c. 260 Total: c. 490

Student Numbers *1999:* Total: c. 4,000

SENGHOR UNIVERSITY ALEXANDRIA

Université Senghor/Université internationale de Langue française au Service du Développement africain
BP 21111-415, 1, Midan Ahmed Orabi, El Mancheya, Alexandria
Tel: +20(3) 484-3371 to 73
Fax: +20(3) 484-3374
EMail: secretariat-general@refer.org.eg
Website: http://www.refer.org.eg

Recteur: Fred Constant (2001-) Tel: +20(3) 484-3504
Fax: +20(3) 484-3479
EMail: rectorat.univ-senghor@refer.org.eg

Secrétaire général: Nahwat Abdalla Tel: +20(3) 484-3458

Departments

Environmental Management *Director*: Rolando Marin, *students:* 25
General Administration (Administration) *Director*: André Courtemanche, *students:* 26
Heritage Management (Heritage Preservation) *Director*: Caroline Gaultier, *students:* 17
Nutrition and Health Studies (Health Administration; Nutrition) *Director*: Souleymane Seck, *students:* 12

Centres

Law and Development *(René-Jean Dupuy)* (Development Studies; Law) *Director*: Ahmed El Kosheri

History: Founded 1990 following a meeting of Heads of State of Francophone Countries. A private postgraduate institution whose objective is to train and assist professionals and higher level teachers.

Governing Bodies: Haut Conseil de l' Université; Conseil d' Administration; Conseil Scientifique

Academic Year: September to May

Admission Requirements: University degree and professional experience

Main Language(s) of Instruction: French

Degrees and Diplomas: *Diplôme d'Etudes professionnelles approfondies*: 2 yrs

Student Services: Foreign Student Adviser, Sports Facilities, Health Services, Canteen

Libraries: Giovanni Agnelli Library, c. 10,000 vols

Publications: Lettres d'Alexandrie; Actes des Conférences; Faits et Chiffres

Student Numbers *2000-2001:* Total: **80**

MISR INTERNATIONAL UNIVERSITY

Ismalia Road, Km 28, Cairo
Tel: +20(2) 477-1560
Fax: +20(2) 477-1566
EMail: miu@miuegypt.com
Website: http://www.miuegypt.com

President: Mahmoud Nagib Hosny

Faculties

Al Alsun (English)

Business Administration and International Trade (Accountancy; Business Administration; Economics; Finance; International Business; Marketing)

Computer and Information Science (Computer Science; Information Technology; Systems Analysis)

Dentistry (Anatomy; Biochemistry; Botany; Chemistry; Dentistry; Microbiology; Pathology; Pharmacology; Physics; Physiology; Surgery; Zoology)

Engineering (Architecture; Engineering)

Languages and Information (Information Technology; Modern Languages)

Mass Communication (Advertising and Publicity; Journalism; Mass Communication; Public Relations; Radio and Television Broadcasting)

Pharmacy (Microbiology; Pharmacology; Pharmacy; Toxicology)

• MISR UNIVERSITY FOR SCIENCE AND TECHNOLOGY

Al Motamayez District, 6th of October City, Giza
Tel: +20(11) 354-685
Fax: +20(11) 354-687
EMail: iu@soticom.eg
Website: http://www.must.edu

President: Ahmed Khodeir Tel: +20(11) 354-708
Fax: +20(11) 354-689

Registrar: Mahmoud Abd El Rahman Tel: +20(11) 354-703

International Relations: Mahmoud El-Diri

Colleges

Business and Economics (Accountancy; Business Administration; Business and Commerce; Computer Science; Economic and Finance Policy; Information Sciences; Political Science)

Engineering (Computer Engineering; Construction Engineering; Electronic Engineering; Engineering; Industrial Engineering) *Dean*: Nabil Saleh

Mass Media and Communication (Mass Communication; Media Studies)

Medicine *Dean*: Salah Eid

Pharmacy *Dean*: Mostafa Sadek Tawakkol

Physiotherapy (Physical Therapy; Physiology)

OCTOBER UNIVERSITY FOR MODERN SCIENCE AND ARTS

14 Amer Street, Dokki, Giza
Tel: +20(2) 360-6324
Fax: +20(2) 360-3811
Website: http://www.msa.eun.eg

President: Hassan Hamdy Ibrahim Tel: +20(2) 336-7844

Secretary-General: Omayma Ouf

Faculties

Computer Science (Computer Science; Software Engineering) *Dean*: Khayri A. M. Ali

Engineering (Architectural and Environmental Design; Computer Engineering; Electrical and Electronic Engineering; Electrical Engineering; Electronic Engineering)

Management Sciences (Accountancy; Economics; International Business; Management; Marketing) *Dean*: Ahmed I. Ghoneim

Mass Communication (Advertising and Publicity; Journalism; Mass Communication; Public Relations; Radio and Television Broadcasting)

History: Founded 1996.

• OCTOBER 6 UNIVERSITY

Giza-Governerate, Central Axis, 6th of October City, Giza
Tel: +20(11) 353-942   +20(11) 353-987
Fax: +20(11) 353-867   +20(11) 353-987
EMail: admoffc@silicon.com.eg

President: Mahmoud Mahfouz

Secretary-General: Talat Kenawy Tel: +20(11) 351-279

Colleges

Auxiliary Medical Sciences (Medical Auxiliaries)

Dentistry

Economics and Management (Economics; Management)

Engineering

Informatics and Computer Sciences (Computer Science)

Languages and Translation (Modern Languages; Translation and Interpretation)

Mass Media and Communication Techniques (Communication Studies; Mass Communication; Media Studies)

Medicine

Pharmacy

Physiotherapy (Physical Therapy; Physiology)

Social Sciences

OTHER UNIVERSITY LEVEL INSTITUTIONS

PUBLIC INSTITUTIONS

* HIGHER INSTITUTE OF TECHNOLOGY-BENHA

New Benha, El-Kaludia, Benha 13512
Tel: +20(13) 229-293
Fax: +20(13) 230-297
EMail: ahuzayyin@gmx.net

Dean: Ahmed Soliman Huzayyin (2000-)
Tel: +20(13) 230-297

Executive Secretary: A.M. Elbahy Tel: +20(13) 231-478

International Relations: A.M. Elhakim

Departments

Basic Sciences (Mathematics and Computer Science; Natural Sciences) *Head*: Hassan Nasr

Civil Engineering *Head*: El Sayed El Kasaby

Electrical Engineering *Head*: Mohamed El Lethy
Mechanical Engineering *Head*: Abdel Moaty El Anwar

History: Founded 1988, a public institution.

Degrees and Diplomas: *Baccalaureos*: Civil Engineering Technology; Electrical Engineering Technology; Mechanical Engineering Technology, 2 yrs following High Diploma; *High Diploma*: Civil Engineering Technology; Electrical Engineering Technology; Mechanical Engineering Technology, 3 yrs; *Magistr*: Civil Engineering Technology; Electrical Engineering Technology; Mechanical Engineering Technology, a further 2 yrs. Also Postgraduate Diploma (2 yrs following Baccalaureos)

Libraries: c. 8100 vols

Academic Staff *2000-2001*	TOTAL
FULL-TIME	128
PART-TIME	143
TOTAL	**271**

Staff with doctorate: Total: **106**

Student Numbers *2000-2001:* Total: **1,529**

OTHER INSTITUTIONS

PUBLIC INSTITUTIONS

COLLEGE OF INDUSTRIAL EDUCATION
Shark-El-Nil , PO Box 65513, Beni-Suef
Tel: +20(82) 240-931

Director: Mohamed Naguib Ahmed Al-Sheikh (1999-)
International Relations: Ibrahim El Tayeb

Architecture
Automation and Electrical Engineering (Automation and Control Engineering; Electrical Engineering)
Civil Works (Civil Engineering)
Electrical and Electronic Engineering
Mechanics of Production (Mechanical Engineering; Production Engineering)
Mechanics of Sophisticated Instruments (Mechanical Engineering)

History: Founded 1992

COLLEGE OF INDUSTRIAL EDUCATION
Al-Sawah, Cairo
Tel: +20(2) 454-7544

Director: Fared Abdel-Aziz Tolba (1998-)
International Relations: Safy El-Ghandour

Electrical Engineering; Electronic Engineering; Heating and Refrigeration; Production Engineering
Automation and Tractors (Industrial Engineering)
Freezing and Air Conditioning Technology (Heating and Refrigeration)

History: Founded 1989

HIGHER INSTITUTE FOR POWER
Aswan

Head: Salama Abdel-Hadi Mohamed

Departments
Electric Power (Electrical Engineering; Power Engineering)
Mechanical Power (Mechanical Engineering; Power Engineering)

PRIVATE INSTITUTIONS

ARTS ACADEMY
Gamal El-Din Al-Afghani Str., Al-Haram Route, Giza
Tel: +20(2) 585-0727
Fax: +20(2) 561-1230
Arts and Humanities

SADAT ACADEMY FOR ADMINISTRATIVE SCIENCES
Corniche El-Nil, Maadi Entrance Road, Cairo
Tel: +20(2) 350-1033
Fax: +20(2) 777-175
Administrative Sciences (Administration; Public Administration)

AKHBAR AL-YOUM ACADEMY FOR ENGINEERING, PRINTING AND PRESS TECHNOLOGY
Fourth Industrial Zone, Akhbar Al-Youm Building, 6th of October City
Tel: +20(11) 334-811

Head: Ahmad Zaki Badr

Departments
Printing and Press Engineering (Printing and Printmaking)

AL-ALSUN HIGHER INSTITUTE OF TOURISM AND HOTEL MANAGEMENT
Block n° 96, Makram Ebeid Ex., 8th District, Nasr City
Tel: +20(2) 287-7522

Head: Nadia Refa'at Abdel-Rahman

Hotel Management; Tourism

AL-MA'AREF HIGHER INSTITUTE FOR LANGUAGE AND TRANSLATION
10, Nasouh Str., Al-Zaytoun
Tel: +20(2) 257-1324

Head: Mervat Mahmoud Ali

Modern Languages; Translation and Interpretation

AL-UBOUR HIGHER INSTITUTE FOR ENGINEERING AND TECHNOLOGY
31 Km, Cairo-Ismaelia High Way
Tel: +20(2) 477-0037
Fax: +20(2) 241-3550

Head: Refa'at Rezq Baseli

Engineering; Technology

AL-UBOUR HIGHER INSTITUTE FOR MANAGEMENT AND INFORMATION SYSTEMS
21, Belbais High Way, Sharquia
Tel: +20(2) 263-6882
Fax: +20(2) 403-0804

Head: Al-Sayed Abdel-Qader Zedan

Computer Science; Information Management; Information Technology; Management Systems

ALEXANDRIA HIGHER INSTITUTE FOR TECHNOLOGY
Victor Emanuel Str., Sidi Gaber, Alexandria
Tel: +20(3) 425-4942

Head: Fouad Nasr Zain

Technology

CAIRO HIGHER INSTITUTE FOR COMPUTER, INFORMATICS AND MANAGEMENT "AL-GOLF"
2, Samir Mokhtar Str., Nabil Al-Waqad Corner, Heliopolis
Tel: +20(2) 417-6550
Fax: +20(2) 417-6551

Head: Mohamed Abdul-Moneim Hashish

Computer Science; Management; Management Systems

CAIRO HIGHER INSTITUTE FOR LANGUAGES, SIMULTANEOUS INTERPRETATION AND ADMINISTRATIVE SCIENCES
5,54 Str., off Route 9, Moqattam, Cairo
Tel: +20(2) 508-1700
Fax: +20(2) 508-1613

Head: Galal Al-Din Mohamed Ashmawy

Administration; Modern Languages; Translation and Interpretation

CAIRO HIGHER INSTITUTE FOR TOURISM AND HOTEL MANAGEMENT
5,54 Str., off Route 9, Moqattam, Cairo
Tel: +20(2) 508-1600
Fax: +20(2) 508-3303

Head: Mohamed Ibrahim Bakr

Hotel Management; Tourism

DELTA HIGHER INSTITUTE FOR COMPUTERS
Mansoura

Computer Science

EGYPTIAN HIGHER INSTITUTE OF ALEXANDRIA ACADEMY FOR MANAGEMENT AND ACCOUNTANCY
Medan Al-Masaged, Alexandria
Tel: +20(3) 484-3384

Head: Adel Abdel-Hamid Ez

Accountancy; Management

EGYPTIAN HIGHER INSTITUTE FOR TOURISM AND HOTEL MANAGEMENT
Final Station of Nozha Metro, behind Sheraton blocks, Cairo
Tel: +20(2) 266-5951
Fax: +20(2) 266-5950

Head: Saad Ahmad Halabo

Hotel Management; Tourism

HIGHER INSTITUTE FOR ADMINISTRATIVE SCIENCES
Division 1/1, Central Route, 6th of October City
Tel: +20(11) 354-271

Head: Mohamed Sayed Hamzawi

Administration

HIGHER INSTITUTE FOR AGRICULTURAL COOPERATIVE STUDIES
Assiut
Tel: +20(88) 322-281

Director: Abdel-Razeq Abdel-Aleem

Agriculture

HIGHER INSTITUTE OF AGRICULTURAL COOPERATIVE STUDIES
Shobra Al-Keima, Cairo
Tel: +20(2) 444-4850
Fax: +20(2) 444-1400

Director: Mostafa Ra'fat Abdel-Zaher

Agriculture

HIGHER INSTITUTE FOR APPLIED ARTS
Distinguished District, 51B, Second Adjacency, 6th of October City
Tel: +20(11) 352-806

Head: Mahmoud Ahmad Abdel A'al

Applied Arts (Graphic Arts; Handicrafts)

HIGHER INSTITUTE FOR ARCHITECTURE
Third District, Second Adjacency, 6th of October City
Tel: +20(11) 356-463
Fax: +20(11) 359-464

Head: Hassan Abdel-Maged Wahbi

Architecture

HIGHER INSTITUTE OF COMPUTER STUDIES
31 Km Al-Kafouri, Cairo Alexandria High Way, King Maryout, Alexandria
Tel: +20(3) 448-3200

Head: Hussein Ahmad Al-Sheikh

Computer Science

HIGHER INSTITUTE FOR COMPUTER AND ADMINISTRATION
Corniche Al-Nile, behind Al-Nile Badrawi Hospital, Al-Maadi, Cairo
Tel: +20(2) 524-7982

Head: Abdel-Aziz Abbas Al-Sherbeni

Administration; Computer Science; Management Systems

HIGHER INSTITUTE FOR COMPUTER AND BUSINESS ADMINISTRATION
High Way, Al-Zarqa City, Damietta
Tel: +20(57) 852-236

Head: Ahmad Deya Mohamed Khames

Business Administration; Business Computing; Computer Science

HIGHER INSTITUTE FOR COMPUTER SCIENCES AND INFORMATICS
Division 1/1, Central Road, 6th of October City
Tel: +20(11) 231-041

Head: Hussein Magdy Zain Al-Din

Computer Science

HIGHER INSTITUTE FOR COMPUTER SCIENCES AND MANAGEMENT TECHNOLOGY
Street n° 304, New Maadi, Cairo
Tel: +20(2) 702-9850
Fax: +20(2) 702-3105

Head: Said Ibrahim Refa'y

Computer Science; Engineering Management; Management Systems

HIGHER INSTITUTE FOR COMPUTER SCIENCES AND MANAGEMENT TECHNOLOGY
Agricultural School Str., Sohag
Tel: +20(93) 605-714

Head: Ahmad Abdel A'al Al-Darder

Computer Science; Management Systems

HIGHER INSTITUTE FOR COOPERATIVE AND ADMINISTRATIVE STUDIES
Al-Mounia, Sayeda Zainab, Cairo
Tel: +20(2) 795-5135
Fax: +20(2) 795-5686

Head: Kamel Hamdi Abou Al-Khair

Administration; Public Administration; Social and Community Services

HIGHER INSTITUTE FOR DEVELOPED STUDIES
Al-Sherif Str., off Al-Haram Str., besides Al-Farouq School, Giza
Tel: +20(2) 386-0008
Fax: +20(2) 388-5405

Head: Lucy Hakem Abou-Saif

Development Studies

HIGHER INSTITUTE FOR ECONOMICS AND ENVIRONMENT
Division 1/1, Central Road, 6th of October City
Tel: +20(11) 231-161

Head: Gaber Abdel-Samea Abou Al-Ainen

Economics; Environmental Studies

HIGHER INSTITUTE FOR ENGINEERING
Adjacency n°13, 10th of Ramadan City
Tel: +20(15) 365-667

Head: Hazem Ali Basiouni

Engineering

HIGHER INSTITUTE FOR ENGINEERING
Corniche Al-Nile, behind Al-Nile Badrawi Hospital, Al-Maadi, Cairo
Tel: +20(2) 524-7982

Head: Ahmad Ahmad Al-Qadi

Engineering

HIGHER INSTITUTE FOR HOTEL MANAGEMENT "EGOTH"
Alexandria
Tel: +20(2) 390-1768

Head: Mena Omar Barakat

Engineering; Hotel Management

HIGHER INSTITUTE FOR HOTEL MANAGEMENT "EGOTH"
Luxor
Tel: +20(2) 391-2688

Head: Saber Mahmoud Abou-Zaid

Hotel Management

HIGHER INSTITUTE FOR INDUSTRIAL ENGINEERING
Division 1/1, Central Route, 6th of October City
Tel: +20(11) 355-275

Head: Ali Mohamed Tal'at

Industrial Engineering

HIGHER INSTITUTE FOR LANGUAGES
Behind Al-Sheraton Blocks, Heliopolis
Tel: +20(2) 266-4472

Head: Salama Mohamed Soliman

Modern Languages

138

HIGHER INSTITUTE FOR LANGUAGES
Division 1/1, Central Route, 6th of October City
Tel: +20(11) 231-161
Fax: +20(2) 231-560

Head: Baher Mohamed Al-Gohary

Modern Languages

HIGHER INSTITUTE FOR LITERARY STUDIES
King Maryout, Alexandria
Tel: +20(2) 484-6155

Head: Farouq Othman Abaza

Literary Studies (Arts and Humanities)

HIGHER INSTITUTE FOR MANAGEMENT AND COMPUTER
Port Said

Head: Zain Al-Albdeen Hassan Faris

Departments
Administration and Computer (Administration; Computer Science; Management)

HIGHER INSTITUTE FOR MANAGEMENT AND INFORMATION TECHNOLOGY
Sakkara, Giza
Tel: +20(2) 381-0318
Fax: +20(2) 381-0313

Head: Sedek Mohamed Afify

Information Technology; Management; Management Systems

HIGHER INSTITUTE FOR MANAGEMENT AND TECHNOLOGY
Shobra Ment

Head: Amr Ghanayem

Management; Management Systems; Technology

HIGHER INSTITUTE FOR MASS MEDIA AND COMMUNICATION ARTS
Division 1/1, Central Route, 6th of October City
Tel: +20(11) 355-281
Fax: +20(2) 266-4472

Head: Layla Mohamed Abdel-Maged

Communication Arts; Mass Communication; Media Studies

HIGHER INSTITUTE FOR OPTICS TECHNOLOGY
Al-Sheraton blocks, Heliopolis
Tel: +20(2) 266-5950
Fax: +20(2) 267-2688

Head: Ahmad Abdel-Samea Al-Hamalawy

Optical Technology

HIGHER INSTITUTE FOR SOCIAL WORK
Al-Almal Str., Al-Sadat City, New Banha
Tel: +20(13) 235-885
Fax: +20(13) 220-554

Head: Al-Sayed Metwali Al-Ashmawi

Social Work

HIGHER INSTITUTE FOR SOCIAL WORK
73, Al-Resafa Street, Moharam Bek, Alexandria
Tel: +20(3) 494-8190
Fax: +20(3) 495-1560

Director: Ahmad Mohamed Fahmi

Social Work

HIGHER INSTITUTE FOR SOCIAL WORK
Aswan
Tel: +20(97) 314-995

Director: Gaber Sayed Ahmad

Social Work

HIGHER INSTITUTE FOR SOCIAL WORK
8th District, Madinet Nasr, Cairo
Tel: +20(2) 272-7325
Fax: +20(2) 272-0556

Director: Ali Al-Din Al-Sayed Mohamed Soliman

Social Work

HIGHER INSTITUTE FOR SOCIAL WORK
Damanhour
Tel: +20(45) 315-386
Fax: +20(45) 318-420

Director: Mohamed Nabil Salem

Social Work

HIGHER INSTITUTE FOR SOCIAL WORK
Al-Guish Street, King Fouad Palace, Kafr Al-Sheikh
Tel: +20(47) 227-835
Fax: +20(47) 223-184

Director: Mohamed Ahmad Abdel-Hadi

Social Work

HIGHER INSTITUTE FOR SOCIAL WORK
Abdel-Salam Aref Str., Mansoura
Tel: +20(50) 367-077

Director: Mohamed Sowelam Al-Baslouni

Social Work

HIGHER INSTITUTE FOR SOCIAL WORK
Port-Said
Tel: +20(66) 324-365

Director: Mohamed Ahmad Abdel-Hadi

Social Work

HIGHER INSTITUTE FOR SOCIAL WORK
Qena
Tel: +20(96) 334-908

Social Work

HIGHER INSTITUTE FOR SOCIAL WORK
Sohag
Tel: +20(93) 640-222

Director: Fawzy Al-Desouki Mohamed

Social Work

HIGHER INSTITUTE FOR SOCIAL WORK
Division 1/1, Central Route, 6th of October City
Tel: +20(11) 355-276

Director: Salah Abdel-Moneim Hawtar

Social Work

HIGHER INSTITUTE FOR SPECIALIZED TECHNOLOGICAL STUDIES
32 Km. Cairo Ismaelia High Way, Ismaelia
Tel: +20(2) 477-2888
Fax: +20(2) 477-1900

Head: Hesham Hassan Makhlouf

Technology

HIGHER INSTITUTE FOR SPECIFIC STUDIES
Nazlet Al-Seman, behind Seyag Hotel, Al-Haram, Giza
Tel: +20(2) 385-9104
Fax: +20(2) 384-5505

Head: Fouad Eskandar Niqola

Specific Studies

HIGHER INSTITUTE FOR TOURISM AND HOTEL MANAGEMENT
Sakkara Route, Al-Haram, Giza
Head: Abdel-Halim Abdel Fattah Ewais

Hotel Management; Tourism

HIGHER INSTITUTE FOR TOURISM AND HOTEL MANAGEMENT
Hurghada
Tel: +20(2) 290-1017
Hotel Management; Tourism

HIGHER INSTITUTE FOR TOURISM AND HOTEL MANAGEMENT
Ra'as Sedr, South Sinai
Tel: +20(62) 400-871
Fax: +20(62) 770-752

Head: Nervana Mokhtar Harraz

Hotel Management; Tourism

HIGHER INSTITUTE FOR TOURISM AND HOTEL MANAGEMENT
6th District, 6th of October City
Tel: +20(11) 330-342

Head: Hassan Abbas Al-Mansouri

Hotel Management; Tourism

HIGHER INSTITUTE FOR TOURISM, HOTEL MANAGEMENT AND COMPUTER
2, Adel Mostafa Shawqi Str., Al-Seouf, Alexandria
Tel: +20(3) 502-1055

Head: Fatouh Mahmoud Abou Al-Azm

Computer Science; Hotel Management; Tourism

HIGHER TECHNOLOGICAL INSTITUTE
Al-Guish Str., King Fouad Palace , Kafr Al-Sheikh, 10th of Ramadan City
Tel: +20(15) 363-497
Fax: +20(15) 364-269

Head: Mostafa Mahmoud Thabet

Technology

LABOUR UNIVERSITY
Al-Nasr Str., Abbas Al-Aquad, Nasr City, Cairo
Tel: +20(2) 275-4646

Head: Emad Al-Din Hassan

Labour and Industrial Relations

POST-GRADUATE HIGHER INSTITUTE FOR ISLAMIC STUDIES
26, Yolyo Str., Meet Oqba, Giza
Tel: +20(2) 346-8547

Head: Baghat Oteba

Islamic Studies

POST-GRADUATE HIGHER INSTITUTE FOR SOCIAL DEFENCE STUDIES
1, Al-Shahed Ra'af Zaki, Polak Al-Dakrour, Giza
Tel: +20(2) 330-5352

Head: Mohamed Shehata Ali

Social Defence Studies (Social and Community Services; Social Policy; Social Problems; Social Welfare)

Eritrea

INSTITUTION TYPES AND CREDENTIALS

Types of higher education institutions:

University
Teacher Training Institute

School leaving and higher education credentials:

Eritrean Secondary Education Certificate Examination (ESECE)
Bachelor's Degree

STRUCTURE OF EDUCATION SYSTEM

Pre-higher education:

Duration of compulsory education:

Age of entry: 7
Age of exit: 14

Structure of school system:

Elementary
Type of school providing this education: Elementary school
Length of programme in years: 5
Age level from: 7 to: 12

Middle
Type of school providing this education: Middle Level School
Length of programme in years: 2
Age level from: 12 to: 14

Secondary
Type of school providing this education: Secondary School
Length of programme in years: 4
Age level from: 14 to: 18
Certificate/diploma awarded: Eritrean Secondary Education Certificate Examination (ESECE)

Technical
Type of school providing this education: Technical School
Length of programme in years: 3
Age level from: 16 to: 19
Certificate/diploma awarded: Eritrean Secondary Education Certificate Examinations (ESECE)

School education:

Elementary education lasts for five years followed by two years of middle education. Secondary education lasts for four years after completion of the basic education cycle (end of middle school). At the end of the course, pupils sit for the Eritrean Secondary Education Certificate Examination. Senior students who leave school at the end of the basic cycle can enter basic-level technical training at the Skill Development Centre. Following completion of training, they may enter intermediate level technical schools after passing an entrance examination. The other route to entry into technical schools is direct, after completing Grade 10 at senior secondary school level and passing an entrance examination. Courses last for three years. They prepare skilled workers for industry, agriculture and other development areas.

Higher education:

Higher education is provided by the University of Asmara. It was founded in 1958 and was granted full university status in 1968. The University consists of four Colleges of Science, Arts and Language Studies, Business and Economics, Agriculture and Aquatic Science. It also offers programmes in Engineering, Education and Law. The governing bodies are the Board of Trustees and the Academic Senate.

Academic year:

Classes from: September *to:* June

Long vacation from: 1 July *to:* 31 August

Languages of instruction:

English

Stages of studies:

Non-university level post-secondary studies (technical/vocational type):

Students completing the full eleven-year cycle may enter diploma-level professional colleges, still in the process of being established.

University level studies:

University level first stage:
Courses for Bachelor's Degrees are generally obtained after four years of regular study for day students and seven years for extension students.

Teacher education:

Training of pre-primary and primary/basic school teachers
The Asmara Teacher Training Institute (TTI) offers a training programme for primary-school teachers. It admits secondary school graduates who have sat for an entrance examination for a one-year course. At the end of this course, trainees are awarded the TTI Certificate. In service courses are also offered during the long vacation, July and August, to upgrade unqualified primary school teachers and school directors. Unqualified elementary teachers can follow the Distance Education programme for Elementary Teachers in Eritrea.

Training of secondary school teachers
Teachers for secondary school level are taught by the University of Asmara at the College of Science and the College of Arts and Social Studies or at the Faculty of Education.

NATIONAL BODIES

Responsible authorities:

Ministry of Education
    Minister: Osman Saleh
    Director, Administration: Haile Alazar
    PO Box 1056
    Asmara
    Tel: +291(1) 11-66-44   +291(1) 12-78-17
    Fax: +291(1) 11-83-51   +291(1) 12-19-13

ADMISSIONS TO HIGHER EDUCATION

Admission to university-level studies

Name of secondary school credential required: Eritrean Secondary Education Certificate Examination (ESECE)
Minimum score/requirement: Five subject passes

Foreign students admission

Admission requirements: Foreign students must hold the Eritrean Secondary School Leaving Certificate Examination or its equivalent.

Entry regulations: A visa is required.

Language requirements: Good knowledge of English is essential.

Application procedures:

Apply to individual institution for entry to: University

Apply to: Registrar's Office, University of Asmara
    PO Box 1220
    Asmara
    Tel: +291(1) 16-19-26
    Fax: +291(1) 16-22-36

References to further information on foreign student admissions and recognition of studies

Title: Study Abroad 2000-2001
Publisher: UNESCO/IBE
Year of publication: 1999

STUDENT LIFE

Main student services at national level

Registrar's Office, University of Asmara
  PO Box 1220
  Asmara
  Tel: +291(1) 16-19-26
  Fax: +291(1) 16-22-36

INTERNATIONAL COOPERATION AND EXCHANGES

Principal national bodies responsible for dealing with international cooperation and exchanges in higher education:

Ministry of Education
  Minister: Osman Saleh
  Director, Administration: Haile Alazar
  PO Box 1056
  Asmara
  Tel: 291(1) 12-78-17
  Fax: +291(1) 12-19-13

GRADING SYSTEM

Usual grading system in secondary school

Full Description: At middle and secondary school 50% and above is the pass mark.

Main grading system used by higher education institutions

Full Description: Letter grades (A,B,C,D, or F) are used to indicate the academic achievement of a student in a course. The value of each grade is as follows: A: excellent (4); B: very good (3); C: good (2); D: unsatisfactory (1); F: failure (0)
Highest on scale: A
Lowest on scale: F

NOTES ON HIGHER EDUCATION SYSTEM

Data for academic year: 2000-2001
Source: University of Asmara, 2001

INSTITUTIONS OF HIGHER EDUCATION

UNIVERSITIES

PUBLIC INSTITUTIONS

*• UNIVERSITY OF ASMARA

PO Box 1220, Asmara
Tel: +291(1) 161-926
Fax: +291(1) 162-236
Telex: 42091 asmuniv et
Cable: Asmuniv
EMail: luul@asmara.uoa.edu.er

President: Wolde-Ab Yisak (1993-) Tel: +291(1)161-935
EMail: wolde.ab@pres.uoa.edu.er

Director of Administration: Tekie Asyhun
Tel: +291(1) 116-141 EMail: tekie@admin.uoa.edu.er

International Relations: Tewolde Zerom, Director of
Strategic Planning/Projects Tel: +291(1) 111-932
EMail: tewelde@IPC.uoa.edu.er

Faculties

Education *Dean:* Belaynesh Araya
Engineering (Civil Engineering; Electrical Engineering; Engineering; Mechanical Engineering) *Dean:* N.V. Rao

Colleges

Agriculture and Aquatic Sciences (Animal Husbandry; Marine Biology; Soil Science) *Director:* Bissrat Ghebru
Arts and Social Sciences (Archaeology; Arts and Humanities; English; Geography; History; Journalism; Mass Communication; Political Science; Social Sciences; Sociology; Statistics) *Director:* Asmerom Kidane
Business and Economics (Accountancy; Business Administration; Business and Commerce; Economics; Finance; Law; Public Administration) *Dean:* Mehari Tewolde
Health Sciences (Biomedicine; Community Health; Health Sciences; Nursing; Pharmacy) *Director:* Asefaw Tekeste
Science (Biology; Chemistry; Mathematics; Natural Sciences; Physics) *Dean:* Ghebrebrhan Ogubazghi

Programmes

Law *Director:* Kibreab Habtemicael

Institutes

Management *Director:* Gafer Abubaker

History: Founded 1958. Dismantled and relocated to Ethiopia 1990. Re-established 1991 as an Autonomous University by the Provisional Government of Eritrea (PGE).

Governing Bodies: Board of Trustees; Academic Senate

Academic Year: September to June (September-January; January-June)

Admission Requirements: Eritrean General Certificate Examination (EGCE) or equivalent

Main Language(s) of Instruction: English

Degrees and Diplomas: *Bachelor's Degree:* Arts; Science, 4 yrs

Libraries: c. 60,000 vols

Publications: Seismic Bulletin (2 per annum)

Academic Staff *2001:* Total: c. 223

Student Numbers *2001:* Total: c. 4,086

145

Ethiopia

INSTITUTION TYPES AND CREDENTIALS

Types of higher education institutions:

University
Institute
College

School leaving and higher education credentials:

Ethiopian School Leaving Certificate
Diploma
Bachelor's Degree
Doctor
Master's Degree
Specialization Diploma
Doctorate (PhD)

STRUCTURE OF EDUCATION SYSTEM

Pre-higher education:

Structure of school system:

Primary
Type of school providing this education: Primary School
Length of programme in years: 8
Age level from: 6 to: 14
Certificate/diploma awarded: Primary School Certificate

First Cycle Secondary
Type of school providing this education: General Secondary School
Length of programme in years: 2
Age level from: 14 to: 16
Certificate/diploma awarded: National examination

Second Cycle Secondary
Type of school providing this education: Preparatory Secondary School
Length of programme in years: 2
Age level from: 16 to: 18
Certificate/diploma awarded: Ethiopian School Leaving Certificate Examination (ESLCE)

Vocational
Type of school providing this education: Vocational School
Length of programme in years: 3
Age level from: 16 to: 19
Certificate/diploma awarded: Ethiopian School Leaving Certificate

School education:

Education is not compulsory. Before 1994, general education was divided into primary (grades 1-6), junior secondary (grades 7 and 8) and senior secondary education (grades 9-12). The new curriculum offers ten years of general education consisting of eight years of primary education (divided into two four-year cycles: basic and general and leading to the Primary School Certificate) and two years of general or first cycle secondary education (grades 9 and 10) followed by two years of second cycle (or preparatory) secondary education (grades 11 and 12). At the end of it, students take the Ethiopian School Leaving Certificate Examination (ESLCE). The second cycle prepares students for continuing their studies at higher education level or selecting their own vocations. Technical and vocational training is separate from the regular system and runs in parallel with it. It takes two to three years to complete.

Higher education:

Higher education is provided by universities, junior colleges and specialized institutions. They are under the responsibility of the Ministry of Education.

Main laws/decrees governing higher education:

Decree: Council of Ministers Regulation N° 197/1994   Year: 1994
Concerns: Administration of Higher Education Institutions in the regions.

Decree: Council of Ministers Regulation No. 113/1993   Year: 1993
Concerns: Addis Ababa University

Decree: Proclamation No. 109 of 1977   Year: 1977
Concerns: Higher Education Institutions

Decree: General Notice No. 284 of 1961   Year: 1961
Concerns: Addis Ababa University

Academic year:

Classes from: September *to:* July

Long vacation from: 8 July *to:* 11 September

Languages of instruction:

English

Stages of studies:

Non-university level post-secondary studies (technical/vocational type):

Higher vocational and technical education are offered by agricultural colleges, teacher training colleges, engineering and technological institutes and commercial institutions. Courses last between two and three years and lead to diplomas. A health sciences institute offers three to six-year diploma and degree courses.

University level studies:

University level first stage: Bachelor's Degree:
The first stage of university level education leads to the Bachelor's Degree after four to five years' study. Examinations are organized at the end of each semester. In Medicine and Veterinary Medicine, the professional qualification of Doctor is conferred after six years' study.

University level second stage: Master's Degree; Specialization:
The second stage leads to a Master's Degree after a minimum of two years' further study. In Medicine and Veterinary Medicine the specialization degree is obtained after a minimum of three years' further study beyond the MD and DVM degrees.

University level third stage: Doctor of Philosophy:
The Doctor of Philosophy is conferred after some three years' study beyond the Master's degree.

Teacher education:

Training of pre-primary and primary/basic school teachers
Primary school teachers follow a one-year course after grade 12 in regional Primary Teacher Training Institutes (TTI).

Training of secondary school teachers
First cycle secondary school teachers are trained in two years at Teacher Training Colleges. Second cycle secondary school teachers are trained at the Faculties of Education of Addis Ababa University, Bahir Dar University, Alemaya University and Debub University (Dila) which offer a four-year course leading to the degree of Bachelor of Education. Technical education teachers follow a two-year diploma and four-year degree course at Nazreth Technical Teachers College.

Training of higher education teachers
Masters and PhD level teacher/staff training is undertaken at Addis Abeba University Graduate School. Many are also trained abroad.

Non-traditional studies:

Lifelong higher education
There are continuing education programmes in almost all institutions of higher education in Ethiopia. They mainly serve the needs of adult students and are offered after regular hours as evening programmes and during the summer season (Kiremt) on a tuition fee paying basis.

NATIONAL BODIES

Responsible authorities:
Department of Higher Education, Ministry of Education
    Head of the Department of Higher Education: Teshome Yizengaw
    Minister of Education: Gennet Zewdie
    PO Box 1367

Addis Ababa
Tel: +251(1) 55-31-33 +251(1) 56-00-63
Fax: +251(1) 55-02-99 +251(1) 56-55-65

Role of governing body: Coordinates tertiary level education in Ethiopia and assists higher education institutions

ADMISSIONS TO HIGHER EDUCATION

Admission to non university higher education studies

Name of secondary school credential required: Ethiopian School Leaving Certificate
Minimum score/requirement: 2.0 out of 4.0 points
For entry to: Technical/Vocational colleges that take 2-3 years

Admission to university-level studies

Name of secondary school credential required: Ethiopian School Leaving Certificate
Minimum score/requirement: 2.0 out of 4.0 points - passes in 5 subjects at C-level.
For entry to: All types of programmes of study at levels that take 2-6 years

Entrance exams required: This will be a requirement as of the 2003/04 academic year.

Other admission requirements: Special privileges for female students and students from disadvantaged/remote regions.

Foreign students admission

Definition of foreign student: A person enrolled at an institution of higher education in a country of which he/she is not permanently resident.

Quotas: The School of Information Studies for Africa (SISA) admits students from the Eastern and Southern African Region on a quota basis.

Admission requirements: Foreign students must provide the academic certificates required by the institution concerned. Foreign qualifications recognized as equivalent to the Ethiopian school-leaving certificate are: the General Certificate of Education of the University of London; the Cambridge Overseas Examination; the West African School Certificate and the Oxford Examination. The Higher Education Department may grant equivalence to other secondary school-leaving certificates in individual cases. All foreign students must cover their living expenses.

Entry regulations: Visas; financial guarantee. In addition, all foreign students, including ECOWAS citizens, are required to secure resident permits for the period of their stay.

Health requirements: Students must present a health certificate.

Language requirements: Students must be proficient in English at TOEFL level.

Application procedures:

Apply to individual institution for entry to: University/College

Apply to: Ministry of Education
    PO Box 30747
    Addis Ababa
    Tel: +251(1) 55-31-33
    Fax: +251(1) 55-02-99

Application closing dates:

    For university level studies: 1 July
    For advanced/doctoral studies: 1 July

Recognition of studies and qualifications:

Studies pursued in home country (System of recognition/accreditation): The University Senate awards credentials which are recognized by the country. The Ministry of Education is mandated to accredit private and public higher education institutions according to whether they fulfil the required standards.

Studies pursued in foreign countries (bodies dealing with recognition of foreign credentials): Department of Higher Education, Ministry of Education
    Head: Teshome Yizengaw
    PO Box 1367
    Addis Ababa
    Tel: +251(1) 55-31-33
    Fax: +251(1) 55-08-77 +251(1) 55-02-99
    Telex: 21435

    Deals with credential recognition for entry to: University and Profession

Special provisions for recognition:

For access to non-university post-secondary studies: It applies to nationals.

For access to university level studies: It applies to nationals who wish to enter medical schools

References to further information on foreign student admissions and recognition of studies

Title: Higher Education in Ethiopia: facts and figures 2000/2001
Author: Ministry of Education
Year of publication: 2001

Title: Study Abroad 2000-2001
Publisher: UNESCO/IBE
Year of publication: 1999

STUDENT LIFE

Student expenses and financial aid

Student costs:

    Home students tuition fees: Minimum: 0 (Ethiopian Birr)
    Foreign students tuition fees: Maximum: 17,730 (Ethiopian Birr)

Bodies providing information on student financial aid:

Office of the Registrar, Addis Ababa University
    PO Box 1176
    Addis Ababa
    Tel: +251(1) 55-08-44
    Fax: +251(1) 55-06-55
    Telex: 21205
    Cable: AAUNV
    Deals with: Grants

Scholarship Unit, Department of Higher Education
    PO Box 1367
    Addis Ababa
    Tel: +251(1) 55-31-33
    Fax: +251(1) 55-02-99
    Deals with: Grants

Publications on student services and financial aid:

    Title: SISA Newsletter
    Publisher: Addis Ababa University

INTERNATIONAL COOPERATION AND EXCHANGES

Principal national bodies responsible for dealing with international cooperation and exchanges in higher education:

Department of Higher Education, Ministry of Education
    PO Box 1367
    Addis Ababa
    Tel: +251(1) 55-31-33
    Fax: +251(1) 55-08-77 +251(1) 55-02-99

GRADING SYSTEM

Usual grading system in secondary school

Full Description: 100-0
Highest on scale: 100
Pass/fail level: 50
Lowest on scale: 1

Main grading system used by higher education institutions

Full Description: It is A-F. The highest on scale is "A" and the lowest is "F". The pass/fail level for undergraduates is "C", and for postgraduates is "B".

Highest on scale: "A"
Pass/fail level: "C" (for undergraduates), "B" (for postgraduates)
Lowest on scale: "F"

Other main grading systems

Marks are sometimes out of 100 with the lowest pass mark set at 60.

NOTES ON HIGHER EDUCATION SYSTEM

Education for both undergraduate and postgraduate level regular programmes is provided free of charge for Ethiopians. This includes free board and lodging in all institutions of higher education. According to the Government's new Education and Training Policy, priority for financial support will depend on the completion of general secondary education and related training. Hence, cost-sharing of higher education is to be implemented in the near future.

Data for academic year: 2000-2001
Source: Ministry of Education, Addis Ababa, 2001

INSTITUTIONS OF HIGHER EDUCATION

UNIVERSITIES

PUBLIC INSTITUTIONS

*• ADDIS ABABA UNIVERSITY (AAU)

PO Box 1176, Addis Ababa
Tel: +251(1) 55-08-44
Fax: +251(1) 55-06-55   +251(1) 55-09-72
Telex: 21205
EMail: kennedy.aau@telecom.net.et

President: Mogessie Ashenafi (1995-)
EMail: mogessie.ashenafi@telecom.net.et

Vice-President: Ato Haile Selassie Wolde-Gerima
Tel: +251(1) 55-74-79

International Relations: Brook Hailu Tel: +251(1) 11-36-48
EMail: ero.aau@telecom.net.et

Faculties

Business and Economics (Accountancy; Economics; Management; Public Administration) *Dean:* Zewdie Shibre, *full-time staff:* 76, *part-time staff:* 21, *students:* 785

Education (Business Education; Curriculum; Education; Educational Psychology) *Dean:* Ayele Meshesha, *full-time staff:* 74, *part-time staff:* 4, *students:* 713

Law *Dean:* Tilahun Teshome, *full-time staff:* 17, *part-time staff:* 1, *students:* 253

Medicine (Anaesthesiology; Anatomy; Biochemistry; Community Health; Gynaecology and Obstetrics; Medicine; Microbiology; Ophthalmology; Orthopedics; Paediatrics; Parasitology; Pathology; Pharmacology; Physiology; Psychiatry and Mental Health; Surgery) *Dean:* Kedebe Oli, *full-time staff:* 112, *students:* 328

Science (Biology; Chemistry; Geology; Geophysics; Mathematics; Natural Sciences; Physics; Sanitary Engineering; Statistics) *Dean:* Sebsibe Demessew, *full-time staff:* 171, *part-time staff:* 4, *students:* 2,737

Technology (Architecture; Building Technologies; Chemical Engineering; Civil Engineering; Electrical Engineering; Mechanical Engineering; Technology) *Dean:* Belay Woldeyes, *full-time staff:* 113, *part-time staff:* 18, *students:* 1,327

Veterinary Medicine *(Debre Zeit)* (Anatomy; Biochemistry; Biology; Embryology and Reproduction Biology; Microbiology; Parasitology; Pathology; Pharmacology; Physiology; Veterinary Science) *Dean:* Getachew Tilahun, *full-time staff:* 65, *part-time staff:* 3, *students:* 313

Colleges

Social Sciences (Geography; History; International Relations; Philosophy; Political Science; Social Sciences; Sociology) *Dean:* Solomon Mulugeta, *full-time staff:* 83, *part-time staff:* 11, *students:* 2,129

Programmes
Distance Education

Schools
Information Studies (Information Sciences; Library Science) *Director:* Getachew Birru, *full-time staff:* 17, *part-time staff:* 5, *students:* 171

Institutes
Language Studies (Linguistics; Literature; Modern Languages; Native Language; Theatre) *Dean:* Zerihun Asfaw, *full-time staff:* 63, *part-time staff:* 20, *students:* 507

Research Institutes
Development Research (Development Studies) *Director:* Tegegne G. Egziabher, *full-time staff:* 7
Education *Director:* Amare Asgedom, *full-time staff:* 8
Ethiopian Studies *Director:* Baye Yimam, *full-time staff:* 18
Pathobiology (Pathology) *Director:* Teshome   J. Michael, *full-time staff:* 17

History: Founded 1961 as Haile Sellassie I University, incorporating University College of Addis Ababa, founded 1950; Imperial College of Engineering, 1953; Ethio-Swedish Institute of Building Technology, 1954; Imperial Ethiopian College of Agricultural and Mechanical Arts, 1951; Public Health College, 1954; and Theological College of the Holy Trinity, 1960. Acquired present title 1975.

Governing Bodies: Board of Governors

Academic Year: September to July (September-February; February-July). Also Summer programme (July-August)

Admission Requirements: Secondary school certificate, or foreign equivalent

Main Language(s) of Instruction: English

International Co-operation: University of Leipzig; University of Osnabruck; University of Mainz; University College Dublin; University of Oslo; University of Berne; University of Edinburgh; University of Sussex; London School of Economics; Michigan State University; Antioch University; Brown University; Washington University

Degrees and Diplomas: *Diploma:* Building Technology; Veterinary Science, 2-3 yrs; *Bachelor's Degree:* Arts (BA); Science (BSc), 4-5 yrs; *Doctor:* Medicine (MD); Veterinary Medecine (DVM), 6 yrs; *Master's Degree:* Arts (MA); Science (MSc), a further 2 yrs; *Specialization Diploma:* a further 2 yrs following MD; *Doctorate (PhD):* History, Languages, Chemistry, Biology, a further 3-4 yrs following MA/MSc

Student Services: Academic Counselling, Social Counselling, Foreign Student Adviser, Cultural Centre, Sports Facilities, Health Services, Canteen

Special Facilities: Archives Museum; Natural Museum. Geophysical Observatory. Cultural Centre. Herbarium. Audio-Visual Centre

Libraries: Total, c. 493,000 vols

Publications: Ethiopian Medical Journal; Ethiopian Journal of Health Development (quarterly); Ethiopian Journal of Engineers and Architects (ZEDE); Journal of Ethiopian Studies; Ethiopian Journal of Development; Bulletin of the Chemical Society of Ethiopia; Ethiopian Journal of Education; Ethiopian Journal of Law; Ethiopian Journal of Science (SINET) (biannually)

Press or Publishing House: Addis Ababa University Press

Academic Staff *1999-2000:* Total: **802**

Student Numbers *1999-2000:* Total: **20,911**

ALEMAYA UNIVERSITY (AU)
PO Box 138, Dire Dawa, Harar
Tel: +251(5) 11-13-99
Fax: +251(5) 11-40-08
EMail: alemaya.univ@telecom.net.et

President: Desta Hamito Tel: +251(5) 11-23-64

Academic Vice-President: Belay Kassa
Tel: +251(5) 11-23-74

Faculties
Agriculture
Education
Health Sciences

Programmes
Continuing Education

Schools
Graduate Studies

Further Information: Also international Research Centres

History: Founded 1954 as College of Agriculture. A State institution. Acquired present status 1985.

Governing Bodies: University Board; Senate

Academic Year: September to July (September-February; February-July)

Admission Requirements: Secondary school certificate or equivalent

Main Language(s) of Instruction: English

Degrees and Diplomas: *Diploma:* 2 yrs; *Bachelor's Degree:* Science (BSc), 4-5 yrs; *Master's Degree:* Science (MSc), a further 2-3 yrs

Student Services: Academic Counselling, Social Counselling, Nursery Care, Cultural Centre, Sports Facilities, Health Services

Student Residential Facilities: For c. 1700 students

Special Facilities: Arboretum. Greenhouse

Libraries: Alemaya University of Agriculture Library

Publications: Annual Research Reports (annually); Newsletter; Working Papers

Academic Staff *1999:* Total: c. 320

Student Numbers *1999:* Total: c. 1,730

154

BAHIR DAR UNIVERSITY (BDU)
PO Box 79, Bahir Dar
Tel: +251(8) 20-01-43
Fax: +251(8) 20-20-27
EMail: bdtc@telecom.net.et

President (Acting): Shimelis Haile Tel: +251(8) 20-01-37

Administrative Vice-President: Gebregziabiher Kahssay
Tel: +251(8) 20-06-98

Faculties
Education
Engineering *Dean:* Wossen Ato, *full-time staff:* 59, *students:* 750
Social Sciences *Dean:* Shimelis Maille, *full-time staff:* 129, *students:* 2,369

History: Founded 1972, acquired present status and title 2000.

Governing Bodies: Regional Board for Higher Education

Academic Year: September to June

Admission Requirements: Ethiopian school leaving certificate (ESLCE) or equivalent

Fees: None for national students

Main Language(s) of Instruction: English

Degrees and Diplomas: *Bachelor's Degree:* Education (BEd), 4 yrs; Science (BSc), 5 yrs

Student Services: Cultural Centre, Sports Facilities, Health Services, Canteen

Libraries: Central Library with computer facilities

Publications: News Letter; Bulletin of University, Research articles on Education, Engineering, Linguistics

Academic Staff *2000:* Total: **129**

Staff with doctorate: Total: **11**

Student Numbers 2000	MEN	WOMEN	TOTAL
All (Foreign Included)	2,126	243	**2,369**

Evening Students, 3,247

DEBUB UNIVERSITY (DU)
PO Box 5, Awassa
Tel: +251(6) 20-06-53
Fax: +251(6) 20-00-72
EMail: acare@padisgn.apc.org

President: Zinabu Glmariam (1999-)

Academic Vice-President: Tesfaye Teshome

Faculties
Education
Health Sciences

Programmes
Agriculture
Forestry

JIMMA UNIVERSITY (JU)
PO Box 378, Jimma
Tel: +251(7) 11-13-40 +251(7) 11-14-58
Fax: +251(7) 11-14-50
EMail: jihs@telecom.net.et
Website: http://www.telecom.net.et-junv.edu/

President: Damtew Woldemariam (2000-)
Tel: +251(7) 11-14-57 Fax: +251(7) 11-14-50

Vice-President for Administration and Development: Kora Tushune Tel: +251(7) 11-09-51

International Relations: Chali Jira Tel: +251(7) 11-22-02

Faculties
Business (Business Administration; Management)
Medical Sciences (Medicine)
Public Health Dean: Sileshi Teklemariam, *full-time staff:* 844, *students:* 3,001
Technology (Civil Engineering; Electrical Engineering; Mechanical Engineering; Technology)

Colleges
Agriculture *Dean:* Kaba Urgessa, *full-time staff:* 285, *students:* 756

History: Founded 1983, acquired present status and title 1999. Jimma University is a national pioneer of community-oriented higher education.

Governing Bodies: Board of Appointees; University Senate

Academic Year: September to June

Admission Requirements: Ethiopia school leaving certificate examination (ESLCE)

Fees: None

Main Language(s) of Instruction: English

International Co-operation: Member of network of community-oriented Educational Institutions of Health Sciences

Degrees and Diplomas: *Bachelor's Degree:* Accountancy (BA); Business Management (BA); Civil Engineering (BSc); Electrical Engineering (BSc); Environmental Health (BSc); Horticulture (BSc); Mechanical Engineering (BSc); Medical Laboratory Technology (BSc); Nursing (BSc); Public Health (BSc); Science (BSc), 3 yrs following successful completion of two years studies; *Doctor:* Medicine (MD), 7 yrs. Also Diplomas in most fields

Student Residential Facilities: Yes

Special Facilities: Computer Centre; Audio-Visual Service

Libraries: University Library

Publications: Innovation, Newsletter (quarterly); Ethiopian Journal of Health Science (2 per annum)

Academic Staff *1999-2000*	MEN	WOMEN	TOTAL
FULL-TIME	289	11	**300**

Staff with doctorate: Total: **4**

Student Numbers *1999-2000*	MEN	WOMEN	TOTAL
All (Foreign Included)	1,661	299	**1,960**

Evening Students, 1,041

• MEKELLE UNIVERSITY (MU)
PO Box 231, Mekelle
Tel: +251(4) 40-08-12   +251(4) 40-08-20
Fax: +251(4) 40-07-93
EMail: mekelle.university@telecom.net.et

President: Mitiku Haile (1999-)

Agriculture; Business and Commerce; Engineering

OTHER INSTITUTIONS

PUBLIC INSTITUTIONS

ADDIS ABABA COMMERCIAL COLLEGE
PO Box 3131, Addis Ababa
Tel: +251(1) 51-80-20
Fax: +251(1) 51-57-86
EMail: aacomcollege@telecom.net.et

Business and Commerce

AMBO COLLEGE OF AGRICULTURE
PO Box 19, Ambo
Tel: +251(1) 36-00-96
Fax: +251(1) 36-15-14
EMail: aca.ethiopia@telecom.net.et

Agriculture

ARBA MINCH WATER TECHNOLOGY INSTITUTE
PO Box 21, Arba Minch, N. Omo
Tel: +251(6) 81-00-97
Fax: +251(6) 81-02-79

Dean (Acting): Bogale Glmariam (2000-)

Engineering; Technology
Water Science

History: Founded 1986

DILLA COLLEGE OF HEALTH SCIENCES
PO Box 419, Dilla
Tel: +251(06) 31-20-30
Fax: +251(06) 31-02-95

Head: Menna Olango

Faculties
Health Sciences (Health Sciences; Hygiene; Laboratory Techniques; Nursing) *Head:* A. Tesfaye, *full-time staff:* 35, *part-time staff:* 5, *students:* 950
Teacher Education (Biology; Chemistry; English; Geography; Health Education; Health Sciences; History; Mathematics;

155

Native Language; Nursing; Physics; Teacher Training) *Lecturer*: T. Bogale, *full-time staff: 85, part-time staff: 5, students: 2,830*

History: Founded 1996

Governing Bodies: Joint Academic Commission; Management Council

Academic Year: September to June

Admission Requirements: Ethiopian School Leaving Certificate Examination (at least 3 on a scale of 5) or equivalent

Fees: (Birr): Tuition, 7711 per annum

Main Language(s) of Instruction: English

Accrediting Agencies: Ministry of Education

Degrees and Diplomas: *Diploma*: Laboratory Technology; Nursing; Sanitation, 2 yrs; *Bachelor's Degree*: Arts (BA); Education (BEd); Science (BSc), 4 yrs

Student Services: Academic Counselling, Nursery Care, Sports Facilities, Canteen

Student Residential Facilities: Yes

Libraries: Main Library

Academic Staff *2000*	MEN	WOMEN	TOTAL
FULL-TIME	105	15	120
PART-TIME	–	–	10
TOTAL	–	–	**130**

Student Numbers *2000*: Total: **3,820**

Part-time Students, 1,560 **Evening Students,** 300 **Distance Students,** 960

ETHIOPIAN CIVIL SERVICE COLLEGE (ECSC)

PO Box 5648, Addis Ababa
Tel: +251(1) 60-17-62
Fax: +251(1) 60-17-64
EMail: ethcscol@excite.com

President: Haile Michael Aberra (1996-)
Tel: +251(1) 60-17-59 EMail: hailem@excite.com

Associate Vice-President for Business and Development: Solomon Fisseha EMail: solomonfis@hotmail.com

International Relations: Negussie Negash
Tel: +251(1) 60-17-10

Schools

Business and Economics (Accountancy; Business Administration; Economics) *Director*: Meshesha Shewarega, *full-time staff: 53, part-time staff: 3, students: 850*

Legal Studies (Law) *Director*: Assefa Fisseha, *full-time staff: 28, students: 570*

Institutes

Urban Development Studies (Town Planning; Urban Studies) *Director*: Assefa Woldem, *full-time staff: 22, part-time staff: 8, students: 200*

History: Founded 1995

Governing Bodies: Board; Senate

Academic Year: September to August

Admission Requirements: Ethiopian School Leaving Certificate and pass in entrance examination

Fees: Cost sharing scheme adopted, students pay 25% of net salary to the college

Main Language(s) of Instruction: English

Accrediting Agencies: Ministry of Education

Degrees and Diplomas: *Bachelor's Degree*: Accountancy (BAcc); Development Administration (BDA); Economics (BEc), 3 yrs; Urban Planning (BSc), 4 years; Law (LLB), 4 yrs. Also Advanced Diploma in Urban Engineering, 3 yrs

Student Services: Academic Counselling, Social Counselling, Sports Facilities, Language Programmes, Health Services, Canteen

Student Residential Facilities: Yes

Special Facilities: Interactive video conferencing centre

Libraries: Three libraries in three campuses

Publications: Interaction (quarterly); Ethiopian Law Review (biannually); ECSC Newsletter

Academic Staff *1999/2000*	MEN	WOMEN	TOTAL
FULL-TIME	128	8	136
PART-TIME	–	–	11
TOTAL	–	–	**147**

Staff with doctorate: Total: **11**

Student Numbers *1999/2000*	MEN	WOMEN	TOTAL
All (Foreign Included)	1,472	166	**1,638**

Evening Students, 296 **Distance Students,** 179

GONDER COLLEGE OF MEDICAL SCIENCES

PO Box 196, Gonder
Tel: +251(8) 11-01-74
Fax: +251(8) 11-14-79
EMail: gcms@eth.healthne.org

Dean: Tesfaye Tessema

Health Sciences; Medicine; Social Sciences

KOTEBE COLLEGE OF TEACHER EDUCATION (KCTE)

PO Box 31248, Addis Ababa
Tel: +251(1) 60-09-21
Fax: +251(1) 60-09-22
EMail: ccte@telecom.net.et

Dean: Zerhihun Kebede Wudie (1994-) Tel: 251(1) 60-12-77

International Relations: Endalew Amenu

Departments

Teacher Education (Biology; Chemistry; English; Geography; Health Education; History; Mathematics Education; Native Language Education; Physical Education; Physics; Primary Education; Teacher Training) *Head*: Zerhihun Kebede, *full-time staff: 89, part-time staff: 5,392*

History: Founded 1969 as Teacher Training College. Acquired present status and title 1989.

Governing Bodies: Administrative Board

Academic Year: September to July. Also Summer sesssion, July- September

Admission Requirements: Ethiopian School Leaving Certificate Examination (ESLCE) or equivalent

Fees: (Birr): Foreign students, 24,953-29,744 per annum

Main Language(s) of Instruction: English

Accrediting Agencies: Ministry of Education

Degrees and Diplomas: *Diploma*: Education, 2 yrs; *Bachelor's Degree*: Education (BEd), 4 yrs. Also Certificate, 1 yr

Student Services: Academic Counselling, Social Counselling, Sports Facilities, Language Programmes, Handicapped Facilities, Health Services, Canteen

Student Residential Facilities: Yes

Special Facilities: Computer Centre. Language Laboratory

Libraries: Main Library with Braille section

Publications: KCTE Newsletter (annually); JOLS, Journal of Language Studies

Academic Staff *1999-2000*	MEN	WOMEN	TOTAL
FULL-TIME	86	3	**89**

Staff with doctorate: Total: **5**

Student Numbers *1999-2000*	MEN	WOMEN	TOTAL
All (Foreign Included)	4,010	1,382	**5,392**

NAZARETH TECHNICAL TEACHERS COLLEGE

PO Box 1888, Nazareth
Tel: +251(2) 11-04-00
Fax: +251(2) 11-04-80
EMail: makoto.manabe@telecom.net.et

Dean: Mesfin Terefe

Teacher Training; Technology

Gabon

INSTITUTION TYPES AND CREDENTIALS

Types of higher education institutions:

Université (University)
Institut (Institute)
Ecole (School)

School leaving and higher education credentials:

Baccalauréat
Capacité en Droit
Brevet de Technicien supérieur
Diplôme d'Etat de Sage-Femme
Diplôme de Technicien supérieur
Diplôme universitaire d'Etudes économiques (DUEE)
Diplôme universitaire d'Etudes juridiques (DUEJ)
Diplôme universitaire d'Etudes littéraires (DUEL)
Diplôme universitaire d'Etudes scientifiques (DUES)
Certificat d'Aptitude au Professorat des Collèges d'Enseignement technique
Licence
Certificat d'Aptitude au Professorat de l'Enseignement secondaire
Certificat d'Aptitude pédagogique des Lycées techniques
Diplôme d'Ingénieur
Diplôme d'Administrateur civil
Diplôme d'Administration de l'Economie et des Finances
Maîtrise
Doctorat

STRUCTURE OF EDUCATION SYSTEM

Pre-higher education:

Structure of school system:

> Primary
> Type of school providing this education: Ecole primaire
> Length of programme in years: 5
> Age level from: 6 to: 11
> Certificate/diploma awarded: Certificat d'Etudes primaires élémentaires (CEPE)

First Cycle Secondary
Type of school providing this education: Premier Cycle secondaire
Length of programme in years: 4
Age level from: 11 to: 15
Certificate/diploma awarded: Brevet d'Etudes du Premier Cycle (BEPC)

Technical Secondary
Type of school providing this education: Enseignement secondaire technique
Length of programme in years: 3
Age level from: 15 to: 18
Certificate/diploma awarded: Brevet de Technicien

Second Cycle Secondary
Type of school providing this education: Deuxième Cycle secondaire
Length of programme in years: 3
Age level from: 15 to: 18
Certificate/diploma awarded: Baccalauréat

Technical
Type of school providing this education: Enseignement Secondaire Technique
Length of programme in years: 4
Age level from: 15 to: 19
Certificate/diploma awarded: Baccalauréat technique

School education:

Primary education lasts for six years and leads to the Certificat d'Etudes primaires élémentaires (CEPE). Secondary-school education covers seven years, divided into a lower (premier) cycle lasting four years and an upper (deuxième) cycle lasting three years. On conclusion of the lower cycle, pupils obtain the Brevet d'Etudes du Premier Cycle (BEPC). During the upper cycle, pupils may specialize in Mathematics, Science or Literature. On completion of this cycle, pupils take the examinations for the Baccalauréat. Pupils who do not qualify for the Baccalauréat are awarded the Certificat de Fin d'Etudes secondaires, a record of attendance and performance in the final year. On completion of the lower cycle pupils may opt to take a 'short' or a 'long' course of technical secondary education. The former leads to the Brevet de Technicien and the latter to the Baccalauréat technique.

Higher education:

Higher education is provided by two universities: Omar Bongo University at Libreville, and the University of Science and Technology of Masuku (USTM at Franceville), as well as various independent institutions. These are all public and receive little or no subsidies from the private sector. The Universities benefit from a certain degree of autonomy. They are headed by Rectors who are solely responsible for the University. Higher education is financed exclusively by public funds.

Academic year:

Classes from: October *to:* June
Long vacation from: 1 July *to:* 30 September

Languages of instruction:

French

Stages of studies:

University level studies:

University level first stage: Premier Cycle:
The entrance requirement for degree studies is the Baccalauréat. The first phase leads, after two years study to the Diplôme universitaire d'Etudes littéraires (DUEL) in Arts and Humanities, Diplôme universitaire d'Etudes scientifiques (DUES) in Scientific subjects, Diplôme universitaire d'Etudes juridiques (DUEJ) in Law, and the Diplôme universitaire d'Etudes économiques (DUEE) in Economics. Most of these qualifications now come under the overall title of Diplôme d'Etudes universitaires générales (DEUG). Students who wish to study Law but do not hold the Baccalauréat may undertake a two-year course leading to the Capacité en Droit.

University level second stage: Deuxième Cycle:
The second stage leads, after a further year of study in Arts and Sciences, Economics and Law, to the Licence. A further year of study leads to the Maîtrise in Arts and Humanities, Law, Economics, Management, Social Communication Techniques, Economics and Finance, Juridical Sciences and General Administration. The Ecole nationale de la Magistrature trains Magistrates in four years after the Baccalauréat and in two years for holders of the Licence in Law. The titles of Ingénieur, Ingénieur informaticien, and Géographe-Aménagiste are awarded on completion of five years' study.

University level third stage: Troisième Cycle:
The Institut d'Economie et des Finances awards a Diplôme d'Administration de l'Economie et des Finances after two years' study following the Maîtrise, or after a preparatory year to those who do not hold the Maîtrise. The Ecole nationale d'Administration (advanced cycle) offers two-year training to holders of a Maîtrise following a competitive examination. Candidates are then awarded the Diplôme d'Administrateur civil (General Administration, Diplomacy, Factory Inspectorate). The Doctorat d'Etat in Medicine is awarded after six years' study. It leads to three post-doctoral specializations: Paediatrics, Surgery, and Gynaecology. A Doctorate is awarded in scientific subjects by the Université des Sciences et Techniques de Masuku.

Teacher education:

Training of pre-primary and primary/basic school teachers
Primary-school teachers are trained in teacher-training colleges. This four-year course leads to the Certificat d'Aptitude pédagogique.

Training of secondary school teachers
Secondary-school teachers are trained in three years for lower-level secondary education and five years for upper-level secondary education at the Ecole normale supérieure. These courses lead to the award of the Certificat d'Aptitude pédagogique des Collèges d'Enseignement général (CAPCEG) and the Certificat d'Aptitude au Professorat de l'Enseignement secondaire (CAPES) respectively. Technical education teachers are trained in five years advanced-level technical secondary education. They are awarded the Certificat d'Aptitude pédagogique des lycées techniques.

Training of higher education teachers
Higher-education teachers are trained abroad, since they must hold a university degree equivalent to the French Diplôme d'Etudes approfondies (DEA), according to the provisions of the Conseil Africain et Malgache pour l'Enseignement supérieur (CAMES). They generally hold a Doctorat de troisième Cycle or an Agrégation.

NATIONAL BODIES

Responsible authorities:

Ministry of Higher Education and Scientific Research (Ministère de l'Enseignement supérieur et de la Recherche scientifique)
  Minister: André Dieudonné Berre
  BP 2217
  Libreville
  Tel: +241 76-07-64
  Fax: +241 76-43-45

ADMISSIONS TO HIGHER EDUCATION

Admission to university-level studies

Name of secondary school credential required: Baccalauréat
For entry to: University

Alternatives to credentials: Capacité en Droit (for studies in law)

Foreign students admission

Admission requirements: For access to University-level studies, foreign students must hold a secondary school leaving Certificate (Baccalauréat) or its equivalent and/or obtain the approval of the teachers' Commission of the department where they wish to be admitted. For access to Postgraduate study and research, they must hold a Maîtrise or its equivalent.

Entry regulations: Foreign students must hold a visa and have financial guarantees. There is no rigid quota system.

Language requirements: Students must have a good command of French.

Application procedures:

Apply to individual institution for entry to: University

Recognition of studies and qualifications:

Studies pursued in foreign countries (bodies dealing with recognition of foreign credentials):
Commission permanente des Equivalences
  BP 17011
  Libreville

Université Omar Bongo
BP 13131
Boulevard Léon M'ba
Libreville
Tel: +241 73-20-45
Fax: +241 73-45-30
Telex: ung 5336

Multilateral agreements concerning recognition of foreign studies

Name(s) of agreement(s): Convention on the Recognition of Studies, Certificates, Diplomas, Degrees and Other Academic Qualifications in Higher Education in the African States
Year of signature: 1981

References to further information on foreign student admissions and recognition of studies

Title: Study Abroad 2000-2001
Publisher: UNESCO/IBE
Year of publication: 1999

STUDENT LIFE

Student expenses and financial aid

Bodies providing information on student financial aid:
Commission nationale des Bourses et Stages
PO Box 165
Libreville
Deals with: Grants

INTERNATIONAL COOPERATION AND EXCHANGES

Principal national bodies responsible for dealing with international cooperation and exchanges in higher education:
Ministère de l'Enseignement et de la Recherche scientifique
B.P. 2217
Libreville
Tel: +241 76-07-64
Fax: +241 76-43-45

Ministère des Affaires Etrangères, de la Coopération et des Affaires francophones
Libreville
Tel: +241 73-94-65 +241 73-94-69

GRADING SYSTEM

Usual grading system in secondary school

Full Description: Marking is on a scale of 0-20 (maximum) per subject, with no official minimum pass mark (though in practice 9 is the minimum pass mark). Overall grades at Baccalauréat are classified: très bien, bien, assez bien, passable.
Highest on scale: 20
Pass/fail level: 9
Lowest on scale: 0

Main grading system used by higher education institutions

Full Description: The Licence is graded as: très bien (very good), bien (good), assez bien (fair), passable (pass)

NOTES ON HIGHER EDUCATION SYSTEM

Data for academic year: 2000-2001
Source: International Association of Universities (IAU)

INSTITUTIONS OF HIGHER EDUCATION

UNIVERSITIES

• UNIVERSITY OMAR BONGO

Université Omar Bongo
BP 13131, Boulevard Léon M'ba, Libreville
Tel: +241 73-20-45   +241 72-69-10
Fax: +241 73-45-30   +241 73-04-17
Telex: 5336 go

Recteur: André Moussavou-Mouyama
Secrétaire général: Pierre Ndong-Meye

Faculties
Law and Economics (Economics; Law)
Letters and Human Sciences (Arts and Humanities; Social Sciences)
Medicine and Health Sciences (Health Sciences; Medicine)

History: Founded 1970 incorporating institutions which were previously part of the Fondation de l'Enseignement supérieur en Afrique Centrale. Renamed 1978. A State institution enjoying financial autonomy with some aid from France.

Academic Year: October to June (October-December; January-Easter; Easter-June)

Admission Requirements: Secondary school certificate (baccalauréat) or equivalent or entrance examination

Main Language(s) of Instruction: French

Degrees and Diplomas: *Diplôme universitaire d'Etudes économiques (DUEE)*: 2 yrs; *Diplôme universitaire d'Etudes juridiques (DUEJ)*: 2 yrs; *Diplôme universitaire d'Etudes littéraires (DUEL)*: 2 yrs; *Diplôme universitaire d'Etudes scientifiques (DUES)*: 2 yrs; *Certificat d'Aptitude au Professorat des Collèges d'Enseignement technique*: (CAPCET); *Licence*: Law; Letters, 3 yrs; Economics, 4 yrs; *Certificat d'Aptitude pédagogique des Lycées techniques*: (CAPLT); *Diplôme d'Ingénieur*: Engineering; *Maîtrise*: Letters, 1 yr following Licence; *Doctorat*: Medicine

Libraries: Central Library, c. 12,000 vols; libraries of the faculties and schools

Academic Staff *1999:* Total: c. 300

Student Numbers *1999:* Total: c. 4,800

HIGHER SCHOOL OF TEACHER TRAINING
ECOLE NORMALE SUPÉRIEURE
BP 17009, Libreville
Tel: +241 76-31-59
Fax: +241 73-20-73
Telex: uob 5336 go

Teacher Training

History: Founded 1972.

NATIONAL INSTITUTE OF MANAGEMENT
INSTITUT NATIONAL DES SCIENCES DE GESTION
BP 190, Libreville
Tel: +241 73-28-45
Fax: +241 73-20-73

Accountancy; Business and Commerce; Finance; Marketing

History: Founded 1973.

NATIONAL SCHOOL OF FORESTRY
ECOLE NATIONALE D'ETUDES FORESTIÈRES DU CAP ESTÉRIAS
BP 3960, Libreville
Tel: +241 76-83-45
Fax: +241 74-84-42

Forestry; Water Science

History: Founded 1957. Acquired present status and title 1975.

NATIONAL SCHOOL OF MAGISTRATURE
ECOLE NATIONALE DE MAGISTRATURE
BP 46, Libreville
Tel: +241 72-00-06

Justice Administration

History: Founded 1971.

NATIONAL SCHOOL OF SECRETARIAL STUDIES
ECOLE NATIONALE DE SECRÉTARIAT
BP 17014, Libreville
Tel: +241 76-18-22

Computer Science; Law; Modern Languages; Secretarial Studies

TECHNICAL TEACHER TRAINING SCHOOL
ECOLE NORMALE SUPÉRIEURE DE L'ENSEIGNEMENT TECHNIQUE
BP 3989, Libreville
Tel: +241 73-29-88
Fax: +241 73-20-73
Telex: uob 5336 go

Automotive Engineering; Civil Engineering; Mechanical Engineering; Metallurgical Engineering; Wood Technology; Technology Education (Automotive Engineering; Civil Engineering; Mechanical Engineering; Metallurgical Engineering; Technology Education; Wood Technology)

• UNIVERSITY OF SCIENCES AND TECHNIQUES OF MASUKU

Université des Sciences et Techniques de Masuku
BP 901, Franceville
Tel: +241 67-77-25   +241 67-74-49
Fax: +241 67-75-20 +241 67-74-49
Telex: 6723 go

Recteur: Jacques Lebibi (1992-) Tel: +241-67-74-49

Secrétaire général: Anselme Punga Tel: +241-67-77-35

International Relations: Jacques Lebibi

Faculties

Sciences (Biology; Chemistry; Computer Science; Geology; Mathematics; Modern Languages; Natural Sciences; Physics)

Schools

Polytechnic (Agricultural Engineering; Automation and Control Engineering; Biotechnology; Civil Engineering; Electrical Engineering; Engineering; Industrial Engineering; Industrial Maintenance; Mechanical Engineering; Technology)

History: Founded 1986, incorporating faculty and school of Université Omar Bongo.

Degrees and Diplomas: *Diplôme de Technicien supérieur:* Agricultural Engineering; Civil Engineering; Electrical Engineering; Industrial Engineering; *Diplôme universitaire d'Etudes scientifiques (DUES):* 2 yrs; *Diplôme d'Ingénieur:* Engineering; *Maîtrise:* Science

Academic Staff *1999:* Total: c. 110

Student Numbers *1999:* Total: c. 550

Gambia (The)

INSTITUTION TYPES AND CREDENTIALS

Types of higher education institutions:

University
Institute
College

School leaving and higher education credentials:

West African Examinations Council Senior Secondary School Leaving Certificate
West African Examinations Council 'A' Level
Gambia Basic Teachers' Certificate
Gambia Higher Teachers' Certificate
Gambia Primary Teachers' Certificate
Bachelor of Arts
Bachelor of Science
Bachelor of Medicine

STRUCTURE OF EDUCATION SYSTEM

Pre-higher education:

Structure of school system:

Primary
Type of school providing this education: Primary School
Length of programme in years: 6
Age level from: 7 to: 13
Certificate/diploma awarded: Primary School Leaving Certificate

Junior Secondary
Type of school providing this education: Junior Secondary School
Length of programme in years: 3
Age level from: 13 to: 16
Certificate/diploma awarded: Junior School Leaving Certificate

Senior Secondary
Type of school providing this education: Senior Secondary School
Length of programme in years: 3
Age level from: 16 to: 19

Certificate/diploma awarded: West African Examinations Council Senior Secondary School Certificate

Sixth Form
Type of school providing this education: Sixth Form
Length of programme in years: 2
Age level from: 19 to: 21
Certificate/diploma awarded: West African Examinations Council 'A' Level

School education:

Primary education lasts for six years and leads to the Primary School Leaving Certificate. Secondary education is divided into junior secondary schools which offer a three-year course leading to the Junior School Leaving Certificate, and Senior Secondary schools which offer a three-year course leading to the West African Examinations Council Senior Secondary School Certificate. This is followed by a further two years in the sixth Form leading to the West African Examinations Council 'A' levels.

Higher education:

Higher education in the Gambia is provided by the University of The Gambia, created in 1999, which comprises four faculties and Gambia College which includes four schools: Agriculture, Education, Nursing and Midwifery, and Public Health.

Main laws/decrees governing higher education:

Decree: Education Act   Year: 1963

Academic year:

Classes from: December *to:* August

Long vacation from: 1 September *to:* 30 November

Languages of instruction:

English

Stages of studies:

Non-university level post-secondary studies (technical/vocational type):

Higher technical and vocational education is offered at the Gambia Technical Training Institute which offers courses leading to the examinations of the City and Guilds of London Institute and the Royal Society of Arts. Gambia College offers courses in Agriculture, Education, Nursing and Midwifery, Public Health, Catering, Management Development and vocational training. Studies lead to Certificates and Diplomas.

University level studies:

University level first stage: *Bachelor's Degree*:
The first stage of university education leads to a Bachelor's Degree after four years of study in Humanities and Social Studies, Economics and Management Science and Nursing and Public Health and six years in Medicine and Surgery.

Teacher education:

Training of pre-primary and primary/basic school teachers
Primary school teachers are trained at the Gambia College School of Education which offers a two-year course leading to the Gambia Primary Teachers' Certificate. A three-year in-service course leading to the award of the Gambia Basic Teachers' Certificate is now offered to unqualified teachers. Admission is based on the Middle School Leaving Certificate.

Training of secondary school teachers
Secondary school teachers are trained at the Gambia College School of Education in a two-year course leading to the Gambia Higher Teachers' Certificate. Students enter with the West African Examinations Council School Certificate.

NATIONAL BODIES

Responsible authorities:

Ministry of Education
    Minister: Satang Jow
    Bedford Place Building
    Banjul
    Tel: +220 22 7236 +220 22 7646
    Fax: +220 22 8140   +220 22 7034

ADMISSIONS TO HIGHER EDUCATION

Admission to non university higher education studies

Name of secondary school credential required: West African Examinations Council Senior Secondary School Leaving Certificate

Admission to university-level studies

Name of secondary school credential required: West African Examinations Council Senior Secondary School Leaving Certificate
Minimum score/requirement: Five credits

Alternatives to credentials: Mature students

Foreign students admission

Admission requirements: Foreign students wishing to enrol at Gambia College should have qualifications equivalent to 3 passes at ordinary level GCE including English, successful completion of an entrance examination and of upgrading courses for service officers.

Entry regulations: A visa is required for non-Commonwealth citizens as well as study or residential permits for all non-Gambians.

Language requirements: Proficiency in English is required.

STUDENT LIFE

Student expenses and financial aid

Student costs:

Home students tuition fees: Minimum: 14,000 (Dalasis)
Maximum: 18,000 (Dalasis)
Foreign students tuition fees: Minimum: 2,500 (US Dollar)
Maximum: 3,000 (US Dollar)

GRADING SYSTEM

Usual grading system in secondary school

Full Description: For the West African Examinations Council Senior Secondary School Certificate: 1-9.
Highest on scale: 1
Pass/fail level: 7-8
Lowest on scale: 9

NOTES ON HIGHER EDUCATION SYSTEM

Data for academic year: 2001-2002
Source: International Association of Universities (IAU)

INSTITUTIONS OF HIGHER EDUCATION

UNIVERSITIES

UNIVERSITY OF THE GAMBIA

PO Box 3530, Administration Building, Kanifing, Serrekunda, Greater Banjul
Tel: +220 372-213
Fax: +220 395-064
EMail: unigambia@ganet.gm

Vice-Chancellor: Donald Ekong
EMail: dekong@unigambia.gm

Registrar: Emmanuel Akopan
EMail: ejakpan@unigambia.gm

Faculties

Economics and Management Sciences (Economics; Finance; Human Resources; Information Technology; Management; Marketing) *Co-Ordinator:* Sulayman Fye, *full-time staff:* 1, *part-time staff:* 4, *students:* 92

Humanities and Social Sciences (Arts and Humanities; English; French; Geography; History; Social Sciences) *Co-ordinator:* Boro Suso, *full-time staff:* 8, *part-time staff:* 2, *students:* 204

Medicine (Medicine; Nursing; Public Health; Surgery) *full-time staff:* 12, *part-time staff:* 1, *students:* 33

Science and Agriculture (Agriculture; Biology; Chemistry; Environmental Studies; Mathematics; Physics; Statistics) *Dean:* Felixtina Josnyn, *full-time staff:* 11, *part-time staff:* 3, *students:* 96

History: Founded 1999. Established by an Act of the National Assembly. Commencement of a 2-year Higher National Diploma (HND) programme in Construction Management in the Gambia Technical Training Institute, GTTI, under a franchise from South Bank University, London. With assistance from the Ministry of Health of Cuba the pre-medical programme with an enrolment of about 25 students also began September 1999.

Governing Bodies: University Council; Senate

Academic Year: December to August (December-April; May-August)

Admission Requirements: West African Senior School Certificate with five credits; General Certificate of Education with five credits

Fees: (Dddalasi): Non-Science, 14,000; Science 16,000; Medicine 18,000.

Main Language(s) of Instruction: English

International Co-operation: Saint Mary's University

Degrees and Diplomas: *Bachelor of Arts:* Development Studies, History, French, Geography, English (BA), 4; *Bachelor of Science:* Environment Science, Agriculture, Biology, Chemistry, Physics, Mathematics/Statistics (BsC), 4; *Bachelor of Medicine:* Nursing, Public Health (BsC), 4; Medicine, Surgery (MB/CHB), 6

Student Services: Academic Counselling, Social Counselling, Sports Facilities, Health Services

Special Facilities: Computer Laboratory

Libraries: Technical Training Institute Library

Academic Staff 2000: Full-Time: c. 35 Part-Time: c. 8 Total: c. 43
Staff with doctorate: Full-Time: c. 16 Part-Time: c. 2 Total: c. 18

Student Numbers 2000: All (Foreign Included): Men: c. 267 Women: c. 66 Total: c. 333
Foreign Only: Men: c. 3 Women: c. 2 Total: c. 5

OTHER INSTITUTIONS

GAMBIA COLLEGE

Brikama
Tel: +220 714

President: N.S.Z. Njie
Registrar: N.S. Manneh

Schools
Agriculture
Education
Nursing and Midwifery
Public Health

History: Founded 1978.

Ghana

INSTITUTION TYPES AND CREDENTIALS

Types of higher education institutions:

University
Polytechnic
Specialized Institution

School leaving and higher education credentials:

Senior Secondary Certificate Examination
WAEC General Certificate of Education Ordinary Level
WAEC General Certificate of Education Advanced Level
Certificate
Diploma
National Diploma
Bachelor's Degree
Bachelor of Dental Surgery
Bachelor of Medecine and Surgery
Graduate Diploma
Master's Degree
Master of Philosophy
Doctorate

STRUCTURE OF EDUCATION SYSTEM

Pre-higher education:

Duration of compulsory education:

    Age of entry: 6
    Age of exit: 15

Structure of school system:

    Primary
    Type of school providing this education: Primary School
    Length of programme in years: 6
    Age level from: 6 to: 12

    Junior Secondary
    Type of school providing this education: Junior Secondary School

Length of programme in years: 3
Age level from: 12 to: 15
Certificate/diploma awarded: Basic Education Certificate Examination (BECE)

Senior Secondary
Type of school providing this education: Senior Secondary School
Length of programme in years: 3
Age level from: 15 to: 18
Certificate/diploma awarded: Senior Secondary School Certificate (SSCE)

Technical
Type of school providing this education: Technical/Vocational School
Length of programme in years: 3
Age level from: 15 to: 18

School education:

The new educational system consists of six years' primary school (compulsory) followed by three years' junior secondary and three years' senior secondary education at the end of which pupils sit for the Senior Secondary Certificate Examination (SSCE). The six years of primary education and the three years of junior secondary school form nine years of basic education. Secondary school is followed by one year of compulsory national service.

Higher education:

The system of higher education includes universities and university colleges; polytechnics; and pre-service training institutes. All higher education institutions are under the National Council for Tertiary Education which forms an advisory and coordinating body at the national level. The Council is under the Minister of Education. Each higher institution has its own Council and its Academic Board or their equivalents. The polytechnics are now in the process of being upgraded to offer university-level courses. A new University of Development Studies has been opened in the North and the University College of Education, Winneba, has been established. Teacher training colleges are becoming tertiary institutions.

Main laws/decrees governing higher education:

Decree: PNDC Law 42   Year: 1983
Concerns: Modifies Education Act of 1961

Decree: NLC Decree 401   Year: 1969
Concerns: Universities and equivalents

Decree: Act 87, the Education Act Parts IV and V   Year: 1961
Concerns: Higher Education

Academic year:

Classes from: September *to:* June

Long vacation from: 22 May *to:* 21 August

Languages of instruction:

English

172

Stages of studies:

Non-university level post-secondary studies (technical/vocational type):

Higher technical education is provided by Regional Colleges of Applied Arts, Science and Technology (RECAAST) and Polytechnics. At the RECAAST, which include Agricultural Colleges, Health Training Institutes, Nursing Training Colleges, a School of Forestry and Teacher Training Colleges, courses generally last for three years and lead to the award of a Certificate. Polytechnics offer Certificate/Diploma courses of varying length depending on the discipline and Higher National Diplomas. These are reserved for students who have completed a Certificate or Diploma course or who have completed the former GCE ' A' level examinations. Courses are offered in Business Studies, Engineering, Fashion, Catering and Pharmaceutical Dispensing Laboratory Technology.

University level studies:

University level first stage: First Degree:

The University of Ghana and the University of Science and Technology offer two-year undergraduate courses leading to the award of the Diploma in a wide range of vocational disciplines. In addition, the University of Cape Coast offers a three-year Diploma course in Laboratory Techniques and two-year Diploma courses in Health Sciences and Basic Education.

There are two types of Bachelor Degree courses: General and Honours. Normally a Bachelor's Degree takes three or four years to obtain, depending on whether the student enrolled with GCE A levels or SSSCE grades. In Medicine and Dentistry, the first degree requires six or seven years depending on whether the student enrolled with GCE 'A' levels or SSSCEs.

University level second stage: Second Degree:

These degrees are open to graduates with the Bachelor's Degree of approved universities. Graduate Diploma courses are of two semesters' full-time or four semesters' part-time. Primary Master's and Master of Philosophy courses last for one to two years. At least two semesters must be spent studying in the University. Candidates are awarded the Graduate Diploma, Master's or Master of Philosophy Degree. The one-year course involves course work and a dissertation. For the MPhil Degree, two years of study, including a year of course work, are required, followed by research work leading to a thesis. It is possible to transfer to Mphil and PhD courses from the one-year Master's.

University level third stage: Doctorate:

The Doctorate Degree is open to graduates of approved universities with Master's or Master of Philosophy Degrees. Candidates must spend the first two years at the university. If the candidate has taken the Master's degree in the same university, this period is one year. Thereafter, subject to approval by the Board of Graduate Studies, candidates may pursue their studies outside the university. Doctorate courses (PhD) are completed entirely by research (i.e. presentation and defence of a thesis) and require a minimum of three years' study. Candidates are awarded the Doctorate Degree at the end of their studies.

The DPhil is also entirely by research and is awarded on consideration of published works of academic merit, the standard being no less than that of a PhD. Only graduates from universities with 10 years standing are eligible.

The Doctor of Medicine (MD degree) covers the medical specialities only. Conditions for the award of the MD are the same as for the D.Phil.

The degrees of LLD, DCL, DLitt and DSc may only be conferred honoris causa.

Teacher education:

Training of pre-primary and primary/basic school teachers

Primary school teacher training is the responsibility of the post-secondary teacher training colleges. Training lasts for three years after the Senior Secondary Certificate Examination at the end of which candidates are awarded the Post-Secondary Teacher's Certificate A. The curriculum of the teacher training colleges was revised to reflect changes in the content and method of basic education.

Training of secondary school teachers

The University College of Education of Winneba offers one-year courses leading to the award of the Certificate in Education for non-professional teachers in technical and vocational subjects; three-year courses for holders of the Certificate A, Specialist Certificate and two level subjects leading to the award of a Diploma; and two-year degree courses for holders of a Certificate or Diploma in educational subjects.

Training of higher education teachers

Higher education teachers are trained in two to three years at the universities where they obtain a Master's or a Doctor's degree.

Non-traditional studies:

Distance higher education

The recently created Ghana National Tertiary Level Distance Education Programme opens up access to higher education; provides an alternative, off-campus channel for tertiary education for qualified people; provides a complementary avenue to higher forms of education provided by the traditional, residential universities; provides an opportunity to those who have the requisite qualifications but have been prevented from having access to tertiary education by various circumstances; and makes the acquisition of a degree more flexible, especially for older adults (such as graduates who want to shift to new areas of studies and lifelong learners). Universities in Ghana offer some of their courses to students outside their walls. Such off-campus students study the same courses and take the same examinations as those in on-campus programmes and are awarded the same degrees when they pass their final examinations. The programme adopts a multi-media approach but the main medium for teaching is self-instructional printed materials sent to students for study. Study centres will be opened in all regional capitals where students can go to for tutorials and counselling. Student assessment is continuous and based on assignments and final examinations.

NATIONAL BODIES

Responsible authorities:

Ministry of Education
    Minister: Christopher Ameyaw-Akumfi
    Deputy Minister: Rashid Bawa
    PO Box M.45

Accra
Tel: +233(21) 662-772
Fax: +233(21) 662-718

Role of governing body: Authority responsible for the administration and financing of education at the National level.

National Council for Tertiary Education (NCTE)
Executive Secretary: Paul Effah
Deputy Executive Secretary: Alhaji Salifu Seidu
Administrative Secretary: Paul Dzadu
PO Box M. 28
Accra
Tel: +233(21) 770-194 +233(21) 770-197
Fax: +233(21) 770-194

Role of governing body: State agency dealing with higher education.

Committee of Vice-Chancellors and Principals of the Universities of Ghana
Chairman: John Sefa K. Ayim
Secretary: S.W. Opoku-Agykwa
PO Box 25
Legon
Accra
Tel: +233(21) 501-967
Fax: +233(21) 502-701
Telex: 2556 UGL GH
EMail: cvcpgh@ug.edu.gh

ADMISSIONS TO HIGHER EDUCATION

Admission to non university higher education studies

Name of secondary school credential required: Senior Secondary Certificate Examination

Other admission requirements: Compulsory National Service after secondary school

Admission to university-level studies

Name of secondary school credential required: Senior Secondary Certificate Examination
Minimum score/requirement: Minimum aggregate of 24 at the SSCE with credit passes in core English, core Mathematics, core Science and any three electives

Name of secondary school credential required: WAEC General Certificate of Education Advanced Level
Minimum score/requirement: 2 or 3 "A" levels, plus 5 "O" levels

Entrance exams required: University Entrance Examination

Other admission requirements: Compulsory National Service after secondary school

Foreign students admission

Definition of foreign student: Any student who is not a Ghanaian

Admission requirements: Foreign students should have good CGE "O" level passes (or their equivalent) in English language and four other subjects plus three "A" level passes (required subjects vary according to degree course).

Entry regulations: Foreign students with the exception of ECOWAS citizens need visas to enter Ghana. All foreign students, including ECOWAS citizens, are required to secure resident permits for the period of their study. Foreign students are required to pay their fees in convertible currency to be drawn on a American or British bank.

Health requirements: Health certificate required.

Language requirements: Good knowledge of English required for all regular university courses. English-language proficiency courses are offered as well as general orientation programmes for all freshmen.

Application procedures:

Apply to individual institution for entry to: Universities, Polytechnics, and other Institutions of Higher Education.

Application closing dates:

> *For non-university level (technical/vocational type) studies:* 30 April
> *For university level studies:* 30 April
> *For advanced/doctoral studies:* 30 April

Recognition of studies and qualifications:

Studies pursued in home country (System of recognition/accreditation): Once the higher institutions from which the credentials are awarded are recognized by the country, the credentials are also recognized. Transfer and recognition of studies and degrees exist between the institutions of a similar type, i.e. university with university, polytechnic with polytechnic.

Other information sources on recognition of foreign studies: The Academic Section of the Universities

Special provisions for recognition:

For access to non-university post-secondary studies: Credentials should be sent to the Executive Secretary, National Accreditation Board P.O.Box M28, Accra. These should be in the form of certificates.

For access to university level studies: Foreign credentials in the form of certificates should be sent to the Academic Registrar of the University. This applies to both nationals with foreign credentials and foreigners.

For access to advanced studies and research: Foreign credentials in the form of certificates, transcripts and Referee's report of two or three people should be sent to the office of the Dean of Graduate Studies of the University. This applies to both nationals and foreigners.

For the exercise of a profession: Access to the professions is subject to the recognition of credentials by the professional associations and to passing professional qualifying examinations. Foreign credentials should be sent to the Board or Institute of the individual professions. In addition, candidates should pass the professional examination conducted by the professional body.

References to further information on foreign student admissions and recognition of studies
Title: University Calendars

STUDENT LIFE

Health/social provisions
Social security for home students: No

Special student travel fares:
By air: Yes
Available to foreign students: Yes

Student expenses and financial aid

Student costs:

   Foreign students tuition fees: Minimum: 11,000,000 (Cedi)
   Maximum: 18,000,000 (Cedi)

Bodies providing information on student financial aid:
Association of African Universities
   PO Box 5744
   Accra North
   Tel: +233(21) 774-495
   Fax: +233(21) 774-821
   WWW: http://www.aau.org
The Scholarship Secretariat
   PO Box M75
   Accra
   Tel: +233(21) 665-461
   Deals with: Grants
   Category of students: All students.

Publications on student services and financial aid:

   Title: Study Abroad 2000-2001
   Publisher: UNESCO/IBE
   Year of publication: 1999

GRADING SYSTEM

Usual grading system in secondary school

Full Description: A-F; 1-9: 1 excellent; 2 very good; 3 good; 4-6 credit; 7-8 pass; 9 fail
Highest on scale: A
Pass/fail level: E
Lowest on scale: F

Main grading system used by higher education institutions

Full Description: 4-0, A-F: 4.00(80-100)=A+; 4.00(70-79)=A; 3.75=A-; 3.50=B+; 3.00=B; 2.50=B-; 2.00=C+; 1.50=C; 1.00=D; 0=F.
Highest on scale: A+
Pass/fail level: D
Lowest on scale: F

Other main grading systems

Honours Degrees: First Class; Second Class, Upper Division; Second Class, Lower Division, Pass

NOTES ON HIGHER EDUCATION SYSTEM

Data for academic year: 2000-2001
Source: University of Ghana, updated by the International Association of Universities (IAU) from IBE website, 2000

INSTITUTIONS OF HIGHER EDUCATION

UNIVERSITIES

• UNIVERSITY OF CAPE COAST (UCC)

University Post Office, Cape Coast
Tel: +233(42) 32440 +233(42) 32449
Fax: +233(42) 32484
Telex: 2552 ucc gh
Cable: University, Cape Coast
EMail: ucclib@ucc.gn.apc.org

Vice-Chancellor: Emmanuel Obeng (2001-)
Tel: +233(42) 32378 EMail: vcucc@ghana.com

Registrar: Kofi Ohene Tel: +233(42) 32139

International Relations: Y.S. Boafo Tel: +233(42) 33807

Faculties

Agriculture (Agricultural Economics; Agriculture; Animal Husbandry; Crop Production; Soil Science) *Dean:* Mensa Bonsu, *full-time staff:* 35, *students:* 655
Arts (Arts and Humanities; Classical Languages; English; French; History; Music; Native Language; Religious Studies) *Dean:* N.N Kofie, *full-time staff:* 49, *students:* 603
Education (Education; Educational Sciences; Health Sciences; Parks and Recreation; Physical Education; Primary Education; Science Education; Social Sciences; Technology Education; Vocational Education) *Dean:* D.K Fobih, *full-time staff:* 74, *students:* 3,904
Graduate Studies (Higher Education) *Dean:* C.K Brown, *full-time staff:* 2
Science (Botany; Chemistry; Mathematics; Natural Sciences; Physics; Zoology) *Dean:* K. Yangson, *full-time staff:* 41, *students:* 696
Social Sciences (Business Administration; Development Studies; Economics; Geography; Social Sciences; Sociology) *Dean:* D.K. Agyeman, *full-time staff:* 49, *students:* 2,408

Units

Consultancy (Agriculture; Educational Research; Industrial Management; Nautical Science; Tourism) *Head:* C.K Brown, *full-time staff:* 1
Laboratory Technician Course (Instrument Making; Laboratory Techniques) *Co-ordinator:* John Blay Jr., *full-time staff:* 2, *part-time staff:* 28

Institutes

Education *Director (Acting):* C.K. Akwesi, *full-time staff:* 6
Educational Planning and Administration *(IEPA)* (Educational Administration; Educational Research) *Director:* S.K. Atakpa

Centres

African Virtual University *(AVU)* (Computer Education; English) *Director:* B.K Gordor
Computer (Computer Science) *Co-ordinator:* Daniel Obuobi

Development Studies *(CDS)* (Development Studies; Economics; Environmental Studies; Rural Planning; Social Studies; Town Planning) *Director (Acting):* J.A Micah
Distance Education *(CDE) Director:* D.K Agyeman
Laser and Fibre Optics *(LAFOC)* (Laser Engineering; Optics) *Co-ordinator:* P.K Buah-Bassuah, *full-time staff:* 4
Research on Improving Quality of Primary Education in Ghana *(CRIQPEG)* (Educational Research; Primary Education) *Co-ordinator:* J.M. Dzinyela, *full-time staff:* 1

History: Founded 1962 as University College of Cape Coast, acquired present status and title 1971.

Governing Bodies: University Council

Academic Year: October to July (October-February; March-July)

Admission Requirements: General Certificate of Education/advanced level or recognized foreign equivalent, or senior secondary school certificate and entrance examination

Fees: (US Dollars): Foreign Students, 600-1500 per semester

Main Language(s) of Instruction: English

International Co-operation: University of Benin; Institute of Social Studies, The Hague; University of Strathclyde; University of Trondheim; Eastern Washington University; North Carolina State University; State University of New York; University of Northern Iowa; Longwood College; Lagos State University

Degrees and Diplomas: *Bachelor's Degree:* Agriculture (BSc); Arts (BA); Education (BEd); Science (BSc); Social Sciences, 3-4 yrs; *Graduate Diploma:* Education (PGDE), 2-3 yrs; *Master's Degree:* Arts (MA); Science (MSc), 1 yr; Education (MEd), 1-2 yrs; Philosophy (MSc), 2 yrs; *Doctorate:* Social Sciences (PhD), 2 yrs; Science (PhD), 3 yrs

Student Services: Academic Counselling, Social Counselling, Employment Services, Nursery Care, Cultural Centre, Sports Facilities, Handicapped Facilities, Health Services, Canteen

Student Residential Facilities: For 7760 students

Special Facilities: Botanical Garden. Technology Village (UCC Farm)

Libraries: Main Library, 750,000 vols

Publications: University Bulletin; University Gazette (monthly); University Calendar (Triannually)

Press or Publishing House: University Printing Press

Academic Staff 1999-2000	MEN	WOMEN	TOTAL
FULL-TIME	213	27	240
PART-TIME	–	–	50
TOTAL	–	–	**290**
STAFF WITH DOCTORATE			
FULL-TIME	103	10	**113**

Student Numbers 1999-2000	MEN	WOMEN	TOTAL
All (Foreign Included)	6,155	2,091	**8,246**
FOREIGN ONLY	6	4	10

*• UNIVERSITY OF GHANA (UG)

PO Box 25, Legon, Accra
Tel: +233(21) 501-967
Fax: +233(21) 502-701
EMail: balme@ug.gn.apc.org
Website: http://www.ug.edu.gh

Vice-Chancellor: Ivan Addae-Mensah (1996-2002)
Tel: +233(27) 554-400 EMail: a-mensah@ug.edu.gh

Registrar: A.T Konu Tel: +233(21) 500-390
EMail: asafo@gh.com

International Relations: S. Sefa-Dedeh
Tel: +233(21) 507-147 Fax: +233(21) 500-389
EMail: crspugl@gh.com

Faculties

Agriculture (Agriculture; Animal Husbandry; Crop Production; Engineering; Soil Science) *Dean:* B. Ahunu, *full-time staff:* 76, *students:* 600

Arts (Arabic; Arts and Humanities; English; French; Modern Languages; Native Language; Philosophy; Religion; Russian; Spanish; Swahili) *Dean:* J.N.D. Dodoo, *full-time staff:* 72, *students:* 3,500

Law (Constitutional Law; Environmental Studies; Family Studies; Human Rights; International Business; International Law; Law) *Dean:* A. Kuenyehia, *full-time staff:* 14, *part-time staff:* 3, *students:* 140

Science (Biochemistry; Botany; Chemistry; Computer Science; Fishery; Food Science; Geology; Marine Science and Oceanography; Mathematics; Natural Sciences; Nursing; Nutrition; Physics; Statistics; Zoology) *Dean:* W.A. Asomaning, *full-time staff:* 85, *part-time staff:* 20, *students:* 1,300

Social Studies (Archaeology; Archiving; Economics; Geography; History; Library Science; Natural Resources; Nursing; Political Science; Psychology; Social Sciences; Social Studies; Sociology) *Dean:* E. Ofori-Sarpong, *full-time staff:* 85, *part-time staff:* 15, *students:* 4,000

Colleges

Health Sciences (Dentistry; Health Sciences; Medicine) *Provost:* A.S. Ayettey, *full-time staff:* 140, *part-time staff:* 25, *students:* 520

Schools

Administration (Accountancy; Administration; Health Administration; Management; Public Administration) *Director:* S.A. Nkrumah, *full-time staff:* 43, *students:* 1,500

Communication Studies (Advertising and Publicity; Communication Studies; Public Relations; Social Psychology) *Director:* Kwame Karikari, *full-time staff:* 8, *part-time staff:* 5, *students:* 40

Medicine (Dentistry; Medicine; Radiology; Surgery) *Director:* P.K. Nyame, *full-time staff:* 47, *part-time staff:* 18, *students:* 408

Performing Arts (Dance; Music; Performing Arts; Theatre) *Director:* M.O. Owusu, *full-time staff:* 17, *students:* 420

Public Health *Director:* S. Ofusu-Amaah, *full-time staff:* 5, *students:* 25

Centres

Languages (Modern Languages) *Director:* A.A. Mante, *full-time staff:* 6, *students:* 2,700

Music and Dance *(International)* (Dance; Music) *Director:* J.N. Nketiah, *full-time staff:* 3

Rehabilitation Medicine and Therapy (Rehabilitation and Therapy)

Tropical Clinical Pharmacology and Therapeutics (Pharmacology; Physical Therapy) *Director:* F. Ofei, *full-time staff:* 2

Further Information: Also United Nations University Institute for Natural Resources in Africa (UNU/INRA). Agricultural research station. English proficiency course for foreign students

History: Founded 1948 as University College of Gold Coast, became University College of Ghana 1957, and acquired present status and title 1961.

Governing Bodies: University Council

Academic Year: August to June (August-September; May-June)

Admission Requirements: General Certificate of Education (GCE) with 5 credits including English, Mathematics, Arts and Science or West Africa School Certificate (WASC) Ordinary ('O') level and three passes at Advanced ('A') level, with a minimum grade D for one. Senior Secondary School Certificate with passes in core English, Mathematics and any 3 elective subjects, with aggregate score of 24 in the WAEC entrance examination

Fees: (US Dollars): Foreign students, 1000-3500 per semester

Main Language(s) of Instruction: English

International Co-operation: Indiana State University; Indiana University; Leiden University; London School of Hygiene and Tropical Medicine; Michigan University; North Carolina Central University; Pennsylvania State University; Southern University-Baton Rouge; Tennessee State University; Tulane University; University of Aalborg; University of Alabama, Birmingham; University of Bergen; University of Bradford; University of Brussels; University of California; University of Copenhagen; University of Leeds; University of Leicester; University of London; University of Manchester; University of Michigan; University of Pennsylvania; University of Texas at Austin; University of Virginia; Free University of Brussels

Degrees and Diplomas: *Diploma:* 4-6 semesters; *Bachelor's Degree:* Administration (BSc); Agriculture (BSc); Arts (BA); Dental Surgery (BOS); Fine Arts (BFA); Home Economies (BSc); Law (LLB); Medical Sciences (BSc); Medicine and Surgery (MBchB); Music (B.Mus); Natural Sciences (BSc); Nursing (BSc), 6-12 semesters; *Master's Degree:* Environmental Studies (Mphil), 1-2 years; Arts (Mphil); Business Administration (MBA); Law (LLM); Public Administration (MPA), a further 1-2 yrs; Philosophy (PhD), a further 2-4 yrs; *Doctorate:* (PhD), 3-7 yrs

Student Services: Academic Counselling, Social Counselling, Foreign Student Adviser, Nursery Care, Cultural Centre, Sports Facilities, Language Programmes, Handicapped Facilities, Health Services, Canteen, Foreign Student Centre

Student Residential Facilities: Yes

Special Facilities: Botanical Garden. Seismological Observatory. Drama Studio

Libraries: Balme Library, 365,000 vols

Publications: University of Ghana Reporter; University Newsletter (monthly); Vice-Chancellor's Annual Report to Congregation (annually); Campus Update (fortnightly)

Press or Publishing House: School of Communication Studies Printing Press; Institute of Adult Education Printing Press; Institute of African Studies Printing Press; Balme Library Tec

Academic Staff *1999:* Total: c. 565
Staff with doctorate: Total: c. 305

Student Numbers *1999:* All (Foreign Included): Men: c. 6,385 Women: c. 2,225 Total: c. 8,610
Foreign Only: Total: c. 220

INSTITUTE OF ADULT EDUCATION
PO Box 31, Legon, Accra
Tel: +233(21) 501-789
Fax: +233(21) 501-391
EMail: gcentre@africaonline.com.gh

Director: Kobina Asiedu (1998-2003)
EMail: iae.ad@libr.ug.edu.gh

Adult Education *full-time staff:* 22, *students:* 120

History: Founded 1948.

INSTITUTE OF AFRICAN STUDIES
PO Box 73, Legon, Accra
Tel: +233(21) 500-152 +233(21) 500-512
EMail: ias@ug.gn.apc.org

Director: Irene Odotei

African Studies *full-time staff:* 27, *students:* 3,500

History: Founded 1961.

INSTITUTE OF STATISTICAL, SOCIAL AND ECONOMIC RESEARCH
PO Box 74, Legon, Accra
Tel: +233(21) 501-182
Fax: +233(21) 500-937
EMail: isser.@gha.healthnet.org

Director: W.K. Asenko-Okyere (1998-2003)
EMail: sadaocgh@ghana.com

Economics; Social Policy; Statistics *full-time staff:* 16, *students:* 118

History: Founded 1962.

NOGUCHI MEMORIAL INSTITUTE FOR MEDICAL RESEARCH
PO Box 25, Legon, Accra
Tel: +233(21) 500-374
Fax: +233(21) 667-701
EMail: noguchi@ncs.com.gh

Director: D. Ofori-Adjei (1998-2003)
EMail: dofori-adjei@noguchi.mimcom.net

Medicine *full-time staff:* 28

History: Founded 1979.

REGIONAL INSTITUTE FOR POPULATION STUDIES
PO Box 96, Legon, Accra
Tel: +233(21) 501-070
Telex: 2164 rips gh

Director: E.O. Tawiah

Demography and Population *full-time staff:* 3, *students:* 20

History: Founded 1972.

UNIVERSITY OF GHANA COLLEGE OF HEALTH SCIENCES
PO Box 4236, Accra
Tel: +233(21) 663-062

Provost: A.S. Ayettey (1998-2003)

Schools
Dentistry *full-time staff:* 7, *part-time staff:* 3, *students:* 38
Medicine *full-time staff:* 45, *part-time staff:* 15, *students:* 370

History: Founded 1964.

*• 'KWAME NKRUMAH' UNIVERSITY OF SCIENCE AND TECHNOLOGY, KUMASI (KNUST)
University Post Office, Kumasi
Tel: +233(51) 60351
Fax: +233(51) 60137
Telex: 2555 ust gh
Cable: kumasitech, kumasi
EMail: ustlib@libr.ug.edu.gh
Website: http://www.knust.edu.gh

Vice-Chancellor: J.S.K. Ayim (1999-2002)
Tel: +233(51) 60334 EMail: jayim.knust@ighmail.com

Registrar and Secretary: Sophia Quashie-Sam
Tel: +233(51) 60331 Fax: +233(51) 60331

International Relations: G. Andy Mensah-Agboh, Senior Assistant Registrar Tel: +233(51) 60021
EMail: ust.uro@ighmail.com

Faculties
Agriculture *Dean:* A.K. Tuah
Environmental and Development Studies (Architecture; Building Technologies; Development Studies; Environmental Studies; Town Planning) *Dean:* E.A. Tackie
Pharmacy *Dean:* J.S.K. Ayim
Science (Biochemistry; Biological and Life Sciences; Chemistry; Computer Science; Mathematics; Natural Sciences; Physics) *Dean:* E. Frempong
Social Sciences (African Studies; Economics; Industrial Management; Modern Languages; Social Sciences) *Dean:* A. Owusu-Sarpong

Colleges
Art (Art Education; Ceramic Art; Design; Fine Arts; Industrial Design; Painting and Drawing; Sculpture; Textile Design) *Dean:* Joyce S. Stuber

Schools

Engineering (Agricultural Engineering; Chemical Engineering; Civil Engineering; Electrical and Electronic Engineering; Engineering; Mechanical Engineering) *Director*: F.O. Akuffo
Medical Sciences (Health Sciences; Medicine) *Director*: G.W. Brobby
Mines (Mining Engineering) *Principal*: E.A. Ofori

Institutes

Land Management and Development *(ILMAD)* (Natural Resources; Rural Planning) *Director*: R.K. Kassanga
Mining and Mineral Engineering *(IMME)* (Geological Engineering; Materials Engineering; Metallurgical Engineering; Mining Engineering) *Director*: K. Sraku-Lartey
Renewable Natural Resources *(IRNR)* (Agronomy; Fishery; Forestry; Natural Resources; Wildlife; Wood Technology) *Director*: S.J. Quashie-Sam
Technical Education *(ITE)* (Technology Education) *Director*: S. Oteng-Seifah

Centres

Technology Consultancy *(TCC)* (Technology Education) *Director*: S. Buatsi

Bureaus

Integrated Rural Development *(BIRD)* (Rural Planning) *Director*: A. Owusu-Bi

History: Founded 1951 as Kumasi College of Technology, acquired present status and title 1961.

Governing Bodies: University Council

Academic Year: September to June (September-January; March-June)

Admission Requirements: General Certificate of Education (GCE), Ordinary ('O') level, with 5 credits, including English, and General Certificate of Education Advanced ('A') level, with 2 passes. Senior Secondary School Certificate (SSCE) with passes in core English and Mathematics and three elective subjects relevant to chosen programme with a total aggregate of 22. Entrance examination

Fees: (Cedi): Foreign students, undergraduate, 11m-16m per annum; postgraduate, 12m-18m

Main Language(s) of Instruction: English

International Co-operation: University of Reading; University of Newcastle upon Tyne; University of Bradford; University of Nottingham; University of Manchester; University of Lancaster; South Bank University; Leeds Metropolitan University; Central State University, Wilberforce; Pennsylvania State University; North Carolina State University; Cornell University, New York; Florida A&M University; Southern University and A&M College; University of California; University of Virginia; Clark-Atlanta University; Washington State University; McGill University; Dalhousie University; University of Regina; Lakehead University; University of British Columbia; Technical University of Berlin; University of Dortmund; Technical University of Clausthal; University of Ulm; University of Besançon; University of Strasbourg; University of Delft; The Osmania University; University of Trondheim; University of Zimbabwe, Harare; United Nations University, Tokyo

182

Degrees and Diplomas: *Diploma*: 2 yrs; *Bachelor's Degree*: 4 yrs; *Master's Degree*: a further 2 yrs; *Doctorate*: a further 3 yrs following Master

Student Services: Academic Counselling, Nursery Care, Cultural Centre, Sports Facilities, Health Services, Canteen

Special Facilities: Botanical Garden

Libraries: Central Library, 270,562 vols; 750 periodicals. Special collections

Publications: Journal of the University of Science and Technology (3 per annum); University Calendar; Newsletter; Recorder (biannually); Annual Report (annually)

Press or Publishing House: University Printing Press. Design Press (College of Art)

Academic Staff *1999*: Total: **532**

Student Numbers 1999	MEN	WOMEN	TOTAL
All (Foreign Included)	6,843	1,730	**8,573**
FOREIGN ONLY	–	–	18

• UNIVERSITY FOR DEVELOPMENT STUDIES, TAMALE (UDS)
PO Box 1350, Tamale
Tel: +233(71) 22078
Fax: +233(71) 22080
EMail: uds@ug.gn.apc.org

Vice-Chancellor: Raymond B. Bening Tel: +233(71) 22080

Registrar (Acting): S.M. Kuu-ire

International Relations: Paul Effah

Faculties

Agriculture (Agriculture; Agronomy; Animal Husbandry; Environmental Studies; Horticulture; Irrigation; Natural Resources; Rural Planning) *Dean*: Saa J. Dittoh
Applied Sciences (Biochemistry; Biological and Life Sciences; Botany; Chemistry; Handicrafts; Modern Languages) *Dean (Acting)*: W.M. Kpikpi
Integrated Development Studies (Development Studies; Economics; History; Management; Social Studies) *Dean*: Z.M.K. Batse
Medicine and Health Sciences (Health Sciences; Medicine) *Dean*: David Nii-Amon-Kotei

Further Information: Also Branches in Nyankpala, Kintampo, Tamale, Wa, Navrongo/Bolgatanga

History: Founded 1992. First students admitted September 1993.

Governing Bodies: University Council

Academic Year: December to November (December-April; May-August; September-November)

Admission Requirements: General Certificate of Education (GCE). Ordinary ('O') level with 5 credits, including English and Mathematics, and General Certificate of Education, Advanced ('A') Level with 3 passes, and a pass in a general paper

Fees: (Cedi): Tuition, 8m-16m per annum

International Co-operation: Clemson University

Degrees and Diplomas: *Bachelor's Degree*: Arts (BA); Sciences (BSc)

Student Residential Facilities: Yes

Libraries: Total, 10,000 vols

Academic Staff *1999:* Total: **69**

Student Numbers *1999*	MEN	WOMEN	TOTAL
All (Foreign Included)	429	74	**503**

• UNIVERSITY COLLEGE OF EDUCATION OF WINNEBA (UCEW)

PO Box 25, Winneba
Tel: +233(432) 22261
Fax: +233(432) 22268
EMail: ucew@ug.gn.apc.org

Principal: Jophus Anamuah-Mensah (1998-2002)
Tel: +233(432) 22361 EMail: pucew@africaonline.com.gh

Registrar: Justice Nii Aryeetey Tel: +233(432) 22269

International Relations: Justice Nii Aryeetey

Divisions

Applied Arts and Technology (Graphic Arts; Handicrafts; Technology Education) *Dean*: J.K.N. Sackey
General Culture and Social Studies (Cultural Studies; Social Studies) *Dean*: S.M. Quartey
Languages (Modern Languages) *Dean*: L. Koranteng
Science (Natural Sciences; Science Education) *Dean*: H.A. Brown-Acquaye
Specialized and Professional Studies in Education (Education; Special Education) *Dean*: J.K. Aboagye

Institutes

Educational Development and Extension *(Distance and continuing education) Director*: S.K.E. Mensah, *full-time staff: 9, students:* 192

Centres

Basic Education *Co-ordinator*: R. Eshun
Educational Policy Studies (Educational Sciences)
Educational Resources *Co-ordinator*: R.K. Biney
School and Community Science and Technology Studies *(SACOST)* (Educational Sciences; Educational Technology; Social and Community Services)

History: Founded 1992, merging seven diploma-awarding colleges.

Academic Year: October to July (October-February; March-July)

Admission Requirements: General Certificate of Education (GCE) with 5 Ordinary ('O') levels at grade 6; Teachers' Certificate ('A'); at least 2 yrs' teaching experience, and entrance examination

Fees: (Cedi): Tuition, 100,000 per annum; foreign students, (US Dollars): 3,928

Main Language(s) of Instruction: English

International Co-operation: University of New York; Eastern Washington University

Degrees and Diplomas: *Certificate*: Education, 1 yr; *Diploma*: 3 yrs; *Bachelor's Degree*: Education (BEd), a further 2 yrs

Student Services: Social Counselling, Sports Facilities, Handicapped Facilities, Health Services, Canteen

Libraries: Osagyefo Library and Kumasi Centre Library, 65,011 vols; 567 periodicals

Publications: Ghana Educational Media and Technology Association (GEMTA) Journal; Journal of Special Education

Academic Staff *1999:* Total: **205**

Student Numbers *1999*	MEN	WOMEN	TOTAL
All (Foreign Included)	–	2,597	**2,597**

OTHER INSTITUTIONS

• GHANA INSTITUTE OF MANAGEMENT AND PUBLIC ADMINISTRATION

PO Box 50, Achimota, Accra
Tel: +233(21) 401-681   +233(21) 401-682   +233(21) 401-338
Fax: +233(21) 405-805
Telex: 2551 gimpa gh
EMail: gimpa@excite.com
Website: http://www.gimpa-edu.org

Director-General/Rector: Stephen Adei (1999-)
Tel: +233(21) 405-801

Director of Administration and Finance: E.A. Cooper
Tel: +233(21) 400-457 Fax: +233(21) 400-457

International Relations: Mercy Bampo Addo
Tel: +233(21) 402-381

Divisions

Consultancy Services (Management)
Human Resources and Private Sector Development (Human Resources; Management; Private Administration)
Public Management and Strategic Studies (Management; Public Administration)

Colleges
Tutorial College

Centres
Distance Learning *(DLC)* (Distance Education)

Graduate Schools
Management

History: Founded 1961

Guinea

INSTITUTION TYPES AND CREDENTIALS

Types of higher education institutions:

Université (University)
Institut supérieur (Higher Institute)
Institut Polytechnique (Polytechnical Institute)

School leaving and higher education credentials:

Baccalauréat 2ème Partie
Diplôme de Technicien supérieur
Diplôme d'Etudes universitaires générales (DEUG)
Diplôme d'Etudes Approfondies (DEA)
Diplôme d'Etudes supérieures (DES)
Diplôme d'Ingénieur
Licence
Maîtrise
Diplôme d'Etat de Docteur

STRUCTURE OF EDUCATION SYSTEM

Pre-higher education:

Duration of compulsory education:

Age of entry: 7
Age of exit: 13

Structure of school system:

Primary
Type of school providing this education: Primary School
Length of programme in years: 6
Age level from: 7 to: 13
Certificate/diploma awarded: Certificat d'Etudes primaires élémentaires (CEPE)

First Cycle Secondary
Type of school providing this education: Collège
Length of programme in years: 4
Age level from: 13 to: 17
Certificate/diploma awarded: Brevet d'Etudes du premier Cycle (BEPC)

Second Cycle Secondary
Type of school providing this education: Lycée
Length of programme in years: 3
Age level from: 17 to: 20
Certificate/diploma awarded: Baccalauréat Deuxième Partie

Vocational
Type of school providing this education: Ecole professionnelle (B type)
Length of programme in years: 3
Age level from: 16 to: 18
Certificate/diploma awarded: Brevet d'Etudes professionnelles (BEP)

School education:

Primary education lasts for six years leading to the Certificat d'Etudes primaires élémentaires (CEPE). First cycle secondary education lasts for four years and is taken at a Collège. It leads to the Brevet d'Etudes du premier Cycle (BEPC). The second cycle lasts for three years and takes place in a Lycée. It leads to the Baccalauréeat 1ère partie (première) and the Baccalauréat 2ème partie the following year (terminale). Students specialize in Experimental Sciences, Mathematics or Social Sciences. Students must pass an entrance examination to enter university. Technical and vocational education lasts three years and leads to the Brevet d'Etudes professionnelles (BEP).

Higher education:

Higher education is provided by two universities and three higher institutes. Higher education institutions are under the responsibility of the Ministère de l'Enseignement supérieur et de la Recherche scientifique.

Academic year:

Classes from: October *to:* June
Long vacation from: 1 July *to:* 15 September

Languages of instruction:

French

Stages of studies:

Non-university level post-secondary studies (technical/vocational type):

National professional schools (A type) train middle-level personnel who have completed Grade 13 and passed an entrance examination. Training lasts three years and leads to the Brevet de Technicien supérieur.

University level studies:

University level first stage: DEUG, Licence:

A Diplôme d'Etudes universitaires générales (DEUG) is awarded after two years in Arts and Humanities. The Licence is awarded after four years and the Diplôme d'Ingénieur after four to five years.

University level second stage: Maîtrise, DES, DEA:
A further year beyond the Licence leads to the Maîtrise/Diplôme d'Etudes supérieures (DES) in various fields or to a Diplôme d'Etudes approfondies (DEA) in Business Administration. Candidates must write a dissertation. A Diplôme de Docteur en Médecine and Docteur en Pharmacie is conferred after six and five years of study respectively.

University level third stage: Doctorat:
This is the third cycle of higher education. Entry to the course is based on the Diplôme d'Etudes supérieures/Maîtrise and it lasts for at least two years. Students must complete a research project and submit a thesis.

Teacher education:

Training of pre-primary and primary/basic school teachers
Primary teacher training colleges (Ecoles nationales d'Instituteurs) offer three-year courses leading to the Certificat d'Aptitude à l'Enseignement élémentaire to those who have reached Baccalauréat level.

Training of secondary school teachers
Secondary school teachers who hold the DEUG are trained in one year at the Institut supérieur des Sciences de l'Education where they obtain a Certificat d'Aptitude. Lycée teachers and ENI teachers must hold a Maîtrise before embarking on the one-year course. Vocational school teachers are trained in two years at the Ecole normale de l'Enseignement technique. Admission is through an entrance examination and the course leads to the Certificat d'Enseignement professionnel.

Training of higher education teachers
Higher education teachers must hold a Diplôme d'Etudes approfondies or a Doctorat.

Non-traditional studies:

Distance higher education
Distance education consists in radio courses produced by the Service national de Télé-enseignement.

Lifelong higher education
Decentralized lifelong education has been developed with the creation of regional and prefectoral centres to upgrade the knowledge of school teachers. Courses last between three and nine months.

NATIONAL BODIES

Responsible authorities:
Ministry of Higher Education and Scientific Research (Ministère de l'Enseignement supérieur et de la Recherche scientifique)
    Minister: Eugène Camara
    PO Box 964
    Conakry

Tel: +224 44-19-50   +224 44-37-02
Fax: +224 41-31-45

ADMISSIONS TO HIGHER EDUCATION

Admission to non university higher education studies

Name of secondary school credential required: Baccalauréat 2ème Partie

Admission to university-level studies

Name of secondary school credential required: Baccalauréat 2ème Partie

Recognition of studies and qualifications:

Studies pursued in foreign countries (bodies dealing with recognition of foreign credentials):
Direction de l'Enseignement supérieur, Ministère de l'Enseignement supérieur et de la Recherche scientifique
   PO Box 964
   Conakry
   Tel: +224 44-19-50   +224 44-37-02
   Fax: +224 41-31-45

Multilateral agreements concerning recognition of foreign studies

Name(s) of agreement(s): Convention on the Recognition of Studies, Certificates, Diplomas, Degrees and Other Academic Qualifications in Higher Education in the African States
Year of signature: 1981

GRADING SYSTEM

Usual grading system in secondary school

Full Description: 0-20: 16-20 très bien; 14-15 bien; 12-13 assez bien; 10-11 passable; 0-10 fail
Highest on scale: 20
Pass/fail level: 11-10
Lowest on scale: 0

Main grading system used by higher education institutions

Full Description: 0-20: 16-20 très bien; 14-15 bien; 12-13 assez bien; 10-11 passable; 0-10 fail
Highest on scale: 20
Pass/fail level: 11-10
Lowest on scale: 0

NOTES ON HIGHER EDUCATION SYSTEM

Data for academic year: 2000-2001
Source: International Association of Universities (IAU), updated from IBE website, 2001

INSTITUTIONS OF HIGHER EDUCATION

UNIVERSITIES

PUBLIC INSTITUTIONS

UNIVERSITY OF CONAKRY

Université de Conakry
BP 1147, Conakry
Tel: +224 46-57-82
Fax: +224 41-48-01

Recteur: Mohamed Lamine Kaba (1991-)
Secrétaire général: Aliou V. Dalio
International Relations: N' Faly Kouyaté

Faculties
Law, Economics and Management (Economics; Law; Management)
Letters and Human Sciences (Arts and Humanities; English; French; Geography; History; Philosophy; Sociology; Spanish)
Medicine and Pharmacy (Biochemistry; Dentistry; Medicine; Paediatrics; Pharmacy; Public Health)
Science (Biochemistry; Biology; Chemistry; Energy Engineering; Mathematics; Microbiology; Natural Sciences; Physics; Physiology; Zoology)

Institutes
Polytechnic (Chemical Engineering; Civil Engineering; Electrical Engineering; Engineering; Food Technology; Technology; Telecommunications Engineering; Telecommunications Services)

Centres
Applied Technology (Technology)
Computer Science
English Studies *(CELA)* (English)
Environmental Studies and Research (Environmental Studies)
French Studies *(CELF)*

Further Information: Also 2 University Hospitals

History: Founded 1962 as Institut Polytechnique, became University 1984. Acquired present status 1989. A State institution under the supervision of the Ministry of Education.
Governing Bodies: Conseil d'Administration; Conseil de l'Université
Academic Year: September to June (September-January; February-June)
Admission Requirements: Secondary school certificate (baccalauréat) and competitive entrance examination
Main Language(s) of Instruction: French

Degrees and Diplomas: *Diplôme de Technicien supérieur*: Computer Science (DTSI), 3 1/2 yrs; *Diplôme d'Etudes universitaires générales (DEUG)*: Human Sciences; *Diplôme d'Etudes Approfondies (DEA)*: Business Administration; Economics; Law; Management; *Diplôme d'Ingénieur*: Engineering, 5 yrs; *Licence*: 3 yrs; *Maîtrise*: 4 yrs; *Diplôme d'Etat de Docteur*: Pharmacy, 5 yrs; Medicine, 6 yrs

Student Residential Facilities: Yes
Special Facilities: Zoo. Meteorology Station. Radiotelescope. Audiovisual Centre
Libraries: Central Library, c. 23,000 vols; libraries of the faculties and departments, c. 11,730
Publications: Bulletin de la Recherche (monthly); Guinée Médicale (quarterly); Annales de l'Université (annually)
Press or Publishing House: Service des Editions Universitaires
Academic Staff *1999*: Full-Time: c. 340 Part-Time: c. 110 Total: c. 450
Student Numbers *1999:* Total: c. 4,685

UNIVERSITY OF KANKAN

Université de Kankan
BP 203, Kankan
Tel: +224 71-20-93

Recteur: Sékou Konaté
Secrétaire général: Aboubacar Cissé
International Relations: Martin Koïvogui

Faculties
Natural Sciences (Mathematics and Computer Science; Natural Sciences)
Social Sciences

History: Founded 1963 as school, became Institut polytechnique 1967 and acquired present status and title 1984. A State institution under the supervision of the Ministry of Education.
Academic Year: October to June (October-December; January-March; April-June)
Admission Requirements: Secondary School Certificate (baccalauréat) and competitive entrance examination
Main Language(s) of Instruction: French
Degrees and Diplomas: *Diplôme d'Etudes supérieures (DES)*: 5 yrs
Student Residential Facilities: Yes
Academic Staff *1999:* Total: c. 75
Student Numbers *1999:* Total: c. 1,050

OTHER INSTITUTIONS

PUBLIC INSTITUTIONS

INSTITUTE OF AGRICULTURE AND VETERINARY MEDICINE
Institut supérieur agronomique et vétérinaire Valéry Giscard d'Estaing
BP 131, Faranah
Tel: +224 81-02-15
Telex: 22331/mdec/ge

Departments
Agriculture
Rural Engineering (Agricultural Engineering)
Stockraising and Veterinary Medicine (Cattle Breeding; Veterinary Science)
Waters and Forestry (Forestry; Water Science)

History: Founded 1978, acquired present status and title 1991

INSTITUTE OF EDUCATIONAL SCIENCES OF MANÉAH
Institut supérieur des Sciences de l'Education de Manéah
BP 795, Conakry

Departments
Continuing Education and Research (Educational Research; Literacy Education) *Head*: Adrian Koffa Kamano, *full-time staff:* 8, *students:* 14
Educational Administration *Head*: Dian Gongoré Djallo, *full-time staff:* 10, *students:* 212
Educational Sciences *Director*: Amadou Tidjiani Diallo, *full-time staff:* 44, *part-time staff:* 8, *students:* 429

Teacher Training (Secondary Education; Teacher Training) *Head*: Lansana Camara, *full-time staff:* 23, *part-time staff:* 4, *students:* 139
Teacher Training Education (Staff Development; Teacher Trainers Education; Teacher Training) *Head*: Amadou Camara, *full-time staff:* 3, *part-time staff:* 4, *students:* 61

History: Founded 1991 by the transformation of the "Ecole Normale Supérieure ".
Governing Bodies: Conseil d' Administration; Conseil de l' Institut
Academic Year: October to July
Admission Requirements: University degree (Maîtrise) and entrance examination. Professional experience may also be required in some sections
Main Language(s) of Instruction: French
International Co-operation: University of Quebec at Montreal
Student Services: Sports Facilities, Health Services, Canteen
Student Residential Facilities: For 300 students
Libraries: Main Library, 3,500 vols
Publications: Faisceau, Educational Sciences (biannually)

Academic Staff 1999-2000	MEN	WOMEN	TOTAL
FULL-TIME	40	4	44
PART-TIME	8	–	8
TOTAL	48	4	52

Staff with doctorate: Total: **16**

Student Numbers 1999-2000	MEN	WOMEN	TOTAL
All (Foreign Included)	399	23	**422**

Distance Students, 635

INSTITUTE OF MINING AND GEOLOGY OF BOKÉ
Institut supérieur des Mines et Géologie de Boké
Boké
Geology; Mining Engineering

History: Founded 1991

Kenya

INSTITUTION TYPES AND CREDENTIALS

Types of higher education institutions:

University
College
Institute
Teachers College
Polytechnic

School leaving and higher education credentials:

Kenya Certificate of Secondary Education
Diploma
Bachelor's Degree
Bachelor of Arts
Bachelor of Education
Bachelor of Science
Bachelor of Technology
Bachelor of Veterinary Medicine
Doctor of Medicine
Postgraduate Diploma
Master's Degree
Master of Philosophy
Doctor's Degree

STRUCTURE OF EDUCATION SYSTEM

Pre-higher education:

Duration of compulsory education:

   Age of entry: 6
   Age of exit: 14

Structure of school system:

   Primary
   Type of school providing this education: Primary School
   Length of programme in years: 8

Age level from: 6 to: 14
Certificate/diploma awarded: Kenya Certificate of Primary Education (KCPE)

Secondary
Type of school providing this education: Secondary School
Length of programme in years: 4
Age level from: 14 to: 18
Certificate/diploma awarded: Kenya Certificate of Secondary Education (KCSE)

School education:

A new system of education, known as the 8-4-4 system, was introduced in 1985. Under this system, eight years of primary schooling (leading to the Kenya Certificate of Primary Education) are followed by four years of secondary schooling (leading to the Kenya Certificate of Secondary Education (KCSE)) and four years of first degree studies at university. This scheme replaces one which was based on the English pattern culminating in A levels and a three-year first degree course. The introduction of the 8-4-4 education system has led to tremendous changes in the secondary school curriculum. This is in line with the need for a broad-based curriculum that prepares students for self-reliance, vocational training and further education. In 1990, the first KCSE students entered university to begin four years of study for a general degree. The KCSE is administered by the Kenya National Examinations Council.

Higher education:

Higher education is offered in public universities that have been granted a royal charter by the Commission for Higher Education (some of them with constituent colleges), private institutions with a charter (fully accredited), private universities with a letter of Interim Authority, and private institutions without a charter. Universities are autonomous. All administrative functions are independently managed through University Councils. Though autonomous, universities receive funding from the Ministry of Education. Alongside these universities, there are several private institutions, without a charter, offering degree courses in Kenya. All of them, except the United States International University, are theologically-oriented. These universities are advised by the Commission for Higher Education to diversify their curricula to meet the needs of Kenyan society. They raise funds from their own sources and do not receive any grants from the State. Apart from the universities, there are a number of post-secondary institutions offering training at diploma and certificate levels. In the field of teacher training, these include diploma colleges for the training of non-graduate secondary school teachers, and teacher training colleges for primary school teachers. For technical education they include national polytechnics, Institutes of technology and technical training institutes. In addition to these, a number of government ministries also offer three years' professional training at diploma level for their middle-level manpower requirements.

Main laws/decrees governing higher education:

Decree: Universities Act   Year: 1985
Concerns: Universities, Colleges

Academic year:

Classes from: October *to:* July

Long vacation from: 1 August *to:* 30 September

Languages of instruction:

English

Stages of studies:

Non-university level post-secondary studies (technical/vocational type):

Institutes of technology have been set up through local and provincial initiatives and they provide training for school leavers with the Kenyan Certificate of Secondary Education, equipping them for employment in medium and large-scale industry. The Government, through the Ministry of Technical Training and Technology, provides some financial assistance as well as soliciting aid from willing donors to establish such institutions. Courses last between two and four years and cover subjects such as construction, engineering, business studies, textiles, agriculture, etc. Technical training institutes offer training at both Craft and Diploma level. The national polytechnics offer Certificate, Diploma and Higher Diploma courses.

University level studies:

University level first stage: *Bachelor's Degree*:
At the University of Nairobi, Bachelor's Degrees with Honours (there are no Ordinary degrees) are generally obtained four years after entering with KCSE, including those in Law and Engineering; Veterinary Medicine takes five years, and Architecture and Medicine six years. At Kenyatta University, most students read for a Bachelor of Education (BEd).

University level second stage: *Master's Degree*:
At the University of Nairobi, Master's Degrees in Architecture, Humanities, Law, Commerce, Science, Engineering, Medicine and Education take between one and three years' further study after the Bachelor's Degree. Kenyatta University offers a two-year Master's Degree.

University level third stage: *Doctorate*:
Holders of a Master's Degree need a minimum of two years' research to obtain a PhD. Kenyatta University offers a one-year Postgraduate Diploma in Education.

Teacher education:

Training of pre-primary and primary/basic school teachers
There are twenty primary teachers' colleges. All students admitted to teacher training colleges must hold the Kenyan Certificate of Secondary Education and have completed four years of secondary education. The teacher training course lasts two years, at the end of which students are awarded a P1, P2 or P3 Certificate, depending on their success in centrally set examinations.

Training of secondary school teachers
Training of secondary school teachers is carried out at two levels. In universities, graduate teachers are trained in four years for the Bachelor of Education Degree (BEd). Graduates holding a BA, BSc or BCom take a one-year post-graduate diploma course in education. Teachers are also trained at two diploma colleges. The three-year course leads to a Diploma in Education. Kenyatta University is a major teacher training institution. It has begun an in-service Postgraduate Diploma programme.

Training of higher education teachers
There is no formal training for higher education teachers who wish to teach in universities. Candidates must hold a first class or upper second class Honours Degree, followed by a Master's Degree.

Non-traditional studies:

Distance higher education
The University of Nairobi offers an external degree programme for the Bachelor of Education in Arts-based subjects.

Higher education training in industry
A number of government Ministries offer three years' professional training at diploma level for their middle-level manpower requirements.

Other forms of non-formal higher education
The University of Nairobi offers external study via six centres located throughout Kenya. Non-degree external study offerings include Community Education, Continuing Education, Cultural programmes, Information and Public Relations programmes, and Leadership and Management training. Instruction and examinations are administered by the University of Nairobi and Kenyatta University and the degree is awarded by the University of Nairobi.

NATIONAL BODIES

Responsible authorities:
Ministry of Education
    Minister: Stephen Kalonzo Musyoka
    Permanent Secretary: W.K.K. Kimalat
    Senior Deputy Director: J.S. O'Bonyo
    PO Box 30040
    Nairobi
    Tel: +254(2) 334-411
    Fax: +254(2) 214-287

Commission for Higher Education
    Secretary: J. Irina
    PO Box 54999
    Nairobi
    Tel: +254(2) 228-753
    Fax: +254(2) 222-218
    Cable: comhigh
    EMail: che@arec.or.ke

    Role of governing body: Regulates and coordinates university and post-secondary education and training. Responsible for accreditation of private universities and post-secondary institutions.

ADMISSIONS TO HIGHER EDUCATION

Admission to non university higher education studies

Name of secondary school credential required: Kenya Certificate of Secondary Education
For entry to: non-university post-secondary programmes

Other admission requirements: Apprenticeship programmes are organized by industries for their employees. Progression depends on passing government trade tests at various levels.

Admission to university-level studies

Name of secondary school credential required: Kenya Certificate of Secondary Education
Minimum score/requirement: C+ in at least ten subjects.
For entry to: University level studies

Alternatives to credentials: Under the Mature Age Scheme, candidates over 25 who do not meet entry requirements may take an entrance examination.

Foreign students admission

Admission requirements: Foreign students should have qualifications equivalent to the Cambridge High School Certificate, GCE or East African Certificate of Education at 'A' level; special one-year courses are arranged under the Mature Age Scheme to allow students over 25 not meeting university requirements to take the entrance examination.

Language requirements: Good knowledge of English is essential.

Application procedures:

Apply to national body for entry to: Universities

Apply to: Joint Admissions Board
PO Box 30197
Nairobi

Recognition of studies and qualifications:

Studies pursued in foreign countries (bodies dealing with recognition of foreign credentials):
Commission for Higher Education
PO Box 54999
Nairobi
Tel: +254 (2) 228-753
Fax: +254 (2) 222-218
Cable: comhigh
EMail: che@arec.or.ke

References to further information on foreign student admissions and recognition of studies

Title: University calendars, catalogues or student's guides

STUDENT LIFE

Student expenses and financial aid

Student costs:

Home students tuition fees: Minimum: 40,000 (Kenyan Shilling)
Maximum: 450,000 (Kenyan Shilling)
Foreign students tuition fees: Maximum: 450,000 (Kenyan Shilling)

Bodies providing information on student financial aid:

African Network of Scientific and Technological Institutions (ANSTI)
PO Box 30592
Nairobi

Category of students: Graduates from ANSTI States who are proficient in French and English

Publications on student services and financial aid:

Title: Study Abroad 2000-2001
Publisher: UNESCO/IBE
Year of publication: 1999

INTERNATIONAL COOPERATION AND EXCHANGES

Principal national bodies responsible for dealing with international cooperation and exchanges in higher education:

Commission for Higher Education
PO Box 54999
Nairobi
Tel: +254 (2) 228-753
Fax: +254 (2) 222-218
Cable: comhigh
EMail: che@arec.or.ke

Ministry of Education
PO Box 30040
Nairobi
Tel: +254(2) 334-411
Fax: +254(2) 214-287
Telex: Education

GRADING SYSTEM

Usual grading system in secondary school

Full Description: In the Kenyan Certificate of Secondary Education candidates are graded on a twelve-point scale as follows: A,A- (distinction/very good); B+,B,B- (credit/good); C+,C,C- (average); D+,D,D- (fair); E (poor).
Highest on scale: A
Lowest on scale: E

Main grading system used by higher education institutions

Full Description: A=70%-100% (First Class Honours), B=60%-69% (Second Class Honours (upper division)), C=50%-69% (Second Class Honours (lower division)), D=40%-49% (Pass), E=0%-39% (Fail).
Highest on scale: A
Pass/fail level: D (for Medicine & Veterinary Medicine : C)
Lowest on scale: E

Other main grading systems

For national polytechnics, institutes of technology: Distinction 70%; Credit 50%-69%; Pass 40%-49%; Fail Below 40%

NOTES ON HIGHER EDUCATION SYSTEM

A major development in the universities' financing has been the introduction of cost-sharing, under which all Kenya nationals are entitled to an annual maximum loan of Kes 1025, repayable when the student starts working, after a grace period.

Data for academic year: 2000-2001
Source: Commission for Higher Education, Nairobi, 2001

INSTITUTIONS OF HIGHER EDUCATION

UNIVERSITIES AND UNIVERSITY LEVEL INSTITUTIONS

PUBLIC INSTITUTIONS

• EGERTON UNIVERSITY

PO Box 536, Njoro
Tel: +254(37) 616-20
Fax: +254(37) 615-27
Telex: (037) 61620 nakuru
Cable: university njoro
EMail: egerton@users.africaonline.co.ke

Head: Ezra Maritim Tel: +254(37) 614-54

Registrar (Academic): Nephat J. Kathuri
Tel: +254(37) 613-32

Faculties
Agriculture (Agriculture; Agronomy; Animal Husbandry; Botany; Horticulture; Natural Resources) *Dean:* F.M. Itulya
Arts and Social Sciences (Anthropology; Arts and Humanities; Geography; History; Linguistics; Literature; Modern Languages; Philosophy; Religious Studies; Social Sciences; Sociology) *Dean (Acting):* C. Demese
Education and Human Resources (Curriculum; Pedagogy; Psychology) *Dean:* A.M. Sindabi
Engineering and Technology (Engineering; Technology)
Environmental Studies and Natural Resources (Environmental Studies; Natural Resources)
Science (Botany; Chemistry; Computer Science; Mathematics; Natural Sciences; Physics; Zoology) *Dean:* E.M. Wathuta

Schools
Continuing Education

Centres
Women's Studies and Gender Analysis (Women's Studies)
Director: R.A. Mwonya

History: Founded 1939 as Egerton Agricultural College, became a University College of University of Nairobi 1986, and acquired present status and title 1987.
Governing Bodies: University Council
Academic Year: September to May
Admission Requirements: Kenya Certificate of Secondary Education (KCSE) or equivalent
Main Language(s) of Instruction: English
International Co-operation: Various institutions in: USA, United Kingdom, Italy, Eastern Africa and the Commonwealth on joint research, secondment of academic staff, and exchange of students and staff

Degrees and Diplomas: *Diploma:* 4 yrs; *Bachelor of Arts:* (BA), 4 yrs; *Bachelor of Science:* (BSc), 4 yrs; *Master's Degree:* a further 2 yrs
Student Residential Facilities: For over 90% of the students
Libraries: c. 90,000 vols
Press or Publishing House: Education Media Centre (EMC)
Academic Staff *1999:* Total: c. 530
Student Numbers: Total: c. 7,280

• INTERNATIONAL CENTRE OF INSECT PHYSIOLOGY AND ECOLOGY (ICIPE)

PO Box 30772, Nairobi
Tel: +254(2) 802-501 +254(2) 861-680
Fax: +254(2) 803-360
EMail: icipe@africaonline.co.ke; icipe@cgnet.com
Website: http://www.icipe.org

Director: Hans Herren (1994-)
Director for Administration: Tina Kuklenski
International Relations: Mudiumbula T. Futa

Units
Animal Rearing and Quarantine
Biomathematics (Biology; Geography (Human); Mathematics; Statistics)

Departments
Behavioural and Chemical Ecology *(BCE)* (Chemistry; Ecology)
Molecular Biology and Biotechnology *(MBB)* (Biotechnology; Molecular Biology)
Population Ecology and Ecosystems Science *(PEES)* (Ecology; Environmental Studies)
Social Sciences *(SSD)*

History: Founded 1970 as a company. Acquired present status and title in mid-80's. Campuses in Nairobi, Kenya West Coast, Ethiopia.
Governing Bodies: Council; ARPIS Academic Board
Fees: (US Dollars): c. 1000 per annum. Scholarships provided for ARPIS students
Main Language(s) of Instruction: English
International Co-operation: Co-operation with 30 African universities
Student Residential Facilities: For c. 100 students
Special Facilities: Biosystematics Unit
Libraries: Information Resource Centre
Publications: Insect Science and its Applications
Press or Publishing House: ICIPE Science Press

*• JOMO KENYATTA UNIVERSITY OF AGRICULTURE AND TECHNOLOGY
PO Box 62000, Nairobi
Tel: +254(2) 1515-2711
Fax: +254(2) 1515-2164
Cable: thika
EMail: jku-lib@nbnet.co.ke
Website: http://www.jkuat.ac.ke

Vice-Chancellor: Ratemo W. Michieka (1994-)
Tel: +254(2) 1515-2165 EMail: jku-vc@nbnet.co.ke

Deputy-Vice-Chancellor (Academic Affairs): Henry M. Thairu Tel: +254(2) 1515-2053 EMail: dvcaca@nbnet.co.ke

Faculties
Agriculture (Agriculture; Crop Production; Engineering; Food Science; Horticulture) *Dean*: Caleb Nindo, *full-time staff:* 62, *students:* 617
Engineering (Architecture; Civil Engineering; Electrical and Electronic Engineering; Engineering; Mechanical Engineering) *Dean*: P. Kioni, *full-time staff:* 105, *part-time staff:* 84, *students:* 808
Science (Botany; Chemistry; Mathematics; Natural Sciences; Physics; Statistics; Zoology) *Dean*: Mabel Imbuga, *full-time staff:* 124, *students:* 790

Programmes
Continuing Education *Head*: S.M. Kangethe, *full-time staff:* 5, *part-time staff:* 19, *students:* 67

Schools
Architecture and Building Sciences (Architecture; Building Technologies) *Director*: P.G. Ngunjiri

Institutes
Computer Science and Information Technology (Computer Science; Information Technology) *Director*: Juma Oketch, *full-time staff:* 8, *part-time staff:* 11
Energy and Environmental Technology (Energy Engineering; Environmental Engineering) *Director*: F.G. Agong, *full-time staff:* 2
Human Resources Development (Human Resources) *Director*: L. A. Oyugi, *full-time staff:* 12, *part-time staff:* 8, *students:* 23

Centres
Biotechnology *Director*: Esther Kahangi, *full-time staff:* 3, *part-time staff:* 2, *students:* 4
Enterprise Development (Business and Commerce) *Director*: Roselyn Gakure, *students:* 24

Further Information: Also Student (Monbusho) Programme in Japan

History: Founded 1981, became Constituent College of Kenyatta University 1988. Acquired present status of University 1994.

Governing Bodies: University Council; University Management Board; University Senate

Academic Year: March to March (March-July; August-December; January-March)

Admission Requirements: Kenya Certificate of Secondary Education (K.S.C.E.)

Fees: (K. Shillings): 280,000-415,000 per annum

Main Language(s) of Instruction: English

International Co-operation: Okayama University; University of Sunderland; Makerere University

Degrees and Diplomas: *Diploma*: 3 yrs; *Bachelor's Degree*: Architecture (BScArch), 6 yrs; *Bachelor of Science*: (BSc), 4 yrs; Engineering (BScE), 5 yrs

Student Services: Academic Counselling, Social Counselling, Employment Services, Nursery Care, Cultural Centre, Sports Facilities, Health Services, Canteen

Student Residential Facilities: For 2500 students

Special Facilities: Botanic Garden

Libraries: Jomo Kenyatta University Library

Publications: Agritechnews (quarterly); Journal of Architecture (biannually); Journal of Agriculture, Science and Technology; Journal of Civil Engineering (annually)

Academic Staff *1999-2000:* Total: c. 305

Staff with doctorate: Total: c. 60

Student Numbers *1999-2000:* All (Foreign Included): Men: c. 1,950 Women: c. 310 Total: c. 2,260

• KENYATTA UNIVERSITY (KU)
PO Box 43844, Nairobi
Tel: +254(2) 810-901 +254(2) 810-912
Fax: +254(2) 810-759
Telex: 25483 kenun ke
Cable: kenuco
Website: http://www.ku.ac.ke

Vice-Chancellor: G.S. Eshiwani (1992-)
Tel: +254(2) 811-231 EMail: kuvc@nbnet.co.ke

Deputy-Vice-Chancellor (Academic): J.J. Ongong'a
Tel: +254(2) 811-380

International Relations: R. Mambo

Faculties
Arts (Arts and Humanities) *Dean*: I. Nbaabu, *full-time staff:* 202, *part-time staff:* 78, *students:* 891
Commerce (Business and Commerce) *Dean*: J.N. Chege, *full-time staff:* 38, *students:* 505
Education *Dean*: P.K. Mutunga, *full-time staff:* 261, *part-time staff:* 29, *students:* 4,394
Environmental Studies *Dean*: K Kerich, *full-time staff:* 35, *part-time staff:* 12, *students:* 268
Home Economics *Dean*: O. Nugenda, *full-time staff:* 28, *part-time staff:* 6
Science (Computer Science; Mathematics; Natural Sciences) *Dean*: S.W. Waudo, *full-time staff:* 235, *part-time staff:* 41, *students:* 683

Board of Studies
Postgraduate *Director*: S.W. Waudo

Centres
African Virtual University *(AVU)* (Computer Education; Distance Education; Mathematics; Software Engineering) *Director*: N. Juna, *students:* 200

199

Computer (Computer Science) *Director*: H.K. Rono, *full-time staff*: 6, *part-time staff*: 1

Bureaus
Educational Research *Director*: R. Karega

History: Founded 1965 as Kenyatta University College, acquired present status and title 1985.

Governing Bodies: Council; Senate

Academic Year: September to June

Admission Requirements: Kenya Certificate of Secondary Education (KCSE)

Fees: (K. Shillings): 16,000 per semester; foreign students, 216,000 per semester; summer term, 8000

Main Language(s) of Instruction: English

Degrees and Diplomas: *Bachelor's Degree*: 3-4 yrs; *Postgraduate Diploma*: Education, 1 yr; *Master's Degree*: a further 2 yrs; *Doctor's Degree*: (PhD), a further 3-4 yrs

Student Services: Academic Counselling, Social Counselling, Employment Services, Nursery Care, Cultural Centre, Sports Facilities, Handicapped Facilities, Health Services, Canteen

Student Residential Facilities: For 6000 students

Libraries: Digital Library, 2000 journals

Publications: Calendar; Directory of Research; Annual Report (annually)

Academic Staff *1999-2000*: Full-Time: c. 420 Part-Time: c. 175 Total: c. 595

Staff with Doctorate: Total: c. 195

Student Numbers *1999-2000*	TOTAL
All (Foreign Included)	**9,500**
FOREIGN ONLY	10

Distance Students, 150

• MASENO UNIVERSITY
PO Box Private Bag, Maseno
Tel: +254(35) 510-08   +254(35) 516-22   +254(35) 510-11
Fax: +254(35) 512-21   +254(35) 511-53
EMail: maseno@arcc.or.ke

Principal: William R. Ochieng (1991-)

Deputy Principal (Administration): T.D.K. Serem

Faculties
Arts and Social Sciences (Arts and Humanities; Economics; Geography; History; Literature; Modern Languages; Music; Religion) *Dean*: F.R. Owino

Education (Education; Psychology; Special Education) *Dean*: J. Agak

Science (Botany; Chemistry; Computer Science; Environmental Studies; Horticulture; Mathematics; Natural Sciences; Physics; Zoology) *Dean*: E.N. Waindi

Schools
Family Consumer Science and Technology (Consumer Studies; Hotel Management; Technology) *Director*: A.J. Sigot

Institutes
Research and Postgraduate Studies *Director*: B.A. Ogot
Undergraduate Studies *Director*: R.T. Ogonda

Centres
Studies of Lake Victoria and the Environment (Environmental Studies) *Director*: P.G. Okoth

Further Information: Also Sandwich Courses, M.Phil

History: Founded 1990 as a Constituent College of Moi University.

Governing Bodies: University College Council; Academic Board

Academic Year: September-May (September-December; January-May)

Admission Requirements: Kenya Certificate of Secondary Education (KCSE), level B

Main Language(s) of Instruction: English

International Co-operation: Northern Arizona University; Iowa State University; Bayreuth University; Umeå University

Degrees and Diplomas: *Bachelor of Education*: (BEd), 4 yrs; *Bachelor of Science*: (BSc), 4 yrs; *Master of Philosophy*: Botany; Cell Biology; Economics and Planning of Education; English; History; Literature; Zoology, a further 2 yrs

Student Services: Academic Counselling, Social Counselling, Employment Services, Cultural Centre, Sports Facilities, Health Services, Canteen

Libraries: University Library

Publications: Equator News (4 per annum); Maseno Journal of Education, Arts and Science (2 per annum)

Press or Publishing House: Maseno University Desktop Publishing Unit

Academic Staff *1999*: Total: c. 180

Student Numbers *1999*: All (Foreign Included): Men: c. 930 Women: c. 900 Total: c. 1,830

• MOI UNIVERSITY
PO Box 3900, Eldoret
Tel: +254(321) 430-01
Fax: +254(321) 430-47
Telex: 254 321 35047
Cable: moi varsity, eldoret

Vice-Chancellor: Raphael M. Munavu (1994-)
Tel: +254(321) 433-63 EMail: rmunavu@irmmoi.com

Chief Administrative Officer: J.K. Sang
Tel: +254(321) 431-84 Fax: +254(321) 432-88
EMail: jksang@irmmoi.com

International Relations: Lilly Takona

Faculties
Agriculture *Dean*: E.O. Auma
Education *Dean*: E.M. Standa
Forest Resources and Wildlife Management (Forestry; Wildlife) *Dean*: B.C.C. Wangila
Health Sciences *Dean*: Khwa Otsyvla
Information Sciences *Dean*: C. Odini
Law *Dean*: F.X. Njenga
Science (Computer Science; Mathematics; Natural Sciences) *Dean*: L.L. Cheruiyot

Social, Cultural and Development Studies (Cultural Studies; Development Studies; Social Studies) *Dean*: J.J. Akonga

Technology *Dean*: P.C. Egau

Schools
Environmental Studies *Director*: W.K. Yabann

Institutes
Human Resources Development (Human Resources) *Director*: Lutta Mukhebi

Centres
Refugee Studies (Demography and Population)

History: Founded 1984.

Governing Bodies: Council; Senate

Academic Year: October to July (October-December; January-March; March-July). Undergraduates, September to May (September-January; February-May)

Admission Requirements: Kenya Certificate of Secondary Education (KCSE)

Main Language(s) of Instruction: English

International Co-operation: University of Amsterdam; University of Limburg; Wageningen Agricultural University; Delft University of Technology; Memorial University of Newfoundland; University of Alberta

Degrees and Diplomas: *Bachelor's Degree*: Medicine, 6 yrs; *Bachelor of Arts*: (BA), 4 yrs; *Bachelor of Science*: (BSc), 4 yrs; *Bachelor of Technology*: (BTech), 5 yrs; *Master of Philosophy*: (MPhil), 2 yrs; *Doctor's Degree*: Philosophy (PhD), 3-6 yrs

Student Services: Academic Counselling, Social Counselling, Nursery Care, Sports Facilities, Handicapped Facilities, Health Services, Canteen

Student Residential Facilities: Yes

Libraries: Margaret Thatcher Library, c. 100,000 vols

Student Numbers *1999*: All (Foreign Included): Men: c. 4,100 Women: c. 1,510 Total: c. 5,610

*• UNIVERSITY OF NAIROBI
PO Box 30197, University Way, Nairobi
Tel: +254(2) 334-244   +254(2) 332-986
Fax: +254(2) 336-885
Telex: 22095 varsity ke
Cable: varsity, nairobi
EMail: vc@uonbi.ac.ke
Website: http://www.uonbi.ac.ke

Vice-Chancellor: Francis J. Gichaga (1996-)
Tel: +254(2) 216-030 Fax: +254(2) 212-604
EMail: vc@ics.uonbi.ac.ke

Deputy-Vice-Chancellor (Administration and Finance):
Crispus Makau Kiamba Tel: +254(2) 336-109
Fax: +254(2) 226-329 EMail: dvcaf@ics.uonbi.ac.ke

International Relations: Kenneth Mavuti, Director
EMail: kmavuti@ics.uonbi.ac.ke

Faculties
Agriculture (Upper Kabete) *Dean*: J.K. Imungi, *full-time staff:* 118, *students:* 596

Architecture, Design and Development (Architecture; Design; Development Studies) *Dean*: P.M. Syagga, *full-time staff:* 72, *students:* 500

Arts (Arts and Humanities) *Dean*: M. Yambo, *full-time staff:* 207, *students:* 2,433

Commerce (Business and Commerce) *Dean*: J.K. Kenduiwo, *full-time staff:* 65, *students:* 1,204

Dentistry *Dean*: J.T. Kaimenyi, *students:* 58

Education *(Kikuyu)* *Dean*: G.N. Kimani, *full-time staff:* 39, *part-time staff:* 1, *students:* 1,478

Engineering *Dean (Acting)*: S.M. Mutuli, *full-time staff:* 113, *students:* 1,146

Law *(Parklands)* *Dean*: E.M. Nderitu, *full-time staff:* 40, *students:* 487

Medicine *Dean*: G.A.O. Magoha, *students:* 737

Pharmacy *Dean*: A.N. Guantai, *full-time staff:* 38, *students:* 156

Science (Mathematics; Natural Sciences) *Dean*: W. Ogana, *full-time staff:* 158, *students:* 1,234

Social Sciences *Dean*: M. Okoth-Okombo, *full-time staff:* 73, *part-time staff:* 11, *students:* 1,478

Veterinary Medicine *(Upper Kabete)* (Veterinary Science) *Dean*: M.M. Kagiko, *full-time staff:* 143, *students:* 207

Schools
Journalism *Director*: Joseph Mbindyo, *full-time staff:* 9, *students:* 25

Institutes
African Studies *Director*: C. Suda, *full-time staff:* 21, *students:* 340

Computer Science *Director*: T. Waema, *full-time staff:* 21, *students:* 128

Development Studies *(IDS)* *Director*: P.O. Alila, *full-time staff:* 16

Diplomacy and International Studies *(IDIS)* (International Relations; International Studies) *Director*: Joshua Olewe-Nyunya, *full-time staff:* 7, *students:* 29

Dryland Research, Development and Utilization *(Upper Kabete)* (Arid Land Studies) *Director*: J.P. Mbuvi, *full-time staff:* 2, *students:* 3

Nuclear Science (Nuclear Engineering) *Director*: A.M. Kinyua, *full-time staff:* 9, *students:* 7

Population Studies and Research *(PSRI)* (Demography and Population) *Director*: A.B.C. Ocholla Alayo, *students:* 51

History: Founded 1956 as Royal Technical College of East Africa, became University College Nairobi 1963 and acquired present status and title 1970. Also branches in Chiromo, Lower Kabete, Upper Kabete, Kikuyu and Parklands.

Governing Bodies: University Senate; University Council; College Academic Boards; College Management Boards; University Management Board

Academic Year: September to June

Admission Requirements: School Certificate or General Certificate of Education (GCE), prior to Higher School Certificate (HSC) or GCE Advanced ('A') level examinations

Fees: (K. Shillings): 80,000-450,000 per annum

Main Language(s) of Instruction: English

Degrees and Diplomas: *Bachelor's Degree*: 4-5 yrs; *Postgraduate Diploma*: Mass Communication; *Master's Degree*: a further 1-3 yrs; *Doctor's Degree*: (PhD), at least 2 yrs

Student Services: Academic Counselling, Social Counselling, Employment Services, Foreign Student Adviser, Cultural Centre, Sports Facilities, Handicapped Facilities, Health Services, Canteen

Student Residential Facilities: For 9322 students

Special Facilities: Biological Garden

Libraries: c. 350,000 vols

Publications: Calendar (1 per annum)

Press or Publishing House: Nairobi University Press

Academic Staff *1999-2000*: Full-Time: c. 430 Part-Time: c. 15 Total: c. 445

Student Numbers *1999-2000*	MEN	WOMEN	TOTAL
All (Foreign Included)	7,914	3,106	**11,020**
FOREIGN ONLY	8	3	11

Distance Students, 1,000

PRIVATE INSTITUTIONS

* CATHOLIC UNIVERSITY OF EASTERN AFRICA
PO Box 24205, Karen, Nairobi
Tel: +254(2) 891-6015
Fax: +254(2) 891-261
EMail: admin@cuea.edu
Website: http://www.cuea.edu

Rector: Caesar Lukudu (1992-) Tel: +254(2) 890-095

Registrar: Br. Ocbamariam Bekit EMail: registrar@cuea.edu

International Relations: Caesar Lukudu, Rector

Faculties
Arts and Social Sciences (Anthropology; Arts and Humanities; Business Administration; Business and Commerce; Economics; Education; Ethics; Geography; History; Mathematics; Philosophy; Political Science; Social Sciences; Social Work; Sociology) *Dean*: Luciano Mattei
Theology *Dean*: John Maviiri

History: Founded 1984 as the Catholic Higher Institute of Eastern Africa. Acquired present status and title 1992.

Governing Bodies: University Council; Senate; Management Boards

Academic Year: August to April (August-December; January-April)

Admission Requirements: Kenya Certificate of Secondary Education (KCSE)

Fees: (K. Shillings): 111,250-126,250 per annum; postgraduate, 131,950-142,300

Main Language(s) of Instruction: English

Degrees and Diplomas: *Bachelor's Degree*: Commerce and Business Administration; Religious Studies; Social Sciences, 3-4 yrs; *Bachelor of Arts*: (BA), 3-4 yrs; *Bachelor of Education*:

(BEd), 3-4 yrs; *Postgraduate Diploma*: Education; Projects Management; *Master's Degree*: Arts in Philosophy and Religious Studies (MA); Arts in Theology (MA), a further 2 yrs; *Doctor's Degree*: Theology (PhD), 3 yrs

Student Services: Academic Counselling, Social Counselling, Employment Services, Cultural Centre, Sports Facilities, Health Services, Canteen

Student Residential Facilities: For c. 160 students

Libraries: Total, 40,618 vols; 8996 periodicals

Publications: African Christian Studies; C.U.E.A., Journal of Humanities and Science (4 per annum)

Press or Publishing House: Catholic University of Eastern Africa Publications

Academic Staff *1999*: Total: **141**

Student Numbers *1999*	MEN	WOMEN	TOTAL
All (Foreign Included)	789	645	**1,434**

• DAYSTAR UNIVERSITY
PO Box 44400, Nairobi
Tel: +254(2) 732-002 to 004
Fax: +254(2) 728-338
Telex: 22615 worgon
EMail: daystar@maf.or.ke
Website: http://www.daystarus.org

Vice-Chancellor: Stephen E. Talitwala (1979-)
Tel: +254(2) 720-650 EMail: tibaga@insight.com

Deputy Vice-Chancellor for Academic Affairs: Samuel K. Katia

International Relations: Rosemary Ngige
Tel: +254(2) 717-309

Faculties
Arts (Arts and Humanities; Bible; English; Literature; Mass Communication; Modern Languages; Theology) *Dean*: Baruck Opiyo, *full-time staff*: 36, *students*: 472
Science (Computer Science; Electronic Engineering) *Dean*: Jon Masso, *full-time staff*: 6
Social Sciences (Accountancy; Business and Commerce; Development Studies; Economics; Education; Information Management; Marketing; Psychology; Social Sciences; Sociology) *Dean*: David Mbiti, *full-time staff*: 30, *students*: 743

Institutes
Christian Ministries and Training *(ICMT)* (Christian Religious Studies; Communication Studies; Development Studies; Management; Missionary Studies; Music; Pastoral Studies) *Director*: Samson Obwa, *full-time staff*: 24, *part-time staff*: 2, *students*: 115

History: Founded 1984, previously Daystar University College. Acquired present status and title 1994. Also 2 branches in Athi River and Nairobi.

Governing Bodies: Daystar Company and Daystar University Council

Academic Year: August to May

Admission Requirements: Kenya Certificate of Secondary Education grade C+, or equivalent

Fees: (K. Shillings): Tuition, Diploma, 102,000; undergraduate, 131,200 ; graduate, 141,000 per annum

Main Language(s) of Instruction: English

Accrediting Agencies: Commission for Higher Education, Kenya

Degrees and Diplomas: *Bachelor's Degree*: Accountancy, Business Administration and Management, Economics and Marketing, 4 yrs; *Bachelor of Arts*: Bible and Religious Studies, Communication, Community Development, English and Psychology, 4 yrs; *Bachelor of Education*: Accountancy, Bible & Religious Studies, Business Administration and Management, Economics, English, Marketing, 4 yrs; *Postgraduate Diploma*: Communication Arts, Christian Ministries in Counselling, Christian Ministries in Missions, Christian Music Communication, Management and Development, 2 yrs. Also Minors in most of the undergraduate courses in addition to Music, Mathematics, Peace and Reconciliation

Student Services: Academic Counselling, Social Counselling, Employment Services, Foreign Student Adviser, Sports Facilities, Language Programmes, Health Services, Canteen

Student Residential Facilities: For 800 students

Libraries: Main Library, 100,00 vols

Publications: Pespectives, An interdisciplinary Academic Journal (2 per annum)

Academic Staff *1999-2000*

	MEN	WOMEN	TOTAL
FULL-TIME	62	47	109
PART-TIME	49	22	71
TOTAL	**111**	**69**	**180**
STAFF WITH DOCTORATE			
FULL-TIME	20	6	26
PART-TIME	4	2	6
TOTAL	**24**	**8**	**32**

Student Numbers *1999-2000*

	MEN	WOMEN	TOTAL
All (Foreign Included)	814	1,139	**1,953**
FOREIGN ONLY	102	122	224

Evening Students, 126

UNIVERSITY OF EASTERN AFRICA, BARATON
PO Box 2500, Eldoret
Tel: +254(326) 2625
Fax: +254(326) 2263
EMail: ueab@tt.gn.apc.org

Vice-Chancellor: Mutuku J. Mutinga (1995-)
Tel: +254(326) 2470 EMail: 1016632423@compuserve.com

Registrar: Gibson S. Moyo

International Relations: Mutuku J. Mutinga

Schools
Business (Business and Commerce; Home Economics) *Dean*: Habtalem Kenea
Education (Curriculum; Education) *Dean*: Danford Musvosvi
Humanities and Social Sciences (Arts and Humanities; Geography; History; Literature; Modern Languages; Religious Studies; Social Sciences; Theology) *Dean*: Wa-Githumo Mwangi
Science and Technology (Agriculture; Biological and Life Sciences; Mathematics; Natural Sciences; Physics; Technology) *Dean*: Asaph Maradufu

History: Founded 1980. Chartered by the Government 1991. A private institution.

Governing Bodies: University Council

Academic Year: September to September (September-December; January-March; April-June; July-September)

Admission Requirements: Kenya Certificate of Secondary Education (KCSE), with C+ average grade in 8 subjects

Main Language(s) of Instruction: English

Degrees and Diplomas: *Bachelor's Degree*: Business Administration (BBA), 4 yrs; *Bachelor of Arts*: (BA), 4 yrs; *Bachelor of Science*: (BSc), 4 yrs; *Bachelor of Technology*: (BTech), 4 yrs

Student Residential Facilities: Yes

Libraries: Central Library, c. 45,000 vols

Academic Staff *1999:* Total: 58

Student Numbers *1999*

	TOTAL
All (Foreign Included)	**1,096**
FOREIGN ONLY	167

SCOTT THEOLOGICAL COLLEGE
PO Box 49, Machakos
Tel: +254(145) 21086
EMail: scott-theol_college@aimint.org
Website: http://www.ozemail.com.an/~anted/scott.html

Principal: Jacob Kibor (1999-)

Deputy Principal for Academic Affairs: Paul Kisau

International Relations: Timothi Kioko Mwangangi

Programmes
Theology

Departments
Biblical and Theological Studies (Bible; Theology) *Head*: Jim Leonard
Church Ministry and Missions (Missionary Studies; Pastoral Studies) *Head*: Esther Kibor

Institutes
Church Renewal (Christian Religious Studies) *Director*: Richard Gehman

History: Founded 1962, acquired present status and title 1997.

Governing Bodies: Governing Council; Academic Council (Senate); Management Board

Academic Year: September to July

Admission Requirements: Kenya Certificate of Secondary Education (KCSE), C+ or above

Main Language(s) of Instruction: English

Accrediting Agencies: Accreditation Council for Theological Education in Africa (ACETEA); Commission for Higher Education (CHE)

Degrees and Diplomas: *Bachelor's Degree*: Theology (BTh), 4 yrs

Student Services: Academic Counselling, Social Counselling, Foreign Student Adviser, Sports Facilities

Publications: African Journal of Evangelical Theology, Academic Journal (biannually)

• UNITED STATES INTERNATIONAL UNIVERSITY (USIU)
PO Box 14634, Nairobi
Tel: +254(2) 802-532
Fax: +254(2) 803-764
EMail: admit@usiu.ac.ke
Website: http://www.usiu.ac.ke

Vice-Chancellor: Freida Brown Fax: +254(2) 862-017
EMail: fbrown@usiu.ac.ke

Deputy Vice-Chancellor: Charles Mutuota
EMail: cmutuota@usiu.ac.ke

International Relations: Catherine Wambui
EMail: cwambui@usiu.ac.ke

Divisions

Arts and Sciences (Arts and Humanities; Natural Sciences)

Business Administration

History: Founded 1999

Lesotho

INSTITUTION TYPES AND CREDENTIALS

Types of higher education institutions:

University
Institute
Polytechnic

School leaving and higher education credentials:

Cambridge Overseas School Certificate
Diploma in Primary Education
Primary Teachers' Certificate
Secondary Teachers' Certificate
Diploma
Bachelor's Degree
Postgraduate Certificate in Education
Master's Degree
Doctorate

STRUCTURE OF EDUCATION SYSTEM

Pre-higher education:

Structure of school system:

Primary
Type of school providing this education: Primary School
Length of programme in years: 7
Age level from: 6 to: 13
Certificate/diploma awarded: Primary School Leaving Examination

Junior Secondary
Type of school providing this education: Junior Secondary School
Length of programme in years: 3
Age level from: 13 to: 16
Certificate/diploma awarded: Junior Certificate Examination

Senior Secondary
Type of school providing this education: High School
Length of programme in years: 2

Age level from: 16 to: 18
Certificate/diploma awarded: Cambridge Overseas School Certificate/GCE

School education:

After seven years of primary school which lead to the Primary School Leaving Examination, pupils enter a junior secondary school which offers three years of secondary schooling leading to the Junior Certificate Examination, followed by a two-year course in a senior secondary school leading to the Cambridge Overseas School Certificate. Various home economics and craft schools offer courses for primary school leavers. Two trade schools offer two- or three-year diploma and certificate courses for holders of the Junior Certificate.

Higher education:

Higher education is provided by the National University of Lesotho and its affiliated institutions. It is a public, autonomous institution sponsored primarily by the government. The government has prime responsibility for the development of higher education which is accomplished through legislation. It also controls most of the budget of the University. The objectives of higher education are communicated through national development plans. The University also draws up its own development plan in consultation with the government. The Council is the supreme governing body of the University whose President and Chancellor is the Head of State. Administrative, academic and non-academic staff are represented on the Council and most members are either elected or nominated. There are several foreign members and one university graduate. The Senate is in charge of all academic matters and is composed of academic and senior administrative staff. Both Council and Senate have a number of committees and boards. All teaching staff have representation in the Senate. Other bodies responsible for academic affairs are the Academic Planning Committee, faculty boards (or advisory boards in the case of institutes), departments and course development committees.

Academic year:

Classes from: August *to:* May

Long vacation from: 15 May *to:* 15 August

Languages of instruction:

English

Stages of studies:

Non-university level post-secondary studies (technical/vocational type):

Higher technical and vocational education are mainly provided by the Lesotho Agricultural College which offers a three-year Diploma course to holders of the Cambridge Overseas School Certificate; schools of Nursing and a Polytechnic which offers two-year Diploma courses in Civil, Electrical and Mechanical Engineering, Business Studies and Secretarial Studies.

University level studies:

University level first stage: Diploma, Bachelor's Degree:
A Diploma is conferred in Theology and Agriculture after two years' study. The Bachelor's Degree is conferred after four years in Arts and Humanities, Science, Commerce and Education, divided into

two two-year cycles. In Law, the Bachelor of Law Degree is conferred after obtaining the Bachelor of Arts Degree and a minimum of two years' full-time study.

University level second stage: *Master's Degree*:

The Master's Degree is conferred in Arts (MA) and Science (MSc) after two years' study beyond the Bachelor's Degree. The Master of Education Degree (MEd) is awarded to holders of a Bachelor's Degree in a teaching subject on submission of a thesis and after one year's full-time study and one-and-a-half years' research work or after two years' part-time study and one or two years' research work.

University level third stage: *Doctorate*:

The Doctorate is conferred in Agriculture, Education and the Humanities after a minimum of two years' study beyond the Master's Degree and three years from the Bachelor's Degree. Candidates must submit a thesis and sit for an oral examination.

Teacher education:

Training of pre-primary and primary/basic school teachers

Primary school teachers are trained in three years at the National Teachers Training College. The entrance requirement is the Junior Certificate of Secondary Education although, in practice, the Cambridge Overseas School Certificate is required. Studies lead to the Primary Teachers' Certificate and to the Diploma in Primary Education.

Training of secondary school teachers

The Secondary Teachers' Certificate for non-specialist teachers of the junior secondary classes is awarded after three years to holders of the Cambridge Overseas School Certificate. The Bachelor of Education Degree, obtained after four years at the University, qualifies teachers for higher secondary classes. Experienced teachers who hold the Primary Teachers' Certificate may obtain the degree after two years. The Secondary Technical Teachers Certificate (STCC) was introduced in 1980 and the Diploma in Technology Education can be obtained by holders of the STCC. The Postgraduate Certificate in Education is a one-year Graduate Certificate.

Non-traditional studies:

Distance higher education

Distance education is provided by the Lesotho Distance Teaching Centre and the Institute of Extra-Mural Studies of the University of Lesotho. The Institute offers short-term courses and off-campus Business studies and Adult Education programmes at certificate and diploma level. The Lesotho Distance Teaching Centre offers Correspondence courses at the Junior Certificate and COSC levels, Radio programmes, Literacy programmes and plays an important part in the Lesotho In-service Education for Teachers programme which is run in cooperation with the National Teacher Training Centre. It is intended to upgrade the academic and pedagogical skills of primary school teachers and head teachers.

207

NATIONAL BODIES

Responsible authorities:

Ministry of Education and Manpower Development
    Chief Executive Officer, Tertiary Education: O.M. Makara
    Minister: Archibald Lesao Lehohla
    Principal Secretary: Tlohang Sekhamane
    PO Box 47
    Maseru 100
    Tel: +266 312-849
    Fax: +266 310-297
    EMail: minedu@Lesotho.com
    WWW: http://www.lesotho.gov.ls/mneducate.htm

ADMISSIONS TO HIGHER EDUCATION

Admission to non university higher education studies

Name of secondary school credential required: Cambridge Overseas School Certificate

Admission to university-level studies

Name of secondary school credential required: Cambridge Overseas School Certificate
Minimum score/requirement: 1st or 2nd division with credit in English and Mathematics (for science)

Alternatives to credentials: Holders of the General Certificate of Education (O' level) with at least four passes including English may also gain entrance to the university under certain conditions.

Foreign students admission

Admission requirements: Foreign students must hold qualifications equivalent to those required for entry to the university.

Application procedures:

Apply to individual institution for entry to: University

Apply to: University Admissions Secretariat
    Roma 180
    Tel: +266 340-601
    Fax: +266 340-000
    WWW: http://www.nul.ls

Application closing dates:
    For university level studies: 1 April
    For advanced/doctoral studies: 1 April

Multilateral agreements concerning recognition of foreign studies

Name(s) of agreement(s): Convention on the Recognition of Studies, Certificates, Diplomas, Degrees and Other Qualifications in Higher Education in the African States

Year of signature: 1981

STUDENT LIFE

Student expenses and financial aid

Student costs:

Home students tuition fees: Minimum: 2,000 (Maloti)
Maximum: 3,400 (Maloti)
Foreign students tuition fees: Minimum: 2,000 (Maloti)
Maximum: 10,500 (Maloti)

GRADING SYSTEM

Usual grading system in secondary school

Full Description: Cambridge Overseas School Certificate is graded: 1-9.
Highest on scale: 1
Pass/fail level: 7-8
Lowest on scale: 9

Main grading system used by higher education institutions

Full Description: A-F
Highest on scale: A
Pass/fail level: D
Lowest on scale: F

NOTES ON HIGHER EDUCATION SYSTEM

Data for academic year: 2000-2001
Source: International Association of Universities (IAU), updated from IBE website, 2000

INSTITUTIONS OF HIGHER EDUCATION

UNIVERSITIES

PUBLIC INSTITUTIONS

*• NATIONAL UNIVERSITY OF LESOTHO
PO 0180, Roma 180
Tel: +266 340-601
Fax: +266 340-000
Telex: (0963) 4303 lo
EMail: info@nul.ls
Website: http://www.nul.ls

Vice-Chancellor: Tefetso Henry Mothibe (2001-2005)
Tel: +266 340-269 Fax: +266 340-702
EMail: th.mothibe@nul.is; vc@nul.ls

Registrar: Anne Masefinela Mphuthing Tel: +266 340-264
Fax: +266 340-269 EMail: registrar@nul.is

International Relations: Khoeli Pholosi

Faculties

Agriculture *(Maseru)* (Agricultural Economics; Agriculture; Animal Husbandry; Ecology; Natural Resources; Rural Planning) *Dean:* Patrick M. Sutlon, *full-time staff:* 21, *students:* 66

Education (Education; Educational Sciences; Modern Languages; Social Studies) *Dean:* Matora Ntimo-Makara, *full-time staff:* 27, *part-time staff:* 1, *students:* 558

Health Sciences *(Maseru) Dean:* Philip O. Odonkor, *full-time staff:* 15, *students:* 150

Humanities (African Languages; Arts and Humanities; Development Studies; English; French; History; Philosophy; Theology) *Dean:* I.M Mokitimi, *full-time staff:* 42, *students:* 310

Law (Justice Administration; Law; Private Law; Public Law) *Dean:* N.L. Mahao Mahao, *full-time staff:* 15, *students:* 259

Postgraduate Studies *Dean:* T.A. Balogun, *students:* 94

Science and Technology (Biology; Geography; Mathematics and Computer Science; Natural Sciences; Physics) *Dean:* K. K. Gopinathan, *full-time staff:* 63, *students:* 320

Social Sciences (Anthropology; Business Administration; Demography and Population; Economics; Political Science; Social Sciences; Sociology; Statistics) *Dean:* M.M. Shale, *full-time staff:* 46, *part-time staff:* 1, *students:* 714

Institutes

Education (Education; Educational Research; Teacher Training) *Director:* Pulane Lefoka, *full-time staff:* 9

Extramural Studies *(Maseru)* (Adult Education; Business Administration; Continuing Education; Management; Media Studies) *Director:* Antony Setšabi, *full-time staff:* 24, *part-time staff:* 70, *students:* 800

Labour Studies *(Maseru)* (Labour and Industrial Relations; Labour Law) *Director:* Sehoai Santho, *full-time staff:* 5

Southern African Studies (African Studies) *Director:* G. Prasad, *full-time staff:* 10

History: Founded 1945 as Pius XII College, became University of Basuto land, Bechuana land Protectorate and Swaziland 1964; part of the trinational University of Botswana, Lesotho and Swaziland 1966. Acquired present status 1975.

Governing Bodies: Council; Senate

Academic Year: August to May (August-December; January-May)

Admission Requirements: Cambridge Overseas School Certificate or equivalent, with credit in English

Fees: (Loti): 2000-3400; foreign students, 2000-10,500

Main Language(s) of Instruction: English

International Co-operation: University of Manchester; Free University Amsterdam

Degrees and Diplomas: *Bachelor's Degree:* Arts (BA); Arts in Law; Arts with Education (BAEd); Commerce (BCom); Education (BEd); Science (BSc); Science in Agriculture (BScAgric); Science with Education (BScEd), 1-4 yrs; *Master's Degree:* Arts (MA); Education (MEd); Laws (LLM); Science (MSc); Social Work (MSW), a further 1-2 yrs; *Doctorate:* (PhD), a further 2-3 yrs

Student Services: Social Counselling, Employment Services, Nursery Care, Sports Facilities, Handicapped Facilities, Health Services, Canteen

Student Residential Facilities: Yes

Special Facilities: Botanical Garden

Libraries: Thomas Mofolo Library, c. 150,000 vols, Roma Campus; IEMS Centre, Maseru, c. 3000 vols

Publications: Lesotho Law Journal (biannually); Academic Calendar (annually); NUL Student Law Review; Lesotho Social Science Review; NUL Journal of Research (occasionally); Mohlomi: Journal of History

Press or Publishing House: NUL Publishing House

Academic Staff *1999:* Total: **350**

Student Numbers 1999	MEN	WOMEN	TOTAL
All (Foreign Included)	997	124	**1,121**
FOREIGN ONLY	–	–	133

OTHER INSTITUTIONS

PUBLIC INSTITUTIONS

LESOTHO AGRICULTURAL COLLEGE
Private Bag A4, Maseru 100
Tel: +266 322-484
Fax: +266 400-022

Departments
Agriculture Mechanization

Agronomy
Animal Science (Animal Husbandry)
Forestry and Resources Management (Forestry; Natural Resources)
Home Economics
Socio-economics and Quantitative Studies (Economics; Social Studies)

Further Information: Also Campus in Leribe

History: Founded 1955.

Academic Year: August to May

Main Language(s) of Instruction: English

Degrees and Diplomas: *Diploma*: 3 yrs

Liberia

INSTITUTION TYPES AND CREDENTIALS

Types of higher education institutions:

University
College

School leaving and higher education credentials:

West African Examination Council (WAEC) Certificate
Bachelor's Degree
Master's Degree
Doctorate

STRUCTURE OF EDUCATION SYSTEM

Pre-higher education:

Structure of school system:

Primary
Type of school providing this education: Elementary School
Length of programme in years: 6
Age level from: 6 to: 12

Junior Secondary
Type of school providing this education: Junior High School
Length of programme in years: 3
Age level from: 12 to: 15
Certificate/diploma awarded: Examination by the West African Examination Council (WAEC)

Senior Secondary
Type of school providing this education: Senior High School
Length of programme in years: 3
Age level from: 15 to: 18
Certificate/diploma awarded: West African Examination Council (WAEC) Certificate

School education:

Elementary education lasts for six years. Secondary education consists of two three-year cycles: three years of Junior secondary (Grades VII-IX) and three years of Senior secondary education (Grades X-XII). At the end of Grade IX, students sit for an examination administered by the West African Examination Council (WAEC). Successful students are eligible to enter Senor High School. Upper secondary education culminates in the WAEC Certificate Examination, which is the basis for access to higher education institutions. An entrance examination is required for access to higher education.

Higher education:

Higher education is mostly provided by the University of Liberia in Monrovia, the African Methodist Episcopal University, Cuttington University College (private and linked to the Episcopalian Church), and William V.S. Tubman College of Technology. More universities and polytechnics have been created recently. Each tertiary institution sets its own standards. Degree-granting institutions are chartered by the National Legislature. Each has a separate Board of Trustees or directors appointed under the terms of its charter. Institutions of higher education are under the authority of the Ministry of Education, the National Commission on Higher Education and the Board of Trustees.

Academic year:

Classes from: March *to:* December

Long vacation from: 1 January *to:* 28 February

Languages of instruction:

English

Stages of studies:

Non-university level post-secondary studies (technical/vocational type):

Non-university level post-secondary education consists of two-year courses offered by junior colleges leading to the award of an Associate Degree. Several colleges also offer middle-level technical training and Liberal Arts education.

University level studies:

University level first stage: *Bachelor's Degree*:
The first stage lasts for four years and leads to the award of the Bachelor's Degree. The curricular structure generally provides for the first two years to include basic and general courses, such as English, introductory Physical and Social Sciences, Physical Education and general Mathematics. This is followed by courses in the student's area of specialization. Entry to legal studies requires at least two years' previous higher education; the degree of Bachelor of Laws is awarded after three years of specialization.

University level second stage: *Master's Degree*:
A second stage leads to the Master of Science Degree, awarded by the University of Liberia after two years' graduate study. In Medicine, the Doctorate is conferred after seven years of study.

Teacher education:

Training of pre-primary and primary/basic school teachers
Primary-school teachers are trained at upper secondary level at a Teacher Training Institute. Courses last for three years and lead to a Primary Teacher's Certificate/Grade C Teaching Certificate.

Training of secondary school teachers
A Grade B Teaching Certificate is required to teach in Junior High Schools. Upper Secondary-school

213

teachers are graduates. They are trained at the Teachers' College of the University of Liberia and the Department of Education at Cuttington University College. Courses last for four years and lead to a Bachelor's Degree in Education. They may also follow a two-year course leading to a Grade A Teaching Certificate if they already hold a degree in another subject.

Training of higher education teachers
A Master's Degree is required to teach in Colleges of Education, together with a teaching qualification. University teachers must hold a Doctorate.

NATIONAL BODIES

Responsible authorities:

Ministry of Education
    Minister: Evelyn S. Kandakai
    PO Box 10-1545
    Broad Street, 4th Floor, Room 413
    Monrovia
    Tel: +231(22) 6216
    Fax: +231(22) 6216 +231(22) 6144

Commission on Higher Education
    Ministry of Education
    PO Box 10-1545
    Broad Street, 4th Floor, Room 413
    Monrovia
    Tel: +231(22) 6216
    Fax: +231(22) 6216 +231(22) 6144

    Role of governing body: Supervises tertiary-level institutions.

ADMISSIONS TO HIGHER EDUCATION

Admission to university-level studies
Name of secondary school credential required: West African Examination Council (WAEC) Certificate
Entrance exams required: Entrance examination.

GRADING SYSTEM

Usual grading system in secondary school
Full Description: Marking is on a percentage scale, the pass mark being 70%.
Highest on scale: 100%

Pass/fail level: 70%
Lowest on scale: 0%

Main grading system used by higher education institutions

Full Description: A=90-100; B=80-89; C=70-79; D=60-69; F=fail
Highest on scale: A
Pass/fail level: D
Lowest on scale: F

NOTES ON HIGHER EDUCATION SYSTEM

Data for academic year: 2000-2001
Source: International Association of Universities (IAU), updated from IBE website, 2001

INSTITUTIONS OF HIGHER EDUCATION

UNIVERSITIES

PUBLIC INSTITUTIONS

• UNIVERSITY OF LIBERIA
PO Box 804, Capital Hill, Monrovia
Tel: +231(22) 4670
Fax: +231(22) 6418

President: Frederic Gbegbe Tel: +231(22) 448

Colleges
Agriculture and Forestry (Agriculture; Forestry)
Business and Public Administration (Business and Commerce; Public Administration)
Medicine *(A.M. Douglas)* (Medicine; Pharmacy; Public Health)
Science and Technology (Natural Sciences; Technology)
Social Sciences and Humanities (Arts and Humanities; Political Science; Social Sciences)
Teacher Training *(William V. S. Tubman)* (Education)

Schools
Law *(Louis Arthur-Grimes)*

Departments
Lifelong Education

Institutes
African Studies and Research (African Studies)

History: Founded 1851 as Liberia College, opened 1862. Became university 1951. The institution is responsible to the Ministry of Education and is financed by the State.

Governing Bodies: Faculty Senate; University Council

Academic Year: March to December (March-July; August-December)

Admission Requirements: Secondary school certificate and entrance examination

Main Language(s) of Instruction: English

Degrees and Diplomas: *Bachelor's Degree*: Laws (LL.B.), 3 yrs, (4 yrs evening course; Arts (B.A.); Science (B.Sc.), 4 yrs; *Doctorate*: Medicine, 7 yrs

Student Residential Facilities: For c. 420 students

Libraries: Total, c. 107,500 vols

Publications: University Spokesman (bimonthly); Research Institute Newsletter (quarterly); Law Journal (biannually); Journal; The Liberian Economic and Management Review; Science Magazine

Academic Staff *1999:* Total: c. 260

Student Numbers *1999:* Total: c. 3,350

PRIVATE INSTITUTIONS

AFRICAN METHODIST EPISCOPAL UNIVERSITY
PO Box 3340, Camp Johnson Road, Monrovia
Tel: +231(22) 7964

Head: Louise C. York
Vice-President for Academic Affairs: William Saa-Salifu
International Relations: Elaine Wilson

Divisions
Biyant Theological Seminary (Theology)
Liberal Arts (Arts and Humanities)
Religious Education *(Theology Seminary)*

Colleges
Business and Public Administration (Business and Commerce; Public Administration)

History: Founded 1997.

OTHER INSTITUTIONS

PRIVATE INSTITUTIONS

• CUTTINGTON UNIVERSITY COLLEGE (CUC)
PO Box 277, Monrovia
Tel: +231(22) 7413 +231(22) 4243
Cable: Pecusam

President: Melvin Mason (1988-)
Vice-President for Academic Affairs: Saaim Naame
International Relations: Thomas K. Gaie

Divisions
Education *students:* 4
Humanities (Arts and Humanities)
Nursing *Head*: Cecilia Morris, *full-time staff:* 4, *part-time staff:* 2, *students:* 120
Science (Biology; Chemistry; Mathematics; Natural Sciences) *Head*: Frankie Cassell, *full-time staff:* 10, *part-time staff:* 3, *students:* 60
Social Sciences (Accountancy; Business Administration; Business and Commerce; Economics; History; Political Science; Public Administration; Social Sciences) *Head*: John Gornuyer, *full-time staff:* 6, *part-time staff:* 2, *students:* 90

Institutes

Rural Development (Agriculture; Rural Studies) *Head*: David Kenkpen, *full-time staff: 2, part-time staff: 2, students: 23*

History: Founded 1889 as Hoffman Institute. Renamed Cuttington College and Divinity School 1897. Closed 1929 to 1949. Acquired present title 1976. Administered by the Protestant Episcopal Church.

Governing Bodies: Board of Trustees, of which the Episcopal Bishop is President, and including the Minister of Education

Academic Year: September to July (September-February; March-July)

Admission Requirements: Secondary school certificate or recognized equivalent, and entrance examination

Fees: (US Dollars): 500 per semester

Main Language(s) of Instruction: English

Accrediting Agencies: Commission for Higher Education in Liberia; Association of Episcopal Colleges, USA; Association of African Universities

Degrees and Diplomas: *Bachelor's Degree*: Arts (BA); Science (BSc), 4 yrs. Also Honoris Causa Doctorate

Student Services: Academic Counselling, Social Counselling, Foreign Student Adviser, Sports Facilities, Health Services, Canteen

Student Residential Facilities: Yes

Special Facilities: Africana Collection

Libraries: William V.S. Tubman Library, c.100,000 vols

Publications: Cuttington Research Journal (biannually)

Academic Staff *2000*	MEN	WOMEN	TOTAL
FULL-TIME	24	1	25
PART-TIME	9	1	10
TOTAL	**33**	**2**	**35**
STAFF WITH DOCTORATE			
FULL-TIME			8
PART-TIME			2
TOTAL			**10**

Student Numbers *2000*	MEN	WOMEN	TOTAL
All (Foreign Included)	176	157	**333**
FOREIGN ONLY	3	2	5

Libya

INSTITUTION TYPES AND CREDENTIALS

Types of higher education institutions:

University
Higher Institute
Research Centre

School leaving and higher education credentials:

Secondary Education Certificate
Bachelor's Degree
Higher Diploma
Master's Degree
Doctorate

STRUCTURE OF EDUCATION SYSTEM

Pre-higher education:

Duration of compulsory education:

Age of entry: 6
Age of exit: 15

Structure of school system:

Basic
Type of school providing this education: Basic School
Length of programme in years: 9
Age level from: 6 to: 15
Certificate/diploma awarded: Basic Education Certificate

Secondary
Type of school providing this education: Intermediate School
Length of programme in years: 4
Age level from: 15 to: 19
Certificate/diploma awarded: Secondary Education Certificate

School education:

The primary and secondary education system consists of nine years basic education, leading to the Basic Education Certificate, followed by four years of "intermediate" education. Intermediate level education extends from three to four years and comprises a number of secondary school types: general secondary schools (Science and Arts sections); specialized secondary schools (in Economics, Biology, Arts and Media, Social Sciences and Engineering), teacher training institutes and intermediate vocational centres. In specialized secondary schools studies last for four years. Secondary studies last for four years in technical education, three years in general secondary and vocational training schools, and three to four years in Teacher Training institutions. Studies lead to the Secondary Education Certificate and to the Intermediate Training Diploma in vocational training centres.

Higher education:

Higher education is offered in Universities, both general and specialized, and higher vocational institutes. These include Teacher Training higher vocational institutes; higher institutes to train trainers and instructors; polytechnic institutes; higher institutes for Technical, Industrial and Agricultural Sciences. Several higher institutes for Teacher Training were founded in 1997. New scientific institutions called Scientific Research Centres have been created in such fields as Health and Pharmacy, Education, the Environment and Basic Sciences. They are both educational and research institutions. The National Authority for Scientific Research is responsible for higher education and research and the University People's Committee, chaired by a Secretary, manages university education. Each faculty also has a People's Committee, chaired by the dean and with heads of departments as members. Each university manages its administration and its budget. University-level education includes three major sections: university education (lasting four to seven years), university vocational and technical education (lasting three to five years), and advanced graduate studies.

Main laws/decrees governing higher education:

Decree: Law 186   Year: 1995
Concerns: Committee for Universities
Decree: Law no. 1 concerning Higher Education   Year: 1992

Academic year:

Classes from: September *to:* June

Languages of instruction:

Arabic, English

Stages of studies:

Non-university level post-secondary studies (technical/vocational type):

Higher vocational and technical education is provided by higher institutes which offer courses of three to five years' duration in such fields as Electricity, Mechanical Engineering, Finance, Computer Studies, Industrial Technology, Social Work, Medical Technology and Civil Aviation. At the end of their studies, graduate technicians are assigned to work in development projects.

University level studies:

University level first stage: Bachelor's Degree:
The Bachelor's Degree is conferred after four to five years' university study.

University level second stage: Master Degree:
A Higher Diploma is conferred after two years' study following the Bachelor's Degree. A Master's

219

Degree (MA or MSc) is conferred after two years' study following the Bachelor's Degree. These programmes are mainly concentrated in the large Universities, such as Garyounis and El-Fateh.

University level third stage: Doctorate:
A Doctorate may be awarded after a further two years of research in such fields as Arabic, Islamic studies and Humanities. The award of this degree is conditional upon the submission of a thesis. Many students are still sent abroad.

Teacher education:

Training of pre-primary and primary/basic school teachers
Primary school teachers are trained in three to four years in State higher teacher training institutes at intermediate school level. A number of centres for in-service training were opened in 1995-96. A training centre was opened to train teachers for technical and vocational basic and intermediate levels.

Training of secondary school teachers
Secondary school teachers are trained in four years at higher education level (Faculty of Education). Teachers at intermediate training centres are graduates of the higher technical institutes.

Training of higher education teachers
MA holders can become assistant lecturers. They can be promoted to lecturer status after three years of teaching. They are promoted to assistant professor status after having taught for four years and submitted three theses evaluated by a scientific committee of three teaching staff members. PhD holders are appointed as lecturers and promoted to assistant professor status after four years of teaching. They are then promoted to joint professor status after four further years of teaching and submission of published scientific theses evaluated by a scientific committee of three teaching staff members. Teachers are promoted to the status of professor after being a joint professor and having taught for five years and presented three published theses evaluated as above.

Non-traditional studies:

Distance higher education
Distance education is provided by the Open University, created in 1987. Its main centre is in Tripoli but it has opened branches in Benghazi, Sebha, Ejdabia, Derna, Misurata and El-Kufra. The number of credits needed for graduation is between 120 and 150 credit hours as per the school year system. Curricula and teaching programmes are conveyed via written and audiovisual material (learning package).

Other forms of non-formal higher education
Non-formal studies consist of short postsecondary courses for training paramedical personnel, inspectors of hygiene, etc.

NATIONAL BODIES

Responsible authorities:
National Authority for Scientific Research
    Chairman: Matoug Mohammed Matoug

PO Box 12312
Tripoli
Tel: +218(21) 462-4350
Fax: +218(21) 462-3353
EMail: salemtog@hotmail.com

ADMISSIONS TO HIGHER EDUCATION

Admission to non university higher education studies

Name of secondary school credential required: Secondary Education Certificate

Alternatives to credentials: Intermediate Training Diploma

Admission to university-level studies

Name of secondary school credential required: Secondary Education Certificate
Minimum score/requirement: A minimum of 65% , 75% for Medicine and Engineering
For entry to: Universities

Foreign students admission

Admission requirements: All foreign students should hold the Libyan Secondary Education Certificate or its equivalent, issued in the same or previous year of application. Grade averages required are the following: in science: medicine 90%, sciences 80%, engineering and veterinary science 85%, agriculture 80%, economy 80%; in liberal arts: law, art and information 85%, languages 80%, education 80%, social sciences, physical education and sports 75%. The original certificate should be submitted. A coordinating committee undertakes the placement of students admitted to the respective faculties in accordance with their total grades and percentage. Students have to pay the tuition fees fixed by the universities.

Language requirements: Language proficiency is required. The language of instruction for undergraduate studies is Arabic for Humanities and Arabic and English for courses in the Science faculties.

Recognition of studies and qualifications:

Studies pursued in home country (System of recognition/accreditation): Convention on the Recognition of Studies, Diplomas and Degrees in Higher Education in the Arab States, 1978.

Studies pursued in foreign countries (bodies dealing with recognition of foreign credentials):
Committee for the Equivalence of Academic Credentials, Secretary of the General People's Committee for Education and Vocational Training
Tripoli
Tel: +218(21) 360-9177
Fax: +218(21) 360-9177

Deals with credential recognition for entry to: University

Multilateral agreements concerning recognition of foreign studies

Name(s) of agreement(s): Convention on the Recognition of Studies, Diplomas and Degrees in Higher Education in the Arab States
Year of signature: 1978

References to further information on foreign student admissions and recognition of studies

Title: Study Abroad 2000-2001
Publisher: UNESCO/IBE
Year of publication: 1999

STUDENT LIFE

Student expenses and financial aid

Student costs:

Home students tuition fees: Minimum: 0 (Libyan Dinar)

Bodies providing information on student financial aid:

Department of Cultural Relations, Secretariat of the General People's Committee for Education and Vocational Training
Tripoli
Tel: +218(21) 604-807
Fax: +218(21) 623-038

GRADING SYSTEM

Usual grading system in secondary school

Full Description: Each subject has minimum and maximum marks appearing on the Certificate (260 for literary subjects with pass at 130; 330 for science subjects with pass at 165)

Main grading system used by higher education institutions

Full Description: 0-100%
Highest on scale: 100%
Pass/fail level: 50%
Lowest on scale: 0%

NOTES ON HIGHER EDUCATION SYSTEM

Data for academic year: 2000-2001
Source: International Association of Universities (IAU), updated from IBE website, 2000

INSTITUTIONS OF HIGHER EDUCATION

UNIVERSITIES

AL-ASMARIA UNIVERSITY
Zlitin

Faculties
Arabic
Shari'a (Islamic Law)

History: Founded 1997.

• AL-FATEH UNIVERSITY
PO Box 13482, Tripoli, Sedi El-Masri
Tel: +218(22) 605-441
Fax: +218(22) 605-460
Telex: 20629

Faculties
Agriculture
Education
Engineering
Graduate Studies
Literature
Medicine
Mining, Petroleum and Gas Engineering
Nuclear Engineering
Pharmacy
Science (Natural Sciences)
Veterinary Science

History: Founded 1957 as University of Libya, reorganized as two separate universities in Tripoli and Benghazi, 1973. Under the jurisdiction of the Ministry of Education and financed by the government.

Academic Year: September to June (September-January; February-June)

Admission Requirements: Secondary school certificate or equivalent

Fees: None

Main Language(s) of Instruction: Arabic, English

Degrees and Diplomas: *Bachelor's Degree*: 4-5 yrs; *Master's Degree*: Science (MSc), a further 2 yrs

Libraries: c. 10,000 vols

Academic Staff *1999:* Total: c. 2,000

Student Numbers *1999:* Total: c. 35,000

AL-TAHADI UNIVERSITY
P.O.Box 674, Sirt
Tel: +218(54) 62150
Fax: +218(54) 4373

Faculties
Agriculture
Economics and Political Science (Economics; Political Science)
Engineering
Mechanical and Electrical Engineering *(Hoon)* (Electrical Engineering; Mechanical Engineering)
Medicine
Science *(Misurata)* (Mathematics and Computer Science; Natural Sciences)

History: Founded 1989.

Academic Year: September to July

BRIGHT STAR UNIVERSITY OF TECHNOLOGY
PO Box 58158, Mersa-El-Brega
Tel: +218(64) 23012 +218(61) 240-851
Fax: +218(21) 600-185

Chancellor: Ali Saleh Elfazzani

Departments
Chemical Engineering
Electrical and Electronic Engineering (Computer Science; Electrical and Electronic Engineering)
Materials Engineering
Mechanical Engineering
Petroleum Engineering (Petroleum and Gas Engineering)
Production Engineering

History: Founded 1981.

Academic Year: October to June

Main Language(s) of Instruction: Arabic, English

Academic Staff *1999:* Total: c. 80

Student Numbers *1999:* Total: c. 1,200

DERNA UNIVERSITY
Derna

Faculties
Accountancy and Economics (Accountancy; Economics)
Fine Arts and Architecture (Architecture; Fine Arts)
Law
Medical Technology
Social Sciences

History: Founded 1995.

Academic Year: September to July

Main Language(s) of Instruction: Arabic, English

UNIVERSITY OF MORAGAB
PO Box 40414-40397, Ain Zara
Tel: 218(31) 629-365
Fax: 218(31) 629-366

Faculties
Economics *(Zlaitin)*
Education and Science (Education; Science Education)
Education and Science *(Tarhuna)* (Education; Science Education)
Engineering
Law *(Tarhuna)*
Literature and Education *(Zlaitin)* (Education; Literature)

History: Founded 1987 as Nasser University.

OMAR-AL-MUKHTAR UNIVERSITY
PO Box 991, Al-Bayda
Tel: +218(84) 6310-719
Fax: +218(84) 632-233

Faculties
Agriculture
Engineering
Literature and Education (Education; Literature)
Science (Natural Sciences)
Veterinary Medicine (Veterinary Science)

History: Founded 1985.

Academic Year: September to July

THE OPEN UNIVERSITY
Tripoli

Departments
Administration
Arabic
Economics
Education and Psychology (Education; Psychology)
Geography
History
Law
Political Science
Sociology and Social Work (Social Work; Sociology)

History: Founded 1987. Curricula and teaching programmes, both theoretical and applied, are conveyed to the student via written, audiovisual materials.

Student Numbers *1999:* Total: c. 9,100

• SEBHA UNIVERSITY
PO Box 18758, Sebha
Tel: +218(71) 21575
Fax: +218(71) 29201
Telex: 30622

Chancellor: Abu Bakr Abdullah Otman

Faculties
Accountancy *(Merzig)* (Accountancy; Economics)
Agriculture
Arts and Education *(Obari)* (Education; Literature)
Engineering and Technology *(Brak)* (Engineering; Technology)
Law
Medicine
Physical Education *(For Men, Ghat)*
Science (Mathematics and Computer Science; Natural Sciences)

History: Founded 1983, incorporating the Faculty of Education of the University of Al-Fateh.

Academic Year: October to August.

Admission Requirements: Secondary school certificate

Main Language(s) of Instruction: Arabic, English

Degrees and Diplomas: *Bachelor's Degree*: 3-4 yrs; *Master's Degree*; *Doctorate*: (PhD)

Student Residential Facilities: Yes

Libraries: Central Library, c. 110,000 vols

Academic Staff *1999:* Total: c. 280

Student Numbers *1999:* Total: c. 3,000

• SEVENTH OF APRIL UNIVERSITY
PO Box 16418, Al-Zawia
Tel: +218(23) 26882

Faculties
Education
Engineering
Physical Education *(For Women)*
Science (Natural Sciences)

History: Founded 1988.

Academic Year: September to July

Main Language(s) of Instruction: Arabic, English

AL-JABAL AL-GHARBI COLLEGE OF TECHNOLOGY
Zintan
Tel: +218 4143-891

Faculties
Accountancy

History: Founded 1991.

• UNIVERSITY OF GARYOUNIS
PO Box 1308, Benghazi
Tel: +218(61) 20148   +218(61) 25007
Fax: +218(61) 20051
Telex: (0901) 40175
EMail: garyounisuniv@lttnet.net

Faculties
Agriculture
Arts and Education (Arts and Humanities; Education)

Dentistry
Economics
Education *(Marg)*
Engineering
Graduate Studies
Law
Science (Mathematics and Computer Science; Natural Sciences)

Research Centres
Social and Economic Sciences (Economics; Social Sciences)

History: Founded 1955 as University of Libya, reorganized as two separate Universities in Benghazi and Tripoli, 1974. Acquired present name 1976. Under the jurisdiction of the Ministry of Education and financed by the government.

Governing Bodies: University Council

Academic Year: October to June (October-January; February-June)

Admission Requirements: Secondary school certificate or equivalent

Fees: None

Main Language(s) of Instruction: Arabic, English

Degrees and Diplomas: *Bachelor's Degree*: 4 yrs

Student Residential Facilities: Yes

Libraries: c. 295,000 vols

Publications: Faculty Journals; Arts; Economics; Law (annually)

Academic Staff *1999:* Total: c. 600

Student Numbers *1999:* Total: c. 15,000

Evening Students, c. 4,050

AL-ARAB MEDICAL COLLEGE
PO Box 18251, Hawari Road, Benghazi
Tel: +218(61) 225-007
Fax: +218(61) 220-051
Telex: (0901) 40204/40437

President: Amer Kahil (1999-)

Faculties
Dentistry (Dentistry; Surgery)
Medicine (Gynaecology and Obstetrics; Medicine; Ophthalmology; Paediatrics; Surgery)
Pharmacy

Institutes
Medical Technology

Further Information: Also 8 Teaching Hospitals; 2 Medical Centres

History: Founded 1984.

Academic Year: September to May

Admission Requirements: Secondary school certificate or equivalent

Main Language(s) of Instruction: Arabic, English

Degrees and Diplomas: *Bachelor's Degree*: Dental Surgery; Medicine and Surgery, 5-7 yrs; *Higher Diploma*: Community Medicine; Dermatology; Laboratory Medicine; Paediatrics, 1-2

yrs following Bachelor; *Master's Degree*: Anaesthesia; Anatomy; Biochemistry; Dermatology; Histology; Laboratory Medicine; Pathology; Pharmacology; Physiology; Public Health, a further 2-3 yrs; *Doctorate*: a further 2-3 yrs

Student Services: Academic Counselling, Foreign Student Adviser, Cultural Centre, Sports Facilities, Health Services, Canteen

Special Facilities: Anatomy Museum

Libraries: Central Library, c. 30,500 vols

Publications: Garyounis Medical Journal (biannually)

Academic Staff *1999:* Total: c. 300

Student Numbers *1999:* Total: c. 2,000

AL-FATEH COLLEGE OF MEDICAL SCIENCES
PO Box 13040, Tripoli

Faculties
Dentistry
Medical Technology *(Misurata)*
Medicine
Pharmacy

History: Founded 1986.

Academic Year: September to June

Degrees and Diplomas: *Bachelor's Degree*: 3-4 yrs; *Master's Degree*

OTHER INSTITUTIONS

FACULTY OF ISLAMIC CALL (FIC)
PO Box 71771, Tariq Assawani, Tripoli
Tel: +218(21) 480-0167 +218(21) 480-1473
Fax: +218(21) 480-0059

Rector: Mokhtar Ahmad Dira

Arabic; Islamic Studies

HIGHER INSTITUTE OF CIVIL AVIATION
Sebha
Civil Aviation (Air Transport)

HIGHER INSTITUTE OF COMPUTER TECHNOLOGY
PO Box 6289, G.S.P.L.A.J, Tripoli
Tel: +218(21) 480-0413
Fax: +218(21) 480-0199

Divisions
Training (Business Computing; Computer Education) *Head:* Kes Housen, *full-time staff:* 6, *part-time staff:* 9, *students:* 300

Departments

Computer Engineering (Computer Engineering; Software Engineering)

Software Engineering (Computer Engineering; Data Processing; Maintenance Technology; Software Engineering)
Head: Moftah Algorni, *full-time staff*: 26, *students*: 1,843

History: Founded 1990

Admission Requirements: High school certificate

Fees: None

Main Language(s) of Instruction: Arabic, English

Student Services: Academic Counselling, Social Counselling, Employment Services, Sports Facilities, Canteen

Libraries: Central Library, fullly computerized with internet facilities

Academic Staff *2000*	MEN	WOMEN	TOTAL
FULL-TIME	21	5	26
PART-TIME	65	16	81
TOTAL	**86**	**21**	**107**
STAFF WITH DOCTORATE			
FULL-TIME			5
PART-TIME			22
TOTAL			**27**

Student Numbers *2000*	MEN	WOMEN	TOTAL
All (Foreign Included)	1,074	769	**1,843**
FOREIGN ONLY	33	17	50

HIGHER INSTITUTE OF ELECTRICITY
Benghazi

Electricity (Electrical Engineering)

HIGHER INSTITUTE OF ELECTRONICS
PO Box 8645, Beni Walid/Souk Jin

Electronics (Electronic Engineering)

History: Founded 1976

HIGHER INSTITUTE OF FINANCE AND ADMINISTRATION
Benghazi

Finance and Administration (Administration; Finance)

HIGHER INSTITUTE OF FINANCE AND ADMINISTRATION
Gadames

Finance and Administration (Administration; Finance)

HIGHER INSTITUTE OF FINANCE AND ADMINISTRATION
Tripoli

Finance and Administration (Administration; Finance)

HIGHER INSTITUTE FOR GENERAL VOCATIONS
Derna

HIGHER INSTITUTE FOR GENERAL VOCATIONS
El-Bayda

HIGHER INSTITUTE FOR GENERAL VOCATIONS
Garyan

HIGHER INSTITUTE FOR GENERAL VOCATIONS
Misurata

HIGHER INSTITUTE FOR GENERAL VOCATIONS
Nalut

HIGHER INSTITUTE FOR GENERAL VOCATIONS
Sebha

HIGHER INSTITUTE FOR GENERAL VOCATIONS
Surman

HIGHER INSTITUTE OF INDUSTRIAL TECHNOLOGY
Misurata

Industrial Technology (Industrial Engineering)

HIGHER INSTITUTE OF INDUSTRIAL TECHNOLOGY
Tripoli

Industrial Engineering

HIGHER INSTITUTE OF MECHANICAL AND ELECTRICAL ENGINEERING
PO Box 61160, Hon
Tel: +218 2154
Telex: 30254 ly

Mechanical and Electrical Engineering (Electrical Engineering; Mechanical Engineering)

History: Founded 1976

HIGHER INSTITUTE FOR MECHANICAL VOCATIONS
Benghazi

Mechanics (Mechanical Engineering)

HIGHER INSTITUTE FOR MECHANICAL VOCATIONS
Tripoli

Mechanics (Mechanical Engineering)

HIGHER INSTITUTE OF MEDICAL TECHNOLOGY
Tripoli

Medical Technology

HIGHER INSTITUTE OF SOCIAL WORK
Benghazi

Social Work

HIGHER INSTITUTE OF TECHNOLOGY
PO Box 68, Brack
Tel: +218 45300

Technology

History: Founded 1976

INDUSTRIAL SAFETY TRAINING INSTITUTE
Tripoli

Industrial Safety (Safety Engineering)

Madagascar

INSTITUTION TYPES AND CREDENTIALS

Types of higher education institutions:

Université (University)
Ecole normale (Teacher Training College)
Institut supérieur technique (Higher Technical Institute)

School leaving and higher education credentials:

Baccalauréat de l'Enseignement secondaire
Baccalauréat de l'Enseignement technique
Diplôme universitaire de Technicien supérieur (DUTS)
Diplôme d'Etudes universitaires générales (DEUG)
Diplôme d'Etudes universitaires littéraires (DEUL)
Diplôme d'Etudes universitaires scientifiques (DEUS)
Diplôme d'Etudes universitaires technologiques (DUET)
Certificat d'Aptitude pédagogique (CAPEN)
Licence
Diplôme d'Ingénieur
Docteur en Chirurgie dentaire
Maîtrise
Diplôme d'Etudes supérieures spécialisées (DESS)
Doctorat en Médecine
Diplôme d'Etudes approfondies (DEA)
Diplôme d'Etudes supérieures (DES)
Doctorat de troisième Cycle
Doctorat Ingénieur
Doctorat d'Etat

STRUCTURE OF EDUCATION SYSTEM

Pre-higher education:

Duration of compulsory education:

Age of entry: 6
Age of exit: 11

Structure of school system:

Primary
Type of school providing this education: Ecole primaire
Length of programme in years: 5
Age level from: 6 to: 11
Certificate/diploma awarded: Certificat d'Etudes Primaires élémentaires (CEPE)

First Cycle Secondary
Type of school providing this education: Collège
Length of programme in years: 4
Age level from: 11 to: 15
Certificate/diploma awarded: Brevet d'Etudes du premier Cycle (BEPC)

Technical Secondary
Type of school providing this education: Technical Secondary School
Length of programme in years: 3
Age level from: 15 to: 18
Certificate/diploma awarded: Baccalauréat de l'Enseignement technique

Second Cycle Secondary
Type of school providing this education: Lycée
Length of programme in years: 3
Age level from: 15 to: 18
Certificate/diploma awarded: Baccalauréat de l'Enseignement secondaire

School education:

Primary education lasts for five years, leading to the Certificat d'Etudes Primaires élémentaires (CEPE). Secondary education then covers seven years divided into a four-year first cycle and a three-year second cycle. On completion of the first cycle of secondary education, pupils obtain the Brevet d'Etudes du premier Cycle (BEPC). On completion of the second cycle, pupils obtain the Baccalauréat de l'Enseignement secondaire. Pupils not wishing to proceed to university may take only the four-year lower cycle programme. Technical secondary education lasts for three years, divided into two cycles. At the end of the lower cycle pupils obtain the Brevet d'Etudes industrielles/commerciales, and at the end of the three-year upper cycle they obtain the Baccalauréat de l'Enseignement technique.

Higher education:

Higher education is mainly provided by universities, technical institutes of higher education and teacher training colleges. The universities are autonomous institutions. Each university is headed by a Rector and administered by a Conseil d'Administration. In January 1999, a National Evaluation Agency (Agence nationale d'Evaluation (Agenate)) was created to evaluate the public and private institutions of higher education.

Main laws/decrees governing higher education:

Decree: Décret n°95-681   Year: 1995
Concerns: Organization of private higher education

Decree: Directive 92-030   Year: 1992
Concerns: Foundation of universities

Academic year:

Classes from: October *to:* July
August September

Languages of instruction:

French, Malagasy

Stages of studies:

Non-university level post-secondary studies (technical/vocational type):

Higher technical studies lead after three years of post-secondary education to the Brevet de Technicien supérieur.

University level studies:

University level first stage: Premier Cycle:

The first stage of higher education comprises a two-year broad-based multidisciplinary course common to all students wishing to study Letters, Science, Law, Economics, Management and Sociology. Students have to obtain a minimum number of credit units at the end of each year and then obtain the Diplôme universitaire d'Etudes littéraires (DUEL) in Humanities, the Diplôme universitaire d'Etudes scientifiques (DUES) in Science, the Diplôme universitaire d'Etudes technologiques or the Diplôme universitaire de Technicien supérieur en Informatique and the Diplôme de Fin d'Etudes du premier Cycle en Droit, Economie et Sociologie. It is foreseen that the first two years of the first cycle of studies will be extended to three years, including in Medicine.

University level second stage: Deuxième Cycle:

A year of specialization leads to the Licence. The Maîtrise is conferred after one year's further study beyond the Licence. If students successfully present a short thesis they are awarded the Maîtrise d'Enseignement. The Diplôme d'Ingénieur is conferred after five years' study. The title of Docteur en Chirurgie dentaire is conferred at the end of five years' study. Studies in Medicine last for seven years (plus one year of hospital practice) and lead to the Doctorat de Médecine.

University level third stage: Troisième Cycle:

A Diplôme d'Etudes approfondies is conferred one year after the Maîtrise. A Diplôme d'Etudes supérieures (DES) may be conferred after two years' study following upon the Maîtrise. Presentation of a thesis then leads to the Doctorat de Troisième Cycle after a minimum of one year's further study beyond the Diplôme d'Etudes approfondies and research work. A Certificat d'Etudes spécialisées (CES) is to be introduced in Medicine and post-university studies in Humanities, Social Sciences and Technical Sciences will be reinforced. A Doctorat Ingénieur is offered to engineers after four years' study after graduating.

University level fourth stage:

A Doctorat d'Etat is now being offered by the University of Antananarivo.

Teacher education:

Training of pre-primary and primary/basic school teachers

Primary school teachers are trained in Ecoles normales d'Instituteurs in courses lasting for two years and five months. Candidates must hold the Brevet d'Etudes du Premier Cycle (BEPC), but this requirement will be upgraded to the Baccalauréat.

Training of secondary school teachers

Secondary school teachers are trained in two years at second level National teacher training colleges. Entry is via a competitive examination and candidates must hold the Baccalauréat. For the second cycle of secondary education (lycées), third level teacher training takes place at the Ecole normale supérieure and at training colleges within the universities. Access is via a competitive examination and training lasts for five years.

Non-traditional studies:

Distance higher education

Distance education courses are provided in Law and Management by the CNTEMAD.

NATIONAL BODIES

Responsible authorities:

Ministry of Higher Education (Ministère de l'Enseignement supérieur)
    Minister: Joseph Sydson
    BP 4163
    Tsimbazaza
    Antananarivo 101
    Tel: +261(2022) 64451
    Fax: +261(2022) 23897
    EMail: spensup@syfed.refer.mg
    WWW: http://www.refer.mg/edu/minesup/minesup/minesup.htm

Universities Communication Centre (Maison de la Communication des Universités)
    Directeur général: Michel Norbert Rejela
    Directeur administratif et financier: John Guy Patrice
    International Relations: Lantoniaina Ralaimidona
    BP 7559
    Antananarivo 101
    Tel: +261(2022) 64409
    Fax: +261(2022) 69284

ADMISSIONS TO HIGHER EDUCATION

Admission to non university higher education studies

Name of secondary school credential required: Baccalauréat de l'Enseignement technique

Admission to university-level studies

Name of secondary school credential required: Baccalauréat de l'Enseignement technique
Minimum score/requirement: 10/20

Name of secondary school credential required: Baccalauréat de l'Enseignement secondaire
Minimum score/requirement: 10/20

Entrance exams required: entrance examination

Foreign students admission

Admission requirements: Foreign students must hold the Baccalauréat or an equivalent qualification.

Entry regulations: They must hold a visa and be officially presented by the competent authorities of their country.

Language requirements: Good knowledge of French.

Recognition of studies and qualifications:

Studies pursued in foreign countries (bodies dealing with recognition of foreign credentials):
Ministry of Higher Education (Ministère de l'Enseignement supérieur)
BP 4163
Tsimbazaza
Antananarivo
Tel: +261(2022) 64451
Fax: +261(2022) 23897
Telex: 22539 mrstd

References to further information on foreign student admissions and recognition of studies

Title: Livret de l'étudiant
Publisher: Université d'Antananarivo

Title: Présentation de l'Université de Madagascar et renseignements pratiques
Publisher: Université de Madagascar

STUDENT LIFE

Main student services at national level

Centre régional des Oeuvres universitaires
Université d'Antananarivo, Campus universitaire Ambohitsaina, PO Box 354
Antananarivo 101

Student expenses and financial aid

Student costs:

Average living costs: 600,000 (Malagasy Franc)
Home students tuition fees: Minimum: 50,000 (Malagasy Franc)
Maximum: 200,000 (Malagasy Franc)

Bodies providing information on student financial aid:

Service de l'Orientation, de l'Information, des Bourses et des Etudiants
  Université d'Antananarivo, PO Box 566
  Ambohitsaina
  Antananarivo 101
  Tel: +261(2022) 241-14

Publications on student services and financial aid:

  Title: Study Abroad 2000-2001
  Publisher: UNESCO/IBE
  Year of publication: 1999

GRADING SYSTEM

Usual grading system in secondary school

Full Description: 0-20
Highest on scale: 20
Pass/fail level: 10
Lowest on scale: 0

Main grading system used by higher education institutions

Full Description: 0-20
Highest on scale: 20
Pass/fail level: 10
Lowest on scale: 0

Other main grading systems

For thesis: passable: 10-12; assez bien: 12-14; bien 14-16; très bien: 16-18; très honorable: 18 or more.

NOTES ON HIGHER EDUCATION SYSTEM

Data for academic year: 2001-2002
Source: Ministère de l'Enseignement supérieur, Antananarivo, 2001

INSTITUTIONS OF HIGHER EDUCATION

UNIVERSITIES AND UNIVERSITY LEVEL INSTITUTIONS

PUBLIC INSTITUTIONS

*• UNIVERSITY OF ANTANANARIVO

Université d'Antananarivo
BP 566, Ambohitsaina, Antananarivo 101
Tel: +261(2022) 24114   +261(2022) 21103
Telex: 22304 recumt mg
EMail: recunivtana@simicro.mg
Website:
http://www.refer.mg/madag_ct/madag_ct/edu/minesup/antana
na/antanana.htm

Recteur: Pascal Rakotobe (2001-) Tel: +261(2022) 32639

Administrative Officer: Roger Andrianasy

International Relations: Christiane Andriamirado

Faculties
Law, Economics, Administration and Sociology *(DEGS)*
(Administration; Economics; Law; Sociology) *Dean*: Rado
Rakotoarison, *full-time staff:* 44, *students:* 5,295
Letters and Humanities (Arts and Humanities; English;
French; Geography; German; History; Literature; Modern Lan-
guages; Philosophy) *Dean*: G. Rabearimanana, *full-time staff:*
100, *students:* 2,781
Medicine (Gynaecology and Obstetrics; Medicine; Paediatrics;
Surgery) *Dean*: Pascal Rakotobe, *full-time staff:* 46, *students:*
1,688
Science (Chemistry; Mathematics; Natural Sciences; Physics)
Dean: M. Rafazy-Andriamampian, *full-time staff:* 169, *students:*
2,500

Schools
Agronomy (Agricultural Engineering; Agricultural Management; Agriculture; Agronomy; Animal Husbandry; Food Technology; Forestry; Water Management) *Director*: Daniel
Razakanindriana, *full-time staff:* 40, *students:* 476

History: Founded 1955 as Institut des hautes Etudes tracing
origins to School of Medicine (1896) and School of Law (1941).
Became Université de Madagascar 1960. Reorganized 1973
with six main divisions, and 1976 as a decentralized institution
with six Regional Centres. Acquired present status as independent university 1988.

Governing Bodies: Administration Council

Academic Year: October to July (October-February;
March-July)

Admission Requirements: Secondary school certificate
(baccalauréat) or equivalent, and entrance examination

Main Language(s) of Instruction: French, Malagasy

International Co-operation: Agreements with Institutions in
France, La Réunion, Germany, Algeria, Switzerland, USA,
South Africa, Netherlands, Belgium, Italy, United Kingdom and
Canada

Degrees and Diplomas: *Diplôme d'Etudes universitaires
littéraires (DEUL)*: 2 yrs; *Diplôme d'Etudes universitaires
scientifiques (DEUS)*: 2 yrs; *Diplôme d'Etudes universitaires
technologiques (DUET)*: 2 yrs; *Licence*: 1 further yr; *Diplôme
d'Ingénieur*: 4 yrs; *Maîtrise*: 1yr following Licence; *Doctorat en
Médecine*: 7 yrs; *Diplôme d'Etudes approfondies (DEA)*: 1yr following Maîtrise; *Diplôme d'Etudes supérieures (DES)*: 2 yrs following Maîtrise; *Doctorat de troisième Cycle*; *Doctorat d'Etat*.
Also teaching qualifications

Student Residential Facilities: Yes

Special Facilities: Museum of Art and Archaeology. Institute of
Civilizations

Libraries: c. 120,000 vols

Publications: Revue de Géographie; Terre Malagache, Sciences Agronomiques; Omaly Sy Anio (Hier et Aujourd'hui)

Academic Staff *1999:* Total: c. 635

Student Numbers *1999:* Total: c. 14,070

GEOPHYSICAL INSTITUTE AND OBSERVATORY OF
ANTANANARIVO
INSTITUT ET OBSERVATOIRE GEOPHYSIQUE
D'ANTANANARIVO
BP 3843 Ambohidempona, Campus Universitaire,
Antananarivo 101
Tel: +261(2022) 25353
Fax: +261(2022) 25353
EMail: ioga@syfed.refer.mg

Directeur: Jean-Bruno Ratsimbazafy

Departments
Geophysics

History: Founded 1989.

HIGHER PEDAGOGICAL SCHOOL
ECOLE NORMALE SUPÉRIEURE
BP 881, Antananarivo 101
Tel: +261(2022) 3562
Fax: +261(2022) 35584
EMail: ens@syfed.refer.mg; ens@dts.mg

Directeur: William R. Ratrema

Departments
Education
Teacher Training

History: Founded 1980. acquired present status 1994.
Academic Staff *1999:* Total: c. 75

Student Numbers *1999:* Total: c. 610

HIGHER POLYTECHNIC
ECOLE SUPÉRIEURE POLYTECHNIQUE
BP 1500, Vontovorona, Antananarivo 101
Tel: +261(2022) 29490
Fax: +261(2022) 27696

Directeur: Benjamin Randrianoelina

International Relations: Nicole Ravelomanantsoa

Departments
Building Technology and Civil Engineering (Building Technologies; Civil Engineering)
Chemical Engineering
Electrical Engineering
Electronic Engineering
Geology
Hydraulic Engineering
Materials Engineering and Metallurgical Engineering (Materials Engineering; Metallurgical Engineering)
Mechanical Engineering
Meteorology
Mining Engineering
Surveying and Mapping
Telecommunications Engineering
Town Planning and Urban Studies (Town Planning; Urban Studies)

History: Founded 1975. Acquired present status 1994.

INSTITUTE OF CIVILIZATIONS, MUSEUM OF ART AND ARCHAEOLOGY
INSTITUT DES CIVILISATIONS, MUSÉE D'ART ET D'ARCHÉOLOGIE
BP 564, 17 rue Docteur Villette, Isoraka, Antananarivo 101
Tel: +261(2022) 1047
EMail: icmaa@dts.mg

Directeur: Jean-Aimé Rakotoarisoa

Anthropology; Archaeology; Arts and Humanities; Cultural Studies; Ethnology; Folklore; Geography; History; Musicology; Prehistory

History: Founded 1964.

INSTITUTE OF ENERGY STUDIES
INSTITUT POUR LA MAÎTRISE DE L'ENERGIE
BP 566, Ambohitsaina, Antananarivo 101
Tel: +261(2022) 30953
Fax: +261(2022) 22316
EMail: enertech@dts.mg

Directeur: Edmond Razafindrakoto

Energy Engineering; Thermal Engineering

History: Founded 1977.

NATIONAL CENTRE OF ENGLISH TEACHING
CENTRE NATIONAL D'ENSEIGNEMENT DE LA LANGUE ANGLAISE
BP 109, Antananarivo 101
Tel: +261(22) 26028
Fax: +261(22) 66462

Directeur: M. Rasoloheritsimba

Centres
English Teaching (Foreign Languages Education)

History: Founded 1985.

RADIO-ISOTOPES LABORATORY
LABORATOIRE DE RADIO-ISOTOPES
BP 3383, Antananarivo 101
Tel: +261(2022) 40488
EMail: lrililia@dts.mg

Directeur: Jean-Rubis Andriantsoa

Nuclear Medicine and Biology *(LRI)* (Biology; Medical Technology)

History: Founded 1956.

* UNIVERSITY OF FIANARANTSOA
Université de Fianarantsoa (UF)
BP 1264, Fianarantsoa 301
Tel: +261(2075) 50802
Fax: +261(2075) 50619
EMail: ufianara@syfed.refer.mg
Website: http://www.misa.mg/univ/fianaran/fianaran.htm

Recteur: Marie Dieu Donné Michel Razafindrandriatsimanir (1998-)

Directeur administratif: Dominique Razafimanampy
Tel: +261(2075) 51092

International Relations: Alphonsine Rasoanirina

Faculties
Law *Dean*: Patrice Goussot, *full-time staff:* 25, *part-time staff:* 5, *students:* 1,247
Science (Chemistry; Mathematics and Computer Science; Natural Sciences; Physics; Social Sciences) *Dean*: Tsilavo Mandresy Razafindrazaka, *full-time staff:* 25, *part-time staff:* 20, *students:* 301

History: Founded 1977 as Regional Centre of the Université de Madagascar. Acquired present status as independent University 1988.

Academic Year: October to June

Admission Requirements: Secondary school certificate (baccalauréat) or equivalent, and entrance examination

Fees: (Malagasy francs-MGF) 1st Cycle, 50,000-90,000; 2nd Cycle, 60,000-90,000; 3rd Cycle, 100,000-200,000

Main Language(s) of Instruction: French, Malagasy

International Co-operation: Université Paris XII; Université de Valenciennes et du Hainaut Cambresis; Université de Picardie Jules Verne; Université de la Réunion

Degrees and Diplomas: *Diplôme universitaire de Technicien supérieur (DUTS)*: Environmental Sciences; Computer Sciences; *Diplôme d'Etudes universitaires générales (DEUG)*: 2 yrs; *Diplôme d'Etudes universitaires scientifiques (DEUS)*: Mathematics; Physics and Chemistry; Mathematics and Computing for Social Sciences, 2 yrs; *Certificat d'Aptitude pédagogique (CAPEN)*: Pedagogy; *Licence*: Mathematics; Physics and Chemistry; Mathematics and Computing for Social Sciences, 3 yrs; *Diplôme d'Ingénieur*: 4 yrs; *Maîtrise*: Mathematics; Physics and Chemistry; Mathematics and Computing for Social Sciences, 4 yrs; *Diplôme d'Etudes supérieures spécialisées (DESS)*: Training for Adult Education, 5 yrs; *Diplôme d'Etudes approfondies (DEA)*: Law; Physics; Environmental Sciences, 5 yrs; *Diplôme d'Etudes supérieures (DES)*: Law (DEJSC), 5 yrs

Student Services: Cultural Centre, Sports Facilities, Language Programmes, Health Services

Academic Staff *1999-2000*			TOTAL
FULL-TIME			68
PART-TIME			93
TOTAL			**161**
STAFF WITH DOCTORATE	MEN	WOMEN	TOTAL
FULL-TIME	–	–	24
PART-TIME	–	33	33
TOTAL	–	–	**57**
Student Numbers *1999-2000*	MEN	WOMEN	TOTAL
All (Foreign Included)	1,072	758	**1,830**

HIGHER PEDAGOGICAL SCHOOL
ECOLE NORMALE SUPÉRIEURE
BP 1264, Fianarantsoa 301
Tel: +261(2075) 50812
Fax: +261(2075) 50619
EMail: ufianara@syfed.refer.mg

Directeur: Roger Ratovonjanahary

Departments
Mathematics
Physics

INSTITUTE OF ENVIRONMENTAL AND TECHNICAL SCIENCES
INSTITUT DES SCIENCES ET TECHNIQUES DE L'ENVIRONNEMENT
BP 1264, Fianarantsoa 301
Tel: +261(2075) 50812
Fax: +261(2075) 50619

Directeur: Pascal Ratalata

Environmental Studies

NATIONAL SCHOOL OF COMPUTER SCIENCE
ECOLE NATIONALE D'INFORMATIQUE
BP 1487, Tanambao, Fianarantsoa 301
Tel: +261(2075) 50801
Fax: +261(2075) 50619
EMail: eni@syfed.refer.mg

Directeur: Josvah Paul Razafimandimby

Computer Science

History: Founded 1980. Acquired present status 1983.

* UNIVERSITY OF MAHAJANGA
Université de Mahajanga
BP 652, Mahajanga 401
Tel: +261(2062) 22724
Fax: +261(2062) 23312
EMail: recifmaj@dts.mg
Website: http://www.misa.mg/univ/mahajang/mahajang.htm

Recteur: Rajabo (2001-) **Tel:** +261(2062) 23312

Directeur Administratif: Jeanette Razafindralinina

International Relations: Claude Hortense Solofoniaina

Faculties
Medicine
Science (Biochemistry; Biology; Botany; Chemistry; Earth Sciences; Environmental Studies; Natural Sciences)

History: Founded 1977 as Regional Centre of the Université de Madagascar. Acquired present status as independent University 1992.

Academic Year: November to July

Admission Requirements: Secondary school certificate (baccalauréat) or equivalent, and entrance examination

Main Language(s) of Instruction: French, Malagasy

Degrees and Diplomas: *Diplôme d'Etudes universitaires littéraires (DEUL)*: 2 yrs; *Diplôme d'Etudes universitaires scientifiques (DEUS)*: 2 yrs; *Diplôme d'Etudes universitaires technologiques (DUET)*: 2 yrs; *Licence*: 1 further yr; *Diplôme d'Ingénieur*: 4 yrs; *Maîtrise*: 1 further yr; *Doctorat en Médecine*: 7 yrs; *Diplôme d'Etudes approfondies (DEA)*: 1 further yr; *Diplôme d'Etudes supérieures (DES)*: a further 2 yrs; *Doctorat de troisième Cycle*. Also teaching qualifications

Student Numbers: Total: c. 1,230

INSTITUTE OF TROPICAL DENTISTRY
INSTITUT D'ODONTO STOMATOLOGIE TROPICALE
BP 453, Mahajanga 401
Tel: +261(2062) 22834
EMail: cdrom@dts.mg

Directrice: Noëline Razanamihaja

Institutes
Tropical Dentistry (Dentistry; Stomatology)

• UNIVERSITY OF NORTH MADAGASCAR
Université Nord Madagascar (UNM)
BP 0, Antsiranana 201
Tel: +261(2082) 21507   +261(2082) 21137   +261(2082) 21483
Fax: +261(2082) 29409
EMail: unm@dts.mg; unm@bow.dts.mg
Website: http://www.misa.mg/univ/antsiran/antsiran.htm

Recteur: Cécile Marie Ange Manorohanta (2001-)

Directeur Administratif: Aly Ahmad Tel: +261(2082) 22095

International Relations: Alex Totomarovario
EMail: atotomar@syfed.refer.mg

Faculties

Letters and Human Sciences (Arts and Humanities; Modern Languages) *Dean*: Cécile Manorohanta, *full-time staff:* 5, *part-time staff:* 7, *students:* 226
Science (Chemistry; Natural Sciences; Physics) *Director*: Jean Victor Randrianohavy, *full-time staff:* 15, *part-time staff:* 8, *students:* 174

Schools

Teacher Training *Director*: André Totohasina, *full-time staff:* 8, *part-time staff:* 5, *students:* 140

History: Founded 1975 as Regional Centre of the Université de Madagascar. Acquired present status as independent university 1992.

Governing Bodies: Board of Governors

Academic Year: November to July

Admission Requirements: Secondary school certificate (baccalauréat) or equivalent, and entrance examination

Main Language(s) of Instruction: French

International Co-operation: Swiss Federal Institute of Technology Lausanne; Ecole normale supérieure (ENS Cachan); University of Le Havre; University of Perpignan; University of Nice-Sophia Antipolis; University of La Réunion; Catholic University of Louvain; Otto-von-Guericke University of Magdeburg; University 'Joseph Fourier' (Grenoble I); Institut national des Sciences appliquées de Lyon (INSA Lyon)

Degrees and Diplomas: *Diplôme d'Etudes universitaires littéraires (DEUL)*: Language Studies, 2 yrs; *Diplôme d'Etudes universitaires scientifiques (DEUS)*: Physics/Chemistry, 2 yrs; *Diplôme d'Etudes universitaires technologiques (DUET)*: 2 yrs; *Certificat d'Aptitude pédagogique (CAPEN)*: Teacher Training, 5 yrs; *Licence*: 3 yrs; *Diplôme d'Ingénieur*: 5 yrs; *Maîtrise*: 4 yrs; *Diplôme d'Etudes approfondies (DEA)*: Technology, a further 2 yrs; *Doctorat Ingénieur*: Engineering, 4 yrs. Also teaching qualifications

Student Services: Academic Counselling, Cultural Centre, Sports Facilities, Health Services

Student Residential Facilities: For c. 1000 students

Libraries: Bibliothèque universitaire, 13,000 vols

Academic Staff 1999	MEN	WOMEN	TOTAL
FULL-TIME	55	8	63
PART-TIME	–	–	29
TOTAL	–	–	**92**
STAFF WITH DOCTORATE			
FULL-TIME	34	3	37
PART-TIME	–	–	13
TOTAL	–	–	**50**
Student Numbers 1999	MEN	WOMEN	TOTAL
All (Foreign Included)	608	200	**808**
FOREIGN ONLY	–	–	31

HIGHER POLYTECHNIC
ECOLE SUPÉRIEURE POLYTECHNIQUE
BP 0, Antsiranana 201
Tel: +261(2082) 21137, Ext. 49
EMail: antenais@syfed.refer.mg

Directeur: Max Andriamanantena

Departments
Electrical Engineering
Electronic Engineering
Hydraulic Engineering
Mechanical Engineering

History: Founded 1977. Acquired present status 1994.

HIGHER SCHOOL OF TECHNICAL STUDIES
ECOLE NATIONALE SUPÉRIEURE DE L'ENSEIGNEMENT TECHNIQUE
BP, Antsiranana 201
Tel: +261(2082) 21137, Ext. 50
Fax: +261(2082) 29409

Directeur: André Totohasina

Departments
Electrical Engineering
Mathematics and Computer Science (Computer Science; Mathematics)
Mechanical Engineering

History: Founded 1991. Acquired present status 1994.

*• UNIVERSITY OF TOAMASINA
Université de Toamasina
BP 591, Barikadimy, Toamasina 501
Tel: +261(2053) 32244
Fax: +261(2053) 33566
EMail: univtoam@dts.mg
Website: http://www.dts.mg/univ-toamasima

Recteur: Eugène Régis Mangalaza (1998-)
EMail: rectorat@univ-toamasina.mg

Directeur administratif: Rachelle Bienvenue Radifison

International Relations: Abraham Latsaka

Faculties
Economics and Management (Economics; Management) *Director*: Raymond Kasave
Letters and Human Sciences (Arts and Humanities) *Director*: Jacques Randrianatoandro

Higher Schools
National Customs (Cultural Studies)

Centres
Applied Modern Language Studies (Modern Languages) *Director*: Germain F. Davidson
Computer-Aided Management (Management) *Director*: Paul Henri Alex
Entrepreneurship Training (Management) *Director*: Ernest Marinasy

Environment and Integrated Development (Development Studies; Environmental Studies; French; Geography; History; Philosophy)

Foreign Languages (Modern Languages) *Director*: Germain Franck Davidson, *full-time staff*: 1, *part-time staff*: 5, *students*: 116

History: Founded 1977 as Regional Centre of the Université de Madagascar. Acquired present status as independent University 1992.

Governing Bodies: Board of Trustees

Academic Year: October to June

Admission Requirements: Secondary school certificate (baccalauréat) or equivalent, and entrance examination

Fees: (Malagasy Francs-MGF): 25,000-30,000 per annum

Main Language(s) of Instruction: French, Malagasy

Degrees and Diplomas: *Diplôme d'Etudes universitaires générales (DEUG)*: 2 yrs; *Diplôme d'Etudes universitaires littéraires (DEUL)*: 2 yrs; *Licence*: 1 further yr; *Diplôme d'Ingénieur*: 4 yrs; *Maîtrise*: 1 yr following Licence; *Diplôme d'Etudes approfondies (DEA)*: 1 further yr; *Diplôme d'Etudes supérieures (DES)*: a further 2 yrs

Special Facilities: Archaeological and Cultural Museum

Libraries: Management Library, 4026 vols; Letters, 4524 vols

Academic Staff *1999:* Total: c. 40

CENTRE FOR ETHNOLOGICAL AND LINGUISTIC STUDIES AND RESEARCH
CENTRE D'ETUDES ET DE RECHERCHES ETHNOLOGIQUES ET LINGUISTIQUES
BP 591, Toamasina
Tel: +261(20) 533-3400
Fax: +261(20) 533-3566
EMail: univtoam@dts.mg

Directeur: Fulgence Fanony

Centres
Ethnology and Linguistics (Ethnology; Linguistics)

History: Founded 1985.

HIGHER PROFESSIONAL INSTITUTE OF MANAGEMENT
INSTITUT SUPÉRIEUR PROFESSIONNEL DE GESTION
BP 591, Toamasina 501
Tel: +261(2053) 33967
Fax: +261(2053) 33615

Directeur: Paul Henri Alex

Departments
Administration
Business Management (Business Administration)

UNIVERSITY OF TOLIARA
Université de Toliara
BP 185, Maninday, Toliara 601
Tel: +261(2041) 033
Fax: +261(2041) 802
EMail: rectul@syfed.refer.mg; rectul@dts.mg
Website: http://www.misa.mg/univ/toliara/toliara.htm

Recteur: Alphonse Dina (2001-)

Directeur administratif et financier: Elysé T. Andriantompoiniarivo

International Relations: Jean Riel

Faculties
Letters and Human Sciences (Arts and Humanities; French; Geography; History; Literature; Philosophy)
Science (Biology; Chemistry; Earth Sciences; Natural Sciences; Physics)

History: Founded 1977 as Regional Centre of the Université de Madagascar. Acquired present status as independent University 1988.

Academic Year: November to July

Admission Requirements: Secondary school certificate (baccalauréat) or equivalent, and entrance examination

Main Language(s) of Instruction: French, Malagasy

International Co-operation: University of Louisville; University of La Réunion; University of Limoges; Ecole normale supérieure agronomique de Rennes; Université des Sciences et Technologies de Lille I; University of Aix-Marseilles III; University of Paris IV; University Louis Pasteur (Strasbourg I); State University of New York at Stony Brook; Université de la Mediterranée (Aix-Marseilles II)

Degrees and Diplomas: *Diplôme d'Etudes universitaires littéraires (DEUL)*: 2 yrs; *Diplôme d'Etudes universitaires scientifiques (DEUS)*: 2 yrs; *Diplôme d'Etudes universitaires technologiques (DUET)*: 2 yrs; *Licence*: 1 further yr; *Diplôme d'Ingénieur*: 4 yrs; *Maîtrise*: 1 further yr; *Diplôme d'Etudes approfondies (DEA)*: 1 further yr; *Diplôme d'Etudes supérieures (DES)*: a further 2 yrs; *Doctorat de troisième Cycle*. Also teaching qualifications

Libraries: Library Calvin Tiesbo, 8000 vols

DOCUMENTATION AND RESEARCH CENTRE FOR ART AND ORAL TRADITIONS OF MADAGASCAR
CENTRE DE DOCUMENTATION ET DE RECHERCHE SUR L'ART ET LES TRADITIONS ORALES À MADAGASCAR
BP 185, Toliara 601
Tel: +261(9) 41033
Fax: +261(9) 41802

Directeur: M. Tsiazonera

Centres
Arts and Oral Traditions (Ethnology; Fine Arts)

History: Founded 1985.

HIGHER PEDAGOGICAL SCHOOL
ECOLE NORMALE SUPÉRIEURE
BP 185, Maninday, Toliara 601
Tel: +261(2094) 41773
Fax: +261(2094) 41802

Directeur: Jean Rakotoarivelo

Departments
Philosophy

INSTITUTE OF MARINE SCIENCE
INSTITUT HALIEUTIQUE ET DES SCIENCES MARINES
BP 141, Toliara 601
Tel: +261(2094) 41612
Fax: +261(2094) 41612
EMail: ihsm@syfed.syfed.refer.mg

Director: Man Wai Rabenievanana

Departments
Aquaculture
Fishery
Safety Engineering

History: Founded 1986.

NATIONAL INSTITUTE OF NUCLEAR SCIENCES AND TECHNIQUES
Institut national des Sciences et Techniques nucléaires (INSTN)
BP 4279, Antananarivo 101
Tel: +261(2022) 61181
Fax: +261(2022) 35583
EMail: official.mail@instn.mg
Website: http://takelaka.dts.mg/instn

Directeur général: Raoelina Andriambololona
Tel: +261(2022) 61180

Directeur administratif: Chrysante Solofoarisina

International Relations: Joël Rajaobelison

Departments
Environmental Engineering
Maintenance Technology
Nuclear Engineering *Head*: Ravelomanantsoa Solofo, *full-time staff:* 2, *students:* 6
Safety Engineering

History: Founded 1976 as Laboratory for Nuclear Physics and Applied Physics (L.P.N.P.A.). Acquired present status and title 1992. A public autonomous institution.

Governing Bodies: Board of Governors

Academic Year: October to September

Admission Requirements: Maîtrise ès Sciences

Fees: (Malagasy Francs-MGF): 50,000

Main Language(s) of Instruction: French, English

International Co-operation: Fachhochschule Giessen-Friedberg, University of Applied Science, Germany

Degrees and Diplomas: *Diplôme d'Etudes approfondies (DEA)*: 1-2 yrs; *Doctorat de troisième Cycle*: 2-3 yrs

Student Services: Employment Services

Libraries: Raoelina Andriambololona Library

Publications: Seminar Raoelina Andriambololona Interdisciplinary

Press or Publishing House: Publishing Unit

Academic Staff *1999*: Full-Time: c. 10 Part-Time: c. 30 Total: c. 40

Staff with Doctorate: Total: c. 10

Student Numbers *1999:* Total: c. 30

PRIVATE INSTITUTIONS

CATHOLIC INSTITUTE OF MADAGASCAR
Institut Catholique de Madagascar (ICM)
BP 6026, Ambatoroka, Antananarivo 101
Tel: +261(2022) 34009
Fax: +261(2022) 34013
EMail: ucm@vitelcom.mg
Website: http://www.misa.mg/univ/prive/icm/icm.htm

Recteur: Germain Rajoelison

General Secretary: Laurent Razafindrazaka

Departments
Economics and Management (Accountancy; Econometrics; Economics; Finance; Management)
Law and Political Science (Commercial Law; International Relations; Law; Political Science)
Philosophy
Social Sciences (Anthropology; Social Psychology; Social Sciences)
Theology

History: Founded 1960, acquired present status and title 1997.

Admission Requirements: Secondary school certificate (Baccalauréat) and entrance examination.

Publications: Aspect du Christianisme à Madagascar

OTHER INSTITUTIONS

PUBLIC INSTITUTIONS

HIGHER INSTITUTE OF TECHNOLOGY, ANTANANARIVO
Institut Supérieur de Technologie (IST)
BP 8122, Ampasapito, Antananarivo 101
Tel: +261(2022) 41423
Fax: +261(2022) 40543

Directeur général: Josoa Ramamonjisoa

Directeur administratif et financier: Antoine Razafindramanana

Departments
Civil Engineering
Industrial Engineering
Tertiary Studies

History: Founded 1989. Acquired present status 2001.

HIGHER INSTITUTE OF TECHNOLOGY, ANTSIRANANA
Institut supérieur de Technologie (IST)
BP 453, Antsiranana 201
Tel: +261(2082) 22431
Fax: +261(2082) 29425
Website: http://www.refer.mg/madag-ct/edu/diego/ist.htm

Directeur général: Fortunat Ramahatandrina

Directeur Administratif et financier: Ederaly

International Relations: Dominique Rakoto

Departments
Maintainance Technology (Maintenance Technology)
Tertiary Studies

History: Founded 1989. Acquired present status 2001.

NATIONAL DISTANCE LEARNING CENTRE OF MADAGASCAR
Centre national de Télé-Enseignement de Madagascar (CNTEMAD)
BP 78, Lot IVC 6, Ambatomitsangana, Antananarivo 101
Tel: +261(2022) 60057
Fax: +261(2022) 36090
EMail: cntemad@syfed.refer.mg

Directeur: Norbert Ralison Tel: +261(2022) 60386

Directeur des Affaires Générales: Jacques Roland Rakotondrasanjy Tel: +261(2022) 64563

Centres
Law and Administration (Administration; Law)

History: Founded 1992

PRIVATE INSTITUTIONS

SOCIAL SERVICE SCHOOL
Ecole de Service Social
BP 7570, 133 Avenue Lénine, Antanimena, Antananarivo 101
Directrice: Phan Van Hien

Departments
Social Sciences (Social and Community Services; Social Sciences)

Malawi

INSTITUTION TYPES AND CREDENTIALS

Types of higher education institutions:

University
College
Polytechnic

School leaving and higher education credentials:

Malawi School Certificate of Education
Teacher's Certificate
Diploma
Bachelor's Degree
Master's Degree
Doctor's Degree

STRUCTURE OF EDUCATION SYSTEM

Pre-higher education:

Duration of compulsory education:

> Age of entry: 5
> Age of exit: 13

Structure of school system:

> *Primary*
> Type of school providing this education: Primary School
> Length of programme in years: 8
> Age level from: 5 to: 13
> Certificate/diploma awarded: Primary School Leaving Certificate of Education
>
> *Junior Secondary*
> Type of school providing this education: Secondary School
> Length of programme in years: 2
> Age level from: 13 to: 15
> Certificate/diploma awarded: Junior Certificate of Education
>
> *Senior Secondary*
> Type of school providing this education: Secondary School
> Length of programme in years: 2

Age level from: 15 to: 17

Certificate/diploma awarded: Malawi School Certificate of Education (MSCE)

School education:

Primary education lasts for eight years, leading to the Primary School Leaving Certificate. Secondary education lasts for four years. At the end of the second year, pupils take the Junior Certificate of Education. Successful students may enter form III. At the end of form IV, pupils take the Malawi School Certificate of Education.

Higher education:

Higher education is provided by the University of Malawi and its five constituent colleges. The university is governed by a Council, most of whose members are appointed by the government. The Senate, composed of academics, is responsible for academic matters. It is mainly supported by government grants and miscellaneous income. The Government has opened the Mzuzu University to train secondary school teachers.

Academic year:

Classes from: September *to:* July

Languages of instruction:

English

Stages of studies:

Non-university level post-secondary studies (technical/vocational type):

Technical and training colleges offer courses in such fields as forestry, marine science, social welfare and hotel management, as well as in various trades. These courses lead to certificates awarded after studies lasting between six months and four years.

University level studies:

University level first stage: *Bachelor's Degree*:
The Bachelor's Degree is generally conferred after five to six years' study. A professional qualification is awarded as a diploma after three years' study.

University level second stage: *Master's Degree*:
A Master's degree or a professional qualification is conferred after one to two years' study beyond the Bachelor's Degree.

University level third stage: *Doctor's Degree*:
The Doctor's Degree is conferred after three to five years' study beyond the Master's Degree. Candidates must submit a thesis and spend at least six months in residence.

Teacher education:

Training of pre-primary and primary/basic school teachers
Primary school teachers are trained in primary teacher training colleges where courses last for two years. Teachers obtain the T2 (senior primary) or T3 (junior primary) Teachers Certificate after one year's study. T2 colleges admit students with the Malawi School Certificate of Education (MSCE) and

T3 colleges admit students with the Junior Certificate of Education (JCE). The Malawi Institute of Education provides introduction courses to give school-leavers the basic skills to act as "assistant" or "pupil teachers".

Training of secondary school teachers
Secondary school teachers are trained at Chancellor College which offers a four-year educational programme and at a secondary teacher training college at Domasi in Zomba. The fifth year consists of professional studies and teaching practice. The course leads to a Bachelor of Education degree. Technical teachers are trained jointly at the Polytechnic and Chancellor College. The government has opened the Mzuzu University which trains secondary school teachers.

NATIONAL BODIES

Responsible authorities:

Ministry of Education
    Minister: Nga Mtafu
    Principal Secretary: O.T. Odala
    PO Box 328
    Lilongwe 3
    Tel: +265 784-800
    Fax: +265 782-873

ADMISSIONS TO HIGHER EDUCATION

Admission to university-level studies

Name of secondary school credential required: Malawi School Certificate of Education
Minimum score/requirement: Excellent results in subjects the candidate wishes to study.

Foreign students admission

Admission requirements: Foreign students should hold qualifications equivalent to the Malawi School Certificate of Education with two of the six credits in English and Mathematics.

Entry regulations: Foreign students must be in possession of a visa. Confirmation of admission to the university must be obtained prior to departure as well as an entry permit from the Chief Immigration Officer, Box. 331, Blantyre.

Language requirements: Good knowledge of English for regular university courses.

Application procedures:

Apply to individual institution for entry to: University

Apply to: The Registrar, University of Malawi
    PO Box 278
    Zomba
    Tel: +265 526-622

Fax: +265 524-760
EMail: university.office@chirunga.sdnp.org.mw

References to further information on foreign student admissions and recognition of studies

Title: Study Abroad 2000-2001
Publisher: UNESCO/IBE
Year of publication: 1999

STUDENT LIFE

Student expenses and financial aid

Student costs:

Home students tuition fees: Minimum: 25,000 (Malawi Kwacha)
Maximum: 50,000 (Malawi Kwacha)
Foreign students tuition fees: Minimum: 7,213 (US Dollar)

GRADING SYSTEM

Usual grading system in secondary school

Full Description: The Malawi Certificate of Education is graded 1-9.
Highest on scale: 1
Pass/fail level: 7,8
Lowest on scale: 9

Main grading system used by higher education institutions

Full Description: 0-100%
Highest on scale: 100%
Pass/fail level: 50-59%
Lowest on scale: 0%

NOTES ON HIGHER EDUCATION SYSTEM

Data for academic year: 2000-2001
Source: University of Malawi, Zomba, 2001

INSTITUTIONS OF HIGHER EDUCATION

UNIVERSITIES

PUBLIC INSTITUTIONS

MZUZU UNIVERSITY
Private Bag 1, Luwinga, Mzuzu 2
Tel: +265 333-575
Fax: +265 333-497
EMail: mzuni@sdnp.org.mw
Website: http://www.mzuzu.leland-mw.org

Vice-Chancellor: Peter Mwanza (2000-)
EMail: gola@sdnp.org.mw

Registrar: Reginald M. Mushani
EMail: rmushani@sdnp.org.mw

Faculties
Education (Continuing Education; Humanities and Social Science Education; Literature; Mathematics; Modern Languages; Natural Sciences; Science Education; Teacher Training) *Dean:* Anacklet G. Phiri
Environmental Sciences (Environmental Engineering; Forestry)

History: Founded 1997 with one faculty.

Academic Year: January to October (January-June; June-October)

Admission Requirements: Malawi Certificate of Education or equivalent

Fees: (Kwacha): Undergraduate, 39,200 per annum; foreign students, 92,500

Degrees and Diplomas: *Bachelor's Degree:* Arts (Education); Science (Education); Science (Forestry); Science (Health Science Education); *Master's Degree; Doctor's Degree*

Academic Staff *1999:* Total: **23**

Student Numbers *1999*	MEN	WOMEN	TOTAL
All (Foreign Included)	81	23	**104**

*• UNIVERSITY OF MALAWI (UNIMA)
PO Box 278, Zomba
Tel: +265 526-622
Fax: +265 524-760
Telex: (0904) 45214 unima
Cable: university zomba
EMail: universityoffice@unima.wn.apc.org

Vice-Chancellor: David Rubadiri (2000-) Tel: +265 524-305
Fax: +265 524-297 EMail: vc@sdnp.org.mlw

Registrar: Geoffrey G. Chipungu Tel: +265 524-754

International Relations: Nita Chivwara Tel: +265 526-561

Faculties
Agriculture *(Lilongwe) Dean:* G.Y. Kanyama-Phiri
Applied Studies *(Blantyre) Dean:* C.R. Mtogolo
Commerce *(Blantyre)* (Business and Commerce) *Dean:* B.J.B. Chiodezka
Education *Dean:* O.J. Kathamalo
Engineering *(Blantyre) Dean:* V.H. Chipofya
Humanities (Arts and Humanities) *Dean:* B.J. Uledi-Kamanga
Law *Dean (Acting):* N.D. Mhura
Medicine *(Blantyre) Dean:* R.L. Broadhead
Nursing *(Lilongwe) Dean:* Maureen L. Chirawa
Science (Natural Sciences) *Dean:* Elizabeth Henry
Social Sciences *Dean:* E.B.D. Silumbu

Units
Agriculture Policy Research (Agronomy)
Gender Studies

Institutes
Education *(Domasi) Director:* N.T. Kaperemera

Centres
Educational Research and Training (Educational Research) *Director:* J.B. Kuthemba Mwale, *full-time staff:* 5
Language Studies
Management *(Blantyre)*
Social Research (Social Studies) *Director:* S.W. Khaila, *full-time staff:* 10

History: Founded 1964, integrating all the country's facilities for further and higher education.

Governing Bodies: University Council

Academic Year: September to June (September-December; January-March; April-June)

Admission Requirements: Malawi Certificate of Education or equivalent

Fees: (Kwacha): 1500 per annum

Main Language(s) of Instruction: English

International Co-operation: Institutions in North America, Europe, and Africa

Degrees and Diplomas: *Bachelor's Degree:* 5-6 yrs; *Master's Degree:* Arts (MA); Education (MEd); Law (LLM); Science (MSc); Science in Agriculture (MSc (Agri)), a further 1-2 yrs; *Doctor's Degree:* (PhD), a further 3-5 yrs

Student Residential Facilities: Yes

Special Facilities: Malawi National Herbarium and Botanical Gardens

Libraries: Total, 338,121 vols; 1074 periodicals

Publications: Advancement of Science in Malawi and Luso; Bunda College Research Bulletin; Calendar; UNIMA Newsletter; Journal of Religious Education; Journal of Social Science; Report on Animal Research Conferences; Physical Scientist; Journal of Humanities

Press or Publishing House: Montfort Press

Academic Staff *1999:* Total: c. 480

Student Numbers *1999:* Total: c. 4,000

BUNDA COLLEGE OF AGRICULTURE
PO Box 219, Lilongwe
Tel: +265 277-222
Fax: +265 277-364
EMail: bcaprincipal@sdnp.org.mw
Website: http://chirunga.sdnp.org.mw/bunda/intro.htm

Principal: G.Y. Kanyama-Phiri (2000-) Tel: +265 277-324
Fax: +265 277-324 EMail: bcaprincipal@sdnp.org.mw

Departments
Agricultural Engineering (Agricultural Engineering; Agriculture)
Animal Science (Animal Husbandry)
Aquaculture and Fisheries (Aquaculture; Fishery)
Crop Science (Crop Production)
Home Economics and Human Nutrition (Home Economics; Nutrition)
Language and Development Communication (Communication Studies; Modern Languages)
Rural Development (Rural Studies)

History: Founded 1964

CHANCELLOR COLLEGE
PO Box 280, Zomba
Tel: +265 524-222
Fax: +265 522-046
Telex: 4742 chancoll mi
Cable: chancoll, zomba
EMail: ccadmin@chirunga.sdnp.org.mw

Principal: Francis Moto (2000-) Tel: +265 525-083
EMail: fmoto@chirunga.sdnp.org.mw

Registrar: Trasinius Nampota

International Relations: Trasinius Nampota
EMail: ccadmi@unima.wn.apc.org

Faculties
Education
Humanities (Arts and Humanities)
Law
Science (Natural Sciences)
Social Sciences

History: Founded 1964

COLLEGE OF MEDICINE
Private Bag 360, Chichiri, Blantyre 3
Tel: +265 671-911
Fax: +265 674-700
Telex: 43744 mi
EMail: com@malawi.net

Principal: John David Chiphangwi (1995-) Tel: +265 674-473
Registrar: B.W. Malunga
International Relations: B.W. Malunga

Colleges
Basic Sciences (Anatomy; Biochemistry; Natural Sciences; Pharmacology; Physiology)
Clinical Medicine (Gynaecology and Obstetrics; Medicine; Paediatrics; Surgery)
Medicine *Principal*: John David Chiphangwi

History: Founded 1991.

Academic Year: January to November

Admission Requirements: ('A') level passes in Biology, Chemistry, Mathematics or Physics

Fees: (Kwacha): 46,000

Main Language(s) of Instruction: English

Degrees and Diplomas: *Master's Degree*: 5 yrs

Student Services: Academic Counselling, Social Counselling, Sports Facilities

Student Residential Facilities: Yes

Libraries: Sharing facilities with The Polytechnic

Academic Staff *1999*	MEN	WOMEN	TOTAL
FULL-TIME	60	8	**68**

Staff with doctorate: Total: **45**

Student Numbers *1999*	MEN	WOMEN	TOTAL
All (Foreign Included)	70	30	**100**

KAMUZU COLLEGE OF NURSING
Private Bag 1, Lilongwe
Tel: +265 721-622
Fax: +265 752-327
Cable: Nursing Lilongwe
EMail: kcnll@sdnp.org.mw

Principal: Christina N. Chihana

Registrar: D.A. Mphepo

International Relations: D.A. Mphepo

Nursing

THE POLYTECHNIC
Private Bag 303, Chichiri, Blantyre 3
Tel: +265 670-411
Fax: +265 670- 578
Telex: 44613 polytech mi
Cable: The Polytechnic, Blantyre

Principal: Henry Chibwana (1996-) Tel: +265 671-637
EMail: hchibwana@sdnp.org.mw

Registrar: F.T.Z Msonthi

International Relations: F.T.Z Msonthi

Faculties
Applied Studies (Environmental Studies; Health Sciences; Journalism; Mathematics; Mathematics and Computer Science; Modern Languages; Technology Education) *Dean*: Y. Alide, *students:* 130

Commerce (Accountancy; Business Administration; Business and Commerce; Commercial Law; Management) *Dean*: M. Chiodzeka, *students:* 530

Engineering (Architecture; Civil Engineering; Electrical Engineering; Engineering; Mechanical Engineering) *Dean*: V. Chipofya, *students:* 400

History: Founded 1964

Academic Year: February to December

Admission Requirements: A minimum of O' levels with at least 6 credits including English or the equivalent from a recognized institution

Fees: (Kwacha): Government sponsored students (local), 50,000; economic fees (local) 20,000; foreign students, $7213. All admissions must be forwarded to the Registrar, University Office, Box 278, Zonta Malawi

Main Language(s) of Instruction: English

International Co-operation: University of Strathclyde (exchange of technical staff)

Degrees and Diplomas: *Bachelor's Degree*: Accountancy (BAc); Arts; Business Administration (BBA); Science, 4 yrs; Engineering, Architecture, 5 yrs. 10 Diplomas in Technology and Business, 3-4 yrs

Student Services: Academic Counselling, Social Counselling, Sports Facilities, Language Programmes, Health Services, Canteen

Student Residential Facilities: Yes

Special Facilities: Audio Visual unit

Libraries: Central Library

Press or Publishing House: The Nation Publication

Student Numbers *1999:* Total: **1,500**

Mali

INSTITUTION TYPES AND CREDENTIALS

Types of higher education institutions:

Université (University)
Ecole normale supérieure (Teacher Training College)
Ecole nationale (National School)
Institut supérieur (Higher Institute)

School leaving and higher education credentials:

Baccalauréat
Baccalauréat technique
Diplôme universitaire de Technicien supérieur
Diplôme
Diplôme d'Ingénieur
Diplôme de Pharmacien
Maîtrise
Doctorat en Médecine
Certificat d'Etudes spécialisées
Diplôme d'Etudes approfondies
Doctorat

STRUCTURE OF EDUCATION SYSTEM

Pre-higher education:

Duration of compulsory education:

    Age of entry: 7
    Age of exit: 13

Structure of school system:

    Basic First Stage
    Type of school providing this education: Enseignement fondamental (Premier Cycle)
    Length of programme in years: 6
    Age level from: 7 to: 13
    Certificate/diploma awarded: Certificat de Fin d'Etudes du premier Cycle de l'Enseignement
    fondamental

Basic Second Stage
Type of school providing this education: Enseignement fondamental (Deuxième Cycle)
Length of programme in years: 3
Age level from: 13 to: 16
Certificate/diploma awarded: Diplôme d'Etudes fondamentales

General Secondary
Type of school providing this education: Lycée
Length of programme in years: 3
Age level from: 16 to: 19
Certificate/diploma awarded: Baccalauréat

Technical Secondary
Type of school providing this education: Lycée technique
Length of programme in years: 3
Age level from: 16 to: 19
Certificate/diploma awarded: Baccalauréat technique

Technical Secondary
Length of programme in years: 2
Age level from: 16 to: 18
Certificate/diploma awarded: Certificat d'Aptitude professionnelle (CAP)

Vocational Secondary
Length of programme in years: 4
Age level from: 16 to: 20
Certificate/diploma awarded: Brevet de Technicien

School education:

Basic education lasts for nine years, divided into two cycles, the first of six years, leading to the Certificat d'Etudes du premier Cycle de l'Enseignement fondamental, and the second of three years leading to the Diplôme d'Etudes fondamentales (DEF). Secondary education lasts for three years and is divided into two streams: one general leading to the Baccalauréat and one technical divided into elementary technical (two years leading to the Certificat d'Aptitude professionnelle) and vocational technical (four years leading to the Brevet de Technicien). Technical Lycées prepare for the Baccalauréat technique in three years.

Higher education:

Higher education is provided by the Université du Mali which was recently created by incorporating some existing higher education centres and the creation of four faculties; Medicine, Pharmacy and Dentistry; Technical Sciences; Juridical and Economic Sciences; Languages, Arts and Humanities; and schools of Administration, Engineering and Teacher Training, and higher Institutes. The Institut supérieur de Formation et de Recherche appliquée (ISFRA) offers post-graduate training.

Main laws/decrees governing higher education:

Decree: A law stipulating the creation of a decentralized and vocationalized university   Year: 1986
Concerns: University

Academic year:

Classes from: October *to:* June

Long vacation from: 1 July *to:* 30 September

Languages of instruction:

French

Stages of studies:

Non-university level post-secondary studies (technical/vocational type):

The Institut Polytechnique rural de Katibougou offers two-year programmes in Stockraising, Forestry, Veterinary Medicine and Animal Husbandry leading to the award of the Diplôme de Technicien Supérieur. A further three years' study lead to the Diplôme d'Ingénieur. The Ecole des Hautes Etudes pratiques offers two-year courses in Business Studies, Bilingual Secretarial Studies and Accountancy leading to the award of the Diplôme de Technicien supérieur.

University level studies:

University level first stage:

The duration of studies varies from four years in Engineering, Management and Teacher Training (Diplôme d'Ingénieur, Diplôme de l'Ecole nationale d'Administration, Diplôme de l'Institut supérieur pour la Formation et la Recherche appliquée) to five and six years in Pharmacy and Medicine (Diplôme de Pharmacien, Diplôme de Docteur en Médecine).

University level second stage:

The Institut supérieur pour la Formation et la Recherche appliquée offers a Diplôme d'Etudes approfondies after two years and a Doctorat after a further three years and a thesis.

Teacher education:

Training of pre-primary and primary/basic school teachers

Teacher training for teachers of the first cycle of Enseignement fondamental takes place at the regional Instituts pédagogiques d'Enseignement général (IPEG). The course lasts for four years for holders of the Diplôme d'Etudes fondamentales and consists of General Education, Pedagogy, Child Psychology and Teaching Practice. Teachers of the second cycle of Enseignement fondamental are trained in Ecoles normales secondaires which offer four-year courses for the holders of the Diplôme d'Etudes fondamentales. Candidates to teacher training schools must hold the Baccalauréat.

Training of secondary school teachers

Higher secondary school teachers are trained in four years after the Baccalauréat (and an entrance examination) in the Ecole normale supérieure where they obtain a Diplôme de l'Ecole normale Supérieure.

NATIONAL BODIES

Responsible authorities:

Ministry of Education (Ministère de l'Education)
    Minister: Moustapha Dicko
    Secretary-General: Salikou Sanogo
    BP 2468
    Bamako
    Tel: +223 22-55-30
    Fax: +223 22-82-97
    Telex: 2412 mini plan

Role of governing body: Manages and administers higher education.

ADMISSIONS TO HIGHER EDUCATION

Admission to non university higher education studies

Name of secondary school credential required: Baccalauréat technique

Entrance exams required: Competitive entrance examination for the Institut Polytechnique rural de Katibougou

Admission to university-level studies

Name of secondary school credential required: Baccalauréat technique

Name of secondary school credential required: Baccalauréat

Application procedures:

Apply to: Ministère de l'Education
    B.P. 2468
    Bamako
    Tel: +223-22 55 30
    Fax: +223-22 82 97
    Telex: 2412 mini plan

STUDENT LIFE

Student expenses and financial aid

Student costs:

    Home students tuition fees: Minimum: 5,000 (CFA Franc)
    Maximum: 150,000 (CFA Franc)
    Foreign students tuition fees: Minimum: 250,000 (CFA Franc)
    Maximum: 300,000 (CFA Franc)

INTERNATIONAL COOPERATION AND EXCHANGES

Principal national bodies responsible for dealing with international cooperation and exchanges in higher education:

Ministry of Education (Ministère de l'Education)
> B.P. 2468
> BAMAKO
> Tel: +223-22 55 30
> Fax: +223-22 82 97
> Telex: 2412 mini plan

GRADING SYSTEM

Usual grading system in secondary school

Full Description: Baccalauréat and school education are graded on a scale of 0-20 (maximum), with 10 as the minimum pass mark. 16-20 très bien; 14-15 bien; 12-13 assez bien; 10-11 passable; 8-9 médiocre; 6-7 faible; 3-5 très faible; 0-2 nul

Highest on scale: 16-20, très bien

Pass/fail level: 10-11, passable

Lowest on scale: 0-2, nul

Main grading system used by higher education institutions

Full Description: Higher education is graded on a scale of 0 to 20.

Highest on scale: 16-20

Pass/fail level: 12

Lowest on scale: 0-2

Other main grading systems

At the Ecole nationale d'Ingénieurs the grading system is 0-5, with 3 as the minimum pass mark.

NOTES ON HIGHER EDUCATION SYSTEM

Data for academic year: 2000-2001

Source: International Association of Universities (IAU), updated from IBE website, 2001

INSTITUTIONS OF HIGHER EDUCATION

UNIVERSITIES

• UNIVERSITY OF MALI
Université du Mali
BP 2528, Rue Baba Diarra Porte 113, Bamako
Tel: +223 22-19-33
Fax: +223 22-19-32
EMail: Universiteaml@refer.org

Recteur: Boubacar Sidiki Cissé (1995-)
Secrétaire général: Mansa Makan Diabate
International Relations: Dauda Diallo

Faculties
Law and Economics (Economics; Law) *Dean*: Ousmane Oumarou Sidibe, *full-time staff:* 28, *students:* 1,259
Letters, Languages, Arts and Humanities (Arts and Humanities; Modern Languages) *Dean*: Drissa Diakite, *students:* 994
Medicine, Pharmacy and Dentistry (Medicine; Pharmacy) *Dean*: Issa Traoré, *full-time staff:* 81, *students:* 1,719
Science and Technology (Natural Sciences; Technology) *Dean*: Abdoul Karim Sanogo, *students:* 636

Schools
Administration *Director*: Ousmane O. Sidibe, *students:* 1,878
Engineering *Director*: Bakary Sininta, *full-time staff:* 58, *students:* 981
Teacher Training *(ENS) Director*: Sekou Boukadary Traoré, *full-time staff:* 152, *students:* 1,554

Institutes
Agricultural Training and Applied Research *Director*: Tahirou Traoré, *full-time staff:* 89, *students:* 811
Management *Director*: Siby Ginette Bellegarde, *full-time staff:* 10, *students:* 891
Training and Applied Research *Director*: N'Golo Diarra, *full-time staff:* 15, *students:* 41

History: Founded 1993.
Governing Bodies: University Council
Academic Year: October to July
Admission Requirements: Secondary school certificate (baccalauréat) or equivalent
Fees: (Franc CFA): 5000-150,000 per annum; foreign students, 250,000-300,000
Main Language(s) of Instruction: French
Degrees and Diplomas: *Diplôme universitaire de Technicien supérieur*: 2 yrs; *Diplôme*: Administration; Economy; Foreign Languages Education; Humanities and Social Science Education; Law; Management; Science Education, 4 yrs; *Diplôme d'Ingénieur*: Applied Sciences, 5 yrs; *Diplôme de Pharmacien*: Pharmacy, 5 yrs; *Maîtrise*: 4 yrs; *Certificat d'Etudes spécialisées*: Dermatology; Ophtalmology; Public Health; Surgery; *Diplôme d'Etudes approfondies*: 1-2 further yrs following Maîtrise; *Doctorat*: a further 2-4 yrs
Academic Staff *1998:* Total: c. 509

Student Numbers *1998*	MEN	WOMEN	TOTAL
All (Foreign Included)	9,284	1,945	**11,229**

Note: Including 479 foreign students.

Mauritania

INSTITUTION TYPES AND CREDENTIALS

Types of higher education institutions:

Université (University)
Institut (Institute)
Centre supérieur (Higher Centre)
Ecole normale supérieure (Teacher Training College)

School leaving and higher education credentials:

Baccalauréat
Diplôme de Fin d'Etudes normales
Diplôme d'Etudes universitaires générales (DEUG)
Diplôme de Technicien supérieur
Certificat d'Aptitude de Professeur de l'Enseignement secondaire
Diplôme d'Ingénieur
Maîtrise

STRUCTURE OF EDUCATION SYSTEM

Pre-higher education:

Duration of compulsory education:

Age of entry: 6
Age of exit: 16

Structure of school system:

Basic
Type of school providing this education: Ecole fondamentale
Length of programme in years: 6
Age level from: 6 to: 12
Certificate/diploma awarded: Certificat d'études fondamentales (CAF) and competitive examination

First Cycle Secondary
Type of school providing this education: Collège
Length of programme in years: 3
Age level from: 12 to: 15
Certificate/diploma awarded: Brevet d'Etudes du Premier Cycle (BEPC)

Technical Secondary
Length of programme in years: 3
Age level from: 15 to: 18
Certificate/diploma awarded: Brevet d'Enseignement professionnel (BEP)

Second Cycle Secondary
Type of school providing this education: Lycée
Length of programme in years: 3
Age level from: 15 to: 18
Certificate/diploma awarded: Baccalauréat

Technical
Length of programme in years: 2
Age level from: 18 to: 20
Certificate/diploma awarded: Brevet de Technicien

School education:

Basic education lasts for six years and leads to the Certificat d'Etudes fondamentales. Access to secondary education is through a competitive entrance examination. Secondary education lasts for six years, divided into three years first cycle secondary (Collège) and three years second cycle secondary (Lycée) education. There is a special entrance examination for access to secondary education (Concours d'Entrée en Première Année secondaire et technique). The lower cycle leads to the Brevet d'Etudes du Premier Cycle. The second cycle culminates in the Baccalauréat in one of the following specializations: Arts/Literature; Mathematics, Physics and Chemistry; Natural Sciences or Koran and Arabic. It gives access to higher education. Technical secondary education also lasts three years and includes two streams: one leading to the Brevet d'Enseignement professionnel (BEP) for those holding the BEPC; and one leading to the Brevet de Technicien after two years' study. Candidates for the latter must have reached the last year of the second cycle secondary.

Higher education:

Higher education is mainly provided by the University of Nouakchott, which comprises faculties of Letters and Humanities, Law and Economics and Science and Technology and other institutions of higher education, such as the Ecole normale supérieure, the Centre supérieur d'Enseignement technique, the Institut supérieur d'Etudes et de Recherches islamiques and the Ecole nationale d'Administration. The University is a public institution managed by an Administrative Board, a Management Committee and a Rector.

Main laws/decrees governing higher education:

Decree: Décret no 95-035   Year: 1995
Concerns: Ecoles normales d'instituteurs

Decree: Décret 86-212   Year: 1986
Concerns: Status of higher education

Decree: Loi 70-243   Year: 1970
Concerns: Higher Education

Academic year:

Classes from: October *to:* June

Languages of instruction:

Arabic, French

Stages of studies:

Non-university level post-secondary studies (technical/vocational type):

Higher technical education is mainly offered at the Centre supérieur d'Enseignement technique which comprises departments of Mechanical and Electrical Engineering.

University level studies:

University level first stage: *Diplôme d'Etudes universitaires générales*:

The first stage of higher education leads to the Diplôme d'Etudes universitaires générales (DEUG) after two years' university study. The Ecole nationale d'administration confers a Diplôme after five years' study.

University level second stage: *Maîtrise*:

The Maîtrise is conferred after two years' study beyond the Diplôme d'Etudes universitaires générales. Postgraduate and doctoral degrees are completed abroad.

Teacher education:

Training of pre-primary and primary/basic school teachers

Holders of the Brevet d'Etudes du Premier Cycle (BEPC) undertake a three-year course at one of the Ecoles normales des Instituteurs. Holders of the Baccalauréat undertake a one-year course. Both courses lead to the Diplôme de Fin d'Etudes normales. There is an entrance examination for both courses.

Training of secondary school teachers

To teach in a Collège, teachers must have followed a one-year course at the Ecole normale supérieure and have obtained the Certificat d'Aptitude aux fonctions de Professeur du premier Cycle (CAPPC). To teach in a Lycée, teachers must have followed a course at the Ecole normale supérieure and have obtained the Certificat d'Aptitude au Professorat de l'Enseignement secondaire (CAPES). Courses lasts for two years for Instituteurs who sit for an external competitive examination and four years for those who sit for an internal competitive examination. Technical secondary schools teachers are recruited on the basis of a direct competitive examination and follow a one-year trainership.

Training of higher education teachers

Higher education teachers must hold a Licence or a Maîtrise and a third cycle Degree. They must sit for a competitive examination.

NATIONAL BODIES

Responsible authorities:

Ministry of National Education (Ministère de l'Education nationale)
Minister: Dedoud Ould Abdallahi
BP 227
Nouakchott
Tel: +222 25-11-25
Fax: +222 25-12-22

ADMISSIONS TO HIGHER EDUCATION

Admission to university-level studies

Name of secondary school credential required: Baccalauréat

Alternatives to credentials: Entrance examination.

GRADING SYSTEM

Usual grading system in secondary school

Full Description: 0-20
Highest on scale: 20
Pass/fail level: 10-11
Lowest on scale: 0

Main grading system used by higher education institutions

Full Description: 0-20
Highest on scale: 20
Pass/fail level: 10-11
Lowest on scale: 0

NOTES ON HIGHER EDUCATION SYSTEM

Data for academic year: 2000-2001
Source: International Association of Universities (IAU), updated from IBE website, 2001

INSTITUTIONS OF HIGHER EDUCATION

UNIVERSITIES

*• UNIVERSITY OF NOUAKCHOTT
Université de Nouakchott
BP 5026, Nouakchott
Tel: +222(2) 513-82
Fax: +222(2) 539-97
Telex: 710
EMail: webmaster@univ-nkc.mr
Website: http://www.univ-nkc.mr
Recteur: Mohamed El Hacen Ould Lebatt

Faculties
Law and Economics (Economics; Law; Management; Private Law; Public Law)
Letters and Humanities (Arabic; Arts and Humanities; English; Geography; History; Linguistics; Native Language; Philosophy; Translation and Interpretation) *Dean:* Diallo Ibrahima
Science and Technology (Biology; Chemistry; Computer Science; Geology; Management; Mathematics; Natural Sciences; Physics; Technology; Technology Education) *Dean:* Ahmedou Ould Haouba

History: Founded 1981.
Governing Bodies: Assemblée de l'Université
Degrees and Diplomas: *Diplôme d'Etudes universitaires générales (DEUG):* Arabic; Chemistry; Economics; English; Geography; History; Law; Modern Languages; Natural Sciences; Philosophy; Physics; Science, 2 yrs; *Diplôme de Technicien supérieur:* Fishery, 2 yrs; *Diplôme d'Ingénieur:* Fishery; *Maîtrise:* Arabic; Biology; Chemistry; Economics; English; Geography; Geology; History; Law; Modern Languages; Philosophy, 2 yrs after DEUG
Academic Staff *1999:* Total: c. 70
Student Numbers *1999:* Total: c. 9,065

OTHER INSTITUTIONS

CENTRE SUPÉRIEUR D'ENSEIGNEMENT TECHNIQUE
BP 986, Nouakchott
Tel: +222(2) 530-17
Fax: +222(2) 544-29
Telex: 719 mtn nktt
Technology

History: Founded 1982

ECOLE NATIONALE D'ADMINISTRATION (ENA)
Nouakchott
Administration

ECOLE NATIONALE DE L'ENSEIGNEMENT MARITIME ET DES PÊCHES
Nouakchott
Fishery; Marine Science and Oceanography

ECOLE NORMALE SUPÉRIEURE
BP 990, Nouakchott
Tel: +222(2) 531-84
Fax: +222(2) 531-72
Education

History: Founded 1970, acquired present status and title 1987

INSTITUT BEN ABASS
Nouakchott
Cultural Studies

INSTITUT SUPÉRIEUR DES ETUDES ET RECHERCHES ISLAMIQUES (ISERI)
Nouakchott
Islamic Studies

INSTITUT SUPÉRIEUR SCIENTIFIQUE
BP 5026, Nouakchott
Tel: +222(2) 511-68
Fax: +222(2) 539-97
Telex: 598 mtn nktt
Biology; Chemistry; Computer Science; English; Geology; Mathematics; Modern Languages; Physics

History: Founded 1986

Mauritius

INSTITUTION TYPES AND CREDENTIALS

Types of higher education institutions:

University
Institute
College

School leaving and higher education credentials:

General Certificate of Education Ordinary Level
School Certificate
General Certificate of Education Advanced Level
Higher School Certificate
Bachelor's Degree
Diploma
Master's Degree
Master of Philosophy
Doctor of Philosophy

STRUCTURE OF EDUCATION SYSTEM

Pre-higher education:

Duration of compulsory education:

Age of entry: 5
Age of exit: 12

Structure of school system:

Primary
Type of school providing this education: Primary School
Length of programme in years: 6
Age level from: 5 to: 12
Certificate/diploma awarded: Certificate of Primary Education

Lower Secondary
Type of school providing this education: Lower Secondary School
Length of programme in years: 5
Age level from: 12 to: 17
Certificate/diploma awarded: General Certificate of Education O-Level/School Certificate

Upper Secondary
Type of school providing this education: Upper Secondary School
Length of programme in years: 2
Age level from: 17 to: 19
Certificate/diploma awarded: General Certificate of Education A-Level/Higher School Certificate

School education:

Primary education lasts for six years and culminates in the Certificate of Primary Education. Secondary education covers seven years: Forms I to V leading to the examinations for the School Certificate, followed by two years leading to the examination for the General Certificate of Education Advanced (A) level or Higher School Certificate. Technical secondary education is provided by a College, Lycées Polytechniques, Institutes and Industrial Trades Training Centres.

Higher education:

Post-secondary and university education are offered by two polytechnics and four tertiary education institutions: the University of Mauritius (UOM), the Mauritius Institute of Education (MIE), the Mahatma Gandhi Institute (MGI) and the Mauritius College of the Air (MCA). The five faculties at UOM (Agriculture, Engineering, Science, Law and Management, and Social Studies and Humanities) offer certificate, diploma, degree, and post-degree courses according to the different fields of studies. UOM is an autonomous institution governed by a Council and a Senate. The University of Technology opened in the year 2000.

Main laws/decrees governing higher education:

Decree: Education Act   Year: 1996
Concerns: Education at all levels

Academic year:

Classes from: August *to:* April

Languages of instruction:

English, French

Stages of studies:

Non-university level post-secondary studies (technical/vocational type):

A number of training centres offer post-secondary training in Electronics, Textiles, Electrical and Mechanical Engineering, Building Construction, Business, and Management. The two polytechnics offer a two-year diploma course in Information Systems or Business Administration, and a three-year course leading to the Brevet de Technicien Supérieur.

University level studies:

University level first stage:
The first stage of higher education leads, usually after one to two years' study to a Diploma or a Certificate. Studies leading to a Bachelor's Degree with Honours last for three to four years, depending on the field of study. Generally, Law, Management and Engineering degrees are of four years' duration.

University level second stage:
A further stage consists of postgraduate degrees, either through taught programmes (Master's degree) or through research (Master of Philosophy (MPhil), or Doctor of Philosophy (PhD). The Master's programmes are normally of one year's duration full-time or two years part-time. The period of study for the M.Phil is two years full-time or three years part-time; for the PhD it is three years full-time or five years part-time.

University level third stage:
Honorary degrees are conferred in Science and Humanities.

Teacher education:

Training of pre-primary and primary/basic school teachers
Teacher training is provided by the Mauritius Institute of Education. A two-year full-time or three-year part-time course leads to a Teacher's Diploma. A two-year course leads to a Teacher's Certificate. Trainee teachers have to earn a minimum of 48 credits out of 50 and obtain a grade point average of at least 2.0.

Training of secondary school teachers
Secondary school teachers must hold a university degree or a non-graduate professional qualification for teaching. The Mauritius Institute of Education runs a one-year full-time/two-year part-time postgraduate certificate in education and a two-year part-time certificate in educational administration. The Bachelor of Education Single Honours is a three-year, part-time post A-level and post-teachers' diploma (three-year part-time training course) run jointly by the Mauritius Institute of Education and the University.

NATIONAL BODIES

Responsible authorities:

Ministry of Education and Scientific Research
    Minister: Louis Steven Obeegadoo
    Permanent Secretary (Acting): Premila Aubeelack
    International Relations: Ram Prakash Ramlugun
    IVTB House (3rd Floor)
    Phoenix
    Tel: +230(698) 0464
    Fax: +230(698) 2550
    EMail: meduhrd@bow.intnet.mu

ADMISSIONS TO HIGHER EDUCATION

Admission to non university higher education studies

Name of secondary school credential required: General Certificate of Education Ordinary Level
Minimum score/requirement: Passes in five subjects including English.

Name of secondary school credential required: School Certificate

Admission to university-level studies

Name of secondary school credential required: General Certificate of Education Advanced Level
Minimum score/requirement: Pass at O' level in English, plus 4 other passes including 2 or 3 at A' level.

Name of secondary school credential required: Higher School Certificate

Foreign students admission

Admission requirements: For higher degrees students must hold a Bachelor Degree (at least 2nd class Honours) or a first degree; for degree courses they must hold GCE O' level passes in five subjects, two of which must be at A level; for diploma courses they must hold five GCE O' level passes including English and Mathematics; for certificate courses they must generally hold a Cambridge SC with passes in five subjects, including English language.

Entry regulations: Foreign students must hold a visa and a residence permit and present financial guarantees.

Health requirements: Foreign students must hold a health certificate.

Language requirements: Students must have a good command of English.

Application procedures:

Apply to national body for entry to: University

Apply to: National Equivalence Council of the Ministry of Education and Scientific Research
   University of Mauritius
   Reduit
   Tel: +230(454) 1041   +230(454) 9958
   Fax: +230(454) 9642
   Telex: 4621 UNIM IW
   Cable: university mauritius
   WWW: http://www.uom.ac.mu

Recognition of studies and qualifications:

Studies pursued in foreign countries (bodies dealing with recognition of foreign credentials):
University of Mauritius
   Reduit
   Tel: +230(454) 1041   +230(454) 9958
   Fax: +230(454) 9642
   Telex: 4621 UNIM IW
   Cable: university mauritius
   WWW: http://www.uom.ac.mu

References to further information on foreign student admissions and recognition of studies

Title: Study Abroad 2000-2001
Publisher: UNESCO/IBE
Year of publication: 1999

Title: University Calendar
Publisher: University of Mauritius

STUDENT LIFE

Main student services at national level

Youth Guidance Unit
    Ministry of Employment
    Reduit

Student expenses and financial aid

Student costs:

Home students tuition fees: Minimum: 0 (Mauritius Rupee)
Maximum: 4,850 (Mauritius Rupee)
Foreign students tuition fees: Minimum: 50,000 (Mauritius Rupee)
Maximum: 60,000 (Mauritius Rupee)

GRADING SYSTEM

Usual grading system in secondary school

Full Description: Overseas School Certificate and CGE Examinations:
A-E with U as Fail
Highest on scale: A very good
Pass/fail level: C or D
Lowest on scale: U

Main grading system used by higher education institutions

Full Description: Bachelor degree: class I; class II division i; class II division ii; class III or pass.

NOTES ON HIGHER EDUCATION SYSTEM

Data for academic year: 2000-2001
Source: International Association of Universities (IAU), updated from IBE website, 2000

INSTITUTIONS OF HIGHER EDUCATION

UNIVERSITIES

*• UNIVERSITY OF MAURITIUS
Reduit
Tel: +230(454) 1041
Fax: +230(454) 9642
Telex: 4621 unim iw
Cable: university mauritius
EMail: mobhai@uom.intnet.mu
Website: http://www.uom.ac.mu

Vice-Chancellor: Goolam Mohamedbhai (1995-)
Tel: +230(465) 6985 Fax: +230(465) 1337
EMail: mobhai@uom.ac.mu

Registrar: S.D. Goordyal Tel: +230(464) 7409
Fax: +230(465) 1336 EMail: sgdyal@uom.ac.mu

International Relations: Indurlall Fagoonee
Fax: +230(465) 9345 EMail: goofa@uom.ac.mu

Faculties

Agriculture (Agricultural Engineering; Agricultural Management; Agriculture; Crop Production; Food Science; Horticulture) *Dean*: Saheed Goburdhun, *full-time staff: 18, part-time staff: 50, students: 454*

Engineering (Chemical Engineering; Civil Engineering; Computer Science; Electrical and Electronic Engineering; Engineering; Food Technology; Industrial Engineering; Mechanical Engineering; Production Engineering; Textile Technology) *Dean*: Brij Kishore Baguant, *full-time staff: 52, part-time staff: 31, students: 1,118*

Law and Management (Accountancy; Business Administration; Business and Commerce; Finance; Human Resources; International Business; Law; Management; Marketing; Public Administration; Tourism) *Dean*: Dharambeer Gokhool, *full-time staff: 31, part-time staff: 32, students: 1,078*

Science (Chemistry; Health Sciences; Mathematics; Medical Technology; Natural Sciences; Physics) *Dean*: Rajindra Choolun, *full-time staff: 44, part-time staff: 53, students: 638*

Social Studies and Humanities (Arts and Humanities; Business and Commerce; Communication Studies; Economics; English; French; Hindi; History; Library Science; Media Studies; Social Studies; Social Work; Statistics) *Dean*: Vidula Nababsing, *full-time staff: 44, part-time staff: 25, students: 978*

Centres

Distance Learning *(J. Baguant)* (Information Technology) *Director*: Camille Pierre François, *full-time staff: 10, students: 5,048*

Information Technology and Systems *(Providing IT services to the University)* (Information Technology; Systems Analysis) *Director*: Anthony J. Rodrigues, *full-time staff: 23*

Medical Research and Studies (Anatomy; Epidemiology; Genetics; Haematology; Medicine; Molecular Biology; Pathology)

Director (Acting): Neera Manraj, *full-time staff: 27, part-time staff: 2*

History: Founded 1965.

Governing Bodies: Council; Senate

Academic Year: August to April (August-November; January-April)

Admission Requirements: General Certificate of Education (GCE) with pass at Ordinary 'O' level or equivalent in English Language, and either passes in 4 other subjects with at least 2 passes at 'A' level or passes in 3 other subjects at 'A' level

Fees: (Mauritius Rupees): None for Mauritian school leavers. Other Mauritian students, 3850-4850. Foreign students, 50,000-60,000

Main Language(s) of Instruction: English

International Co-operation: University of Birmingham; University of Manchester; Aston University; University of Dundee; University of London; University of Reading; University of Sheffield. Informal working arrangements with Brunei University and University of Warwick. Memorandum of understanding on student and staff exchange for Faculty of Agriculture, Forestry and Veterinary Medicine in the SADC Region

Degrees and Diplomas: *Bachelor's Degree*: 3-4 yrs; *Diploma*: 2-3 yrs; *Master's Degree*: 2-3 yrs; *Master of Philosophy*: (MPhil); *Doctor of Philosophy*: (PhD), 3-5 yrs. Also Certificates, 1-2 yrs

Student Services: Sports Facilities, Health Services, Canteen

Special Facilities: 21 acre University Farm. Crop Museum

Libraries: 125,000 vols including bound vols and periodicals

Publications: Newsletter (3 per annum); Annual Report; Calendar (annually); Journal

Press or Publishing House: University Library Printing Section

Academic Staff *1999-2000*	MEN	WOMEN	TOTAL
FULL-TIME	133	67	200
PART-TIME	100	33	133
TOTAL	**233**	**100**	**333**
STAFF WITH DOCTORATE			
FULL-TIME	34	13	47
PART-TIME	24	7	31
TOTAL	**58**	**20**	**78**

Student Numbers *1999-2000*		TOTAL
All (Foreign Included)		**5,048**
FOREIGN ONLY		37

SIR SEEWOOSAGUR RAMGOOLAM CENTRE FOR MEDICAL STUDIES AND RESEARCH
Moka
Tel: +230(433) 2929 +230(433) 2931
Fax: +230(433) 2400

Director (Acting): Meera Manraj Tel: +230(433) 8436
EMail: madhav@dove.ac.mu

Centres
Medical Research (Medicine)

History: Founded 1986.

UNIVERSITY OF TECHNOLOGY
La Tour Koenig, Pointe-aux-Sables
Tel: +230(234) 7624
Fax: +230(234) 1660
EMail: registrar@utm.intnet.mu
Website: http://ncb.intnet.mu/utm/

Chairman: F. Currimjee

Director (Acting): R.S. Lutchmeah

Schools
Business Informatics and Software Development (Business Computing; Software Engineering)
Public Sector Policy and Management (Management; Public Administration)
Sustainable Development Science (Natural Sciences)

History: Founded 2000.

OTHER INSTITUTIONS

HIGHER INSTITUTE OF TECHNOLOGY
Institut Supérieur de Technologie
Rue de la Concorde, Camp Levieux, Rose-Hill
Technology

LYCÉE POLYTECHNIQUE SIR GUY FORGET
Rue François Mitterrand, Central Flacq
Tel: +230(413) 2959
Fax: +230(413) 2938
EMail: Lpsgf@intnet.mu

Manager: B. Lotun Tel: +230(413) 2420

Departments
Automobile Mechanics (Automotive Engineering)
Building Construction (Building Technologies; Construction Engineering)
Electrotechnics and Electronics (Electronic Engineering)
Maintenance and Production Mechanics (Maintenance Technology; Production Engineering)

History: Founded 1982.

MAHATMA GANDHI INSTITUTE
Moka
Tel: +230(433) 1277
Fax: +230(433) 2235
EMail: asibmgi@intnet.mu

Director: Asha Sibartie (1982-) Tel: +230(433) 2166
Fax: +230(433) 2160

Schools
Fine Arts (Fine Arts; Painting and Drawing; Sculpture) *Head (Acting)*: Mala Ramyead, *full-time staff:* 6, *part-time staff:* 5, *students:* 150
Indian Music and Dance (Dance; Fine Arts; Music; Musical Instruments; Singing) *Head*: Indurduth Deerpaul, *full-time staff:* 21, *part-time staff:* 6, *students:* 282
Indian Studies (Curriculum; Hindi; Indic Languages; Literature; Philosophical Schools; Philosophy; Teacher Trainers Education; Urdu) *Head*: Cassam Heerah, *full-time staff:* 24, *part-time staff:* 1, *students:* 540
Mauritian, African and Asian Studies (African Studies; Arts and Humanities; Asian Studies; Comparative Literature; Continuing Education; Cultural Studies; Development Studies; Economic History; Ethnology; Geography (Human); Indigenous Studies; International Relations; Island Studies; Social Problems; Social Psychology; Social Sciences; Translation and Interpretation) *Associate Professor*: Sooryankanti Nirsimloo-Gayan, *full-time staff:* 8, *part-time staff:* 1, *students:* 125

Departments
Folklore and Oral Traditions (Cultural Studies; Folklore) *Head*: Suchita Ramdin

History: Founded 1970

Governing Bodies: Ministry of Education and Scientific Research

Main Language(s) of Instruction: English, French

Degrees and Diplomas: *Bachelor's Degree*: Fine Arts (BA Hons); Fine Arts with Education (BA Hons); Hindi (BA Joint Hons); Hindi (BA Hons); Hindi with Education (BA Hons); Indian Philosophy with Education (BA Hons); Marathi with Education (BA Hons); Performing Arts with Education (BA Hons); Tamil with Education (BA Hons); Telugu with Education (BA Hons); Urdu with Education (BA Hons); *Diploma*: Fine Arts; Indian Philosophy with Sanskrit; Vocational Hindustani, 2 yrs

Student Services: Cultural Centre, Language Programmes

Student Residential Facilities: Guest House

Special Facilities: Museum. Art Gallery

Libraries: Central Library

Publications: Rimjhim, Children's Creative Writings (Hindi); Vasant, Creative Writings (Hindi) (quarterly); Journal of Mauritian Studies, Mauritian Studies (English, French) (biannually)

Academic Staff *2000*: Full-Time: c. 224 Part-Time: c. 22 Total: c. 246

Staff with doctorate: Full-Time: c. 13

Student Numbers *2000*: All (Foreign Included): Men: c. 390 Women: c. 431 Total: c. 821
Foreign Only: Men: c. 5 Women: c. 7 Total: c. 12

MAURITIUS COLLEGE OF THE AIR
Reduit
Tel: +230(464) 7106
Fax: +230(464) 8854
Website: http://www.mcawebcast.org

Director: Meenakshi Seetulsingh (1986-)
Tel: +230(464) 6662 Fax: +230(465) 9440
EMail: meena@bow.intnet.mu

Administrative Secretary: Leela Devi Ramburuth
Tel: +230(465) 9480 EMail: leelaram@bow.intnet.mu

Divisions
Distance Education (Business and Commerce; Preschool Education; Teacher Trainers Education; Tourism) *Senior Lecturer*: Issawar Jheengut, *full-time staff:* 18, *part-time staff:* 70, *students:* 1,300

Centres
National Resources *Head*: Christine Ah Fat, *full-time staff:* 9
Media (Media Studies; Printing and Printmaking) *Director*: Shakuntala Hawoldar, *full-time staff:* 70, *part-time staff:* 100

History: Founded 1985.

Fees: (Mauritius Rupees): 300-120,000 depending on the course

Main Language(s) of Instruction: English, French

International Co-operation: Indira Gandhi National Open University

Degrees and Diplomas: *Bachelor's Degree*: Commerce; Computer Applications; Tourism Studies, 36 months. Also Certificates (12-15 months); Diplomas (12-24 months)

Student Services: Academic Counselling

Libraries: Central Library

Distance Students, 1,300

MAURITIUS INSTITUTE OF EDUCATION
Reduit
Tel: +230(454) 1031
Fax: +230(454) 1037

Director: Prem Saddul (2000-)

Registrar (Acting): Diwakar Ramyead

International Relations: George Arekion
Tel: +230(466) 1940

Education

History: Founded 1974.

SWAMI DAYANAND INSTITUTE OF MANAGEMENT
Round About Beau Plan SE, Pamplemousses
Management

Morocco

INSTITUTION TYPES AND CREDENTIALS

Types of higher education institutions:

Université (University)
Ecole normale supérieure (Higher Teacher-Training College)
Grande Ecole (Higher College)
Etablissement de Formation des Cadres (Training Institution for Executives)

School leaving and higher education credentials:

Baccalauréat
Capacité en Droit
Diplôme universitaire de Technologie (DUT)
Certificat d'Aptitude à l'Enseignement secondaire
Certificat universitaire
Diplôme d'Etudes universitaires générales (DEUG,
Diplôme de Technicien supérieur
Diplôme d'Architecte (DENA)
Diplôme d'Ingénieur d'Etat
Diplôme/Diplôme supérieur
Licence
Maîtrise
Diplôme d'Etudes supérieures spécialisées (DESS)
Diplôme d'Etudes supérieures (DES)
Certificat d'Etudes spécialisées (CES)
Diplôme d'Etudes supérieures approfondies (DESA)
Diplôme de Professeur agrégé
Diplôme de Professeur de deuxième Cycle
Doctorat

STRUCTURE OF EDUCATION SYSTEM

Pre-higher education:

Duration of compulsory education:

    Age of entry: 7
    Age of exit: 14

Structure of school system:

Basic First Stage
Type of school providing this education: Ecole primaire
Length of programme in years: 6
Age level from: 6 to: 12

Basic Second Stage
Type of school providing this education: Collège
Length of programme in years: 3
Age level from: 12 to: 15
Certificate/diploma awarded: Certificat d'Enseignement secondaire

General Secondary
Type of school providing this education: Lycée
Length of programme in years: 3
Age level from: 15 to: 18
Certificate/diploma awarded: Baccalauréat

Technical Secondary
Type of school providing this education: Technical Secondary School
Length of programme in years: 3
Age level from: 15 to: 18
Certificate/diploma awarded: Baccalauréat Technique

Technical
Type of school providing this education: Technical institutions
Length of programme in years: 2
Age level from: 18 to: 20
Certificate/diploma awarded: Brevet de Technicien supérieur

School education:

Primary education lasts for six years and, together with the first three years of secondary education, form the basic (fondamental) education. After nine years' basic education, students enter general secondary education where they are offered three options: letters, sciences, or mathematics. Upon completion, they are awarded the Baccalauréat. They may also choose a technical path, leading to the Baccalauréat technique. Some technical schools offer two years' training after the Baccalauréat leading to the Brevet de Technicien supérieur (BTS).

Higher education:

Higher education is provided by universities, Grandes Ecoles, institutes, teacher-training schools and centres under the supervision of the Ministère de l'Enseignement supérieur. A characteristic feature of training is the existence, besides the traditional system of higher education, of institutions of higher education (Etablissements de Formation des Cadres) which provide specialized training for high-level personnel in Science/Technology; Law/Economics/Administration/Social Sciences and Teacher Training under the direct control of ministerial departments. There are also eight Grandes Ecoles d'Ingénieurs (engineering schools). University councils rule on important questions related to university life. Universities are public institutions with budgetary autonomy.

Main laws/decrees governing higher education:

Decree: N° 2-96-796   Year: 1997
Concerns: Organization of the Doctorate, DESA and DESS and Accreditation of institutions

Decree: Dahir portant loi N° 1-75-87   Year: 1987
Concerns: Organization of Universities

Decree: 1.59.072   Year: 1959
Concerns: All institutions

Decree: 2.59.0364   Year: 1959
Concerns: All institutions

Academic year:

Classes from: September *to:* July

Languages of instruction:

Arabic, French

Stages of studies:

Non-university level post-secondary studies (technical/vocational type):

Postsecondary technical institutes offer two to four-year programmes in Law, Economics, Administration, Social Sciences and Engineering. Some offer a Brevet de Technicien supérieur (BTS) after two years' training. Most private technical institutions offer programmes in Computer Science and Business and Management. Private institutions confer engineering degrees. Secondary schools offer two years of post-Baccalauréat preparatory training for the Grandes Ecoles, after which students may pass the competitive entrance examination of the school(s) they have opted for.

University level studies:

University level first stage: 1er Cycle:
The first stage at university lasts for two years and is devoted to broadly-based studies; it leads to a Certificat universitaire d'Etudes littéraires in Arts and Humanities (CUEL) and a Certificat universitaire d'Etudes scientifiques (CUES) in Science and Economics. At the Facultés des Sciences et Techniques a Diplôme d'Etudes universitaires générales (DEUG) in Applied Sciences and a Diplôme d'Etudes universitaires de Technologie (DEUT) are conferred after two years' study. A two-year preparatory programme in Engineering and Agriculture is offered by the Grandes Ecoles d'Ingénieurs. A Diplôme de Technicien supérieur is awarded after two years' study.

University level second stage: 2ème Cycle:
The second stage is a phase of in-depth training lasting two years and leading to the Licence. A further two years' study beyond the DEUG and the DEUT lead to the Maîtrise. The Diplôme d'Ingénieur d'Etat is conferred after a total of five years' study by the Grandes Ecoles d'Ingénieurs in Engineering and Agriculture. A Diplôme supérieur is conferred in Business after four years' study and

a Diplôme d'Architecte after six years. The Doctorat in Medicine is conferred after seven years, the Doctorat in Pharmacy after six years and the Doctorat in Dentistry after five years.

University level third stage: *3ème Cycle*:

The third stage leads to the Dipôme d'Etudes supérieures approfondies (DESA) which is conferred after one to two years' further study beyond the Licence. A Diplôme d'Etudes supérieures (DES) (Takhsis) in Arts, Science, Law and Economics is usually awarded at the end of two to three years' study beyond the Licence. It includes theoretical courses, individual research work and the submission of a dissertation. The Diplôme d'Etudes supérieures spécialisées (DESS) also requires two years' study.

University level fourth stage: *Doctorat*:

The Doctorat is obtained by holders of a DES or DESA in Arts, Science, Law, Economics and Education after three to five years' study and defence of a thesis.

Teacher education:

Training of pre-primary and primary/basic school teachers

Primary-school teachers (first cycle of basic education) are trained in Centres de Formation des Instituteurs (CFI). Two-year training programmes are offered to Baccalauréat holders. They must sit for an entrance examination. Holders of a Certificat universitaire, a DEUG or a Licence follow a one-year course.

Training of secondary school teachers

Lower secondary-school teachers (second cycle of basic education) are trained in Centres pédagogiques régionaux (CPR). They follow a two-year programme and must hold the Baccalauréat. Upper secondary school teachers follow one- to two-year post-graduate courses at Ecoles normales supérieures and are awarded the Diplôme de Professeur de deuxième Cycle. They must hold a DEUG (at least) or a Licence and sit for an entrance examination or hold a Junior Secondary Teaching Diploma and sit for an entrance examination. Holders of the Baccalauréat study for four years after passing an entrance examination. The Diplôme de Professeur agrégé is conferred after a further two years' study plus four years' teaching experience and an entrance examination to the Professeur de deuxième Cycle. Technical secondary school teachers go to the Ecole normale supérieure technique (ENSET).

Training of higher education teachers

Higher education teachers must hold a post-graduate degree.

NATIONAL BODIES

Responsible authorities:

Ministry of Higher Education, Professional Training & Research (Ministère de l'Enseignement supérieur,de la Formation des Cadres & de la Recherche scientifique)

Minister: Najib Zerouali Ouariti

BP 707

35 Ave. Ibn Sina, Agdal

Rabat
Tel: +212(37) 77-47-17
Fax: +212(37) 77-80-28
EMail: des@dfc.gov.ma
WWW: http://www.dfc.gov.ma

Conférence des Recteurs des Universités marocaines
President: Mohamed Knidiri
BP 511
Rectorat de l'Université Cadi Ayad
Avenue Prince Abdellah
Marrakech
Tel: +212(4) 43-48-13
Fax: +212(4) 43-44-94
EMail: rectorat@ucam.ac.ma
WWW: http://www.ucam.ac.ma

ADMISSIONS TO HIGHER EDUCATION

Admission to non university higher education studies

Name of secondary school credential required: Baccalauréat

Alternatives to credentials: Baccalauréat technique

Admission to university-level studies

Name of secondary school credential required: Baccalauréat

Other admission requirements: There is an entrance examination for the faculties of Medicine, Pharmacy, Dentistry, higher schools of Technology, the School for Translation and Interpreting and the Grandes Ecoles d'Ingénieurs.

Foreign students admission

Entry regulations: Foreign students must hold the Baccalauréat or an equivalent qualification. Within the framework of agreements or conventions concluded with other countries, foreign applicants may be admitted to the Ecoles normales supérieures on the basis of their academic record, provided they hold a Licence entitling them to practise as a teacher.

Language requirements: Good knowledge of Arabic or French

Recognition of studies and qualifications:

Studies pursued in foreign countries (bodies dealing with recognition of foreign credentials):
Division de la Réglementation et des Equivalences de Diplômes, Ministère de l'Education nationale
24 rue du Sénégal-Océan
Rabat
Tel: +212(37) 77-18-22

Fax: +212(37) 77-20-34
Telex: 31016 meps-mes

Multilateral agreements concerning recognition of foreign studies

Name(s) of agreement(s): Convention on the Recognition of Studies, Diplomas and Degrees in Higher Education in the Arab States
Year of signature: 1978

International Convention on the Recognition of Studies, Certificates, Diplomas and Degrees in Higher Education in the Arab and European States Bordering on the Mediterranean.
Year of signature: 1976

STUDENT LIFE

Main student services at national level

Direction de la Recherche scientifique et de la Coopération universitaire
Service des Etudiants étrangers
Rabat
Tel: +212(37) 73-72-22

Student expenses and financial aid

Student costs:

Home students tuition fees: Minimum: 0 (Moroccan Dirham)
Maximum: 18,000 (Moroccan Dirham)
Foreign students tuition fees: Minimum: 4,700 (US Dollar)

Publications on student services and financial aid:

Title: Study Abroad 2000-2001
Publisher: UNESCO/IBE
Year of publication: 1999

GRADING SYSTEM

Usual grading system in secondary school

Full Description: 16-20 très bien; 14-15 bien; 12-13 assez bien; 10-11 passable; 0-9 insuffisant.
Highest on scale: 20
Pass/fail level: 10
Lowest on scale: 0

Main grading system used by higher education institutions

Full Description: 16.0-20.0 Très bien; 14.0-15.9 Bien; 12.0-13.9 Assez bien; 10.0-11.9 Passable
Highest on scale: 20

Pass/fail level: 10
Lowest on scale: 0

NOTES ON HIGHER EDUCATION SYSTEM

Data for academic year: 2000-2001
Source: International Association of Universities (IAU), updated from IBE website, 2001

INSTITUTIONS OF HIGHER EDUCATION

UNIVERSITIES

PUBLIC INSTITUTIONS

IBN ZOHR UNIVERSITY AGADIR

Université Ibn Zohr Agadir
BP 32/S, Agadir
Tel: +212(48) 22-70-17
Fax: +212(48) 22-72-60
EMail: ibnzohr@marocnet.net.ma

Recteur: Ahmed Jebli (1997-) Tel: +212(8) 22-74-69

Secrétaire général: Abderrahmane Rida
Tel: +212(8) 23-32-25

Faculties
Letters and Humanities (Arts and Humanities)
Science (Mathematics and Computer Science; Natural Sciences)

Schools
Commerce and Management (Business and Commerce; Management)
Technology *(Advanced Studies)*

History: Founded 1989.

Academic Year: September to July (September-December; January-March; April-July)

Admission Requirements: Secondary school certificate (baccalauréat)

Fees: None

Main Language(s) of Instruction: Arabic, French

Degrees and Diplomas: *Diplôme universitaire de Technologie (DUT)*: 2 yrs; *Certificat universitaire*: Arab Literature (CUEL); Biology-Geology (CUES); English Literature (CUEL); French Literature (CUEL); History-Geography (CUEL); Islamic Studies (CUEL); Mathematics-Physics (CUES); Physics-Chemistry (CUES); Spanish Literature (CUEL), 2 yrs; *Diplôme/Diplôme supérieur*: Business and Management, 4 yrs; *Licence*: 4 yrs; *Diplôme d'Etudes supérieures (DES)*: a further 3-4 yrs; *Diplôme d'Etudes supérieures approfondies (DESA)*: a further 2 yrs following Licence; *Doctorat*

Academic Staff *1999:* Total: c. 350

Student Numbers *1999:* Total: c. 10,850

HASSAN II UNIVERSITY AÏN CHOCK CASABLANCA

Université Hassan II Aïn Chock Casablanca
BP 9167, Rue Tarik Bnou Ziad, Casablanca
Tel: +212(22) 27-37-37
Fax: +212(22) 27-51-60
EMail: rectorat@rectorat-uh2.ac.ma
Website: http://www.facsc-achok.ac.ma

Recteur: Aziz Hasbi (1997-) Tel: +212(2) 29-78-64

Secrétaire général: Noreddine Siraj

Faculties
Dentistry
Law, Economics, Social Studies and Political Science (Economics; Law; Political Science; Social Studies)
Letters and Humanities *(Aïn Chock)* (Arabic; Arts and Humanities; English; French; Geography; German; History; Islamic Studies; Spanish)
Medicine and Pharmacy (Medicine; Pharmacy)
Science *(Aïn Chock)* (Biology; Chemistry; Geology; Mathematics; Natural Sciences; Physics)

Schools
Advanced Electrical and Mechanical Engineering (Electrical Engineering; Mechanical Engineering)
Technology (Electrical Engineering; Engineering Management; Mechanical Engineering; Technology)

History: Founded 1975.

Academic Year: September to July

Admission Requirements: Secondary school certificate (baccalauréat)

Fees: None

Main Language(s) of Instruction: Arabic, French

International Co-operation: Université de Tours; University of Dakar; Université de Provence (Aix-Marseille I); Université de Paris V; Université de Paris VII; Université de Paris X; Université de Paris XIII; Université de Lille II; Université de Nancy I; Université de Toulouse II; Université de Nantes; Université de Picardie; Université de Lyon; Université du Québec à Hull; University of Tunis I. Also Ecoles techniques supérieures d'Ingénieurs in France and Spain

Degrees and Diplomas: *Capacité en Droit*: Law, 2 yrs; *Diplôme universitaire de Technologie (DUT)*: Chemical Engineering; Electrical Engineering; Mechanical Engineering; Secretarial Studies, 2 yrs; *Certificat universitaire*: Arab Language and Literature (CUEL); Biology-Geology (CUES); English Language and Literature (CUEL); History and Geography (CUEL); Islamic Studies (CUEL); Mathematics (CUES); Physics-Chemistry (CUES), 2 yrs; *Diplôme d'Ingénieur d'Etat*: Electrical Engineering; Mechanical Engineering, 5 yrs; *Licence*: Biology; Chemistry; Communication; Computer Science; Economics; Geology; Islamic Studies; Languages and Literatures; Letters;

Linguistics; Mathematics; Physics; Private Law; Public Law, 4 yrs; *Diplôme d'Etudes supérieures (DES)*: 1-2 yrs following Licence; *Doctorat*: Biology; Chemistry; Economics; Mathematics; Physics; Private Law; Public Law; Dentistry, 6 yrs; Medicine, 7 yrs

Student Services: Academic Counselling, Cultural Centre, Sports Facilities, Handicapped Facilities, Canteen, Foreign Student Centre

Student Residential Facilities: Yes

Libraries: Central Library, libraries of the Faculties and Schools, total, 150,317 vols

Publications: Revue Tribune; Revue marocaine de Droit et de l'Economie de Développement; Annales de la Faculté de Lettres Aïn Chok

Academic Staff *1999:* Total: c. 1,160

Student Numbers *1999*: All (Foreign Included): c. 33,215 Foreign Only: c. 495

Evening Students, c. 2,300

UNIVERSITY CHOUAÏB DOUKKALI EL JADIDA

Université Chouaïb Doukkali El Jadida

BP 299, 2bis, avenue Mohamed ben Larbi Alaoui, Koudiate ben Driss, 24000 El Jadida
Tel: +212(23) 34-44-47, Ext. 48
Fax: +212(23) 34-44-49
Website: http://www.ucd.ac.ma

Recteur: Abdelhamid Ahmady (1997-)

Faculties

Letters and Human Sciences (Arabic; Arts and Humanities; Communication Studies; English; French; Geography; History; Islamic Studies; Literature)
Science (Biology; Chemistry; Geology; Mathematics; Natural Sciences; Physics)

History: Founded 1989, following the decentralization of higher education.

Governing Bodies: Rectorat

Academic Year: September to July

Admission Requirements: Secondary school certificate (baccalauréat)

Fees: None

Main Language(s) of Instruction: Arabic, French, English

Degrees and Diplomas: *Certificat universitaire*: Arab Language and Literature; Biology; Chemistry; English Language and Literature; French Language and Literature; Geography; Geology; History; Islamic Studies; Mathematics; Physics, 2 yrs; *Diplôme d'Etudes universitaires générales (DEUG)*: Applied Biology and Agro-Food Science; Applied Chemistry and Environment; Applied Geology; Applied Mathematics and Computer Science; Electrical and Mechanical Engineering, 2 yrs; *Licence*: Letters; Science, 4 yrs; *Maîtrise*: a further 2 yrs following Licence; *Diplôme d'Etudes supérieures (DES)*: 2-3 yrs following DEUG; *Doctorat*: Arab Language and Literature; English Language and Literature; French Language and Literature; Geography; History; Islamic Studies; Science and Technology

Student Services: Cultural Centre, Sports Facilities, Health Services

Student Residential Facilities: For c. 10,000 students

Libraries: Faculty Libraries, total, 14,460 vols

Publications: Revue de la Faculté des Lettres; Magazine de la Faculté des Lettres parallèles

Academic Staff *1999:* Total: c. 440

Staff with doctorate: Total: c. 25

Student Numbers *1999:* Total: c. 8,070

• UNIVERSITY QUARAOUIYINE FÈS

Université Quaraouiyine Fès

A.C. 2509, Fès
Tel: +212(55) 64-10-06
Fax: +212(55) 64-10-13
Telex: 31016

Recteur: Abledwahab Tazi Saoud

Secrétaire général: Mohamed Bennani Zoubir

International Relations: Mohamed El Badri
Tel: +212(5) 64-10-16

Faculties

Arabic Language and Literature *(Marrakech)* (Arabic; Literature)
Islamic Law
Islamic Law *(Agadir, Aït Melloul)*
Theology and Philosophy *(Tétouan)* (Philosophy; Theology)

Centres

Islamic Studies and Research (Islamic Studies)

History: Founded 859, reorganized 1788-89 by Mohammed III. Became Moroccan State institution 1947.

Academic Year: November to June (November-December; January-March; April-June)

Admission Requirements: Secondary school certificate (baccalauréat) or equivalent

Fees: None

Main Language(s) of Instruction: Arabic

International Co-operation: Al-Azhar University, Cairo; Azzaïtouna University, Tunisia; Institut catholique de Paris

Degrees and Diplomas: *Licence*: Arab Language and Literature; Islamic Law; Theology and Philosophy, 4 yrs; *Diplôme d'Etudes supérieures (DES)*: a further 2 yrs; *Doctorat*: 4 yrs

Student Residential Facilities: Yes

Libraries: Central Library; faculty libraries

Publications: Revues (quarterly); Bulletin Universitaire

Academic Staff *1999:* Total: c. 120

Student Numbers *1999:* Total: c. 5,595

UNIVERSITY SIDI MOHAMMED BEN ABDELLAH FÈS

Université Sidi Mohammed Ben Abdellah Fès
BP 2626, Fès Almohades, Fès
Tel: +212(55) 62-55-85
Fax: +212(55) 62-36-41

Recteur: Rachid Bel Mokhtar (1991-) Tel: +212(5) 65-04-52

Secrétaire général: Mohamed Ferhane
Tel: +212(5) 65-07-80 Fax: +212(5) 62-24-01

International Relations: Hassan Chergui
Tel: +212(5) 62-55-86

Faculties

Law, Economics and Social Sciences (Economics; Law; Social Sciences)

Letters and Human Sciences *(Dhar El Mehraz)* (Arts and Humanities; Geography; History; Islamic Studies; Literature; Modern Languages; Philosophy; Psychology; Sociology)

Letters and Human Sciences *(Saïs)* (Arts and Humanities; Geography; History; Islamic Studies; Literature; Modern Languages)

Science *(Dhar Mehrez)* (Biological and Life Sciences; Chemistry; Geology; Mathematics; Natural Sciences; Physics)

Science and Technology *(Saïs)* (Biology; Chemistry; Geology; Mathematics; Natural Sciences; Physics; Technology)

Schools

Advanced Technology (Electrical Engineering; Engineering Management; Industrial Engineering; Management; Mechanical Engineering; Production Engineering)

History: Founded 1975.

Governing Bodies: Conseil

Academic Year: September to June (September-February; February-June)

Admission Requirements: Secondary school certificate (baccalauréat) or equivalent

Fees: None

Main Language(s) of Instruction: Arabic, French

International Co-operation: Université d'Aix Marseille; Université de Paris V; Université de Franche Comté, Besançon; Université Paul Sabatier Toulouse III; Université Catholique de Louvain; Université de Mons-Hainaut; Université libre de Bruxelles; Universidad de Córdoba; Universitat Autónoma de Barcelona; Universitá degli Studi di Roma; Universitá degli Studi di Firenze; Universidad de Guadalajara; University of Khartoum; University of Aleppo; Université du Centre, Sousse

Degrees and Diplomas: *Diplôme universitaire de Technologie (DUT)*: Chemical Engineering; Electrical Engineering; Industrial Maintenance; Management Technology; Mechanical Engineering, 2 yrs; *Certificat universitaire*: Biology and Geology; Economics; Law; Mathematics and Physics; Physics and Chemistry, 2 yrs; *Licence*: Arab Language and Literature; Biology; Chemistry; Economics; English Language and Literature; French Language and Literature; Geography; Geology; German Language and Literature; History; Islamic Studies; Mathematics; Philosophy; Physics; Private Law; Public Law; Spanish Language and Literature, 4 yrs; *Maîtrise*: a further 2 yrs;

Diplôme d'Etudes supérieures (DES): (DES), a further 2 yrs; *Doctorat*: Science, a further 2-4 yrs

Student Services: Social Counselling, Employment Services, Cultural Centre, Sports Facilities, Health Services, Canteen

Student Residential Facilities: For c. 5000 students

Libraries: c. 170,000 vols

Academic Staff *1999:* Total: c. 1,010

Staff with doctorate: Total: c. 935

Student Numbers *1999:* Total: c. 31,090

AL AKHAWAYN UNIVERSITY IFRANE

Université Al Akhawayn Ifrane
BP 104, Hassan II Avenue, 53000 Ifrane
Tel: +212(55) 86-20-00
Fax: +212(55) 56-71-50
EMail: info@alakhawayn.ma
Website: http://www.alakhawayn.ma

Président: Ahmed Kerkour (1994-) Tel: +212(5) 86-20-01
Fax: +212(5) 56-71-42 EMail: president@alakhawayn.ma

Secretaire-Général: Wail Benjelloun Tel: +212(5) 86-20-25
Fax: +212(5) 56-71-46 EMail: vpaa@alakhawayn.ma

International Relations: Amy Fishburn
Tel: +212(5) 86-29-05 Fax: +212(5)56-71-47
EMail: a.fishburn@alakhawayn.ma

Schools

Business Administration (Business Administration; Finance; International Business; Management; Marketing)

Humanities and Social Sciences (Arts and Humanities; Communication Studies; Media Studies; Social Sciences)

Science and Engineering (Biological and Life Sciences; Computer Science; Engineering; Environmental Studies; Natural Sciences)

Institutes

Economic Analysis and Prospective Studies (Economics)

Centres

Environmental Issues and Regional Development (Environmental Studies; Regional Planning)

Executive Education (Leadership)

Women and Empowerment *(Hillary Rodham Clinton)* (Women's Studies)

Further Information: Also Arabic courses for foreign students

History: Founded 1995 as an English language institution based on the American higher education model.

Governing Bodies: Board of Trustees

Academic Year: September to May (September-December; January-May). Also optional Summer Session (June-July)

Admission Requirements: Secondary school certificate (baccalauréat) with excellent academic credentials and an interview

Fees: (US Dollars): Foreign students, 4700

Main Language(s) of Instruction: English

International Co-operation: Georgetown University, Washington; The American University, Washington; Boston College, Chestnut Hill; State University of New York at Binghamton

Degrees and Diplomas: *Licence*: 4 yrs; *Maîtrise*: a further 2 yrs

Student Services: Academic Counselling, Social Counselling, Nursery Care, Cultural Centre, Sports Facilities, Health Services, Canteen, Foreign Student Centre

Student Residential Facilities: For c. 1000 students

Libraries: University Library, c. 30,000 vols

Publications: AUI Horizons; AUI News

Academic Staff *1999*: Full-Time: c. 60 Part-Time: c. 10 Total: c. 70
Staff with Doctorate: Total: c. 55

Student Numbers *1999*: All (Foreign Included): c. 780 Foreign Only: c. 20

Evening Students, c. 10

UNIVERSITY IBN TOFAIL KENITRA
Université Ibn Tofail Kénitra
BP 242, Bir Rami, Est Route 41, Villa 302, 14000 Kenitra
Tel: +212(37) 37-28-09
Fax: +212(37) 37-40-52

Recteur: Chaouki Serghini (1992-)

Secrétaire général: Abdallah El Maliki

International Relations: Souad Guelzim

Faculties
Letters and Humanities (Arabic; Arts and Humanities; English; French; Geography; History; Islamic Studies; Literature)
Science (Biology; Chemistry; Geology; Mathematics; Natural Sciences; Physics)

History: Founded 1989.

Academic Year: September to July

Admission Requirements: Secondary school certificate (baccalauréat)

Fees: None

Main Language(s) of Instruction: Arabic, French

International Co-operation: Université de Grenoble I; Université de Paris I; Université de Paris XIII; Université d'Aix-Marseille III; Université de Metz; Université de Lyon; Université de Nice; Université de Nancy; Université de Strasbourg; Université de Bruxelles; Université de Louvain; Université de Montréal; Sherbrooke University; Rice University

Degrees and Diplomas: *Certificat universitaire*: Islamic Studies; Arab Language and Literature; Biology and Geology; English Language and Literature; French Language and Literature; History and Geography; Mathematics and Physics; Physics and Chemistry, 2 yrs; *Licence*: Biology; Chemistry; Geology; Letters; Mathematics; Physics, 4 yrs; *Diplôme d'Etudes supérieures (DES)*: Biology; Chemistry; Mathematics; Physics, a further 2 yrs; *Doctorat*: Letters; Science, 3 yrs

Student Residential Facilities: Yes

Libraries: Total, 21,289 vols

Academic Staff *1999*: Full-Time: c. 400 Part-Time: c. 5 Total: c. 405
Staff with Doctorate: Total: c. 330

Student Numbers *1999*: All (Foreign Included): c. 8,405 Foreign Only: c. 60

UNIVERSITY CADI AYYAD MARRAKECH
Université Cadi Ayyad Marrakech
BP 511, Avenue Prince Abdellah, Marrakech
Tel: +212(44) 43-48-13
Fax: +212(44) 43-44-94
Telex: 74869
Website: http://www.ucam.ac.ma

Recteur: Mohamed Knidiri

Faculties
Law, Economics, and Social Sciences *(FSJES)* (Economics; Law; Social Sciences)
Letters and Humanities *(Beni-Mellal)* (Arts and Humanities)
Letters and Humanities *(FLSH)* (Arabic; Arts and Humanities; English; French; Geography; History; Islamic Studies)
Medecine and Pharmacy (Medicine; Pharmacy)
Science and Technology (Biology; Chemistry; Geology; Mathematics; Natural Sciences; Physics; Technology)
Science and Technology *(Beni Mellal)* (Biology; Chemistry; Geology; Mathematics; Natural Sciences; Physics; Technology)
Science Semlalia *(FSSM)* (Biology; Chemistry; Computer Science; Geology; Mathematics; Natural Sciences; Physics)

Higher Schools
Technology *(Safi)* (Industrial Maintenance; Management Systems; Production Engineering; Technology)

History: Founded 1978.

Academic Year: September to June (September-December; January-April; May-June)

Admission Requirements: Secondary school certificate (baccalauréat) or equivalent

Fees: None

Main Language(s) of Instruction: French

Degrees and Diplomas: *Capacité en Droit*: Law, 2 yrs; *Diplôme universitaire de Technologie (DUT)*: Analysis Technology and Quality Control; Industrial Maintenance; Management Technology, 2 yrs; *Certificat universitaire*: Arabic; Bioscience and Earth Sciences; Economics; English; French; History and Geography; Islamic Studies; Law; Mathematics and Physics; Physics and Chemistry, 2 yrs; *Licence*: Agricultural Management; Applied Management; Applied Mathematics; Arab Literature; Biology; Chemistry; Computer Science; Computer Science and Management; Economics; English Literature; French Literature; Geography; Geology; History; Islamic Studies; Local and Regional Planning; Mathematics; Optics; Physics; Private Law; Public Law; Tourism, 4 yrs; *Maîtrise*: Science and Technology, 2 yrs following Licence; *Diplôme d'Etudes supérieures (DES)*: Arab Literature; Biology; Chemistry; French Literature; Geology; Mathematics, 2 yrs following Licence; *Doctorat*: Science

Academic Staff *1999*: Total: c. 630

Student Numbers *1999*: Total: c. 29,000

UNIVERSITY MOULAY ISMAIL MEKNÈS

Université Moulay Ismail Meknès
BP 298, 1, place Andalous, Meknès
Tel: +212(55) 52-63-78
Fax: +212(55) 52-73-14

Recteur: Mohamed Bennani (1997-)

Secrétaire général: El Houssine Mejdoul

Faculties

Law, Economics and Social Studies (Economics; Law; Social Studies)

Letters and Human Sciences (Arabic; Arts and Humanities; Modern Languages; Oriental Languages)

Science (Mathematics and Computer Science; Natural Sciences)

Science and Technology (Natural Sciences; Technology)

Science and Technology *(Errachidia)* (Natural Sciences; Technology)

Institutes
Technology

History: Founded 1981.

Academic Year: September to July (September-December; January-March; April-July)

Admission Requirements: Secondary school certificate (baccalauréat)

Fees: None

Main Language(s) of Instruction: Arabic, French

International Co-operation: University of Indiana; University of Austin, Texas; Université Montpellier II; Université de Franche Comté; University of Catania

Degrees and Diplomas: *Diplôme universitaire de Technologie (DUT)*: Business Management; Secretarial Studies, 2 yrs; *Certificat universitaire*: Arabic Language and Literature; Biology and Geology; Chemistry; Economics; English Language and Literature; French Language and Literature; History and Geography; Islamic Studies; Law; Mathematics; Physics, 2 yrs; *Diplôme d'Etudes universitaires générales (DEUG)*: Biology; Bioscience and Earth Sciences; Geology; Physics and Chemistry, 2 yrs; *Diplôme d'Ingénieur d'Etat*: Electrical Engineering; Mechanical Engineering; Occupational Arts, 5 yrs; *Licence*: Biology; Chemistry; Economics; Geology; Letters; Mathematics; Physics; Private Law; Public Law, 4 yrs; *Maîtrise*: Science and Technology; Social Sciences, a further 2 yrs; *Diplôme d'Etudes supérieures spécialisées (DESS)*: Biology; Community Law and Management; Letters; Mathematics; Public Law, a further 2 yrs; *Doctorat*: Biology; Chemistry; Mathematics; Physics, 2 yrs following Maîtrise

Student Services: Social Counselling, Employment Services, Cultural Centre, Sports Facilities, Health Services, Foreign Student Centre

Academic Staff *1999:* Total: c. 635

Student Numbers *1999:* Total: c. 23,060

HASSAN II UNIVERSITY MOHAMMEDIA

Université Hassan II Mohammedia
BP 150, 279 Cité Yassmina, Mohammedia
Tel: +212(23) 31-46-35
Fax: +212(23) 31-46-34
Website: http://www.uh2m.ac.ma

Recteur: Mohamed Ferhat

Faculties

Law (Economics; Law; Social Studies)

Letters and Humanities (Arabic; Arts and Humanities; English; French; Geography; History; Islamic Studies)

Letters and Humanities *(Ben M'Sik)* (Arabic; Arts and Humanities; English; French; Geography; History; Islamic Studies)

Science *(Ben M'Sik)* (Natural Sciences)

Science and Technology (Biological and Life Sciences; Chemistry; Communication Studies; Electrical Engineering; Environmental Studies; Natural Sciences; Physics; Technology)

History: Founded 1992.

Main Language(s) of Instruction: Arabic, French, English

International Co-operation: Université d'Oran; University of Karlsruhe; Université de Clermont-Ferrand; Université de Nice; Université de Bordeaux II; Université de Paris; University of Granada; Laval University; Montreal Polytechnic

Degrees and Diplomas: *Licence*: 4 yrs; *Doctorat*

Libraries: c. 97,665 vols

Publications: Basamat; Bahuth; Aqlam al-Jamia

Academic Staff *1999:* Full-Time: c. 550 Part-Time: c. 30 Total: c. 580

Student Numbers *1999:* Total: c. 14,100

*• MOHAMMED I UNIVERSITY OUJDA

Jami'at Muhammad al-Awwal Oujda
BP 724, 60000 Oujda
Tel: +212(56) 50-06-12 +212(56) 50-06-14
Fax: +212(56) 50-06-09
EMail: rectorat@univ-oujda.ac.ma
Website: http://www.univ-oujda.ac.ma

Recteur: El-Madani Belkhadir (1997-)
EMail: recteur@univ-oujda.ac.ma

Secrétaire général: Abderrahman Houtch
EMail: houtch@univ-oujda.ac.ma

International Relations: Youssef Smiri
EMail: smiri@univ-oujda.ac.ma

Faculties

Law, Economics and Social Sciences (Economics; Law; Political Science; Social Sciences) *Dean*: Larbi M'Rabet, *full-time staff:* 86, *part-time staff:* 9,711

Letters and Human Sciences (Arts and Humanities; English; French; Geography; History; Islamic Studies) *Dean*: Mohammed Laamiri, *full-time staff:* 176, *students:* 5,465

Science (Natural Sciences) *Dean*: Benaïssa Nciri, *full-time staff:* 290, *students:* 3,737

Institutes

Technology (Engineering; Technology) *Director*: Mohammed Barboucha, *students*: 376

Centres

Migration Studies (Demography and Population)

History: Founded 1978.

Governing Bodies: Conseil

Academic Year: October to June

Admission Requirements: Secondary school certificate (baccalauréat) or equivalent

Fees: None

Main Language(s) of Instruction: Arabic, French

International Co-operation: Laval University; University of Ottawa. Links with institutions in France, Belgium, Italy, Spain, Netherlands, Germany, United Kingdom, Irak, Algeria, Tunisia and Romania

Degrees and Diplomas: *Diplôme universitaire de Technologie (DUT)*: Electrical Engineering; Management, 2 yrs; *Certificat universitaire*: Arab Language and Literature; Biology and Geology; Economics; English Language and Literature; French Language and Literature; History and Geography; Islamic Studies; Law; Mathematics and Physics; Physics and Chemistry, 2 yrs; *Licence*: Arab Language and Literature; Biology; Chemistry; Economics; English Language and Literature; French Language and Literature; Geography; Geology; History; Islamic Studies; Mathematics; Physics; Private Law; Public Law, 4 yrs; *Diplôme d'Etudes supérieures (DES)*: Arab Language and Literature; Biology; Chemistry; Economics; French Language and Literature; Geography; Geology; History; Islamic Studies; Law; Mathematics, 1-2 yrs; *Doctorat*: Arab Language and Literature; Biology; Chemistry; Economics; English Language and Literature; French Language and Literature; Geography; Geology; History; Islamic Studies; Law; Mathematics; Physics

Student Residential Facilities: Yes

Libraries: Faculty libraries, total, c. 128,612 vols

Publications: University Info; Moroccan Revue of International Relations; Journal of Juridical, Economic and Social Studies; Journal of Administrative Studies (1 per annum)

Academic Staff *1999-2000:* Total: **589**

Student Numbers *1999-2000*	MEN	WOMEN	TOTAL
All (Foreign Included)	11,135	8,244	**19,379**
FOREIGN ONLY	–	–	314

*• MOHAMMED V AGDAL UNIVERSITY RABAT

Jamiât Mohammed al Khamis-Agdal

BP 554, 3, rue Michlifen, Agdal, Rabat-Chellah
Tel: +212(37) 67-13-18
Fax: +212(37) 67-14-01
Telex: recuniv 32603
EMail: belkeziz@onpt.net.ma
Website: http://www.emi.ac.ma

Recteur par intérim: Saïd Bensaid Alaoui (2001-)
Tel: +212(37) 67-33-45

Secrétaire général: Mohammed Maniar
Tel: +212(37) 67-43-90

Faculties

Law, Economics and Social Sciences *(Agdal)* (Economic and Finance Policy; Economics; Human Resources; International Relations; Law; Management; Political Science; Social Sciences) *Dean*: Abdelghani Kadmiri, *full-time staff:* 188, *students:* 13,168

Letters and Humanities *(Agdal)* (Arts and Humanities; English; French; Geography; German; History; Islamic Studies; Philosophy; Psychology; Sociology; Spanish) *Dean*: Saïd Bensaïd Alaoui, *full-time staff:* 276, *students:* 6,190

Science (Biology; Chemistry; Computer Science; Earth Sciences; Mathematics; Natural Sciences; Physics) *Dean*: Hassan Chlyah, *full-time staff:* 456, *students:* 4,443

Schools

Engineering (Chemistry; Civil Engineering; Computer Science; Electrical Engineering; Engineering; Mathematics; Mechanical Engineering; Mining Engineering; Physics) *Director*: Khalid Ramdane, *full-time staff:* 177, *students:* 1,105

Technology *(Salé)* (Building Technologies; Industrial Maintenance; Management; Sales Techniques; Technology) *Director*: Ahmed Zbakhe, *full-time staff:* 51, *students:* 315

Institutes

Scientific Research (Botany; Geography (Human); Natural Sciences; Physics; Surveying and Mapping; Zoology) *Director*: Mohamed Saghi, *full-time staff:* 41

History: Founded 1957 incorporating former Institutes of Letters (1912), Law (1920), and Science (1940). Reorganized 1975 and 1993. A State Institution.

Governing Bodies: Conseil de l'Université

Academic Year: September to June (September-December; January-March; April-June)

Admission Requirements: Secondary school certificate (baccalauréat) or equivalent. Entrance examination for Engineering

Fees: None

Main Language(s) of Instruction: Arabic, French

International Co-operation: Exchange programmes of academic staff and students, and research projects with institutions in: Belgium; Canada; France; Germany; Iraq; Tunisia; Mauritania; USA; Russian Federation; Syria; Italy; Spain

Degrees and Diplomas: *Diplôme universitaire de Technologie (DUT)*: Engineering; Technology, 2 yrs; *Certificat universitaire*: Science (CUES), 2 yrs; *Diplôme d'Etudes universitaires générales (DEUG)*: Economics; Law; Letters and Human Sciences, 2 yrs; *Diplôme d'Ingénieur d'Etat*: Engineering, 5 yrs; *Licence*: Economics; Letters and Human Sciences; Private Law; Public Law; Science, 4 yrs; *Diplôme d'Etudes supérieures spécialisées (DESS)*: Engineering; Letters and Human Sciences; Science, 2 yrs; *Diplôme d'Etudes supérieures approfondies (DESA)*: Economics; Engineering; Law; Letters and Human Sciences; Science, 2 yrs; *Doctorat*: Economics; Engineering; Letters and Human Sciences; Private Law; Public

Law; Science. Also Diplôme de Spécialité de 3e cycle in Science.

Student Services: Academic Counselling, Sports Facilities, Language Programmes, Health Services, Canteen, Foreign Student Centre

Student Residential Facilities: Yes

Special Facilities: Scientific Research Institute Museum

Libraries: Rectorate, c. 28,000 vols; Faculty libraries, 427,168 vols, 40,998 periodicals

Publications: Langues et Littératures; Revue de la Faculté des Lettres et des Sciences Humaines; Hespéris Tamuda; Revue Juridique, Politique, Economique du Maroc; Revue Attadriss; Journal marocain d'Automatique d'Informatique et de Traitement de Signal; Travaux de l'Institut scientifique; Bulletin de l'Institut scientifique; Signes du Présent; Annales du Centre des Etudes stratégiques de Rabat; La Recherche scientifique; Bulletins du Département de Physique du Globe

Academic Staff *1999-2000*	MEN	WOMEN	TOTAL
FULL-TIME	859	330	**1,189**

Student Numbers *1999-2000*	MEN	WOMEN	TOTAL
All (Foreign Included)	13,606	11,615	**25,221**
FOREIGN ONLY	–	–	440

• MOHAMMED V SOUISSI UNIVERSITY RABAT

Jâmiât Mohammed El Khâmiss Rabat
BP 8007, N.U. Agdal-Rabat, Agdal-Rabat
Tel: +212(37) 68-11-60
Fax: +212(37) 68-11-63
EMail: um5souissi@ac.ma

Recteur: Mohammed Tahar Alaoui
EMail: um5souissi@ac.ma

Secrétaire Général: Mohammed Belfquih

Faculties

Dentistry *Dean:* Bouchaib Jidal
Educational Sciences *Dean:* M'Hammed Zgor
Law, Economics and Social Sciences *(Salé)* (Economics; Law; Social Sciences) *Dean:* Mohammed Benallal
Law, Economics and Social Sciences *(Souissi)* (Economics; Law; Social Sciences) *Dean:* Moulay Rachid Abderrazzak
Medicine and Pharmacy (Medicine; Pharmacy) *Dean:* Abdelmajid Belmahi

Schools

Computer Science and Systems Analysis *(Advanced)* (Computer Science; Systems Analysis) *Director:* Adelfdil Bennani

Institutes

African Studies *Director:* Halima Ferhat
Scientific Research (Natural Sciences) *Director:* Abdelkébir Khatibi
Studies and Research on Arabization (Middle Eastern Studies; North African Studies) *Director:* Abdelkader Fassi-Fihri

History: Founded 1992 incorporating faculties which were originally part of the Université Mohammed V, after division of this institution.

280

Degrees and Diplomas: *Diplôme d'Etudes supérieures spécialisées (DESS):* 2 yrs; *Diplôme d'Etudes supérieures approfondies (DESA):* 2 yrs; *Doctorat:* 3 to 5 yrs

Student Services: Cultural Centre, Sports Facilities, Canteen

Student Residential Facilities: Yes

Academic Staff *1999-2000:* Total: **661**

Staff with doctorate: Total: **280**

Student Numbers *1999-2000*	MEN	WOMEN	TOTAL
All (Foreign Included)	6,850	7,798	**14,648**
FOREIGN ONLY	205	88	293

HASSAN I UNIVERSITY SETTAT

Université Hassan 1er
BP 539, 50 rue Ibn Al Haithem, 26000 Settat
Tel: +212(23) 72-12-75
Fax: +212(23) 72-12-74
EMail: essaid@onpt.net.ma
Website: http://www.uh1.ac.ma

Recteur: Abderrahmane Essaid

Faculties

Law, Economics and Social Sciences (Economics; Law; Social Sciences)
Science and Technology (Biological and Life Sciences; Chemistry; Computer Science; Earth Sciences; Electronic Engineering; Mathematics; Mechanical Engineering; Physics; Technology)

Schools

Commerce and Management *(National)* (Accountancy; Business Administration; Business and Commerce; Economics; Law; Management)

UNIVERSITY ABDELMALEK ESSAÂDI TÉTOUAN

Université Abdelmalek Essaâdi Tétouan
BP 211, Martil-Tétouan
Tel: +212(39) 97-90-99
Fax: +212(39) 97-91-51

Recteur: Saâd Daoudi (1993-)

Secrétaire général: Larbi Kabbab

International Relations: Ahmed El Moussaoui

Faculties

Law, Economics and Social Sciences *(Tanger)* (Economics; Law; Social Sciences)
Letters and Humanities (Arts and Humanities)
Science (Biology; Chemistry; Geology; Mathematics; Natural Sciences; Physics)
Science and Technology *(Tanger)* (Natural Sciences; Technology)

Schools

Business Administration and Management *(Tanger)* (Business Administration; Management)
Translation *(Tanger)* (Arabic; English; French; Spanish; Translation and Interpretation)

History: Founded 1989.

Academic Year: September to July (September-December; January-March; April-July)

Admission Requirements: Secondary school certificate (baccalauréat)

Fees: None

Main Language(s) of Instruction: Arabic, French

International Co-operation: University of Granada; University of Alicante; University of Malaga; University of Seville; University of Cadiz; Federal University of Rio de Janeiro; University of Huelva; University of Castilla la Mancha

Degrees and Diplomas: *Licence*: 4 yrs; *Diplôme d'Etudes supérieures (DES)*: 2-3 yrs; *Doctorat*: 3-4 yrs

Libraries: Libraries of the Faculties and Schools

Publications: Tourjouman, Journal of School of Translation

Academic Staff *1999:* Total: c. 555

Student Numbers *1999:* Total: c. 9,530

OTHER UNIVERSITY LEVEL INSTITUTIONS

PUBLIC INSTITUTIONS

NATIONAL INSTITUTE OF ARCHEOLOGY AND CULTURAL HERITAGE SCIENCES
Institut national des Sciences de l'Archéologie et du Patrimoine
Avenue Kennedy, Route des Zaers, 10 000 Rabat-Souissi
Tel: +212(37) 75-09-61
Fax: +212(37) 75-08-84
EMail: archeo@iam.net.ma

Directeur: Joudia Hassar-Benslimane (1985-)

Secrétaire Général: Abdelfettah El Rhazoui

Departments
Anthropology (Anthropology; Ethnology; Social Sciences) *Head*: Mustapha Nhaila, *full-time staff:* 3, *students:* 8
Archaelogy, Anthropology and Cultural Heritage (Anthropology; Archaeology; Heritage Preservation; Museum Studies) *Head*: M. Abdeljalil El Hajraoui, *full-time staff:* 6, *students:* 8
Heritage Studies (Fine Arts; Heritage Preservation; Restoration of Works of Art) *Head*: Elarbi Erbati, *full-time staff:* 4, *students:* 10
Prehistory, Antiquity, and Islamic Studies (Ancient Civilizations; Art History; Ceramic Art; Geology; Islamic Studies; Prehistory; Surveying and Mapping) *Head*: Armar Akerraz, *full-time staff:* 13, *students:* 24

History: Founded 1986

Admission Requirements: Secondary school certificate (baccalauréat)

Fees: None

Main Language(s) of Instruction: Arabic, French

International Co-operation: With Universities in USA and Europe

Degrees and Diplomas: *Diplôme d'Etudes supérieures (DES)*: Sciences de l'Archéologie et du Patrimoine, 1st and 2nd cycles, 2 yrs each; *Diplôme d'Etudes supérieures approfondies (DESA)*: Sciences de l'Archéologie et du Patrimoine, 3rd cycle, 5 yrs

Student Services: Cultural Centre, Sports Facilities, Health Services, Foreign Student Centre

Student Residential Facilities: Dormitory or Housing

Special Facilities: Museum

Libraries: Central Library

Publications: Bulletin d'Archéologie Marocaine (1 per annum)

Press or Publishing House: Nouvelles d'Archéologie et du Patrimoine

Academic Staff *1999-2000*	MEN	WOMEN	TOTAL
FULL-TIME	19	7	**26**

Student Numbers *1999-2000*	MEN	WOMEN	TOTAL
All (Foreign Included)	50	25	**75**

NATIONAL SCHOOL OF ARCHITECTURE
Ecole nationale d' Architecture (ENA)
BP 6372, Rabat
Tel: +212(37) 77-52-94
Fax: +212(37) 77-52-61
EMail: ena@maghrebnet.net.ma

Directeur: Abderrahmane Chorfi Tel: +212(37) 77-52-41 Fax: +212(37) 77-52-76

Secrétaire Général: Abdeljabar Lakhmiri Tel: +212(37) 77-52-30

International Relations: Naïma El Haouzaki, Responsable du Service de Coopération Tel: +212(37) 77-52-29

Architecture *Director*: Abderrahmane Chorfi, *full-time staff:* 53, *part-time staff:* 13, *students:* 403
Regional Town Planning and Housing (House Arts and Environment; Regional Planning; Town Planning) *Head*: Abederrahmane Chorfi, *full-time staff:* 53, *part-time staff:* 13, *students:* 403

History: Founded 1980.

Admission Requirements: Secondary school certificate (baccalauréat) and entrance examination

Main Language(s) of Instruction: French

International Co-operation: Links with institutions in France, Italy, Spain

Accrediting Agencies: Ministère de l' Aménagement du Territoire, de l' Urbanisme et de l' Habitat

Degrees and Diplomas: *Diplôme d'Architecte (DENA)*: Architecture, 6 yrs

Student Services: Sports Facilities, Language Programmes

Student Residential Facilities: None

Libraries: Documentation Centre

Academic Staff *1999-2000*	TOTAL
FULL-TIME	43
PART-TIME	14
TOTAL	**57**

Staff with doctorate: Total: **1**

Student Numbers *1999-2000*	TOTAL
All (Foreign Included)	**403**
FOREIGN ONLY	30

NATIONAL SCHOOL OF ARTS AND CRAFTS

Ecole nationale supérieure des Arts et Métiers (ENSAM)

BP 4024, Marjane II, Meknès Ismailia, Beni M'Hamed, Meknès
Tel: +212(55) 45-20-22
Fax: +212(55) 45-20-26
EMail: ensam@aim-net.ma
Website: http://www.dfc.gov.ma/ensam.htm

Directeur: Mohamed Bouidida

Directeur-Adjoint: Youssef Benghabrit

Departments

Energy Engineering *Head*: M'hamed Mouqallid, *full-time staff:* 3, *students:* 224

Engineering (Automation and Control Engineering; Electronic Engineering; Engineering) *Head*: Jalal Sabor, *full-time staff:* 7, *students:* 224

Industrial and Production Engineering (Industrial Engineering; Production Engineering) *Head*: Mounir El Maghri, *full-time staff:* 7, *students:* 224

Materials Engineering *Head*: Mohammed Alami, *full-time staff:* 4, *students:* 224

Mathematics and Sociology (Mathematics and Computer Science; Sociology) *Head*: Mohamed Douimi, *full-time staff:* 6, *students:* 224

Mechanical and Structural Engineering (Mechanical Engineering; Structural Architecture) *Head*: Bouchaib Radi, *full-time staff:* 9, *students:* 224

History: Founded 1997.

Accrediting Agencies: Ministère de l' Enseignement, de la Formation des Cadres et de la Recherche Scientifique

Admission Requirements: Secondary school certificate (baccalauréat Maths A or B, or sections Mechanical Engineering or Electrical Engineering), and entrance examination

Main Language(s) of Instruction: French

International Co-operation: Ecole nationale supérieure des Arts et Métiers; Université de Technologie de Compiègne; Ecole nationale d' Ingénieurs de Saint-Etienne

Degrees and Diplomas: *Diplôme d'Ingénieur d'Etat*: Mechanical and Industrial Engineering, 5 yrs

Student Services: Academic Counselling, Social Counselling, Nursery Care, Sports Facilities, Language Programmes

Student Residential Facilities: Yes

Libraries: None

282

Academic Staff *1999-2000*	MEN	WOMEN	TOTAL
FULL-TIME	35	6	41
PART-TIME	6	–	6
TOTAL	**41**	**6**	**47**

Staff with doctorate: Total: **20**

Student Numbers *1999-2000*	MEN	WOMEN	TOTAL
All (Foreign Included)	181	43	**224**

PRIVATE INSTITUTIONS

HIGHER SCHOOL OF FOOD INDUSTRY

Ecole supérieure de l'Agro-Alimentaire (Sup Agro)

22, rue Catelet, Belvedère, Casablanca
Tel: +212(22) 24-54-05
Fax: +212(22) 24-53-99
EMail: supagro@casanet.net.ma
Website: http://www.casanet.net.ma/users/supagro

Directeur Pédagogique: Abderrazak Mounis

Administrative Officer: Hicham Arsaoui

International Relations: Hicham Arsaoui

Schools

Food Industry (Food Technology) *Director*: Abderrazak Mounis

History: Founded 1997

Governing Bodies: Administrative Board

Academic Year: October to July

Admission Requirements: Secondary school certificate (baccalauréat)

Fees: (Moroccan Dirhams): Registration, 3,000 per annum; tuition, 19,900 per annum

Main Language(s) of Instruction: French

International Co-operation: Links with institutions in France

Degrees and Diplomas: *Diplôme universitaire de Technologie (DUT)*: Contrôle Qualité des Aliments, 2 yrs; *Maîtrise*: Technologie Alimentaire, 4 yrs; *Diplôme d'Etudes supérieures spécialisées (DESS)*: Gestion, Commerce, Qualité (DESS), 5 yrs

Student Services: Social Counselling, Language Programmes, Canteen

Libraries: Central Library

Academic Staff *2000*	MEN	WOMEN	TOTAL
FULL-TIME	5	5	10
PART-TIME	70	10	80
TOTAL	**75**	**15**	**90**
STAFF WITH DOCTORATE			
FULL-TIME	2	–	2
PART-TIME	50	7	57
TOTAL	**52**	**7**	**59**

Student Numbers *2000*: All (Foreign Included): Men: c. 40 Women: c. 30 Total: c. 70
Foreign Only: Men: c. 3 Women: c. 5 Total: c. 8

HIGHER SCHOOL OF MANAGEMENT, COMMERCE AND COMPUTER SCIENCE, FÈS

Ecole supérieure de Management, du Commerce et d'Informatique, Fès (Sup' Management)
28, place du 11 Janvier et rue Patrice Lumumba, Ville Nouvelle, Fès
Tel: +212(55) 65-35-31 +212(55) 94-08-25
Fax: +212(55) 65-27-32
EMail: supmgt@extranet.net.ma
Président: Abdesselam Erkik (1985-) Tel: 212(1) 21-64-72
Sécretaire Générale: Laila El Alaoui El Mdagari
International Relations: Rachida Erkik

Departments

Computer Science (Computer Science; Information Sciences; Management) *Head*: Abdelmajid Benyakhlef
Financial Management (Accountancy; Finance) *Head*: Amina Bourassi
International Commerce and Marketing (Business and Commerce; International Business; Marketing) *Head*: Mahmoud Belamhitou
Management (Accountancy; Finance; Management; Marketing) *Head*: Ahmed Maghni

History: Founded 1995.
Governing Bodies: Conseil d' Administration
Academic Year: September to June
Admission Requirements: Secondary school certificate (baccalauréat; bac + 4 for Financial Management and International Commerce)
Fees: (Moroccan Dirham): 18,050 per annum
Main Language(s) of Instruction: French, English, German, Spanish
International Co-operation: Newport University
Degrees and Diplomas: *Diplôme/Diplôme supérieur*: Computer Engineering; Management and Commerce, 4 yrs; *Diplôme d'Etudes supérieures (DES)*: Commerce and Marketing; Finance, 6 yrs. Certificats de formation continue (CFC). Certificats de Cycles Spéciaux (CCS)
Student Services: Academic Counselling, Social Counselling, Employment Services, Foreign Student Adviser, Sports Facilities, Language Programmes, Foreign Student Centre
Student Residential Facilities: Yes
Libraries: Central Library and computer facilities
Publications: Flash Managers, Cultural Studies, Management, Economics and Leisure (3 per annum)

Academic Staff *1999-2000*	MEN	WOMEN	TOTAL
FULL-TIME	4	7	11
PART-TIME	3	–	3
TOTAL	**7**	**7**	**14**
STAFF WITH DOCTORATE			
FULL-TIME	8	2	10
PART-TIME	12	1	13
TOTAL	**20**	**3**	**23**

Student Numbers *1999-2000*	MEN	WOMEN	TOTAL
All (Foreign Included)	111	70	**181**
FOREIGN ONLY	63	15	78

Part-time Students, 7 **Evening Students,** 280

OTHER INSTITUTIONS

PUBLIC INSTITUTIONS

CENTRE DE FORMATION DES TECHNICIENS DE L'AÉRONAUTIQUE CIVILE ET DE LA MÉTÉOROLOGIE

BP 8088, Km. 7 Route d'El Jadida, Casablanca-Oasis
Tel: +212(2) 23-06-55
Fax: +212(2) 23-06-52
Directeur: Amal Kabbaj

Aeronautics (Aeronautical and Aerospace Engineering)
Meteorology
Telecommunications (Telecommunications Engineering)

COMPLEXE HORTICOLE

BP 18/S, Agadir
Tel: +212(48) 24-10-06
Fax: +212(48) 24-22-43
Directeur: Brahim Hafidi

Horticulture

ECOLE HASSANIA DES TRAVAUX PUBLICS ET DES COMMUNICATIONS

BP 8108, Km. 7, Route d'El Jadida, Casablanca
Tel: +212(22) 23-07-10
Fax: +212(22) 23-07-17
Directeur: Abdessalam Messaoudi

Public Works and Communications (Civil Engineering; Transport and Communications)

ECOLE MOHAMMEDIA D'INGÉNIEURS

BP 765, Avenue Ibn Sina, Agdal-Rabat
Tel: +212(37) 77-19-05
Fax: +212(37) 77-88-53
EMail: diremi@emi.ac.ma
Website: http://www.emi.ac.ma
Directeur: Khalid Ramadane

Engineering

ECOLE NATIONALE D'ADMINISTRATION

1, avenue de la Victoire, Rabat
Tel: +212(37) 72-44-00
Fax: +212(37) 73-09-29
Directeur: Mostafa Taimi

Administration

ECOLE NATIONALE D'AGRICULTURE
BPS/40, Meknès
Tel: +212(55) 30-02-39
Fax: +212(55) 30-02-38
Telex: 421 54
EMail: ena@enameknes.ac.ma
Website: http://www.enameknes.ac.ma
Directeur: Abdelhafid Debbarh

Programmes
Agricultural Pedagogy (Agriculture; Pedagogy)
Agriculture
Animal Production (Animal Husbandry)
Fruit Production Techniques (Fruit Production)
Plant Protection (Plant and Crop Protection)
Rural Economics (Agricultural Economics)
Vegetable Production

ECOLE NATIONALE DE COMMERCE ET DE GESTION D' AGADIR (ENCG, AGADIR)
BP S37/s, Hay Salem, 80 000 Agadir
Tel: +212(48) 22-57-39
Fax: +212(48) 22-57-41
EMail: info@encg-agadir.ac.ma
Website: http://www.encg-agadir.ac.ma/
Directeur: Mohamed Marzak (1994-) Tel: +212(8) 22-57-48
EMail: marzak.m@encg-agadir.ac.ma

Departments
Commerce (Business and Commerce)
Information Technology
Languages and Communication (Communication Studies; Modern Languages)
Management

History: Founded 1994.

Academic Year: September to July

Admission Requirements: Secondary school certificate (baccalauréat scientifique), and entrance examination

Fees: None

Main Language(s) of Instruction: French

Degrees and Diplomas: *Maîtrise*: Commerce et Gestion; *Diplôme d'Etudes supérieures spécialisées (DESS)*; *Diplôme d'Etudes supérieures approfondies (DESA)*; *Doctorat*. Also Diploma in Accountancy

Student Services: Employment Services, Foreign Student Adviser, Nursery Care, Sports Facilities, Language Programmes, Health Services

Student Residential Facilities: Yes

Libraries: Documentation Centre

Academic Staff *1999-2000*	MEN	WOMEN	TOTAL
FULL-TIME	53	27	**80**
STAFF WITH DOCTORATE			
FULL-TIME	22	13	**35**

Student Numbers *1999-2000*	MEN	WOMEN	TOTAL
All (Foreign Included)	420	300	**720**
FOREIGN ONLY	22	11	33

ECOLE NATIONALE DE COMMERCE ET DE GESTION DE SETTAT (ENCG)
BP 658, Km 3 Route de Casa, Settat
Tel: +212(23) 40-10-63
Fax: +212(23) 40-13-62
Directeur: Hassan Ibn Ismail

Business and Commerce; Management

ECOLE NATIONALE DE COMMERCE ET DE GESTION DE TANGER (ENCG)
BP 125, Ancienne route de l'aéroport, Tanger princip., Tanger
Tel: +212(39) 31-34-87 +212(39) 31-34-89
Fax: +212(39) 31-34-93
Directeur: Abdelbaqui Agrar

Business and Commerce; Management

ECOLE NATIONALE FORESTIÈRE D'INGÉNIEURS
BP 511, Tabriquet, Salé
Tel: +212(37) 78-97-04
Fax: +212(37) 78-71-49
Directeur: Omar Mkhirit

Forestry

ECOLE NATIONALE DE L'INDUSTRIE MINÉRALE (ENIM)
BP 753, Avenue Hadj Ahmed, Cherkaoui, Agdal, Rabat
Tel: +212(7) 68-02-30
Fax: +212(7) 77-10-55
EMail: info@enim.ac.ma
Website: http://www.enim.ac.ma
Directeur: Omar Debbaj

Programmes
Computer Engineering
Electro-mechanical Engineering (Electronic Engineering; Mechanical Engineering)
Energy Systems (Energy Engineering)
Exploitation and Production of the Substratum (Geology; Soil Conservation)
Geological Engineering
Industrial Maintenance (Maintenance Technology)
Materials and Quality Control (Materials Engineering)
Mineralogy
Process Engineering (Production Engineering)
Production Systems (Production Engineering)

ECOLE NORMALE SUPÉRIEURE, CASABLANCA (ENS)

Route de Casablanca, Casablanca
Tel: +212(22) 23-22-77
Fax: +212(22) 98-53-26

Directeur: Lahcen Oubahamou

Education; Mathematics; Physics

ECOLE NORMALE SUPÉRIEURE, FÈS (ENS)

BP 5206, Kariat Ben Souda Ahouaz-Oued Fès, Fès
Tel: +212(55) 65-50-83
Fax: +212(55) 65-50-69

Directeur: Abdenbi Rejouani

Education; Islamic Studies; Mathematics; Physics

ECOLE NORMALE SUPÉRIEURE, MARRAKECH (ENS)

BP S41, Douar El Askar, Route d'Essaouira, Marrakech
Tel: +212(44) 34-01-25 +212(44) 34-22-58
Fax: +212(44) 34-22-87

Directeur: Mohamed Fliou

Computer Science; Mathematics; Physics

ECOLE NORMALE SUPÉRIEURE, MEKNÈS (ENS)

BP 3104, Toulal, Meknès
Tel: +212(55) 53-38-85
Fax: +212(55) 53-38-83

Directeur: Mbarek Hanoun (2000-)

Directeur-Adjoint: Hammani Akefli Tel: +212(5) 53-388

Departments

Arabic (Arabic; Teacher Training) *Head*: Hassan Youssif
French (French; Teacher Training) *Head*: Mohammed Faragi
Philosophy (Philosophy; Teacher Training) *Head*: Mohammed Kechkech
Translation (Translation and Interpretation) *Head*: Nour Eddine Denkir

Institutes

Teacher Training (Education; Teacher Training) *Director*: Mbarek Hanoun, *full-time staff*: 20

History: Founded 1983.
Governing Bodies: Ministry of Education
Fees: None
Main Language(s) of Instruction: Arabic, French
Student Services: Academic Counselling, Employment Services, Nursery Care, Sports Facilities, Language Programmes, Health Services, Canteen
Student Residential Facilities: Yes
Special Facilities: Local audio-visual equipments

Libraries: Local and National Libraries
Academic Staff *2000-2001:* Total: **20**

ECOLE NORMALE SUPÉRIEURE, RABAT (ENS)

BP 5118, Av. Oued Akrach, Takaddoum, Rabat
Tel: +212(37) 75-00-25 +212(37) 75-22-61
Fax: +212(37) 75-00-47

Directeur: Abdeltif Mogine

Computer Science; English; Geography; History; Physics

ECOLE NORMALE SUPÉRIEURE, TÉTOUAN (ENS)

BP 209, Martil, Tétouan
Tel: +212(39) 97-91-75 +212(39) 97-90-48
Fax: +212(39) 97-91-80

Directeur: Arid Eljalali

Arabic; Education; French

ECOLE DE PERFECTIONNEMENT DES CADRES DU MINISTÈRE DE L'INTÉRIEUR

Kenitra
Tel: +212(37) 37-13-66

Executives Training (Leadership)

ECOLE DES SCIENCES DE L' INFORMATION (ESI)

Avenue Maa Al Aïnaïne, Haut Agdal, Rabat
Tel: +212(37) 77-49-04 +212(37) 77-49-07
Fax: +212(37) 77-02-32
EMail: esi@cnd.mpep.gov.ma
Website: http://www.mpep.gov.ma/esi/index.htm

Directeur: Mohamed Benjelloun Tel: +212(37) 68-12-90
EMail: mbenjelloun@cnd.mpep.gov.ma
Directeur Adjoint: Abdelmoula El Hamdouchi
Tel: +212(37) 68-12-91 Fax: +212(37) 68-12-91
International Relations: Nazha Hachad
Tel: +212(37) 77-49-13 EMail: n-hachad@yahoo.com

Information Sciences *Director*: Mohamed Benjelloun, *full-time staff*: 21, *part-time staff*: 42, *students*: 301

History: Founded 1974 to meet the needs of the country for professionnals by ensuring their training in the areas of Documentation Techniques, Information Sciences, Science and Librarianship.
Governing Bodies: Ministry of Economic Prevision and Planning
Admission Requirements: Secondary school certificate (baccalauréat)
Fees: None
Main Language(s) of Instruction: French

International Co-operation: Agreements with institutions in United Kingdom, USA, Spain, Canada, France, Algeria, Tunisia, Denmark, Senegal, Egypt

Accrediting Agencies: Ministry of Higher Training

Degrees and Diplomas: *Maîtrise*: Information Sciences, 4 yrs. Also Specialist Diploma, 2 yrs

Student Services: Employment Services, Sports Facilities, Language Programmes, Canteen

Student Residential Facilities: Yes

Libraries: Central Library

Publications: Revue de la Science de l' information (biannually)

Academic Staff 2000	MEN	WOMEN	TOTAL
FULL-TIME	8	13	21
PART-TIME	34	8	42
TOTAL	**42**	**21**	**63**
STAFF WITH DOCTORATE			
FULL-TIME	3	1	4
PART-TIME	8	1	9
TOTAL	**11**	**2**	**13**

Student Numbers 2000	MEN	WOMEN	TOTAL
All (Foreign Included)	104	197	**301**
FOREIGN ONLY	12	14	26

INSTITUT AGRONOMIQUE ET VÉTÉRINAIRE HASSAN II
BP 6202, Madinat al Irfane, Chariaa Maa Al Aïnaïne, Rabat
Tel: +212(37) 77-17-58
Fax: +212(37) 77-81-35

Directeur: Fouad Guessouss

Agriculture; Veterinary Science

INSTITUT DAR-AL-HADITH AL-HASSANIA
BP 7844, 2, rue Dahomey, Rabat
Tel: +212(37) 72-25-87
Fax: +212(37) 72-62-01

Directeur: Ahmed El Khamlichi

Islamic Studies

INSTITUT DE FORMATION AUX CARRIÈRES DE SANTÉ, AGADIR
Hôpital Hassan II, Agadir
Tel: +212(8) 84-14-77

Health Sciences

INSTITUT DE FORMATION AUX CARRIÈRES DE SANTÉ, CASABLANCA
Rue Jenner, Casablanca
Tel: +212(22) 26-02-85

Head: Mohamed Achiri

Health Sciences

INSTITUT DE FORMATION AUX CARRIÈRES DE SANTÉ, FÈS
Hôpital Ibnou El Khatib, Fès
Tel: +212(55) 62-29-76

Head: Thami Merrouni

Health Sciences

INSTITUT DE FORMATION AUX CARRIÈRES DE SANTÉ, MARRAKECH
Riad Si Aissa Moussine, Marrakech
Tel: +212(44) 44-21-95

Head: Said El Amiri

Health Sciences

INSTITUT DE FORMATION AUX CARRIÈRES DE SANTÉ, MEKNÈS
Hôpital Mohamed V, Meknès
Tel: +212(55) 52-09-27

Head: Ahmed Oalla

Health Sciences

INSTITUT DE FORMATION AUX CARRIÈRES DE SANTÉ, OUJDA
Hôpital Farabi, Oujda
Tel: +212(56) 68-49-73

Head: Benyounes Benhaala

Health Sciences

INSTITUT DE FORMATION AUX CARRIÈRES DE SANTÉ, RABAT
Km. 4, Route de Casa, Rabat
Tel: +212(37) 69-19-38

Head: Mohamed Boulgana

Health Sciences

INSTITUT DE FORMATION AUX CARRIÈRES DE SANTÉ, TÉTOUAN
Hôpital Civil, Tétouan
Tel: +212(39) 97-10-92

Head: Mohamed Khbiez

Health Sciences

INSTITUT NATIONAL DE L'ACTION SOCIALE
Ruel Hariri, Tanger
Tel: +212(39) 94-09-71
Fax: +212(39) 94-07-96
Directeur: Mohammed Zanouny

Social Work

INSTITUT NATIONAL D'AMÉNAGEMENT ET D'URBANISME
BP 6215, Avenue Maa Al Aïnaïne, Rabat
Tel: +212(37) 77-16-24
Fax: +212(37) 77-50-09
Directeur: Abdellah El Hazam

Development Studies; Town Planning

INSTITUT NATIONAL D'ADMINISTRATION SANITAIRE (INAS)
College de Santé publique, KM 4,5 Route de Casa, Rabat
Tel: +212(37) 69-16-26
Fax: +212(37) 69-16-26
EMail: inas@mtds.com
Directeur: Fikri Benbrahim Tel: +212(37) 29-98-34

Health Sciences

History: Founded 1989

INSTITUT NATIONAL DES BEAUX-ARTS (INBA)
BP 89, Av. Med V , Cité scolaire, Tétouan
Tel: +212(39) 96-15-45
Fax: +212(39) 96-42-92
Directeur: Abdel Karim Ouazzani

Fine Arts

INSTITUT NATIONAL D' ETUDES JUDICIAIRES (INEJ)
PO Box 1007, Boulevard Mehdi Ben Berka, Souissi, Rabat
Tel: +212(37) 75-19-92 +212(37) 75-39-16
Fax: +212(37) 75-25-13
Website: http://www.justice.gov.ma
Directeur: Abdelkébir Zeroual Fax: +212(37) 75-49-02
Assistant Directeur: Abdeslam Hassi-Rahou
Tel: +212(37) 75-25-46

Institutes
Legal Studies *(National)* (Law) *Director:* Abdelkebir Zeroual, *students:* 167

History: Founded 1969, acquired present status and title 1970.
Admission Requirements: Secondary school certificate (baccalauréat) and competitive entrance examination

Fees: None
Main Language(s) of Instruction: Arabic
Accrediting Agencies: International Agency of Cooperation
Degrees and Diplomas: *Capacité en Droit*: Law, 2 yrs
Student Services: Nursery Care, Sports Facilities, Canteen
Student Residential Facilities: Yes
Libraries: Central Library
Publications: The Judicial Attaché

Academic Staff *1999-2000*	MEN	WOMEN	TOTAL
FULL-TIME	33	14	**47**

Staff with doctorate: Total: **6**

Student Numbers *1999-2000*	MEN	WOMEN	TOTAL
All (Foreign Included)	126	41	**167**
FOREIGN ONLY	6	–	6

INSTITUT NATIONAL DES POSTES ET TÉLÉCOMMUNICATIONS (INPT)
Avenue Allal Al Fasse, Madinat Al Irfane, Rabat
Tel: +212(37) 77-30-79
Fax: +212(37) 77-30-44
EMail: riouch@inpt.ac.ma
Website: http://www.inpt.ac.ma
Directeur: Mohamed Abdelfettah Chefchaouni

Telecommunications Engineering

INSTITUT NATIONAL DES STATISTIQUES ET D'ECONOMIE APPLIQUÉE
BP 6217, Madinat El Irfane, Rabat
Tel: +212(7) 77-48-60
Fax: +212(7) 77-94-57
EMail: insea@insea.ac.ma
Website: http://www.insea.ac.ma
Directeur: Abdelaziz El Ghazali

Programmes
Computer Science
Demography
Economics
Statistics

INSTITUT ROYAL DE FORMATION DES CADRES DE LA JEUNESSE ET DES SPORTS
Belle-Vue, Avenue Ibn Sina, Agdal, Rabat
Tel: +212(37) 72674
Directeur: Mohammed Kaach

Executives Training (Leadership)

INSTITUT SUPÉRIEUR D'ART DRAMATIQUE ET D'ANIMATION CULTURELLE
BP 1355, Chariaa Al Mansour, Rabat
Tel: +212(37) 72-17-02
Fax: +212(37) 70-34-23

Directeur: Ahmed Massaia

Cultural Studies; Theatre

INSTITUT SUPÉRIEUR DE COMMERCE ET D'ADMINISTRATION DES ENTREPRISES
Km. 9500 Route de Nouasseur Oasis, Casablanca
Tel: +212(22) 33-54-82
Fax: +212(22) 33-54-96
EMail: iscac@iscac.ac.ma
Website: http://www.iscac.ac.ma

Directeur: Rachid Mirabet

Business Administration; Business and Commerce

INSTITUT SUPÉRIEUR DES ETUDES MARITIMES
Km 7, Route d'El Jadida, Casablanca
Tel: +212(22) 23-07-40
Fax: +212(22) 23-15-68

Directeur: Miloud Loukili

Marine Science and Oceanography

INSTITUT SUPÉRIEUR D'INFORMATION ET DE COMMUNICATION
BP 6205, Avenue Alla Al Fassi, Rabat
Tel: +212(37) 77-33-40
Fax: +212(37) 77-27-89

Directeur: Mohamed Lamouri

Journalism

INSTITUT SUPÉRIEUR INTERNATIONAL DE TOURISME
BP 651, Baie de Tanger, Tanger
Tel: +212(39) 94-59-04
Fax: +212(39) 94-59-05

Directrice: Souad Hassoune

Tourism

288

PRIVATE INSTITUTIONS

ECOLE D' ADMINISTRATION ET DE DIRECTION DES AFFAIRES, RABAT (EAD)
2, avenue Prince Moulay Youssef, Rabat
Tel: +212(37) 70-19-95
Fax: +212(37) 70-81-36
EMail: ead@mail.sis.net.ma

Directeur: Ahne Berrezel (1984-) Tel: +212(37) 70-19-23
Study Director: Abdelah Chriai Tel: +212(37) 70-81-36
International Relations: M. Jamila

Institutes
Business, Finance and Management (Business Administration; Finance; Management) *Director*: Ahmed Berrezel, *full-time staff*: 12, *part-time staff*: 35, *students*: 200

History: Founded 1984

Academic Year: September to June

Admission Requirements: Secondary school certificate (baccalauréat)

Fees: (Moroccan Dirhams): 34,000; US$ 3,400

Main Language(s) of Instruction: French, English

International Co-operation: Links with Institutions in France, Canada, USA, United Kingdom

Degrees and Diplomas: *Maîtrise*: Finance, 4 yrs; *Diplôme d'Etudes supérieures spécialisées (DESS)*; *Diplôme d'Etudes supérieures (DES)*: Management and Commerce, 4 yrs

Student Services: Academic Counselling, Employment Services, Foreign Student Adviser, Nursery Care, Cultural Centre, Sports Facilities, Language Programmes, Canteen, Foreign Student Centre

Student Residential Facilities: Yes

Libraries: Central Library

Publications: La Vie Economique; Le Matin; L'Opinion

Academic Staff *2000*: Total: **c.**50

Student Numbers 2000	MEN	WOMEN	TOTAL
All (Foreign Included)	120	80	**200**
FOREIGN ONLY	20	30	50

Evening Students, 60

ECOLE D' ENSEIGNEMENT SUPÉRIEUR DE MANAGEMENT, CASABLANCA (ECO-SUP)
Casablanca
Management

ECOLE DES HAUTES ETUDES DE BIOTECHNOLOGIE, CASABLANCA (EHEB)
118, avenue Atlantide Polo, Casablanca
Tel: +212(2) 21-43-99
Fax: +212(2) 52-15-50

Biotechnology

ECOLE DES HAUTES ETUDES DE COMMERCE, CASABLANCA
Angle rue de Strasbourg et boulevard de la Résistance, Casablanca
Tel: +212(22) 44-00-40
Fax: +212(22) 44-00-57

Directeur: A. Sekkaki

Business and Commerce

ECOLE DES HAUTES ETUDES DE COMMERCE, FÈS
1, rue Jaber Al Ansari et boulevard Hamza, Bnou Abdel Moutalib, Fès
Tel: +212(55) 64-33-28
Fax: +212(55) 64-04-56
EMail: hec@fesnet.net.ma

Directrice: Ilham Skalli

Business and Commerce

ECOLE DES HAUTES ETUDES DE COMMERCE, RABAT
67, rue Jaafar Assadiq, Agdal, Rabat
Tel: +212(37) 67-12-76
Fax: +212(37) 67-12-77

Directeur: Khalil El Kouhen

Business and Commerce

ECOLE DES HAUTES ETUDES COMMERCIALES ET INFORMATIQUES, AGADIR (HECI)
Avenue Hassan II, Immeuble Inbiaat, Stade Hassania, Agadir
Tel: +212(48) 84-71-74
Fax: +212(48) 82-11-03

Directeur: Driss Benserighe

Business and Commerce; Computer Science

ECOLE DES HAUTES ETUDES COMMERCIALES ET INFORMATIQUES, CASABLANCA (HECI)
25, rue Poincaré, Immeuble Librairie des Sciences, Casablanca
Tel: +212(22) 26-25-68
Fax: +212(22) 20-22-10

Directeur: Fayçal Ghissassi

Business and Commerce; Computer Science

ECOLE DES HAUTES ETUDES COMMERCIALES ET INFORMATIQUES, FÈS (HECI)
Avenue Allal Ben Aboulevardellah, rue No. 134, Fès
Tel: +212(55) 93-12-03
Fax: +212(55) 93-12-03

Business and Commerce; Computer Science

ECOLE DES HAUTES ETUDES COMMERCIALES ET INFORMATIQUES, KENITRA (HECI)
535, boulevard Mohammed V, Kénitra
Tel: +212(37) 37-93-25

Business and Commerce; Computer Science

ECOLE DES HAUTES ETUDES COMMERCIALES ET INFORMATIQUES, MEKNÈS (HECI)
9, rue de Chinon, Es-Saada, Meknès
Tel: +212(55) 53-84-43
Fax: +212(55) 55-01-34

Business and Commerce; Computer Science

ECOLE DES HAUTES ETUDES COMMERCIALES ET INFORMATIQUES, MOHAMMADIA (HECI)
Bd Yacoub Al Mansour, Lot. Al Wafaa Mohammadia, Mohammadia
Tel: +212(23) 30-49-10

Business and Commerce; Computer Science

ECOLE DES HAUTES ETUDES COMMERCIALES ET INFORMATIQUES, RABAT (HECI)
89, rue Sebou, Agdal, Rabat
Tel: +212(37) 77-07-05
Fax: +212(37) 77-11-62

Directeur: Moulay Hachem Kacimi

Business and Commerce; Computer Science

ECOLE DES HAUTES ETUDES COMMERCIALES ET INFORMATIQUES, TANGER (HECI)
Place des Nations, avenue Mohammed V, Résidence Molk Allah, 1er Etage, Tanger
Tel: +212(39) 94-06-91

Directeur: Mohamed Fikri

Business and Commerce; Computer Science

ECOLE DES HAUTES ETUDES ÉCONOMIQUES ET COMMERCIALES, MARRAKECH (EHEEC)

Avenue Allal El Fassi, Rue Abou Oubaida Daoudiate, Marrakech
Tel: +212(44) 34-31-33
Fax: +212(44) 43-63-09

Directeur: Adnan Toughrai

Business Administration

ECOLE DES HAUTES ETUDES EN GESTION, INFORMATIQUE ET COMMUNICATION DE CASABLANCA (EDHEC)

201, boulevard de Bordeaux et 7, rue de Boulmane, Casablanca
Tel: +212(22) 49-14-98
Fax: +212(22) 49-25-53
Communication Studies; Computer Science; Management

ECOLE MAROCAINE DES SCIENCES DE L'INGÉNIEUR EN INFORMATIQUE DE GESTION ET EN INFORMATIQUE INDUSTRIELLE, CASABLANCA (EMSI)

44, rue de Soissons, Belvedère, Casablanca
Tel: +212(22) 24-43-39
Fax: +212(22) 40-46-52
Computer Engineering; Management

History: Founded 1986.

ECOLE MAROCAINE DES SCIENCES DE L'INGÉNIEUR EN INFORMATIQUE DE GESTION ET EN INFORMATIQUE INDUSTRIELLE, RABAT

49, rue Patrice Lumumba (Place Pietri), Rabat
Tel: +212(37) 76-40-50
Fax: +212(37) 76-40-51
Computer Engineering; Management

History: Founded 1996.

ECOLE POLYFINANCE, CASABLANCA

309, boulevard Ziraoui, Casablanca
Tel: +212(22) 47-63-63
Fax: +212(22) 47-63-65

Finance

ECOLE POLYVALENTE SUPÉRIEURE D'INFORMATIQUE ET DU GÉNIE ÉLECTRIQUE, FÈS (EPSIEL)

4, Immeuble 'Abbou', avenue Allal Ben Abdellah, 30000 Fès
Tel: +212(55) 65-40-37
Fax: +212(55) 62-52-68

Head: Abdelilah Benani

Computer Science; Electrical Engineering

ECOLE SUPÉRIEURE D'ARCHITECTURE D'INTÉRIEUR (ESAI)

3, rue Amir Sidi Mohammed Souissi, Rabat
Tel: +212(37) 75-58-20
Fax: +212(37) 75-58-20

ECOLE SUPÉRIEURE DE COMMERCE, MARRAKECH (ESC)

BP 529, Avenue Prince Moulay Abdellah, Gueliz, 40000 Marrakech
Tel: +212(44) 43-33-93
Fax: +212(44) 43-60-67
EMail: supdeco@esc.marrakech.ac.ma

President: Bennis Ahmed (1986-)

Business and Commerce *President*: Bennis Ahmed

History: Founded 1987

Admission Requirements: Secondary school certificate (baccalauréat), entrance examination and interview

Fees: (Moroccan Dirhams): Registration, 3200; tuition, 9900 per term, 26,500 per annum

Main Language(s) of Instruction: French

International Co-operation: Washington University; Delaware State University

Degrees and Diplomas: *Maîtrise*: Management, 4 yrs

Student Services: Academic Counselling, Social Counselling, Employment Services, Foreign Student Adviser, Nursery Care, Cultural Centre, Sports Facilities, Language Programmes, Health Services, Canteen, Foreign Student Centre

Student Residential Facilities: Yes

Libraries: Central Library, c. 3000 vols

Academic Staff 2000	MEN	WOMEN	TOTAL
FULL-TIME	2	–	2
PART-TIME	38	9	47
TOTAL	**40**	**9**	**49**
STAFF WITH DOCTORATE			
FULL-TIME	–	–	1
PART-TIME	16	5	21
TOTAL	**–**	**–**	**22**

Student Numbers 2000	MEN	WOMEN	TOTAL
All (Foreign Included)	192	138	**330**
FOREIGN ONLY	42	24	66

ECOLE SUPÉRIEURE DE COMMERCE ET DES AFFAIRES, CASABLANCA (ESCA)

55, rue Jaber Ben Hayan, boulevard d'Anfa, Casablanca
Tel: +212(22) 20-91-20
Fax: +212(22) 20-91-15
Business and Commerce

ECOLE SUPÉRIEURE DE COMMUNICATION, CASABLANCA (ESC)

73, rue Pierre Parent, Casablanca
Tel: +212(22) 31-09-09
Fax: +212(22) 31-09-39
Communication Studies

ECOLE SUPÉRIEURE DE COMMUNICATION ET DE PUBLICITÉ, CASABLANCA (COM CUP)

18, rue Bachir Al Ibrahimi, Quartier Belair, Casablanca
Tel: +212(2) 26-34-20
Fax: +212(2) 27-46-02
Advertising and Publicity; Communication Studies

ECOLE SUPÉRIEURE DE L'ECONOMIE SCIENTIFIQUE ET DE GESTION, RABAT (ESES)

34, rue Mediouna, Hay Aviation, Rabat
Tel: +212(37) 75-04-94
Fax: +212(37) 75-04-95
Directeur pédagogique: Younies Naciri

Business and Commerce; Management

ECOLE SUPÉRIEURE DU GÉNIE ÉLECTRIQUE, CASABLANCA (ISGE)

Electrical Engineering

ECOLE SUPÉRIEURE DE GESTION D'ENTREPRISE, CASABLANCA

Avenue de la Résistance, Angle Puissesseau, Casablanca
Tel: +212(22) 30-81-50

ECOLE SUPÉRIEURE DE GESTION MAROC, CASABLANCA (ESG)

4, 18, rue Colbert, Casablanca
Tel: +212(22) 31-55-55
Fax: +212(22) 31-56-26
Président délégué: Jacques Knafo

Management

ECOLE SUPÉRIEURE DE GESTION ET DE COMMERCE, RABAT (EGICO)

2, rue Chouaib Doukkali, angle boulevard Ibn Toumart, Quartier les Orangers, Rabat
Tel: +212(37) 73-25-64
Fax: +212(37) 73-25-70
Directeur: Khalid Tarik

Business Administration; Management

ECOLE SUPÉRIEURE D'INFORMATIQUE APPLIQUÉE, CASABLANCA (ESIA)

Avenue de la Résistance, angle rue Puissesseau, Casablanca
Tel: +212(22) 30-59-82
Fax: +212(22) 30-32-86
EMail: esma@casanet.net.ma
Directeur: Mohamed Ziani

Computer Science

ECOLE SUPÉRIEURE D'INFORMATIQUE APPLIQUÉE À LA GESTION, MARRAKECH (ESIAG)

Villa Thérèse 1, Quartier Saadia, Gueliz, Marrakech
Tel: +212(44) 43-39-82
Fax: +212(44) 43-72-95
Directeur: Mohammed Kabbaj

Computer Science; Management

ECOLE SUPÉRIEURE D'INFORMATIQUE ET DE MANAGEMENT DES AFFAIRES, EL JADIDA (ESIMA)

Place Hansali, Imm. Mounia, El Jadida
Tel: +212(23) 34-04-04
Fax: +212(23) 34-06-61
Business Administration
Computer Science

ECOLE SUPÉRIEURE INTERNATIONALE DE GESTION, CASABLANCA (ESIG)

6, rue Ampère et boulevard de Bordeaux, Casablanca
Tel: +212(22) 27-91-10
Fax: +212(22) 20-43-27
EMail: esigcasa@open.net.ma
Directeur: Azzedine Bennani

Management

ECOLE SUPÉRIEURE INTERNATIONALE DE GESTION, FÈS (ESIG)
Km 3, route d'Immouzer, Fès
Tel: +212(55) 60-10-37
Fax: +212(55) 62-65-01
EMail: esig.fes@casanet.net.ma

Management

ECOLE SUPÉRIEURE INTERNATIONALE DE GESTION, MARRAKECH (ESIG)
Boulevard Mansour Eddahbi, angle rue Mohammed Baqual, Marrakech
Tel: +212(44) 44-71-43
Fax: +212(44) 44-71-45

Management

ECOLE SUPÉRIEURE INTERNATIONALE DE GESTION, RABAT (ESIG)
32, Zankat Moulay Ali Cherif Hassan, Rabat
Tel: +212(37) 76-94-57
Fax: +212(37) 76-28-09
EMail: esigraba@elau.net.ma

Directeur: Mohamed Kabbaj Tel: +212(37) 76-94-58

International Relations: Merieme Drissi

Accountancy; Administration; Finance; Information Management; International Business; Marketing
Management *Directeur:* Mohamed Kabbaj, *full-time staff:* 15, *part-time staff:* 46, *students:* 184

History: Founded 1991

Academic Year: October to June

Admission Requirements: Secondary school certificate (baccalauréat), and entrance examination

Main Language(s) of Instruction: French

International Co-operation: Université Panthéon Sorbonne; Université du Québec

Degrees and Diplomas: *Maîtrise:* Administration; Computer Science, 4 yrs

Student Services: Academic Counselling, Social Counselling, Employment Services, Foreign Student Adviser, Cultural Centre, Sports Facilities, Language Programmes, Health Services, Canteen, Foreign Student Centre

Student Residential Facilities: Yes

Libraries: Central Library

Publications: Revue de l' Ecole (quarterly)

ECOLE SUPÉRIEURE DE MANAGEMENT, CASABLANCA (ESM)
Boulevard de la Résistance, rue Puissesseau, Casablanca
Tel: +212(22) 30-81-30
Fax: +212(22) 30-32-86

Directeur: Mohammed Ali Cherif Kettani

Management

ECOLE SUPÉRIEURE DE MANAGEMENT APPLIQUÉ, MARRAKECH (ESMA)
Avenue Prince Moulay Aboulevardellah, Immeuble Berrada Rouidate II, Marrakech
Tel: +212(44) 30-86-22
Fax: +212(44) 30-02-23

Directeur: Mohammed Berrada Elazizi

Management

ECOLE SUPÉRIEURE DE MANAGEMENT DE LA QUALITÉ, CASABLANCA (ESIMAQ)
56, rue Ibn Hamdis, Casablanca
Tel: +212(22) 36-92-27
Fax: +212(22) 29-44-03

Directeur: Mohamed Afif

Industrial Management

ECOLE SUPÉRIEURE D'OPTIQUE ET DE LUNETTERIE, FÈS (ESOL)
5, rue Bizert, route d'Immouzer, Ville Nouvelle, Fès
Tel: +212(55) 60-11-87
Fax: +212(55) 60-76-42

Directeur: Farouk Blidi

Optical Technology

ECOLE SUPÉRIEURE DE PROTHÈSE, CASABLANCA (ESP)
5, rue Casablanca, Casablanca
Tel: +212(22) 40-52-88
Fax: +212(22) 40-33-63

Directeur: Nabil Daoudi

Dental Technology
Prosthetics (Medical Technology)

ECOLE SUPÉRIEURE DE SECRÉTARIAT, INFORMATIQUE ET COMPTABILITÉ, FÈS (ESSIC)

Angle Avenue Abdelkrim Al Khattabi et Houssein Khadar, Fès
Tel: +212(55) 51-41-65

Directeur: Abdelaziz Badaoui

Accountancy; Computer Science; Secretarial Studies

ECOLE SUPÉRIEURE DE SECRÉTARIAT, INFORMATIQUE ET COMPTABILITÉ, KENITRA (ESSIC)

40, Avenue Hassan II, Kenitra
Tel: +212(37) 68-19-41
EMail: essic@france.mail.com

Accountancy; Computer Science; Secretarial Studies

History: Founded 1999

ECOLE SUPÉRIEURE DE SECRÉTARIAT D' INFORMATIQUE ET DE COMPTABILITÉ, MEKNÈS (ESSICM)

132, avenue des FAR, 50000 Meknès
Tel: +212(55) 51-41-64
Fax: +212(55) 51-41-63
EMail: essic@caramail.com

Directeur: Abdelaziz Badaoui

Higher Schools

Secretarial Studies, Computer Science and Accountancy (Accountancy; Computer Science; Finance; Management; Secretarial Studies) *President*: Fouad Benchekroune, *full-time staff:* 30, *students:* 100

Systems Analysis *Head*: Abdel Aziz Badaoui, *students:* 30

History: Founded 1990

Admission Requirements: Secondary school certificate (baccalauréat)

Main Language(s) of Instruction: French, English

Degrees and Diplomas: *Maîtrise*: Finance and Management; Informatics, 4 yrs

Student Services: Foreign Student Adviser, Nursery Care, Cultural Centre, Sports Facilities, Language Programmes, Foreign Student Centre

Student Residential Facilities: Yes (free of charge)

Libraries: Central Library; Photographic library

Publications: Le Guide, Studies in Morocco

Academic Staff *1999-2000*	MEN	WOMEN	TOTAL
FULL-TIME	5	2	7
PART-TIME	18	1	19
TOTAL	**23**	**3**	**26**
STAFF WITH DOCTORATE			
FULL-TIME	2	2	**4**

Student Numbers *1999-2000*	MEN	WOMEN	TOTAL
All (Foreign Included)	45	55	**100**

ECOLE SUPÉRIEURE DE SECRÉTARIAT D'INFORMATIQUE ET DE COMPTABILITÉ, RABAT (ESSIC)

80, rue de Sebou, Agdal, Rabat
Tel: +212(37) 68-19-41
Fax: +212(37) 51-41-63

Directeur: Mohammed Toma

Accountancy; Computer Science; Secretarial Studies

ECOLE TECHNIQUE DES RÉSEAUX ET SYSTÈMES, SETTAT (ETRS)

46, avenue Mohammed V (2ème et 3ème Etages), Settat
Tel: +212(23) 40-27-05
Fax: +212(23) 40-27-67

Directeur: Abdelaly Guissj

Networks and Systems Technology (Computer Networks; Telecommunications Engineering)

HIGH TECHNOLOGY SCHOOL IN MOROCCO, RABAT (HIGH-TECH)

10 bis, rue El Yamana, Rabat
Tel: +212(37) 76-93-97
Fax: +212(37) 20-12-50
Website: http://www.hightech.edu

Technology

INSTITUT D'ADMINISTRATION DES ENTREPRISES, KÉNITRA (IAE)

422, Bir Rami, Est, Kénitra
Tel: +212(37) 37-74-06
Fax: +212(37) 37-74-23

Business Administration

INSTITUT DE FORMATION AUX FONCTIONS SOCIALES ET ÉDUCATIVES SPÉCIALISÉES, CASABLANCA (IFFSES)

Rue 9 Avril, Maârif, Casablanca
Tel: +212(22) 21-57-00
Fax: +212(22) 25-57-11

Social Work
Special Education

INSTITUT DES HAUTES ETUDES BANCAIRES ET FINANCIÈRES, CASABLANCA (HBF)

4, rue Van Zeeland, Casablanca
Tel: +212(22) 47-65-54
Fax: +212(22) 47-65-97

Directeur: Tayeb Rhafes

Banking; Finance

INSTITUT DES HAUTES ETUDES BANCAIRES ET FINANCIÈRES, OUJDA

Rue Al Khalil, Quartier El Qods, Oujda
Tel: +212(56) 74-60-60

Directeur: Moulay Abdelhamid Smaili

Banking; Finance

INSTITUT DES HAUTES ETUDES ÉCONOMIQUES ET SOCIALES, CASABLANCA (IHEES)

3, rue Caporal Corras, Anfa, Casablanca
Tel: +212(22) 30-01-95
Fax: +212(22) 30-28-90

Directeur: Abdelhamid Lazrak

Economics; Social Studies

INSTITUT DES HAUTES ETUDES DE MANAGEMENT, CASABLANCA (HEM)

52, avenue de Nador, Polo, Casablanca
Tel: +212(22) 52-52-52
Fax: +212(22) 21-55-30
EMail: hem@hem.ac.ma
Website: http://www.hem.ac.ma

Président: Abdelali Benamour

Administrative Officer: Mouloud Sadat
EMail: m.sadat@hem.ac.ma

Academic Affairs Director: Hassan Sayarh
EMail: hassan.sayarh@hem.ac.ma

Schools

Business *(Casablanca, Rabat)* (Business Administration; Finance; Information Management; Management; Marketing) *President*: Abdelali Benamour, *full-time staff:* 20, *part-time staff:* 85, *students:* 600

History: Founded 1988. HEM has set as its major goal the promotion of ethics and the pursuit of scholarly work of high quality. A private Institution

Governing Bodies: Board of Directors

Academic Year: September to June

Admission Requirements: Secondary school certificate (baccalauréat), and entrance examination

Main Language(s) of Instruction: French

International Co-operation: Université Paris Dauphine; Institut d' Etudes politiques de Paris; Université Jean Moulin; Faculté des Sciences économiques de Montpellier I; Ecole supérieure de Commerce, Lyon; Université d' Ottawa

Accrediting Agencies: Ministry of Higher Education and Research

Degrees and Diplomas: *Maîtrise*: Management, 4 yrs; *Diplôme d'Etudes supérieures spécialisées (DESS)*: Finance, Marketing (MBA/DESS), 2 yrs. Also Diploma in Management, 1 yr

Student Services: Academic Counselling, Social Counselling, Employment Services, Foreign Student Adviser, Nursery Care, Cultural Centre, Sports Facilities, Language Programmes, Canteen

Student Residential Facilities: Yes

Special Facilities: Conference Hall. Computer Centre. Workshops (Painting, Theatre, Dance, Music)

Libraries: Central Library, c. 1000 vols

Publications: Penser l' Entreprise, Revue Marocaine de Management (biannually)

Academic Staff 2000	TOTAL
FULL-TIME	20
PART-TIME	100
TOTAL	**120**

INSTITUT DES HAUTES ETUDES DE MANAGEMENT, RABAT (HEM)

8, rue Hamza, Agdal, Rabat
Tel: +212(37) 67-42-56
Fax: +212(37) 67-42-56

Président: Abdellatif Homy

Management

INSTITUT MAROCAIN D'ETUDES SUPÉRIEURES, OUJDA (IMES)

181, boulevard Derfoufi, Oujda
Tel: +212(56) 68-78-12
Fax: +212(56) 68-78-11

Directeur: Hassan Jaali

Higher Education

INSTITUT MAROCAIN DE MANAGEMENT, CASABLANCA (IMM)

33, rue Allal Ben Abdellah, angle rue Foucauld, Casablanca
Tel: +212(22) 20-22-88
Fax: +212(22) 20-26-39

Directeur: Mustapha Benchehla

Management

INSTITUT SUPÉRIEUR EN ADMINISTRATION ET MANAGEMENT, KÉNITRA (ISHAM)

Palais de la Foire, route Sidi Allal, Al Bahraoui, Kénitra
Tel: +212(73) 37-10-80
Fax: +212(73) 37-15-44

Administration; Management

INSTITUT SUPÉRIEUR DES ARTS ET MÉTIERS, CASABLANCA (ISAM)

Angle rue de la Plage, boulevard Sidi Abderrahmane Ibnou Majid El Bahar, Casablanca
Tel: +212(22) 26-54-93
Fax: +212(22) 44-90-40

Directeur: Mohamed Jaouad Marrakchi

Engineering

INSTITUT SUPÉRIEUR DE BIOLOGIE ET DE BIOCHIMIE, CASABLANCA (ISBB)

34, boulevard Mohammed V, Casablanca
Tel: +212(22) 26-26-01
Fax: +212(22) 20-22-12
EMail: export@mbox.azure.net

Directeur: Ahmed Essadki

Biochemistry; Biology

INSTITUT SUPÉRIEUR DE BIOLOGIE ET DE BIOCHIMIE, MARRAKECH (ISBB)

Lotissement Semlalia, Lot No.100, Marrakech
Tel: +212(44) 44-87-34
Fax: +212(44) 44-87-32

Directrice: Saida Chahbouni

Biochemistry; Biology

INSTITUT SUPÉRIEUR DE BIOLOGIE ET DE BIOCHIMIE, TÉTOUAN (ISBB)

Tétouan
Tel: +212(39) 68-83-46
Fax: +212(39) 68-82-15

Directeur: Nard Bennas

Biochemistry; Biology

INSTITUT SUPÉRIEUR DU COMMERCE INTERNATIONAL, CASABLANCA (CNCD)

13, rue Lavoisier (en Face de l'Hôpital 20 Août), Casablanca
Tel: +212(22) 82-61-26
Fax: +212(22) 28-89-42
EMail: cncd@casanet.net.ma

Directeur: Mohamed Aoune

International Business

INSTITUT SUPÉRIEUR DE COMPTABILITÉ, AUDIT ET FINANCE, CASABLANCA (ISCAF)

21, rue de l'Olympe, Maarif, Casablanca
Tel: +212(22) 80-20-40
Fax: +212(22) 80-20-40

Directeur: Mohamed Douch

Accountancy; Finance

INSTITUT SUPÉRIEUR D'ELECTRONIQUE ET DES RÉSEAUX DE TÉLÉCOMMUNICATION, CASABLANCA (ISERT)

30, rue Kamel Mohammed, Casablanca
Tel: +212(22) 45-08-45
Fax: +212(22) 45-08-47
EMail: isert@open.net.ma

Directeur: Boujemaâ Charoub

Telecommunications Engineering

INSTITUT SUPÉRIEUR DES ETUDES INFORMATIQUES, CASABLANCA (IN. SUP. INFO)

3, rue Ibrahim Ibnou El Adham, Maarif, Casablanca
Tel: +212(22) 98-25-25
Fax: +212(22) 99-39-39

Directeur: Soûad Bhanimi

Computer Science

INSTITUT SUPÉRIEUR DE FORMATION AUX TECHNIQUES DE GESTION, TANGER (ISFOTEG)

47, boulevard Pasteur, Tanger
Tel: +212(39) 93-71-01
Fax: +212(39) 93-17-71
EMail: isfoteg@marocnet.net.ma

Management

INSTITUT SUPÉRIEUR DE FORMATION EN TECHNOLOGIE ALIMENTAIRE, CASABLANCA (ISFORT)

94, rue Allal Ben Aboulevardellah, 2000 Casablanca
Tel: +212(22) 44-88-28
Fax: +212(22) 44-88-26
EMail: isfortdirection@isfort.ac.ma
Website: http://www.isfort.ac.ma

Directeur: Mounir Diouri

Food Technology

INSTITUT SUPÉRIEUR DU GÉNIE APPLIQUÉ, CASABLANCA (IGA)

Place de la Gare, angle boulevard Ba Hmad, Ain Sbaa, Hay Mohammadi, Casablanca
Tel: +212(22) 24-06-05
Fax: +212(22) 40-40-38

Engineering

INSTITUT SUPÉRIEUR DU GÉNIE APPLIQUÉ, RABAT (IGA)

27, rue Oqba, angle Rue Al Battani et Ibnou Al Haitam, Agdal, Rabat
Tel: +212(37) 77-14-70
Fax: +212(37) 77-14-72

Directeur: Naoufal Bennouna

Accountancy; Business and Commerce; Electronic Engineering; Marketing

INSTITUT SUPÉRIEUR DE GESTION, CASABLANCA (ISG)

23, rue Houssein Benali, Anfa, Casablanca
Tel: +212(22) 27-71-22
Fax: +212(22) 27-71-22

Directeur: Driss Skalli

Management

INSTITUT SUPÉRIEUR DE GESTION ET DE COMMERCE, CASABLANCA (ISGC)

23, rue Hafid Ibrahim, Quartier Gauthier, Casablanca
Tel: +212(22) 26-63-12
Fax: +212(22) 47-46-43

Directeur: Azzedine Chraibi

Business and Commerce; Management

INSTITUT SUPÉRIEUR DE GESTION ET DU DROIT DES ENTREPRISES, MEKNÈS

24, rue Badi El Kobra, Meknès
Tel: +212(55) 40-32-29

Business Administration
Law (Medicine)

296

INSTITUT SUPÉRIEUR D'INFORMATIQUE APPLIQUÉE ET DE MANAGEMENT, AGADIR (ISIAM)

Lotissement Dakhla No. 479, HF, Agadir
Tel: +212(8) 22-32-21
Fax: +212(8) 22-33-68
EMail: isiam@marocnet.net.ma
Website: http://www.isiam.org

Directeur: Aziz Bouslikhane

Computer Science; Management

INSTITUT SUPÉRIEUR D'INFORMATIQUE ET DE MANAGEMENT, NADOR (ISIM)

BP 641, 34, avenue Toyko, 3ème Etage, No.9, Nador
Tel: +212(56) 60-22-00
Fax: +212(56) 33-34-03

Directeur: Bensalem El Hanafi

Computer Science; Management

INSTITUT SUPÉRIEUR D'OPTIQUE 'IBN AL HAITAM', TÉTOUAN (ISOPIH)

Zone Industrielle, Lot No.176, Tétouan
Tel: +212(39) 68-88-52
Fax: +212(39) 68-88-54

Directeur: Adil Khayat

Optics

INSTITUTE FOR LANGUAGE AND COMMUNICATION STUDIES (ILCS)

29, rue Oukaimeden, Agdal, 10100 Rabat
Tel: +212(37) 67-59-68
Fax: +212(37) 67-59-65
EMail: ilcs@acdim.net.ma
Website: http://www.fusion.net.ma/ilcs

Directrice: Amal Daoudi

Language and Communication Studies (Advertising and Publicity; Arts and Humanities; Business Administration; Communication Studies; English; French; Human Resources; Management; Marketing; Mass Communication; Modern Languages; Public Relations; Translation and Interpretation) *Head*: Abderrafi Benhallam, *full-time staff:* 5, *part-time staff:* 25, *students:* 50

History: Founded 1996 to train operational individuals in the fields of Business Communication and Languages.
Governing Bodies: Board of Advisers
Academic Year: October to June (October-January; February-June)
Admission Requirements: Secondary school certificate (baccalauréat)
Fees: (Moroccan Dirham): Registration, 900; tuition, 12,000 per semester

Main Language(s) of Instruction: English, French

Accrediting Agencies: Ministère de l' Enseignement Supérieur

Degrees and Diplomas: *Maîtrise*: Language and Communication, 4 yrs

Student Services: Academic Counselling, Employment Services, Foreign Student Adviser, Language Programmes, Canteen

Student Residential Facilities: None

Special Facilities: Multimedia Laboratory

Libraries: Central Library

STAFF WITH DOCTORATE	MEN	WOMEN	TOTAL
PART-TIME	7	3	10

Student Numbers *2000-2001*	MEN	WOMEN	TOTAL
All (Foreign Included)	15	35	**50**
FOREIGN ONLY	4	5	9

INTERNATIONAL INSTITUTE FOR HIGHER EDUCATION, RABAT (IIHE)
Km 4, 2 rue des Ziars, Souissi, Rabat
Tel: +212(37) 75-19-20
Fax: +212(37) 65-97-70
EMail: info@iihe.ac.ma
Website: http://www.iihe.ac.ma

Directeur: Dina Tidjani

Higher Education

INTERNATIONAL SCHOOL OF BUSINESS ADMINISTRATION, CASABLANCA (ISBA)
24, boulevard Mohammed V, Casablanca
Tel: +212(22) 26-30-53
Fax: +212(22) 26-29-98
EMail: isba@mail.cbi.net.ma

Directeur: Mammar El Mansari

Business Administration

Mozambique

INSTITUTION TYPES AND CREDENTIALS

Types of higher education institutions:

Universidade (University)
Instituto Superior (Higher Institute)

School leaving and higher education credentials:

Certificado de Habilitações Literárias
Bacharelato
Licenciatura

STRUCTURE OF EDUCATION SYSTEM

Pre-higher education:

Duration of compulsory education:

Age of entry: 6
Age of exit: 13

Structure of school system:

Primary
Type of school providing this education: Primary School
Length of programme in years: 7
Age level from: 6 to: 13
Certificate/diploma awarded: Carta de Ensino Primário de Segundo Grau

General Secondary
Type of school providing this education: Secondary School
Length of programme in years: 5
Age level from: 13 to: 18
Certificate/diploma awarded: Certificado de Habilitações Literárias (Secondary School Leaving Certificate)

Technical Secondary
Type of school providing this education: Technical Secondary School
Length of programme in years: 3
Age level from: 13 to: 16

Technical
Length of programme in years: 2

Age level from: 16 to: 18
Certificate/diploma awarded: Technician Diploma

School education:

Primary education lasts for seven years, subdivided into two levels: the first (EP1), of five years, and the second (EP2), of two years, leading to the Carta de Ensino Primário de Segundo Grau. Secondary education is offered in secondary, technical and agricultural schools. Ten per cent of students from primary education go on to this level. Under the National Education System, the best graduates of primary education follow five years of general secondary education, divided into the first cycle, lasting three years and the second, lasting two years. In the final year of secondary education students study Mathematics, Physics, Chemistry, Biology, Portuguese, Geography, History, Physical Education and English. The course leads to the Certificado de Habilitações Literárias (Secondary School Leaving Certificate). An entrance examination is necessary to enter university. Technical and professional education take place in technical schools and institutes. Basic technical education (equivalent to the first cycle of general secondary) trains skilled workers; mid-level technical education (equivalent to the second cycle of general secondary) trains technicians.

Higher education:

Higher education is provided by public and private universities and higher institutes. Higher education is the responsibility of the Ministry of Education and is financed by the State. Universities have a high degree of autonomy and coodinate their actions with the National Council of Higher Education. Their internal governing body is the Conselho Universitário composed of the Rector and the deans of the faculties.

Main laws/decrees governing higher education:

Decree: Law no. 1/93   Year: 1993
Concerns: Public higher education institutions

Decree: Decree no. 11/90   Year: 1990
Concerns: Private education

Academic year:

Classes from: August *to:* June

Languages of instruction:

Portuguese

Stages of studies:

University level studies:

University level first stage:
The first stage of higher education leads to the Bacharelato after two to three years' study in most subjects.

University level second stage:
The second stage leads to the Licenciatura after two years' study following upon the Bacharelato. Licentiate degrees are offered in Agriculture, Veterinary Science, Engineering, Architecture, and

Medical Sciences. In Veterinary Medicine the degree is conferred after five years' study following upon the Bacharelato and in Medicine after seven years. Only students having obtained the grades "good" or "very good" in the Bacherelato may proceed to this level.

Teacher education:

Training of pre-primary and primary/basic school teachers

At present, the initial training of primary school teachers is done in primary school teacher training colleges where admission is seven years of schooling for the CFPP (EP1 teachers) and ten years of schooling for the IMP (EP2 teachers). The government advocates that primary school teachers will be trained at primary teacher training institutes for two years after having completed grade 10. In coordination with the Pedagogical University, courses leading to a Bachelor's Degree or Licenciatura in primary education will be implemented.

Training of secondary school teachers

Teachers of grade 7 to 9 are trained at the Faculty of Education of "Eduardo Mondlane" University. Academic requirements for entry are grade 9 plus two years of training in two disciplines. Teachers of grades 10-11 are trained at the Faculty of Education of "Eduardo Mondlane" University. Academic requirements for entry are grade 11 plus two years of training in two disciplines. There are also higher level courses for teachers in general education given at the Pedagogical University. Physical education teachers are trained at the Physical Education Institute. Entrance requirements are grade 9 plus two years of training after which they can teach physical education in EP2 and ESG schools. The training of teachers in technical subjects takes place in the middle-level industrial, commercial and agricultural pedagogical institutes. Courses last for two years and include psycho-pedagogical training and teaching practice. Students must have completed a middle-level or higher technical-professional course in the field in which they will teach.

Training of higher education teachers

Higher education teachers are recruited among holders of the Licenciatura.

NATIONAL BODIES

Responsible authorities:

Ministry of Education (Ministério da Educação)
    Minister: Alcido Eduardo Nguenha
    Permanent Secretary: Zefanias Senete Mabie Muhate
    International Relations: Cremildo Ezequias Ricardo Binana
    Caixa Postal 34
    Av. 24 de Julho no. 167
    Maputo
    Tel: +258(1) 490-249
    Fax: +258(1) 490-979
    Telex: 6.148 MEC MO

EMail: vpt@mined.gov.mz
WWW: http://www.mined.gov.mz

Ministry of Higher Education, Science and Technology
Minister: Lidia Brito
1586 Av. Julius Nyrere
Maputo
Tel: +258(1) 499-491

ADMISSIONS TO HIGHER EDUCATION

Admission to university-level studies

Name of secondary school credential required: Certificado de Habilitações Literárias

Entrance exams required: Access to higher education is based on the Secondary-School Leaving Certificate and an entrance examination. Completion of middle level technical courses may also qualify a student for undergraduate entry.

GRADING SYSTEM

Usual grading system in secondary school

Full Description: 0-20
Highest on scale: 20
Pass/fail level: 10
Lowest on scale: 0

Main grading system used by higher education institutions

Full Description: Bacharelato: pass, good, very good; Licenciatura: marked on a scale of 1-20, 13 is considered satisfactory.

NOTES ON HIGHER EDUCATION SYSTEM

The academic year is divided into two semesters and varies: February-June and July-December for some institutions; and August-December and January-June for others.

Data for academic year: 2000-2001
Source: International Association of Universities (IAU), updated from IBE website, 2000

INSTITUTIONS OF HIGHER EDUCATION

UNIVERSITIES AND UNIVERSITY LEVEL INSTITUTIONS

PUBLIC INSTITUTIONS

*• EDUARDO MONDLANE UNIVERSITY
Universidade Eduardo Mondlane (UEM)
Caixa postal 257, Praça 25 de Junho, Maputo
Tel: +258(1) 425-976   +258(1) 424-429
Fax: +258(1) 426-426   +258(1) 428-411
Telex: 6718 uem mo
EMail: aalberto@rei.uem.mz
Website: http://www.uem.mz

Rector: Brazao Mazula (1995-) Tel: +258(1) 427-851
EMail: bmazula@rei.uem.mz

Vice-Rector: Venâncio Massingue

International Relations: Gracinda Andre Mataveia
Tel: +258(1) 303-214 Fax: +258(1) 304-405
EMail: gmataveia@nei.uem.mz

Faculties
Agronomy and Forest Engineering (Agronomy; Forestry) *Dean*: Rui Brito
Architecture and Physical Planning (Architecture and Planning) *Dean*: José Forjáz
Arts (Arts and Humanities; Geography; History; Linguistics) *Dean*: Armindo Ngunga
Economics *Dean*: Fernando Licucha
Education (Adult Education; Curriculum; Education; Educational Psychology) *Dean*: Mouzinho Mário
Engineering (Chemical Engineering; Civil Engineering; Electrical Engineering; Engineering; Hydraulic Engineering; Mechanical Engineering) *Dean*: Gabriel Amós
Law *Dean*: Taibo Mocobora
Medicine *Dean*: João Schwalbach
Science (Biology; Chemistry; Computer Science; Geology; Natural Sciences; Physics) *Dean*: Francisco Viera
Veterinary Science *Dean*: Luis Bernardo Gil das Neves

Units
Social Sciences *Director*: Obede Suarte Baloi

Centres
African Studies *Director*: Teresa Cruz e Silva
Electronics and Instrumentation (Electronic Engineering; Instrument Making) *Director*: Venâcio Matusse
Engineering Studies *(UP)* (Engineering) *Director*: Jorge Oliveira Nhambiu
Habitat Studies and Development *(CEDH)* (Town Planning) *Director*: Júlio Carrilho

Industrial Studies, Safety and Environment (Environmental Engineering; Industrial Engineering; Safety Engineering) *Director*: Joaquim Langa
Population Studies *(CEP)* (Demography and Population) *Director*: Manuel de Araújo

History: Founded 1962 as Estudios Gerais Universitários, became Universidade de Lourenço Marques 1968, acquired present title 1976. A State institution responsible to the Ministry of Education.

Governing Bodies: Conselho Universitário

Academic Year: August to June (August-December; February-June)

Admission Requirements: Secondary school certificate or equivalent, and entrance examination

Fees: (Metical): Home students: 21,000,000 per annum plus 10,000,000 enrolment fee. International students: 70,000,000 per annum plus 100,000,000 enrolment fee

Main Language(s) of Instruction: Portuguese

International Co-operation: University of Lisbon; University of Porto; University of Poitiers; Utrecht University; Delft University; Autonomous University of Barcelona

Degrees and Diplomas: *Bacharelato*: Law, 2 yrs; Agriculture; Biology; Chemistry; Economics; Engineering; Geography; Geology; History; Letters; Mathematics; Physics, 3 yrs; *Licenciatura*: 2 yrs following Bacharelato; Veterinary Medicine, 5 yrs; Medicine, 7 yrs

Student Services: Sports Facilities, Health Services, Canteen

Student Residential Facilities: For 926 students

Special Facilities: Natural History Museum. Castle

Libraries: c. 85,000 vols; faculty libraries

Publications: Estudos Moçambicanos (biannually); Boletim informativo (annually)

Press or Publishing House: UEM Press

Academic Staff *1999-2000:* Total: **808**

Student Numbers *1999-2000*	MEN	WOMEN	TOTAL
All (Foreign Included)	5,124	1,676	**6,800**
FOREIGN ONLY	–	–	53

HIGHER INSTITUTE FOR INTERNATIONAL RELATIONS
Instituto Superior de Relaçoes Internacionais (ISRI)
Rua Damião de Góis 100, Sommerchild, Maputo
Tel: +258(1) 493-133
Fax: +258(1) 493-213
EMail: ccei@isri.uem.mz
Website: http://www.isri.imoz.com

Rector: Taimo Wilson Jamisse Tel: +258(1) 491-233

Administrator: Jerónimo Inguane Tel: +258(1) 491-800
Fax: +258(1) 491-506
International Relations: Valter Fainda Tel: +258(1) 491-109
Fax: +258(1) 491-179

Departments
Economics
International Relations
Languages (Modern Languages)
Law
Pedagogy
Social Sciences
Teacher Training

Centres
Strategic and International Studies (Cultural Studies; Development Studies; Economics; International Studies; Peace and Disarmament; Political Science; Social Policy)

History: Founded 1986 to train diplomats and those concerned with international relations, acquired present status 1997.

Academic Year: August to June (August-December; January-June)

Admission Requirements: Secondary school certificate and entrance examination

Main Language(s) of Instruction: Portuguese

International Co-operation: Göteborg University; University of Brasilía

Degrees and Diplomas: *Licenciatura*: 5 yrs

Student Services: Academic Counselling, Handicapped Facilities, Canteen

Libraries: c. 5000 vols

Academic Staff *1999*: Full-Time: c. 20 Part-Time: c. 10 Total: c. 30

Staff with doctorate: Total: c. 2

Student Numbers *1999:* Total: c. 160

• HIGHER INSTITUTE FOR SCIENCE AND TECHNOLOGY
Instituto Superior de Ciências e Tecnologia de Moçambique (ISCTEM)
Rua 1394, Zona da Facim 322, Maputo
Tel: +258(1) 312-014   +258(1) 497-658
Fax: +258(1) 312-993   +258(1) 497-648
EMail: isctem@isctem.com
Website: http://www.isctem.com
Reitor: Paulo Ivo Garrido Tel: +258(1) 312-015

Higher Schools
Computer Science (Mathematics and Computer Science)
Economics and Management (Economics; Management)
Health Sciences
Law

History: Founded 1996.
Governing Bodies: Conselho Directivo
Main Language(s) of Instruction: Portuguese

• PEDAGOGICAL UNIVERSITY
Universidade Pedagógica
Com. Augusto Cardoso 135, Maputo
Tel: +258(1) 420-860
Fax: +258(1) 422-113

Reitor: Carlos Machili (1989-)
Administrator: Rosita Alberto
International Relations: Ana Paula Manso

Faculties
Languages (English; French; Modern Languages; Portuguese)
Natural Sciences and Mathematics (Biology; Chemistry; Mathematics; Natural Sciences; Physics)
Pedagogical Sciences (Educational Sciences; Pedagogy; Psychology; Special Education)
Physical Education and Sports (Physical Education; Sports)
Social Sciences (Anthropology; Geography; History; Philosophy; Social Sciences)

Departments
Chemistry *(Beira)*
Geography *(Beira)*
Mathematics *(Beira)*
Physics *(Beira)*

History: Founded 1986.

Academic Year: August to June (August-December; January-June)

Admission Requirements: Secondary school certificate or equivalent, and entrance examination

International Co-operation: University of Education of Heidelberg; Monash University; University of Montpellier; University of Porto; University of Bergen

Degrees and Diplomas: *Bacharelato*: 3 yrs; *Licenciatura*: 5 yrs

Student Services: Sports Facilities, Health Services, Canteen

Academic Staff *1999:* Total: c. 215

Staff with Doctorate: Total: c. 12

Student Numbers *1999*: All (Foreign Included): c. 1,305 Foreign Only: c. 5

PRIVATE INSTITUTIONS

• HIGHER POLYTECHNIC AND UNIVERSITY INSTITUTE
Instituto Superior Politécnico e Universitário (ISPU)
Caixa postal 17, Avenida Albert Liphuli 438, Maputo
Tel: +258(1) 305-953
Fax: +258(1) 305-298
EMail: ispu@ispu.ac.mz
Website: http://www.ispu.ac.mz

Rector: Lourenço Joaquim Costa do Rosário
Tel: +258(1) 305-993 Fax: +258(1) 305-992
EMail: reitor@ispu.ac.mz

International Relations: Rosânia da Silva
EMail: rosania@ispu.ac.mz

Schools
Business and Management (Business and Commerce; Management)
Distance Education
Languages and Communication (Communication Studies; Modern Languages)
Science and Technology (Mathematics and Computer Science; Natural Sciences; Technology)

Departments
Business and Management (Business and Commerce; Management)
Communication (Communication Studies)
Informatics Management (Business Computing)
Legal Sciences (Law)
Psychology

History: Founded 1996.
Main Language(s) of Instruction: Portuguese

Accrediting Agencies: Universidade Lusófona

MOZAMBIQUE CATHOLIC UNIVERSITY
Universidade Católica de Moçambique (UCM)
Res. Maristas 353, Rua Gov. Sousa Pinto-Macúti, Beira
Tel: +258(3) 311-569
Fax: +258(3) 313-077
EMail: ucm.beira@teledata.mz
Website: http://www.ucm.mz

Rector: Filipe José Couto Tel: +258(3) 313-077
Fax: +258(3) 311-520 EMail: fjcouto@teledata.mz

Secretary-General: Francisco Ponci

Faculties
Economics
Educational Sciences *(Nampula)*
Health Sciences
Law *(Nampula)*
Management

History: Founded 1986.
Main Language(s) of Instruction: Portuguese

Namibia

INSTITUTION TYPES AND CREDENTIALS

Types of higher education institutions:

University
Polytechnic
College of Education
Vocational Training Centre

School leaving and higher education credentials:

International General Certificate of Secondary Education
Certificate
National Diploma
Baccalaureus Juris
Bachelor's Degree
Diploma
Master's Degree
Doctorate

STRUCTURE OF EDUCATION SYSTEM

Pre-higher education:

Structure of school system:

> *Primary*
> Type of school providing this education: Primary School
> Length of programme in years: 7
> Age level from: 5 to: 12

> *Junior Secondary*
> Type of school providing this education: Junior Secondary School
> Length of programme in years: 3
> Age level from: 12 to: 15
> Certificate/diploma awarded: Namibian Junior Secondary Certificate

> *Senior Secondary*
> Type of school providing this education: Senior Secondary School
> Length of programme in years: 2

Age level from: 15 to: 17

Certificate/diploma awarded: International General Certificate of Secondary Education (IGCSE)

School education:

Primary education lasts for seven years divided into lower primary (four years) and upper primary (three years). Junior secondary education lasts for three years and leads to the Namibian Junior Secondary Certificate. Admission to senior secondary education is based on the six best subjects in the Junior Secondary Certificate. Senior secondary education lasts for two years and leads to the International General Certificate of Secondary Education (IGCSE) which gives access to higher education. Vocational training centres offer technical subjects at the junior secondary level: options include Bricklaying and Plastering, Electricity, Motor Mechanics, Metalwork and Welding and Woodwork etc....

Higher education:

Higher education is mainly provided by the University of Namibia, the Polytechnic of Namibia, Colleges of Education and Colleges of Agriculture.

Academic year:

Classes from: February *to:* November

Languages of instruction:

English

Stages of studies:

Non-university level post-secondary studies (technical/vocational type):

Vocational Institutes offer Diploma courses that last for three to four years. Studies at the Polytechnic of Namibia lead to Certificates and Diplomas in Accounting, Information Systems, Law, Management and Natural Resources Management.

University level studies:

University level first stage: Diploma, Certificate, Bachelor's Degree:
Diplomas are conferred after three years' study in Humanities, Science, Education, Commerce, Economics, Administration, Nursing and Law. In Social Work, studies last for four years. Honours Degrees are conferred after one year's full-time or two years' part-time study in such fields as Nursing, Diagnostic Radiography and Education. Certificates are awarded after studies lasting between two and three years. The Bachelor's Degree is conferred after one year's full-time or two year's part-time study.

University level second stage: Master's Degree:
The Master's Degree is conferred after one year's full-time and two years' part-time study following upon the Bachelor's Degree by research in an approved topic or thesis and an oral or written examination or a mini thesis and a comprehensive written examination.

University level third stage: Doctorate:
A PhD is conferred after a minimum of two years' full-time or four years' part-time study in Administration, Political Studies, Adult Education, Humanities and Nursing. Students must present a dissertation and sit for an examination based on the dissertation.

Teacher education:

Training of pre-primary and primary/basic school teachers
Primary school teachers are trained at one of the four Colleges of Education at Windhoek, Ongwediva, Rundu and Caprivi. They are awarded the Basic Education Teacher Diploma (BETD) after three years of study. The minimum requirement for the BETD is a grade 12 with IGCSE passes or the equivalent.

Training of secondary school teachers
Junior secondary school teachers receive the same training as primary school teachers and take the Basic Education Teacher Diploma. The BETD is a unified general preparation for all basic education teachers (primary and junior secondary), combining a common core foundation for all, with opportunities for specialization in relation to phases of schooling and subject areas. Senior secondary school teachers are trained at the Faculty of Education of the University of Namibia.

Non-traditional studies:

Distance higher education
The College of Distance Education offers courses for those in full-time employment. There are also outreach centres and satellite campuses.

NATIONAL BODIES

Responsible authorities:

Ministry of Higher Education, Training and Employment Creation
    Minister: Nahas Angula
    Permanent Secretary: Vitalis Ankama
    Private Bag 13391
    Windhoek
    9000
    Tel: +264(61) 270-6111
    Fax: +264(61) 253-672
    WWW: http://www.op.gov.na/Decade_peace/h_edu.htm

ADMISSIONS TO HIGHER EDUCATION

Admission to non university higher education studies

Name of secondary school credential required: International General Certificate of Secondary Education
Minimum score/requirement: 5 subjects passed in not more than the 3rd examination sitting and with a minimum of 25 points in the university scale
For entry to: University

Admission to university-level studies

Name of secondary school credential required: International General Certificate of Secondary Education

Alternatives to credentials: Higher International General Certificate of Secondary Education

Entrance exams required: Entrance Examination or interview

Other admission requirements: English IGCSE compulsory

Foreign students admission

Admission requirements: Foreign students must hold qualifications required of Namibian students. Applications should be made to the university registrar before 30 September in Health Sciences and 31 October for all other courses.

Language requirements: Students whose language of education is not English may be required to pass an approved test in English.

Application procedures:

Apply to individual institution for entry to: University

Application closing dates:

   For university level studies: 31 October

References to further information on foreign student admissions and recognition of studies

Title: Study Abroad 2000-2001
Publisher: UNESCO/IBE
Year of publication: 1999

STUDENT LIFE

Student expenses and financial aid

Student costs:

   Home students tuition fees: Minimum: 3,700 (Namibian Dollar)
   Maximum: 5,390 (Namibian Dollar)

GRADING SYSTEM

Usual grading system in secondary school

Full Description: A, B, C, D, E, F and G.
Highest on scale: A
Pass/fail level: G

Main grading system used by higher education institutions

Full Description: A-E or 4.00-0.0
Highest on scale: A Distinction
Pass/fail level: D Satisfactory
Lowest on scale: E Fail

NOTES ON HIGHER EDUCATION SYSTEM

Data for academic year: 2000-2001

Source: International Association of Universities (IAU), updated from Ministry of Higher Education and IBE websites, 2000

INSTITUTIONS OF HIGHER EDUCATION

UNIVERSITIES

PUBLIC INSTITUTIONS

*• UNIVERSITY OF NAMIBIA

Private Bag 13301, 340 Mandume Ndemufayo Avenue,
Pioneerspark, Windhoek
Tel: +264(61) 206-3111
Fax: +264(61) 206-3866
Telex: (50) 908 7271
EMail: postmaster@grumpy.cs.unam.na
Website: http://www.unam.na

Vice-Chancellor: Peter H. Katjavivi (1992-)
Tel: +264(61) 206-3937 EMail: pkatjavivi@unam.na

Registrar: Z.J.N. Kazapua Tel: +264(61) 206-3082
EMail: zkazapua@unam.na

International Relations: Itah Kandjii-Murangi, Director
Tel: +264(61) 206-3068 Fax: +264(61) 206-3820
EMail: ikandjii@unam.na

Faculties
Agriculture and Natural Resources (Agriculture; Natural Resources) *Dean*: O.D. Mwandemele, *students:* 142
Economics and Management Sciences (Economics; Management; Public Administration) *Dean*: A. du Pisani, *students:* 775
Education *Dean*: R. Auala, *students:* 1,199
Humanities and Social Sciences (Arts and Humanities; Christian Religious Studies; Social Sciences) *Dean*: F. Becker, *students:* 437
Law (Human Rights; Justice Administration; Law) *Dean*: M.O. Hinz, *students:* 108
Medical and Health Sciences (Health Sciences; Medicine) *Dean*: A. van Dyk, *students:* 697
Science (Natural Sciences) *Dean*: G.E. Kiangi, *students:* 379

Centres
External Studies *Director*: J.A. Dodds, *students:* 466
Language (Modern Languages) *Director*: R.K. Ndjoze-Ojo
Multidisciplinary Research *Director*: L. Hangula

History: Founded 1992; to provide a University responsive to the needs, culture and values of Namibia through highest quality education and research for students who may benefit from them, regardless of race, colour, gender, ethnic origin, religion, creed, social and economic status or physical condition.

Governing Bodies: University Council; Senate

Academic Year: January to November

Admission Requirements: International general certificate of secondary education, with 5 subjects passed normally in not more than 3 examination sittings, and with a minimum of 25 points on the UNAM evaluation scale. English IGCSE (English as First, or Second, Language) compulsory. Entrance examination and/or interview

Fees: (Namibian Dollars): Registration, 140; First year, 3700-5390 per annum

Main Language(s) of Instruction: English

Accrediting Agencies: Ministry of Education

Degrees and Diplomas: *National Diploma*: Radiography (Diagnostic), 3 yrs; *Baccalaureus Juris*: Law, 3 yrs; *Bachelor's Degree*: Laws (LLB), 2 yrs; Accountancy; Administration; Adult Education; Business Administration; Economics; Education; Science (BSc); Science (Population and Development), 4-6 yrs; Science (Engineering), 5 yrs; Agriculture and Natural Resources; Arts (BA); Arts (Library Science and Archiving); Arts (Media Studies); Arts (Social Work); Arts (Theology and Religion); Arts (Tourism), 6 yrs; *Diploma*: Comprehensive Nursing and Midwifery Science, 4 yrs; Adult Education, 4-6 yrs; *Master's Degree*: 1 yr following Bachelor; *Doctorate*: 2-3 yrs following Master. Also undergraduate and postgraduate Certificates and Diplomas.

Student Residential Facilities: Yes (4 hostels)

Libraries: Central Library, 86,137 vols; 40,000 UNIN books and documents

Academic Staff *1999-2000*	MEN	WOMEN	TOTAL
FULL-TIME	189	128	**317**

Student Numbers *1999-2000*	MEN	WOMEN	TOTAL
All (Foreign Included)	1,711	2,491	**4,202**

OTHER INSTITUTIONS

PUBLIC INSTITUTIONS

CAPRIVI COLLEGE OF EDUCATION
Private Bag 1069, Katima Mulilo
Tel: +264(66) 253-422
Fax: +264(66) 253-934

Rector: A. Mushe (1992-) Tel: +264(66) 252-053

Education

Governing Bodies: College Council

Academic Year: January to December

Admission Requirements: Certificate, grade 12 or equivalent

Fees: (Namibian Dollars): 1st and 2nd year students, 3250; 3rd year students, 4550

Main Language(s) of Instruction: English

Degrees and Diplomas: *Bachelor's Degree*: Teacher Education, 3 yrs

Student Services: Academic Counselling, Sports Facilities, Language Programmes, Health Services, Canteen

Student Residential Facilities: For 280 students

Libraries: Central Library

ONGWEDIVA COLLEGE OF EDUCATION
Private Bag X5507, Oshakati
Tel: +264(65) 230-001
Fax: +264(65) 230-006

Rector: M. Hatutale

Education

POLYTECHNIC OF NAMIBIA
13 Storch Street, Private Bag 13388, Windhoek
Tel: +264(61) 207-9111
Fax: +264(61) 207-2100
Telex: (50) 908-727
EMail: polytech@polytechnic.edu.na
Website: http://www.polytechnic.edu.na

Rector: Tjiama Tjivikua (1995-2003) Tel: +264(61) 207-2000 Fax: +264(61) 207-2053 EMail: tjivikua@polytechnic.edu.na

Registrar: Corneels Jafta Tel: +264(61) 207-2008 Fax: +264(61) 207-2113 EMail: cjafta@polytechnic.edu.na

Schools

Business and Management (Accountancy; Business Administration; Human Resources; Management; Marketing) *Director*: Kofi Boamah, *students: 2,653*

Communication, Legal and Secretarial Studies (Communication Studies; Law; Police Studies; Secretarial Studies) *Director*: Tara Elyssa, *students: 1,712*

Engineering and Information Technology (Business Computing; Civil Engineering; Electrical Engineering; Electronic Engineering; Engineering; Information Technology) *students: 5,304*

Natural Resources and Tourism (Ecology; Hotel and Restaurant; Natural Resources; Rural Studies; Tourism) *Director*: Willen Jankowitz, *students: 454*

History: Founded 1985 as Academy of Tertiary Education, the first Black college of higher learning in Namibia. Reorganized 1994, incorporating the Technikon Namibia and College for Out-of-School Training. Acquired present status 1994.

Governing Bodies: Council

Academic Year: February to November (February-June; July-November)

Admission Requirements: Senior certificate

Fees: (Namibian Dollars): Registration and Board, 5670 per semester; tuition, 220-11700 (depending on courses)

Main Language(s) of Instruction: English

Accrediting Agencies: Certification Council for Technical Education

Degrees and Diplomas: *Bachelor's Degree*: Nature Conservation (BTech), 4 yrs

Student Services: Academic Counselling, Social Counselling, Employment Services, Cultural Centre, Sports Facilities, Health Services, Canteen

Student Residential Facilities: For 470 students

Libraries: Central Library

Publications: Poly Quil (quarterly)

Academic Staff *2000*	MEN	WOMEN	TOTAL
FULL-TIME	95	51	146
PART-TIME	55	26	81
TOTAL	**150**	**77**	**227**
STAFF WITH DOCTORATE			
FULL-TIME	7	2	9
PART-TIME	–	–	4
TOTAL	**–**	**–**	**13**

Student Numbers *2000*	MEN	WOMEN	TOTAL
All (Foreign Included)	1,667	1,924	**3,591**
FOREIGN ONLY	34	19	53

Part-time Students, 1,724 **Evening Students,** 958 **Distance Students,** 909

RUNDU COLLEGE OF EDUCATION
PO Box 88, Rundu
Tel: +264(66) 255-699
Fax: +264(66) 255-564

Education

WINDHOEK COLLEGE OF EDUCATION
Private Bag 13317, Andrew Kloppers Road, Khomasdal, Windhoek
Tel: +264(61) 270-3111
Fax: +264(61) 212-169

Rector: M. Mbudje Tel: +264(61) 270-3201

Administrative Officer: J. Nitschke Tel: +264(61) 270-3253

Education

Niger

INSTITUTION TYPES AND CREDENTIALS

Types of higher education institutions:

Université (University)
Centre régional (Regional Centre)
Ecole (School)

School leaving and higher education credentials:

Baccalauréat
Diplôme de Technicien supérieur
Diplôme d'Aptitude pédagogique au Professorat des Colleges d'Enseignement Général
Diplôme d'Etudes universitaires générales (DEUG)
Diplôme universitaire d'Etudes économiques générales (DUEEG)
Diplôme universitaire d'Etudes juridiques générales (DUEJG)
Diplôme universitaire d'Etudes littéraires (DUEL)
Diplôme universitaire d'Etudes scientifiques (DUES)
Diplôme d'Ingénieur des Techniques agricoles
Licence
Diplôme d'Agronomie approfondie/d'Ingénieur Agronome
Maîtrise
Docteur en Médecine
Diplôme d'Etudes approfondies (DEA)
Diplôme d'Etudes supérieures spécialisées (DESS)
Doctorat de 3e Cycle
Doctorat d'Etat

STRUCTURE OF EDUCATION SYSTEM

Pre-higher education:

Duration of compulsory education:

   Age of entry: 6
   Age of exit: 12

Structure of school system:

   Primary
   Type of school providing this education: Ecole primaire

Length of programme in years: 6
Age level from: 6 to: 12
Certificate/diploma awarded: Certificat de fin d'Etudes du premier Degré (CFEPD)

First Cycle Secondary
Type of school providing this education: Collège d'Enseignement général
Length of programme in years: 4
Age level from: 12 to: 16
Certificate/diploma awarded: Brevet d'Etudes du premier Cycle (BEPC)

Second Cycle Secondary
Type of school providing this education: Lycée
Length of programme in years: 3
Age level from: 16 to: 19
Certificate/diploma awarded: Baccalauréat

Technical
Type of school providing this education: Lycée technique
Length of programme in years: 3
Age level from: 16 to: 19
Certificate/diploma awarded: Baccalauréat/Bachelier technicien

School education:

Primary education lasts for six years and leads to the Certificat de fin d'Etudes du premier Degré (CFEPD). Secondary school education comprises three types of training: general secondary education, divided into two cycles; technical and vocational education and Ecoles normales which train primary school teachers. Studies culminate with the Baccalauréat. In technical fields, pupils follow a technical upper secondary course and sit for the Baccalauréat/Bachelier technicien.

Higher education:

Postsecondary-level education, for the most part, takes place at the Université Abdou Moumouni, Niamey, and the Islamic University. The Université Abdou Moumouni is a state institution under the jurisdiction of the Ministère de l'Enseignement supérieur, de la Recherche et de la Technologie. Its Council defines the guidelines for teaching, curricula and study systems and the organization of examinations and votes the budget. There are also specialized institutions of higher education such as the Ecole normale supérieure or the Ecole nationale d'Administration which come under the responsibility of the corresponding ministries, as well as several Grandes Ecoles régionales, such as the Ecole des Mines, des Industries et de la Géologie (EMIG) which are sub-regional or continental institutions.

Main laws/decrees governing higher education:
Decree: Loi d'Orientation du Système éducatif   Year: 1998
Concerns: Organization of the educational system

Decree: N° 95-20/PRN   Year: 1995
Concerns: Reorganization of the Ministry of Education and creation of the Ministry of Higher Education and Research

Academic year:

Classes from: October *to:* June
Long vacation from: 1 July *to:* 30 September

Languages of instruction:

French

Stages of studies:

Non-university level post-secondary studies (technical/vocational type):

Technical education remains separate from the universities and is usually provided at the postsecondary level by institutes or centres falling under the responsibility of the relevant Ministry. Le Centre régional d'Application en Agrométéorologie (AGRHYMET) offers a Diplôme de Technicien supérieur after two years' study, and the Ecole nationale de la Santé publique and the Ecole des Mines et de la Géologie after three years' study after the Baccalauréat and an entrance examination.

University level studies:

University level first stage: *Premier Cycle*:
The first cycle is a two-year period of general university studies. It leads to the Diplôme universitaire d'Etudes littéraires (DUEL) in Arts and Humanities; to the Diplôme universitaire d'Etudes scientifiques (DUES) in Science; to the Diplôme universitaire d'Etudes économiques générales (DUEEG) in Economics and to the Diplôme universitaire d'Etudes générales (DEUG).

University level second stage: *Deuxième Cycle*:
The second cycle lasts for a further two years, the first leading to the Licence, and the second to the Maîtrise. In Engineering, the Diplôme d'Ingénieur des Techniques agricoles is conferred after two years' post-first cycle studies. Longer studies in Agriculture lead to the Diplôme d'Ingénieur agronome/Diplôme d'Agronomie approfondie. The title of Docteur en Médecine is conferred after six to seven years' study.

University level third stage: *Troisième Cycle*:
The third cycle is open to holders of the Maîtrise. The Diplôme d'Etudes supérieures spécialisées (DESS) is conferred after one year's specialized study following upon the Maîtrise in a particular field, combined with a special training session. The Diplôme d'Etudes approfondies (DEA) is conferred after one and sometimes two years beyond the Maîtrise. The Doctorat de 3ème Cycle is conferred after a minimum of two and a maximum of three years' study, with the first year spent working on the DEA. The Doctorat d'Etat is the most advanced third cycle degree. It is mainly awarded in sciences. The course normally lasts for five years. Candidates must carry out original research. They must hold the DEA or the DESS and defend their thesis in front of a jury.

Teacher education:

Training of pre-primary and primary/basic school teachers

Primary school teachers are trained at Ecoles normales. They must hold the BEPC and sit for an entrance examination. After three years' study they obtain the Diplôme de Fin d'Etudes normales (DFEN). Instituteurs adjoints are trained in two years after which they obtain the Certificat de Fin d'Etudes normales (CFEN).

Training of secondary school teachers

Teachers for first cycle secondary schools are trained at the Ecole normale supérieure. A one-year programme after the DEUG and an entrance examination lead to a professional diploma, the Diplôme d'Aptitude professionnelle au Professorat des Collèges d'Enseignement général (DAP/CEG). Teachers of Lycées are trained in one year after the Maîtrise (and the passing of an entrance exam) and obtain the Certificat d'Aptitude professionnelle à l'Enseignement secondaire (CAPES). The Ecole normale supérieure also trains inspectors and advisers for primary and secondary levels.

NATIONAL BODIES

Responsible authorities:

Ministry of Higher Education, Research and Technology (Ministère de l'Enseignement supérieur, de la Recherche et de la Technologie)
    Minister: Amadou Laousal Edmond
    PO Box 628
    10896 Niamey
    Tel: +227 72-26-20

ADMISSIONS TO HIGHER EDUCATION

Admission to non university higher education studies

Name of secondary school credential required: Baccalauréat
For entry to: All institutions

Alternatives to credentials: Baccalauréat de Technicien

Entrance exams required: Competitive entrance examination for access to BTS in most schools.

Admission to university-level studies

Name of secondary school credential required: Baccalauréat
For entry to: University

Entrance exams required: Entrance Examination

Foreign students admission

Admission requirements: Foreign students should hold a Baccalauréat or an equivalent qualification. They also have to sit for a special entrance examination.

Language requirements: Good knowledge of French or English is required.

Recognition of studies and qualifications:

Studies pursued in foreign countries (bodies dealing with recognition of foreign credentials):
Direction des Examens, Concours et Equivalences, Ministère de l'Enseignement supérieur, de la Recherche et de la Technologie
    PO Box 628
    10896 Niamey
    Tel: +227 72-26-20

Multilateral agreements concerning recognition of foreign studies

Name(s) of agreement(s): Convention on the Recognition of Studies, Certificates, Diplomas, Degrees and Other Academic Qualifications in Higher Education in the African States
Year of signature: 1981

STUDENT LIFE

Student expenses and financial aid

Student costs:

    Home students tuition fees: Minimum: 0 (CFA Franc-O)

Bodies providing information on student financial aid:
Université Abdou Moumouni
    B.P. 237
    10896 Niamey
    Tel: +227 73 27 13
    Fax: +227 73 38 62
    Telex: UNINIM(975) 5258 NI

Deals with: Grants
Category of students: Students from all countries holding a Secondary School Leaving Certificate and with a good knowledge of French and English. Applications have to go through their Government or through international organizations.

Publications on student services and financial aid:

    Title: Study Abroad 2000-2001
    Publisher: UNESCO/IBE
    Year of publication: 1999

GRADING SYSTEM

Usual grading system in secondary school

Full Description: 16-20=Très bien; 14-15=Bien; 12-13=Assez Bien; 10-11=Passable; 0-9=Ajourné.
Highest on scale: 20
Pass/fail level: 10
Lowest on scale: 0

Main grading system used by higher education institutions

Full Description: 16-20=Très bien; 14-15=Bien; 12-13=Assez bien; 10-11=Passable.
Highest on scale: 20
Pass/fail level: 10
Lowest on scale: 0

NOTES ON HIGHER EDUCATION SYSTEM

Data for academic year: 2000-2001
Source: Université de Niamey, Service des Equivalences de Diplômes, updated by the International Association of Universities from IBE website, 2001

INSTITUTIONS OF HIGHER EDUCATION

UNIVERSITIES

ISLAMIC UNIVERSITY OF NIGER
Université Islamique du Niger
11507 Niamey, Say
Tel: +227 72-39-03
Fax: +227 73-37-96
Vice-Chancellor: Abdelali Oudrhiri (1994-)

Faculties
Arabic Language and Islamic Studies (Arabic; Islamic Studies)

History: Founded 1987 by the Islamic Conference Organization.

Academic Year: October to June (October-February; March-June)

Admission Requirements: High school leaving certificate or equivalent

Fees: None

Main Language(s) of Instruction: Arabic (French, English optional)

Degrees and Diplomas: *Licence*: Arabic; Shari'a, 4 yrs

Academic Staff *1999:* Total: c. 20

Student Numbers *1999:* Total: c. 350

• UNIVERSITY ABDOU MOUMOUNI
Université Abdou Moumouni
BP 237, 10896 Niamey
Tel: +227 73-27-13 +227 73-27-14
Fax: +227 73-38-62
Telex: UNINIM(975) 5258 NI
EMail: resadep@ilimi.uam.ne
Website: http://www.ird.ne/resadep
Recteur: Bouli Ali Diallo Fax: +227 73-39-43
Secrétaire général: Maïga Djibo
International Relations: Boukari Dodo

Faculties
Agronomy
Economics and Law (Economics; Law)
Health Sciences
Letters and Humanities (Arts and Humanities; English; Geography; History; Philosophy; Psychology; Sociology)
Pedagogy (Pedagogy; Teacher Training)
Science (Agronomy; Biology; Chemistry; Geology; Mathematics; Natural Sciences; Physics)

Schools
Teacher Training *(ENS)*

318

Research Institutes
Humanities (Arts and Humanities; Social Sciences)
Mathematics Education

History: Founded 1971 as Centre d'Enseignement supérieur. Became university 1973. Under the jurisdiction of the Ministry of Higher Education and Research.

Governing Bodies: Conseil, composed of the Rector, Deans and Directors of the faculties and institutes, representatives of the academic staff and student body, and representatives of the government

Academic Year: October to June (October-December; January-March; April-June)

Admission Requirements: Secondary school certificate (baccalauréat) or special entrance examination

Main Language(s) of Instruction: French

International Co-operation: University of Orléans; University of Toulouse; University of Montpellier; University of Paris VI; University of Clermont-Ferrand; University of Aix-Marseilles; University of Dijon; University of Grenoble; University of Bordeaux; University of Toulon; University of Tours; University of Tunis; University of Würzburg

Degrees and Diplomas: *Diplôme d'Etudes universitaires générales (DEUG)*: Law and Economics, 2 yrs; *Diplôme universitaire d'Etudes économiques générales (DUEEG)*: Economics, 2 yrs; *Diplôme universitaire d'Etudes juridiques générales (DUEJG)*: Law, 2 yrs; *Diplôme universitaire d'Etudes littéraires (DUEL)*: English; Geography; History; Letters; Linguistics; Philosophy; Psychology; Sociology, 2 yrs; *Diplôme universitaire d'Etudes scientifiques (DUES)*: Agronomy; Biology and Geology; Chemistry and Biology; Mathematics and Physics; Physics and Chemistry, 2 yrs; *Diplôme d'Ingénieur des Techniques agricoles*: Agricultural Engineering; *Licence*: Economics; Law; Letters, 1 yr following DUEL; Chemistry; Mathematics; Natural sciences; Physics, 1 yr following DUES; *Diplôme d'Agronomie approfondie/d'Ingénieur Agronome*: 5 yrs; *Maîtrise*: Agronomy; Chemistry; Mathematics; Natural Sciences; Physics, 1 yr following Licence; *Docteur en Médecine*: Medicine; *Diplôme d'Etudes approfondies (DEA)*: Science; *Doctorat de 3e Cycle*: Letters; Science; *Doctorat d'Etat*: Science. Also diplomas in school counselling and teaching (lower level)

Student Residential Facilities: Yes

Libraries: c. 62,000 vols

Academic Staff *1999:* Total: c. 260

Student Numbers *1999:* Total: c. 3,630

OTHER INSTITUTIONS

AGRHYMET REGIONAL CENTRE
Centre Regional Agrhymet (CRA/ARC)
BP 11011, Niamey
Tel: +227 73-31-16
Fax: +227 73-22-35
EMail: admin@sahel.agrhymet.ne
Website: http://www.agrhymet.ne

Director-General: Alhassane Adama Diallo
EMail: adiallo@sahel.agrhymet.ne

Administrative Officer: Sankung Bangally Sagnia

Units

Hydrology and Crop Protection (Agricultural Equipment; Meteorology; Plant and Crop Protection; Water Science) *Head:* B. Sagnia Sankung, *full-time staff:* 12, *part-time staff:* 20, *students:* 77

History: Founded 1974 as specialized institute of the Permanent Interstate Committee for drought control in the Sahel (CILSS). Offers training and information in the fields of food security and sustainable natural resources management.

Governing Bodies: Technical and Management Committee; Scientific and Pedagogic Committee

Academic Year: October to June

Admission Requirements: Secondary school certificate (baccalaureat, Science option) or equivalent for the higher diploma; and higher diploma or equivalent for the "Ingénieur" diploma

Fees: (CFA Francs): 2,000,000 per annum

Main Language(s) of Instruction: French

International Co-operation: University Abdou Moumouni; Ecole Africaine et Malgache de l' Aviation civile; Haute Ecole de la Communauté française du Luxembourg 'Robert Schuman'

Accrediting Agencies: Conseil Africain et Malgache pour l' Enseignement Supérieur (CAMES)

Degrees and Diplomas: *Diplôme de Technicien supérieur:* Agrometeorology, Hydrology, Instrument Maintenance, Crop Protection, 2 yrs; *Diplôme d'Ingénieur des Techniques agricoles:* Agrometeorology, Hydrology, 3 yrs

Student Services: Academic Counselling, Cultural Centre, Sports Facilities, Language Programmes, Health Services

Student Residential Facilities: 110-Room Residence Halls

Special Facilities: Specialized Laboratories (Entomology, Phytopathology, Phytopharmacy, Electronics, Hydrology, Geographic Information Systems and Remote Sensing)

Libraries: Central Library, 28,000 references completely computerized and connected to Internet

Publications: Agrhymet Info, Information Bulletin on the Agrhymet Regional Centre (quarterly); Bulletin du Programme Majeur Formation, Liaison Bulletin specially designed for former students (2 per annum); Year book, Annuaire des Diplômes (once every 3 years)

Academic Staff *1999-2000*	TOTAL
FULL-TIME	12
PART-TIME	20
TOTAL	**32**
STAFF WITH DOCTORATE	
FULL-TIME	3
PART-TIME	5
TOTAL	**8**

Student Numbers *1999-2000*	MEN	WOMEN	TOTAL
All (Foreign Included)	41	36	**77**

Note: In addition to long term students, our Centre trains every year more than 200 trainees through short term programs

ÉCOLE AFRICAINE ET MALGACHE DE L'AVIATION CIVILE (EAMAC)
BP 746, Niamey
Tel: +227 72-36-61

Air Transport

ÉCOLE DES MINES ET DE LA GÉOLOGIE (EMIG)
BP 732, Niamey
Tel: +227 73-37-97
Fax: +227 73-51-37

Departments

Civil and Environmental Engineering (Civil Engineering; Environmental Engineering)
Electricity (Electrical Engineering)
General Studies
Management Studies (Management)
Mechanics
Mining and Geology (Geology; Mining Engineering)

ÉCOLE NATIONALE D'ADMINISTRATION NIVEAU SUPÉRIEUR (ENA)
BP 542, Niamey
Tel: +227 72-28-53

Administration

ÉCOLE NATIONALE DE LA SANTÉ PUBLIQUE NIVEAU SUPÉRIEUR (ENSP)
BP 290, Niamey
Tel: +227 72-30-01

Public Health

Nigeria

INSTITUTION TYPES AND CREDENTIALS

Types of higher education institutions:

Federal University
State University
University of Technology
University of Agriculture
Polytechnic
College

School leaving and higher education credentials:

Senior School Certificate
West African GCE "O" Level
West African GCE "A" Level
National Diploma
Higher National Diploma
Bachelor's Degree
Bachelor Honours Degree
Doctor of Veterinary Medicine
Postgraduate Diploma
Master's Degree
Master of Philosophy
Doctor of Philosophy

STRUCTURE OF EDUCATION SYSTEM

Pre-higher education:

Duration of compulsory education:

    Age of entry: 6
    Age of exit: 15

Structure of school system:

    Primary
    Type of school providing this education: Primary School
    Length of programme in years: 6
    Age level from: 6 to: 12

Junior Secondary
Type of school providing this education: Junior School
Length of programme in years: 3
Age level from: 12 to: 15
Certificate/diploma awarded: Junior School Certificate (JSSC)

Senior Secondary
Type of school providing this education: Senior Secondary School
Length of programme in years: 3
Age level from: 15 to: 18
Certificate/diploma awarded: Senior School Certificate (SSSC)

Technical
Type of school providing this education: Technical Secondary School
Length of programme in years: 6
Age level from: 12 to: 18
Certificate/diploma awarded: Senior School Certificate (SSSC)

School education:

Primary education lasts for six years. Entrance to secondary education is based on an examination. Secondary education is divided into junior and senior secondary, and technical and vocational education. The Junior School Certificate is awarded after three years of junior school. The Senior School Certificate is awarded after three years of senior secondary education. It replaced the West African GCE "O" level in 1989. Pupils who complete junior secondary school are streamed into senior secondary school, technical college, out of school vocation training centre or an apprenticeship. Technical secondary education is offered in secondary commercial schools which offer six-year courses including academic subjects and specialization. At the end of the course, students may take the examinations for the Senior School Certificate. Vocational education produces low level manpower and is offered in technical colleges or business and engineering skills training centres. Technical colleges are the only alternative to senior secondary schools as a route to further formal education and training after junior secondary education. To enter university, students have to pass the University Matriculation examination (UME).

Higher education:

Higher education is provided by universities, polytechnics ,institutions of technology, colleges of education (which form part of the universities and polytechnical colleges or are affiliated to these) and professional institutions. Universities can be established either by federal or state governments. Each university is administered by a Council and a Senate. Within the universities, the institutes and colleges are more or less autonomous.

Main laws/decrees governing higher education:

Decree: Decree n.9, Education Amendment Decree   Year: 1993

Academic year:

Classes from: October *to:* July

Long vacation from: 15 July *to:* 30 September

Languages of instruction:

English

Stages of studies:

Non-university level post-secondary studies (technical/vocational type):

Higher technical education is offered in technical colleges, polytechnics and colleges of education. They offer two-stage National Diplomas and Higher National Diplomas of two years' duration. The colleges also offer various Certificates in technology which may be obtained after one, two or three years. Students are expected to have at least one year industrial attachment after obtaining the National Diploma to proceed to the Higher National Diploma course. The colleges of education in this sector train technical teachers.

University level studies:

University level first stage: *Bachelor's Degree*:

First degree courses in Arts, Social Sciences and Pure Sciences are usually of four years' duration (three years for students holding good GCE "A" levels), whilst professional degrees tend to last for five years. Degree courses in Medicine and Dentistry last for six years. The Bachelor's Degree may be awarded as an Honours degree: students take either a single subject Honours degree course or combined Honours.

University level second stage: *Master's Degree*:

Master's Degree courses usually last for one year after the Bachelor's Degree but, increasingly, where the qualification depends on research, it becomes a two-year course.

University level third stage: *Doctorate*:

The Doctorate Degree is usually conferred two to three years after the Master's Degree. Some first generation universities require students to complete a Master of Philosophy degree before being admitted to the PhD programme.

Teacher education:

Training of pre-primary and primary/basic school teachers

Four years' post primary study at a grade 2 teacher training college leads to a Grade 2 Certificate/Higher Elementary Teacher's Certificate. Holders of the former Grade 3 Certificate may take an upgrading course to become grade 2 teachers. As from 1998, the Nigerian Certificate in Education conferred by colleges of education is required for teaching in primary schools.

Training of secondary school teachers

Holders of the Nigerian Certificate of Education may teach in junior secondary schools and technical colleges. Senior secondary school teachers are trained at the universities. They must hold the BEd or a Bachelor's plus a Postgraduate Diploma in Education. Most students study for three years at an advanced teachers' college for the Nigerian Certificate of Education, which also gives access to university. As from 1998, no teacher with a qualification below this level will be able to teach in any school.

Non-traditional studies:

Distance higher education
Distance education is offered in Open Studies Centres of certain universities.

Lifelong higher education
Extension services are provided mainly in the area of Agriculture. In Education, vacation courses have become a very popular path for teachers wishing to obtain a Bachelor's or a Master's degree.

NATIONAL BODIES

Responsible authorities:

Federal Ministry of Education
Minister: Babalola Borishade
Federal Secretariat, PMB 146, Shehu Shagari Way-Maitama
Abuja
Tel: +234(9) 52-32-800
Fax: +234(9) 53-37-839

Role of governing body: Ministerial responsibility for Education at Secondary and Tertiary levels in Universities, Polytechnics, Colleges of Education and Federal Government Colleges.

National Universities Commission
Executive Secretary: Idris A. Abdulkadir
Aja Nwachukwu House, Plot 430 Aguiyi-Ironsi St., Maitama District PMB 237 Garki GPO
Abuja
Tel: +234(9) 52-33-176
Fax: +234(9) 52-33-250

Role of governing body: Allocates funds to Federal universities; examines the curricula so that it corresponds to professional requirements; develops university education.

Committee of Vice-Chancellors of Nigerian Federal Universities
Chairman: Placid C. Njoku
Secretary-General: Gabriel M. Umerzurike
PMB 12002
Idowu Taylor Street, Victoria Island
Lagos
12022
Tel: +234(1) 26-12-425
Telex: 23555 comvic ng
Cable: nivicom lagos

Role of governing body: Acts as coordinating body and offers advice to government and universities governing councils on matters of general concern.

ADMISSIONS TO HIGHER EDUCATION

Admission to non university higher education studies

Name of secondary school credential required: Senior School Certificate

Numerus clausus/restrictions: For most fields of study as determined by the National Board for Technical Education and as conditioned by the availability of instructional facilities in different programmes in each institution.

Admission to university-level studies

Name of secondary school credential required: Senior School Certificate
For entry to: Bachelor's degree

Name of secondary school credential required: West African GCE "A" Level
Minimum score/requirement: good grades allow for direct entry to universities
For entry to: Bachelor's degree

Name of secondary school credential required: West African GCE "O" Level
Minimum score/requirement: Credit passes in 5 subjects including English Language, Mathematics and Science.
For entry to: Bachelor's Degree

Alternatives to credentials: National Certificate of Education passes at Credit or Merit levels or Ordinary National Diploma at upper credit level.

Entrance exams required: Universities Matriculation Examination (UME) for all first Degrees. Good GCE 'A' level results give direct access to universities.

Numerus clausus/restrictions: For most fields as determined by the National Universities Commission and conditioned by availability of instructional facilities available in different programmes at the level of institution.

Other admission requirements: None

Foreign students admission

Definition of foreign student: Student who is not a citizen of Nigeria, where citizenship is defined in terms of being born in Nigeria after 1960, or both parents being Nigerian, and not being a citizen of another country.

Admission requirements: Foreign students should have qualifications equivalent to the General Certificate of Education in at least 5 subjects, after 6 years of secondary school. At postgraduate level, foreign students must have an appropriate first degree with upper second class honours. Those with a lower grade have to take admission exams.

Entry regulations: Resident permits required of ECOWAS Nationals. Visas and resident permits required of Nationals of other countries.

Health requirements: Certificate of medical fitness at Medical Centre of Institution

Application procedures:

Apply to individual institution for entry to: Post-Graduate Studies.

Apply to national body for entry to: First Degree Programmes.

Apply to: Joint Admissions and Matriculation Board (JAMB)
PMB 12748
11/13 Ojoro Road, IKOYI
Lagos
Telex: 28708 JAMB NG

Application closing dates:

For non-university level (technical/vocational type) studies: 31 March
For university level studies: 31 March
For advanced/doctoral studies: 31 March

Recognition of studies and qualifications:

Studies pursued in home country (System of recognition/accreditation): Accreditation of Higher Vocational / Technical programmes in Polytechnics and Colleges of Education is performed by the National Board of Technical Education (NBTE). The National Universities Commission does the same for university level programmes.

Studies pursued in foreign countries (bodies dealing with recognition of foreign credentials):
National Standing Committee for the Evaluation of Foreign Qualifications, Federal Ministry of Education
Director, E.S.S.: S.A.B. Atolagbe
Deputy Director (E&A): S.O. Okunola
International Relations: Marie Uko
Educational Support Services Department
Evaluation and Accreditation Division
Federal Secretariat Phase III
Shehu Shagari Way
Abuja
Tel: +234(9) 31-41-215
Fax: +234(9) 31-41-215

Services provided and students dealt with: Deals with the broad principles and sets the criteria for the evaluation of foreign certificates and diplomas; receives and considers representations from aggrieved persons on the day-to-day evaluation carried out by officials of the Federal Ministry of Education; compiles an up-to-date register of foreign qualifications and their Nigerian equivalents.

Other information sources on recognition of foreign studies: Universities, the Nigerian Law School, etc. where each department often decides on the status of foreign credentials submitted by applicants.

Special provisions for recognition:

For the exercise of a profession: Access to the Medicine, Pharmacy, Accountancy, Law and related professions is regulated by professional associations/societies. The associations/societies are supported by statutes and moderate qualifying examinations.

Multilateral agreements concerning recognition of foreign studies

Name(s) of agreement(s): Convention on the Recognition of Studies, Certificates, Diplomas, Degrees and Other Academic Qualifications in Higher Education in the African States
Year of signature: 1981

References to further information on foreign student admissions and recognition of studies

Title: Study Abroad 2000-2001
Publisher: UNESCO/IBE
Year of publication: 1999

Title: Universities calendars

STUDENT LIFE

National student associations and unions

National Association of Nigerian Students
    Federal University of Technology
    PO Box 1526
    Oweri
    Imo State
    Tel: +234(83) 233-974
    EMail: root@futo.edu.ng

Health/social provisions

Social security for home students: No

Social security for foreign students: No

Foreign student social security provisions: None

Special student travel fares:

By road: No
By rail: No
By air: No
Available to foreign students: No

Student expenses and financial aid

Student costs:

    Home students tuition fees: Minimum: 2,000 (Naira)
    Maximum: 8,000 (Naira)
    Foreign students tuition fees: Minimum: 6,000 (Naira)
    Maximum: 35,000 (Naira)

Bodies providing information on student financial aid:

Scholarships Division, Federal Ministry of Education
    Federal Secretariat, PMB 146, Shehu Shagari Way-Maitama

Abuja
Tel: +234(9) 52-32-800
Fax: +234(9) 53-37-839

Deals with: Grants
Category of students: Commonwealth students.

Publications on student services and financial aid:

Title: Nigerian Awards-Commonwealth Scholarships
Publisher: Federal Ministry of Education, Scholarships Division

GRADING SYSTEM

Usual grading system in secondary school

Full Description: For the West African Senior School Certificate: 1-9
Highest on scale: A 1
Pass/fail level: P 8
Lowest on scale: F 9

Main grading system used by higher education institutions

Full Description: For the Ordinary National Diploma(OND):GPA 3.50+ (Distinction; 3.00-3.49(Upper Credit); 2.50-2.99(Lower Credit); 2.00-2.49(Pass)
Highest on scale: 3.50+(Distinction)
Pass/fail level: 2.00-2.49(Pass)
Lowest on scale: 2.00

Other main grading systems

For the Bachelor' degree: 1st class(70-100), 2nd class upper division(60-69), 2nd class lower division(50-59), 3rd class pass(40-49).

NOTES ON HIGHER EDUCATION SYSTEM

Data for academic year: 2000-2001
Source: University of Ibadan, updated by the International Association of Universities (IAU) from IBE website, 2000

INSTITUTIONS OF HIGHER EDUCATION

UNIVERSITIES AND TECHNICAL UNIVERSITIES

• ABIA STATE UNIVERSITY (ABSU)
PMB 2000, Uturu, Abia State
Tel: +234(82) 220-785 +234(82) 440-291 to 93
Vice-Chancellor: Ogwo E. Ogwo (2000-)
EMail: vc@absu.edu.ng
Registrar: Madubuike Okoronkwo

Faculties
Engineering and Environmental Studies (Architecture; Construction Engineering; Engineering; Environmental Studies; Geography; Real Estate; Regional Planning; Urban Studies) *Dean*: Innocent Mbadiwe, *full-time staff: 33, part-time staff: 3, students: 802*
Humanities and Social Sciences (Arts and Humanities; English; French; Government; History; Library Science; Linguistics; Literature; Public Administration; Social Sciences; Sociology) *Dean*: Afam Ebeogu, *full-time staff: 58, part-time staff: 6, students: 3,011*
Legal Studies (Civil Law; Commercial Law; Constitutional Law; International Law; Law; Private Law; Public Law) *Dean*: Ernest Ojukwu, *full-time staff: 17, part-time staff: 2, students: 1,310*
Medicine and Health Sciences (Health Sciences; Medicine; Optometry) *Provost*: Frank Akpuaka, *full-time staff: 60, part-time staff: 6, students: 1,201*
Postgraduate Studies (Architecture; Arts and Humanities; Biological and Life Sciences; Business Administration; Education; Environmental Studies; Law; Social Sciences) *Dean*: Geoffrey Nwaka, *full-time staff: 1, students: 950*

Colleges
Agriculture and Veterinary Medicine (Agricultural Economics; Agriculture; Animal Husbandry; Food Science; Food Technology; Soil Science; Veterinary Science) *Dean*: L.C. Nwaigbo, *full-time staff: 20, part-time staff: 2, students: 371*
Biological and Physical Sciences (Biochemistry; Biological and Life Sciences; Botany; Industrial Chemistry; Mathematics; Microbiology; Physics; Statistics; Zoology) *Dean*: Michael Oleka, *full-time staff: 52, part-time staff: 5, students: 1,211*
Business Administration (Accountancy; Banking; Business Administration; Economics; Finance; Management; Marketing) *Dean*: Igwe Aja-Nwachuku, *full-time staff: 31, part-time staff: 3, students: 2,024*
Education (Accountancy; Biology; Economics; English; Ethnology; French; Geography; Government; History; Mathematics; Religion; Social Studies) *Dean*: Michael Maduabum, *full-time staff: 39, part-time staff: 4, students: 625*

Institutes
Distance Education (Accountancy; Economics; Finance; Government; Marketing; Mass Communication; Public Administration) *Director*: Chinyere Nwahunanya, *full-time staff: 1, students: 8,562*
Pre-Science (Biology; Chemistry; Economics; English; Government; History; Literature; Mathematics; Physics; Religion) *full-time staff: 340, part-time staff: 34, students: 45*

Centres
Igbo Studies (Archaeology; Cultural Studies; Dance; Environmental Studies; Ethnology; Geography; Government; History; Law; Political Science; Religion; Social Studies; Theatre) *Director*: Adiele Afigbo, *full-time staff: 1*

History: Founded 1981. The University operates a collegiate system with related disciplines clustered into Schools and Schools grouped into Colleges. Interdisciplinary in structure and mission, each school is flexible in function.
Governing Bodies: Council; Senate
Academic Year: October to July (October-March; April-July)
Admission Requirements: Universities Matriculation Examination (UME) following secondary school education
Main Language(s) of Instruction: English
Degrees and Diplomas: *Bachelor's Degree*: Arts (BA); Education (BEd); Science (BSc), 4 yrs; *Postgraduate Diploma*: 1 yr; *Master's Degree*: Arts (MA); Business Administration (MBA); Education (MEd); Laws (LLM); Library Studies (MLS); Public Administration (MPA); Science (MSc), a further 1-3 yrs; *Doctor of Philosophy*: Education (PhD), 2-3 yrs
Student Residential Facilities: Yes
Academic Staff *1999:* Total: c. 340
Student Numbers *1999:* Total: c. 7,010

• ABUBAKAR TAFAWA BALEWA UNIVERSITY OF TECHNOLOGY (ATBU)
PMB 0248, Bauchi, Bauchi State
Tel: +234(77) 592-964   +234(77) 543-500
Fax: +234(77) 542-065
Cable: Televarsity Bauchi
EMail: vc@atbu.edu.ng
Vice-Chancellor: Abubakar Sani Sambo (1995-)
Tel: +234(77) 543-500 EMail: sambo@atbu.edu.ng
Registrar: Ibrahim Musa Tel: +234(77) 542-092

Units
Industrial Training Coordination *Head*: J.O. Ajayi

Programmes
Agriculture (Agricultural Economics; Agriculture; Cattle Breeding; Crop Production) *Coordinator*: S. Kushwaha, *full-time staff: 15, students: 226*
Architecture *Coordinator*: I.U. Hussaini, *full-time staff: 6, part-time staff: 2, students: 226*

Biological Sciences (Biological and Life Sciences) *Coordinator:* I.A. Jideani, *full-time staff: 28, students:* 380
Building (Building Technologies) *Coordinator:* S.A. Sumaila, *full-time staff: 5, part-time staff: 4, students:* 216
Chemistry *Coordinator:* I.O. Akpabio, *full-time staff: 15, students:* 150
Civil Engineering *Coordinator:* J.A. Egwurube, *full-time staff: 18, students:* 56
Electrical and Electronic Engineering *Coordinator:* H.A. Guda, *full-time staff: 20, students:* 78
Estate Management (Real Estate) *Coordinator:* I.I. Adaminda, *full-time staff: 5, students:* 116
General Studies, Remedial and Foundation (Continuing Education) *Coordinator:* O.C. Ogidi, *full-time staff: 7, students:* 558
Geology *Coordinator:* D.M. Orazulike, *full-time staff: 10, students:* 134
Industrial Design *Coordinator:* A.D. Umar, *full-time staff: 9, students:* 38
Land Surveying (Surveying and Mapping) *Coordinator:* I.I. Adaminda, *full-time staff: 4, part-time staff: 4, students:* 41
Mathematics *Coordinator:* E.J.A Edemenang, *full-time staff: 17, students:* 219
Mechanical and Production Engineering (Mechanical Engineering; Production Engineering) *Coordinator:* M.H. Muhammad, *full-time staff: 17, students:* 81
Physics *Coordinator:* M.F. Haque, *full-time staff: 16, students:* 111
Quantity Surveying (Mathematics) *Coordinator:* S.A. Sumaila, *part-time staff: 2, students:* 74
Science Education *Coordinator:* V.O. Oloyede, *full-time staff: 12, students:* 268
Urban and Regional Planning (Regional Planning; Town Planning) *Coordinator:* I.I. Adaminda, *full-time staff: 8, students:* 96

Schools

Agriculture and Agricultural Technology (Agricultural Equipment; Agriculture) *Director:* T.A. Adegbola, *full-time staff: 74, students:* 775
Engineering *Director:* A.U. Elinwa, *full-time staff: 55, students:* 215
Environmental Technology (Environmental Engineering) *Director:* S. Suleiman, *full-time staff: 43, part-time staff: 16, students:* 691
Management Technology (Management; Management Systems) *Director:* S.L. Kela
Science and Science Education (Natural Sciences; Science Education) *Director:* E.J.D. Garba, *full-time staff: 111, part-time staff: 16, students:* 1,816

Centres

Computer Science *Director:* M.H. Alhassan, *full-time staff: 23*
Distance Learning *Director:* A.B. Mohammed
Industrial Studies (Industrial Management) *Director:* J.S. Jatau, *full-time staff: 10*
Research *(FEPA) Director:* M.O. Agho

History: Founded 1980 as the Federal University of Technology, Bauchi. Acquired present status 1988.
Governing Bodies: University Council

Academic Year: October to August (October-April; April-August)
Admission Requirements: Senior Secondary Certificate of Education (SSCE) or General Certificate of Education (GCE) ('O') levels with at least 5 credits
Main Language(s) of Instruction: English
International Co-operation: Oklahoma State University; University of N'Djamena
Degrees and Diplomas: *Bachelor's Degree:* Technology (BTech), 5 yrs; *Master's Degree:* Science (MSc), a further 1-2 yrs; Engineering (MEng), a further 2 yrs; *Doctor of Philosophy:* (PhD), 2-3 yrs
Student Services: Academic Counselling, Social Counselling, Employment Services, Nursery Care, Sports Facilities, Health Services
Student Residential Facilities: For c. 1500 students
Libraries: University Library, 45,000 vols
Publications: University Bulletin (monthly); ATBU Annual Report (annually)
Press or Publishing House: ATBU Printing Press
Academic Staff *1999:* Total: **233**

Student Numbers 1999	MEN	WOMEN	TOTAL
All (Foreign Included)	4,853	1,038	**5,891**
FOREIGN ONLY	–	–	47

• AHMADU BELLO UNIVERSITY
PMB 1044, Zaria
Tel: +234(69) 50-581
Fax: +234(69) 50-022
Telex: 75244 con ng
Cable: unibello, zaria
EMail: vc@abu.edu.ng

Vice-Chancellor: Abdullahi Mahadi (1998-)
Tel: +234(69) 50-691
Registrar: Alhaji Mairiga Mani Tel: +234(69) 51-294
EMail: registrar@abu.edu.ng
International Relations: S.S. Mayaki Tel: +234(69) 51-144

Faculties
Administration Dean: Alhaji Abdullahi
Agriculture (Agriculture; Animal Husbandry; Economics; Rural Studies) Dean: E.B. Amans
Arts (Arts and Humanities; English; French; History) Dean: Tanimu N. Abubakar
Education (Education; Health Education; Information Sciences; Library Science; Physical Education) Dean: K. Venkateswarlu
Engineering (Agricultural Engineering; Chemical Engineering; Civil Engineering; Electrical Engineering; Engineering; Surveying and Mapping) Dean: S.S. Adefila
Environmental Design (Architectural and Environmental Design; Architecture; Fine Arts; Industrial Design; Regional Planning; Town Planning) Dean: James B. Kaltho
Law Dean: Kharisu Chukkol
Medicine (Gynaecology and Obstetrics; Medicine; Midwifery; Paediatrics; Psychiatry and Mental Health) Dean: Iliyasu Muhammed

Pharmaceutical Sciences (Pharmacy) *Dean*: E.M. Abdulrahman

Science (Biochemistry; Biological and Life Sciences; Chemistry; Geology; Mathematics; Microbiology; Natural Sciences; Physics; Textile Technology) *Dean*: C.O. Ajayi

Social Sciences *Dean*: J. De-Goshie

Veterinary Medicine (Veterinary Science) *Dean*: A. Ghaji

Schools

Postgraduate *Head*: Julius Olayemi

Institutes

Administration *Director*: B.M. Shani

Agricultural Research (Agriculture) *Director*: D.O.A. Philip

Animal Production Research (Animal Husbandry; Cattle Breeding) *Director*: J.P. Alawa

Education (Distance Education; Education) *Director*: Aliyu Mohammed

Health Studies (Health Sciences) *Director*:

Centres

Agricultural Extension and Research Liaison Services (Agriculture)

Energy Research and Training (Energy Engineering) *Head*: S.B. Elegba, *full-time staff*: 2

Islamic Legal Studies (Islamic Law) *Head*: B. Mohammed, *full-time staff*: 6

Further Information: Also Teaching Hospitals and Veterinary Teaching Hospital

History: Founded 1962, acquired present status and title 1975.

Governing Bodies: Council; Senate

Academic Year: October to July

Admission Requirements: Direct entry for holders of the Higher School Certificate (General Certificate of Education, Advanced ('A') level). Evidence of minimum standard in English

Main Language(s) of Instruction: English

International Co-operation: University of Reading; University of Bristol; University of Manchester; University of Belfast; University of Bradford; University of Pittsburgh; Kansas State University; University of Utrecht

Degrees and Diplomas: *Bachelor's Degree*: Arts (BA); Education (BEd); Law (LLB); Library Science (BLS); Medicine and Surgery (MB BS); Pharmacy (BPharm); Science (BSc); *Doctor of Veterinary Medicine*: Veterinary Science (DVM), 3-5 yrs; *Master's Degree*: 1-2 yrs following Bachelor; *Doctor of Philosophy*: (PhD), 3-5 yrs

Special Facilities: Museums. Art Gallery. Biological Garden

Libraries: Kashim Ibrahim Library, c. 313,000 vols; President Kennedy Library and Departmental libraries, c. 84,000 vols

Publications: University Annual Report (annually); Calendar; University Calendar; Prospectus; Research Report; Student Hand Book; History of Ahmadu Bello University at 25

Press or Publishing House: Ahmadu Bello University Press Ltd

Academic Staff *1999*: Full-Time: c. 730 Part-Time: c. 15 Total: c. 745

Student Numbers *1999*: Total: c. 18,600

330

• AMBROSE ALLI UNIVERSITY
PMB 14, Ekpoma
Tel: +234(55) 984-48 +234(55) 984-46
Telex: 98448
Cable: edo varsity, ekpoma
EMail: root@edosu.edu.ng

Vice-Chancellor: Dennis E. Agbonlahor

Registrar: G.T. Olawole

Faculties

Agriculture (Agricultural Economics; Agriculture; Agronomy; Botany) *Dean*: J.O. Omueti

Arts and Social Sciences (Arts and Humanities; Social Sciences; Sociology) *Dean*: T.A. Imobighe

Education *(Abraka)* (Education; Vocational Education) *Dean*: D.O. Aigbomian

Engineering and Technology (Civil Engineering; Electrical and Electronic Engineering; Engineering; Mechanical Engineering; Technology) *Dean*: S.K. Momoh Engu

Environmental Sciences (Environmental Studies)

Law (Commercial Law; International Law; Law; Public Law) *Dean*: K.A. Apori

Medicine *(Ekpoma)* (Anatomy; Medicine) *Dean*: C.P. Aloamaka

Natural Sciences (Microbiology; Natural Sciences; Pharmacology) *Dean*: I.O. Eguavoen

Further Information: Abraka campus

History: Founded 1981 as Bendel State University. Formerly known as Edo State University.

Governing Bodies: Council; Senate

Academic Year: October to June

Admission Requirements: Universities Matriculation Examination (UME) following secondary school training, or direct entry for holders of the Higher School Certificate (General Certificate of Education, Advanced ('A') level)

Main Language(s) of Instruction: English

Degrees and Diplomas: *Bachelor's Degree*: 3-4 yrs; *Master's Degree*: a further 2 yrs

Libraries: Central Library, 14,000 items; Abraka campus library, 80,000 vols

Publications: Gazette; Calendar; Faculty Journals

Press or Publishing House: University Press

Academic Staff: Total: c. 390

Student Numbers: Total: c. 8,180

BAGAUDA UNIVERSITY OF SCIENCE AND TECHNOLOGY
PMB 3469, Kano State
Tel: +234(64) 646-600

Vice-Chancellor (Acting): Alhaji Hafiz S. Wali

Registrar: Alhaji A. Hassan

• BAYERO UNIVERSITY
PMB 3011, Kano, Kano State
Tel: +234(64) 666-021   +234(64) 666-023
Fax: +234(64) 665-904   +234(64) 661-480
Telex: 77189 unibayro ng
EMail: root@bayero.edu.ng
Vice-Chancellor: Musa Abdullahi (2000-)

Registrar: Faruk M. Yanganau **EMail:** registrar@buk.edu.ng

Faculties
Arts and Islamic Studies (Arabic; English; French; History; Islamic Studies; Mass Communication) *Dean*: Abdulkadir Dangambo
Education (Adult Education; Education; Health Education; Library Science; Physical Education) *Dean*: Mansur Malumfashi
Law (Commercial Law; Islamic Law; Law; Private Law; Public Law) *Dean*: Haruna Alhaji
Medicine (Anaesthesiology; Anatomy; Biochemistry; Community Health; Gynaecology and Obstetrics; Haematology; Medicine; Microbiology; Paediatrics; Parasitology; Pathology; Pharmacology; Physiology; Psychiatry and Mental Health; Surgery) *Dean*: I. Dutse Abdulhameed
Science (Biological and Life Sciences; Chemistry; Mathematics; Natural Sciences; Physics) *Dean*: Wahab L.O. Jimoh
Social and Management Sciences (Accountancy; Business Administration; Economics; Geography; Management; Political Science; Public Law; Social Sciences; Sociology) *Dean*: Kabiru Ahmed
Technology (Civil Engineering; Electrical Engineering; Mechanical Engineering; Technology) *Dean*: Umaru Dambatta

Units
General Studies *Director*: Matthew Ajibero

Centres
Study of Nigerian Languages (African Languages; Native Language) *Director*: Abba Rufai, *full-time staff:* 9

Further Information: Also Aminu Kano Teaching Hospital

History: Founded 1960 as Ahmadu Bello College, renamed Abdullahi Bayero College 1962. Acquired present status 1975 and title 1977.

Governing Bodies: University Governing Council

Academic Year: October to July (October-February; March-July)

Admission Requirements: Universities Matriculation Examination (UME) following secondary school education, or direct entry for holders of the Higher School Certificate (General Certificate of Education, Advanced ('A') level)

Fees: None for Nigerian students

Main Language(s) of Instruction: English

Degrees and Diplomas: *Bachelor's Degree*: Arts (BA); Engineering (BEng); Science (BSc), 4 yrs; Law (LLB); Medicine and Surgery (BMed), 5 yrs; *Master's Degree*: a further 1-2 yrs; *Doctor of Philosophy*: (PhD). Also undergraduate and postgraduate Diplomas.

Student Services: Academic Counselling, Social Counselling, Employment Services, Nursery Care, Sports Facilities, Health Services, Canteen

Student Residential Facilities: Yes
Libraries: Central Library, c. 200,000 vols; 1000 periodicals
Publications: Prospectus; Calendar
Academic Staff *1999-2000:* Total: **873**

Student Numbers *1999-2000*	MEN	WOMEN	TOTAL
All (Foreign Included)	6,270	2,869	**9,139**
FOREIGN ONLY	15	5	20

Part-time Students, 875

BENUE STATE UNIVERSITY
PMB 102119, Makurdi, Benue State
Tel: +234(44) 533-811
Fax: +234(44) 534-040
Cable: unibenue
EMail: root@bensu.edu.ng
Vice-Chancellor: I. David
Registrar: W.I. Mozeh

Faculties
Arts (Arts and Humanities)
Education
Management Science (Management)
Science (Natural Sciences)
Social Sciences

History: Founded 1992.

DELTA STATE UNIVERSITY
PMB 1, Abraka, Delta State
Tel: +234(54) 66-027
Cable: delta versity
EMail: root@desu.edu.ng
Vice-Chancellor: F.M.A. Ukoli
Registrar: E.E. Avbiorokoma

Agriculture; Arts and Humanities; Education; Management; Natural Sciences; Social Sciences

History: Founded 1992.

*• ENUGU STATE UNIVERSITY OF SCIENCE AND TECHNOLOGY
PMB 01660, Independence Layout, Enugu, Enugu State
Tel: +234(42) 451-319
Fax: +234(42) 455-705
Telex: 51440 esutech ng
Cable: unitech, enugu
EMail: esut@compuserve.com
Vice-Chancellor: Julius O. Onah (2000-)
Registrar: Festus C. Eze

Faculties
Agricultural Sciences *(Abakaliki)* (Agricultural Economics; Agriculture; Soil Science) *Dean*: Cletus J.C. Akubuilo

331

Applied Natural Sciences *(Nsukka)* (Biochemistry; Biology; Geological Engineering; Microbiology; Mining Engineering; Physical Engineering; Statistics) *Dean*: Ethel-Doris Umeh

Basic Medical Sciences (Anatomy; Biochemistry; Medicine; Pathology; Physiology) *Head (Acting)*: A.O.C. Akpa

Clinical Medicine (Medicine)

Education *Dean*: Jonathan O. Mogbo

Law *Dean*: Martin Okany

Management Sciences (Management) *Dean*: Samuel C. Chukwu

Social Sciences (Anthropology; Social Sciences; Sociology) *Dean*: Daniel O. Okanya

Divisions
General Studies *Director*: Richard C. Okafor

Colleges
Health Sciences *(Abakaliki)* (Biochemistry; Community Health; Health Sciences; Pharmacology; Physiology; Rehabilitation and Therapy)

Programmes
Pre-Science *Director*: Benjamin Marire

Schools
Engineering (Agricultural Engineering; Chemical Engineering; Civil Engineering; Electrical and Electronic Engineering; Engineering; Materials Engineering; Mechanical Engineering) *Dean*: Linus Aneke

Environmental Sciences (Environmental Studies) *Dean*: Ernest C. Adibe

Postgraduate Studies *Dean*: Stephen O. Alaku

Institutes
Education *Director*: Aaron Eze

Centres
Biotechnology and Pest Management (Biotechnology; Pest Management) *Director*: Ethel-Doris Umeg

Industrial Development (Industrial Management) *Director*: Boniface A. Okorie, *full-time staff*: 3

History: Founded 1991, following creation of new States in Nigeria, and incorporating the Enugu and Abakaliki campuses of the former Anambra State University of Technology, founded 1980.

Governing Bodies: Council

Academic Year: September to August (September-March; April-August)

Admission Requirements: Universities Matriculation Examination (UME) following secondary school education, or direct entry for holders of the Higher School Certificate (General Certificate of Education, Advanced Level); or pre-science internal exams (science exams only).

Fees: (Naira): Tuition, undergraduate, 2000 per semester; graduate, 4000- 5000. Foreign students, US$, 5000

Main Language(s) of Instruction: English

Degrees and Diplomas: *Bachelor's Degree*: 4 yrs; *Master's Degree*: a further 1-1 1/2 yrs; *Doctor of Philosophy*: (PhD)

Student Services: Sports Facilities, Health Services, Canteen

Libraries: Total, 35,000 vols; 1200 periodicals

Academic Staff *1999:* Total: **865**

Student Numbers 1999	MEN	WOMEN	TOTAL
All (Foreign Included)	4,974	4,702	**9,676**

• FEDERAL UNIVERSITY OF TECHNOLOGY AKURE
PMB 704, Akure, Ondo State
Tel: +234(34) 200-090
Fax: +234(34) 230-450
Telex: 32492 futatel-ng
Cable: Fedunitech, Akure
EMail: root@futa.edu.ng

Vice-Chancellor: Lawrence B. Kolawole (1998-)
Tel: +234(34) 243-060 EMail: vce@futa.edu.ng

Registrar: Babatunde A. Adebayo Tel: +234(34) 230-190

Schools
Agriculture and Agricultural Technology (Agricultural Economics; Agricultural Engineering; Animal Husbandry; Crop Production; Fishery; Wildlife; Wood Technology) *Dean*: Adebisi M. Balogun

Engineering and Engineering Technology (Agricultural Engineering; Civil Engineering; Electrical and Electronic Engineering; Materials Engineering; Mechanical Engineering; Mining Engineering) *Dean*: Cornelius O. Ademosun

Environmental Technology (Architecture; Design; Environmental Engineering; Industrial Design; Real Estate; Regional Planning; Surveying and Mapping; Town Planning) *Dean*: Rufus B. Fatuyi

Postgraduate Studies Olatunji Kadeba

Science (Biochemistry; Biology; Chemistry; Computer Science; Meteorology; Natural Sciences; Physics) *Dean*: Aladesanmi A. Oshodi

History: Founded 1981

Governing Bodies: Council, comprising 17 members; Senate

Academic Year: February to October (February-June; July-October)

Admission Requirements: Minimum 5 credits at GCE (General Certificate of Education), Ordinary ('O') level. Admission is through Universities Matriculation Examinations conducted by Joint Admissions and Matriculation Board (JAMB).

Fees: (Naira): Foreign students 10,000

Main Language(s) of Instruction: English

International Co-operation: The Johns Hopkins University; International Higher School for Advanced Studies Trieste

Degrees and Diplomas: *Bachelor's Degree*: Agricultural Technology (BAgricTech); Engineering (BEng); Technology (BTech), 5 yrs; Architecture (BArch), 6 yrs; *Master's Degree*: a further 1-2 yrs; *Doctor of Philosophy*: (PhD), a further 2-3 yrs

Student Residential Facilities: For c. 45% of students. It is the policy of the University to accommodate all foreign students

Libraries: c. 49,100 vols; 237 periodicals. Special collection: UN Food and Agricultural Organisation's depositary library.

Publications: Bulletin (monthly); Handbook; Calendar

Academic Staff *1999:* Total: **1,123**

За.....

Student Numbers *1999*

	MEN	WOMEN	TOTAL
All (Foreign Included)	3,945	854	**4,799**
FOREIGN ONLY	–	–	46

• FEDERAL UNIVERSITY OF TECHNOLOGY MINNA

PMB 65, Minna, Niger State
Tel: +234(66) 222-422 +234(66) 222-397
Fax: +234(66) 224-482
Cable: futech minna
EMail: info.futma@alpha.link.serve.com

Vice-Chancellor: Muhammad Abdullahi Daniyan (1998-2003)
Tel: +234(66) 222-887 Fax: +234(66) 625-426

Registrar: Alhaji U.A. Sadiq Fax: +234(66) 224-305

Schools

Agriculture and Agricultural Technology (Agricultural Equipment; Agriculture; Cattle Breeding; Fishery; Soil Science) *Director*: S.L. Lamai, *full-time staff: 26, students: 250*

Engineering and Engineering Technology (Agricultural Engineering; Chemical Engineering; Civil Engineering; Electrical Engineering; Electronic Engineering; Mechanical Engineering) *Director*: R.H. Khan, *full-time staff: 58, students: 1,851*

Environmental Technology (Architecture; Building Technologies; Environmental Engineering; Real Estate; Regional Planning; Surveying and Mapping; Town Planning) *Director*: Olajide Solanke, *full-time staff: 40, students: 1,183*

Postgraduate *Director*: J.O. Adeniyi, *students: 606*

Science and Science Education (Biological and Life Sciences; Chemistry; Geography; Geology; Industrial Engineering; Mathematics and Computer Science; Natural Sciences; Physics; Science Education) *Director*: K.R. Adeboye, *full-time staff: 83, students: 2,556*

History: Founded 1981, acquired present status and title 1983.

Governing Bodies: Council; Senate

Admission Requirements: Universities Matriculation Examination (UME) following secondary school education

Fees: (Naira): Nationals, 3,855-17,355; foreign students, 17,855-27,855. Postgraduate, 11,955-19,955 part-time; 12,955-20,955 full-time

Main Language(s) of Instruction: English

Accrediting Agencies: National Universities Commission

Degrees and Diplomas: *Bachelor's Degree*: 5 yrs; *Master's Degree*: a further 2 yrs; *Doctor of Philosophy*: (PhD), 3 yrs

Student Residential Facilities: Yes

Libraries: c. 20,000 vols

Publications: News Bulletin (weekly); Minna at a Glance (1985); Federal University of Technology

Academic Staff *1999-2000:* Total: **207**

Student Numbers *1999-2000:* Total: **6,446**

• FEDERAL UNIVERSITY OF TECHNOLOGY OWERRI

PMB 1526, Owerri, Imo State
Tel: +234(83) 230-974 +234(83) 230-564
Fax: +234(83) 233-228
Cable: fedunitech, owerri
EMail: root@futo.edu.ng

Vice-Chancellor: Chuka O.G. Obah (1992-)
Tel: +234(83) 232-430 +234(83) 232-456
EMail: vc@futo.edu.ng
Registrar: M.O. Okoye

Units
General Studies *Head*: L.C. Asiegbu

Schools
Agriculture and Agricultural Technology (Agricultural Equipment; Agriculture) *Dean*: C.E. Onyenweaku

Engineering and Engineering Technology (Engineering; Technology) *Dean*: G.U. Ojiako

Management Technology (Management Systems) *Dean*: T.Y. Obah

Postgraduate *Dean*: M.E. Enyiegbulem

Science (Natural Sciences) *Dean*: B.N. Onwuagba

Departments
Agricultural Economics and Extension (Agricultural Economics) *Head*: C.C. Asiabaka

Agricultural Engineering *Head*: S.N. Asoegwu

Animal Husbandry *Head*: C.E. Onyenweaku

Biological Sciences (Biological and Life Sciences) *Head*: P.T.E. Ozoh

Chemical and Petroleum Engineering (Chemical Engineering; Petroleum and Gas Engineering) *Head*: K.O. Okpala

Chemistry *Head*: A.I. Onuchukwu

Civil Engineering *Head*: H.I. Agha

Crop Production

Electrical and Electronic Engineering *Head*: S.O.E. Ogbogu

Food Science and Technology (Food Science; Food Technology) *Head*: J.O. Uzuegbu

Geology *Head*: C.J. Iwuagwu

Materials and Metallurgical Engineering (Materials Engineering; Metallurgical Engineering) *Head*: O.O. Onyemaobi

Mathematics and Computer Science *Head*: U.B.C.O. Ejike

Mechanical Engineering

Physics *Head*: F.C. Ezeh

Polymer and Textile Engineering (Polymer and Plastics Technology; Textile Technology) *Head*: A.E. Iheonye

Project Management Technology *Head*: G.E. Nworuh

Transport Management Technology (Transport Engineering; Transport Management) *Head*: D.U. Ekwenna

Institutes
Erosion Studies (Soil Science) *Director*: C.I. Ijioma

Centres
Computer Science

Industrial Studies (Industrial Management) *Head*: V.O. Nwoko, *full-time staff: 4*

History: Founded 1980, acquired present status and title 1981.

333

Governing Bodies: Governing Council; Senate; Convocation

Academic Year: October to July (October-February; March-July)

Admission Requirements: At least 5 credits in General Certificate of Education (GCE), or Senior School Certificate (SSC), in relevant subjects

Fees: (Naira): Tuition, none

Main Language(s) of Instruction: English

International Co-operation: Wageningen Agricultural University

Degrees and Diplomas: *Bachelor's Degree*: Agricultural Technology (BAgricTech); Engineering (BEng); Technology (BTech), 5 yrs; *Postgraduate Diploma*: 1 yr; *Master's Degree*: Business Administration (MBA); Engineering (MEng); Science (MSc), a further 1-2 yrs; *Doctor of Philosophy*: (PhD), 2-3 yrs

Student Services: Academic Counselling, Social Counselling, Employment Services, Sports Facilities, Health Services, Foreign Student Centre

Student Residential Facilities: For c. 1950 students

Special Facilities: Comskiptec

Libraries: c. 50,000 vols

Publications: Newsletter (monthly); FUTNOTES, FUTO Library (annually); Calendar

Press or Publishing House: FUTO Press

Academic Staff: Total: c. 240

Staff with Doctorate: Total: c. 220

Student Numbers: All (Foreign Included): c. 5,900 Foreign Only: c. 30

• FEDERAL UNIVERSITY OF TECHNOLOGY YOLA (FUTY)
PMB 2076, Yola, Adamawa State
Tel: +234(75) 625-532
Cable: futy yola

Vice-Chancellor: Salihu Mustafa (1995-)
Tel: +234(75) 625-426 +234(75) 624-416
Fax: +234(75) 625-176 EMail: vc@futy.edu.ng

Registrar: M. Aminu

Schools
Agriculture and Agricultural Technology (Agricultural Economics; Agricultural Engineering; Agriculture; Animal Husbandry; Forest Management; Forestry) *Director*: Allen Kadams, *full-time staff: 98, students: 1,011*

Engineering and Engineering Technology (Agricultural Engineering; Civil Engineering; Electrical Engineering; Electronic Engineering; Mechanical Engineering; Technology) *Director*: E. Smekhounov, *full-time staff: 94, students: 1,057*

Environmental Sciences (Architecture; Building Technologies; Environmental Studies; Geography; Industrial Design; Surveying and Mapping) *Director*: O. Owoale, *full-time staff: 89, students: 902*

Management and Information Technology (Information Technology; Management) *Director*: Kavin Nwogu, *full-time staff: 31, students: 51*

Postgraduate Studies

Pure and Applied Sciences (Biochemistry; Biological and Life Sciences; Chemistry; Computer Science; Geology; Mathematics; Mathematics and Computer Science; Microbiology; Natural Sciences; Operations Research; Physics; Statistics) *Director*: Gregory Wajia, *full-time staff: 268, students: 1,637*

Technology and Science Education (Science Education; Technology Education) *Director*: R. Uyanga, *full-time staff: 62, students: 935*

Centres
Computer and Biotechnology *(CEMIT)* (Biotechnology; Computer Science; Maintenance Technology; Technology Education)

History: Founded 1981, acquired present title and status 1988

Governing Bodies: Council; Senate

Academic Year: October to August (October-February; April-August)

Admission Requirements: Universities Matriculation Examination (UME) following secondary school education, or direct entry for holders of the Higher School Certificate (General Certificate of Education, Advanced ('A') level)

Main Language(s) of Instruction: English

Accrediting Agencies: National University Commission (NUC)

Degrees and Diplomas: *Bachelor's Degree*: 4-6 yrs; *Master's Degree*: (BTech), a further 2 yrs; *Doctor of Philosophy*: (PhD), 3 yrs

Student Services: Academic Counselling, Social Counselling, Employment Services, Sports Facilities, Health Services, Canteen

Student Residential Facilities: Yes

Libraries: 20,000 vols

Publications: Information Brochure, University prospectus; Journal of Technology (annually); FUTY News (Occasional)

Academic Staff *1999:* Total: c. 2,285

Student Numbers *1999:* Total: c. 7,015

• IGBINEDION UNIVERSITY
PMB 006, Okada, 69, Airport Road, Benin City, Edo State
Tel: +234(52) 254-942
Fax: +234(52) 251-504

IMO STATE UNIVERSITY
PMB 2000, Owerri, Imo State
Tel: +234(83) 231-433
Fax: +234(83) 232-716
Cable: imsu

Vice-Chancellor: T.O.C. Ndubizu EMail: vc@imosu.edu.ng

Registrar: C.G. Ukaga

Faculties
Education
Humanities and Social Sciences (Arts and Humanities; Social Sciences)

Colleges
Agriculture
Business Administration
Engineering and Environmental Sciences
Legal Studies (Law)
Medical and Health Sciences (Health Sciences; Medicine)
Sciences (Mathematics and Computer Science; Natural Sciences)

History: Founded 1981.

LADOKE AKINTOLA UNIVERSITY OF TECHNOLOGY
PMB 4000, Ogbomoso, Oyo State
Tel: +234(38) 720-285
Fax: +234(38) 720-750
EMail: lautech-dvc@informatics.com.ng

Vice-Chancellor (Acting): Akinola M. Salau
Registrar: J.A. Oladokun

Faculties
Agriculture
Engineering and Technology (Engineering; Technology)
Environmental Sciences (Environmental Studies)
Medical Sciences (Health Sciences; Medicine)
Pure and Applied Sciences (Applied Chemistry; Applied Mathematics; Applied Physics; Engineering; Mathematics and Computer Science; Natural Sciences)

History: Founded 1990 as Oyo State University of Technology, acquired present title 1991.

LAGOS STATE UNIVERSITY
PMB 1087, Badagry Expressway, Ojo, Apapa, Lagos State
Tel: +234(1) 588-4048
Fax: +234(1) 588-4048
EMail: lasu-alpha@linkserve.com

Vice-Chancellor: Fatiu Ademola Akesode (1997-)
Registrar: Owolabi Amisu

Faculties
Arts (Arts and Humanities) *Head*: C.O. Oshun, *full-time staff: 78, students: 1,217*
Education *Head*: I. Osafehinti, *full-time staff: 39, students: 1,583*
Engineering and Technology (Engineering; Environmental Studies; Technology) *Head*: A. Noah, *full-time staff: 22, students: 1,044*
Law *Head*: O.A. Osunbor, *full-time staff: 29, part-time staff: 3, students: 1,165*
Science (Natural Sciences) *Head*: V.A. Adisa, *full-time staff: 82, students: 1,196*
Social Sciences *Head*: Adele Jinadu, *full-time staff: 46, students: 2,504*

Institutes
Education *Head*: S.O.A. Olaniyonu, *full-time staff: 16*

Centres
Educational Technology *Head*: Shodeinde, *full-time staff: 5*
Environmental Sciences and Education (Environmental Studies) *Head*: P.A.O. Okebukola, *full-time staff: 5*

History: Founded 1983, acquired present status and title 1984.
Governing Bodies: Council; Senate
Academic Year: June to December
Admission Requirements: Universities Matriculation Examination (UME) following secondary school education, or direct entry for holders of the Higher School Certificate (General Certificate of Education, Advanced ('A') Level)
Main Language(s) of Instruction: English
International Co-operation: Austin Peay State University; University of Cape Coast
Degrees and Diplomas: *Bachelor's Degree*: 3-5 yrs; *Postgraduate Diploma*; *Master's Degree*: Business Administration (MBA); Educational Management (MEdM); Public Administration (MPA); Science (MSc); Town Planning (MTP); Urban and Regional Planning (MURP), a further 1-2 yrs; *Master of Philosophy*: Philosophy (MPhil), a further 1-2 yrs; *Doctor of Philosophy*: (PhD), 2-3 yrs
Student Services: Academic Counselling, Nursery Care, Cultural Centre, Sports Facilities, Health Services, Canteen, Foreign Student Centre
Special Facilities: Fish Pond. Fish Hatchery
Libraries: University Library and Law Library, total, c. 40,000 vols
Publications: Lasu Bulletin (monthly); Academic Calendar
Press or Publishing House: Lasu Press
Academic Staff: Total: c. 330
Staff with doctorate: Total: c. 85
Student Numbers: Total: c. 12,850

'MICHAEL OKPARA' UNIVERSITY OF AGRICULTURE UMUDIKE
PMB 7267, Umuahia, Abia State
Tel: +234(82) 440-555
Fax: +234(82) 440-555
EMail: root@undusok.edu.ng; asagwara@fuau.edu.ng

Vice-Chancellor: Ogbonnaya C. Onwudike (2000-)
EMail: vc@fuau.edu.ng
Registrar (Acting): F. Ike

Colleges
Agricultural Economics, Rural Sociology and Extension (Agricultural Economics; Development Studies; Rural Planning) *Director*: Aloysius C. Nwosu
Animal Husbandry and Health (Animal Husbandry) *Director*: J.A. Ibeawuchi
Biological and Physical Sciences (Biological and Life Sciences) *Director (Acting)*: V.O Chiboka
Crop and Soil Science (Crop Production; Soil Science) *Director*: S. Emosairue
Food Processing and Storage Technology (Food Technology) *Director*: Enoch N. Akobundu

Natural Resources and Environmental Management (Environmental Management; Natural Resources) *Director*: Eme A. Akachuku

Schools
General and Remedial Studies *Director (Acting)*: N. Oke

History: Founded 1992.

Governing Bodies: Governing Council

Main Language(s) of Instruction: English

Accrediting Agencies: National Universities Commission

Degrees and Diplomas: *Bachelor's Degree*: Agriculture (BSc)

Student Services: Academic Counselling, Social Counselling, Sports Facilities, Language Programmes, Health Services, Canteen

Student Residential Facilities: Yes

Libraries: Central Library

Publications: Journal of Sustainable Agriculture and the Environment (biannually)

NNAMDI AZIKIWE UNIVERSITY
PMB 5025, Awka, Anambra State
Tel: +234(46) 550-018
Fax: +234(46) 550-018
Cable: unizik, awka

Vice-Chancellor: Pita N. Ejiofor (1998-2003)

Registrar (Acting): Tim Obi Umeasiegbu

International Relations: R.I. Egwuatu

Faculties
Arts and Social Sciences (Arts and Humanities; Economics; Mass Communication; Political Science; Psychology; Social Sciences; Sociology) *Dean*: A.W. Obi

Education (Education; Health Education; Physical Education; Vocational Education) *Dean*: G.I. Ndinechi

Engineering (Civil Engineering; Computer Engineering; Electrical Engineering; Electronic Engineering; Engineering; Materials Engineering; Metallurgical Engineering) *Dean*: E.L.C. Nnabuife

Law *Dean (Acting)*: Ilochi Okafor

Management Sciences (Accountancy; Banking; Finance; Management) *Dean (Acting)*: E.S. Ekezie

Medicine (Anatomy; Gynaecology and Obstetrics; Medicine; Paediatrics; Pathology; Pharmacology; Physiology; Surgery) *Dean*: B.U.O. Umeh

Natural Sciences (Biology; Chemistry; Geology; Mathematics; Mathematics and Computer Science; Natural Sciences; Physics; Statistics) *Dean*: G.U. Okereke

Units
General Studies (Arts and Humanities; English; Social Sciences) *Co-ordinator*: I.C. Okoye

Programmes
Continuing Education *Director*: B.C.E. Eqboka

Centres
Biotechnology Research (Biomedical Engineering; Biotechnology) *Director*: I.E. Nwana

Further Information: Also Teaching Hospital, Nnewi

History: Founded 1980 as Anambra State University of Technology. Acquired present title 1991.

Governing Bodies: Council

Academic Year: November to August (November-March; April-August)

Admission Requirements: Five credits in West African School Certificate (WASC), Senior Secondary Certificate Examination (SSCE) or General Certificate of Education (GCE) 'O' level, with minimum grade C and including English language. For direct entry, candidates must possess a higher qualification from an accredited university or polytechnic

Fees: (Naira): Tuition, undergraduate, 1500-2750 per annum

Main Language(s) of Instruction: English

International Co-operation: Saginaw Valley State University; California State University, Northridge

Degrees and Diplomas: *Bachelor's Degree*: 3-4 yrs; *Master's Degree*: a further 1-2 yrs; *Doctor of Philosophy*: (PhD), 3-4 yrs. Also postgraduate Diploma, 1-2 yrs.

Student Services: Academic Counselling, Sports Facilities, Health Services, Canteen

Libraries: Main Library, c. 50,000 vols; 70 periodicals

Publications: 'Unizik News' (quarterly)

Academic Staff: Total: c. 370

• OBAFEMI AWOLOWO UNIVERSITY
Ile-Ife, Osun State
Tel: +234(36) 230-290 to 299
Fax: +234(36) 233-971
Telex: 34261 oau ife nigeria
Cable: ifevarsity ile-ife, nigeria
EMail: omole@oauife.edu.ng
Website: http://www.oauife.edu.ng

Vice-Chancellor: Roger Makanjuola (2001-)
Tel: +234(36) 230-661 Fax: +234(36) 232-401

Registrar: D.O. Oyeyemi

International Relations: D.O. Kolawole

Faculties
Administration (Accountancy; Administration; Business Administration; Government; International Relations; Management; Public Administration) *Dean*: Oladimeji Aborisade

Agriculture (Agricultural Economics; Agriculture; Animal Husbandry; Plant and Crop Protection; Rural Studies; Soil Science) *Dean*: P.O. Aina

Arts (African Languages; Archaeology; Arts and Humanities) *Dean*: O. Omosini

Basic Medical Sciences (Anaesthesiology; Anatomy; Cell Biology; Child Care and Development; Community Health; Dental Technology; Dermatology; Epidemiology; Forensic Medicine and Dentistry; Gynaecology and Obstetrics; Haematology; Health Sciences; Immunology; Medicine; Microbiology;

Nursing; Nutrition; Orthopedics; Paediatrics; Parasitology; Physiology; Psychiatry and Mental Health; Radiology; Rehabilitation and Therapy; Surgery; Venereology) *Dean*: V.C.B. Nwuga

Dentistry *Dean*: S.A. Odusanya

Education *Dean*: J. Ibitoye Agun

Environmental Design and Management (Architectural and Environmental Design) *Dean*: J.R.O. Ojo

Law *Dean*: M.O. Adediran

Pharmacy *Dean*: A. Lamikanra

Science (Chemistry; Computer Science; Natural Sciences) *Dean*: P.O. Olutiola

Social Sciences *Dean*: B.O. Oloruntimehin

Technology (Agricultural Engineering; Chemical Engineering; Civil Engineering; Electrical and Electronic Engineering; Materials Engineering; Mechanical Engineering; Metallurgical Engineering; Technology) *Dean*: M.T. Ige

Institutes

Agricultural Research and Training (Agriculture; Animal Husbandry; Crop Production; Farm Management; Soil Management; Water Management)

Cultural Studies *Head*: A. Ogunba

Ecology and Environmental Studies (Ecology; Environmental Studies)

Education

Centres

Energy Research and Development (Energy Engineering) *Director (Acting)*: A.O. Adegbulugbe

Industrial Research and Development (Industrial Engineering) *Director*: Josephine O. Abiodun

Space Research (Aeronautical and Aerospace Engineering)

Space Science and Technology Education (Aeronautical and Aerospace Engineering)

Technology Management *(National)* (Technology)

Training in Aerospace Surveys *(Regional)*

History: Founded 1961 as University of Ife, acquired present title 1987.

Governing Bodies: Council; Senate

Academic Year: January to December (January-June; July-December)

Admission Requirements: Universities Matriculation Examination (UME), or five credits passes in relevant subjects at Senior Secondary Certificate (SSC) level, or at School Certificate/General Certificate of Education 'O' level in no more than two sittings.

Fees: Foreign students, US$ 1000-2000 per annum

Main Language(s) of Instruction: English

International Co-operation: University of Wisconsin; University of Leeds

Degrees and Diplomas: *Bachelor's Degree*: 3 yrs; *Master's Degree*: a further 1 1/2-2 yrs; *Doctor of Philosophy*: (PhD), a further 2 yrs

Student Residential Facilities: Yes

Libraries: Total, 400,919 vols; 7003 periodicals; Africana collection; audio-visual materials; government documents

Publications: Obafemi Awolowo University Law Reports (quarterly); Postgraduate Handbook; Handbooks; Odu: a Journal of West African Studies; African Journal of Philosophy; Calendar (biannually); Quarterly Journal of Administration

Press or Publishing House: University Press

Academic Staff *1999:* Total: **908**

Student Numbers *1999:* Total: **21,712**

Part-time Students, 1,753

• OGUN STATE UNIVERSITY
PMB 2002, Ago-Iwoye, Ogun State
Tel: +234(37) 390-660   +234(37) 390-147
Cable: ogunvasity

Vice-Chancellor: Afolabi Soyode

Registrar: Bola Taiwo

Faculties

Arts (Arts and Humanities) *Dean (Acting)*: Sola O. Adebajo

Basic Medical Sciences (Health Sciences) *Dean*: Julius O. Olowookere

Clinical Sciences (Health Sciences) *Dean*: M.R.C. Oyegunle

Education *Dean*: Taiwo Ajayi

Law *Dean (Acting)*: Mojisola O. Ogungbe

Science (Natural Sciences) *Dean*: O.A. Sosanwo

Social and Management Sciences (Management; Social Sciences) *Dean*: Kayode Oyesiku

Colleges

Agricultural Sciences (Agriculture) *Provost*: B.O. Durojaiye

Health Sciences *(Obefami Alowolo)* *Provost*: Olalekan O. Adetoro

Schools

Postgraduate Studies *Dean*: Victor A. Awoderu

Further Information: Also Teaching Hospital

History: Founded 1982. One of the University's distinctive characteristics is the adoption of an innovative programme of compulsory credit-earning courses on modern agricultural and rural life, Nigerian life and culture for all students in their first 2 years of study.

Governing Bodies: Council

Academic Year: October to July (October-March; March-July)

Admission Requirements: Universities Matriculation Examination (UME) following secondary school training, or direct entry for holders of the Higher School Certificate (General Certificate of Education, Advanced 'A' Level)

Main Language(s) of Instruction: English

Degrees and Diplomas: *Bachelor's Degree*: 3-5 yrs; *Master's Degree*: 1 further yr

Libraries: Main Library, c. 20,000 vols

Publications: Annual Report (annually); Handbook; University Calendar

Academic Staff: Total: c. 370

Student Numbers: Total: c. 4,090

Part-time Students, c. 30

• RIVERS STATE UNIVERSITY OF SCIENCE AND TECHNOLOGY

PMB 5080, Nkpolu Oroworukwo, Port Harcourt, Rivers State
Tel: +234(84) 335-823
Fax: +234(84) 230-720
Cable: riverstech port harcourt

Vice-Chancellor: Steven Odi-Owei Tel: +234(84) 230-720 Fax: +234(84) 233-288

Registrar: Markson B. Mieyebo

Faculties

Agriculture (Agriculture; Animal Husbandry; Fishery; Food Technology; Forestry; Horticulture; Soil Science; Viticulture; Water Science)

Engineering (Chemical Engineering; Civil Engineering; Computer Engineering; Construction Engineering; Electrical Engineering; Electronic Engineering; Engineering; Industrial Engineering; Marine Engineering; Materials Engineering; Metallurgical Engineering; Mining Engineering; Telecommunications Engineering; Transport Engineering)

Environmental Sciences (Environmental Studies)

Law

Management Sciences (Management)

Science (Natural Sciences)

Technology and Education (Technology Education)

Institutes

Agricultural Research and Training *(Rivers)* (Agriculture)

Foundation Studies (Construction Engineering)

Geosciences and Space Technology (Astronomy and Space Science; Geophysics)

Pollution Studies (Ecology; Sanitary Engineering)

Centres

Computer Science

Continuing Education

History: Founded as College of Science and Technology, acquired present status and title 1980.

Governing Bodies: Council; Senate

Academic Year: October to July (October-March; March-July)

Admission Requirements: Universities Matriculation Examination (UME) following secondary school education, or direct entry for holders of the Higher School Certificate (General Certificate of Education, Advanced ('A') Level)

Main Language(s) of Instruction: English

Degrees and Diplomas: *Bachelor's Degree:* 4 yrs; *Master's Degree:* a further 2 yrs; *Doctor of Philosophy:* (PhD), a further 2 yrs

Student Residential Facilities: Yes

Libraries: c. 90,200 vols

Publications: News Letter (monthly); Gazette (3 per annum); Annual Report; Calendar/Prospectus (annually)

Press or Publishing House: Rivers State University Press

Academic Staff: Full-Time: c. 370 Part-Time: c. 210 Total: c. 580

Student Numbers: Total: c. 4,310

• UNIVERSITY OF ABUJA

PMB 117, Abuja, Federal Capital Territory
Tel: +234(9) 882-1379
Fax: +234(9) 882-1605
Cable: unibuja
EMail: vc@uniabuja.edu.ng

Vice-Chancellor: A.L. Gambo (1999-)

Registrar: Alhaji Yakubu Habi

Colleges

Arts and Education (Arts and Humanities; Education; History; Modern Languages; Theatre) *Dean:* U. Bappah

Law, Management and Social Sciences (Business Administration; Economics; Islamic Law; Law; Management; Social Sciences; Sociology) *Dean:* Amdii

Science and Agriculture (Agriculture; Chemistry; Mathematics; Physics) *Dean:* Ikeotuonye

Centres

Computer Science *Director:* M.C. Hussaimi

Distance Learning and Lifelong Education *Director:* S.Y. Ingawa

History: Founded 1988. A single-campus University with strong distance learning components. In process of development.

Governing Bodies: Council; Senate

Academic Year: October to September

Admission Requirements: Senior School Certificate (SSC) with credits in 5 relevant subjects obtained at no more than 2 sittings, or General Certificate of Education (GCE) O level in 5 subjects, or equivalent qualification; and University Matriculation Examination (UME) in 3 relevant subjects and knowledge of English

Main Language(s) of Instruction: English

Degrees and Diplomas: *Bachelor's Degree:* 4 yrs; *Bachelor Honours Degree:* 4-5 yrs; *Master's Degree:* a further 1-2 yrs; *Doctor of Philosophy:* (PhD), a further 2-5 yrs

Special Facilities: Open Air Theatre

Publications: University of Abuja News Journal (quarterly); Abuja Journal of Education; Abuja Journal of Humanities (annually)

• UNIVERSITY OF ADO-EKITI

PMB 5363, Ado-Ekiti, Ekiti State
Tel: +234(30) 250-026   +234(30) 240-711
Fax: +234(30) 240-188
Cable: ondovarsity ado-ekiti

Vice-Chancellor: Akindele B Oyebode

Registrar: M.O. Ogunniyi

Faculties

Agriculture (Agriculture; Forestry) A.A. Agboola

Arts (Arts and Humanities; History; Modern Languages; Philosophy; Religious Studies) *Dean:* L.O. Bamikole

Education *Dean:* M.F. Alonge

Engineering (Civil Engineering; Electrical Engineering; Engineering; Mechanical Engineering; Physical Engineering) *Dean*: O.O. Ogunlade

Law *Dean (Acting)*: G.D. Oke

Science (Botany; Chemistry; Geography; Microbiology; Natural Sciences; Zoology) *Dean*: M.A. Faluyi

Social Sciences (Accountancy; Economics; Psychology; Social Sciences; Sociology) *Dean*: F.I. Afolabi

Schools
Postgraduate

History: Founded 1982 as Obafemi Awolowo University, and renamed Ondo State University 1985. Acquired present status 1985, and present name 1999.

Academic Year: October to July (October-March; April-July)

Admission Requirements: Senior School Certificate (SSC) or General Certificate of Education (GCE) 'O' levels, with credits in 5 relevant subjects, obtained at no more than 2 sittings; and University Matriculation Examination (UME). Some courses have additional requirements. International applicants: equivalent qualifications and UME

Fees: Home students: $35 - 51.25 (humanities); $ 43.6 - 59.2

Main Language(s) of Instruction: English

Degrees and Diplomas: *Bachelor's Degree*: 4 yrs; *Master's Degree*: 1 further yr; *Doctor of Philosophy*: (PhD), 2 yrs

Libraries: c. 100,000 vols

Publications: Annual Report (annually); Handbook; Calendar

Academic Staff *1999-2000:* Total: c. 200

Student Numbers *1999-2000*: All (Foreign Included): Men: c. 7,085 Women: c. 4,275 Total: c. 11,360

• UNIVERSITY OF AGRICULTURE, ABEOKUTA
PMB 2240, Abeokuta, Ogun State
Tel: +234(39) 245-291   +234(39) 240-768
Fax: +234(39) 243-045   +234(39) 244-299
Telex: 24676 unaab ng
EMail: root@unaab.edu.ng

Vice-Chancellor: Julius A. Okojie (1996-)

Registrar (Acting): Ademola Oyerinde

Colleges
Agricultural Management, Rural Development, and Consumer Studies (Agricultural Management; Consumer Studies; Dietetics; Food Science; Home Economics; Nutrition; Rural Planning)

Animal Husbandry and Livestock Production (Animal Husbandry; Cattle Breeding; Genetics)

Environmental Resources Management (Environmental Studies; Fishery; Forestry; Meteorology; Toxicology; Water Management; Wildlife)

Natural Sciences and General Studies (Biology; Chemistry; Mathematics; Natural Sciences; Physics)

Plant Science and Crop Production (Botany; Crop Production)

Schools
Postgraduate

Centres
Agricultural Media Resources and Extension (Agriculture)
Research and Development (Development Studies)

History: Founded 1983 as Federal University of Technology, Abeokuta, merged with University of Lagos 1984, acquired present status 1988.

Governing Bodies: Council

Academic Year: October to July (October-February; March-July)

Admission Requirements: Universities Matriculation Examination (UME) following secondary school education, or direct entry for holders of the Higher School certificate (General Certificate of Education, Advanced ('A') level)

Fees: None

Main Language(s) of Instruction: English

International Co-operation: University of Reading; University of Edinburgh. Participates in the British Council-Sponsored Academic Programme

Degrees and Diplomas: *Bachelor's Degree*: Science (BSc), 3-5 yrs

Student Residential Facilities: For c. 30% of the students

Libraries: c. 22,000 vols

Publications: UNAAB News; Student Handbook; UNAAB Conference Proceedings Series; UNAAB Special Lecture Series

Academic Staff: Total: c. 120

Student Numbers: Total: c. 3,500

Note: Also c. 560 students in Science Laboratory Technology Training Programme (SLTTP)

UNIVERSITY OF AGRICULTURE, MAKURDI
PMB 2373, Makurdi, Benue State
Tel: +234(44) 533-204
Telex: 85304

Vice-Chancellor: Erastus O. Gyang (1996-)
Fax: +234(44) 531-455 EMail: vc@fuam.edu.ng

Registrar (Acting): Eraer Kureve

Faculties
Agricultural Economics and Extension (Agricultural Economics) *Dean*: C.P.O. Obinne

Agricultural Engineering and Engineering Technology (Agricultural Engineering; Technology) *Dean*: E.I. Kucha

Agronomy *Dean*: E.O. Ogunwolu

Animal Science (Animal Husbandry) *Dean*: N.G. Ehiobu

Food Technology *Dean*: Charles C. Ariahu

Science, Agriculture and Science Education (Agricultural Education; Natural Sciences; Science Education) *Dean*: O. Amali

Colleges
Forestry and Fisheries (Fishery; Forestry) *Dean*: Iorysa Verinumbe

Schools
Postgraduate *Dean*: M.C. Njike

Centres
Seed Technology (Crop Production) *Director*: B.A. Kalu

Research Centres
Co-operative Extension *Director*: D.K. Adedzwa
Food and Agricultural Strategy (Agriculture; Food Science; Food Technology)

History: Founded 1988

Academic Year: March to September (March-June; June-September)

Admission Requirements: 5 credits in Senior Secondary School Certificate (SSSC) or West African School Certificate (WASC) or General Certificate of Education (GCE) ('O') level or equivalent, and English language. Entrance examination

Fees: (Naira): Tuition, undergraduate, 265 per annum. Postgraduate (international): 6915

Main Language(s) of Instruction: English

Degrees and Diplomas: *Bachelor's Degree*: 4-5 yrs; *Master's Degree*: a further 1-4 yrs; *Doctor of Philosophy*: (PhD), 3-6 yrs

Libraries: Total, 30,000 vols; 699 periodicals; Nigerian/Canadian soil science documents

Academic Staff *2000*: Total: **223**

Student Numbers *2000*	MEN	WOMEN	TOTAL
All (Foreign Included)	1,548	352	**1,900**

*• UNIVERSITY OF BENIN
PMB 1154, Benin City, Edo State
Tel: +234(52) 600-443
Fax: +234(52) 600-273
Telex: 41365 uniben ng
Cable: uniben, benin
Website: http://www.uniben.edu

Vice-Chancellor: Abhulimen R. Anao (1999-2004)
EMail: vc@uniben.edu

Registrar: Mary N. Idehen

Faculties
Agriculture (Agricultural Economics; Agriculture; Animal Husbandry; Botany; Crop Production; Fishery; Forestry; Soil Science) *Dean*: John O. Igene
Arts (Applied Chemistry; Arts and Humanities; Fine Arts; Graphic Arts) *Dean*: Aigbona I. Igbafe
Dentistry (Dentistry; Surgery) *Dean*: Michael Ojo
Education (Curriculum; Education; Educational Administration; Health Education; Physical Education; Psychology; Vocational Education) *Dean*: David Awanbor
Engineering (Chemical Engineering; Civil Engineering; Electrical Engineering; Engineering; Mechanical Engineering) *Dean*: Thomas O. Audu
Law *Dean*: Patrick E. Oshio
Pharmacy (Chemistry; Microbiology; Pharmacology; Pharmacy; Toxicology) *Dean*: Augustine O. Okhamafe

Science (Biochemistry; Botany; Chemistry; Computer Science; Geology; Mathematics; Microbiology; Natural Sciences; Optometry; Physics; Zoology) *Dean*: John A. Okhunoya
Social Sciences (Accountancy; Anthropology; Business Administration; Economics; Geography; Political Science; Public Administration; Regional Planning; Social Sciences; Sociology; Statistics) *Dean*: Amorosu B. Agbadudu

Colleges
Medical Sciences (Gynaecology and Obstetrics; Medicine; Ophthalmology; Psychiatry and Mental Health; Surgery) *Dean*: Friday E. Okonofua

Schools
Postgraduate Studies (Anaesthesiology; Arts and Humanities; Business Administration; Chemical Engineering; Computer Science; Education; Engineering; Finance; Fine Arts; Health Administration; History; International Relations; Law; Petroleum and Gas Engineering; Pharmacy; Philosophy; Public Administration; Science Education)

Institutes
Adult Education and Extramural Studies (Educational Research) *Head*: Akpovire B. Oduaran
Child Health (Health Sciences) *Director*: Osawaru Oriawe
Education *Director*: A.O. Orubu
Public Administration and Extension Services (Public Administration) *Director (Acing)*: Samuel U. Akpovi

Centres
Educational Technology *Director*: Akinyele Odebunmi

Further Information: Also Teaching Hospital

History: Founded 1970 as the Institute of Technology Benin City, acquired present title 1972 and status 1975.

Governing Bodies: Council; Senate

Academic Year: October to June

Admission Requirements: Universities Matriculation Examination (UME) plus 5 General Certificate of Education (GCE) 'O' level passes, or 2 A level passes plus appropriate diploma/certificate

Main Language(s) of Instruction: English

International Co-operation: University of Kansas; University of Pittsburgh; Université du Bénin, Lomé; University of Illinois

Degrees and Diplomas: *Bachelor's Degree*: 3-5 yrs; *Master's Degree*: a further 1 1/2-2 yrs; *Doctor of Philosophy*: (PhD), at least 2 yrs following Master's Degree

Student Residential Facilities: Yes

Libraries: c. 200,500 vols; c. 250 periodicals

Publications: University Newsletter (bimonthly); Faculty of Arts Journal (quarterly); University Report (biannually); Faculty of Education Journal (2 per annum); Calendar; Prospectus (annually); Bini Journal of Educational Studies; Nigerian Journal of Educational Research Association; Physical Health Education and Recreational Journal; Nigerian Bulletin of Contemporary Law

Academic Staff *1999-2000*: Total: c. 800

Student Numbers *1999-2000*: All (Foreign Included): Men: c. 13,641 Women: c. 7,760 Total: c. 21,401

Part-time Students, c. 22,430

• UNIVERSITY OF CALABAR
PMB 1115, Calabar, Cross River State
Tel: +234(87) 222-790
Fax: +234(87) 221-766
Telex: (0905) 6510 unical ng
Cable: unical, calabar
EMail: root@unical.anpa.net.ng

Vice-Chancellor (Acting): E. Ivara

Registrar (Acting): E. Effiom

International Relations: E. Effiom, Registrar (Acting)

Faculties

Agriculture (Agriculture; Animal Husbandry; Crop Production; Economics; Soil Science) *Dean:* A.I. Essien

Arts (Arts and Humanities; History; Linguistics; Modern Languages; Philosophy; Religion; Theatre) *Dean:* D. Orisawayi

Education (Adult Education; Continuing Education; Curriculum; Education; Special Education; Vocational Education) *Dean:* D.N. Nwachukwu

Law (International Law; Law; Private Law; Public Law) *Dean:* N.O. Ita

Science (Biological and Life Sciences; Chemistry; Computer Science; Geology; Mathematics; Natural Sciences; Physics; Statistics) *Dean:* John O. Offem

Social Sciences (Accountancy; Banking; Business Administration; Economics; Finance; Management; Marketing; Political Science; Social Sciences; Sociology) *Dean:* J.G. Otong

Colleges

Medical Sciences (Anaesthesiology; Anatomy; Biochemistry; Community Health; Gynaecology and Obstetrics; Haematology; Health Sciences; Medicine; Microbiology; Ophthalmology; Paediatrics; Parasitology; Pathology; Pharmacology; Physiology; Psychiatry and Mental Health; Radiology; Surgery) *Provost:* S.E. Efem

Schools

Graduate Studies *Dean:* Elerius E. John

Institutes

Education (Distance Education; Education) *Director:* John U. Emeh

Oceanography (Marine Science and Oceanography) *Director:* Augustine I. Obiekezie

Public Policy and Administration (Rural Studies) *Director:* Okon E. Uya

History: Founded 1975. Also campus at Ogoja.

Governing Bodies: University Council; Senate; Committee of Deans

Academic Year: October to July (October-February; March-July)

Admission Requirements: Senior School Certificate (SSC) or its equivalent, with 5 passes at credit level, taken at no more than 2 sittings, and either University Matriculation Examination (UME) or (for direct entry) General Certificate of Education (GCE) 'A' level in 3 subjects or equivalent

Fees: (Naira): Tuition per annum: Undergraduate, 4440-5000 (Medicine, Science); 4090 (Non-science subjects). Postgraduate, 6000 (Arts), 4000 (part-time); 6000 (Science), 5000 (part-time); 8000 (MPA). Overseas students, undergraduate, 6000 (Arts, Law, Social Sciences); 8000 (Science); 12,000 (Medicine); postgraduate 24,800 (Arts, Science); 25,000 (MPA)

Main Language(s) of Instruction: English

Degrees and Diplomas: *Bachelor's Degree:* 4-5 yrs; *Master's Degree:* a further 1-2 yrs; *Doctor of Philosophy:* (PhD), 2-3 yrs following Master's Degree

Student Services: Academic Counselling, Social Counselling, Sports Facilities, Health Services, Canteen

Student Residential Facilities: for c. 3100 students

Special Facilities: Geography Observatory. Biological Garden. Theatre. Arts Gallery. Audiovisual Studio

Libraries: Total, 150,000 vols

Publications: News Bulletin (monthly); Introducing the University of Calabar; Calendar

Press or Publishing House: University of Calabar Press

Academic Staff *1999:* Total: **639**

Student Numbers 1999	MEN	WOMEN	TOTAL
All (Foreign Included)	7,767	4,389	**12,156**

Part-time Students, 11,800

*• UNIVERSITY OF IBADAN
Ibadan, Oyo State
Tel: +234(2) 810-1100-4 +234(2) 810-1188
Fax: +234(2) 810-3043 +234(2) 810-2921
Telex: campus 31128 ng
Cable: university ibadan
EMail: registrar@kdl.ui.edu.ng
Website: http://www.ui.edu.ng

Vice-Chancellor: Omoniyi Adewoye (1996-)
Tel: +234(2) 810-3168 Fax: +234(2) 810-3043

Registrar: Mojisola O. Ladipo Tel: +234(2) 810-4031
EMail: moji.ladipo@kdl.ui.edu.ng

Faculties

Agriculture and Forestry (Agricultural Economics; Agricultural Engineering; Agriculture; Agronomy; Forestry) *Dean:* S.O. Adesiyan

Arts (African Studies; Arabic; Arts and Humanities; Classical Languages; Communication Arts; English; History; Islamic Studies; Philosophy; Religious Studies; Theatre) *Dean:* S.O. Odunuga

Education (Adult Education; Education) *Dean:* J.A. Ajala

Law *Dean:* J.D. Ojo

Pharmacy *Dean:* H.A. Odelola

Science (Archaeology; Botany; Chemistry; Computer Science; Crop Production; Geology; Mathematics; Microbiology; Natural Sciences; Physics; Statistics; Zoology) *Dean:* I. Iweibo

Social Sciences (Economics; Geography (Human); Political Science; Psychology; Social Sciences; Sociology) *Dean:* J.A.A. Ayoade

Technology (Agricultural Engineering; Civil Engineering; Electrical Engineering; Engineering Management; Food

341

Technology; Mechanical Engineering; Petroleum and Gas Engineering; Technology) *Dean*: O. Ofi
Veterinary Science (Animal Husbandry; Veterinary Science) *Dean*: R.O. A. Arowolo

Schools
Postgraduate *Dean*: B.O. Fagbemi

Institutes
African Studies *Director*: C.O. Adepegba
Child Health (Health Sciences) *Director*: Foladale M. Akinkugbe
Education *Director*: S.T. Bajah

Centres
Bio-Medical Communications (Biomedicine) *Head*: O.S. Ndekwu
Information Sciences *Director (Acting)*: F.A. Ehikhamenor
Further Information: Also Teaching Hospital

History: Founded as a college of the University of London 1948, acquired present status and title 1962.

Governing Bodies: University Council; University Senate

Academic Year: September to June

Admission Requirements: Universities Matriculation Examination (UME). Secondary School Certificate of Education (SSCE) with 5 credits, including English.

Fees: (Naira): Foreign students, undergraduate, 600-1000 per annum; postgraduate, 2500-35,000

Main Language(s) of Instruction: English

International Co-operation: University of Birmingham, United Kingdom; University of Bénin, Lomé; University of Harvard; The Johns Hopkins University; University of Pennsylvania; Pushkin Institute, Moscow

Degrees and Diplomas: *Bachelor's Degree*: 4-5 yrs; *Master's Degree*: a further 1-2 yrs; *Doctor of Philosophy*: (PhD), 3-4 yrs

Student Services: Academic Counselling, Social Counselling, Employment Services, Cultural Centre, Sports Facilities, Handicapped Facilities, Health Services, Foreign Student Centre

Student Residential Facilities: Yes

Libraries: Main Library, c. 560,000 vols; c. 6000 journals and other serials

Publications: African Notes (3 per annum); Student Handbook; Annual Report; Calendar (annually)

Press or Publishing House: University Press

Academic Staff *1999:* Total: **1,156**

Student Numbers 1999	MEN	WOMEN	TOTAL
All (Foreign Included)	13,839	7,482	**21,321**
FOREIGN ONLY	–	–	946

Note: Also c. 1200 evening students

*• UNIVERSITY OF ILORIN (UNILORIN)
PMB 1515, Ilorin, Kwara State
Tel: +234(31) 221-694
Fax: +234(31) 222-561
Telex: 33144 unilon ng
Cable: unilorin

Vice-Chancellor: S.O. Abdul Raheem (1997-2002)
Tel: +234(031) 221-911 EMail: vc@unilorin.edu.ng
Registrar: M.T. Balogun Tel: +234(31) 221-937
EMail: registrar@unilorin.edu.ng

Faculties
Agriculture (Agriculture; Cattle Breeding; Crop Production; Farm Management; Rural Planning) *Dean*: R.O. Fadayomi, *full-time staff: 52, students: 684*
Arts (Arabic; Arts and Humanities; Christian Religious Studies; English; French; History; Islamic Studies; Linguistics; Performing Arts; Social Sciences) *Dean*: E.E. Adegbija, *full-time staff: 92, students: 1,308*
Business and Social Sciences (Accountancy; Business Administration; Finance; Geography; Law; Political Science; Social Sciences; Sociology) *Dean*: I.O. Taiwo, *full-time staff: 64, students: 3,552*
Education (Education; Educational and Student Counselling; Health Education; Physical Education) *Dean*: I.A. Idowu, *full-time staff: 60, students: 1,970*
Engineering and Technology (Agricultural Engineering; Civil Engineering; Electrical Engineering; Engineering; Mechanical Engineering; Technology) *Dean*: K.C. Oni, *full-time staff: 52, students: 1,980*
Law (International Law; Islamic Law; Law) *Dean*: M.T. Abdul Rasaq, *full-time staff: 26, students: 595*
Science (Biochemistry; Biological and Life Sciences; Botany; Chemistry; Geology; Mathematics; Microbiology; Mineralogy; Natural Sciences; Physics; Statistics; Zoology) *Dean*: S.O. .Akande, *full-time staff: 117, students: 3,450*

Divisions
General Studies *Head*: M.A. Akanji

Colleges
Medicine (Anatomy; Medicine; Physiology; Surgery) *Director*: A.O. Soladoye, *full-time staff: 102, students: 1,562*

Schools
Postgraduate School *Director*: I.A. Awogun, *students: 1,124*

Institutes
Education *Director*: S.A. Jimoh, *students: 1,242*

Research Institutes
Sugar Technology (Food Technology) *Director*: J.A. Olofintoye

History: Founded 1975 as University College, acquired present status and title 1977. Under the jurisdiction of the Federal Government.

Governing Bodies: University Council

Academic Year: October to July (October-January; March-July)

Admission Requirements: Universities Matriculation Examination (UME) following secondary school education, or direct entry for holders of the Higher School Certificate (General Certificate of Education, Advanced ('A') level)

Fees: (Naira): Foreign students, 750-1200; postgraduate, 500-700; foreign students, US$ 2000-3000

Main Language(s) of Instruction: English

International Co-operation: University of Calgary; University of New Brunswick; University of Reading

Degrees and Diplomas: *Bachelor's Degree*: Arts in Education (BAEd); Science in Education (BSCEd), 3-4 yrs; Agriculture (BAgric), 4-5 yrs; Medicine and Surgery (MB BS), 5-6 yrs; *Bachelor Honours Degree*: Arts (BA(Hons)); Science (BSc(Hons)), 3-4 yrs; Engineering (Beng(Hons)), 4-5 yrs; *Master's Degree*: a further 1-2 yrs; *Doctor of Philosophy*: (PhD), 2-3 yrs

Student Residential Facilities: For 3607 students

Special Facilities: Biological Garden

Libraries: University Library, 129, 798 vols

Publications: News Bulletin (weekly); Ilorin Lectures; University Calendar (annually)

Press or Publishing House: University Press

Academic Staff *1999-2000*	MEN	WOMEN	TOTAL
FULL-TIME	507	58	**565**
STAFF WITH DOCTORATE			
FULL-TIME	246	28	**274**

Student Numbers *1999-2000*	MEN	WOMEN	TOTAL
All (Foreign Included)	11,020	5,205	**16,225**
FOREIGN ONLY	67	16	83

Part-time Students, 1,242

*• UNIVERSITY OF JOS

PMB 2084, Jos, Plateau State
Tel: +234(73) 610-936
Fax: +234(73) 610-514
Telex: 81136 unijos ng
Cable: unijos, nigeria 2019
EMail: unijos@aol.com

Vice-Chancellor (Acting): Monday Y. Mangvwat (1999-)
Tel: +234(73) 453-724 +234(73) 612-513
Fax: +234(73) 611-928 EMail: vc@unijos.edu.ng

Registrar: Z.D. Galam

Faculties

Arts (Arts and Humanities) *Dean*: S. Aje, *full-time staff:* 91, *students:* 1,250
Education *Dean*: C.T.O. Akinmade, *full-time staff:* 60, *students:* 1,366
Environmental Sciences (Environmental Studies) *Dean*: J.O. Kolawole, *full-time staff:* 48, *students:* 1,058
Law *Dean*: I.I. Gabriel, *full-time staff:* 23, *students:* 1,276
Medical Sciences (Health Sciences; Medicine) *Dean*: Abraham O. Malu, *full-time staff:* 58, *students:* 760
Natural Sciences (Botany; Geology; Natural Sciences; Zoology) *Dean*: C.O.E. Omwliri, *full-time staff:* 118, *students:* 1,610
Pharmaceutical Sciences (Pharmacology; Pharmacy) *Dean*: T.A. Iranloye
Social Sciences (Economics; Psychology; Social Sciences; Sociology) *Dean*: A. Nweze, *full-time staff:* 82, *students:* 3,272

Schools

Postgraduate Studies *Director*: J.O.A. Onyeka, *students:* 805

Institutes

Education *Director*: M.A. Adewole, *full-time staff:* 20, *students:* 3,266

Centres

Computer Science *Director*: E.G. Eseyin, *full-time staff:* 13
Development Studies *Director (Acting)*: Victor A.O. Adetula, *full-time staff:* 10

Further Information: Also Teaching Hospital

History: Founded 1971 as campus of University of Ibadan, acquired present status and title 1975.

Governing Bodies: Council; Senate

Academic Year: March to December (March-July; August-December)

Admission Requirements: Universities Matriculation Examination (UME) following secondary school education, or direct entry for holders of the Senior Secondary School Certificate (SSSC) or General Certificate of Education (GCE) with ('O') levels with at least 5 credits

Fees: (Naira): 1500-3000 per session; foreign students, 4000-8000

Main Language(s) of Instruction: English

Degrees and Diplomas: *Bachelor's Degree*: 4-6 yrs; *Master's Degree*: a further 2 yrs; *Doctor of Philosophy*: (PhD), a further 2 yrs

Student Services: Academic Counselling, Social Counselling, Employment Services, Nursery Care, Sports Facilities, Handicapped Facilities, Health Services

Student Residential Facilities: Yes

Special Facilities: Anatomy Museum. Geography Observatory. House of Animal Pharmacology. Botanical Garden; Zoological Garden

Libraries: Total, 150,104 vols; 23,155 periodicals

Publications: News Flash (weekly); News Bulletin (monthly)

Press or Publishing House: University Press

Academic Staff *1999-2000*	MEN	WOMEN	TOTAL
FULL-TIME	491	132	**623**

Student Numbers *1999-2000*	MEN	WOMEN	TOTAL
All (Foreign Included)	6,926	4,119	**11,045**
FOREIGN ONLY	56	29	85

Part-time Students, 3,266

*• UNIVERSITY OF LAGOS

Lagos, Lagos State
Tel: +234(1) 821-945
Fax: +234(1) 822-644
Telex: 26983
Cable: university. lagos

Vice-Chancellor: Jelili Adebisi Omotola (1995-)
Tel: +234(1) 821-111 EMail: vc@unilag.edu.ng

Registrar: O.A. Aderibigbe Tel: +234(1) 820-310

International Relations: Solomon Thomas
Tel: +234(1)823-336 EMail: omotola@unilag.edu.ng

Faculties
Arts (Arts and Humanities)
Business Administration
Dentistry
Education

Engineering
Environmental Sciences (Environmental Studies)
Law
Science (Natural Sciences)
Social Sciences

Colleges
Medicine

Schools
Postgraduate Studies

Institutes
Distance Learning
Further Information: Also Teaching Hospital

History: Founded 1962.
Academic Year: October to July (October-February; March-July)
Admission Requirements: Universities Matriculation Examination (UME) following secondary school education, or direct entry for holders of the Higher School Certificate (General Certificate of Education, GCE, Advanced ('A') level)
Main Language(s) of Instruction: English
Degrees and Diplomas: *Bachelor's Degree*: Architecture (BArch); Arts (BA); Education (BEd); Environmental Science (BES); Pharmacy, 4 yrs; Science (BSc), 4-5 yrs; Dental Surgery (BDS); Medicine and Surgery (MB BS), 5 yrs; Laws, 5-7 yrs; *Master's Degree*: Arts in Translation; International Law and Diplomacy, a further 1-2 yrs; Banking and Finance (MBF); Business Administration (MBA); Public Administration (MPA), a further 3-5 sem; *Doctor of Philosophy*: (PhD), 2-3 yrs. Also undergraduate and postgraduate Diplomas.
Student Services: Academic Counselling, Social Counselling, Employment Services, Nursery Care, Cultural Centre, Sports Facilities, Health Services, Canteen, Foreign Student Centre
Student Residential Facilities: Yes
Special Facilities: Biological Garden
Libraries: c. 270,000 vols
Publications: Faculty prospectuses; Calendar
Press or Publishing House: University of Lagos Press
Academic Staff *1999*: Full-Time: c. 650 Part-Time: c. 100 Total: c. 750
Student Numbers *1999:* Total: c. 13,930

• UNIVERSITY OF MAIDUGURI
PMB 1069, Bama Road, Maiduguri, Borno State
Tel: +234(76) 231-730
Fax: +234(76) 231-639
Telex: 82102 unimai ng
Cable: university maiduguri
Vice-Chancellor: Abubakar Mustapha (1998-2003)
Registrar: Umaru Ibrahim

Faculties
Agriculture (Agriculture; Crop Production; Food Science) *Dean*: A.O. Folorunso

Arts (Arts and Humanities; Fine Arts; History; Linguistics; Modern Languages) *Dean*: B.R. Badejo
Education *Dean*: P.F.C. Carew
Engineering (Civil Engineering; Electrical and Electronic Engineering; Engineering; Mechanical Engineering) *Dean*: M.A. Haque
Law *Dean*: Isa H. Chiroma
Science (Biological and Life Sciences; Chemistry; Geography; Mathematics; Natural Sciences) *Dean*: M.Y. Balla
Social and Management Sciences (Anthropology; Economics; Management; Political Science; Social Sciences; Sociology) *Dean*: H.D. Dlakwa
Veterinary Science *Dean*: T.I.O. Osiyemi

Colleges
Medical Sciences (Health Sciences; Medicine) *Dean*: M.I.A. Khalil

Schools
Postgraduate Studies *Dean*: Abdulhamid Abubakar

Centres
Arid Zone Studies (Arid Land Studies) *Director*: Pender O. Ugherughe
Trans-Saharan Studies (Arid Land Studies) *Director*: K. Tijani
Further Information: Also Teaching Hospital

History: Founded 1975.
Governing Bodies: Governing Council
Academic Year: October to June (October-February/March; March-June)
Admission Requirements: Either Senior School Leaving Certificate (SSLC) or General Certificate of Education (GCE) 'O' level with at least 5 credits in relevant subjects and good scores in the University Matriculation Examination; or GCE 'A' level with minimum C grade in at least 3 relevant subjects. Application is through Joint Admission and Matriculation Board (JAMB).
Main Language(s) of Instruction: English
International Co-operation: Virginia Polytechnic and State University; University of Frankfurt; University of Oxford; University of Hull
Degrees and Diplomas: *Bachelor's Degree*: Engineering (BEng), 3-4 yrs; Medicine and Surgery (MB BS), 5 yrs; *Bachelor Honours Degree*: Arts (BAHons); Education (BEdHons); Library Science Studies (BLS(Hons)); Science (BSc(Hons)); Sharia (Islamic Law) (LLB(Hons)), 3-4 yrs; *Doctor of Veterinary Medicine*: Veterinary Medicine (DVM), 5 yrs; *Master's Degree*: Arts (MA); Education (MEd); Law (LLM); Library Science Studies (MLS); Performing Arts (MPA); Science (MSc), a further 1-2 yrs; *Master of Philosophy*: Philosophy (MPhil), a minimum of 12 months' full-time study following Master's Degree; *Doctor of Philosophy*: (PhD), 2-5 yrs. Also Diplomas.
Student Services: Academic Counselling, Social Counselling, Nursery Care, Cultural Centre, Sports Facilities, Health Services, Foreign Student Centre
Student Residential Facilities: Yes
Libraries: Main Library, c. 116,360 vols
Publications: The Annals of Borno (Multidisciplinary Yearbook of Research) (annually); University Calendar

Press or Publishing House: University of Maiduguri Printing Press

Academic Staff: Total: c. 650

Student Numbers: Total: c. 9,200

• UNIVERSITY OF NIGERIA

Nsukka, Enugu State
Tel: +234(42) 771-911
Fax: +234(42) 770-644
Telex: 51496 u-lions ng
Cable: nigersity nsukka
EMail: misun@aol.com

Vice-Chancellor (Acting): Ginigeme F. Mbanefoh (1998-)
Tel: +234(42) 770-095 Fax: +234(42) 771-997

Registrar (Acting): Grace I. Adichie Tel: +234(42) 771-920

Faculties

Agriculture *Dean:* Ignatius U. Obi

Arts (Archaeology; Arts and Humanities; Fine Arts; History; Modern Languages; Music; Performing Arts; Philosophy) *Dean:* Sylvanus A. Ekwelie

Biological Sciences (Biological and Life Sciences) *Dean:* Ogugua C. Nwankiti

Education *Dean:* Violet F. Harbor-Peters

Engineering (Civil Engineering; Electrical and Electronic Engineering; Engineering; Mechanical Engineering) *Dean:* David C. Onyejekwe

Pharmaceutical Sciences (Pharmacology; Pharmacy) *Dean:* Cletus N. Aguwa

Physical Sciences (Physics) *Dean:* Celestine O. Okogbue

Social Sciences (Anthropology; Economics; Political Science; Psychology; Social Sciences; Sociology) *Dean:* R.C. Bob-Duru, *full-time staff:* 185, *students:* 2,928

Veterinary Science *Dean:* Samuel N. Chiejina

Schools

Postgraduate Studies *Dean:* Charles C. Okafor

Departments

Adult Education and Extramural Studies *Head:* Judith D.C. Osuala

General Studies *Head:* Stephen O. Olaitan

Institutes

African Studies *Head:* Osmond O. Enekwe

Education *Director:* Anthony Ali

Centres

Energy Research and Development (Energy Engineering) *Director:* Samuel O. Onyegegbu

Rural Development and Cooperatives (Rural Studies) *Director:* Festus C. Obioha, *full-time staff:* 10

Further Information: Also 2 Teaching Hospitals

History: Founded 1960. The former Nigerian College of Arts, Science and Technology, Enugu, was incorporated into the University 1961 and its buildings now form the Enugu campus of the University.

Governing Bodies: Governing Council, comprising 17 members; Senate

Academic Year: March to December (March-June; June-December)

Admission Requirements: Universities Matriculation Examination (UME) following secondary school education, or direct entry for holders of the Higher School Certificate (General Certificate of Education, Advanced ('A') level)

Fees: (Naira): Tuition, undergraduate, 4,320-4980 per annum; postgraduate, 6,000-8,000; foreign students, African students, 8,000-16,000; students from Europe and North America, US$ 500-750

Main Language(s) of Instruction: English

International Co-operation: Michigan State University; Dublin University; Catholic University of Louvain; Colgate University

Degrees and Diplomas: *Bachelor's Degree*: 3-6 yrs; *Master's Degree*: a further 1-3 yrs; *Doctor of Philosophy*: (PhD), 2-5 yrs

Student Services: Academic Counselling, Nursery Care, Sports Facilities, Health Services, Canteen, Foreign Student Centre

Student Residential Facilities: for c. 11,230 students

Special Facilities: Zoo

Libraries: Nnamdi Azikiwe Library, c. 700,500 vols

Publications: Annual Report (annually); Undergraduate Prospectus; Calendar

Press or Publishing House: University of Nigeria Press Ltd; University of Nigeria Bookshop

Academic Staff *1999:* Total: **1,051**

Student Numbers 1999	MEN	WOMEN	TOTAL
All (Foreign Included)	–	–	**21,957**
FOREIGN ONLY	80	25	105

ENUGU CAMPUS
Enugu, Anambra State
Tel: +234 252-080
Cable: nigersity enugu
EMail: uinec@aol.com

Faculties

Business Administration *Dean:* Uche Modum

Environmental Studies *Dean:* Sammy I. Agajelu

Health Sciences and Technology (Health Sciences; Technology) *Dean:* Ernest O. Ukaejiofo

Law *Dean:* D.I.O. Ewelukwa

Colleges

Medical Sciences and Dentistry (Dentistry; Medicine) *Dean:* Martin A.C. Aghaji

Institutes

Development Studies *Director:* E.U.L. Imaga

• UNIVERSITY OF PORT HARCOURT

PMB 5323, Port Harcourt, Rivers State
Tel: +234(84) 330-883   +234(84) 335-218
Fax: +234(84) 230-903
Telex: 61183 phuni ng
Cable: university pharcourt

Vice-Chancellor: Nimi Briggs (2000-) Tel: +234(84) 230-902

Registrar (Acting): C.A. Tamuno

International Relations: C.U. Oyegun

Faculties

Education (Curriculum; Education; Educational Administration; Educational Psychology; Educational Technology) *Dean*: J.M. Kosemani

Engineering (Chemical Engineering; Civil Engineering; Electrical and Electronic Engineering; Engineering; Mechanical Engineering; Petroleum and Gas Engineering; Surveying and Mapping) *Dean*: I.L. Nwaogazie

Graduate *Dean*: E.N. Elechi

Humanities (Archaeology; Arts and Humanities; Fine Arts; History; Modern Languages; Theatre) *Dean*: C.E. Nnolim

Management Sciences (Business Administration; Management) *Dean*: D.O.N. Baridam

Science (Biochemistry; Botany; Chemistry; Geology; Natural Sciences; Physics; Zoology) *Dean*: E.S. Okoli

Social Sciences (Economics; Political Science; Social Sciences; Sociology) *Dean*: S. Ekpenyong

Colleges

Health Sciences (Anaesthesiology; Anatomy; Gynaecology and Obstetrics; Haematology; Health Sciences; Medicine; Microbiology; Paediatrics; Pathology; Pharmacology; Physiology; Psychiatry and Mental Health; Social and Preventive Medicine; Surgery) *Provost*: D.D. Datubo-Brown

Institutes

Agricultural Research Development (Agriculture) *Director*: N.H. Igwiloh

Education (Education; Educational Psychology) *Director*: J.M. Kosemani

History: Founded 1975 as University College, acquired present status 1977.

Academic Year: October to July (October-February; April-July)

Admission Requirements: Universities Matriculation Examination (UME) following secondary school education

Main Language(s) of Instruction: English

International Co-operation: University of Texas at Austin

Degrees and Diplomas: *Bachelor's Degree*: 2-6 yrs; *Master's Degree*: a further 1-2 yrs; *Doctor of Philosophy*: (PhD), 3 yrs following Master's Degree

Student Residential Facilities: Yes

Libraries: Total, 77,622 vols

Publications: News Bulletin (monthly); Kiabara: A Journal of the Humanities (biannually); Diary; Calendar; Prospectus

Press or Publishing House: University Press

Academic Staff *2000:* Total: **532**

Student Numbers *2000:* Total: **18,924**

• UNIVERSITY OF UYO

PMB 1017, Uyo, Akwa Ibom State
Tel: +234(85) 200-303   +234(85) 201-111
Fax: +234(85) 202-694
Cable: uniuyo
EMail: root@uniuyo.edu.ng

Vice-Chancellor: Afolabi Lasisi (1991-)
Tel: +234(85) 202-693 EMail: vc@uniuyo.edu.ng

Registrar: J.S. Aborisade Tel: +234(85) 202-699

International Relations: A.H. Ekpo

Faculties

Agriculture (Agricultural Economics; Agriculture; Agronomy; Animal Husbandry; Fishery; Forestry) *Dean*: Okon A. Ansa

Arts (Arts and Humanities; Communication Arts; English; History; Modern Languages; Music; Philosophy; Religious Studies; Theatre) *Dean*: Ime S. Ikiddeh

Business Administration (Business Administration; Hotel Management; Tourism) *Dean*: E.R. Iwok, *full-time staff:* 36, *part-time staff:* 12, *students:* 1,198

Education (Curriculum; Education; Educational Administration; Educational and Student Counselling; Educational Technology; Health Education; Physical Education; Preschool Education; Science Education; Vocational Education) *Dean*: Okon E. Ekpo, *full-time staff:* 80, *part-time staff:* 12, *students:* 1,423

Law *Dean*: Osita C. Eze

Natural and Applied Sciences (Biochemistry; Botany; Brewing; Chemistry; Computer Science; Mathematics; Microbiology; Natural Sciences; Physics; Statistics; Zoology) *Dean*: Tunde Bamgboye

Pharmacy (Pharmacology; Pharmacy) *Dean*: E.E. Essien

Social Sciences (Anthropology; Economics; Geography (Human); Political Science; Public Administration; Social Sciences) *Dean*: Akpan H. Ekpo

Centres
Development Studies

Further Information: Also Commercial Farm; Educational Technology Unit; Science laboratory Technology Training Unit

History: Founded 1983 as University of Cross River State. Acquired present status and title 1991.

Governing Bodies: Council; Senate

Academic Year: January to October (January-May; July-October)

Admission Requirements: Senior Secondary Certificate/West African School Certificate/General Certificate of Education (GCE), Ordinary ('O') level, or equivalent, with credit passes in at least 5 subjects, including English Language. Credit pass in Mathematics is required for Science-based and Social Science Courses

Fees: None

Main Language(s) of Instruction: English

Degrees and Diplomas: *National Diploma*: Fine Arts; French; Public Administration; Theatre Arts; *Bachelor's Degree*: Arts (BA); Education (BEd); Science (BSc); Science Education (BScEd), 4 yrs; Agriculture (BAgr); Forestry (BForestry); Law (LLB); Pharmacy (BPharm), 5 yrs; *Master's Degree*: a further

1-2 yrs; *Doctor of Philosophy*: (PhD), a further 3-4 yrs. Also Engineering and Environmental Courses, 5 yrs

Student Residential Facilities: Yes

Special Facilities: Geographical Observatory

Libraries: c. 44,150 vols

Academic Staff: Full-Time: c. 595 Part-Time: c. 115 Total: c. 710

Staff with Doctorate: Total: c. 295

Student Numbers: All (Foreign Included): c. 14,150 Foreign Only: c. 90

• USMANU DANFODIYO UNIVERSITY SOKOTO

PMB 2346, Sokoto
Tel: +234(60) 233-221   +234(60) 234-039
Fax: +234(60) 236-688
Telex: 73134 udusok, nigeria
Cable: udusok, sokoto

Vice-Chancellor: Aminu Salihu Mikailu (1999-2004)
Tel: +234(60) 236-688 Fax: +234(60) 235-519
EMail: vc@udusok.edu.ng

Registrar: Abubakar Usman

Faculties
Arts and Islamic Studies (Arts and Humanities; Islamic Studies; Modern Languages) *Dean*: Mohammed Dangana
Education and Extension Services (Education) *Dean*: F.A. Kalgo
Law (Islamic Law; Law) *Dean*: M.I. Said
Science (Biochemistry; Chemistry; Mathematics; Natural Sciences; Physics) *Dean*: Usman Abubakar
Social Sciences and Administration (Administration; Economics; Management; Political Science; Social Sciences; Sociology) *Dean*: S.A. Diyo
Veterinary Science *Dean*: A.I. Daneji

Colleges
Health Sciences *Provost*: E.E.K. Opara

Centres
Energy Research *(Sokoto)* (Energy Engineering)
Islamic Studies

Bureaus
University Translation *(UNESCO)* (Translation and Interpretation)

Further Information: Also Teaching Hospital

History: Founded 1975 as University of Sokoto, acquired present title 1985.

Governing Bodies: Council; Senate

Academic Year: November to July (November-March; March-July)

Admission Requirements: Universities Matriculation Examination (UME) following secondary school education, or direct entry for holders of the Higher School Certificate (General Certificate of Education, Advanced ('A') level)

Fees: (Naira): Foreign students, postgraduate, 5000-7000 per annum

Main Language(s) of Instruction: English, Hausa, Arabic

Degrees and Diplomas: *Bachelor's Degree*: 3 yrs; *Master's Degree*: a further 1-2 yrs; *Doctor of Philosophy*: (PhD), a further 3-5 yrs

Libraries: 233,000 vols; 3699 periodicals

Publications: Calendar; Prospectus

Press or Publishing House: University Press

Academic Staff: Total: c. 310

Student Numbers: Total: c. 7,080

OTHER INSTITUTIONS

AKANU IBIAM FEDERAL POLYTECHNIC, UNMANA

PMB 1007, Afikpo, Abia State
Tel: +234(88) 521-574

Rector: Zak A. Obanu

Schools
Business (Business Administration)
Engineering
Science and General Studies (Mathematics and Computer Science; Natural Sciences)

History: Founded 1981.

BENUE STATE POLYTECHNIC, UGBOKOLO

PMB 2215, Otukpo, Benue State

Rector: Y.W. Awodi
Registrar: D.O. Ona

Schools
Art and Design (Design; Fine Arts)
Business and Administration (Administration; Business and Commerce)
Engineering
Technology

History: Founded 1976.

FEDERAL POLYTECHNIC, ADO-EKITI

PMB 5351, Ado-Ekiti, Ekiti State
Tel: +234(30) 250-523

Rector: G.O.S. Adejinmi
Registrar: A.B. Omodele

Schools
Business Studies (Business and Commerce)
Engineering
Environmental Studies
Science and Computer Studies (Computer Science)

347

History: Founded 1977.

FEDERAL POLYTECHNIC, AUCHI

PMB 13, Auchi, Edo State
Tel: +234(57) 200-148

Schools

Applied Sciences and Technology (Applied Chemistry; Applied Mathematics; Applied Physics; Computer Science; Engineering; Technology)
Art and Design (Design; Fine Arts)
Business Studies (Business and Commerce)
Engineering
Environmental Studies

History: Founded 1973.

FEDERAL POLYTECHNIC, BAUCHI

PMB 0231, Bauchi, Bauchi State
Tel: +234(77) 543-630
Fax: +234(77) 540-465
Telex: 83273
Website: http://www.bauchipoly.edu.ng

Rector: M.L.I.S. Jahun (2000-) Tel: +234(77) 543-487
Fax: +234(77) 541-393 EMail: rector@bauchipoly.edu.ng
Registrar: Y.M. Maskano Tel: +234(77) 543-481
EMail: registrar@bauchipoly.edu.ng

Schools

Business Studies (Business Administration; Management) *Director:* R.C. Mamman, *full-time staff: 31, students: 1,252*
Engineering Technology (Engineering; Graphic Design; Industrial Design) *Director:* Samuel Sule, *full-time staff: 52, students: 456*
Environmental Studies *Director:* J.K. Tumba, *full-time staff: 29, students: 273*
General Studies (Teacher Training) *Director:* Ishaya Ludu, *full-time staff: 42, students: 655*
Technology (Engineering; Management; Technology) *Director:* I.S. Shinga, *full-time staff: 56, students: 266*

History: Founded 1979.

Governing Bodies: Governing Council

Academic Year: October to June (October-February; March-June)

Admission Requirements: Higher school certificate, with 4 passes including English and Mathematics

Main Language(s) of Instruction: English

Accrediting Agencies: National Board for Technical Education (NBTE)

Degrees and Diplomas: *National Diploma:* 2 yrs; *Higher National Diploma:* 2 yrs

Student Residential Facilities: Yes (limited)

Libraries: Central Library

Publications: Prospectus (biannually); Annual Report (annually)

Academic Staff *2000*	MEN	WOMEN	TOTAL
FULL-TIME	174	44	**218**
STAFF WITH DOCTORATE			
FULL-TIME	2	1	**3**
Student Numbers *2000*	MEN	WOMEN	TOTAL
All (Foreign Included)	1,967	935	**2,902**

Part-time Students, 466 **Evening Students,** 466

FEDERAL POLYTECHNIC, BIDA

PMB 55, Bida, Niger State
Tel: +234(66) 461-707

Rector: Umaru Sani-Ango
Registrar: S.F. Iko

Schools

Applied Arts and Science (Fine Arts; Natural Sciences)
Business and Management (Business and Commerce; Management)
Engineering
Environmental Studies
Preliminary Studies

History: Founded 1977.

FEDERAL POLYTECHNIC, IDAH

PMB 1037, Idah, Kogi State
Tel: +234(58) 800-128

Rector: Y.W. Awodi
Registrar: S.A. Ogunleye

Schools

Business Studies (Business and Commerce)
Engineering
General Studies
Metallurgy and Materials Technology (Materials Engineering; Metallurgical Engineering)
Technology

Departments

Accountancy
Business Administration
Civil Engineering
Continuing Education
Electrical Engineering
Food Technology
Foundry Technology (Industrial Engineering)
Hotel and Catering Management (Hotel and Restaurant)
Languages and Liberal Studies (Artificial Intelligence; Modern Languages)
Marketing
Mathematics and Statistics (Mathematics; Statistics)
Mechanical Engineering
Metallurgy (Metallurgical Engineering)
Science Technology (Technology)
Secretarial Studies
Social Science and Humanities (Arts and Humanities; Social Sciences)
Surveying (Surveying and Mapping)

History: Founded 1977.

FEDERAL POLYTECHNIC, ILARO

PMB 50, Ilaro, Ogun State
Tel: +234(39) 440-005

Rector: S.A. Olateru-Olagbegi

Registrar: R.O. Egbeyemi

Schools

Applied Sciences (Applied Chemistry; Applied Mathematics; Applied Physics; Computer Science; Engineering; Natural Sciences)
Business Studies (Business and Commerce)
Engineering

History: Founded 1979.

FEDERAL POLYTECHNIC, KAURA NAMODA

PMB 1012, Kaura Namoda, Sokoto State

Schools

Business Management (Management)
Engineering
Environmental Studies
General Studies
Science and Technology (Natural Sciences; Technology)

History: Founded 1983.

FEDERAL POLYTECHNIC, MUBI (FPM)

PMB 35, Mubi, Adamawa State
Tel: +234(75) 882-771

Rector: Aminu Muhammad Tel: +234(75) 882-771

Registrar: Bello Buba Tel: +234(75) 882-529

International Relations: Bakari Inuwa

Colleges

Technology (Business Administration; Engineering; Technology) *Rector*: Aminu Muhammad, *full-time staff:* 716, *part-time staff:* 8, *students:* 2,156

History: Founded 1979.

Governing Bodies: Governing Council

Admission Requirements: Higher school certificate, with 4 passes in relevant subjects, including Mathematics and English

Main Language(s) of Instruction: English

Accrediting Agencies: National Board for Technical Education

Degrees and Diplomas: *National Diploma*: Engineering and Management (ND), 2 yrs; *Higher National Diploma*: Engineering and Management (HND), 2 yrs

Student Services: Academic Counselling, Social Counselling, Employment Services, Nursery Care, Sports Facilities, Health Services, Canteen

Academic Staff 2000	MEN	WOMEN	TOTAL
FULL-TIME	163	27	190
PART-TIME	8	–	8
TOTAL	**171**	**27**	**198**

Staff with doctorate: Total: **1**

Student Numbers 2000: Total: **2,156**

FEDERAL POLYTECHNIC, NEKEDE

PMB 1036, Owerri, Imo State
Tel: +234(83) 231-516

Rector: C.I. Osuoji

Registrar: G.T.U. Chiaha

Schools

Business and Public Administration (Business Administration; Public Administration)
Engineering and Technology (Engineering; Technology)
Environmental Design (Environmental Studies)
General Studies
Industrial Sciences (Industrial Engineering)

History: Founded 1978 as College of Technology, Owerri. Acquired present status and title 1993.

Governing Bodies: Federal Ministry of Education

Admission Requirements: General Certificate of Education; West African School Certificate with 4 passes

Fees: (Nairas): 2000 per session; evening, 3200

Main Language(s) of Instruction: English

Accrediting Agencies: National Board for Technical Education (NBTE)

Degrees and Diplomas: *National Diploma*: 2 yrs; *Higher National Diploma*: 2 yrs

Student Residential Facilities: For men and women students

Libraries: Central Library

Publications: Fedpno Bulletin, News and Information (quarterly)

Academic Staff 2000	MEN	WOMEN	TOTAL
FULL-TIME	121	21	**142**
STAFF WITH DOCTORATE FULL-TIME	10	1	**11**
Student Numbers 2000	MEN	WOMEN	TOTAL
All (Foreign Included)	2,818	2,875	**5,693**

Evening Students, 678

FEDERAL POLYTECHNIC, OKO

PMB 21, Aguata, Anambra State
Tel: +234(48) 911-144

Rector: U.C. Nzewi

Registrar: O.C.A. Ofochebe

Accountancy; Architecture; Banking; Building Technologies; Business Administration; Environmental Studies; Information Technology; Library Science; Marketing; Mass Communication; Secretarial Studies; Technology

History: Founded 1979.

HASSAN USMAN KATSINA POLYTECHNIC
PMB 2052, Katsina, Katsina State
Tel: +234(65) 32816

Colleges
Administration and Management (Administration; Business Administration; Management; Public Administration)
Legal and General Studies (Islamic Law; Law; Modern Languages; Private Law; Public Law)
Science and Technology (Agriculture; Applied Chemistry; Applied Mathematics; Applied Physics; Civil Engineering; Computer Science; Electrical Engineering; Engineering; Food Science; Hotel Management; Mathematics; Mechanical Engineering; Natural Sciences; Surveying and Mapping; Technology)

History: Founded 1983.

INSTITUTE OF MANAGEMENT AND TECHNOLOGY
PMB 01079, Enugu, Enugu State
Tel: +234(42) 250-416

Rector: C.C. Njeze
Registrar: C.A. Attah

Schools
Business Studies (Business and Commerce)
Communication Arts
Continuing Education and Distance Learning
Engineering
Financial Studies (Finance)
General Studies
Science, Vocational and Technical Education (Science Education; Technology Education; Vocational Education)
Technology

History: Founded 1973.

KADUNA POLYTECHNIC
PMB 2021, Kaduna, Kaduna State
Tel: +234(62) 211-551
EMail: mis@kadpoly.edu.ng
Website: http://www.kadpoly.edu.ng

Rector (Acting): J.D.J. Dashe
Registrar: Alh. Garba I. Bakori

Colleges
Administrative and Business Studies (Administration; Business and Commerce)
Engineering
Environmental Studies
Science and Technology (Natural Sciences; Technology)

History: Founded 1956 as Kaduna Technical Institute. Acquired present status and title 1968.

KANO STATE POLYTECHNIC
PMB 3401, Kano, Kano State
Tel: +234(64) 625-658

Schools
Agriculture *(Audo Bako)*
Islamic Legal Studies *(Aminu)* (Islamic Law; Islamic Studies)
Management Studies (Management)
Social and Rural Development (Rural Studies; Social Studies)
Technology

History: Founded 1976.

KEBBI STATE POLYTECHNIC
PMB 1034, Birnin Kebbi, Kebbi State

Schools
Accounting and Finance (Accountancy; Finance)
Business and Public Administration (Business Administration; Public Administration)
Environmental Design (Environmental Studies)
Industrial Engineering
Natural Resources Engineering (Engineering; Natural Resources)
Science (Mathematics and Computer Science; Natural Sciences)
Surveying and Land Administration (Surveying and Mapping)
Vocational and Technical Education

History: Founded 1976.

KWARA STATE POLYTECHNIC
PMB 1375, Ilorin, Kwara State
Tel: +234(31) 221-441

Institutes
Administration
Basic and Applied Sciences (Applied Chemistry; Applied Mathematics; Applied Physics; Computer Science; Engineering; Natural Sciences)
Business and Vocational Studies (Business Administration)
Environmental Studies
General Studies
Technology

History: Founded 1972.

LAGOS STATE POLYTECHNIC
PMB 21606, Ikeja, Lagos State
Tel: +234(65) 523-528
Natural Sciences; Technology

History: Founded 1977.

350

OGUN STATE POLYTECHNIC

PMB 2210, Abeokuta, Ogun State
Tel: +234(39) 231-274

Departments
Accountancy
Architecture
Business Administration
Business Studies (Business and Commerce)
Civil Engineering
Continuing Education
Electrical and Electronic Engineering
Estate Management (Real Estate)
Financial Studies (Finance)
Food Science and Technology (Food Science; Food Technology)
Liberal Studies (Arts and Humanities)
Marketing
Mass Communication
Science Laboratory Technology (Laboratory Techniques)
Secretarial Studies
Town and Regional Planning (Regional Planning; Town Planning)

History: Founded 1977.

ONDO STATE POLYTECHNIC

PMB 1019, Owo, Ondo State

Colleges
Business Studies (Business and Commerce)
Engineering
Environmental Studies
Food Technology

History: Founded 1980

PETROLEUM TRAINING INSTITUTE

PMB 20, Effurun, Delta State

Departments
Electrical and Electronic Engineering
General Studies
Industrial Continuing Education
Industrial Safety and Environmental Engineering (Environmental Engineering; Safety Engineering)
Mechanical Engineering
Petroleum Engineering and Geosciences (Earth Sciences; Geological Engineering; Petroleum and Gas Engineering)
Petroleum Processing Technology (Petroleum and Gas Engineering)
Welding and Underwater Operations (Hydraulic Engineering; Metal Techniques)

History: Founded 1972.

PLATEAU STATE POLYTECHNIC, BARKIN LADI

PMB 02023, Barakin Ladi, Buruku, Plateau State

Rector: Alexander A.T. Kebang

Registrar: Timothy A. Anjide

Schools
Administration and General Studies (Administration)
Engineering and Environmental Studies (Engineering; Environmental Studies)
Management Studies (Management)
Science and Technology (Mathematics and Computer Science; Natural Sciences; Technology)

History: Founded 1978.

POLYTECHNIC, CALABAR

PMB 1110, Calabar, Cross River State
Tel: +234(87) 222-303

Rector: R.E. Ekanem

Registrar: G.F.A. Onugba

Schools
Agriculture
Applied Sciences (Natural Sciences)
Business and Management (Business and Commerce; Management)
Communication Arts
Education
Engineering
Environmental Studies

Centres
Computer Science
Continuing Education
General and Preliminary Studies
Industrial Co-ordination and Public Relations (Industrial Management; Public Relations)

History: Founded 1973

POLYTECHNIC, IBADAN

PMB 22, U.I. Post Office, Ibadan, Oyo State
Tel: +234(22) 410-451
Telex: 31222 polyib ng

Rector: A.O. Alabi

Registrar: R.G. Olayiwola

Business and Commerce; Communication Studies; Engineering; Environmental Studies; Natural Sciences; Teacher Training

History: Founded 1960, acquired present status and title 1970.

YABA COLLEGE OF TECHNOLOGY

PMB 2011, Yaba, Lagos State
Tel: +234(1) 800-160
Fax: +234(1) 860-211
Cable: tekinst
EMail: yabatech@anpa.net.ng
Website: http://www.yabatech.edu.ng

Rector: F.A. Odugbesan EMail: rector@yabatech.edu.ng

Registrar (Acting): F.F. Taiwo

Programmes

Technical Teachers Training (Teacher Training)

Schools

Applied Sciences (Applied Chemistry; Applied Mathematics; Applied Physics; Computer Science; Engineering)

Art, Design and Printing (Design; Fine Arts; Printing and Printmaking)

Engineering

Environmental Studies

Management and Business Studies (Business Administration; Management)

History: Founded 1947.

Rwanda

INSTITUTION TYPES AND CREDENTIALS

Types of higher education institutions:

Université (University)
Institut (Institute)

School leaving and higher education credentials:

Diplôme de Fin d'Etudes secondaires
Technicien supérieur
Baccalauréat
Bachelor's Degree
Diplôme d'Ingénieur des Travaux statistiques
Diplôme d'Ingénieur
Maîtrise
Docteur en Médecine

STRUCTURE OF EDUCATION SYSTEM

Pre-higher education:

Duration of compulsory education:

    Age of entry: 7
    Age of exit: 13

Structure of school system:

    Primary
    Type of school providing this education: Primary School
    Length of programme in years: 6
    Age level from: 7 to: 13
    Certificate/diploma awarded: Certificat national de sixième Année primaire (competitive examination)

    First Cycle Secondary
    Type of school providing this education: Tronc commun/Cycle d'Orientation
    Length of programme in years: 3
    Age level from: 13 to: 16

    Second Cycle Secondary
    Type of school providing this education: Sections moyennes générales
    Length of programme in years: 3

Age level from: 16 to: 19
Certificate/diploma awarded: Diplôme de Fin d'Etudes secondaires

School education:

Primary education is compulsory and lasts for six years. There is a competitive entrance examination at the end, the Certificat national de sixième Année primaire, to enter secondary school. Secondary education is divided into two three-year cycles. The first cycle is common to all pupils. The second cycle covers Modern or Classical Humanities. On successful completion of the second cycle, pupils are awarded the Diplôme de Fin d'Etudes secondaires. There is a variety of two-year technical secondary courses for pupils who have completed two to three years of academic secondary education, although pupils could also enter directly from primary school. Four-year technical courses are also offered.

Higher education:

Higher education is mainly provided by universities and specialized institutes, both public and private. Most institutions of higher education come under the jurisdiction of the Ministère de l'Education. The National University of Rwanda is an autonomous institution governed by a Council which is made up of a representative of the President of the Republic, the Minister of Education, the Rector and deans, the Secretary-General, the Treasurer and the Administrator. The Council proposes the creation of faculties, institutes, centres of research and university extension. It establishes the budget of the University and approves grants and donations. The Academic Senate coordinates academic activities. Members include the Vice-Rector, the deans of faculties, the heads of institutes, tenured professors and student representatives. The President of the Republic is Honorary President of the University. The Rector of the University is nominated by the President of the Republic for a three-year term which can be renewed, as are the Secretary-General and the Treasurer.

Main laws/decrees governing higher education:

Decree: Loi organique N° 1/1985 sur l'Education nationale   Year: 1985
Concerns: Organization of Education

Academic year:

Classes from: September *to:* June

Languages of instruction:

French

Stages of studies:

Non-university level post-secondary studies (technical/vocational type):

Higher technical and vocational studies are offered in universities and vocational institutions in Finance, Management, Computer Studies, Statistics, Economics and Secretarial Studies. Studies consist in short-term technical and professional education and lead to the title of Technicien supérieur after two years in Accountancy, Management, Computer Studies, to the title of Ingénieur technicien or Diplôme d'Ingénieur des Travaux statistiques after three years in Statistics at the Statistics Institute.

University level studies:

University level first stage: *Premier Cycle*:

The first stage of university-level studies lasts for two years (to be extended to three years) and leads to the Baccalauréat in Law, Science, Letters, Economics, Social Sciences, Human Biology, Management, Agriculture, Education, Nutrition, Public Health, and Pharmacy. In Engineering, the Baccalauréat takes three years.

University level second stage: *Deuxième Cycle*:

The second stage lasts between two and four years and leads to the Licence (to be changed to Maîtrise) or to the title of Ingénieur agronome or Ingénieur civil (five years). The title of Docteur en Médecine is conferred after a total of seven years' study (one year of general studies in the Faculty of Science and two years' general study in the Faculty of Medicine, followed by four years of specialization).

Teacher education:

Training of pre-primary and primary/basic school teachers

Primary school teachers are trained in secondary school teacher training institutions (Ecoles normales primaires) in a three-year post-tronc commun course (nine years of schooling). They obtain an A2 Diploma.

Training of secondary school teachers

Secondary school teachers are trained in four years at the Faculty of Education of the Université nationale du Rwanda where they obtain the Agrégation. They may also follow refresher courses. Since 1999, secondary school teachers are also trained at the new Institut supérieur de Pédagogie (ISP) of Kigali. Training at ISP include two cycles: for admission to the first, students must hold a Diplôme de Fin d'Etudes secondaires. For the second cycle, they must hold a Baccalauréat in Pedagogy.

Training of higher education teachers

Higher education teachers are trained at the Université nationale du Rwanda. They must hold a Maitrîse or a Doctorat. They often go abroad to complete their training.

Non-traditional studies:

Lifelong higher education

Continuing education is mainly offered by the Extension Study Centre of the National University. It consists essentially in evening classes.

NATIONAL BODIES

Responsible authorities:

Ministry of Education (Ministère de l'Education (Mineduc))
   Minister: Emmanuel Mudidi
   PO Box 624
   Kigali

Tel: +250 82-745
Fax: +250 82-162

ADMISSIONS TO HIGHER EDUCATION

Admission to non university higher education studies

Name of secondary school credential required: Diplôme de Fin d'Etudes secondaires

Admission to university-level studies

Name of secondary school credential required: Diplôme de Fin d'Etudes secondaires

Foreign students admission

Admission requirements: Foreign students must hold a secondary school leaving certificate or an equivalent qualification. They must pay registration fees that are higher than those payed by nationals.

Entry regulations: Students must have a valid passport, a visa, financial guarantees.

Health requirements: Students must have a health certificate

Language requirements: Students must be fluent in French but should also have some knowledge of English.

Application procedures:

Apply to: Université nationale du Rwanda
   PO Box 56
   Butare
   Tel: +250 530122
   Fax: +250 530121
   EMail: rectorat@nur.ac.rw
   WWW: http://www.nur.ac.rw

Recognition of studies and qualifications:

Studies pursued in foreign countries (bodies dealing with recognition of foreign credentials):
Ministry of Education (Ministère de l'Education (Mineduc))
   Minister: Emmanuel Mudidi
   PO Box 624
   Kigali
   Tel: +250 82-745
   Fax: +250 82-162

   Deals with credential recognition for entry to: University

Multilateral agreements concerning recognition of foreign studies

Name(s) of agreement(s): Convention on the Recognition of Studies,Certificates, Diplomas, Degrees and Other Academic Qualifications in Higher Education in the African States
Year of signature: 1981

References to further information on foreign student admissions and recognition of studies

Title: Annuaire de l'Université
Publisher: Université nationale du Rwanda

Title: Guide de l'Etudiant
Publisher: Université nationale du Rwanda

GRADING SYSTEM

Usual grading system in secondary school

Full Description: 50%-90%
Highest on scale: 90% plus grande distinction
Pass/fail level: 50% satisfaction

Main grading system used by higher education institutions

Full Description: 50%-90%
Highest on scale: 90% plus grande distinction
Pass/fail level: 50%-69% satisfaction

NOTES ON HIGHER EDUCATION SYSTEM

Data for academic year: 2000-2001
Source: International Association of Universities (IAU), updated from IBE website, 2001

INSTITUTIONS OF HIGHER EDUCATION

UNIVERSITIES

PUBLIC INSTITUTIONS

*• NATIONAL UNIVERSITY OF RWANDA
Université nationale du Rwanda
BP 56, Butaré
Tel: +250 530-122   +250 530-302
Fax: +250 530-121   +250 530-858
EMail: rectorat@nur.ac.rw
Website: http://www.nur.ac.rw
Recteur: Emile Rwamasirabo (1998-) Tel: +250 30121
Vice-Recteur académique: Jean-Bosco Butera

Faculties
Agronomy (Agronomy; Animal Husbandry; Crop Production; Rural Studies; Soil Science) *Dean*: Salvator Kaburungu
Arts and Humanities (African Studies; Arts and Humanities; English; French Studies; Geography; History; Literature) *Dean*: Deo Byanafashe
Economics Management and Social Sciences (Accountancy; Anthropology; Banking; Business Administration; Development Studies; Economics; Finance; Human Resources; International Business; Management; Marketing; Political Science; Public Administration; Social Sciences; Social Work; Sociology; Tourism; Transport and Communications) *Dean*: Gérard Rutazibwa
Education (Arts and Humanities; Continuing Education; Education; Educational Sciences; Pedagogy; Psychology; Science Education) *Dean*: Ferdinand Kayoboke
Law (Administration; Business and Commerce; Economics; Law) *Dean*: J.M. Kamatali
Medicine (Anaesthesiology; Anatomy; Biochemistry; Biology; Chemistry; Entomology; Epidemiology; Ethics; Gynaecology and Obstetrics; Immunology; Medical Technology; Medicine; Orthopedics; Paediatrics; Pharmacology; Philosophy; Physics; Physiology; Psychology; Surgery; Virology) *Dean*: Emmanuel Gasakure
Science and Technology (Biology; Chemistry; Civil Engineering; Computer Science; Electronic Engineering; Mathematics; Mechanical Engineering; Natural Sciences; Pharmacy; Physics; Technology) *Dean*: Safari Bonfils

Schools
Journalism and Communication *(ESTI)* (Journalism; Mass Communication)
Modern Languages *(EPLM)* (English; French; Modern Languages) *Director (Acting)*: Ildephonse Kereni
Public Health and Nutrition *(ESPN)* (Nutrition; Public Health) *Director*: Munyanshongore Cyprien

Centres
Conflict Management (Peace and Disarmament)
Mental Health *(UCMH)* (Psychiatry and Mental Health)

History: Founded 1963 as a national institution and its initial organization and direction entrusted to the Dominican Order, Province of St. Dominic, Canada. Reorganized 1976 and Institut pédagogique national incorporated 1981.

Governing Bodies: Conseil universitaire, including a representative of the President of the Republic, the Minister of Education, the Rector, Vice-Rector and Deans; Sénat académique; Conseil de Faculté

Academic Year: May to February (May-September; October-February)

Admission Requirements: Secondary school certificate (Diplôme des Humanités complètes) or equivalent, or foreign equivalent

Fees: (Rwanda Francs): c. 3800 per annum; foreign students, c. 2800 plus 1000 per credit

Main Language(s) of Instruction: French, English

International Co-operation: University of Burundi; University of Sheffield; Autonomous University of Madrid; University of Quebec at Montreal; University of Alabama; Université libre des Grands Lacs, Goma

Degrees and Diplomas: *Baccalauréat*: Agriculture; Economics; Education; Human Biology; Law; Letters; Management; Nutrition; Pharmacy; Public Health; Science; Social Sciences, 2 yrs; *Diplôme d'Ingénieur*: Engineering, 3 yrs; Agriculture, 5 yrs; *Maîtrise*: Economics; Education; Law; Letters; Management; Pharmacy; Science; Social Sciences, 4-5 yrs; *Docteur en Médecine*: Médecine, 6 yrs

Student Services: Social Counselling, Employment Services, Nursery Care, Cultural Centre, Handicapped Facilities, Health Services, Canteen

Student Residential Facilities: For c. 1620 students

Libraries: Central Library, 169,209 vols; Faculty of Medicine, 13,310

Academic Staff 1999: Full-Time: c. 165 Part-Time: c. 360 Total: c. 525

Student Numbers 1999: All (Foreign Included): c. 4,180 Foreign Only: c. 95

Evening Students, c. 2,560

PRIVATE INSTITUTIONS

ADVENTIST UNIVERSITY IN RWANDA
Université adventiste au Rwanda
BP 2461, Kigali
Tel: +250 86616
Fax: +250 87147
EMail: aum@maf.org

Recteur: Gerald Vyhmeister Tel: +250 83718
EMail: geraldvyh@maf.org
Administrateur-Trésorier: Moses Banuag Tel: +250 85677
EMail: mbanuag@juno.com
International Relations: Gerald Vyhmeister
EMail: geraldvyh@maf.org

Faculties
Business and Administration (Administration; Business and Commerce)
Education
Theology

History: Founded 1984.
Governing Bodies: Senate; Executive Committee
Academic Year: January to December (January-April; May-August; September-December)
Admission Requirements: Secondary school certificate or equivalent, or foreign equivalent
Fees: (Rwanda Francs) c. 49,600-89,280 per semester
Main Language(s) of Instruction: French
Degrees and Diplomas: *Bachelor's Degree*: Business Administration; Education; Theology, 4 yrs
Student Residential Facilities: For c. 400 students
Libraries: 17,500 vols
Academic Staff *1999*: Full-Time: c. 10 Part-Time: c. 20 Total: c. 30
Student Numbers *1999*: All (Foreign Included): c. 150 Foreign Only: c. 5

OTHER INSTITUTIONS

INSTITUT AFRICAIN ET MAURICIEN DE STATISTIQUES ET D'ÉCONOMIE APPLIQUÉE
BP 1109, Kigali
Tel: +250 84989
Economics; Statistics

History: Founded 1976

INSTITUT SAINT FIDÈLE (ECOLE SUPÉRIEURE DE GESTION ET D'INFORMATION)
BP 210, Gisenyi
Tel: +250 40306
Information Sciences; Management

History: Founded 1985

• INSTITUT DES SCIENCES, DE TECHNOLOGIE ET DE GESTION DE KIGALI
BP 3900, Avenue de l'Armée, Kigali
Tel: +250 74696 +250 71931
Fax: +250 71925 +250 71924
EMail: kist@avu.org; kist@rwandatel.rwandal.com
Recteur: Silas Lwakabamba
Management; Mathematics and Computer Science; Natural Sciences; Technology

INSTITUT SUPÉRIEUR CATHOLIQUE DE PÉDAGOGIE APPLIQUÉE
BP 37, Ruhengeri
Pedagogy

History: Founded 1986

INSTITUT SUPÉRIEUR D'AGRICULTURE ET D'ÉLEVAGE DE BUSOGO
BP 210, Ruhengeri
Tel: +250 46045
Agriculture; Cattle Breeding

History: Founded 1989

INSTITUT SUPÉRIEUR DES FINANCES PUBLIQUES
BP 1514, Kigali
Tel: +250 72513
Public Administration; Taxation

History: Founded 1986

Senegal

INSTITUTION TYPES AND CREDENTIALS

Types of higher education institutions:

Université (University)
Grande Ecole (Higher School)
Ecole normale supérieure (Teacher Training College)
Ecole supérieure de Technologie (Technological College)
Institut (Institute)

School leaving and higher education credentials:

Baccalauréat
Baccalauréat technique
Capacité en Droit
Diplôme d'Etudes économiques générales (DEEG)
Diplôme d'Etudes juridiques générales (DEJG)
Diplôme d'Etudes universitaires générales (DEUG)
Diplôme universitaire d'Etudes littéraires (DUEL)
Diplôme universitaire d'Etudes scientifiques (DUES)
Diplôme universitaire de Technologie (DUT)
Certificat d'Aptitude à l'Enseignement dans les Collèges d'Enseignement moyen
Diplôme de Bibliothécaire/Archiviste/Documentaliste
Diplôme supérieur de Journalisme
Licence
Section des Normaliens-Instituteurs
Certificat d'Aptitude à l'Enseignement moyen
Certificat d'Aptitude à l'Enseignement moyen technique et professionnel
Certificat d'Aptitude aux fonctions de Professeur d'Education physique et sportive
Diplôme d'Ingénieur
Diplôme de Pharmacien
Maîtrise
Certificat d'Aptitude à l'Enseignement secondaire
Certificat d'Aptitude à l'Enseignement secondaire technique et professionnel
Certificat d'Aptitude aux fonctions de Psychologue-Conseiller
Certificat d'Etudes supérieures
Diplôme d'Etat de Docteur
Diplôme d'Etudes supérieures spécialisées (DESS)
Diplôme supérieur en Sciences de l'Information

Diplôme d'Etudes Approfondies (DEA)
Certificat d' Etudes spéciales (CES)
Doctorat d'Ingénieur
Doctorat de Troisième Cycle
Doctorat d'Etat

STRUCTURE OF EDUCATION SYSTEM

Pre-higher education:

Structure of school system:

Primary
Type of school providing this education: Ecole élémentaire
Length of programme in years: 6
Age level from: 6 to: 12
Certificate/diploma awarded: Certificat de Fin d'Etudes élémentaires (CFEE) and competitive examination

Middle Secondary
Type of school providing this education: Collège d'Enseignement général (CEG); Collège d'Enseignement moyen (CEM); Lycée.
Length of programme in years: 4
Age level from: 12 to: 16
Certificate/diploma awarded: Brevet de Fin d'Etudes moyennes (BFEM)

Technical Secondary
Length of programme in years: 3
Age level from: 16 to: 19
Certificate/diploma awarded: Brevet de Technicien du Développement rural (BTDR)/de l'Industrie (BTI)/de Maintenance hospitalière (BTMH).

Upper Secondary
Type of school providing this education: Lycée d'Enseignement général or Lycée Technique
Length of programme in years: 3
Age level from: 16 to: 19
Certificate/diploma awarded: Baccalauréat/Baccalauréat Technique

Vocational
Type of school providing this education: Centre de Formation professionnelle
Length of programme in years: 3
Age level from: 16 to: 19
Certificate/diploma awarded: Brevet d'Etudes Professionnelles (BEP):After 2 yrs/Certificat d'Aptitude Professionnelle (CAP)/Brevet Professionnel (BP)

School education:

Primary education lasts for six years, leading to the Certificat de Fin d'Etudes élémentaires (CFEE). Secondary schooling lasts for seven years, divided into four-year lower secondary and three-year upper secondary education. The lower cycle (called "moyen") is offered by CEGs and CEMs (lower secondary only) or Lycées, and ends with the Brevet de Fin d'Etudes moyennes (BFEM). The three-year upper cycle has four options (general, short and long technical and professionnal) and ends with the Baccalauréat, which may be taken in five series depending on the specialization taken in the last two years. In technical tracks, the Centres de Formation professionnelle train non-BFEM holders in three years leading to a CAP, and BFEM holders in two years leading to a Brevet d'Etudes professionnelles (BEP). One further year leads to the Brevet professionnel (BP). In Lycées techniques, three years' upper secondary education lead to a Baccalauréat technique. The Baccalauréat gives access to higher education. Various Brevets de Technicien, of Baccalauréat level, are offered in three years, but do not give access to university.

Higher education:

Access to higher education is based on the Baccalauréat or an equivalent qualification. Those who do not hold the Baccalauréat may enrol in universities if they have passed a special entrance examination or if they have received dispensation from a special committee. In addition, each establishment lays down its own requirements. Higher education is provided by three universities (which are responsible to the Ministry of Education), and other institutions (e.g. Ecole normale supérieure) founded for the training of scientific, technical, teaching and administrative personnel. There are also research institutes and Grandes Ecoles - entry to which involves a special examination - which are similar to those in France and offer specialized courses.

Main laws/decrees governing higher education:

Decree: loi 91-22 d'Orientation de l'Education nationale   Year: 1991
Concerns: Education as a whole

Decree: Law   Year: 1971
Concerns: University

Decree: Law   Year: 1970
Concerns: University

Academic year:

Classes from: October *to:* July

Long vacation from: 1 August *to:* 1 October

Languages of instruction:

French

Stages of studies:

University level studies:

   University level first stage: *Premier Cycle*:
   The first stage or cycle of higher education offers multidisciplinary and basic studies. Two years

study in Humanities lead to the Diplôme universitaire d'Etudes littéraires (DUEL), in Science to the Diplôme universitaire d'Etudes scientifiques (DUES), in Law and Economics to the Diplôme d'Etudes juridiques générales (DEJG) ou économiques générales (DEEG). No qualification is awarded in Medicine and Pharmacy. Holders of the DUES may take the competitive entrance examination for the Grandes Ecoles of Engineering. Studies at the Ecole Nationale supérieure de Technologie (ENSUT) lead after two years to a Diplôme universitaire de Technologie (DUT). In Law, students may enter the university without the Baccalauréat, for a two-year course leading to the qualification of Capacité en Droit. They may then enrol in the three-year Law degree course.

University level second stage: *Deuxième Cycle*:
The second stage (one further year of specialization) leads to the Licence "d'Enseignement" in teaching subjects or Licence "de Recherche" in Linguistics, Psychology and Sociology). Students holding the Licence may undertake a one-year postgraduate course leading to the Maîtrise. In Law and Economics, studies lead to the Maîtrise in two years directly after the DEJG or DEEG. In Pharmacy and Dentistry the first qualifications, obtained after five years, are the Diplôme de Pharmacien and the Diplôme d'Etat de Docteur en Chirurgie Dentaire respectively. In Medicine, the Diplôme d'Etat de Docteur en Médecine is obtained after seven years.

University level third stage: *Troisième Cycle*:
At least one year's research following the Maîtrise leads to the Diplôme d'Etudes approfondies (DEA) and at least a further two years to the Doctorat de troisième Cycle. With either qualification students may undertake a minimum of two years research and presentation of a thesis in Law, Economics, Arts and Science, leading to the Doctorat d'Etat. This qualification is necessary to teach in higher education.

Teacher education:

Training of pre-primary and primary/basic school teachers
Primary school teachers (Instituteurs) take a four-year course at one of the Ecoles normales régionales leading to a Certificat d'Aptitude pédagogique (CAP). Assistant teachers holding a Brevet de Fin d'Etudes moyennes (BFEM) and having professional experience may take a one-year course at the Centre de formation pédagogique, also leading to the CAP.

Training of secondary school teachers
Secondary school teachers are trained at Ecoles normales supérieures which were partly integrated to the University of Dakar in 1971. Licence holders follow a one-year course leading to a Certificat d'Aptitude à l'Enseignement moyen (CAEM); Baccalauréat holders follow a two-year course leading to a Certificat d'Aptitude à l'Enseignement des Collèges d'Enseignement moyen (CAECEM). Upper secondary teachers who hold a Maîtrise follow a two-year course leading to a Certificat d'Aptitude à l'Enseignement secondaire (CAES). Vocational trainers pass their own Certificats d'Aptitude four or five years after the Baccalauréat (CAEMTP and CAESTP) or two years after a Licence.

Training of higher education teachers
Assistants and Maîtres assistants must hold a Doctorat de 3ème Cycle. The latter must also be listed on a "liste d'aptitude" maintained by the Conseil Africain et Malgache pour l'Enseignement supérieur (CAMES). Maîtres de Conférence and Professors must hold a Doctorat d'Etat and be listed on a

"liste d'aptitude". In Law, Economics and Medical fields, the Agrégation (delivered by the CAMES) is necessary.

Non-traditional studies:

Lifelong higher education
Non-formal education is provided in the form of short courses in : Mechanics, Rural Engineering, Child Health Protection, Law and Economics.

NATIONAL BODIES

Responsible authorities:

Higher Education Division, Ministry of Education (Direction de l'Enseignement supérieur, Ministère de l'Education nationale)
Minister of Education: Moustapha Sourang
Directeur: Marème Dieng
B.P. 11.009
Dakar
Tel: +221 821-0881
Fax: +221 821-4755
Telex: 3239 miensup sg
EMail: omardieng@moncourrier.com
WWW: http://www.refer.sn/sngal_ct/edu/edu.htm

ADMISSIONS TO HIGHER EDUCATION

Admission to university-level studies

Name of secondary school credential required: Baccalauréat technique

Name of secondary school credential required: Baccalauréat

Alternatives to credentials: Examen spécial d'entrée (Special entrance examination).

Foreign students admission

Admission requirements: Foreign students should hold the Baccalauréat or its equivalent. They must not be over 22 to enter Medicine and not over 23 for the other faculties.

Entry regulations: Students must be in possession of a visa. Applications by African candidates must be sponsored by their national governments. Students of the Sudano-Sahelian area are given priority. Applications from outside Africa are considered individually, although the university requirements may not be waived.

Language requirements: Students must have a good command of French. Courses are provided by the Institut français pour les étudiants étrangers, Université Cheikh, Anta Diop, Dakar.

Recognition of studies and qualifications:

Studies pursued in foreign countries (bodies dealing with recognition of foreign credentials):
Rectorat, Université Cheikh Anta Diop (University of Dakar)

B.P. 5005
Dakar
Tel: +221 825-0530
Fax: +221 825-5219
Telex: 51262 sg
Cable: unidak.sg
EMail: info@ucad.sn
WWW: http://www.ucad.sn

Multilateral agreements concerning recognition of foreign studies

Name(s) of agreement(s): Convention on the Recognition of Studies, Certificates, Diplomas, Degrees and Other Academic Qualifications in Higher Education in the African States
Year of signature: 1981

References to further information on foreign student admissions and recognition of studies

Title: Guide de l'Etudiant
Publisher: Université Cheikh Anta Diop

Title: Study Abroad 2000-2001
Publisher: UNESCO/IBE
Year of publication: 1999

STUDENT LIFE

Main student services at national level
Centre des Oeuvres universitaires de Dakar

B.P. 2056
Route de Ouakam
Dakar

Services available to foreign Students: Yes

Student expenses and financial aid

Bodies providing information on student financial aid:
Direction des Bourses

Building Maginot, 1er étage
Dakar
Tel: +221 821-38-22

Institut Culturel Africain

B.P. 01

13, avenue Bourguiba
Dakar
Deals with: Grants

INTERNATIONAL COOPERATION AND EXCHANGES

Principal national bodies responsible for dealing with international cooperation and exchanges in higher education:

Direction de l'Enseignement supérieur, Ministère de l'Education nationale.
Dakar
Tel: +221 821- 0881
Fax: +221 821- 4755
Telex: 3239 miensup sg

GRADING SYSTEM

Usual grading system in secondary school

Full Description: Marking is on scale 0-20 (maximum); 10 is the minimum pass mark (16-20: très bien/very good; 14-15: bien/good; 12-13: assez bien/quite good; 10-11: passable/average).
Highest on scale: 20
Pass/fail level: 10
Lowest on scale: 0

Main grading system used by higher education institutions

Full Description: Grades : 0-20 (16-20 : Très Bien; 14-15 : Bien; 12-13 : Assez Bien; 10-11 : Passable)
Highest on scale: 20
Pass/fail level: 10
Lowest on scale: 0

NOTES ON HIGHER EDUCATION SYSTEM

Data for academic year: 2000-2001
Source: International Association of Universities (IAU), updated from IBE website, 2001

INSTITUTIONS OF HIGHER EDUCATION

UNIVERSITIES

*• GASTON BERGER UNIVERSITY OF SAINT-LOUIS

Université Gaston Berger de Saint-Louis
BP 234, Saint-Louis
Tel: +221 961-1906
Fax: +221 961-1884
Telex: 75 128 univ.sl/sg
EMail: ndoye@bu.univ.stl.sn
Website: http://www.ugb.sn

Recteur: Ndiawar Sarr (1999-) Tel: +221 961-2270
Fax: +221 961-5139

Secrétaire général: Abdoulaye Diagne Tel: +221 961-2271
Fax: +221 961-1884 EMail: diagne.secgen@minitel-refer-org

International Relations: Issiaka Prosper Laleye

Units
Applied Mathematics and Computer Science (Applied Mathematics; Computer Science; Physics)
Economics and Management (Agricultural Business; Economics; Management)
Legal and Political Sciences (Law; Political Science)
Letters and Human Sciences (Applied Linguistics; Arts and Humanities; English; French; Geography; Modern Languages; Sociology)

History: Founded 1990.

Governing Bodies: Assemblée

Academic Year: October to July

Admission Requirements: Secondary school certificate (baccalauréat)

Main Language(s) of Instruction: French

International Co-operation: University of Wisconsin, Madison; Université de Nouakchott; University of Montana; University of Kansas; Université de Toulouse II Le-Mirail

Degrees and Diplomas: *Diplôme d'Etudes universitaires générales (DEUG)*: 2 yrs; *Licence*: 3 yrs; *Maîtrise*: 1 further yr; *Diplôme d'Etudes Approfondies (DEA)*: 5 yrs; *Doctorat de Troisième Cycle*; *Doctorat d'Etat*

Student Services: Academic Counselling, Social Counselling, Cultural Centre, Sports Facilities, Handicapped Facilities, Health Services, Canteen, Foreign Student Centre

Libraries: 18,500 vols

Publications: URED (Revue Scientifique)

Academic Staff *1999*: Full-Time: c. 70 Part-Time: c. 120 Total: c. 190

Student Numbers *1999*: Total: c. 2,095

• UNIVERSITY CHEIKH ANTA DIOP OF DAKAR

Université Cheikh Anta Diop de Dakar
BP 5005, Dakar-Fann
Tel: +221 825-7528
Fax: +221 825-3724
EMail: info@ucad.sn
Website: http://www.ucad.sn

Recteur: Abdel Kader Boye Tel: +221 257-584

Secrétaire général: Abdoul Wahab Kâ Tel: +221 240-586

International Relations: Amadou Ly

Faculties
Arts and Humanities (Arts and Humanities; Social Sciences)
Economics and Management (Economics; Management)
Law and Political Science (Law; Political Science) *Dean*: Moustapha Sourang
Medicine, Pharmacy and Odonto-Stomatology (Dentistry; Medicine; Pharmacy; Stomatology) *Dean*: René D. Ndoye
Science and Technology (Natural Sciences; Technology)

Schools
Librarians, Archivists and Documentalists *(EBAD)* (Archiving; Documentation Techniques; Information Sciences; Library Science)
Teacher Training *(ENS) Directeur:* Valdiodio Ndiaye

Higher Schools
Polytechnic *(ESP)* (Artificial Intelligence; Automation and Control Engineering; Biochemistry; Biology; Biotechnology; Building Technologies; Chemical Engineering; Civil Engineering; Computer Science; Construction Engineering; Electrical Engineering; Engineering; Heating and Refrigeration; Management; Materials Engineering; Microbiology; Technology; Telecommunications Engineering) *Directeur:* Oumar Sock
Technology *(ENSUT)*

Institutes
Applied Nuclear Technology *(ITNA)* (Nuclear Engineering)
Applied Tropical Medicine *(IMTA)* (Tropical Medicine)
French for Foreign Students *(IFE)* (French)
Health and Development *(ISD)* (Development Studies; Health Sciences)
Human Rights and Peace *(IDHP)* (Human Rights; Peace and Disarmament)
Social Paediatrics *(IPS)* (Paediatrics)

Higher Institutes
Popular Education and Sport *(INSEPS)* (Physical Education; Sports)

Centres
Applied Linguistics *(CLAD)* (Applied Linguistics; English; French)

Information Sciences and Techniques *(CESTI)* (Cinema and Television; Information Sciences; Journalism; Photography; Radio and Television Broadcasting)

Psychological Research *(CRPP)* (Psychiatry and Mental Health; Psychology)

Renewable Energies Studies Research *(CERER)* (Natural Resources)

Research Institutes

Mathematics, Physics and Technology Teaching *(IREMPT)* (Mathematics Education; Physics; Science Education; Technology Education)

History: Founded 1918 as Ecole de Médecine, became Institut des hautes Etudes 1950 and University by decree 1957. A State institution.

Governing Bodies: Assemblée

Academic Year: October to July (October-February; March-July)

Admission Requirements: Secondary school certificate (baccalauréat) or recognized equivalent, and entrance examination

Main Language(s) of Instruction: French

Degrees and Diplomas: *Capacité en Droit*; *Diplôme d'Etudes économiques générales (DEEG)*: Economics, 2 yrs; *Diplôme d'Etudes juridiques générales (DEJG)*: Law, 2 yrs; *Diplôme universitaire d'Etudes littéraires (DUEL)*: Arts and Humanities, 2 yrs; *Diplôme universitaire d'Etudes scientifiques (DUES)*: 2 yrs; *Diplôme universitaire de Technologie (DUT)*: 2 yrs; *Certificat d'Aptitude à l'Enseignement dans les Collèges d'Enseignement moyen*; *Diplôme de Bibliothécaire/Archiviste/Documentaliste*: Library Science, 2 yrs; *Diplôme supérieur de Journalisme*: Journalism; *Licence*: Arts and Humanities; Science, 1 yr following DUES; *Certificat d'Aptitude à l'Enseignement moyen*; *Diplôme d'Ingénieur*: 3 yrs following DUT; *Diplôme de Pharmacien*: Pharmacy, 5 yrs; *Maîtrise*: Arts and Humanities; Science, 1 yr following Licence; Economics; Law, a further 2 yrs; *Certificat d'Aptitude à l'Enseignement secondaire*; *Certificat d'Etudes supérieures*: Economics; Law, 1 yr following Maîtrise; *Diplôme d'Etat de Docteur*: Dental Surgery, 5 yrs; *Diplôme d'Etudes supérieures spécialisées (DESS)*: Financial Management, 2 yrs following Maîtrise; *Diplôme supérieur en Sciences de l'Information*: Information Sciences; *Diplôme d'Etudes Approfondies (DEA)*: Arts and Humanities; Economics; Engineering; Law; Science, 2 yrs following Maîtrise; *Certificat d' Etudes spéciales (CES)*: 4 yrs following Doctor of Medicine; *Doctorat de Troisième Cycle*: Arts and Humanities, 2 yrs following Maîtrise; Dentistry, 7-8 yrs; *Doctorat d'Etat*: Veterinary medicine, 6 yrs; Medicine, 7 yrs; Pharmacy, 8-9 yrs. Also technical qualifications.

Student Residential Facilities: Yes

Special Facilities: Ethnology Museum; History Museum; Marine Museum

Libraries: c. 400,000 vols; faculty libraries

Publications: L'Enfant en Milieu tropical (monthly); Cancérologie tropicale (biannually); Annales de la Faculté des Sciences; Bulletin et Mémoires de la Faculté de Médecine et Pharmacie; Annales africaines (Faculty of Law) (annually); Afrique médicale; Notes africaines; Bulletin de l'Institut français d'Afrique noire; Revue de Géographie d'Afrique Occidentale; Psychopathologie africaine; Médecine d'Afrique noire; Bulletin de la Société médicale d'Afrique noire de Langue française

Press or Publishing House: Presses Universitaires de Dakar

Academic Staff *1999:* Total: c. 700

Student Numbers *1999:* Total: c. 22,000

INSTITUTE OF BLACK AFRICAN STUDIES AND
RESEARCH
INSTITUT FONDAMENTAL D'AFRIQUE NOIRE CHEIKH
ANTA DIOP (IFAN/CAD)
BP 206, Dakar
Tel: +221 250-090
Fax: +221 244-918

Directeur: Djibril Sahib

Departments

African Literature and Civilization (African Studies; Anthropology; Islamic Studies; Linguistics)

Animal Biology (Biology; Marine Biology; Zoology)

Botany and Geology (Botany; Geology)

Human Sciences (Anthropology; Arts and Humanities; Geography; History; Prehistory; Social Sciences; Sociology)

Scientific Information (Information Sciences)

History: Founded 1936.

UNIVERSITY OF THE SAHEL

Université du Sahel (UNIS)
BP 5355 33, Mermoz, Dakar
Tel: +221 824-9975
Fax: +221 824-9975
EMail: unis@cyg.sn
Website: http://www.cyg.sn/unis

Président: Issa Sall

Programmes
Communication Studies

Documentation Studies (Documentation Techniques)

Enquiries and Statistics (Statistics)

History of Science (History; Natural Sciences)

Office Management

Religious Studies

Schools
Economics and Administration (Accountancy; Business Administration; Business and Commerce; Computer Science; Economics; Finance; Health Administration; Marketing)

Educational Sciences (Curriculum; Educational Sciences; Educational Testing and Evaluation; Literacy Education; Pedagogy)

Law and Political Science (International Relations; Law; Political Science)

Letters and Civilizations (African Studies; American Studies; Arabic; Asian Studies; English; European Studies; French; Linguistics; Modern Languages; Philosophy)

Science and Engineering (Agronomy; Architecture; Biology; Chemical Engineering; Chemistry; Civil Engineering; Computer Science; Electrical Engineering; Engineering; Environmental

Studies; Forestry; Genetics; Geology; Mathematics; Mechanical Engineering; Physics; Rural Studies; Science Education; Telecommunications Engineering)
Social Sciences (Anthropology; Geography; History; Psychology; Social Sciences; Sociology)
Admission Requirements: Baccalauréat or equivalent

OTHER UNIVERSITY LEVEL INSTITUTIONS

ÉCOLE NATIONALE SUPÉRIEURE D' AGRICULTURE (ENSA)
Thiès
Tel: +221 511-257
Fax: +221 511-551
EMail: ensath@telecomplus.sn

Directeur: Moussa Fall
Directeur des Etudes: Aliou Coly

Agriculture *Head*: Moussa Fall
Academic Year: January to November
Admission Requirements: Secondary school certificate (baccalauréat séries C, D, E)
Fees: (CFA Francs): 1,850,000 per annum
Main Language(s) of Instruction: French
Degrees and Diplomas: *Diplôme d'Ingénieur*. Agronomy, 5 yrs
Student Services: Academic Counselling, Social Counselling, Foreign Student Adviser, Cultural Centre, Sports Facilities, Language Programmes, Health Services, Canteen

Academic Staff *1999-2000*	MEN	WOMEN	TOTAL
FULL-TIME	9	1	10
PART-TIME	54	2	56
TOTAL	**63**	**3**	**66**
STAFF WITH DOCTORATE			
FULL-TIME	7	–	7
PART-TIME	50	2	52
TOTAL	**57**	**2**	**59**

Student Numbers *1999-2000*	MEN	WOMEN	TOTAL
All (Foreign Included)	95	20	**115**
FOREIGN ONLY	18	3	21

OTHER INSTITUTIONS

CENTRE AFRICAIN D'ÉTUDES SUPÉRIEURES EN GESTION
BP 3802, Boulevard Général de Gaulle, Dakar
Tel: +221 228-022
Fax: +221 213-215

Departments
Audit Procedures (Accountancy)
Business Management (Management)
Health Services Management (Health Administration)

History: Founded 1978

CENTRE DE FORMATION ET DE PERFECTIONNEMENT ADMINISTRATIF
Boulevard Dial Diop, Dakar
Tel: +221 250-058
Fax: +221 248-744
Administration

History: Founded 1965

CENTRE DE PERFECTIONNEMENT EN LANGUE ANGLAISE
35, rue Jules Ferry, Dakar
Tel: +221 210-359
English

History: Founded 1973

CONSERVATOIRE NATIONAL DE MUSIQUE, DE DANSE ET D'ARTS DRAMATIQUES
Dakar
Tel: +221 224-673
Dance; Music; Theatre

ÉCOLE INTER-ÉTATS DES SCIENCES ET MÉDECINE VÉTÉRINAIRE (EISMV)
BP 5077, Dakar
Tel: +221 865-1008
Fax: +221 825-4283
EMail: mariamd@eismv.refer.sn
Website: http://www.refer.sn/sngal_et/edu/eismv/eismv.htm
Directeur: François Adebayo Abiola (1994-)

Programmes
Veterinary Science (Anatomy; Biology; Embryology and Reproduction Biology; Ethnology; Food Technology; Genetics; Histology; Immunology; Microbiology; Parasitology; Pathology; Pharmacy; Physiology; Rural Planning; Toxicology; Veterinary Science; Zoology)

ÉCOLE NATIONALE D'ADMINISTRATION ET DE MAGISTRATURE
Rue Dial Diop, Dakar
Tel: +221 250-058
Fax: +221 258-744
Administration
Magisterial Studies (Justice Administration)

ÉCOLE NATIONALE DES BEAUX ARTS
124/126, avenue A. Peytavin, Dakar
Fine Arts

History: Founded 1979

ÉCOLE NATIONALE DES CADRES RURAUX DE BAMBEY (ENCR)
BP 54, Bambey
Tel: +221 973-6195
Fax: +221 973-6061
EMail: encrbbey@cyg.sn

Directeur: Sidy Harou Camara (1987-) **Tel:** +221 973-6060
EMail: encrbbey@cyg.sn

Directeur des Etudes: Cheikh M. Mboup

Departments
Animal Husbandry (Cattle Breeding) *Head*: Pap Sher Diop, *full-time staff:* 4, *part-time staff:* 3, *students:* 11
Applications and Production (Crop Production) *Head*: Saliou Diouf, *full-time staff:* 5, *students:* 141
Counsel, Training, Development (Agricultural Economics; Development Studies; Rural Planning) *Head*: Diakho Makha, *full-time staff:* 3, *part-time staff:* 4, *students:* 141
Forestry *Head*: Birahim Fall, *full-time staff:* 4, *part-time staff:* 3, *students:* 18
Vegetal Production (Vegetable Production) *Head*: Ibrahima Mbodj, *full-time staff:* 5, *part-time staff:* 9, *students:* 67

History: Founded 1960

Governing Bodies: Ministère de l'Enseignement Supérieur et de la Recherche Scientifique

Academic Year: September to June

Admission Requirements: Secondary school certificate (baccalauréat toutes séries), or diplôme d'agent technique and 2 yrs experience

Fees: (CFA Francs): Registration, 995,000

Main Language(s) of Instruction: French

Degrees and Diplomas: *Diplôme d'Ingénieur*: Agriculture (ITA); Stockbreeding, Water and Forestry (ITE), 3 yrs

Student Services: Employment Services, Sports Facilities, Language Programmes, Health Services

Student Residential Facilities: Yes

Libraries: Central Library; Library of the Centre National de Recherches Agricoles

Publications: None

Academic Staff *1999-2000*	TOTAL
FULL-TIME	49
PART-TIME	17
TOTAL	**66**

Staff with doctorate: Total: 14

Student Numbers *1999-2000*	MEN	WOMEN	TOTAL
All (Foreign Included)	120	21	**141**
FOREIGN ONLY	43	8	51

ÉCOLE NATIONALE DES DOUANES
Avenue Carde-Rue René Ndiayé, Dakar
Tel: +221 212-879

Customs (Taxation)

History: Founded 1970

ÉCOLE NATIONALE D'ÉCONOMIE APPLIQUÉE
Avenue Cheikh A. Diop, Dakar
Tel: +221 247-928

Economics

History: Founded 1968

• ÉCOLE NATIONALE DE FORMATION MARITIME
Km 4, 5 Route de Rufisque, Dakar
Tel: +221 213-823

Maritime Studies (Marine Science and Oceanography)

ÉCOLE NATIONALE D'HORTICULTURE CAMBÉRÈNE
Dakar
Tel: +221 357-821
Fax: +221 353-991

Horticulture

ÉCOLE NATIONALE DE POLICE ET DE LA FORMATION PERMANENTE
BP 5025, Dakar-Fann
Tel: +221 252-818
Fax: +221 242-557

Police Studies

History: Founded 1954

ÉCOLE NATIONALE DES POSTES ET TÉLÉCOMMUNICATIONS
Rue Ousmane Socé Diop, Rufisque
Tel: +221 360-029

Post and Telecommunications (Postal Services; Telecommunications Services)

ÉCOLE NORMALE SUPÉRIEURE D'ÉDUCATION ARTISTIQUE
124-126, avenue A. Peytavin, Dakar
Tel: +221 230-343
Fax: +221 221-638

Communication (Communication Studies)
Environmental Studies
Plastic Arts (Painting and Drawing; Sculpture)

ÉCOLE POLYTECHNIQUE DE THIÈS
BP 10, Thiès
Tel: +221 511-632
Fax: +221 511-476

Departments
Civil Engineering
Electro-mechanical Engineering (Electronic Engineering; Mechanical Engineering)

History: Founded 1973.

ÉCOLE SUPÉRIEURE MULTINATIONALE DES TÉLÉCOMMUNICATIONS (ESMT)
B.P. 10000, Dakar Liberté
Tel: +221 824-9806
Fax: +221 824-6890
Website: http://www.esmt.sn

Directeur: Idrissa Touré **Tel:** +221 869-0301
EMail: Idrissa.Toure@esmt.sn

Telecommunications (Telecommunications Engineering)

History: Founded 1981

INSTITUT NATIONAL SUPÉRIEUR DE L'ÉDUCATION POPULAIRE ET DU SPORT
Stade Iba Mar Diop, Dakar
Tel: +221 233-384
Education and Sport (Education; Sports)

History: Founded 1979.

INSTITUT SÉNÉGALAIS DE RECHERCHES AGRICOLES (ISRA)
BP 3120, Dakar
Tel: +221 211-913
Fax: +221 223-413
Agriculture

History: Founded 1974

INSTITUT SÉNÉGALO-BRITANNIQUE D'ENSEIGNEMENT DE L'ANGLAIS
BP 35, rue du 18 juin, Dakar
Tel: +221 224-023
English

History: Founded 1976

Sierra Leone

INSTITUTION TYPES AND CREDENTIALS

Types of higher education institutions:

University
University College
Technical Institute
Teacher Training College

School leaving and higher education credentials:

Senior School Certificate Examination
General Certificate of Education Advanced Level
Certificate
Diploma
Higher Teacher's Certificate
Bachelor's Degree
Bachelor Honours Degree
Postgraduate Diploma in Education
Master's Degree
Doctor's Degree

STRUCTURE OF EDUCATION SYSTEM

Pre-higher education:

Structure of school system:

Primary
Type of school providing this education: Primary School
Length of programme in years: 6
Age level from: 6 to: 12
Certificate/diploma awarded: National Primary School Examination

Junior Secondary
Type of school providing this education: Junior Secondary School
Length of programme in years: 3
Age level from: 12 to: 15
Certificate/diploma awarded: Basic Education Certificate Examination (BECE)

Senior Secondary
Type of school providing this education: Senior Secondary School
Length of programme in years: 3
Age level from: 15 to: 18
Certificate/diploma awarded: Senior School Certificate Examination

School education:

In the 6-3-3-4 education system, primary education lasts for six years followed by secondary education which is divided into two three-year cycles. The first leads to the Basic Education Certificate Examination and the second to the Senior School Certificate Examination which gives access to higher education. Candidates may also sit for the General Certificate of Education Ordinary Level/Cambridge Overseas School Certificate and the General Certificate of Education Advanced Level/Cambridge Overseas School Certificate, which is conferred after five years lower secondary education and two years sixth form.

Higher education:

Higher education is offered by one university and its constituent colleges, teacher training colleges and a technical institute. They come under the jurisdiction of the Ministry of Education, Youth and Sports. The University is governed by the Court, composed of non-university and university members, and the Senate, which is composed of academic members and is responsible for academic matters.

Main laws/decrees governing higher education:

Decree: University of Sierra Leone Act   Year: 1972

Academic year:

Classes from: October *to:* June

Long vacation from: 1 July *to:* 7 October

Languages of instruction:

English

Stages of studies:

Non-university level post-secondary studies (technical/vocational type):

Higher vocational and technical education is provided by technical institutes which train technicians and clerks and prepare candidates for examinations of the City and Guilds of London Institute, the Royal Society of Arts and the United Kingdom Ordinary National Diploma in technical studies.

University level studies:

University level first stage: Undergraduate:
The first stage of higher education leads, after a period of three years (or four, in the case of not sufficiently qualified entrants), to the Bachelor's Degree (general). A Bachelor's Degree with Honours is awarded after four years' study. A Diploma in Engineering is conferred after three years' study at undergraduate level. A Certificate in Agriculture and Home Economics is awarded after two years' study at undergraduate level. These are professional qualifications.

University level second stage: *Graduate*:
The Master's Degree is awarded one year following the Bachelor's Degree with Honours and two years following a general degree.

University level third stage: *Doctor of Philosophy*:
The Ph.D. is conferred after a minimum of three years' study following upon the Bachelor's Degree, and the submission of a thesis. A Postgraduate Diploma in Education is awarded after one year's postgraduate study.

Teacher education:

Training of pre-primary and primary/basic school teachers
Primary school teachers are trained in teacher training colleges in three years after junior secondary school. They are awarded the Teacher's Certificate (TC).

Training of secondary school teachers
Junior secondary school teachers are trained at teacher's colleges where studies lead to a Higher Teachers' Certificate. Senior secondary school teachers hold a four-year Bachelor Degree. The Faculty of Education at Njala University College offers a four-year course leading to a BA in Education, and a BSc in Education, Agricultural Education, and Home Economics Education. Fourah Bay College offers a one-year graduate diploma in Education to graduates who have studied at least two subjects taught in secondary schools.

NATIONAL BODIES

Responsible authorities:
Ministry of Education, Youth and Sports
    Minister: Alpha Wurie
    Freetown
    New England
    Tel: +232(22) 240560
    Fax: +232(22) 240560

ADMISSIONS TO HIGHER EDUCATION

Admission to university-level studies

Name of secondary school credential required: General Certificate of Education Advanced Level

Name of secondary school credential required: Senior School Certificate Examination

Alternatives to credentials: Provisions are made for entry for mature students with special aptitudes and experience.

Other admission requirements: The choice of subject is based on the type of course students wish to follow in higher education. Faculties have their own special entrance requirements and students are selected from among suitably qualified candidates.

Foreign students admission

Admission requirements: Foreign students should hold qualifications equivalent to the requirements of national students. An orientation programme is provided for all students during the first week of each session.

Language requirements: Proficiency in English is required.

Application procedures:

Apply to individual institution for entry to: University

Application closing dates:

  For university level studies: 31 March

References to further information on foreign student admissions and recognition of studies

Title: Commonwealth Universities Yearbook
Author: Association of Commonwealth Universities
Publisher: ACU

Title: Guide for Prospective Foreign Student
Author: University of Sierra Leone

GRADING SYSTEM

Usual grading system in secondary school

Full Description: For Secondary school leaving certificate A' level: A, B, C, D, E, O (subsidiary pass), F or 1-9 with 1 as maximum.
Highest on scale: A
Pass/fail level: O
Lowest on scale: F

Main grading system used by higher education institutions

Full Description: First Class Honours: A+; Second Class Honours, Upper Division: A-/B+; Second Class Honours, Lower Division: B; Third Class Honours: B-C/+; Pass: C
Highest on scale: A+
Pass/fail level: C
Lowest on scale: F

Other main grading systems

Degrees are classified :
Honours Degrees: Class I, Class II (upper and lower), Class III
Pass Degrees: Division I, II, III; general degrees

NOTES ON HIGHER EDUCATION SYSTEM

Data for academic year: 1999-2000
Source: International Association of Universities (IAU)

INSTITUTIONS OF HIGHER EDUCATION

UNIVERSITIES

• UNIVERSITY OF SIERRA LEONE

Private Mail Bag, Tower Hill, A.J. Momoh Street, Freetown
Tel: +232(22) 6859
Fax: +232(22) 2334
Cable: unisal, freetown

Vice-Chancellor: Ernest H. Wright (1998-)
EMail: wrighteh@sierratel.sl
Registrar: J.A.G. Thomas Tel: +232(22) 4921

Institutes

Education *Director (Acting)*: Melisa F. Jonah
Librarianship and Information Studies (Administration; Archiving; Documentation Techniques; Information Sciences; Library Science) *Director*: G. Jusu-Sheriff, *full-time staff: 2, part-time staff: 12, students: 67*
Public Administration and Management (Accountancy; Business and Commerce; Finance; Management; Public Administration) *Director*: Ibi I. May-Parker, *full-time staff: 21, part-time staff: 9, students: 420*

History: Founded 1967.

Governing Bodies: Court; Senate

Academic Year: October to June (October-December; January-March; April-June)

Admission Requirements: General Certificate of Education (GCE) at Ordinary ('O') level or Advanced ('A') level

Main Language(s) of Instruction: English

International Co-operation: University of Manchester; South Carolina State University; University of Hohenheim; Technical University of Nova Scotia

Degrees and Diplomas: *Bachelor's Degree*: 3-4 yrs; *Bachelor Honours Degree*: 4-5 yrs; *Master's Degree*; *Doctor's Degree*. Also Diplomas and Certificates, 1-2 yrs.

Student Residential Facilities: For c. 3000 students

Special Facilities: Botanical Garden. Herbarium

Publications: Bulletin of African Studies (quarterly); Journal of Pure and Applied Sciences (annually)

Academic Staff *1999:* Total: c. 45

Student Numbers *1999:* Total: c. 490

COLLEGE OF MEDICINE AND ALLIED HEALTH SCIENCES
Private Mail Bag, Freetown
Tel: +232(22) 240884

Principal: Ahmed M. Taqi (1992-)

Faculties

Basic Medical Sciences (Anatomy; Biochemistry; Dentistry; Haematology; Health Sciences; Medicine; Microbiology;

Pharmacy; Physiology) *Dean*: J.K. George, *full-time staff: 9, part-time staff: 3, students: 84*
Clinical Sciences (Community Health; Dental Hygiene; Gynaecology and Obstetrics; Medicine; Paediatrics; Surgery) *Dean*: L.G.O. Gordon-Harris, *full-time staff: 35, part-time staff: 1, students: 72*
Pharmaceutical Sciences (Pharmacology; Pharmacy) *Dean*: Ayiteh Smith, *full-time staff: 11, part-time staff: 3, students: 8*

History: Founded 1988 as a Constituent College of University of Sierra Leone.

Academic Staff *1999:* Total: c. 60

Student Numbers *1999:* Total: c. 165

FOURAH BAY COLLEGE
PO Box 87, Freetown
Tel: +232(22) 223258
Cable: fourahbay

Principal: V.E. Strasser-King (1993-)

Faculties

Arts (Accountancy; Arts and Humanities; Demography and Population; Education; English; Linguistics; Mass Communication; Modern Languages; Political Science; Sociology; Theology) *Dean*: L.E.T. Shyllon, *full-time staff: 40, part-time staff: 11, students: 504*
Economics and Social Studies (Accountancy; Demography and Population; Economics; Political Science; Social Sciences; Sociology) *Dean*: A. Abraham, *full-time staff: 19, part-time staff: 4, students: 455*
Engineering (Civil Engineering; Electrical Engineering; Electronic Engineering; Engineering; Maintenance Technology; Mechanical Engineering) *Dean*: O.R. Davidson, *full-time staff: 20, part-time staff: 8, students: 135*
Law (International Law; Law) *Dean*: H.M.J. Smart, *full-time staff: 6, part-time staff: 1, students: 52*
Pure and Applied Sciences (Botany; Chemistry; Geography; Geology; Marine Biology; Marine Science and Oceanography; Natural Sciences; Physics; Zoology) *Dean*: V.E. Godwin, *full-time staff: 40, part-time staff: 4, students: 174*

Institutes

Adult Education and Extramural Studies (INSTADEX) (Environmental Studies; Rural Planning) *Director*: E.D.A. Turay, *full-time staff: 6, part-time staff: 1, students: 39*
African Studies *Director*: A. A. Abraham
Marine Biology and Oceanography (Marine Science and Oceanography) *Director*: I.O.W. Findlay, *full-time staff: 7, part-time staff: 1, students: 10*
Population Studies (Demography and Population; Economics; Statistics) *Director*: Armand C. Thomas, *full-time staff: 5, students: 21*

History: Founded 1827 by the Church Missionary Society, became affiliated to University of Durham 1876 and incorporated as independent Institution under Royal Charter 1960. Became Constituent College of University of Sierra Leone 1966.

Academic Year: October to June (October-December; January-March; April-June)

Admission Requirements: General Certificate of Education (GCE) with Ordinary ('O') level passes in 5 approved subjects, including English Language

Main Language(s) of Instruction: English

Degrees and Diplomas: *Bachelor's Degree*: 3-4 yrs; *Master's Degree*: a further 1-2 yrs; *Doctor's Degree*: (PhD), a further 3-4 yrs

Student Residential Facilities: Yes

Libraries: c. 120,000 vols

Publications: Prospectus (biennially); Gazette

Academic Staff *1999:* Total: c. 155

Student Numbers *1999:* Total: c. 1,450

NJALA UNIVERSITY COLLEGE
Private Mail Bag, Freetown
Tel: +232(22) 8788
Cable: njalun

Principal (Acting): H. M. Turay

Faculties

Agriculture (Agricultural Economics; Agricultural Engineering; Agriculture; Animal Husbandry; Home Economics; Soil Science) *Dean*: A.M. Alghali, *full-time staff: 39, part-time staff: 3, students: 299*

Education (Agricultural Education; Education; Physical Education; Teacher Trainers Education) *Dean*: P.K. Saidu, *full-time staff: 32, part-time staff: 6, students: 636*

Environmental Sciences (Biological and Life Sciences; Chemistry; Environmental Studies; Geography; Physics) *Dean*: B.J. Tucker, *full-time staff: 21, students: 73*

Centres

Educational Services (Educational Technology) *Director*: P.K. Saidu, *full-time staff: 2, students: 229*

Science Curriculum Development *Director*: M.J. Cole, *full-time staff: 5, part-time staff: 1, students: 229*

History: Founded 1964. Became a Constituent College of University of Sierra Leone 1966.

Academic Year: October to June (October-December; January-March; April-June)

Admission Requirements: General Certificate of Education (GCE) with Ordinary ('O') level passes in 5 approved subjects, including English Language

Main Language(s) of Instruction: English

Degrees and Diplomas: *Certificate*: Agriculture; *Bachelor's Degree*: 3-4 yrs; *Master's Degree*: a further 3-4 yrs; *Doctor's Degree*: (PhD), a further 3-4 yrs

Student Residential Facilities: Yes

Special Facilities: Herbarium with rare collections

Libraries: c. 50,000 vols

Publications: Handbook; Education and Agricultural Development in Sierra Leone

Academic Staff *1999:* Total: c. 115

Student Numbers *1999:* Total: c. 1,600

OTHER INSTITUTIONS

BO TEACHERS' COLLEGE
PO Box 162, Bo
Teacher Training

History: Founded 1972

BUNUMBU TEACHERS' COLLEGE
Private Mail Bag, Kenema
Teacher Training

History: Founded 1933

FREETOWN TEACHERS' COLLEGE
PO Box 1049, Freetown
Tel: +232(22) 263010
Teacher Training

History: Founded 1964

MAKENI TEACHERS' COLLEGE
Private Mail Bag, Makeni, Northern Provinces
Teacher Training

MILTON MARGAI TEACHERS' COLLEGE
Goderich
Teacher Training

History: Founded 1960

PORT LOKO TEACHERS' COLLEGE
Port Loko
Tel: +232(22) 229903
Teacher Training

TECHNICAL INSTITUTE
Congo Cross, Freetown
Tel: +232(22) 31368
Technology

Somalia

INSTITUTION TYPES AND CREDENTIALS

Types of higher education institutions:
University
Institute
Teacher Training College

School leaving and higher education credentials:
Secondary School Leaving Certificate
Laurea

STRUCTURE OF EDUCATION SYSTEM

Pre-higher education:

Duration of compulsory education:
    Age of entry: 6
    Age of exit: 14

Structure of school system:
    Primary
    Type of school providing this education: Primary School
    Length of programme in years: 8
    Age level from: 6 to: 14

    Secondary
    Type of school providing this education: Secondary School
    Length of programme in years: 4
    Age level from: 14 to: 18
    Certificate/diploma awarded: Secondary School Leaving Certificate

    Technical
    Type of school providing this education: Technical Secondary School
    Length of programme in years: 4
    Age level from: 14 to: 18

School education:

Primary education lasts for eight years. Secondary education lasts for four years. All main subjects are taught. Studies lead to the Secondary School Leaving Certificate. Technical secondary education is offered in technical/vocational secondary schools. The curriculum is being revised.

Higher education:

Higher education is mainly provided by the National University of Somalia and specialized postsecondary institutions. The University is administered by the Ministry of Higher Education and Culture. The Chancellor, who is the head of State, is also the statutory head of the University. The Rector is the chief executive officer. He is assisted by two Vice-Rectors responsible for administrative and academic affairs. The two main administrative committees of the University are the Council and the Senate. The Chairman of the Council is the Minister for Higher Education. The Senate committee is chaired by the Rector and includes two academic staff members selected by their deans from each of the faculties. The academic staff in each faculty is responsible for the design and implementation of the curriculum for their students. Each faculty is headed by a dean. Institutions of higher education are financed by the State but are not all under the supervision of the Ministry of Higher Education.

Languages of instruction:

Arabic, English, Italian, Somali

Stages of studies:

Non-university level post-secondary studies (technical/vocational type):
Higher technical and vocational education is offered in specialized institutions which provide courses that last between one and four years in such subjects as Industrial Studies, Public Health, Veterinary Medicine, Telecommunications, and Commerce.

University level studies:

University level first stage: Bachelor's Degree/Laurea:
The first stage lasts for four years and leads to the Bachelor's Degree or Laurea. Students must first spend two years in national service and sit for a competitive entrance examination.

University level second stage: Master's Degree:
The University is introducing Master's Degrees.

Teacher education:

Training of pre-primary and primary/basic school teachers
Primary school teachers are trained at Scuole Magistrali one year after completion of secondary education. They are awarded a Diploma.

Training of secondary school teachers
Secondary school teachers are trained in three years at the University or at the Technical Teacher Training College for vocational and technical education. Entrants to the TTTC are selected from among those who have completed three and four years of technical secondary education. Graduates are expected to serve as vocational and/or technical teachers for five years.

Training of higher education teachers
The minimum requirement for the rank of lecturer is a Master Degree and a minimum of three years teaching experience. The rank of Professor requires a PhD, scholarly publications and a minimum of five years' service at the University.

NATIONAL BODIES

Responsible authorities:

Ministry of Higher Education
    Minister: Mohamed Ali Ahmed
    Mogadishu

ADMISSIONS TO HIGHER EDUCATION

Admission to non university higher education studies

Name of secondary school credential required: Secondary School Leaving Certificate

Admission to university-level studies

Name of secondary school credential required: Secondary School Leaving Certificate

Entrance exams required: Entrance examination.

Other admission requirements: Two years' national youth service.

Foreign students admission

Admission requirements: Foreign students must have completed secondary education and pass the university entrance examination. Services available to foreign students include accommodation, health and teaching facilities. They may also be awarded fellowships.

Entry regulations: Students must hold a resident's permit.

Health requirements: Health certificates are required.

GRADING SYSTEM

Usual grading system in secondary school

Full Description: For the Secondary School Certificate: 0-100%.
Highest on scale: 100%
Pass/fail level: 60%
Lowest on scale: 0

Main grading system used by higher education institutions

Full Description: In the faculties that follow the Italian system all subjects are marked out of a possible maximum of 30 with 18 as the pass mark.

Highest on scale: 30
Pass/fail level: 18
Lowest on scale: 0

NOTES ON HIGHER EDUCATION SYSTEM

Data for academic year: 1999-2000
Source: International Association of Universities (IAU)

INSTITUTIONS OF HIGHER EDUCATION

UNIVERSITIES

SOMALI NATIONAL UNIVERSITY

Jaamacadda Ummadda Soolaaliyeed
PO Box 15, Mogadishu
Tel: +252(1) 80404

Rector: Mohamed Ganni Mohamed

Vice-Rector: Mohamed Elmi Bullale

International Relations: Nureyn Sheikh Abrar, Registrar

Faculties

Agriculture *Dean*: Mohamed Ali Mohamed
Arabic and Islamic Studies (Arabic; Islamic Studies) *Dean*: Sharif Mohamed Ali Isaak
Economics *Dean*: Mohamed Ismail Sheikh
Education *Dean*: Hussein Musa Ali
Engineering *Dean*: Abdullahi Jimale Mohamed
Geology *Dean*: Mohammoud Abdi Arush
Industrial Chemistry *Dean*: Ahmed Maye Abdurahman
Journalism *Dean*: Mohamoud Ismail Abdirahman
Languages (Modern Languages)
Law *Dean*: Abud Musad Abud
Medicine *Dean*: Abdi Ahmed Farah
Political Science *Dean*: Aden Abdullahi Nur
Technical Teacher Education (Teacher Trainers Education) *Dean*: Abdullahi Mohamud Warsamme

Veterinary Medicine (Veterinary Science) *Dean*: Abdulhamid Haji Mohamed

Colleges
Technical Sciences (Engineering; Technology)
Veterinary Science

Schools
Industrial Studies (Industrial Engineering)
Islamic Studies (Islamic Law; Islamic Studies)
Nautical Science and Fishing (Fishery; Nautical Science)
Public Health

Institutes
Development Administration and Management (Administration; Management) *Dean*: Ibrahim Mohamud Abyan

History: Founded 1954 as Institute of Law, Economics, and Social Sciences. Became Istituto Universitario della Somalia 1969, Università nazionale della Somalia 1970, and acquired present title 1979. A State Institution.

Academic Year: July to June (July-December; January-June)

Admission Requirements: Secondary school certificate and entrance examination

Main Language(s) of Instruction: Somali, Italian, English, Arabic

Degrees and Diplomas: *Laurea*

Academic Staff *2001:* Total: c. 550

Student Numbers *2001:* Total: c. 4,700

South Africa

INSTITUTION TYPES AND CREDENTIALS

Types of higher education institutions:

University
Technikon
College (Teacher Training, Nursing, Technical Colleges)

School leaving and higher education credentials:

Senior Certificate
Matriculation Endorsement
National Certificate
National Higher Certificate
National Diploma
National Higher Diploma
Bachelor of Technology
Bachelor's Degree
Honours Bachelor's Degree
Postgraduate Diploma
Master of Technology
Master's Degree
Doctor of Technology
Doctorate

STRUCTURE OF EDUCATION SYSTEM

Pre-higher education:

Duration of compulsory education:

Age of entry: 6
Age of exit: 15

Structure of school system:

Primary
Type of school providing this education: Primary School
Length of programme in years: 6
Age level from: 6 to: 12

Junior Secondary
Type of school providing this education: Junior Secondary School (first year still placed under primary school)
Length of programme in years: 3
Age level from: 12 to: 15
Certificate/diploma awarded: General Education and Training Certificate

Technical Secondary
Type of school providing this education: Technical Level Secondary School
Length of programme in years: 2
Age level from: 15 to: 17
Certificate/diploma awarded: Senior Certificate 1-3 years (depending on N programmes followed)

Senior Secondary
Type of school providing this education: Senior Secondary School
Length of programme in years: 3
Age level from: 15 to: 18
Certificate/diploma awarded: Senior Certificate

School education:

Primary education lasts for six years, divided into junior primary and senior primary. Until now, secondary school lasted for five years, the first year of the junior secondary phase being followed in primary school. At the end of junior secondary (three years), pupils are awarded the General Education and Training Certificate. At the end of the senior secondary phase (lasting three years), pupils sit for the Senior Certificate Examination. The 1996 Constitution confirms the right to basic education and that the Government must progressively make available and accessible through reasonable measures further education (i.e. the senior secondary phase preceding higher education). Compulsory education lasts for nine years (until age 15), followed by non-compulsory further education. In the senior cycle, students may study subjects either at Higher Grade, Standard Grade, or Lower Grade. N-courses are also offered by some technical school and college candidates. A Senior Certificate is awarded by the SA Certification Council after externally moderated examinations on completion of senior secondary school. Technical secondary education is provided by technical centres and secondary and vocational schools. Matriculation endorsements are also offered by this Council to students who have satisfied the ministerially approved overlay on the Senior Certificate. Provision is also made for further education colleges in terms of the Further Education and Training Act. Technical high schools may inter alia offer courses leading to Senior Certificates with matriculation endorsements, which statutorily constitute the minimum general admission requirement for access to universities. Technikons require Senior Certificates but not necessarily with matriculation endorsements.

Higher education:

The higher education system consists of State Universities, a Technikon sector and a College sector. The Higher Education Act (December 1997) provides for the appointment of a Registrar of Private Higher Education Institutions and a number of private institutions have registered or are in the process of registering in terms of these provisions. The South African universities offer Bachelor, Bachelor

Honours, Master and Doctorate Degrees, as well as Undergraduate and Postgraduate Diplomas. Course work is structured in modules, with students registering in a unit/credit system. Technikons and Universities, as autonomous institutions, are subsidized by the Department of Education, and provide training at the post senior certificate level. Technikon courses lead to National Diplomas and Certificates and as from 1995 to Degrees with a minimum duration of four years. The Certification Council for Technikons (SERTEC) is responsible for conferring Technikon Diplomas. The Higher Education Act stipulates that higher education at Universities, Technikons and Colleges comes directly under the responsibility of the national government, whilst further education colleges report to the nine provincial governments. It has recently been planned to reduce the number of Colleges of Education and to incorporate them in the higher education system. In most cases they will be linked to universities and technical institutes.

Main laws/decrees governing higher education:

Decree: Higher Education Act   Year: 1997

Academic year:

Classes from: January *to:* December

Languages of instruction:

Afrikaans, English

Stages of studies:

Non-university level post-secondary studies (technical/vocational type):

Higher technical/vocational studies are provided by Technical Colleges and Technikons. Apprenticeship training for technicians is offered by Technical Colleges. Apprentices study for the National (Technical) Certificate (N training). N-3 courses can also be taken as credits for the Senior Certificate. The programme consists of three parts (N-1, N-2, N-3), each lasting for four months, six months or a year depending on the course concerned. The N-training is a pre-senior Certificate level and the N-3 credits are considered for the Senior Certificate (with pass in English and Afrikaans) for entry to Technikon and National Certificate studies, but not for university studies. Most tertiary-level vocational programmes lead to a three-year National Diploma as basic qualification. Technikons also provide vocationally oriented education and training in a variety of disciplines leading to amongst other Diplomas, first and advanced Degrees. Diplomas at technical-vocational level lead to BTech, MTech and Dtech Degrees. There are other types of specialist colleges, such as Nursing Colleges and Agricultural Colleges, which do not offer Degree studies unless offered in cooperation with Universities or Technikons. In such cases the Degree-awarding institution/authority's name will appear on the Certificate.

University level studies:

University level first stage: *First stage*:

The Bachelor Degree is awarded both by Universities and Technikons. (The latter structure came into effect in January 1995). Universities award the Bachelor Degree after three to six years of study. Humanities, Commerce, Science - 3 years; Agriculture, Law, Engineering, Pharmacy and Education, four years; Veterinary Medicine and Architecture, five years; Dentistry , five and a half years;

Medecine and Theology, six years. Students in Humanities, Commerce and Science wishing to proceed to a Master Degree are required to take a Bachelor Honours Degree, which is awarded after a further year's study. Technikons award the Bachelor Degree of Technology (BTech), which is a four-year Degree which includes one year of experiencial training. Universities also confer a Professional Bachelor Degree after four years.

University level second stage: *Second stage*:

The Master Degree is awarded both by Universities and Technikons. This Degree requires a minimum of one to two years research after the award of an Honours Degree in the case of universities, and a Bachelor Degree in the case of Technikons. The Master Degree in Technology (MTech) may be obtained at least one year after the BTech. This is an advanced qualification comprising taught subjects and research, or only research. The thesis must relate to an industry specific problem. Some university Master Degrees, e.g. the Master Degree in Business Leadership (MBusAdministration), are partly taught and partly research Degrees, where the thesis must relate to an industry or subject specific problem.

University level third stage: *Third stage*:

Doctorates and research Degrees are also awarded both by Universities and Technikons. They are conferred to holders of Master Degrees, after a minimum of two years' study. A Doctor in Technology (DTech) is awarded after successful completion of a thesis at Technikons. This degree is research based and studies last at least two years. It comprises an advanced research project.

Teacher education:

Training of pre-primary and primary/basic school teachers

Training Colleges that previously reported to the provinces are currently in the process of transfer to the National Department of Education and certain Universities run three-or four-year Diploma courses qualifying holders to teach in primary schools. This also applies to some universities and technikons. The general admission requirement for Diploma studies at any of these colleges is a Senior Certificate with pass marks in one of the two languages of instruction (i.e. English and Afrikaans).

Training of secondary school teachers

Degree-level courses for secondary school teachers are run by all universities and technikons. A Senior Certificate with a matriculation endorsement or a Certificate of complete or conditional exemption is required for university study, whilst technikons have different requirements (usually Senior Certificates and further requirements as stipulated in their joint statute).

Training of higher education teachers

Forty per cent of academic staff obtained their highest qualification at the University in which they are employed, 30 per cent at another South African University and 30 per cent at a foreign University.

Non-traditional studies:

Distance higher education

Distance teaching, which is mainly by correspondence, provides courses for about 35 per cent of enrolled students. The University of South Africa (UNISA) offers correspondence courses, either in English or in Afrikaans, for Bachelor Degree and Postgraduate qualification. Course work is structured in modules. A maximum of 10 years is allowed to obtain a Bachelor Degree, an additional year for Bachelor Honours Degree, 3 years for Postgraduate qualifications, 2 further years for a Master Degree and 2 years for a Doctorate. The Degrees are considered to be equivalent in standard to those awarded by other Universities. The Technikon South Africa offers distance education either through the medium of English or Afrikaans for Diplomas, Bachelor Degrees and Postgraduate qualifications provided such Bachelor Degrees include an in-service training component.

NATIONAL BODIES

Responsible authorities:

Department of Education
　　Minister: Kader Asmal
　　Director-general: T.D. Mseleku
　　International Relations: G. Jeppie
　　Private Bag X9034
　　Cape Town 8000
　　Tel: +27(21) 465-7350
　　Fax: +27(21) 461-4788
　　EMail: webmaster@educ.pwv.gov.za
　　WWW: http://education.pwv.gov.za

South African Universities' Vice-Chancellors' Association (SAUVCA)
　　Chief executive: Piyushi Kotecha
　　Director, Administrative Services: Tessa Yeowart
　　PO Box 27392
　　Sunnyside
　　Pretoria 0132
　　Tel: +27(12) 481-2842
　　Fax: +27(12) 481-2843
　　EMail: admin@sauvca.org.za
　　WWW: http://www.sauvca.org.za

　　Role of governing body: Umbrella body for the 21 South African public universities

Committee of Technikon Principals (CTP)
　　Executive Director: R.H. du Pré
　　Executive Secretary: Marianne Haettingh
　　Executive Officer: Kogie Pretorius
　　Private Bag X680
　　Pretoria 0001
　　Tel: +27(12) 3261066
　　Fax: +27(12) 3257387

EMail: CTPdupre@techpta.ac.za
WWW: http://www.technikons.co.za

ADMISSIONS TO HIGHER EDUCATION

Admission to non university higher education studies

Name of secondary school credential required: Senior Certificate
For entry to: Technikons, technical colleges, and other colleges.

Alternatives to credentials: Senior Certificate with N-courses obtained at technical colleges or technical high schools.

Admission to university-level studies

Name of secondary school credential required: Senior Certificate
Minimum score/requirement: Pass marks in two Higher Grade languages, two additional Higher Grade subjects, at least a further Standard Grade subject and a minimum aggregate of 45 % for six subjects.
For entry to: Universities.

Alternatives to credentials: Certificate of exemption from the matriculation endorsement required as issued by the Matriculation Board on behalf of SAUVCA or a conditional admission certificate issued by a technikon.

Entrance exams required: Matriculation endorsements are required for admission to first degree studies at university level and senior certificates for first degree studies at Technikon or college level.

Foreign students admission

Admission requirements: Prospective students coming from a non-South African schooling system must for benchmark purposes hold qualifications that must be at least equivalent to the local system. For university studies candidates apply to the university which will forward the application to the Matriculation Board which issues a certificate of exemption in terms of other specified provisions. Conditions must be satisfied on completion of degrees in the case of foreign conditional exemption certificates.

Entry regulations: Students must hold a valid passport, a duly completed application form B1-159 available from the Department of Home Affairs, a standard letter of provisional acceptance to a South African institution, a letter of motivation and proof that the student is in a situation to pay the tuition fees and has adequate means of support.

Language requirements: Students must be proficient in English or Afrikaans.

References to further information on foreign student admissions and recognition of studies

Title: A Guide of South African Universities
Publisher: South African Universities Vice-Chancellors' Association

Title: University calendars
Publisher: South African Universities Vice-Chancellors' Association

STUDENT LIFE

National student associations and unions

South African Students' Representative Council (SAU-SRC)
Private Bag
Students' Union. University of Cape Town
Rondebosch 7700
Tel: +27(21) 650-9111
Fax: +27(21) 650-2138
WWW: http://www.uct.ac.za

Student expenses and financial aid

Student costs:

Home students tuition fees: Minimum: 4,320 (Rand)
Maximum: 25,000 (Rand)

Publications on student services and financial aid:

Title: Guide to Distance Education in South Africa
Publisher: HSRC Publishers

Title: Guide to Higher Education in South Africa
Publisher: HSRC Publishers

Title: Study Abroad 2000-2001
Publisher: UNESCO/IBE
Year of publication: 1999

INTERNATIONAL COOPERATION AND EXCHANGES

Principal national bodies responsible for dealing with international cooperation and exchanges in higher education:

South African Universities' Vice Chancellors' Association (SAUVCA)
Chief Executive: Piyushi Kotecha
Director, Administrative Services: Tessa Yeowart
PO Box 27392
Sunnyside, Pretoria 0132
Tel: +27(12) 481-2842
Fax: +27(12) 481-2843
EMail: admin@sauvca.org.za
WWW: http://www.sauvca.za

The International Education Association of South Africa (IEASA)
Head: Amalia Altin
PO Box 11029

Hatfield, Pretoria 0028
Tel: +27(12) 4202049
Fax: +27(12) 4202029
EMail: aaltin@ccnet.up.ac.za
WWW: http://sunsite.wits.ac.za/ieasa

GRADING SYSTEM

Usual grading system in secondary school

Full Description: Marking is alphabetical or expressed as a percentage. The usual pass mark in all higher grade subjects is 40% (with 2 exceptions). The pass mark in all standard grade subjects is 33%.
Highest on scale: A 80-100%
Pass/fail level: E 40-49%
Lowest on scale: F 33-39%

Main grading system used by higher education institutions

Full Description: Classification at some universities: 1st class (75-100%); 2nd class division 1 (70-74); 2nd class division 2 (60-69); 3rd class (50-59); fail (below 50). Other universities only distinguish: Distinction (75-100%); Pass (50-74%).
Highest on scale: 1st class
Pass/fail level: 3rd class
Lowest on scale: F

NOTES ON HIGHER EDUCATION SYSTEM

Data for academic year: 2000-2001
Source: South African Universities Vice-Chancellors' Association (SAUVCA), 2001

INSTITUTIONS OF HIGHER EDUCATION

UNIVERSITIES

• UNIVERSITY OF CAPE TOWN (UCT)

Bremner Bldg., Private Bag, Rondebosch, Cape Town 7701
Tel: +27(21) 650-9111
Fax: +27(21) 650-2138
Telex: 5-22208
EMail: aeshta@bremner.uct.ac.za
Website: http://www.uct.ac.za

Vice-Chancellor: Njabulo S. Ndebele (2000-2004)
Tel: +27(21) 650-2105 Fax: +27(21) 689-2440
EMail: vc@bremner.uct.ac.za

Registrar: Hugh Theodore Amoore Tel: +27(21) 650-2115
Fax: +27(21) 650-2138 EMail: aeshta@bremner.uct.ac.za

International Relations: Lesley Shackleton
Tel: +27(21) 650-2822 Fax: +27(21) 686-5444
EMail: lys@education.uct.ac.za

Faculties

Commerce (Accountancy; Actuarial Science; Business and Commerce; Computer Science; Economics; Industrial and Organizational Psychology; Information Sciences; Law; Management; Marketing; Statistics) *Dean:* Brian N Kantor, *full-time staff:* 233, *part-time staff:* 248, *students:* 4,736

Engineering and Built Environment (Architecture and Planning; Building Technologies; Chemical Engineering; Civil Engineering; Computer Engineering; Economics; Electrical and Electronic Engineering; Engineering; Management; Mechanical Engineering; Town Planning) *Dean:* C.T O'Connor, *full-time staff:* 221, *part-time staff:* 126, *students:* 2,520

Health Sciences (Health Sciences; Medicine; Nursing; Physical Therapy; Speech Therapy and Audiology; Surgery) *Dean:* N. Padayachee, *full-time staff:* 466, *part-time staff:* 198, *students:* 2,438

Humanities (Arts and Humanities; Dance; Fine Arts; Music; Performing Arts; Social Sciences) *Dean:* Royston Pillay, *full-time staff:* 312, *part-time staff:* 168, *students:* 4,684

Law (Law; Philosophy) *Dean:* H. Corder, *full-time staff:* 59, *part-time staff:* 23, *students:* 837

Science (Applied Mathematics; Archaeology; Astronomy and Space Science; Biochemistry; Botany; Chemistry; Computer Science; Environmental Studies; Geography; Marine Science and Oceanography; Mathematics; Microbiology; Natural Sciences; Physics; Statistics; Zoology) *Dean:* B. Daya Reddy, *full-time staff:* 372, *part-time staff:* 237, *students:* 1,910

History: Founded 1829 as College by local community, acquired official status 1873. Became University by Act of Parliament 1916 and granted Charter 1918. An autonomous Institution receiving financial support (70%) from the State. Open to all who meet the academic requirements, regardless of colour, race, sex or religion.

Governing Bodies: University Council; University Senate

Academic Year: February to December (February-April; April-June; July-September; September-December)

Admission Requirements: Matriculation Certificate or certificate of exemption issued by the Joint Matriculation Board

Main Language(s) of Instruction: English

Degrees and Diplomas: *Bachelor's Degree:* Education (BEd), 1 yr following first degree; Chemical Engineering, 1yr full first degree; Arts (BA); Commerce (BCom); Laws (LLB); Social Sciences (BSocSc), 3 yrs; Allied Health Professions and Sciences; Business Science (BBusSc); Library and Information Sciences (BBibl); Medicine and Surgery (MBChB); Music; Primary Education (BPrimEd), 4 yrs; Electrical Engineering; Electro-Mechanical Engineering; Logopaedics and Physiotherapy; Science (BSc), 4-5 yrs; Civil Engineering; Engineering (BScEng), 5 yrs; Architecture and Planning (BArch), 6 yrs; *Honours Bachelor's Degree:* a further yr; *Master's Degree:* a further 1-2 yrs; *Doctorate:* 1-2 yrs. The Bachelor (Honours) Degree is awarded in the same fields of study as the Bachelor's Degree. Also Undergraduate and Postgraduate Diplomas

Student Services: Academic Counselling, Social Counselling, Employment Services, Foreign Student Adviser, Cultural Centre, Language Programmes, Handicapped Facilities, Health Services, Canteen, Foreign Student Centre

Student Residential Facilities: For c. 2200 students

Special Facilities: Irma Stern Museum (Fine Arts Collection). Archaeological Museum. P.A. Wagner Museum (Mineralogical and Geological Specimens). Herbarium

Libraries: J.W. Jagger Library, 7 branch Libraries, total, c. 1m. vols

Publications: Journal of Energy in Southern Africa (quarterly); Sea Changes; Social Dynamics (biannually); Responsa Meridiane; General and Faculty Prospectuses; Mathematics Colloquium; Research Report; UCT News; Jagger Journal; Acta Juridica; Bolus Herbarium Contributions; Centre for African Studies Communications; Studies in History of Cape Town; Oceanography Yearbook (annually)

Academic Staff 2000			TOTAL
FULL-TIME			1,663
PART-TIME			1,000
TOTAL			**2,663**

Student Numbers 2000	MEN	WOMEN	TOTAL
All (Foreign Included)	9,050	8,075	**17,125**

• UNIVERSITY OF DURBAN-WESTVILLE

Private Bag X54001, Durban 4000
Tel: +27(31) 204-4111
Fax: +27(31) 204-4383
Telex: 6-23338 SA
Cable: udwest
EMail: knaicker@pixie.udw.ac.za
Website: http://www.udw.ac.za

Vice-Chancellor and Principal: Mapule F. Ramashala
Tel: +27(31) 204-5000 Fax: +27(31) 622-2192
EMail: vc@pixie.udw.ac.za

Registrar (Academic): E. Mneney Tel: +27(31) 204-8656
Fax: +27(31) 204-4824 EMail: emneney@pixie.udw.ac.za

International Relations: Prem Ramlachan
Tel: +27(31) 204-4253 Fax: +27(31) 204-4808
EMail: diggers@pixie.udw.ac.za

Faculties

Health Sciences (Anatomy; Dentistry; Health Sciences; Occupational Therapy; Optometry; Pharmacology; Pharmacy; Physiology; Social Work; Speech Therapy and Audiology; Sports) *Dean*: S.S. Mokoena

Humanities (Afrikaans; Anthropology; Arts and Humanities; Economics; Education; English; History; Native Language; Psychology; Religious Studies; Social Sciences; Sociology)

Law, Economics and Management (Accountancy; Commercial Law; Criminology; Economics; Industrial and Organizational Psychology; Law; Management; Private Law; Public Law) *Dean*: J.G. Mowatt

Science and Engineering (Applied Physics; Biochemistry; Botany; Chemical Engineering; Chemistry; Civil Engineering; Computer Science; Electrical Engineering; Geology; Information Technology; Marine Science and Oceanography; Mathematics; Mechanical Engineering; Microbiology; Physics; Zoology) *Dean*: R.G. Ori

Further Information: Also Legal Aid Clinic. Advice desk for abused women

History: Founded 1961 as University College under the aegis of the University of South Africa, became University 1972. An autonomous Institution receiving financial support from the State.

Governing Bodies: University Council, comprising 20 members; University Senate

Academic Year: February to December (February-March; April-June; July-September; October-December)

Admission Requirements: Matriculation Certificate or certificate of exemption issued by the Joint Matriculation Board

Fees: (Rand): 8000-10, 000 per annum

Main Language(s) of Instruction: English

International Co-operation: Michigan State University

Degrees and Diplomas: *Bachelor's Degree*: Accountancy (BAcc); Administration (BAdmin); Arts (BA); Business Science (BBusSc); Commerce (BCom); Dental Therapy; Engineering (BEng); Financial Law (BProcLaw); Home Economics (BHomeEcon); Jurisprudence (BJuris); Law (LLB); Library Science (BBibl); Medical Science (BMedSc); Music (BMus); Occupational Therapy (BOT); Optometry (BOptom); Oral Health; Pedagogy (BPaed); Pharmacy (BPharm); Physiotherapy (BPhysio); Science (BSc); Speech and Hearing Therapy; Theology (BTheol), 3-4 yrs; *Honours Bachelor's Degree*: a further yr; *Master's Degree*: a further 1-2 yrs; *Doctorate*: (PhD), 1-2 yrs. The Bachelor (Honours) Degree is awarded in the same fields of study as the Bachelor's Degree. Also Undergraduate and Postgraduate Diplomas

Student Services: Academic Counselling, Social Counselling, Employment Services, Nursery Care, Cultural Centre, Sports Facilities, Handicapped Facilities, Health Services, Canteen, Foreign Student Centre

Student Residential Facilities: For c. 1200 students

Special Facilities: Documentation Centre on Indian Culture and History

Libraries: 208,000 vols

Publications: Renaissance (quarterly); University Journal (annually)

Press or Publishing House: University of Durban-Westville Press

Academic Staff *1999:* Total: **435**

Student Numbers *1999:* Total: **10,000**

• UNIVERSITY OF FORT HARE
Private Bag X1314, Alice, Eastern Cape Province 5700
Tel: +27(40) 602-2011
Fax: +27(40) 653-1643
Cable: unifort
EMail: dmc@ufh.ac.za
Website: http://www.ufh.ac.za

Vice-Chancellor: Derrick Swartz Tel: +27(40) 653-2312
Fax: +27(40) 653-1338 EMail: dbotha@ufh.ac.za

Registrar: A.W. Shaw Tel: +27(40) 602-2181
Fax: +27(40) 653-2314 EMail: ashaw@ufh.ac.za

Faculties
Agriculture
Arts (Arts and Humanities)
Economics
Education
Law
Science (Natural Sciences)
Social Sciences
Theology

Units
English Language Curriculum Renewal (English)

Divisions
External Studies *(Bisho)* (Education)
Nursing *(Mdantsane)*

Institutes
Agricultural and Rural Development Research (Agriculture; Rural Studies)
Government *(Fort Hare)*
Management (FHIM) *(Fort Hare)* (Management)

Centres
Academic Development (Education)
Adult Basic Education
Cultural Studies
Educational Policy (Educational Administration)
Human Rights *(Olivier Tambo Chair)*
Research Resource *(Govan Mbeki)* (Natural Resources)
Xhosa Dictionary (Native Language Education)

History: Founded 1916 as South African Native College by the United Free Church of Scotland. Affiliated to Rhodes University

1951-1959. Transferred to Department of Bantu Education 1960. Acquired present status and title 1970.

Governing Bodies: University Council; University Senate

Academic Year: January to December (January-April; April-June; July-September; September-December)

Admission Requirements: Matriculation Certificate or certificate of exemption issued by the Joint Matriculation Board

Main Language(s) of Instruction: English

Degrees and Diplomas: *Bachelor's Degree*: Arts (BA); Commerce (BComm); Financial Law (BProcLaw); Jurisprudence (BJuris); Law (LLB); Nursing (BCur); Pedagogy (BPaed); Science (BSc); Theology (BTheol); *Honours Bachelor's Degree*: a further yr; *Master's Degree*: a further 1-2 yrs; *Doctorate*: 1-2 yrs. The Bachelor (Honours) Degree is awarded in the same fields of study as the Bachelor's Degree. Also Undergraduate and Postgraduate Diplomas

Student Residential Facilities: Yes

Special Facilities: F.S. Malan Museum. De Beers Centenary Art Gallery

Libraries: Central Library (Howard Pimm collection of Africana)

Publications: Fort Harian (3 per annum); Papers

Academic Staff *1999*: Full-Time: c. 230 Part-Time: c. 15 Total: c. 245

Student Numbers *1999:* Total: c. 5,520

Evening Students, c. 1,180

• MEDICAL UNIVERSITY OF SOUTHERN AFRICA (MEDUNSA)
PO Box 197, Medunsa 0204
Tel: +27(12) 521-4222 +27(12) 521-4111
Fax: +27(12) 521-4349
Telex: 320580 sa
EMail: berndt@medunsa.ac.za
Website: http://www.medunsa.ac.za

Principal and Vice-Chancellor (Acting): M.D. Bomela
Tel: +27(12) 521-4112 Fax: +27(12) 560-0274

Registrar: Carl W. Berndt EMail: berndt@medunsa.ac.za

Faculties
Dentistry (Dentistry; Oral Pathology; Orthodontics; Stomatology) *Dean (Acting)*: C. Peter Owen
Medicine (Anaesthesiology; Anatomy; Cardiology; Clinical Psychology; Community Health; Dermatology; Forensic Medicine and Dentistry; Gastroenterology; Haematology; Medicine; Nursing; Nutrition; Pathology; Pharmacy; Surgery) *Dean (Acting)*: James R. la Rose
Sciences (Biological and Life Sciences; Chemistry; Mathematics; Natural Sciences; Physics; Psychology; Statistics; Technology) *Dean*: J. Viljoen Groenewald

History: Founded 1976. An autonomous institution receiving financial support from the Central Government.

Governing Bodies: University Council, comprising 28 members; University Senate, comprising 81 members

Academic Year: January to November (January-June; June-November)

Admission Requirements: Matriculation Certificate or certificate of exemption issued by the Joint Matriculation Board

Main Language(s) of Instruction: English

International Co-operation: Bristol University; Ben Gurion University; Curtin University of Technology; Tulane University of Louisiana; University of Ulm; Free University Amsterdam; University of Kentucky; University of Nairobi

Degrees and Diplomas: *Bachelor's Degree*: Nursing Science (BCur), 4 1/2 yrs; Nursing Education and Administration (BCur(1and A)); Occupational Therapy (BOccTher); Science (BSc); Science (Medical) (BSc(Med)); Science in Dietetics (BSc(Diet)); Science in Physiotherapy (BSc(Physio)), 4 yrs; Dental Surgery (BChD); Medicine and Surgery (MB ChB); Veterinary Medicine and Surgery (BVMCh), 6 yrs; *Master's Degree*; *Doctorate*

Student Services: Academic Counselling, Social Counselling, Nursery Care, Cultural Centre, Sports Facilities, Health Services, Canteen, Foreign Student Centre

Student Residential Facilities: For c. 2400 students

Libraries: Medunsa Library, 76,297 vols; 710 periodicals

Publications: Medunsa Yearbook; Principal's Annual Report; Exploration (Medunsa Annual Research Report) (annually); Echo; Medunsa Brief

Academic Staff *1999:* Total: c. 187

Student Numbers 1999	MEN	WOMEN	TOTAL
All (Foreign Included)	1,868	1,576	**3,444**

*• UNIVERSITY OF NATAL
King George V Avenue, Durban 4041
Tel: +27(31) 260-2206
Fax: +27(31) 260-2204
Telex: 621231 sa
EMail: malgasp@nu.ac.za
Website: http://www.nu.ac.za

Vice-Chancellor (Acting): D.A. Maughan Brown (2002-)

General Secretary (Acting): R. Suchipersadh

International Relations: Roshen Kishun
Tel: +27(31) 260-2230 Fax: +27(31) 260-2967
EMail: kishun@nu.ac.za

Faculties
Community and Development Disciplines (Anthropology; Architecture; Development Studies; Education; Nursing; Psychology; Social and Community Services; Social Work) *Dean*: R. Miller, *full-time staff: 66, part-time staff: 17, students: 2,451*
Engineering (Agricultural Engineering; Chemical Engineering; Civil Engineering; Construction Engineering; Electrical Engineering; Electronic Engineering; Engineering; Real Estate; Surveying and Mapping) *Dean*: L.W. Roberts, *full-time staff: 61, part-time staff: 10, students: 1,661*
Human Sciences *(Durban Campus)* (African Languages; Afrikaans; Arts and Humanities; Classical Languages; Communication Arts; Dutch; Economic History; English; European Studies; Gender Studies; History; Industrial and Organizational Psychology; Labour and Industrial Relations; Linguistics; Media Studies; Music; Performing Arts; Philosophy; Social Sciences;

Theatre; Translation and Interpretation) *Dean*: M. Chapman, *full-time staff*: 89, *students*: 1,667

Human Sciences *(Pietermaritzburg)* (Accountancy; Adult Education; African Languages; Afrikaans; Arts and Humanities; Business Administration; Business and Commerce; Classical Languages; Communication Arts; Dutch; Economic History; Education; English; European Studies; Fine Arts; Greek; Hebrew; History; Library Science; Linguistics; Literature; Management; Marketing; Media Studies; Philosophy; Primary Education; Secondary Education; Social Sciences; Theology; Translation and Interpretation) *Dean*: R. Nicolson, *full-time staff*: 89, *students*: 2,760

Law *(Durban and Pietermaritzburg)* (Commercial Law; Labour Law; Law; Maritime Law; Private Law; Public Law) *Dean*: A. Rycroft, *full-time staff*: 41, *part-time staff*: 3, *students*: 1,343

Management Studies (Accountancy; Business Administration; Economics; Finance; Management) *Dean*: A. Lumby, *full-time staff*: 46, *students*: 2,871

Medicine (Health Sciences; Medicine; Occupational Health; Public Health; Sports Medicine) *Dean*: B.M. Kistnasamy, *full-time staff*: 219, *part-time staff*: 168, *students*: 1,154

Science (Applied Chemistry; Applied Mathematics; Biology; Chemistry; Environmental Studies; Geography; Geology; Information Technology; Mathematics; Natural Sciences; Physics) *Dean*: J. van den Berg, *full-time staff*: 84, *part-time staff*: 20, *students*: 904

Science and Agriculture (Agricultural Business; Agricultural Management; Agriculture; Agronomy; Animal Husbandry; Applied Chemistry; Botany; Chemistry; Crop Production; Environmental Studies; Food Technology; Information Technology; Mathematics; Natural Resources; Natural Sciences; Nutrition; Physics; Rural Planning; Statistics; Zoology) *Dean*: R. Haines, *full-time staff*: 84, *part-time staff*: 20, *students*: 1,626

History: Founded 1909 by Act of Parliament as University College, became independent University 1949. An autonomous institution with branches in Durban and Pietermaritzburg receiving financial support from the State.

Governing Bodies: University Council; University Senate

Academic Year: February to November

Admission Requirements: Matriculation Certificate or certificate of exemption issued by the Joint Matriculation Board

Main Language(s) of Instruction: English

Degrees and Diplomas: *Bachelor's Degree*: Education (BEd), 1 yr following first degree; Laws (LLB), 3 yrs following first degree; Accountancy (BAcc); Agricultural Management (MAgricMgt); Agriculture (BAgric); Arts (BA); Commerce (BComm); Community Development (BCommunDev); Engineering (BSc(Eng)); Music (BMus); Science (BSc); Social Sciences (BSocSc); Social Work (BSocWK), 3-4 yrs; Architecture (BArch), 6 yrs; Medicine (MBChB), 7 yrs; *Honours Bachelor's Degree*: a further yr; *Master's Degree*: a further 1-2 yrs; *Doctorate*: a further 1-2 yrs. The Bachelor (Honours) Degree is awarded in the same fields of study as the Bachelor's Degree. Also Undergraduate and Postgraduate Diplomas

Student Services: Academic Counselling, Employment Services, Foreign Student Adviser, Cultural Centre, Sports Facilities, Language Programmes, Handicapped Facilities, Health Services, Canteen, Foreign Student Centre

Student Residential Facilities: For c. 1960 students

Special Facilities: Campbell Collections (Africana)

Libraries: Total, c. 918,000 vols

Academic Staff *1999-2000:* Total: c. 1,100

Student Numbers *1999-2000:* Total: c. 22,000

PIETERMARITZBURG CAMPUS
Private Bag X10, Scottsville, Kwazulu Natal 3209

Faculties

Agriculture (Agricultural Economics; Agriculture; Agronomy; Animal Husbandry; Dietetics; Genetics; Horticulture; Microbiology; Plant Pathology) *Dean*: F.H.J. Rijkenberg, *full-time staff*: 46, *students*: 688

Commerce (Accountancy; Business Administration; Business and Commerce) *Dean*: B.S. Stobie, *full-time staff*: 22, *students*: 1,347

Human Sciences (Arts and Humanities; Social Sciences)

Humanities and Education (Art History; Arts and Humanities; Classical Languages; Education; English; Fine Arts; French; German; History; Modern Languages; Philosophy; Religious Studies; Theatre; Theology) *Dean*: R. Nicolson, *full-time staff*: 70, *students*: 1,755

Law (Environmental Studies; Law) *Dean*: J.R. Lund, *full-time staff*: 16, *students*: 377

Science (Applied Mathematics; Biochemistry; Botany; Chemical Engineering; Chemistry; Computer Science; Entomology; Geology; Mathematics; Natural Sciences; Physics; Statistics; Zoology) *Dean*: R.J. Haines, *full-time staff*: 86, *students*: 935

Science and Agriculture (Agriculture)

Social Sciences (Economics; Information Sciences; Political Science; Psychology; Social Sciences; Sociology) *Dean*: P. Stopforth, *full-time staff*: 40, *students*: 709

*• UNIVERSITY OF THE NORTH
Private Bag X1106, Sovenga 0727
Tel: +27(15) 268-9111
Fax: +27(15) 267-0152
Telex: 331813 SA
Cable: unikol sovenga
EMail: ndebele-ns@univl.unorth.ac.za
Website: http://www.unorth.ac.za

Vice-Chancellor and Principal: P.T Fitzgerald (2002-)
Tel: +27(15) 268-2100 Fax: +27(15) 267-0142
EMail: moagin@unin.unorth.ac.za

Registrar (Acting): KMA Nhlane Tel: +27(15) 268-2407
Fax: +27(15) 268-3048 EMail: malgasp@unin.unorth.ac.za

International Relations: J.M. Wiltshire
Tel: +27(15) 268-2625 Fax: +27(15) 268-0485
EMail: majai@unin.unorth.ac.za

Faculties

Agriculture (Agricultural Economics; Agriculture; Animal Husbandry; Aquaculture; Environmental Studies; Soil Science) *Dean*: N.M. Mokgalong

Arts (Arts and Humanities) *Dean*: Sr. Motshologane

Education *Dean*: Ma Rampedi

Health Sciences (Health Sciences; Medicine; Nursing; Nutrition; Optometry; Pharmacology; Pharmacy) *Dean*: D.D.D. Sheni

Humanities (African Languages; African Studies; Ancient Civilizations; Asian Studies; Behavioural Sciences; Communication Studies; Education; Linguistics; Mathematics; Science Education; Social Sciences; Technology) *Dean*: L.J. Teffo

Law (Commercial Law; Labour Law; Law; Private Law; Public Law) *Dean*: P.F. Breed

Management Sciences (Accountancy; Administration; Business Administration; Development Studies; Economics; Industrial and Organizational Psychology; Leadership; Management; Public Administration) *Dean*: P.E. Franks

Mathematics and Natural Sciences (Applied Mathematics; Aquaculture; Biochemistry; Biology; Botany; Chemistry; Computer Science; Materials Engineering; Mathematics; Microbiology; Natural Sciences; Physiology; Zoology) *Dean*: M.M. Sibara

Theology and Religious Studies (Christian Religious Studies; Missionary Studies; Religious Studies; Theology) *Dean*: R.T.H. Dolamo

Units

Aquacultural Research (Aquaculture)
Statistics and Operations Research (Statistics)

Further Information: Also Branches at Qwaqwa and Giyani

History: Founded 1959 as College to serve the Tsonga, Sotho, Vedda, Xitsonga and Tswana communities. Acquired present status and title 1970. An autonomous, non-racial institution receiving financial support from the State.

Governing Bodies: University Council; University Senate

Academic Year: January to December (January-March; April-July; July-December)

Admission Requirements: Matriculation Certificate or certificate of exemption issued by the Joint Matriculation Board

Main Language(s) of Instruction: English

International Co-operation: Free University Amsterdam

Degrees and Diplomas: *Bachelor's Degree*: Administration (BAdmin); Arts (BA); Commerce (BComm); Jurisprudence (BJuris); Science (BSc), 3 yrs; Agricultural Management (BAgricAdmin); Agriculture in Pedagogy (BAgricPaed); Arts in Pedagogy (BAPaed); Nursing (BCur); Theology (BTh), 3-4 yrs; Arts in Social Work (BA(SW)); Commerce in Pedagogy (BCommPaed); Financial Law (BProcLaw); Library Information Sciences (BBibl); Optometry (BOptom); Pharmacy (BPharm); Roman Law (LLB(Roman)); Science in Agriculture (BScAgric); Science in Medical Laboratory Sciences (BSc(MedLabSci)), 4 yrs; *Honours Bachelor's Degree*: a further yr; *Master's Degree*: a further 1-2 yrs; *Doctorate*. The Bachelor (Honours) Degree is awarded in the same fields of study as the Bachelor's Degree

Student Residential Facilities: Yes

Special Facilities: Biological Museum. Herbarium. Experimental Farm

Libraries: Unin Library, 140,000 vols

Publications: Educationis (biannually); Theologica Viatorum (annually)

Academic Staff *1999:* Total: c. 600

Student Numbers *1999:* Total: c. 9,850

Evening Students, c. 300

• UNIVERSITY OF NORTH WEST
Private Bag X2046, Mmbatho, North-West 2735
Tel: +27(18) 389-2111
Fax: +27(18) 392-5775
Telex: (0140) 3072 BP
Cable: unibo mmabatho
Website: http://www.uniwest.ac.za

Vice-Chancellor: M.N. Takalo Tel: +27(18) 392-1189
Fax: +27(18) 392-3434
EMail: takalomn@unw001.uniwest.ac.za

Registrar: D. Setsetse Tel: +27(18) 389-2156
Fax: +27(18) 392-4285 EMail: mgtreh@unw001.uniwest.ac.za

Faculties

Administration and Management (Accountancy; Economics; Management) *Dean*: E.I. Simbo

Agriculture (Agricultural Economics; Agriculture; Animal Husbandry; Botany; Plant and Crop Protection) *Dean*: S.M. Funnah

Education (Education; Teacher Training)

Health and Social Sciences (Development Studies; Health Sciences; Industrial and Organizational Psychology; Nursing; Political Science; Psychology; Social Sciences) *Dean*: D.B.T. Milazi

Human Sciences (Arts and Humanities; English; Fine Arts; Geography; History) *Dean*: J. Buscop

Law *Dean*: R.L. Kettles

Science and Technology (Biology; Chemistry; Communication Studies; Information Technology; Mathematics; Natural Sciences; Physics; Technology) *Dean*: S.H. Taole

Institutes

African Studies
Development Research (Development Studies) *Director (Acting)*: M.P. Maaga
Education *Director*: M.I. Mahape

Centres

Academic Development (Education) *Director (Acting)*: M.C. Rakubutu

Business and Management Development (Business Administration; Management) *Director*: I. Bootha

Medicine and Law (International) (Law; Medicine)

History: Founded 1980 as University of Bophuthatswana, acquired present title 1996.

• UNIVERSITY OF FREE STATE/UNIVERSITEIT VAN DIE VRYSTAAT (UFS)
PO Box 339, Bloemfontein, Free State 9300
Tel: +27(51) 401-9111
Fax: +27(51) 401-2117
EMail: aag@rs.uovs.ac.za
Website: http://www.uovs.ac.za

Rector and Vice-Chancellor: S.F. Coetzee (1997-)
Fax: +27(51) 444-0740

Registrar: W.S. Malherbe Tel: +27(51) 401-2112
EMail: bewm@admin.uovs.ac.za

International Relations: H. Barnard Tel: +27(51) 401-2501
EMail: ardp@rs.uovs.ac.za

Faculties
Commerce (Business and Commerce) *Dean*: M.J. Crous, *full-time staff:* 56, *part-time staff:* 97, *students:* 2,082
Health Sciences (Health Sciences; Pharmacy) *Dean*: C.J.C. Nel, *full-time staff:* 456, *part-time staff:* 104, *students:* 1,936
Humanities (Arts and Humanities; Education; Political Science; Social Sciences) *Dean*: D.F.M. Strauss, *full-time staff:* 170, *part-time staff:* 261, *students:* 3,041
Law *Dean*: Jozeph J. Henning, *full-time staff:* 21, *part-time staff:* 25, *students:* 670
Natural and Agricultural Sciences (Agriculture; Animal Husbandry; Natural Sciences) *Dean*: G.N. van Wyk, *full-time staff:* 284, *part-time staff:* 176, *students:* 2,058
Theology *Dean*: P.C. Potgieter, *full-time staff:* 15, *part-time staff:* 15, *students:* 119

Units
Agricultural Biometrics *(On Campus)* (Statistics) *Head*: Mike D. Fair, *full-time staff:* 1, *students:* 4
Business Ethics (Ethics) *Head*: D.S. Lubbe, *full-time staff:* 1
Professional Development in Human Sciences (Development Studies; Social Sciences) *Head*: A. Weyers, *full-time staff:* 5, *part-time staff:* 4
Small Business Development (Small Business) *Head*: W.J.C. van der Merwe, *full-time staff:* 7, *part-time staff:* 12

Programmes
Open Learning Distance Education *(OLDEAP)* *Head*: A.H. Strydam, *full-time staff:* 17, *part-time staff:* 4, *students:* 25

Schools
Management *Director*: D.A. Viljoen, *full-time staff:* 9, *part-time staff:* 1, *students:* 257

Institutes
Contemporary History *Director*: A.M. Dippenar, *part-time staff:* 9
Groundwater Studies (Water Science) *Director*: F.D.I. Hodgson, *full-time staff:* 11, *part-time staff:* 5, *students:* 20
Research in Educational Planning (Educational Research) *Director*: H.J. van der Linde, *full-time staff:* 2, *part-time staff:* 3

Centres
Accountancy *Director*: Hentie A. van Wyk, *full-time staff:* 9, *part-time staff:* 43, *students:* 1,505
Agricultural Management *(On Campus)* *Director*: Wimpie T. Nell, *full-time staff:* 1, *students:* 102
Business Law
Business Law (Commercial Law) *Director*: Jozeph J. Henning, *full-time staff:* 5, *part-time staff:* 10
Construction Entrepreneurship (Real Estate) *Director*: J.J.P. Verster, *full-time staff:* 7, *part-time staff:* 11
Continued Legal Training *(On Campus)* (Law) *Director*: Mouritz C.J. Bobbert, *full-time staff:* 1
Development Support (Development Studies) *Director*: Lucius C. Botes, *full-time staff:* 1, *part-time staff:* 3, *students:* 36

Environmental Management *(On Campus)* *Director*: Maitland T. Seaman, *full-time staff:* 2, *students:* 48
Human Rights Studies (Human Rights) *Director*: Jan L. Pretorius, *full-time staff:* 2
Professional Ethics *(On Campus)* (Ethics) *Director*: Mouritz C.J. Bobbert, *full-time staff:* 1
Sustainable Agriculture *(On Campus)* (Agriculture) *Director*: Izak B. Groenewald, *full-time staff:* 2, *students:* 121

Research Centres
Farmous *Director*: B.H. Meyer, *full-time staff:* 131

History: Founded 1855 by Sir George Grey and established as University College 1904. Became University under present title 1950. An autonomous Institution receiving financial support from the State.

Governing Bodies: University Council, comprising c. 30 members

Academic Year: February to December (February-March; April-June; July-September; October-December)

Admission Requirements: Matriculation Certificate or certificate of exemption issued by the Joint Matriculation Board

Fees: (Rand): 5550-8070; postgraduate, 5230-5708

Main Language(s) of Instruction: Afrikaans, English

International Co-operation: Catholic University Leuven; Nottingham Trent University; Griffith University; University of Denver; Uppsala University; South Carolina State University; North Dakota State University; University of Ghent; Virginia Polytechnic Institute and State University; University of Murcia; DePaul University; University of Wroclaw; University of Mysore; Sambalpur University

Degrees and Diplomas: *Bachelor's Degree*: Education (BEd), 1 yr following first degree; Law (LLB), 2-3 yrs following first degree; Theology (BTh), 3 yrs following first degree; Accountancy (BAcc); Administration (BAdmin); Agriculture (BAgric); Arts (BA); Civil Law (BClur.civil law); Commerce (BCom); Economics (BEcon); Financial Law (BProcLaw); Jurisprudence (BJuris); Library Science (BBibl); Medical Science (BMedSc); Occupational Therapy; Personnel Guidance (BPL); Radiography (BRad); Science (BSc); Social Science (BSocSc), 3-4 yrs; Architecture (BArch), 4 1/2 yrs; Medicine and Surgery (MBChB), 6 yrs; *Honours Bachelor's Degree*: a further yr; *Master's Degree*: a further yr; *Doctorate*. The Bachelor (Honours) Degree is awarded in the same fields of study as the Bachelor's Degree. Also Postgraduate Diplomas

Student Services: Academic Counselling, Social Counselling, Employment Services, Nursery Care, Cultural Centre, Sports Facilities, Handicapped Facilities, Health Services, Canteen, Foreign Student Centre

Student Residential Facilities: For maximum 3190 students

Special Facilities: Drama and Theatre Studio. Johannes Stegmann Art Gallery

Libraries: Central Library, c. 436,340 vols. Libraries of: Medicine, Music, Agriculture

Publications: Acta Varia; Acta Academica

Press or Publishing House: University Press

Academic Staff *1999* — TOTAL
FULL-TIME — 680
PART-TIME — 650
TOTAL — **1,330**

Student Numbers *1999*	MEN	WOMEN	TOTAL
All (Foreign Included)	5,025	5,435	**10,460**
FOREIGN ONLY	–	–	255

UNIVERSITY OF PORT ELIZABETH/UNIVERSITEIT VAN PORT ELIZABETH (UPE)

PO Box 1600 Summerstrand, Port Elizabeth 6000
Tel: +27(41) 504-2111
Fax: +27(41) 504-2574
EMail: topnyw@upe.ac.za
Website: http://www.upe.ac.za

Vice-Chancellor and Principal: Rolf Stumpf (1994-)
Tel: +27(41) 504-2101 Fax: +27(41) 504-2699

Registrar: Jenny Bishop Tel: +27(41) 504-2108
EMail: samjmb@upe.ac.za

International Relations: A.J. Havenga
Tel: +27(41) 504-2572 Fax: +27(41) 504-2333
EMail: bsamee@upe.ac.za

Faculties

Arts (African Languages; Anthropology; Arts and Humanities; English; History; Management; Modern Languages; Music; Philosophy; Political Science; Public Administration; Religious Studies; Sociology) *Dean*: H.M. Thipa

Economic and Building Sciences (Accountancy; Architecture; Building Technologies; Business Administration; Computer Science; Economics; Industrial and Organizational Psychology; Labour and Industrial Relations) *Dean*: Martheanne Finnemore

Education (Curriculum; Education; Educational Administration) *Dean*: W.E. Morrow

Health Sciences (Health Sciences; Nursing; Pharmacy; Psychology; Social Work; Sociology) *Dean*: N.T. Naidoo

Law *Dean*: C. Van Loggerenberg

Science (Biochemistry; Botany; Chemistry; Computer Science; Geology; Mathematics; Microbiology; Natural Sciences; Physics; Statistics; Textile Technology; Zoology) *Dean*: C.A.B. Ball

Units

Community Development (Social and Community Services) *Head*: J.H. Senekal
Cyclic Peptide
Economic Processes (Economics)
Labour Relations and Human Resources (Human Resources; Labour and Industrial Relations)
Language Education (Modern Languages)
Student Counselling (Educational and Student Counselling)
Study of Learning Problems and Rendering of Remedial Therapy
Terrestrial Ecology Research (Ecology)
Tourism Law (Law; Tourism)

Institutes

Construction Processes (Building Technologies)

Environmental and Coastal Management *(SAB)* (Environmental Management; Marine Science and Oceanography) *Director*: G.C. Bate
Social and Systemic Change (Social Sciences)
Statistical Consultation and Methodology (Statistics) *Director*: D.J.L. Venter
Study and Resolution of Conflict (Peace and Disarmament; Political Science) *Director*: G.J. Bradshaw

Centres

Applied Business Management (Business Administration)
Biokinetics and Sports Science (Sports; Sports Medicine)
Eastern Cape Studies (Regional Studies)
Management Development (Management)
Organizational and Academic Development (Development Studies)

Research Institutes

Health and Development (Development Studies; Health Sciences)

Research Units

Metal Ion Separation Research (Physics) *Director*: J.G.H Du Preez, *students*: 10

History: Founded 1964 by Act of Parliament and financially supported by the State.

Governing Bodies: University Council; University Senate

Academic Year: February to November (February-June; July-November)

Admission Requirements: Matriculation Certificate or certificate of exemption issued by the Joint Matriculation Board

Fees: (Rand): Undergraduate, 4500-10,000 per annum; Honours and postgraduate, 1120-6890 per course

Main Language(s) of Instruction: Afrikaans, English

International Co-operation: University of Missouri, Kansas City; University of Wisconsin, Milwaukee; Vrije Universiteit Amsterdam

Degrees and Diplomas: *Bachelor's Degree*: Education (BEd), 1 yr following first degree; Architecture (BArch), 2 yrs; Law (LLB), 2 yrs following first degree; Arts (BA); Commerce (BComm); Jurisprudence (BJuris); Science (BSc), 3 yrs; Physical Education (BPhysEd), 3-4 yrs; Arts in Social Work (BA(SW)); Commerce Education (BCom(Ed)); Financial Law (BProc); Music (BMus); Music Education (BMusEd); Nursing (BCur); Pharmacy (BPharm); Primary Education (BPrimEd); Science in Quantity Surveying (BSc(QS)), 4 yrs; Science in Construction Management (BSc(Man)), 5 yrs; *Honours Bachelor's Degree*: a further yr; *Master's Degree*: a further 1-2 yrs; *Doctorate*: Curationis (DCurNursing); Education (DEd); Law (LLD); Literature (DLitt); Music (DMus); Nursing (DCur); Philosophy (DPhil); Science (DSc), 1-2 yrs. The Bachelor (Honours) Degree is awarded in the same fields of study as the Bachelor's Degree. Also Undergraduate and Postgraduate Diplomas.

Student Residential Facilities: For c. 1200 students

Special Facilities: Nature Reserve and Environmental Trail

Libraries: Albert Delport Library, c. 385,000 vols; 1271 periodicals

Publications: UPE Focus (biannually); Obiter; Labour Turnover in Port Elizabeth; Building Management Journal (annually); Institute for Planning Research publications; Publications Series

Academic Staff *1999:* Total: c. 280

Staff with doctorate: Total: c. 125

Student Numbers *1999*	TOTAL
All (Foreign Included)	**15,000**
FOREIGN ONLY	350

Distance Students, 9,000

• POTCHEFSTROOM UNIVERSITY FOR CHRISTIAN HIGHER EDUCATION

Potchefstroomse Universiteit vir Christelike Hoër Onderwys

Private Bag X6001, 11 Hoffman Street, Potchefstroom 2520
Tel: +27(18) 299-1111
Fax: +27(18) 299-2799
Telex: 4-21363 sa
Cable: puk
EMail: regjr@puknet.puk.ac.za
Website: http://www.puk.ac.za

Vice-Chancellor and Principal: T. Eloff
Tel: +27(18) 299-2601 Fax: +27(18) 299-2603
EMail: rktsjhvr@puknet.puk.ac.za

Registrar: C.F.C. Van der Walt Tel: +27(18) 299-2609
Fax: +27(18) 299-2603

International Relations: C.F.C. Van der Walt
EMail: regcfvdw@puknet.puk.ac.za

Faculties

Arts (African Languages; Afrikaans; Ancient Civilizations; Art History; Arts and Humanities; Communication Studies; Dutch; English; French; German; Graphic Design; Latin; Modern History; Music; Philosophy; Political Science; Public Administration; Sociology; Translation and Interpretation) *Dean:* Annette L. Combrink

Economics and Management Sciences (Accountancy; Actuarial Science; Banking; Economics; International Business; Management; Marketing; Tourism) *Dean:* G.J. de Klerk

Education Sciences (Education; Teacher Trainers Education) *Dean:* H.J. Steyn

Engineering (Chemical Engineering; Electrical and Electronic Engineering; Energy Engineering; Engineering; Materials Engineering; Mechanical Engineering) *Dean:* G.P. Greyvenstein

Health Sciences (Behavioural Sciences; Consumer Studies; Health Sciences; Nursing; Nutrition; Pharmacology; Pharmacy; Physical Therapy; Psychology; Psychotherapy; Social Work) *Dean:* H.A. Koeleman

Law *Dean:* F. Venter

Natural Sciences (Applied Mathematics; Biochemistry; Chemistry; Computer Science; Environmental Studies; Geography; Geology; Mathematics; Natural Sciences; Physics; Regional Planning; Statistics; Technology; Town Planning; Zoology) *Dean:* D.J. Van Wyk

Theology (Bible; Greek; New Testament; Theology) *Dean:* Aler du Plooy

Institutes

Biokinetics
Communication Research
Future Studies
Industrial Pharmacy
Reclamation Ecology Research (Ecology)
Reformational Studies
Sport Science and Development (Sports)
Tourism and Leisure Studies (Leisure Studies; Tourism)

Centres

Regional Development (Regional Planning) *Director:* A. Nierwadt

History: Founded 1869, became Constituent College of University of South Africa 1921, and by Act of Parliament became independent University 1951. An autonomous institution receiving financial support from the State.

Governing Bodies: University Council, comprising 22 members; University Senate, comprising 160 members

Academic Year: February to December (February-April; April-July; July-September; October-December)

Admission Requirements: Matriculation Certificate or certificate of exemption issued by the Joint Matriculation Board

Fees: (Rand): c. 8000 per annum

Main Language(s) of Instruction: Afrikaans, English

International Co-operation: Baylor University, Waco; California State University; Kosin University, Pusan; Leiden University; Tunghai University, Taichung

Degrees and Diplomas: *Bachelor's Degree:* Curationis (BCur); Education (BEd), 1 yr following first degree; Arts (BA); Commerce (BCom); Dietetics (BSc(Dietetics)); Domestic Science; Education, primary level (BEd); Engineering (BEng); Library Science (BLibSc); Music (BMus); Pharmacy (BPharm); Science (BSc), 3-4 yrs; Theology (ThB), 4 yrs following B.A; *Honours Bachelor's Degree:* a further yr; *Master's Degree:* a further 1-2 yrs; *Doctorate:* 1-2 yrs. The Bachelor (Honours) Degree is awarded in the same fields of study as the Bachelor's Degree. Also Undergraduate and Postgraduate Diplomas

Student Services: Academic Counselling, Cultural Centre, Sports Facilities, Health Services, Canteen, Foreign Student Centre

Student Residential Facilities: For c. 340 students in 17 hostels

Special Facilities: Pu-Kanamuseum

Libraries: Ferdinand Postma Library, 512,047 vols; 115,466 periodicals; 131,247 other materials

Publications: Kampusnuus (bimonthly); Koers, Skriflig, Word and Action (4 per annum); Litterator (3 per annum); PU-kaner Skakelblad

Academic Staff *1999:* Total: **654**

Student Numbers *1999*	MEN	WOMEN	TOTAL
All (Foreign Included)	3,356	4,506	**7,862**
FOREIGN ONLY	361	785	1,146

Part-time Students, 7,818

VAAL TRIANGLE CAMPUS
VAALDRIEHOEK KAMPUS
PO Box 1174, Van Eck Boulevard, Vanderbijlpark 1900
Tel: +27(016) 807-3111
Fax: +27(016) 807-3116
EMail: vvdjeur@puknet.puk.ac.za
Website: http://www.puk.ac.za

Vice-Principal: P.J.J. Prinsloo

Units

Accounting Sciences (Accountancy) *Director*: P. Locouw
Basic Sciences (Natural Sciences) *Director*: J.W.N. Tempelhoff
Behavioural Sciences *Director*: C. de W. Van Wick
Economics and Management (Economics; Management) *Director*: J.B. Pretorius
Education *Director*: A.M.C. Theron
Modelling Sciences *Director*: L.M. Venter

History: Founded 1966.

Academic Staff *1999*: Full-Time: c. 55 Part-Time: c. 40 Total: c. 95

Student Numbers *1999*: All (Foreign Included): Men: c. 870 Women: c. 785 Total: c. 1,655

• UNIVERSITY OF PRETORIA/UNIVERSITEIT VAN PRETORIA (TUKS)

Lynnwood Road, Hillcrest, Pretoria 0002
Tel: +27(12) 420-4111
Fax: +27(12) 342-2712
Telex: 322723
Cable: puniv
EMail: lenie@admin-1.up.ac.za; jvanzyl@ccnet.up.ac.za
Website: http://www.up.ac.za

Vice-Chancellor and Principal: Calie W.I. Pistorius (2001-)
Tel: +27(12) 420-2900 Fax: +27(12) 420-3696
EMail: rektor@postino.up.ac.za

Registrar: N.J. Grove Tel: +27(12) 420-4273
Fax: +27(12) 420-3696 EMail: njgrove@ccnet.up.ac.za

International Relations: V. Rajah Tel: +27(12) 420-3237
Fax: +27(12) 420-4025 EMail: yrajah@ccnet.up.ac.za

Faculties

Economics and Management Sciences (Communication Studies; Computer Science; Economics; Human Resources; Management; Marketing; Statistics; Tourism) *Dean*: C. Thornhill, *full-time staff*: 153, *part-time staff*: 40, *students*: 6,564
Education (Education; Educational Sciences) *Dean*: J.D. Jansen, *full-time staff*: 40, *part-time staff*: 35, *students*: 2,286
Engineering, the Built Environment and Information Technology (Building Technologies; Engineering; Information Technology; Town Planning) *Dean*: C.W.I. Pistorius, *full-time staff*: 212, *part-time staff*: 213, *students*: 5,843
Health Sciences (Health Sciences; Pathology; Sports Medicine) *Dean*: D. J. Du Plessis, *full-time staff*: 492, *part-time staff*: 93, *students*: 3,584
Humanities (Arts and Humanities; Modern Languages; Social Sciences) *Dean*: M.E. Muller, *full-time staff*: 182, *part-time staff*: 222, *students*: 3,803

Law (Administrative Law; Civil Law; Comparative Law; Constitutional Law; Criminal Law; History of Law; Human Rights; International Law; Labour Law; Law) *Dean*: D.G. Kleyn, *full-time staff*: 52, *part-time staff*: 68, *students*: 2,098
Natural and Agricultural Sciences (Agriculture; Biological and Life Sciences; Mathematics; Natural Sciences; Physics) *Dean*: R.M. Crewe, *full-time staff*: 214, *part-time staff*: 209, *students*: 2,961
Theology (Bible; Christian Religious Studies; Missionary Studies; New Testament; Theology) *Dean*: C.J.A. Vos, *full-time staff*: 20, *part-time staff*: 34, *students*: 433
Veterinary Science (Anatomy; Animal Husbandry; Community Health; Pharmacology; Toxicology; Veterinary Science) *Dean*: N.P.J. Kriek, *full-time staff*: 125, *part-time staff*: 20, *students*: 619

Schools

Agricultural Sciences (Agricultural Economics; Animal Husbandry; Food Science; Home Economics; Soil Science) *Dean*: J.F. Kirsten, *students*: 1,423
Arts (Music; Visual Arts) *Dean*: M.D. Sauthoff, *students*: 527
Biological Sciences (Biochemistry; Biological and Life Sciences; Botany; Entomology; Genetics; Microbiology; Physiology; Plant Pathology; Zoology) *Dean*: T.E. Cloete, *students*: 470
Built Environment (Architecture; Interior Design; Landscape Architecture; Regional Planning; Town Planning) *Dean*: H.M. Single, *students*: 988
Community Health
Economic Science (Banking; Econometrics; Economics) *Director*: J.H. Van Heerden, *students*: 904
Educational Sciences (Teacher Trainers Education) *students*: 1,435
Engineering (Aeronautical and Aerospace Engineering; Chemical Engineering; Civil Engineering; Computer Engineering; Electrical and Electronic Engineering; Engineering; Food Technology; Industrial Engineering; Mechanical Engineering; Metallurgical Engineering; Mining Engineering) *Dean*: J.L. Steyn, *students*: 2,872
Financial Science (Accountancy; Finance; Taxation) *Dean*: Q. Vorster, *students*: 2,807
Health Care Science (Nursing; Occupational Therapy; Physical Therapy) *students*: 1,383
Health Systems and Public Health (Community Health; Public Health) *students*: 139
Information Technology (Information Technology; Management) *Dean*: J.D. Roode, *students*: 1,983
Languages (African Languages; Ancient Languages; English) *Dean*: J.H. Potgieter, *students*: 272
Management Sciences (Human Resources; Management; Marketing; Public Administration; Tourism) *Dean*: R.S. Rensburg, *students*: 2,524
Mathematical Sciences (Actuarial Science; Applied Mathematics; Mathematics; Statistics) *students*: 383
Medicine (Anaesthesiology; Anatomy; Cardiology; Dermatology; Epidemiology; Forensic Medicine and Dentistry; Gynaecology and Obstetrics; Medicine; Neurology; Orthopedics; Otorhinolaryngology; Paediatrics; Pharmacology; Physiology; Psychiatry and Mental Health; Radiology; Sports Medicine; Surgery; Urology) *students*: 2,091

Pathology Sciences (Genetics; Immunology; Pathology) *students:* 53

Physical Sciences (Chemistry; Earth Sciences; Geography; Physics) *Dean*: J.B. Malherbe, *students:* 653

Social Sciences (Anthropology; Archaeology; Communication Disorders; Criminology; Cultural Studies; Leisure Studies; Philosophy; Political Science; Psychology; Social Sciences; Social Work; Sports) *Dean*: S.R. Hugo, *students:* 2,019

Centres

Academic Development (Education) *Director*: A. De Boer

Augmentative and Alternative Communication (Communication Studies) *Director*: E. Alant

Child and Adult Guidance (Educational Psychology) *Director*: L.J. Jacobs

Child Law *Director*: T. Davel

Community Education (Educational Research) *Director*: L.J. Jacobs

Computer Science for Education *(Golgfields)* (Educational Technology) *Director*: J.C. Van Staden

Continued Theological Education (Theology) *Director*: J .H. Le Roux

Education Law and Education Policy *(CELP)* (Educational Administration) *Director*: J.L. Beckmann

Environmental Biology and Biological Control (Biology) *Director*: J.M. Kotze

Equine Research *Director*: A.J. Guthrie

Gender Studies *Director*: M. De Waal

Human Rights *Director*: C.H. Heyns

Information Development (Information Sciences) *Director*: T.J.D. Bothma

Interlanguage Communication (Communication Studies)

International Political Studies (International Relations) *Director*: M.E. Muller

Land Development Housing and Construction (Construction Engineering; Landscape Architecture) *Director*: A.C. Hauptfleisch

Legal Aid (Law) *Director*: F.E. Van der Merwe

Mammal Research (Zoology) *Director*: J.T. Du Toit

Music *Director*: C. Van Niekerk

New Electricity Studies *(CNES)* (Electrical and Electronic Engineering) *Director*: G.J. Delport

Population Studies (Demography and Population) *Director*: J.L. Van Thonder

Science Education *Director*: M.W.H. Braun

Stomatological Research (Dentistry) *Director*: S.J. Botha

Wildlife Research (Wildlife) *Director*: J. du P. Bothma

Bureaus

Economic Politics and Analysis (Political Science) *Head*: N.J. Schoeman

Financial Analysis (Finance)

Statistics and Methodology *(STATOMET)* (Statistics)

Graduate Schools
Management

History: Founded 1908 by Transvaal Government, became separate University College 1910 and autonomous University 1930. Financially supported by the State.

Governing Bodies: University Council, comprising 26 members; University Senate

Academic Year: January to November (January-June; July-November)

Admission Requirements: Matriculation Exemption Certificate. Matriculation subjects passed with at least 50% on the Higher Grade for admission in Science branches. Accessible to members of all race and language groups

Fees: (Rands): 7 500-12 500 per annum

Main Language(s) of Instruction: Afrikaans, English

Degrees and Diplomas: *Bachelor's Degree*: 3-4 yrs; *Honours Bachelor's Degree*: a further yr; *Master's Degree*: a further 2 yrs; *Doctorate*: (PhD), a further 2 yrs. The Honours Degree is awarded in the same fields of study as the Bachelor's Degree. Also, Professional Bachelor Degrees, 4 yrs, and Undergraduate and Postgraduate Diplomas, 1-2 yrs

Student Services: Academic Counselling, Social Counselling, Employment Services, Nursery Care, Cultural Centre, Sports Facilities, Handicapped Facilities, Health Services, Canteen, Foreign Student Centre

Student Residential Facilities: For 6000 students

Special Facilities: Anton van Wouw House Museum. Van Tilburg Collection. Van Gybland-Oosterhoff Collection. Kya Rosa (historical landmark) University Art Collection

Libraries: Academic Information Service, c. 1.1m. vols

Publications: Perdeby, Students' newspapers (name could be translated as "wasp") (1 per week); Prospectus, Corporate profile; Research Report, Report on research outputs; Annual Report; Guide to Expertise, Providing Information on the field of expertise of academic personnel at the University (annually); Ad-Destinatum, Commemorative Volumes of the University of Pretoria (3-4 per annum); Tukkievaria, Staff Newsletter (24 per annum)

Academic Staff *2000*			TOTAL
FULL-TIME			1,500
PART-TIME			979
TOTAL			**2,479**
STAFF WITH DOCTORATE	MEN	WOMEN	TOTAL
FULL-TIME	–	–	563
PART-TIME	–	130	130
TOTAL	–	–	**693**
Student Numbers *2000*	MEN	WOMEN	TOTAL
All (Foreign Included)	13,473	14,620	**28,093**
FOREIGN ONLY	610	357	967

Evening Students, 6,810

• RAND AFRIKAANS UNIVERSITY/RANDSE AFRIKAANSE UNIVERSITEIT (RAU)
PO Box 524, Auckland Park 2006
Tel: +27(11) 489-2911
Fax: +27(11) 489-2191
Telex: 424526 sa
Cable: rauniv
EMail: ath@raul.rau.ac.za
Website: http://www.rau.ac.za

Rector: T.R. Botha (1995-) **Tel:** +27(11) 489-3000
Fax: +27(11) 726-8373 **EMail:** rektor@bestuur.rau.ac.za

Registrar (Academic): P.M.S. Von Staden
Tel: +27(11) 489-3008 EMail: regacad@bestuur.rau.ac.za
International Relations: J.H.P. Ellis Tel: +27(11) 489-2417
Fax: +27(11) 489-2632

Faculties

Arts (Arts and Humanities) *Dean:* J.A. Naudé, *full-time staff:* 104, *part-time staff:* 22, *students:* 3,975
Economics and Management Sciences (Economic History; Economics; Management) *Dean:* I.V.W. Raubenheimer, *full-time staff:* 65, *part-time staff:* 27, *students:* 4,899
Education and Nursing (Education; Nursing) *Dean (Acting):* J.C. Kok, *full-time staff:* 44, *part-time staff:* 5, *students:* 6,799
Engineering *Dean:* P. van der Merwe, *full-time staff:* 25, *part-time staff:* 5, *students:* 679
Law *Dean:* D. van der Merwe, *full-time staff:* 29, *students:* 972
Natural Sciences (Natural Sciences; Optometry) *Dean:* D.D. Van Reenen, *full-time staff:* 105, *part-time staff:* 23, *students:* 1,507

Institutes

Child and Adult Guidance (Social and Community Services) *Director:* A. Burke, *full-time staff:* 8, *part-time staff:* 11

Centres

Distance Education *Director:* Izak J. Broere, *full-time staff:* 40, *part-time staff:* 10, *students:* 6,000
Metropolitan and Regional Administration (Public Administration) *Head:* W. Zybrands, *full-time staff:* 2

Research Centres

Islamic Studies *Director:* J.A. Naudé

Research Institutes

Energy Studies (Energy Engineering) *Director:* C. Cooper, *full-time staff:* 2
European Studies *Head:* G.C. Olivier

History: Founded 1966 by Act of Parliament, first students admitted 1968. Financially supported by the State.
Governing Bodies: University Council; Management Committee; University Senate
Academic Year: January to November (January-June; July-November)
Admission Requirements: Matriculation Certificate or certificate of exemption issued by the Joint Matriculation Board
Fees: (Rand): 8500 per annum; Honours, 8500; postgraduate, 4200
Main Language(s) of Instruction: Afrikaans, English
International Co-operation: Links with Universitites in USA, Europe and Far Eastern Countries
Degrees and Diplomas: *National Diploma:* Education, 2 yrs; *Bachelor's Degree:* Education (BEd), 1 yr following first degree; Arts (BA); Arts in Law; Commerce (BCom); Information Science (BInf); Science (BSc), 3 yrs; Commercial Law (BCom(Law)); Engineering (BIng); Law (LLB); Nursing (BCur); Optometry (BOptom), 4 yrs; *Honours Bachelor's Degree:* a further yr; *Postgraduate Diploma:* Information Science, 1 yr following Bachelor's Degree; Education; Human Resource Management; Language and Text Guidance; Transport Economics, 1 yr

following Bachelor's Degree; *Master's Degree:* Humanities, Natural Sciences, Economics and Management Sciences, Education, Engineering and Law (MA; MSc; MMcom; MEd; MIng; LLM; MPhil), a further 1-2 yrs; *Doctorate:* Humanities, Natural Sciences, Economic and Management Sciences, Education, Engineering and Law (DLitt; Dcom; DEd; DIng; LLD; DPhil), 2-4 yrs. The Bachelor (Honours) Degree is awarded in the same fields of study as the Bachelor's Degree

Student Services: Academic Counselling, Social Counselling, Employment Services, Foreign Student Adviser, Cultural Centre, Sports Facilities, Language Programmes, Handicapped Facilities, Canteen
Special Facilities: Museums: Geology; Zoology and Anthropology. Art Collection
Libraries: 420,448 vols
Publications: Higher Education Bulletin (bimonthly); Ekklesiastikos Pharos; Quarterly Econometric Forecast; RAU-Rapport (quarterly); Medieval Studies; Anvil-Aambeeld: Opinion Journal (biannually); Communicare, (Communication Studies) (annually)
Academic Staff *2000:* Total: **320**
Staff with doctorate: Total: **192**

Student Numbers *2000*

	MEN	WOMEN	TOTAL
All (Foreign Included)	7,615	11,216	**18,831**
FOREIGN ONLY	–	–	300

Evening Students, 1,500 **Distance Students,** 6,000

• RHODES UNIVERSITY

POB 94, Drostdy Road, Grahamstown, Eastern Cape 6140
Tel: +27(46) 603-8111
Fax: +27(46) 622-8444
EMail: adsf@ru.ac.za
Website: http://www.ru.ac.za

Vice-Chancellor: David R. Woods (1996-)
Tel: +27(46) 603-8148 EMail: d.woods@ru.ac.za
Registrar: S. Fourie Tel: +27(46) 603-8101
Fax: +27(46) 603-8127 EMail: s.fourie@ru.ac.za
International Relations: R.A. de Villiers
Tel: +27(46) 603-3851 Fax: +27(46) 636-1902
EMail: a.devilliers@ru.ac.za

Faculties

Commerce (Accountancy; Business and Commerce; Commercial Law; Economics; Information Technology; Management; Statistics)
Education
Humanities (African Languages; Afrikaans; Anthropology; Arts and Humanities; Dutch; English; English Studies; Fine Arts; French; German; Greek; History; International Relations; Italian; Journalism; Latin; Media Studies; Political Science; Psychology; Social Work; Sociology; Theatre)
Law (Commercial Law; Law) *Dean:* R. Midgley, *students:* 80
Pharmacy
Science (Applied Mathematics; Biochemistry; Biological and Life Sciences; Botany; Chemistry; Earth Sciences; Economics; Environmental Studies; Ergotherapy; Fishery; Geography; Geology; Information Sciences; Journalism; Linguistics;

Management; Marine Biology; Mathematics; Microbiology; Musicology; Physical Therapy; Physics; Psychology; Statistics; Zoology)

Departments

Accountancy *Head*: E.M. Stack, *full-time staff*: 12, *students*: 231

Anthropology *Head*: C.J. de Wet, *full-time staff*: 4, *part-time staff*: 1, *students*: 56

Biochemistry and Microbiology (Biochemistry; Microbiology) *Head*: Chris Whiteley, *students*: 88

Botany *Head*: R.A. Lubke, *full-time staff*: 9, *students*: 32

Chemistry *Head*: P.T. Kaye, *full-time staff*: 14, *students*: 83

Drama (Theatre) *Head*: A.F. Bucklano, *students*: 55

Education *Head*: P.R. Irwin, *full-time staff*: 19, *students*: 152

English *Head*: P.S. Walters, *full-time staff*: 10, *students*: 128

Environmental Sciences (Environmental Studies) *Head*: C. Fabricius, *full-time staff*: 3, *students*: 6

Geology *Head*: J.S. Marsh, *full-time staff*: 9, *students*: 42

History *Head*: P. Maylam, *full-time staff*: 4, *part-time staff*: 1, *students*: 42

Human Kinetics and Ergonomics (Ergotherapy; Physical Therapy) *Head*: P.A. Scott, *full-time staff*: 6, *students*: 61

Ichthyology and Fisheries Science (Fishery; Zoology) *Head*: Peter Britz, *students*: 23

Journalism and Media Studies (Journalism; Media Studies) *Head*: G. Berger, *full-time staff*: 12, *students*: 198

Linguistics and English Language (English; Linguistics) *Head*: V.A. de Klerk, *students*: 81

Management *students*: 172

Mathematics *(Pure and Applied) Head*: W.J. Kotze, *students*: 50

Political Studies (Political Science) *Head*: P.H. Bischoff, *students*: 79

Psychology *Head*: C. Stones, *students*: 266

Institutes

Water Research (Water Management) *Director*: J. O'Keefe

Aeronomy *(Herman Ohlthaver) Director*: A.W.V. Poole

Range and Forage *(ARC)* (Surveying and Mapping)

Study of English in Africa (English; Literacy Education; Writing)

Centres

Mathematics Education Projects (Mathematics Education) *Director*: J. Stoker, *full-time staff*: 4

Research Institutes

Biopharmaceutics (Biology; Pharmacology; Pharmacy)

History: Founded 1904 as University College, became Constituent College of the University of South Africa 1916 and incorporated as independent University 1951. An autonomous institution receiving financial support from the State.

Governing Bodies: University Council; Senate

Academic Year: February to November (February-April; April-June; July-September; September-November)

Admission Requirements: Matriculation Certificate or certificate of exemption issued by the Joint Matriculation Board

Fees: (Rands): 11,500 per annum

Main Language(s) of Instruction: English

International Co-operation: Rhodes College; Washington College; Boston College; Bishop University

Degrees and Diplomas: *Bachelor's Degree*: Education (Bed), 1 yr following first degree; Arts (BA); Arts (Human Movement Studies) (BA); Commerce (Bcom); Economics (Becon); Science (BSc); Social Sciences (BSocSc), 3 yrs; Fine Arts (BFineArt); Journalism and Media Studies (BJourn); Laws (LLB); Music (BMus); Pharmacy (BPharm); Primary Education (BPrimEd), 4 yrs; *Honours Bachelor's Degree*: a further yr; *Master's Degree*: a further 1-2 yrs; *Doctorate*: 2 yrs. The Bachelor (Honours) Degree is awarded in the same fields of study as the Bachelor's Degree. Also Undergraduate and Postgraduate Diplomas

Student Services: Academic Counselling, Social Counselling, Employment Services, Foreign Student Adviser, Nursery Care, Cultural Centre, Sports Facilities, Language Programmes, Handicapped Facilities, Health Services, Canteen, Foreign Student Centre

Student Residential Facilities: For 2039 students

Special Facilities: Rhodes University Museum; National English Literary Museum; Albany Museum

Libraries: Central Library, 33,108 vols; Cory Library for Historical Research, 40,000; International Library of African Music

Publications: Rhodes Review (biannually)

Academic Staff *1999*: Full-Time: c. 345 Part-Time: c. 25 Total: c. 370

Staff with doctorate: Total: c. 135

Student Numbers *1999*: All (Foreign Included): Men: c. 2,250 Women: c. 2,850 Total: c. 5,100
Foreign Only: Total: c. 915

EAST LONDON CAMPUS
50 Church Street, East London 5201
Tel: +27(431) 22-539
Fax: +27(431) 35-3645
EMail: director@dolphin.ru.ac.za

Director: T.A. Marsh

Departments
Accountancy
African Languages
Afrikaans and Dutch Studies (Afrikaans; Dutch)
Economics and Economic History (Economics)
Education
English
History
Informations Systems (Information Technology)
Law
Management
Psychology
Social Work
Sociology
Statistics

Institutes
Leadership Development *(Johnson and Johnson) full-time staff*: 4
Social and Economic Research (Economics; Social Studies)

History: Founded 1981.

• UNIVERSITY OF SOUTH AFRICA/UNIVERSITEIT VAN SUID-AFRIKA (UNISA)

PO Box 392, Preller Street Nieu, Muckleneuk, Pretoria, Transvaal 0003
Tel: +27(12) 429-3111
Fax: +27(12) 429-3221
Cable: unisa
EMail: msimact@alpha.unisa.ac.za
Website: http://www.unisa.ac.za

Vice-Chancellor and Principal (Acting): Barney Pityana (2001-) Tel: +27(12) 429-2550 Fax: +27(12) 429-2565

Registrar: Louis Molamu

International Relations: P.J.N. Steyn Tel: +27(12) 429-6889 Fax: +27(12) 429-3551 EMail: steynpjn@alpha.unisa.ac.za

Faculties

Arts (African Languages; African Studies; Afrikaans; Ancient Civilizations; Anthropology; Archaeology; Archiving; Art History; Arts and Humanities; Bible; Chinese; Classical Languages; Communication Studies; Criminal Law; Criminology; English; Environmental Studies; French; Gender Studies; Geography; German; Greek; Hebrew; History; Information Sciences; International Studies; Islamic Studies; Italian; Latin; Linguistics; Musicology; Nursing; Philosophy; Political Science; Psychology; Public Administration; Romance Languages; Russian; Social Work; Sociology; Spanish; Visual Arts) *Dean*: W.F. Meyer
Economics and Management (Accountancy; Business Administration; Economics; Industrial and Organizational Psychology; Management; Tourism) *Dean*: M. Shania
Education *Dean*: L.R. MacFarlane
Law (Commercial Law; Law) *Dean*: Johann Neethling
Science (Applied Mathematics; Astronomy and Space Science; Biological and Life Sciences; Chemistry; Computer Science; Geography; Information Sciences; Mathematics; Natural Sciences; Operations Research; Physics; Psychology; Statistics) *Dean*: E.C. Reynhardt
Theology and Religious Studies (Missionary Studies; New Testament; Religious Studies; Theology) *Dean*: J.N.J. Kritzinger

Institutes

Adult Basic Education and Training *(ABET)* (Education)
All African Languages Redevelopment (African Languages)
Continuing Education *Head*: Evelyn Nonyongo
Criminology *Director*: J.H. Prinsloo
Educational Research *Director*: C.H. Swanepoel
Foreign and Comparative Law (Comparative Law) *Director*: A.E.A.M. Thomashausen
Gender Studies *Coordinator*: Jennifer Lemon
Social and Health Sciences (Health Sciences; Peace and Disarmament; Social Sciences) *Director*: Mohamed Seedat
Theology and Religion *Director*: C.W. Du Toit

Centres

Accounting Studies (Accountancy) *Head*: J.B.J. van Rensburg

Applied Psychology (Psychology)
Applied Statistics (Statistics)
Arts, Culture and Heritage Studies *(African)* (Cultural Studies; Fine Arts; Heritage Preservation) *Director*: Chris van Vuuren
Bible *(C.B. Powell)*
Business Law (Commercial Law; Labour Law)
Business Management (Business Administration; Management) *Head*: B.J. Erasmus
Community Training and Development (Social Welfare)
Development Administration (Administration)
Improvement of Mathematics, Science and Technology Education (Mathematics Education; Science Education; Technology)
Indigenous Law (Law)
Industrial and Organizational Psychology
Latin American Studies *Head*: Zélia Roelofse-Campbell
Legal Aid Clinic *(Western Cape)*
Legal Terminology in African Languages (Law)
Peace Education (Peace and Disarmament)
Public Law Studies *(Verloren van Themaat)* (Public Law)
Software Engineering

Bureaus

Market Research (Marketing) *Director*: J.H. Martins
University Teaching (Higher Education Teacher Training; Pedagogy)

History: Founded 1873 as University of Cape of Good Hope. Incorporated by Act of Parliament as the University of South Africa 1916. Since 1951 concerned only with external students for whom it provides tuition by correspondence.

Governing Bodies: University Council, comprising 21 members; University Senate

Academic Year: January to December (january-May; June-November)

Admission Requirements: Matriculation Certificate or certificate of exemption issued by the Joint Matriculation Board

Fees: (Rand): Undergraduate, 840-1300 per annum; postgraduate, 2500-3500

Main Language(s) of Instruction: English, Afrikaans

International Co-operation: Adam Mickiewicz University, Poznan; National Open University, Taiwan; Open Universiteit, Heerlen; University of Hull; Vrije Universiteit van Brussels; University of Toledo, Ohio; University of Zimbabwe; University of New England; Makerere University; South Valley University, Aswan; University of Malaya

Degrees and Diplomas: *Bachelor's Degree*: Education (BEd), 1 yr following first degree; Law (LLB), 2-4 yrs following first degree; Divinity (BD), 3 yrs following BA; Accountancy (BCompt); Administration (BAdmin); Arts (BA); Commerce (BCom); Diaconiology (BDiac); Financial Law (BProcLaw); Jurisprudence (BJuris); Library Science (BBibl); Music (BMus); Primary Education (BPrimEd); Science (BSc); Theology (BTh), 3-4 yrs; *Honours Bachelor's Degree*: a further yr; *Master's Degree*: a further 1-2 yrs; *Doctorate*: 1-2 yrs. The Bachelor (Honours) Degree is awarded in the same fields of study as the Bachelor's Degree. Also Undergraduate and Postgraduate Diplomas

Student Services: Academic Counselling, Employment Services, Nursery Care, Handicapped Facilities, Health Services, Canteen

Special Facilities: Museums: Anthropology; Theology; Education; Nursing Science. Art Gallery. Archives and Special Collection

Libraries: Central Library, c. 1.5m. vols; 7000 periodicals

Publications: Theologia Evangelica (3 per annum); English Usage in South Africa; Unisa English Studies; Codicillus; Communicatio; Educare; Unisa Psychologia; De Arte; Politeia; Progressio; Mousaion; Musicus (biannually); Kleio; Ars Nova; Africanus; Dynamica (annually)

Press or Publishing House: Unisa Press

Academic Staff *1999:* Total: **1,311**

Student Numbers *1999*	TOTAL
All (Foreign Included)	**132,790**
FOREIGN ONLY	7,875

Note: Also c. 5700 evening students

ST AUGUSTINE UNIVERSITY OF SOUTH AFRICA

PO Box 436, Bedfrodview 2008
Tel: +27(11) 487-0301
Fax: +27(11) 648-1877
EMail: admin@staugustine.ac.za
Website: http://www.staugustine.ac.za

Chancellor: Buti Tlhagale

Vice-Chancellor: Edith Raidt

Degrees and Diplomas: *Master's Degree:* Applied Ethics

• UNIVERSITY OF STELLENBOSCH

Universiteit van Stellenbosch

Private Bag X1, Matieland 7602
Tel: +27(21) 808-9111
Fax: +27(21) 808-3800
Telex: 52-0383
EMail: interoff@maties.sun.ac.za; mts@maties.sun.ac.za
Website: http://www.sun.ac.za

Vice-Chancellor and Rector: C. Brink
Tel: +27(21) 808-4490 Fax: +27(21) 808-3714
EMail: abe@sun.ac.za

Registrar: Johan Aspeling Tel: +27(21) 808-4516
Fax: +27(21) 808-4576 EMail: jaa@sun.ac.za

International Relations: Robert Kotze
Tel: +27(21) 808-4628 EMail: rk@maties.sun.ac.za

Faculties

Agricultural and Forestry Sciences (Agricultural Economics; Agriculture; Agronomy; Animal Husbandry; Ecology; Entomology; Food Science; Forestry; Genetics; Horticulture; Oenology; Plant Pathology; Soil Science; Viticulture; Water Science; Wood Technology) *Dean:* L. van Huyssteen, *full-time staff:* 54, *students:* 938

Arts (African Languages; Afrikaans; Arts and Humanities; Classical Languages; Dutch; English; Environmental Studies; Fine Arts; Geography; History; Information Sciences; Journalism; Linguistics; Modern Languages; Music; Philosophy; Political Science; Psychology; Religion; Religious Studies; Social Work; Sociology; Theatre) *Dean:* I.J. van der Merwe, *full-time staff:* 153, *students:* 3,790

Dentistry *(Tygeberg)* (Dental Hygiene; Dentistry; Oral Pathology; Orthodontics; Periodontics; Radiology; Surgery) *Dean:* W.P. Dreyer, *full-time staff:* 22, *students:* 692

Economics and Management (Accountancy; Business Administration; Economics; Industrial and Organizational Psychology; Management; Rural Planning; Statistics; Town Planning; Transport Economics) *Dean:* J.A. Matthee, *full-time staff:* 118, *students:* 4,895

Education (Education; Educational Psychology; Special Education) *Dean:* T. Park, *full-time staff:* 42, *students:* 4,312

Engineering (Applied Mathematics; Chemical Engineering; Civil Engineering; Electrical and Electronic Engineering; Engineering; Industrial Engineering; Mechanical Engineering) *Dean:* P.W. van der Walt, *full-time staff:* 91, *students:* 1,495

Law (Commercial Law; Law; Private Law; Public Law) *Dean:* J.S.A. Fourie, *full-time staff:* 28, *students:* 799

Medicine *(Tygerberg)* (Anatomy; Biochemistry; Cardiology; Community Health; Dermatology; Forensic Medicine and Dentistry; Gynaecology and Obstetrics; Haematology; Histology; Medicine; Microbiology; Nursing; Nutrition; Occupational Therapy; Oncology; Ophthalmology; Orthopedics; Otorhinolaryngology; Paediatrics; Pathology; Pharmacology; Physical Therapy; Physiology; Plastic Surgery; Psychiatry and Mental Health; Radiology; Speech Therapy and Audiology; Surgery; Urology; Virology) *Dean:* J.D.V. Lochner, *full-time staff:* 98, *students:* 2,340

Military Science *(Saldanha) Dean:* D.J. Malan, *full-time staff:* 41, *students:* 216

Science (Biochemistry; Botany; Chemistry; Computer Science; Consumer Studies; Geology; Home Economics; Mathematics; Microbiology; Natural Sciences; Nutrition; Physics; Physiology; Zoology) *Dean:* F.J.W. Hahne, *full-time staff:* 137, *students:* 1,961

Theology (Bible; Missionary Studies; Religious Studies; Theology) *Dean:* H.J.B. Combrink, *full-time staff:* 13, *students:* 318

Units

Advanced Manufacturing *(SENROB)* (Production Engineering) *Director:* C.J. Fourie

Cranio-Facial Unit *Head:* C.S.F. Smit

Drug Research (Toxicology) *Director:* J.R. Joubert

Educational Psychology *(Social Science Psychology) Director:* P.J. Normand, *full-time staff:* 3

Experimental Phonology (Speech Therapy and Audiology) *Director:* J.C. Roux, *part-time staff:* 9

Mathematics Education *Head:* A.I. Olivier

Perinatal Mortality (Paediatrics; Toxicology) *Head:* H.J. Odendaal

Institutes

Applied Computer Science (Computer Science) *Director:* A.E. Krzesinski

Future Studies Research *(Bellville)* (Futurology) *Director:* A. Roux, *full-time staff:* 12, *part-time staff:* 5

Geographical Analysis (Geography) *Director:* H.L. Zietsman

Industrial Engineering *Director:* N.D. du Preez

Mathematics and Science Education (Mathematics Education; Science Education) *Director*: J.H. Smit

Oral and Dental Research *(Tygerberg)* (Dentistry) *Director*: P. van der Bijl, *full-time staff:* 5, *part-time staff:* 4

Plant Biotechnology (Botany) *Director*: F.C. Botha

Polymer Science (Polymer and Plastics Technology) *Director*: R.D. Sanderson, *full-time staff:* 6, *part-time staff:* 5

Sports and Movement Studies (Sports) *Director*: J.H. Malan

Structural Engineering (Building Technologies) *Director*: J.V. Retief

Theoretical Physics (Physics) *Director*: H.B. Geyer

Thermodynamics and Mechanics (Mechanics; Physics) *Director*: N.J. Theron

Transport Technology (Transport Engineering) *Director*: N.J. Theron

Wine Bio-Technology *Director*: I.S. Pretorius

Centres

Afrikaans Usage *Director*: L.G. de Stadler

Applied Ethics (Ethics) *Director*: A.A. van Niekerk

Bible Translation in Afrikaans (Bible; Translation and Interpretation) *Director*: C.H.J. van der Merwe

Care and Rehabilitation of the Disabled (Rehabilitation and Therapy) *Director*: J.A. Hendry

Children's Literature and Media (Literature; Media Studies) *Director*: A.E. Carl, *full-time staff:* 1

Contextual Hermeneutics (Translation and Interpretation) *Director*: J. Kinghorn

Educational Development (Educational Sciences) *Director*: Y. Waghid

Effective Medicine Cost *Director*: J.R. Joubert

Electrical and Electronic Engineering *Director*: F.S. van der Merwe

Geographical Analysis (Geography) *Director*: J.H. van der Merwe, *full-time staff:* 4

Global Competitiveness *Director*: N.D. du Perez

Higher and Adult Education (Adult Education; Higher Education) *Director*: C.A. Kapp

Interdisciplinary Studies *Director*: J. Mouton, *full-time staff:* 2, *part-time staff:* 2

International and Comparative Labour and Social Security Law (International Studies; Labour and Industrial Relations) *Director*: G. Giles

International and Comparative Politics (Comparative Politics; International Studies) *Director*: H.J. Kotzé

International Business *Director (Acting)*: M. Leibold, *full-time staff:* 1

Leadership Studies *(Bellville)* *Director*: H. Spangenberg

Military Studies *(Saldanha)* (Military Science) *Director*: L. du Plessis, *full-time staff:* 3

Molecular and Cellular Biology *(Tygerberg)* (Cell Biology; Molecular Biology) *Director*: P.D. van Helden

Theatre and Performance Studies (Performing Arts; Theatre) *Director*: T. Hauptfleisch

Bureaus

Bioengineering *(Tygerberg)* *Head*: J.F. Coetzee, *full-time staff:* 1

Chemical Engineering *Head*: C. Nel, *part-time staff:* 1

Continuing Theological Training and Research (Theology) *Head*: M.A.V. Van der Merwe, *full-time staff:* 2, *part-time staff:* 1

Economic Research (Economics) *Head*: B.W. Smit, *full-time staff:* 11

Industrial Mathematics (Mathematics and Computer Science) *Head*: W.F.D. Theron

History: Founded 1866 as College, became independent University 1918. An autonomous institution receiving financial support from the State.

Governing Bodies: University Council; University Senate

Academic Year: February to December (February-March; April-June; July-September; October-December)

Admission Requirements: Matriculation Certificate or Certificate of Exemption issued by the Joint Matriculation Board

Fees: (Rand): Registration, 150; tuition, 10,000 - 25,000

Main Language(s) of Instruction: Afrikaans, English

International Co-operation: Catholic University of Louvain; University of Rennes I; Ecole supérieure de Commerce de Grenoble (ESC Grenoble); Institute of Political Studies Paris-'Sciences Po'; University Centre of Antwerp; University of Ghent; Catholic University of Leuven; Free University, Amsterdam; University of Nijmegen; University of Amsterdam; Leiden University; Erasmus University Rotterdam; Maastricht University; Technical University Berlin; University of Hamburg; University of Leipzig; Philipps-University of Marburg; University of Tübingen; University of Salzburg; University of Malaya; University of Technology Malaysia; University of Gezira; University of Florida; University of Wyoming; University of Texas, Austin; Colorado State University; Youngsan University of International Affairs

Degrees and Diplomas: *Bachelor's Degree*: Education (Bed), 1 yr following first degree; Law (LLB), 2 yrs following first degree; Agricultural Management (BAgricManagement); Military Science (BMil); Science (BSc), 3 yrs; Accountancy (BAcc); Arts (BA); Commerce (Bcomm); Economics (BEcon); Music (BMus), 3-4 yrs; Agricultural Education (BScAgricEd); Consumer Science (BScConsumerSc); Drama (Bdram); Engineering (Beng); Food Science (BScFoodSc); Forestry (BScFor); Nursing (BNursing); Occupational Therapy (BOccTher); Primary Education (BPrimEd), 4 yrs; Theology (BTh), 4-5 yrs; Dentistry (BChD), 5 1/2 yrs; Medicine and Surgery (MBChB), 6 yrs; *Honours Bachelor's Degree*: a further yr; *Master's Degree*: a further 1-2 yrs; *Doctorate*: at least 2 yrs. The Bachelor (Honours) Degree is awarded in the same fields of study as the Bachelor's Degree. Also Undergraduate and Postgraduate Diplomas

Student Residential Facilities: For 6100 students

Special Facilities: University Museum; John R. Ellerman Museum (Zoology). University Gallery. Botanical Garden

Libraries: J.S. Gericke Library, total, 955,466 vols

Publications: University of Stellenbosch Annales; Rector's Report; Research Report; Matieland

Academic Staff *1999-2000*	MEN	WOMEN	TOTAL
FULL-TIME	575	222	**797**

Student Numbers *1999-2000*	MEN	WOMEN	TOTAL
All (Foreign Included)	10,314	11,442	**21,756**

Evening Students, 845

UNIVERSITY OF TRANSKEI/UNIVERSITEIT VAN TRANSKEI (UNITRA)

Private Bag X1, Umtata 5117
Tel: +27(471) 302-2111
Fax: +27(471) 268-20
EMail: Postmaster@getafix.utr.ac.za
Website: http://www.utr.ac.za

Vice-Chancellor and Principal (Acting): E.D. Malaza

Registrar: Peggy Luswazi

Faculties

Arts (African American Studies; African Languages; Afrikaans; Anthropology; Classical Languages; Criminology; English; Geography; History; Information Sciences; Modern Languages; Philosophy; Political Science; Psychology; Religious Studies; Social Work; Sociology)

Economics (Accountancy; Economics; Information Technology; Management; Public Administration)

Education (Adult Education; Business and Commerce; Education; Educational Research; Mathematics Education; Music Education; Science Education)

Law (Criminal Law; History of Law; Law; Private Law; Public Law)

Medicine and Health Sciences (Anaesthesiology; Anatomy; Biomedicine; Dermatology; Embryology and Reproduction Biology; Gynaecology and Obstetrics; Haematology; Health Education; Health Sciences; Medicine; Microbiology; Nursing; Ophthalmology; Orthopedics; Otorhinolaryngology; Paediatrics; Pharmacology)

Science (Applied Mathematics; Botany; Chemistry; Computer Science; Mathematics; Physics; Statistics; Zoology)

Departments

Educational Research *(EDRES)*

History: Founded 1976 as branch of the University of Fort Hare and acquired present status 1977.

Governing Bodies: Council

Academic Year: February to November (February-June; July-November)

Admission Requirements: Matriculation Certificate of exemption issued by the Joint Matriculation Board

Main Language(s) of Instruction: English

International Co-operation: University of Bristol

Degrees and Diplomas: *Bachelor's Degree*: 3 yrs; Laws (LLB), 3 yrs following first degree; Medicine and Surgery (BM), 6 yrs; *Honours Bachelor's Degree*: a further yr; *Master's Degree*: a further 2-3 yrs; *Doctorate*. The Bachelor (Honours) Degree is awarded in the same fields of study as the Bachelor's Degree

Student Residential Facilities: For c. 1850 students

Academic Staff: Total: c. 240

Student Numbers: Total: c. 6,800

• UNIVERSITY OF VENDA FOR SCIENCE AND TECHNOLOGY

Private Bag X5050, Thohoyandou, State Northern Province 0950
Tel: +27(159) 624-757
Fax: +27(159) 624-791
EMail: prd@univen.ac.za
Website: http://www.univen.ac.za

Vice-Chancellor and Principal: G.M. Nkondo
Tel: +27(15) 962-8316 Fax: +27(15) 962-4742
EMail: gnkondo@uneven.ac.za

Registrar: J.N. Matidza

Schools

Agriculture, Rural Development and Forestry (Forestry; Rural Studies) *Dean*: M.O. Makinde

Business, Economics and Administrative Sciences (Administration; Business and Commerce; Economics) *Dean*: H.P.M. Simukonda

Education *Dean*: E.L.M. Bayona

Environmental Sciences (Environmental Studies) *Dean*: P.H. Omara-Ojungu

Health Sciences *Dean*: N.S. Shai-Mahoko

Human Sciences (Afrikaans; Anthropology; English; History; Music; Philosophy; Political Science; Psychology; Social Sciences; Social Work; Theology) *Dean*: K.F. Netshiombo

Integrated Studies (African Studies; Gender Studies)

Law *Dean*: P.R. Mawila

Mathematics and Natural Sciences (Biochemistry; Biological and Life Sciences; Botany; Chemistry; Mathematics; Physics; Statistics) *Head*: G.D. Djolov

History: Founded 1982. Acquired present title 1996.

Governing Bodies: Council, comprising 28 members

Academic Year: February to December (February-March; April-June; July-September; September-December)

Admission Requirements: Matriculation Certificate or certificate of exemption issued by the Joint Matriculation Board

Fees: (Rand): Tuition, undergraduate, 4490-5430 per annum; postgraduate, 4220-5040

Main Language(s) of Instruction: English

Degrees and Diplomas: *Bachelor's Degree*: Education (BEd), 1 yr following first degree; Laws (LLB), 2 yrs following first degree; Administration (BAdmin); Agriculture (BAgric); Arts (BA); Commerce (BCom); Economics (BEcon); Jurisprudence (BJuris); Science (BSc), 3-4 yrs; *Honours Bachelor's Degree*: a further yr; *Master's Degree*: a further 1-2 yrs; *Doctorate*: 1-2 yrs. The Bachelor (Honours) Degree is awarded in the same fields of study as the Bachelor's Degree. Also Undergraduate and Postgraduate Diplomas

Student Residential Facilities: For 1100 students

Special Facilities: Experimental Farm

Libraries: University of Venda Library, c. 80,000 vols; 900 periodicals

Academic Staff *1999:* Total: **246**

Student Numbers *1999*	MEN	WOMEN	TOTAL
All (Foreign Included)	2,975	3,147	**6,122**
FOREIGN ONLY	4	7	11

• VISTA UNIVERSITY (DECENTRALIZED CAMPUSES)

Private Bag X634, 63 Skinner Street, Pretoria 0001
Tel: +27(12) 322-8967
Fax: +27(12) 320-0528
Cable: vista university
Website: http://www.vista.ac.za

Vice-Chancellor: C.T. Keto (2001-) Tel: +27(12) 322-2400
Fax: +27(12) 320-3521 EMail: evc@vista.ac.za

Registrar: R.J. Mbuli

Faculties

Arts (Afrikaans; Arts and Humanities; English; History; Native Language; Psychology; Religious Studies; Sociology)
Education *(Port Elizabeth)* (Curriculum; Education; Vocational Education)
Law *(Bloemfontein)* (Commercial Law; Law; Private Law; Public Law)
Management *(Port Elizabeth)* (Accountancy; Business Administration; Economics; Industrial and Organizational Psychology; Management; Public Administration)
Science (Agriculture; Biological and Life Sciences; Chemistry; Computer Science; Geography; Information Sciences; Mathematics; Natural Sciences; Physics; Statistics)

Centres

Agricultural Sciences *(VUDEC)* (Agriculture)
Biological Sciences *(VUDEC)* (Biological and Life Sciences)
Chemistry *(Soweto)*
Community Development (Development Studies)
Community Resources Technology *(VUDEC)* (Urban Studies)
Computer Science and Information Systems *(Bloemfontein)* (Computer Science)
Education *(Postgraduate, Port Elizabeth)*
Industrial Psychology (Industrial and Organizational Psychology)
Nguni Languages *(Port Elizabeth)* (Native Language)
Physics *(Port Elizabeth)*
Procedural Law *(Port Elizabeth)* (Law)
Professional Education *(Soweto)* (Education)
Religious Education and Biblical Studies *(VUDEC)*
School Subject Education *(Sebokeng)* (Curriculum)
Sotho Languages *(Soweto)*
Statistics *(Bloemfontein)*

Research Units

Employment *(Port Elizabeth)* (Labour and Industrial Relations)
Indigenous Languages *students:* 31

Further Information: Also campuses in Bloemfontein, East Rand, Mamelodi, Port Elizabeth, Sebokeng, Soweto, and Welkom

History: Founded 1982. An urban University catering primarily to local matriculants at eight decentralized campuses: Bloemfontein Campus, Mamelodi Campus (near Pretoria), East Rand Campus (Daveyton), Port Elizabeth Campus (Zwide), Sebokeng Campus (Vanderbijlpark), Soweto Campus (Johannesburg), VUDEC (Vista Distance Education Campus, previously Further Training in Pretoria) and Welkom Campus

(Thabong). An autonomous institution receiving financial support from the State.

Governing Bodies: University Council; University Senate

Academic Year: January to December (January-March; April-June; July-September; September-December)

Admission Requirements: Matriculation Certificate or certificate of exemption issued by the Joint Matriculation Board

Main Language(s) of Instruction: English

Degrees and Diplomas: *Bachelor's Degree*: Education (BEd), 1 yr after first degree; Accountancy (BCompt); Administration (BAdmin); Arts (BA); Commerce (BCom); Science (BSc), 2 yrs; Law (LLB), 2-4 yrs following first degree; Financial Law (BProcLaw); Jurisprudence (BJuris); Science Education (BScEd), 3-4 yrs; Commerce Education (BComEd), 4 yrs; *Honours Bachelor's Degree*: 2 yrs; *Master's Degree*: Arts (MA); Commerce (MCom); Education (MEd), 4 yrs; *Doctorate*: 1-2 yrs. The Bachelor (Honours) Degree is awarded in the same fields of study as the Bachelor's Degree. Also Undergraduate and Postgraduate Diplomas

Student Services: Academic Counselling, Employment Services, Sports Facilities, Canteen

Libraries: Library Services, c. 42,000 vols

Publications: Vital; Vista Occasional Papers (annually)

Press or Publishing House: Mutualpark (Production and Dispatch)

Academic Staff: Total: c. 865

Student Numbers: Total: c. 28,180

Distance Students, c. 10,180

UNIVERSITY OF WESTERN CAPE/UNIVERSITEIT VAN WES-KAAPLAND (UWC)

Private Bag X17, Bellville, Western Cape 7535
Tel: +27(21) 959-2911
Fax: +27(21) 959-3126
Telex: 5226661
Cable: UNIBELL
Website: http://www.uwc.ac.za

Rector (Acting): Ikey Van de Rheede Tel: +27(21) 959-2101
Fax: +27(21) 959-2973 EMail: rector@uwc.ac.za

Registrar: Ingrid Muller EMail: imiller@uwc.ac.za

Faculties

Arts (Afrikaans; Anthropology; Arts and Humanities; English; Gender Studies; Geography; History; Information Sciences; Library Science; Linguistics; Native Language; Philosophy; Religion; Sociology; Theology; Women's Studies) *Dean:* Tony Parr
Community and Health Sciences (Community Health; Dietetics; Ecology; Health Sciences; Nursing; Occupational Therapy; Physical Education; Physical Therapy; Psychology; Public Health; Social Work; Sports) *Dean:* Ratie Mpofu
Dentistry *Dean:* Martin H. Hobdell
Economics and Management (Accountancy; Computer Science; Economics; Industrial and Organizational Psychology; Management; Political Science; Public Administration) *Dean:* Fatimah Abrahams

Education *Dean*: Harold D. Herman
Law *Dean*: Darcy du Toit
Religion and Theology (Religion; Theology) *Dean*: R.H. Botman
Science (Biology; Biomedicine; Biotechnology; Chemistry; Computer Science; Environmental Studies; Geology; Mathematics; Natural Sciences; Pharmacy; Physics; Statistics; Zoology) *Dean*: Jan van Beverdonker

Units
Education Policy (Educational Research)
Enterprise Development (Business Administration)
Teaching and Learning Technologies (Pedagogy)

Divisions
Lifelong Learning (Continuing Education)

Programmes
Land and Agrarian Studies *(PLAAS)* (Agriculture)
Social Law

Schools
Government

Institutes
Bioinformatics *(South African National)* (Biology; Computer Science)
Child and Family Development (Child Care and Development; Family Studies) *Director*: F.C.T. Sonn
Historical Research (History) *Director*: H.C. Bredekamp
Ocean Regional Operational Centre for Southern Africa *(International)* (Marine Science and Oceanography)

Centres
Adult and Continuing Education *Director*: S.C. Walters
Community Law (Law)
Community Law (Law) *Director*: N.C. Steyler
Mayibuye (Archiving)
Southern African Studies (African Studies) *Director*: P. Vale

History: Founded 1959 as University College of the University of South Africa, became independent University 1984. An autonomous institution receiving financial support from the State.

Governing Bodies: University Council, comprising the Rector, 2 Vice-Rectors, 8 members appointed by the State President, 2 elected by the Senate, 4 elected by Convocation, 1 elected by Donors, 1 nominated by the City Council of Bellville, 2 elected by Principals of secondary schools

Academic Year: February to December (February-July; July-December)

Admission Requirements: Matriculation Certificate or certificate of exemption issued by the Joint Matriculation Board

Fees: (Rands): Tuition, undergraduate, 6300-6900 per annum; foreing students, 9100-9500

Main Language(s) of Instruction: English, Afrikaans

International Co-operation: University of Missouri; Wesleyan University; Yale University; Penn State University; Rijksuniversiteit Utrecht; Universiteit van Amsterdam; Vrije Universiteit van Amsterdam; University of Zimbabwe; University of Namibia; University Eduardo Mondlane, Maputo

Degrees and Diplomas: *Bachelor's Degree*: Education (BEd), 1 yr following first degree; Law (LLB); Theology (BTh), 3 yrs following first degree; Administration (BAdmin); Arts (BA); Commerce (BComm); Economics (BEcon); Financial Law (BProcLaw); Jurisprudence (BJuris); Library Science (BBibl); Pharmacy (BPharm); Science (BSc), 3-4 yrs; Nursing (BCur), 4 1/2 yrs; Dental Surgery (BChD), 5 1/2 yrs; *Honours Bachelor's Degree*: a further yr; *Master's Degree*: a further 1-2 yrs; *Doctorate*: by thesis. The Bachelor (Honours) Degree is awarded in the same fields of study as the Bachelor's Degree. Also Diplomas

Student Residential Facilities: For c. 3120 students

Special Facilities: Cape Flats Nature Reserve. Archives. Mayibuye Historical and Cultural Centre

Libraries: Central Library and specialized libraries, total, 258,724 vols; 1440 periodicals

Publications: UWC News; Campus Bulletin

Press or Publishing House: Publications Committee (in association with David Philip, Publisher)

Academic Staff *1999:* Full-Time: c. 450 Part-Time: c. 40 Total: c. 490

Student Numbers *1999:* Total: c. 11,460

*• UNIVERSITY OF THE WITWATERSRAND
Private Bag 3, Wits, 2050
Tel: +27(11) 716-3200
Fax: +27(11) 716-8030
Telex: 42 7125 wits sa
Cable: uniwits
EMail: 086wendy@atlas.wits.ac.za
Website: http://www.wits.ac.za

Vice-Chancellor and Principal: Norma Reid (2001-)
Tel: +27(11) 717-1101 Fax: +27(11) 339-8215
EMail: 160vc1@atlas.wits.ac.za

Registrar (Academic): Derek K. Swemmer
Tel: +27(11) 717-1201 Fax: +27(11) 403-7593
EMail: 160acadr@atlas.wits.ac.za

International Relations: Sharon Groenemeyer-Edigheji
Tel: +27(11) 717-1052 Fax: +27(11) 403-1385

Faculties
Arts (African Languages; Afrikaans; Anthropology; Archaeology; Art History; Arts and Humanities; Classical Languages; Comparative Literature; Dutch; English; Fine Arts; History; International Relations; Linguistics; Literature; Modern Languages; Music; Philosophy; Political Science; Psychology; Religious Studies; Social Sciences; Speech Studies; Speech Therapy and Audiology; Theatre; Translation and Interpretation) *Dean*: Gerrit Olivier, *full-time staff*: 266, *part-time staff*: 5, *students*: 3,023
Built Environment (Architecture; Building Technologies; Regional Planning; Surveying and Mapping; Town Planning) *Dean*: Lindsay Jill Bremner, *full-time staff*: 41, *part-time staff*: 5, *students*: 714
Commerce (Accountancy; Business and Commerce; Economics; Information Technology) *Dean*: Merton B. Dagut, *full-time staff*: 81, *part-time staff*: 10, *students*: 2,800

Education *Dean (Acting):* A.D. Lelliott, *full-time staff:* 57, *part-time staff:* 5

Engineering (Civil Engineering; Electrical Engineering; Engineering; Engineering Management; Materials Engineering; Mechanical Engineering; Mining Engineering) *Dean:* Jan Peter Reynders, *full-time staff:* 179, *part-time staff:* 3, *students:* 1,974

Health Sciences (Dentistry; Health Sciences; Medicine; Nursing; Pharmacy) *Dean:* Max Price, *full-time staff:* 450, *part-time staff:* 15, *students:* 3,172

Law *Dean:* Andrew Skeen, *full-time staff:* 80, *part-time staff:* 7, *students:* 848

Management (Business Administration; Development Studies; Management) *Dean:* Keith A. Yeomans, *full-time staff:* 126, *part-time staff:* 8, *students:* 1,066

Science (Applied Mathematics; Archaeology; Biochemistry; Environmental Studies; Genetics; Geography; Geology; Geophysics; Mathematics and Computer Science; Microbiology; Natural Sciences) *Dean:* Colin J. Wright, *full-time staff:* 444, *part-time staff:* 5, *students:* 2,357

Centres

Continuing Education *Director:* D.D Russell

Nuclear Sciences (Nuclear Engineering)

Further Information: Also 80 Research Units, Institutes, Groups and Programmes

History: Founded 1896 as School of Mines at Kimberley. Incorporated in Transvaal Technical Institute 1904, renamed South African School of Mines and Technology 1910. Became University College 1920 and University 1922. An autonomous institution receiving financial support from the State.

Governing Bodies: University Council; University Senate

Academic Year: February to November (February-June; July-November)

Admission Requirements: Matriculation Certificate or certificate of exemption issued by the Matriculation Board

Fees: (Rands): First year, 4320-16,550

Main Language(s) of Instruction: English

International Co-operation: Florida State University; Ben-Gurion University of the Negev; University of Cambridge; Columbia University; DePaul University; Technical University of Dresden; Eduardo Mondlane University Maputo; Erasmus University Rotterdam; Free University Amsterdam; Indiana University; La Trobe University; Leiden University; Macquarie University; Pennsylvania State University; Soka University; Aachen University of Technology; University of Queensland; Université de Montpellier I; University of Birmingham; California State University, Los Angeles; Technical University of Dresden; University of Swaziland; University of Warwick; University of Zimbabwe; Brown University; Colorado State University; Florida Atlantic University; Oxford University; University of Manitoba; University of Sussex; University of Texas; West Virginia University

Degrees and Diplomas: *Bachelor's Degree:* Education (BEd), 1 yr following first degree; Laws (LLB), 2-3 yrs following first degree; Arts (BA); Commerce (BCom); Economic Science (BEconSc); Engineering (BSc(Eng)); Financial Law (BProcLaw); Music (BMus); Pharmacy (BPharm); Primary Education (BPrimEd); Science (BSc), 3-4 yrs; Dental Science, 5 1/2 yrs; Accountancy (BAcc); Architecture (BArch), 5 yrs; Medicine and Surgery (MBBCh), 6 yrs; *Honours Bachelor's Degree:* a further yr; *Master's Degree:* a further 1-2 yrs; *Doctorate:* 1-2 yrs. The Bachelor (Honours) Degree is awarded in the same fields of study as the Bachelor's Degree. Also Undergraduate and Postgraduate Diplomas

Student Services: Academic Counselling, Social Counselling, Employment Services, Nursery Care, Cultural Centre, Sports Facilities, Handicapped Facilities, Health Services, Canteen, Foreign Student Centre

Student Residential Facilities: For 3100 students

Special Facilities: Adler Museum of the History of Medicine; Archaeology Museum; Bleloch Museum (Geology); Brebner Museum (Surgery); Robert Broom Museum (Sterkfontein Caves); Dental Museum; Hunterian Museum (Anatomy); Museum of Obstetrics and Gynaecology; Palaeontology Museum; Social Anthropology Museum; Sutherland Strachan Museum (Pathology); Museum of Wireless, Radio and Electronics; Zoology Museum. Gertrude Posel Gallery. Standard Bank Collection of African Art. Planetarium. Moss Herbarium

Libraries: Wartenweiler Library, total 1.5m vols

Publications: English Studies in Africa; Urban Forum (biannually); Palaeontologia Africana (annually)

Press or Publishing House: Wits University Press

Academic Staff *1999-2000*	TOTAL
FULL-TIME	951
PART-TIME	141
TOTAL	**1,092**

Student Numbers *1999-2000:* Total: **17,308**

UNIVERSITY OF ZULULAND/UNIVERSITEIT VAN ZULULAND (UNIZUL)

Private Bag X1001, Kwa-Dlangezwa, Natal 3886
Tel: +27(351) 93-911
Fax: +27(351) 93-130
Telex: 631311
Website: http://www.uzulu.ac.za

Vice-Chancellor and Rector: Charles R.M. Dlamini (1993-)

Registrar (Acting): T.A. Dube

Faculties

Arts (African Languages; Afrikaans; Arts and Humanities; Communication Studies; Criminal Law; Development Studies; English; History; Library Science; Linguistics; Music; Nursing; Philosophy; Psychology; Social Work; Sociology; Theatre; Tourism)

Commerce and Administration *(Umlazi Campus)* (Accountancy; Business Administration; Economics; Political Science; Public Administration) *Dean:* N.J. Smith

Education *(Umlazi Campus)* (Education; Educational Administration; Educational Psychology; Educational Sciences)

Law

Science (Agriculture; Animal Husbandry; Biochemistry; Botany; Chemistry; Computer Science; Consumer Studies; Geography; Hydraulic Engineering; Mathematics; Microbiology; Natural Sciences; Physics; Zoology) *Dean:* M.F. Coetsee

Theology and Religious Studies (Bible; Ethics; Religious Practice; Theology) *Dean:* Arthur Song

History: Founded 1959 as University College for Zulu and Swazi students. Became University 1970. An autonomous institution receiving financial support from the State.

Governing Bodies: Council; Senate

Academic Year: February to December (February-June; July-December)

Admission Requirements: Matriculation Certificate or certificate of exemption issued by the Joint Matriculation Board

Main Language(s) of Instruction: English

Degrees and Diplomas: *Bachelor's Degree*: Education (BEd), 1 yr following first degree; Laws (LLB), 2 yrs following first degree; Arts (BA); Commerce (BCom); Financial Law (BProcLaw); Jurisprudence (BJuris); Library Science (BBibl); Pedagogy (BPaed); Science (BSc); Theology (BTh), 3-4 yrs; *Honours Bachelor's Degree*: a further yr; *Master's Degree*: a further 1-2 yrs; *Doctorate*: 1-2 yrs. The Bachelor (Honours) Degree is awarded in the same fields of study as the Bachelor's Degree. Also Undergraduate and Postgraduate Diplomas

Libraries: c. 95,000 vols

Publications: Journal of Psychology; Paedonomia (biannually)

Academic Staff: Total: c. 290

Student Numbers: Total: c. 5,170

OTHER INSTITUTIONS

ANN LATSKY COLLEGE OF NURSING
Private Bag 40, Auckland Park 2006
Tel: +27(11) 726-3170/8

Principal: E. Harms

Nursing

BARAGWANATH NURSING COLLEGE
Private Bag X05, Bertsham 2013
Tel: +27(11) 933-1535

Principal: N.M.N. Mayekiso

Registrar: G. Angelides

Nursing

B.G. ALEXANDER COLLEGE OF NURSING
Private Bag X43, Johannesburg 2000
Tel: +27(11) 488-3219
Fax: +27(11) 643-1036

Principal: C. Campbell (1995-)

Registrar: A. du Plessis

Nursing

History: Founded 1961

BLOEMFONTEIN COLLEGE
Douglas Street, Bloemfontein 9301
Tel: +27(51) 448-1525
Fax: +27(51) 447-0486
EMail: info@bfncol.co.za
Website: http://www.connix.co.za/bfncol/

Rector: FNJ Fourie

Faculties
Business Studies (Business Administration)
Continuing Education
Engineering
General Studies
Management

BONALESEDI NURSING COLLEGE
Private Bag X1001, Luipaardsvlei 1743
Tel: +27(11) 410-1402

Principal: L.T. Phore

Nursing

BORDER TECHNIKON
Private Bag 1421, East London 5200
Tel: +27(403) 708-5200
Fax: +27(403) 708-5331
EMail: bormain@indlovu.bortech.ac.za
Website: http://www.bortech.ac.za

Rector: L.R. Brunyee Fax: +27(403) 63-3729

Registrar: J. Bhana Fax: +27(403) 63-1165

Faculties
Applied Technology (Civil Engineering; Communication Studies; Construction Engineering; Electrical Engineering; Engineering; Fashion Design; Fine Arts; Information Technology; Mathematics; Mechanical Engineering; Physics; Technology; Tourism)
Human Sciences (Accountancy; Arts and Humanities; Business Administration; Finance; Journalism; Marketing; Secretarial Studies; Taxation)

History: Founded 1988.

BUSINESS MANAGEMENT TRAINING COLLEGE
Denavo House, 5 King Street, Kensington B, Randburg
Tel: +27(11) 886-4096
Fax: +27(11) 886-4245
EMail: bmtc@global.co.za
Website: http://www.global.co.za/business/bmtc/
Management

History: Founded 1973 in association with the Institute of Business Management.

Degrees and Diplomas: Diplomas in Business Management, Financial Management and Computer Education

CAPE TECHNIKON

PO Box 652, Cape Town 8000
Tel: +27(21) 460-3911
Fax: +27(21) 460-3695
Telex: 521666 sa
Cable: teccom
Website: http://www.ctech.ac.za

Rector and Vice-Chancellor: M.M. Balintulo (1997-)
Tel: +27(21) 460-3352 Fax: +27(21) 460-3700
EMail: rector@ctech.ac.za

Vice-Rector: J. Van Zyl Tel: +27(21) 460-3355
EMail: jvzyl@ctech.ac.za

Faculties

Applied Sciences (Applied Chemistry; Applied Mathematics; Applied Physics) *Dean:* Lionel Slammert, *students:* 1,294
Built Environment and Design (Architectural and Environmental Design) *Dean:* Mel Hagan, *students:* 1,020
Business Informatics (Business Computing) *Dean:* Lotter, *students:* 2,573
Engineering *Dean:* Nico Beute, *students:* 2,715
Management *Dean:* Mohamed Bayat, *students:* 2,616
Teacher Education (Teacher Training) *Dean:* Willie Smith, *students:* 335

History: Founded 1923, acquired present title 1979. Granted degrees 1995
Governing Bodies: Council
Academic Year: January to December
Main Language(s) of Instruction: English, Afrikaans
Accrediting Agencies: Certification Council for Technikon Education (SERTEC)
Student Services: Academic Counselling, Social Counselling, Employment Services, Cultural Centre, Sports Facilities, Language Programmes, Health Services, Foreign Student Centre
Student Residential Facilities: Yes
Libraries: Central Library

CARINUS NURSING COLLEGE

Private Bag XI, Groote Schuur 7937
Tel: +27(21) 404-6151 +27(21) 404-6152
Fax: +27(21) 404-4400

Head: E. Kilian

Nursing

CEDARA COLLEGE OF AGRICULTURE

Private Bag X6008, Hilton, Kwazulu-Natal 3245
Tel: +27(33) 355-9304
Fax: +27(33) 355-9303
EMail: college@dae.kzntl.gov.za
Website: http://agriculture.kzntl.gov.za

Principal: A. Van Niekerk (1997-)
EMail: vanniekerka@dae.kzntl.gov.za
Vice-Principal: Berno Lütge (1999-)
EMail: lütgeb@ome.kzntl.gov.za

Colleges

Agriculture *Director:* Alison Van Niekerk, *full-time staff:* 18, *part-time staff:* 8, *students:* 150

History: Founded 1905.
Academic Year: January to November
Admission Requirements: Senior certificate
Fees: (Rands): 8500-00 per annum (includes accommodation)
Main Language(s) of Instruction: English
Accrediting Agencies: Certification Council for Technikon Education (SERTEC)
Degrees and Diplomas: *National Higher Certificate*: Agriculture, 2 yrs; *National Diploma*: Agriculture, 3 yrs
Student Services: Sports Facilities
Student Residential Facilities: For 150 students
Special Facilities: Farm
Libraries: Central Library

Academic Staff 2000	MEN	WOMEN	TOTAL
FULL-TIME	8	6	14
PART-TIME	6	2	8
TOTAL	**14**	**8**	**22**

Staff with doctorate: Total: **1**

Student Numbers 2000	MEN	WOMEN	TOTAL
All (Foreign Included)	61	57	**118**

CISKEI COLLEGE OF NURSING

Private Bag 13003, Cambridge 5206
Tel: +27(403) 611-802
Fax: +27(403) 611-158

Principal (Acting): M.V. Yoli

Nursing

COLLEGE OF AGRICULTURE, POTCHEFSTROOM

Private Bag X804, Potchefstroom, Northwest 2520
Tel: +27(18) 299-6556
Fax: +27(18) 293-3925
EMail: oplkirk@potchli.agric.za

Deputy-Director: Les Kirkland (1997-)
EMail: oplkirk@potch1.agric.za
Assistant Director and Registrar: J.L. Venter (1997-)
Tel: +27(18) 299-6608 EMail: opljlv@potch1.agric.za
International Relations: Philip Nel, Student Affairs (1995-)
Tel: +27(18) 299-6636 EMail: oplpwn@potch1.agric.za

Colleges

Agriculture (Agricultural Education; Agriculture)

History: Founded 1909.
Admission Requirements: Senior Certificate or equivalent
Fees: (Rands): 14,500 per annum
Main Language(s) of Instruction: Afrikaans
Accrediting Agencies: Certification Council for Technikon Education (SERTEC)

Degrees and Diplomas: *National Diploma*: Agriculture, 3 yrs

Student Services: Academic Counselling, Social Counselling, Foreign Student Adviser, Sports Facilities, Canteen

Student Residential Facilities: Yes

Special Facilities: Computer Centre

Libraries: Central Library

Academic Staff 2000	MEN	WOMEN	TOTAL
FULL-TIME	25	9	**34**

Staff with doctorate: Total: **1**

Student Numbers 2000	MEN	WOMEN	TOTAL
All (Foreign Included)	325	25	**350**
FOREIGN ONLY	7	–	7

CORONATION COLLEGE OF NURSING
Private Bag X01, Newclare 2112
Tel: +27(11) 470-9000
Fax: +27(11) 673-4256

Principal: M. Nizamdin

Registrar: R.C. Pugin

Nursing

EASTERN COLLEGE OF NURSING, CHARLOTTE SEARLE CAMPUS
Private Bag, Korsten 6014
Tel: +27(41) 405-2150

Head: M.W. Kingsley

Nursing

EASTERN CAPE COLLEGE OF NURSING
Sharley Cribb Campus, Private Bag X6047, Port Elizabeth 6000
Tel: +27(41) 343-000
Fax: +27(41) 332-614

Head: E.P. du Perez

Nursing

EASTERN CAPE TECHNIKON
Private Bag X 3182, Butterworth, Eastern Cape 4960
Tel: +27(474) 401-2000
Fax: +27(474) 492-0735
EMail: vido@garfield.tktech.ac.za
Website: http://www.tktech.ac.za

Principal and Vice-Chancellor: Q.T. Mjoli
Fax: +27(474) 620-721

Vice-Rector: Alfred Bomvu

International Relations: Andrew Christoffels

Faculties
Applied Technology (Cooking and Catering; Education; Fashion Design; Technology)

Business Science (Accountancy; Communication Studies; Human Resources; Law; Management; Public Administration; Secretarial Studies) *Dean:* C.J. Posthumus

Engineering (Civil Engineering; Construction Engineering; Electrical Engineering; Engineering; Information Technology; Mathematics; Mechanical Engineering) *Dean:* S.P.K. Boni

EDENDALE NURSING COLLEGE
Private Bag X 9099, Pietermaritzburg 3200
Tel: +27(331) 95-4161
Fax: +27(331) 81-721

College Principal: S. Ndlovu

Nursing

ELSENBURG AGRICULTURAL COLLEGE
PO Box 54, Elsenburg 7607
Tel: +27(21) 808-5018
Fax: +27(21) 884-4319
Website: http://www.elsenburg.com

Principal: M.J. Paulse

Vice-Principal: G.J.O. Marincowitz

International Relations: A. Marais, Head

Agriculture

History: Founded 1898.

EXCELSIUS NURSING COLLEGE
Private Bag A 19, Klerksdrop 2570
Tel: +27(18) 462-1030
Fax: +27(18) 462-1030

Principal: A.J. Senekal

Nursing

FORT COX AGRICULTURAL COLLEGE (FCC)
PO Box 2187, King William's Town, Eastern Cape 5600
Tel: +27(40) 653-8034
Fax: +27(40) 653-8336

Principal: R.C.Y. Awumey (1996-) Tel: +27(40) 653-8038
Fax: +27(40) 653-8040 EMail: rawumey@iafrica.com

Deputy-Principal: M. Mankazana

International Relations: Mbeko Pityane

Departments
Agriculture and Natural Resources Management (Agriculture; Forestry; Natural Resources) Richard Awumey, *full-time staff:* 20, *part-time staff:* 2, *students:* 234

Crop Production and Community Forest (Agricultural Business; Cattle Breeding; Crop Production; Forest Management)

History: Founded in 1930, acquired present status and title 1993.

Governing Bodies: Board of Governors; Academic Council

Academic Year: January to December

Admission Requirements: Grade 12 with one Science subject

Main Language(s) of Instruction: English

International Co-operation: Oregon State University; University of Guelph

Accrediting Agencies: Certification Council for Technikon Education (SERTEC)

Degrees and Diplomas: *National Diploma*: Agriculture; Community Forest, 3 yrs. Also Diplomas, 1 yr

Student Services: Academic Counselling, Social Counselling, Sports Facilities, Canteen

Student Residential Facilities: Yes

Libraries: Central Library, c. 5000 vols; Audio Visual Centre

Academic Staff 2000	MEN	WOMEN	TOTAL
FULL-TIME	16	4	20
PART-TIME	2	–	2
TOTAL	**18**	**4**	**22**

Staff with doctorate: Total: **1**

Student Numbers 2000	MEN	WOMEN	TOTAL
All (Foreign Included)	142	92	**234**

FRERE NURSING COLLEGE
Private Bag X9023, East London 5200
Tel: +27(43) 709-1136
Fax: +27(43) 743-4265
EMail: frerenc@iafrica.com

Head: P. Bellad-Ellis (1984-)

Nursing (Midwifery; Nursing; Psychiatry and Mental Health) *Director*: Penelope Bellad-Ellis, *full-time staff:* 35, *students:* 500

History: Founded 1975

Governing Bodies: Senate; Council

Academic Year: January to November

Admission Requirements: Senior Certificate

Main Language(s) of Instruction: English

Accrediting Agencies: South African Nursing Council

Degrees and Diplomas: *National Higher Diploma*: Nursing, 4 yrs. Diploma in Midwifery; Diploma in Psychiatric Nursing Science

Student Services: Academic Counselling, Social Counselling, Health Services

Libraries: Local Health Resource Centre

Academic Staff 2000	MEN	WOMEN	TOTAL
FULL-TIME	–	26	**26**

Student Numbers 2000	MEN	WOMEN	TOTAL
All (Foreign Included)	48	432	**480**

GA-RANKUWA COLLEGE
Private Bag X 422, Pretoria 0001
Tel: +27(12) 529-3111

Nursing

414

GERMISTON COLLEGE
Corner of Sol Street and Driehoek Road, Germiston 1401
Tel: +27(11) 825-3524
Fax: +27(11) 873-1769
EMail: gercoll@global.co.za
Website: http://www.home.global.co.za

History: Established 1928. The Germiston Technical Institution was one of the 12 branches of the Witwatersrand Technical College. The College was granted autonomy in 1983. It now caters for more than 3000 students and the number of registrations per year is close to 10,000.

GLEN AGRICULTURAL COLLEGE
Private Bag X 01, Glen 9360
Tel: +27(51) 861-1256
Fax: +27(51) 861-1122
Telex: 267690 sa

Principal: T.P. Ntili **EMail:** paul@glen.agric.za

Agriculture

GOLD FIELDS NURSING COLLEGE
Private Bag XII, Westonaria 1783
Tel: +27(11) 752-1145
Fax: +27(11) 752-1109

Nursing Superintendent: Hertie De Mendonca
EMail: hertie.demendonca@goldfields.co.za

Principal: Erika Kotze (1996-)
EMail: erika.kotze@goldfields.co.za

Human Resource Manager: Louise Wienard
EMail: louise.wienard@goldfields.co.za

Nursing *Head*: Louise Wienard

Academic Year: January to December

Admission Requirements: Senior school certificate (English)

Fees: (Rands): 5800 per annum; 2900 per semester

Main Language(s) of Instruction: English

Accrediting Agencies: South African Nursing Council

Degrees and Diplomas: *National Diploma*: Nursing, 4 yrs. Also Diploma in Nursing (bridging course), 2 yrs

Student Services: Academic Counselling, Social Counselling

Student Residential Facilities: None

Libraries: Central Library

Academic Staff 2000	MEN	WOMEN	TOTAL
FULL-TIME	2	7	9
PART-TIME	1	–	1
TOTAL	**3**	**7**	**10**

GROOTFONTEIN AGRICULTURAL COLLEGE
Private Bag X 529, Middelburg 5900
Tel: +27(49) 842-1113
Fax: +27(49) 842-1477

Principal (Acting): F. Roux EMail: w612@kardo1.agric.za

Vice-Principal (Acting): S. Schoonraad
EMail: ople19@karco1.agric.za

Agriculture

History: Founded 1911.

GROOTHOEK COLLEGE OF NURSING
Private Bag X 1122, Sovenga 0727

Nursing

HENRIETTA STOCKDALE NURSING COLLEGE
Private Bag X5051, Kimberley 8300
Tel: +27(531) 81-4659
Fax: +27(531) 81-4346

Principal: M. du Plessis

Nursing

INTEC COLLEGE
PO Box 19, Cape Town 8000
Tel: +27(21) 460-6700
Fax: +27(21) 447-9569
EMail: info@intec.edu.za
Website: http://www.intec.edu.za

Programmes
Business Studies (Accountancy; Business and Commerce; Human Resources; Management; Marketing; Public Relations)
Computer Studies (Computer Science; Data Processing; Information Management; Software Engineering)
Creative Studies (Cosmetology; Fashion Design; Graphic Arts; Journalism; Psychology; Sports)
Technical Studies (Architectural and Environmental Design; Chemistry; Civil Engineering; Construction Engineering; Electrical Engineering; Electronic Engineering; Mechanical Engineering)
Vocational Studies (Business Administration; Child Care and Development; Cooking and Catering; Health Education; Hotel and Restaurant; Safety Engineering; Tourism)

History: Founded 1906, INTEC specializes in Distance Education, also known as correspondence study or home study. Specialist tutors provide guidance and support to students.

LEBONE COLLEGE OF NURSING
Private Bag X 751, Pretoria 0001
Tel: +27(12) 373-8452
Fax: +27(12) 373-8607

Nursing

LOWVELD AGRICULTURAL COLLEGE
Private Bag X 11283, Nelspruit 1200
Tel: +27(13) 753-3064
Fax: +27(13) 753-1110

Principal: S.E. Terblanche EMail: fanie@laeveld1.agric.za
Registrar: C.J. Louw EMail: bom@laeveld1.agric.za

Agriculture

History: Founded 1991.

MADZIVHANDILA AGRICULTURAL COLLEGE
Private Bag X2377, Hohoyandou 0950
Tel: +27(159) 21-109
Fax: +27(159) 31-414
EMail: madzivha@mweb.co.za

Principal: E.F. Kolajo

Agriculture

History: Founded 1982.

MANGAUNG NURSING COLLEGE OF THE FREE STATE
Private Bag X 20556, Bloemfontein 9300
Tel: +27(51) 405-1397
Fax: +27(51) 432-4402

Principal: M.A. Mabandla

Nursing

MANGOSUTHU TECHNIKON
PO Box 12363, Jacobs 4026
Tel: +27(31) 907-7111
Fax: +27(31) 907-2892
EMail: principal@julian.mantec.ac.za

Vice-Chancellor and Principal: A.M. Ndlovu (1997-)
Fax: +27(31) 906-5470

Registrar: E.C. Zingu

International Relations: A. M. Ndulovu

Faculties
Engineering
Management Sciences (Management)
Natural Sciences

History: Founded 1979

M.L. SULTAN TECHNIKON
Durban 4000
Tel: +27(31) 308-5111
Fax: +27(31) 308-5194
Cable: sulkon
EMail: chaina@wpo.mlsultan.ac.za.
Website: http://www.mlsultan.ac.za

Principal and Vice-Chancellor (Acting): Daniel Ncayiyana (2000-) Fax: +27(31) 308-5103

Registrar: S. Naidoo

International Relations: R. Naran

Faculties

Arts (Arts and Humanities; Communication Studies; Cooking and Catering; Fashion Design; Graphic Design; Hotel Management; Journalism; Library Science; Public Relations; Textile Design)

Commerce (Accountancy; Business and Commerce; Computer Science; Economics; Marketing; Public Administration)

Engineering (Architecture; Building Technologies; Chemical Engineering; Civil Engineering; Engineering; Surveying and Mapping)

Science (Analytical Chemistry; Biological and Life Sciences; Biomedicine; Biotechnology; Chemistry; Food Technology; Health Sciences; Natural Sciences)

History: Founded 1946

MPUMALANGA COLLEGE OF NURSING
Pte Bag X1005, Kabokweni 1245
Tel: +27(13) 7961-352 to 355
Fax: +27(13) 7961-342

Principal: B.P Mkwanazi (1997-) Tel: +27(13) 7961-352 Fax: +27(13) 7961-342 EMail: patriciam@social.mpu.gov.200

Registrar: V.B Mashabane Tel: +27(13) 7961-808

Colleges

Nursing *(Kabokweni)* (Community Health; Midwifery; Nursing; Psychiatry and Mental Health) *Director*: B. Patricia Mkwanazi, *full-time staff: 25, students: 524*

History: Founded 1974, acquired present status and title 1986

Governing Bodies: Senate; Council; Students' Representative Council

Admission Requirements: Matriculation certificate

Fees: (Rands): 500 per annum

Main Language(s) of Instruction: English

International Co-operation: Links with institutions in Sweden

Accrediting Agencies: South African Nursing Council

Degrees and Diplomas: *National Higher Diploma*: Nursing, 4 yrs. Also Bridging diploma in Nursing, 2yrs; diploma in Midwifery, 1 yr

Student Services: Academic Counselling, Social Counselling, Employment Services, Cultural Centre, Sports Facilities, Health Services

Student Residential Facilities: For 228 Students

Special Facilities: Clinical Laboratory; Model Room

Libraries: Central Library

Academic Staff 2000	MEN	WOMEN	TOTAL
FULL-TIME	–	25	**25**

NATAL COLLEGE OF NURSING
Grey's Campus, Private Bag 9089, Pietermaritzburg 3200
Tel: +27(331) 95-2689
Fax: +27(331) 42-6744

Principal (Acting): L. Ruiters

Nursing

NGWELEZANA NURSING COLLEGE
Private Bag X20016, Empangeni 3880
Tel: +27(351) 94-2570

Principal: H.L. Felepe

Nursing

NICO MALAN NURSING COLLEGE
Private Bag, Surwell 7762
Tel: +27(21) 637-1313
Fax: +27(21) 638-6988

Head: D.C. Mostert

Nursing

NORTHERN PROVINCE COLLEGE OF NURSING, GIYANI CAMPUS
Private Bag X 9658, Giyani 0826
Tel: +27(158) 20-330
Fax: +27(158) 20-330

Principal: R.C. Tlakula (1988-)

Colleges

Nursing (Anatomy; Applied Chemistry; Applied Physics; Biology; Community Health; Midwifery; Nursing; Physiology; Psychiatry and Mental Health; Social and Community Services) *Director*: Rachel Cecilia Tlakula, *full-time staff: 23, students: 268*

History: Founded 1983, acquired present status and title 1996

Governing Bodies: Senate; Council

Admission Requirements: Matriculation Exemption Certificate issued by the Joint Matriculation Board. Higher Grade in English or in Biology

Main Language(s) of Instruction: English

Accrediting Agencies: South African Nursing Council

Degrees and Diplomas: *National Higher Diploma*: Nursing, 4 yrs

Student Services: Academic Counselling, Sports Facilities, Health Services

Student Residential Facilities: Yes

Libraries: Central Library

Academic Staff 2000	MEN	WOMEN	TOTAL
FULL-TIME	1	22	**23**

Staff with doctorate: Total: **1**

NURSING COLLEGE OF THE FREE STATE

Private Bag X20520, Bloemfotein 9300
Tel: +27(51) 405-2345
Fax: +27(51) 30-6469

Principal: S. Fourie

Nursing

OTTO DU PLESSIS NURSING COLLEGE

Private Bag 7, Tygerberg 7505
Tel: +27(21) 938-4118
Fax: +27(21) 938-4269

Assistant Director: J.M. Viljoen (1984-)

Administrative Officer: A. Rust

Nursing

History: Founded 1957

OWEN SITHOLE AGRICULTURAL COLLEGE

Private Bag X 20013, Empangeni 3830
Tel: +27(35) 795-1345
Fax: +27(35) 795-1379
Website: http://www.agriculture.kzntl.gov.za

Principal: J. Foli **EMail:** principl@osca1.kzntl.gov.za

Vice-Principal: M. Hoosen
EMail: mhoosen@osca1.kzntl.gov.za

Agriculture

PENINSULA TECHNIKON

PO Box 1906, Bellville 7535
Tel: +27(21) 959-6121
Fax: +27(21) 951-6069
EMail: postmaster@pentech.ac.za
Website: http://www.pentech.ac.za

Principal and Vice-Chancellor: B. Figaji (1995-)
Fax: +27(21) 951-5422

Vice-Rector (Administration): A.M. Slabbert

International Relations: Vuyisa Mazwi-Tanga

Faculties
Business (Accountancy; Business Administration; Human Resources; Management; Marketing; Public Administration; Retailing and Wholesaling) *Dean*: Norman Jacobs
Engineering (Building Technologies; Civil Engineering; Clothing and Sewing; Construction Engineering; Electrical Engineering; Fashion Design; Graphic Design; Information Technology; Journalism; Mechanical Engineering; Multimedia; Photography; Textile Technology) *Dean*: Anthony Staak
Science (Analytical Chemistry; Chemical Engineering; Chemistry; Dental Technology; Education; Food Technology; Health Sciences; Horticulture; Management; Natural Sciences; Nursing; Radiology; Technology) *Dean*: Dhiro Giwhala

Centres
Continuing Education

History: Founded 1967, acquired present status and title 1979

PORT ELIZABETH TECHNIKON

Private Bag X6011, Port Elizabeth, Eastern Cape Province 6000
Tel: +27(41) 504-3911
Fax: +27(41) 533-644
EMail: grimbeek@petech.ac.za
Website: http://www.petech.ac.za

Rector and Vice-Chancellor: Hennie Snyman (1989-)
Tel: +27(41) 504-3211 Fax: +27(41) 583-1558

Registrar: Hugo Grimbeek Tel: +27(41) 504-3370
EMail: grimbeek@ml.petech.ac.za

International Relations: Pieter Swart Tel: +27(41) 504-3339
Fax: +27(41) 504-3423 EMail: pswart@ml.petech.ac.za

Faculties
Applied Science (Biomedicine; Chemistry; Health Sciences; Mathematics; Radiology) *Dean*: D.W. Sharwood
Art and Design (Ceramic Art; Design; Fashion Design; Fine Arts; Glass Art; Graphic Design; Photography; Textile Design) *Dean*: N.P.L. Allen
Civil Engineering, Building, Architecture and Agriculture (Agricultural Management; Agriculture; Architecture; Building Technologies; Business Administration; Civil Engineering; Interior Design) *Dean*: J.J. Van Wyk
Commerce and Governmental Studies (Business and Commerce; Economics; Government; Law; Management; Marketing; Public Administration; Sports Management; Tourism; Transport Management) *Dean*: H.F. Wissink
Communication and Educational Studies (Administration; Adult Education; Business and Commerce; Education; Information Sciences; Journalism; Library Science; Modern Languages; Natural Sciences; Public Relations; Telecommunications Services) *Dean*: M.A. Fouché
Computer Studies (Business Computing; Computer Science; Information Technology) *Dean*: E.F. du Preez
Electrical Engineering (Electrical Engineering; Electronic Engineering; Power Engineering)
Management (Accountancy; Business Administration; Finance; Human Resources; Management) *Dean*: N.J. Dorfling
Mechanical Engineering (Engineering Management; Industrial Design; Industrial Engineering; Mechanical Engineering) *Dean*: H.L.T. Jeffery

Units
Catalysis Research (Chemistry)
Corrosion Prevention *(ECCP)* (Mechanical Equipment and Maintenance)
Electron Microscopy *(Sanlam)* (Electronic Engineering)
Productivity Growth and Development (Development Studies; Production Engineering)

Institutes
Building Research and Support *(IBRS)* (Building Technologies)

History: Founded 1882, this tertiary Institution offers both formal and non-formal career-oriented courses in nine Faculties located across three campuses. Long recognized for its partnerships with industry and other Eastern Cape institutions of higher education, the PE Technikon continues to maintain a reputation for research, cooperative education, and community service.

Governing Bodies: Council

Academic Year: January to December

Admission Requirements: Matriculation Certificate or School Leaving Certificate issued by the Joint Matriculation Board

Main Language(s) of Instruction: English

Degrees and Diplomas: *National Higher Certificate*: Computer Studies: Foundation Studies- Information Technology; *National Diploma*: Applied Sciences: Analytical Chemistry, Biomedical Technology, Environmental Health, Fire Service Technology, Rubber Technology, Radiography (Diagnostic) (NDip); Art and Design: Ceramic Design, Fashion, Fine Arts, Graphic Design, Photography, Textile Design and Technology (NDip); Civil Engineering: Agricultural Management, Architectural Technology, Building, Interior Design (NDip); Commerce and Govermental Studies: Inventory and Stores Management, Marketing, Public Management, Purchasing Management, Sports Administration and Management, Tourism (NDip); Communication and Educational Studies: Commercial Administration, Journalism, Library and Information Studies, Public Relations Management, Adult Basic Education and Training, Education-Commerce, Education-Natural Sciences, Education-Post School (NDdip); Computer Studies: Information Technology (NDip); Electrical Engineering (NDip); Management: Cost and Management Accountancy, Financial Information System, Human Resources Management, Internal Auditing, Management (NDip); Mechanical Engineering: Industrial Engineering, Mechanical Engineering, Metallurgical Engineering, Production Management, Safety Management (NDip); *National Higher Diploma*: Applied Science: Fire Service Technology (NHDip); Communication and Educational Studies: Technical Education (NHDip); *Bachelor of Technology*: Applied Science: Biomedical Technology, Environmental Health, Chemistry, Radiography (BTech); Art and Design: Ceramic Design, Fashion, Fine Arts, Graphic Design, Photography, Textile Design and Technology (BTech); Civil Engineering: Agricultural Management, Architectural Technology, Construction Management , Quantity Surveying, (BTech); Commerce and Govermental Studies: Marketing, Public Management, Tourism (BTech); Communication and Educational Studies: Commercial Administration, Library and Information Studies, Public Relations Management, Commerce, Natural Sciences, Continuing Education (BTech); Computer Studies: Information Technology (BTech); Electrical Engineering (BTech); Management: Business Administration, Cost and Management Accountancy, Financial Information System, Human Resources Management, Internal Auditing (BTech); Mechanical Engineering: Quality Engineering, Industrial Engineering, Mechanical Engineering, Production Management (BTech); *Master of Technology*: Applied Science: Biomedical Technology, Chemistry, Environmental Health (MTech); Art and Design: Fashion, Fine Arts, Graphic Design, Photography, Textile Design and Technology (MTech); Civil Engineering: Agriculture, Architectural Technology, Business Administration, Construction Management, Quantity Surveying (MTech);

Commerce and Govermental Studies: Logistics, Marketing, Public Management (MTech); Communication and Educational Studies: Library and Information Studies, Public Relations Management, Education (MTech); Computer Studies: Information Technology (MTech); Electrical Engineering (MTech); Management: Business Administration, Human Resources Management (MTech); Mechanical Engineering: Industrial Engineering, Mechanical Engineering, Production Management (MTech); *Doctor of Technology*: Applied Science: Chemistry, Environmental Health (DTech); Art and Design: Fine Arts, Photography (DTech); Civil Engineering: Agriculture, Architectural Technology, Construction Management, Quantity Surveying (DTech); Commerce and Govermental Studies: Logistics, Marketing, Public Management (DTech); Communication and Educational Studies: Library and Information Studies, Public Relations Management, Education (DTech); Computer Studies: Information Technology (DTech); Electrical Engineering (DTech); Management: Human Resources Management, Business Administration (DTech); Mechanical Engineering: Industrial Engineering, Mechanical Engineering, Production Management (DTech)

Student Services: Academic Counselling, Sports Facilities, Language Programmes, Health Services

Student Residential Facilities: Yes

Libraries: Central Library and two branch Libraries

Publications: Annual Report; Impetus, General Liaison Magazine (annually)

Academic Staff 2000	MEN	WOMEN	TOTAL
FULL-TIME	159	93	252
PART-TIME	68	53	121
TOTAL	**227**	**146**	**373**
STAFF WITH DOCTORATE			
FULL-TIME	22	8	30
PART-TIME	2	–	2
TOTAL	**24**	**8**	**32**

Student Numbers 2000	MEN	WOMEN	TOTAL
All (Foreign Included)	4,637	3,708	**8,345**
FOREIGN ONLY	125	49	174

Part-time Students, 2,366

QWA-QWA NURSING COLLEGE
Private Bag X883, Witzieshoek 9870
Tel: +27(58) 713-1881
Fax: +27(58) 713-0660

Principal (Acting): M.F.A. Maja

Nursing

SAMS NURSING COLLEGE
Private Bag X1026, Voortrekkerhogte 0143
Tel: +27(12) 314-0999
Fax: +27(12) 71-3333

Principal: J.M. Kruger

Nursing

SARICH DOLLIE NURSING COLLEGE

Private Bag X14, Tygerberg 7505
Tel: +27(21) 938-4313
Fax: +27(21) 938-4314

Head: D.I. Govin

Nursing

S.G. LOURENS COLLEGE OF NURSING

Private Bag X755, Pretoria 0001
Tel: +27(12) 329-4817
Fax: +27(12) 329-4822

Principal: H.S.C. de Jager

Nursing

TAUNG AGRICULTURAL COLLEGE

Private Bag X532, Taung 8584
Tel: +27(053) 994-1832
Fax: +27(053) 994-1130

Principal (Acting): L. Kirkland
Registrar: E. Coetzee

Agriculture

TECHNIKON FREE STATE

Private Bag X20539, 20 President Brand Street, Bloemfontein 9300
Tel: +27(51) 507-3911
Fax: +27(51) 507-3199
EMail: dsmuts@tofs.ac.za
Website: http://www.tofs.ac.za

Principal and Vice Chancellor: A.S. Koorts (1996-)
Tel: +27(51) 507-3001 Fax: +27(51) 507-3310
EMail: askoorts@tofs.ac.za

Vice Rector for Financial Administration: J.J. Hamman
Tel: +27(51) 507-3006 Fax: +27(51) 507-3318
EMail: jhamman@tofs.ac.za

International Relations: H.S. Wolvaardt
Tel: +27(51) 507-3554 Fax: +27(51) 507-3315
EMail: manie@tofs.ac.za

Faculties
Engineering (Civil Engineering; Electrical Engineering; Engineering; Mechanical Engineering) *Dean*: G. D. Jorrie Jordaai, *students:* 1,600
Health and Environmental Sciences (Agriculture; Environmental Studies; Health Sciences; Natural Sciences) *Dean*: Barry Frey, *students:* 600
Human Sciences (Communication Studies; Fine Arts; Teacher Trainers Education) *Dean*: Moss Thulare, *students:* 500
Management (Accountancy; Hotel and Restaurant; Management; Sports) *Dean*: Piet Le Raix, *students:* 3,300

History: Founded 1981
Governing Bodies: Technikon Council

Academic Year: January to November
Admission Requirements: School leaving certificate and specific subject requirements
Main Language(s) of Instruction: English, Africaans
International Co-operation: Links with Universities in Sweden, Netherlands, Germany, United Kingdom and China
Accrediting Agencies: Certification Council for Technikon Education
Degrees and Diplomas: *Bachelor of Technology*; *Master of Technology*; *Doctor of Technology*
Student Services: Academic Counselling, Social Counselling, Employment Services, Foreign Student Adviser, Cultural Centre, Sports Facilities, Language Programmes, Health Services, Canteen
Student Residential Facilities: For Women and Men Students
Special Facilities: Art gallery
Libraries: Main Library, c. 60000 vols; four branch libraries
Publications: Gratia (biannually); Annual Report (annually)

Academic Staff *2000*	MEN	WOMEN	TOTAL
FULL-TIME	102	75	177
PART-TIME	188	108	296
TOTAL	**290**	**183**	**473**
STAFF WITH DOCTORATE			
FULL-TIME	13	4	**17**

Student Numbers *2000*	MEN	WOMEN	TOTAL
All (Foreign Included)	3,281	2,946	**6,227**
FOREIGN ONLY	–	–	61

Part-time Students, 765 **Evening Students,** 765

TECHNIKON NATAL

PO Box 953, 70 Mansfield Road, Berea, Durban 4000
Tel: +27(31) 204-2111
Fax: +27(31) 22-3405
Telex: 620187 sa
Cable: nattechnikon
Website: http://www.ntech.ac.za

Vice-Chancellor and Principal: B. Khoapa
Fax: +27(31) 204-2663

Vice-Rector: Nico de Koker

International Relations: Andre du Preez

Faculties
Arts (Communication Studies; Education; Fashion Design; Fine Arts; Graphic Design; Interior Design; Jewelry Art; Journalism; Music; Photography; Textile Design; Theatre; Video) *Dean*: A.R. Starky
Commerce (Accountancy; Business and Commerce; Economics; Environmental Studies; Finance; Food Science; Human Resources; Leisure Studies; Management; Nutrition; Public Relations; Software Engineering; Taxation; Tourism) *Dean*: Terry Dagnall-Quinn
Engineering and Science (Architecture; Biotechnology; Chemical Engineering; Chemistry; Civil Engineering; Clothing and Sewing; Construction Engineering; Electrical Engineering; Electronic Engineering; Engineering; Food Technology; Marine Science and Oceanography; Mathematics; Mechanical

419

Engineering; Paper Technology; Physics; Surveying and Mapping; Textile Technology) *Dean*: Mike J.M. Stewart
Health (Biology; Child Care and Development; Chiropractic; Dental Technology; Homeopathy; Nursing; Public Health; Radiology; Stomatology) *Dean*: Angela Milne

History: Founded 1907, acquired present status and title 1968

Academic Staff *2000*	MEN	WOMEN	TOTAL
FULL-TIME	50	80	130
PART-TIME	33	18	51
TOTAL	**83**	**98**	**181**

Staff with doctorate: Total: **4**

Student Numbers *2000:* Total: **3,622**

Part-time Students, 617

TECHNIKON NORTHERN GAUTENG
Private Bag X07, Pretoria North 0116
Tel: +27(12) 799-9000
Fax: +27(12) 793-0966

Principal: C.S.K. Lenyai (1994-) Fax: +27(12) 793-0975

Vice-Principal: M.A. Mashego

International Relations: C.H.J. vander Westheizen

Computer Science; Economics; Engineering; Health Sciences; Management; Nutrition; Teacher Training

History: Founded 1979

TECHNIKON NORTH-WEST
Private Bag X31, Rosslyn 200
Tel: +27(1461) 31166
Fax: +27(1461) 31166

Principal and Vice-Chancellor: Itumeleng Mosala (1997-)
EMail: imosala@mweb.co.za

Registrar: R. Maphal

International Relations: Ricky Olipant
EMail: moumi@tnw.ac.za

Faculties
Economics and Management (Accountancy; Economics; Human Resources; Management; Marketing; Public Administration) *Dean*: George Moatsne
Humanities (Arts and Humanities; Communication Arts; Education; Secretarial Studies; Teacher Training; Tourism) *Dean*: M. Maimane
Technology (Analytical Chemistry; Business Administration; Chemistry; Computer Engineering; Computer Science; Fashion Design; Information Technology; Management; Secretarial Studies; Systems Analysis; Technology; Tourism)

History: Founded 1975, acquired present status and title 1986
Governing Bodies: Council
Admission Requirements: Matriculation Certificate (grade 12)
Fees: (Rand): 828 per annum
Main Language(s) of Instruction: English
Student Services: Academic Counselling, Social Counselling, Sports Facilities, Health Services, Canteen
Student Residential Facilities: Yes
Special Facilities: Computer Centre. Laboratories
Libraries: Central Library
Publications: TNW News, International Newsletter (quarterly); Vice Chancellor's Annual Report, Highlights of the Year

TECHNIKON PRETORIA
Private Bag X680, Pretoria 0001
Tel: +27(12) 318-5911
Fax: +27(12) 318-5114
Cable: techpret
Website: http://www.techpta.ac.za

Rector and Vice-Chancellor: R.L. Ngcobo (2001-)
Fax: +27(12) 318-5422

Registrar: N.J. vdM Stofberg

Faculties
Agriculture, Horticulture and Nature Conservation (Agricultural Management; Animal Husbandry; Crop Production; Environmental Studies; Farm Management; Horticulture; Landscape Architecture)
Arts (Arts and Humanities; Dance; Fashion Design; Fine Arts; Graphic Design; Music; Opera; Photography; Textile Design; Theatre) *Dean*: Eric Dinkelmann
Economics (Accountancy; Economics; Human Resources; Industrial Engineering; Management; Marketing; Production Engineering; Public Administration) *Dean*: Maynard van der Merwe
Engineering (Architecture; Engineering; Mechanical Engineering; Polymer and Plastics Technology; Surveying and Mapping)
Health Sciences (Dentistry; Health Sciences; Nursing; Paramedical Sciences; Pharmacy; Sports) *Dean*: M.M.J. Lowes
Information Sciences (Advertising and Publicity; Business Administration; Information Management; Information Technology; Journalism; Radio and Television Broadcasting; Systems Analysis; Teacher Training; Tourism) *Dean*: P.J. Rall
Natural Sciences (Analytical Chemistry; Biomedical Engineering; Ceramics and Glass Technology; Chemical Engineering; Chemistry; Environmental Management; Fire Science; Food Technology; Geology; Metallurgical Engineering; Natural Sciences; Veterinary Science; Water Management) *Dean*: PJJG Marais

Institutes
Clothing, Design and Interior Design *(CLODEC)* (Clothing and Sewing; Fashion Design; Interior Design)
Quality Management and Statistics *(TIQMS)* (Statistics)

Centres
Drama Spectrum (Theatre)
Entrepreneurship (Business Administration)
Food Service Management (Food Science)
Industrial Health and Safety (Safety Engineering)
Language and Leadership Dynamics (Leadership)

Outdoor Development Training and Leisure Activities (Leisure Studies; Sports)
Pharmaceutical and Chemical Services (Chemistry; Pharmacology)

History: Founded 1979

• TECHNIKON SA
Private Bag X6, Florida 1710
Tel: +27(11) 471-2000
Fax: +27(11) 471-2134
EMail: wmaster@tsamail.trsa.ac.za
Website: http://www.tsa.ac.za

Principal and Vice-Chancellor (Acting): Neo Mathabe
Fax: +27(11) 471-2554
Registrar: Tony Links

Divisions
Applied Community Sciences (Law; Public Administration)
Economics and Management (Accountancy; Business Administration; Economics; Human Resources; Information Technology; Management; Marketing; Real Estate; Tourism)
Public Safety and Criminal Justice (Criminal Law; Police Studies; Public Law)

Centres
Lifelong Learning (Continuing Education)

History: Founded 1980

TECHNIKON WITWATERSRAND
PO Box 17011, Doornfontein 2028
Tel: +27(11) 406-2911
Fax: +27(11) 402-0475
EMail: amanda@twrinet.twr.ac.za
Website: http://www.twr.ac.za

Vice-Chancellor and Principal: Connie Mogale (1998-)
Fax: +27(11) 402-7575
Registrar (Administration): F. Van den Berg
International Relations: J.L. Stead

Faculties
Art, Design and Architecture (Architecture; Ceramic Art; Clothing and Sewing; Design; Fashion Design; Fine Arts; Graphic Design; Interior Design; Jewelry Art)
Business Management (Accountancy; Banking; Business Administration; Finance; Food Technology; Information Technology; Management; Marketing; Public Relations; Retailing and Wholesaling; Tourism)
Engineering (Analytical Chemistry; Building Technologies; Chemical Engineering; Civil Engineering; Computer Engineering; Construction Engineering; Electrical Engineering; Electronic Engineering; Engineering; Geology; Industrial Engineering; Mechanical Engineering; Metallurgical Engineering; Mining Engineering; Real Estate; Regional Planning; Town Planning)

Health Sciences (Biotechnology; Chiropractic; Food Technology; Health Sciences; Homeopathy; Nursing; Occupational Therapy; Optometry; Podiatry; Radiology; Stomatology)
Mining and Metallurgy (Metallurgical Engineering; Mining Engineering)

Schools
Accountancy
Administration
Architecture
Biotechnology
Building (Building Technologies)
Chiropractic Studies (Chiropractic)
Civil Engineering
Electrical Engineering
HealthTechnology (Medical Technology)
Hotel Management
Human Technology (Technology)
Information Technology
Logistics (Transport Management)
Mechanical and Chemical and Industrial Engineering (Industrial Chemistry; Industrial Engineering; Mechanical Engineering)
Mining (Mining Engineering)
Operations Management (Operations Research)
Optometry
Radiography (Radiology)
Town Planning

Centres
Career Development

History: Founded 1980

TOMPI SELEKA AGRICULTURAL COLLEGE
Private Bag X9619, Marble Hall 0450
Tel: +27(013) 268-9300
Fax: +27(013) 268-9309

Manager: M.H. Ramabofa (1999-)
Administrative Officer: E.M. Buys
International Relations: M.J. Dladla

Agriculture

History: Founded 1960.

VAAL TRIANGLE TECHNIKON
Private Bag X021, Vanderbijlpark 1900
Tel: +27(16) 950-9000
EMail: webmaster@nt.tritek.ac.za
Website: http://www.tritek.ac.za

Rector and Vice-Chancellor: A.T Mokadi (1996-)
Vice-Rector: I.N Steyn
International Relations: J.M Grov

Faculties

Applied and Computer Science (Biological and Life Sciences; Chemistry; Computer Science; Information Technology; Mathematics; Physics; Software Engineering) *Dean*: B.R. Mabuza

Business (Business Administration)

Engineering (Civil Engineering; Electronic Engineering; Engineering; Industrial Engineering; Metallurgical Engineering; Power Engineering; Production Engineering) *Dean*: Henk de Jager

Humanities (Arts and Humanities; Ceramic Art; Clothing and Sewing; Fine Arts; Food Science; Graphic Design; Photography)

Management Sciences (Accountancy; Business Administration; Law; Management; Marketing; Public Relations; Retailing and Wholesaling; Staff Development; Tourism) *Dean (Acting)*: A.S. Dhlamini

Teaching Development (Staff Development)

Units

Lifelong Learning (Continuing Education)

History: Founded 1966

VENDA NURSING COLLEGE
Private Bag X919, Shayandima 0945
Tel: +27(159) 41-516

Principal: M.A. Mogashoa

Nursing

Sudan

INSTITUTION TYPES AND CREDENTIALS

Types of higher education institutions:

University
Institute
College

School leaving and higher education credentials:

Sudan School Certificate
Diploma
Bachelor's Degree
Bachelor Honours Degree
Postgraduate Diploma
Master's Degree
Doctor of Philosophy
Higher Doctorate

STRUCTURE OF EDUCATION SYSTEM

Pre-higher education:

Duration of compulsory education:

   Age of entry: 6
   Age of exit: 14

Structure of school system:

   Basic
   Type of school providing this education: Basic School
   Length of programme in years: 8
   Age level from: 6 to: 14
   Certificate/diploma awarded: Basic Education Certificate Examination

   Secondary
   Type of school providing this education: General Secondary School
   Length of programme in years: 3
   Age level from: 14 to: 17
   Certificate/diploma awarded: Sudan School Certificate Examination

Vocational
Type of school providing this education: Technical and Vocational School
Length of programme in years: 3
Age level from: 14 to: 17
Certificate/diploma awarded: Sudan School Certificate Examination

School education:

Basic education lasts for eight years and is compulsory. It leads to the Basic Education Certificate Examination. General (academic) secondary education lasts for three years leading to the Sudan School Certificate Examination. In the first two years, students follow the same curriculum. In the final year, they choose between arts and science streams. The technical secondary schools include Industrial, Commercial and Agricultural schools for boys and some Home Economics schools for girls. They offer three-year courses leading to the Sudan Secondary School Certificate. Vocational Training Centres offer two-year vocational courses. Admission is based on completion of basic education. Admission to higher education is based on the results of the Sudan School Certificate Examination.

Higher education:

Higher education is provided by universities, both public and private, and institutes and colleges of technical and professional education. All universities are autonomous and government financed. The National Council of Higher Education is the government body responsible for higher education. Since 1990, many government universities have been created, mostly in the provinces. A few private tertiary institutions have also opened.

Main laws/decrees governing higher education:

Decree: 1991 Higher Education Act   Year: 1991
Concerns: Higher Education

Academic year:

Classes from: July *to:* March

Long vacation from: 1 April *to:* 30 June

Languages of instruction:

Arabic, English

Stages of studies:

Non-university level post-secondary studies (technical/vocational type):

Specialized higher education institutions offer courses in music, hygiene, nursing, radiography and mechanical engineering.

University level studies:

University level first stage: Bachelor's Degree:
The first year of university studies is devoted to basic studies and the major stage is reached with the award of the Bachelor's Degree in science, humanities and social sciences after another three years. A more specialized Bachelor's Degree with Honours requires a further year of study. Professional qualifications need five to six years' study.

University level second stage: *Master's Degree*:

This stage represents an in-depth knowledge at a certain degree of specialization and requires individual research; it is reached after two to three years' study. A Postgraduate Diploma is also offered in certain disciplines, following one or two years' study after the Bachelor's Degree.

University level third stage: *Doctor of Philosophy*:

The PhD may be reached after at least three years' study following the Master's Degree and requires individual research work and the presentation of a thesis.

University level fourth stage: *Higher Doctorate*:

It is awarded in humanities, law and science at the University of Khartoum only, in respect of published work contributing significantly to the advancement of knowledge.

Teacher education:

Training of pre-primary and primary/basic school teachers

Basic education teachers are trained in colleges of basic education teachers that are affiliated to the Faculties of Education of the universities. Basic level teachers holding a Teacher's Certificate can return to BEd studies after a period of teaching in schools.

Training of secondary school teachers

Secondary-school teachers are trained at colleges for secondary school teachers or at the Faculties of Education of the universities. Graduates are awarded a BEd Degree. Since 1990, a postgraduate Diploma in Teaching English at Secondary Level (DIPTEASL) has been offered in Khartoum North.

Non-traditional studies:

Distance higher education

The University of Khartoum has a School of Extramural Studies and there is also a private Open University.

NATIONAL BODIES

Responsible authorities:

Ministry of Higher Education and Scientific Research
  Minister: Mubarak Mohammed Al Maghzoub
  PO Box 2081
  Khartoum
  Tel: +249(11) 779-312
  Fax: +249(11) 779-312
  EMail: mhesr@sudanmail.net

National Council for Higher Education
  President: Ibrahim Ahmed Omar
  Under-Secretary: Hassan Mohamed Salih
  International Relations: Mirghani Yousif Mohammed Ahmed
  PO Box 2081

Khartoum
Tel: +249(11) 779-312
Fax: +249(11) 779-312

Role of governing body: Planning, coordinating and financing higher education.

The Association of Sudanese Universities
c/o University of Khartoum, P.O. Box 321
Khartoum
Tel: +249(11) 772-601
Fax: +249(11) 780-295
EMail: info@uofk.edu

ADMISSIONS TO HIGHER EDUCATION

Admission to non university higher education studies

Name of secondary school credential required: Sudan School Certificate
Minimum score/requirement: 50%

Admission to university-level studies

Name of secondary school credential required: Sudan School Certificate
Minimum score/requirement: 73% for the University of Khartoum; 88% for the medical faculty

Foreign students admission

Admission requirements: Foreign students seeking admission as undergraduates to higher education institutions should have a minimum of 5 credits (45%) in the Sudan School Certificate or equivalent and must fulfil the admission requirements of the University of Karthoum. Only foreign students residing in the Sudan and foreign scholarship holders are accepted in Sudanese universities.

Entry regulations: Students must obtain a visa.

Language requirements: Good knowledge of either Arabic or English. Orientation programme arranged by universities.

Recognition of studies and qualifications:

Studies pursued in home country (System of recognition/accreditation): The Namibia Qualification Authority establishes and maintains a comprehensive national qualification framework.

Studies pursued in foreign countries (bodies dealing with recognition of foreign credentials):
Committee for the Evaluation and Equivalency of Diplomas and Academic Degrees, Ministry of Education and Scientific Research
PO Box 2081
Khartoum
Tel: +249(11) 772-515   +249(11) 779-312
Fax: +249(11) 779-312
Telex: 22115QRANT

Deals with credential recognition for entry to: University and Profession

Multilateral agreements concerning recognition of foreign studies

Name(s) of agreement(s): UNESCO Convention on the Recognition of Studies, Certificates, Diplomas, Degrees and Other Academic Qualifications in Higher Education in the African States
Year of signature: 1981

UNESCO Convention on the Recognition of Studies, Diplomas and Degrees in Higher Education in the Arab States
Year of signature: 1978

References to further information on foreign student admissions and recognition of studies

Title: Annual Admissions Guide
Publisher: National Council of Higher Education

STUDENT LIFE

Main student services at national level

Department of Foreign Cultural Relations, National Council for Higher Education
PO Box 2081
Khartoum

Category of services provided: Special services/Centre for foreign students

Student expenses and financial aid

Student costs:

Foreign students tuition fees: Minimum: 1,500 (US Dollar)
Maximum: 3,000 (US Dollar)

Bodies providing information on student financial aid:

Department of Foreign Relations and Training, Ministry of Higher Education and Scientific Research
PO Box 2081
Khartoum
Tel: +249(11) 772-515
Fax: +242(11) 779-312
Telex: 22115QRANT

Deals with: Grants
Category of students: Students knowing Arabic, aged 19 to 26 from various countries in Europe, Asia and Africa. Scholarship awarded according to cultural agreements.

Publications on student services and financial aid:

Title: Study Abroad 2000-2001
Publisher: UNESCO/IBE
Year of publication: 1999

GRADING SYSTEM

Usual grading system in secondary school

Full Description: Sudan School Certificate: A: 80-100%; B: 70-79%; C: 60-69%; D: 50-59%; F: 49-0 fail:
Highest on scale: 100
Pass/fail level: 50
Lowest on scale: 0

Main grading system used by higher education institutions

Full Description: A+-F
The Bachelor of Arts is graded: 80-100: Division I; 60-79: Division II; 40-59: Division III
Highest on scale: A+
Pass/fail level: C
Lowest on scale: F

NOTES ON HIGHER EDUCATION SYSTEM

Data for academic year: 2000-2001
Source: International Association of Universities (IAU), updated from IBE website, 2000

INSTITUTIONS OF HIGHER EDUCATION

UNIVERSITIES

PUBLIC INSTITUTIONS

• AL FASHIR UNIVERSITY
Jameat Al-Fashir
PO Box 125, El Fashir, North Darfur
Tel: +249(527) 43394
Fax: +249(527) 52111

Vice-Chancellor: Abd Elbagi Mohammed Kabir
Tel: +249(527) 43394

Administrative Officer: Yahia Ali Abdalla
Tel: +249(527) 43432

International Relations: Adam Haroun

Faculties
Education
Environment Study and Natural Resources (Environmental Studies; Natural Resources)
Medicine and Health Science (Health Sciences; Medicine)

Centres
Scientific Research and Documentation (Documentation Techniques)
Society Development and Extramural Studies (Social Studies)

History: Founded 1975.

*• AL-ZAIEM AL-AZHARI UNIVERSITY
Jameat Al-Zaiem Al-Azhari (AAU)
PO Box 1933, Omdurman, El-Abassia
Tel: +249(15) 560-501
Fax: +249(15) 562-536
EMail: alazhariuniv@sudanmail.net
Website: http://www.alazhari-univ.net

Vice-Chancellor: Mohamed Ali Qurashi (1998-2002)
Tel: +249(13) 344-511 Fax: +249(13) 344-520
EMail: qurashi@sudanmail.net

International Relations: Alsheik Magzoub, Deputy
Vice-Chancellor Tel: +249(13) 344-514
Fax: +249(13) 344-513
EMail: elsheikmagzoub@maktoob.com

Faculties
Agriculture *(Bashir)* (Agriculture; Food Technology)
Economics and Administration (Administration; Economics)
Education
Engineering
Medical Laboratory Sciences (Laboratory Techniques)

Medicine (Health Sciences; Medicine)
Political Science and Strategic Studies (Military Science; Political Science)
Public and Environment Health (Environmental Studies; Public Health)
Radiological Science and Medical Imaging (Medical Technology; Radiology)
Shari'a and Law (Islamic Law; Law)
Technical and Developmental Studies (Development Studies; Technology)
Urban Sciences (Urban Studies)

History: Founded 1993.

Governing Bodies: University Council

Admission Requirements: Secondary school certificate

Fees: (US Dollars): International Students, Undergraduate 3000-4000; Graduate 4000-6000

Main Language(s) of Instruction: Arabic, English

Degrees and Diplomas: *Diploma*: 2-3 yrs; *Bachelor's Degree*: 4-5 yrs; *Bachelor Honours Degree*: 5 yrs

Student Residential Facilities: For 800 students

Academic Staff *2001:* Total: **239**

Student Numbers *2001:* Total: **5,109**

BAHR-AL-GHAZAL UNIVERSITY
Jameat Bahr Al-Ghazal
Wau Town, West Bahr-Al Gazal 10739
Tel: +249(841) 22-311

Vice-Chancellor: Mathew Atem (1991-)
Administrative Officer: Lotan Wool Wool

Faculties
Education
Medicine
Veterinary Science

History: Founded 1991.

BAKHET EL-RUDDA UNIVERSITY
Jameat Bakhet El-Rudda
PO Box 16722, Khartoum, Eldewaym/White Nile
Tel: +249(531) 2440

Vice-Chancellor: Anaas A. El-Hafeez

Faculties
Agriculture and Natural Resources (Agriculture; Natural Resources)
Economics and Administration (Administration; Economics)
Education
Medicine

History: Founded 1997.

BLUE NILE UNIVERSITY
Jameat Al-Neel Alazarg
PO Box 143, Damazeen, Blue Nile
Tel: +249(11) 785-614

Vice-Chancellor: Mohammed El-Hassan Abdul El-Rahman

Faculties
Education
Engineering

Centres
Extramural Studies and Continuing Education

History: Founded 1995.

DONGOLA UNIVERSITY
Jameat Dongola
Dongola
Tel: +249(241) 21515

Vice-Chancellor: Mohammed Osman Ahmed
Administrative Officer: Hassan Ibrahim

Faculties
Agriculture
Arts (Arts and Humanities)
Education
Law and Islamic Law (Shari'a) (Islamic Law)
Medicine
Mining and Earth Sciences (Earth Sciences; Mining Engineering)

History: Founded 1994.

EL-DALANG UNIVERSITY
Jameat El-Dalang
El-Dalang, South Kordofan
Tel: +249(11) 785-614

Vice-Chancellor: Kamess Kago Kunda (1993-)

Faculties
Agriculture
Education
Social Development (Social Studies)
Teacher Training

Centres
Computer Study (Computer Education)
Peace Studies (Peace and Disarmament)

History: Founded 1990.

430

EL-GADARIF UNIVERSITY
Jameat El-Gadarif
El-Gadarif 449
Tel: +249(441) 43680
Fax: +249(441) 43120

Vice-Chancellor: Omer Ibrahim Elkordey (1994-)
Administrative Officer: Mohamed Said Zaroug

Faculties
Agriculture and Natural Resources (Agriculture; Natural Resources)
Economics and Administration (Administration; Economics)
Education
Medicine

Centres
Extramural Studies

History: Founded 1990, acquired present status 1994

EL-MAHADI UNIVERSITY
Jameat Elman El-Mahadi
Kosti 11588
Tel: +249(571) 22545
Fax: +249(571) 22222

Vice-Chancellor: Alazeem A. Abas (1997-)
Administrative Officer: Sirag Eldin Mohamed El-Amin

Faculties
Arabic and Islamic Sciences (Arabic; Islamic Studies)
Arts (Arts and Humanities)
Engineering and Technical Studies (Engineering; Technology)
Law and Islamic Law (Shari'a) (Islamic Law; Law)
Medicine and Health Sciences (Health Sciences; Medicine)

Centres
Computer Studies (Computer Science)
Extramural Studies (Distance Education)

History: Founded 1993.

*• AL-NEELAIN UNIVERSITY
Jameat Al-Neelain
PO Box 12702, Khartoum 12702
Tel: +249(11) 780-055
Fax: +249(11) 776-338
Telex: 23027 nilun sd b
EMail: awadha@sudanmail.net
Website: http://www.neelain.8m.net/ARABIC2.htm

Vice-Chancellor: Awad Haj Ali Ahmed (1997-)
EMail: awadha@sudanmail.net

Deputy-Vice-Chancellor: Yaseen Osman Ahmed El Nugomi
Tel: +249(11) 780-907

International Relations: Abdal Mageed Ahmad Abdal Rahman Tel: +249(11) 777-653
EMail: aaamageed@yahoo.com

Faculties

Agriculture, Animal Production and Fisheries (Agriculture; Cattle Breeding; Fishery) *Dean*: Mohamed Saeed El-Tahir, *full-time staff:* 12

Arts (Arabic; Archaeology; Arid Land Studies; Art Education; Art History; Art Management; Arts and Humanities; Comparative Religion; English; Geography; History; Library Science; Meteorology; Middle Eastern Studies; North African Studies; Philosophy; Sociology) *Dean*: Khougali Suliman Hamid, *full-time staff:* 36, *part-time staff:* 34, *students:* 5,866

Commerce and Socio-Economic Studies (Accountancy; Administration; Administrative Law; African Studies; Anthropology; Automation and Control Engineering; Banking; Behavioural Sciences; Business Administration; Business and Commerce; Business Computing; Business Education; Commercial Law; Communication Arts; Cultural Studies; Data Processing; Economic and Finance Policy; Economics; Educational Administration; Educational Technology; Engineering Management; Finance; Human Resources; Industrial and Organizational Psychology; Industrial and Production Economics; Industrial Management; Information Management; Information Sciences; Institutional Administration; Insurance; International Business; Labour and Industrial Relations; Leadership; Management; Management Systems; Marketing; Mathematics; Political Science; Private Administration; Public Administration; Rural Planning; Rural Studies; Safety Engineering; Sales Techniques; Secretarial Studies; Small Business; Social Studies; Sociology; Store Management; Systems Analysis; Transport Economics; Transport Management; Welfare and Protective Services) *Dean*: M. Salih El-Tigani Mustafa, *part-time staff:* 9, *students:* 8,659

Engineering (Computer Engineering; Electronic Engineering; Engineering; Technology; Telecommunications Engineering) *Dean*: Mohammed Ismail El-Ashari, *full-time staff:* 4, *students:* 163

Graduate Studies (Arts and Humanities; Natural Sciences) *Dean*: Ahmed Ali Al-Sauri, *students:* 1,985

Law (Air and Space Law; Civil Law; Commercial Law; Comparative Law; Constitutional Law; Criminal Law; Criminology; Fiscal Law; History of Law; International Law; Islamic Law; Justice Administration; Labour Law; Law; Maritime Law; Private Law; Public Law) *Dean*: Mustafa Hilmi, *full-time staff:* 28, *part-time staff:* 3, *students:* 9,659

Medicine (Anaesthesiology; Anatomy; Biochemistry; Cardiology; Dermatology; Embryology and Reproduction Biology; Gastroenterology; Gynaecology and Obstetrics; Haematology; Health Administration; Health Education; Immunology; Medicine; Microbiology; Neurology; Occupational Health; Ophthalmology; Pharmacology; Physiology; Public Health; Radiology; Surgery; Urology; Venereology; Virology) *Dean*: Ahmed Bayumi Al-Sayih, *full-time staff:* 2, *students:* 137

Optometry and Visual Sciences (Anatomy; Arabic; Biochemistry; Biology; Chemistry; English; Islamic Studies; Ophthalmology; Optics; Optometry; Pharmacology; Physics; Physiology) *Dean*: Hashim Abdalla Mangell, *full-time staff:* 12, *part-time staff:* 10, *students:* 240

Science and Technology (Actuarial Science; Agricultural Engineering; Aquaculture; Astrophysics; Automation and Control Engineering; Automotive Engineering; Biochemistry; Biological and Life Sciences; Biology; Biophysics; Biotechnology; Botany; Cell Biology; Chemical Engineering; Chemistry; Coastal Studies; Computer Science; Crop Production; Earth Sciences; Ecology; Electrical Engineering; Electronic Engineering; Energy Engineering; Engineering; Entomology; Environmental Studies; Farm Management; Fire Science; Fishery; Food Science; Forestry; Genetics; Geography; Geology; Geophysics; Graphic Arts; Handicrafts; Harvest Technology; Heating and Refrigeration; Heritage Preservation; Homeopathy; Horticulture; Hydraulic Engineering; Industrial Design; Irrigation; Laboratory Techniques; Landscape Architecture; Laser Engineering; Limnology; Maintenance Technology; Marine Biology; Marine Science and Oceanography; Mathematics; Mathematics and Computer Science; Measurement and Precision Engineering; Medical Technology; Meteorology; Microelectronics; Mineralogy; Mining Engineering; Molecular Biology; Mountain Studies; Multimedia; Museum Studies; Music Theory and Composition; Natural Resources; Natural Sciences; Nuclear Physics; Optical Technology; Parasitology; Peace and Disarmament; Petrology; Physics; Radio and Television Broadcasting; Radiology; Safety Engineering; Soil Science; Statistics; Surveying and Mapping; Technology; Telecommunications Engineering; Textile Technology; Thermal Physics; Town Planning; Tropical Agriculture; Waste Management; Water Science; Wildlife; Wood Technology) *Dean*: Badr Eldin Khalil Aamid, *part-time staff:* 25, *students:* 2,181

Statistical, Population Studies and Information Technology (Accountancy; Computer Graphics; Computer Science; Demography and Population; Economic and Finance Policy; Economics; Information Technology; Mathematics; Operations Research; Software Engineering; Statistics; Systems Analysis) *Dean*: Husain Hasan Ayoub, *full-time staff:* 8, *students:* 568

Centres

Computer (Computer Science) *Director*: Mohamed Higazi, *part-time staff:* 9

Research Centres

Nile Basin Studies (Arts and Humanities; Natural Sciences) *Director*: Issam Abdd Wahab Muhamed

History: Founded 1955 as Khartoum Branch of Cairo University. Acquired present status and title 1993.

Academic Year: July to April (July-October; November-April)

Admission Requirements: Secondary school certificate (passes in 7 subjects) or recognized foreign equivalent

Fees: (Sudanese Dinar): 200-250 per annum

Main Language(s) of Instruction: Arabic

Degrees and Diplomas: *Bachelor Honours Degree*: 4 yrs; *Master's Degree*: a further 2 yrs; *Doctor of Philosophy*: (PhD), a further 3-4 yrs. Also High Diploma, 1 yr; General Diploma (Undergraduate)

Student Services: Academic Counselling, Social Counselling, Employment Services, Nursery Care, Cultural Centre, Sports Facilities, Health Services, Canteen

Special Facilities: Al-Neelain University Theatre

Libraries: Central Library, Library of the Faculty of Science and Technology, Library of the Faculty of Arts, Library of the Faculty of Law, Library of the Faculty of Commerce, Library of the Faculty of Optometry and Visual Science, Graduate College

Library, Faculty of Engineering Library, English Language Library, Computer Centre Library, Faculty of Medicine Library

Press or Publishing House: Al-Neelain University Press

Academic Staff *1999-2000*	MEN	WOMEN	TOTAL
FULL-TIME	169	37	206
PART-TIME	51	5	56
TOTAL	**220**	**42**	**262**
STAFF WITH DOCTORATE			
FULL-TIME	–	–	78
PART-TIME	31	1	32
TOTAL	–	–	110

Student Numbers *1999-2000:* Total: **35,735**

KASSALA UNIVERSITY
Jameat Kassala
Kassala 266
Tel: +249(411) 22095
Fax: +249(411) 23501

Vice-Chancellor: Mustafa Ali Abasher (1998-2002)

Administrative Officer: Abdelmoneim Abdelrahman

Faculties
Agriculture and Natural Resources (Agriculture; Natural Resources)
Economics and Administration (Administration; Economics)
Education
Medicine and Health Sciences (Medicine)

History: Founded 1990.

• KORDOFAN UNIVERSITY
Jameat Kordofan
El Obeid, North Kordofan 517
Tel: +249(611) 23319
Fax: +249(611) 23108
Telex: 6001

Vice-Chancellor: Osman Adam Osman (1994-)

Registrar: Kamal Mohamed Khier

International Relations: Al-Taj Fadlalla Abdel-Rahim
Tel: +249(11) 471-269

Faculties
Education
Engineering and Technical Science (Engineering; Technology)
Medicine and Health Sciences (Health Sciences; Medicine)
Natural Resources
Science and Humanities Studies (Humanities and Social Science Education; Natural Sciences)

Centres
Arabic Gum
Further Education

History: Founded 1990.

432

• NILE VALLEY UNIVERSITY
Jameat Wadi Al-Neel
PO Box 52, Eldamer 163
Tel: +249(216) 24433
Fax: +249(216) 24370
EMail: nilevu@sudanmail.net

Vice-Chancellor: Faisal Abdalla Alhag

Academic Secretary: Mohammed Yasin

Faculties
Agricultural Sciences (Agriculture)
Commerce and Business Administration (Business Administration; Business and Commerce)
Earth Sciences and Mining (Earth Sciences; Mining Engineering)
Education
Engineering and Technology (Engineering; Technology)
Islamic and Arabic Studies (Arabic; Islamic Studies)
Islamic Law (Shari'a) and Law (Islamic Law)
Medicine and Health Sciences (Health Sciences; Medicine)
Teacher Training

Centres
Extramural Studies

History: Founded 1990, incorporating two existing faculties.

Governing Bodies: University Council, comprising 50 members

Academic Year: April to December

Admission Requirements: Secondary school certificate or equivalent

Main Language(s) of Instruction: Arabic, English (subsidiary)

Degrees and Diplomas: *Bachelor's Degree; Bachelor Honours Degree; Postgraduate Diploma; Master's Degree.* Also Diploma

Libraries: c. 16,000 vols

Academic Staff *1999:* Total: c. 120

Student Numbers *1999:* All (Foreign Included): Men: c. 1,200 Women: c. 500 Total: c. 1,700

• NYALA UNIVERSITY
Jameat Nyala
PO Box 155, Nyala, South Darfur
Tel: +249(711) 33122
Fax: +249(711) 33123
EMail: nyala@un.com

Vice-Chancellor: Adam Hassan Sulaiman

Principal: Yousif Shambal Tel: +249(711) 33124

Faculties
Economics and Commerce (Business and Commerce; Economics)
Education
Engineering
Veterinary Science

Centres
Extramural Studies
Peace Studies (Peace and Disarmament)

History: Founded 1994.

*• OMDURMAN ISLAMIC UNIVERSITY
Jameat Omdurman Islamic
PO Box 382, Omdurman
Tel: +249(11) 511-524   +249(11) 784-375
Fax: +249(11) 775-253
Telex: (0984) 22527 oui sd

President: Mohammed Osman Salih (2001-)

Secretary: Ahmed Mohammed El-Hassan

International Relations: Hashim M.M. Salih
Tel: +249(11) 775-253

Faculties
Agriculture
Al-Da'awah Al-Islamia (Islamic Studies)
Arabic Language (Arabic)
Arts (Arts and Humanities)
Business Administration
Economics and Political Science (Economics; Political Science)
Education
Engineering (Educational Sciences; Engineering)
Further Education
Islamic Law (Shari'a) and Law (Islamic Law)
Islamic Principles (Islamic Studies)
Medicine and Health Sciences (Health Sciences; Medicine)
Pharmacy
Science (Natural Sciences)

Centres
Further Education

History: Founded 1912 as Islamic Institute, became college 1924 and university 1965. Acquired present status 1975. A State institution under the jurisdiction of and financially supported by the National Council for Higher Education. Branches in Damascus and Elginan.

Governing Bodies: University Council; Senate; Faculty Boards

Academic Year: July to April (July-November; December-April)

Admission Requirements: Secondary school certificate or recognized equivalent

Main Language(s) of Instruction: Arabic

Degrees and Diplomas: *Bachelor's Degree*: Arts (BA); Law (LLB); Science (BSc), 4 yrs; *Postgraduate Diploma*: Education, 1 yr; *Master's Degree*: Arts (MA), a further 2-3 yrs; *Doctor of Philosophy*: (PhD), 3 yrs. Also Diplomas in-Education; Islamic Economics, 1 yr.

Student Residential Facilities: For c. 1500 students

Libraries: Central Library, c. 90,000 vols; Girls College, c. 10,000 vols

Publications: Journals of the Faculties

Press or Publishing House: The University Press
Academic Staff *1999:* Total: c. 200
Student Numbers *1999:* Total: c. 4,000

RED SEA UNIVERSITY
Jameat Al-Bahar Al-Ahmar
PO Box 24, Port Sudan, Red Sea
Tel: +249(311) 27878
Fax: +249(311) 27778

Vice-Chancellor: Abdel Gadir Dafalla Elhag (1994-)
Registrar: Alsir Ahmed Babiker

Faculties
Applied Sciences (Natural Sciences)
Earth Sciences
Economics and Administration (Administration; Economics)
Education
Engineering (Chemical Engineering; Civil Engineering; Engineering; Mechanical Engineering)
Marine Science and Fisheries (Fishery; Marine Science and Oceanography)
Maritime Transport Economics (Economics; Marine Transport)
Medicine and Health Sciences (Health Sciences; Medicine)
Teacher Training *(Primary Level)*

Units
Continuing Education

Institutes
Oceanography (Marine Science and Oceanography)

History: Founded 1994.

Governing Bodies: University Council; Senate; Faculty Boards

Academic Year: September to June (September-December; March-June)

Admission Requirements: Secondary school certificate

Main Language(s) of Instruction: Arabic and English

International Co-operation: Hamburg University

Degrees and Diplomas: *Bachelor's Degree*: Arts; Science, 4 yrs; *Bachelor Honours Degree*: 5 yrs; *Postgraduate Diploma*: 3 yrs

Student Residential Facilities: For 25 students

Libraries: c. 1550 vols Marine Science; Faculty Libraries

Academic Staff *1999*: Full-Time: c. 50 Part-Time: c. 30 Total: c. 80
Student Numbers *1999:* Total: c. 800

SHANDI UNIVERSITY
Jameat Shandi
PO Box 14 and 143, Shandi, River Nile
Tel: +249(261) 721-84
Fax: +249(261) 725-09

Vice-Chancellor and President: Ali Abdel Abdel Rahman Barri (1994-) EMail: ali-barri@hotmail.com

Registrar: Yahia Fadlalla

International Relations: Ali Ahmed

Faculties

Arts (Arabic; Archaeology; Arts and Humanities; English; Hotel Management; Modern Languages; Tourism) *Dean*: Awad Alkarim Bakhet, *full-time staff:* 27, *part-time staff:* 10, *students:* 442

Community Development *(Taybat Al Khawad)* (Development Studies; Gender Studies; Social Studies; Women's Studies) *Dean*: Afaf Abdel Rahman, *full-time staff:* 10, *part-time staff:* 6, *students:* 213

Economics, Commerce and Business Administration *(Al-Magawir)* (Business Administration; Business and Commerce; Business Education; Economics; Finance; Management; Statistics) *Dean*: Rugaia Ahmed, *full-time staff:* 7, *part-time staff:* 11, *students:* 237

Education for Primary School Teachers (Foreign Languages Education; Geography; History; Humanities and Social Science Education; Mathematics; Natural Sciences; Primary Education) *Dean*: Malik Mohd-Kheir, *full-time staff:* 41, *part-time staff:* 15, *students:* 1,054

Islamic Law (Shari'a) and Law *(Al Matama)* (Islamic Law; Law) *Dean*: Seif Aldin Hamatu, *full-time staff:* 14, *part-time staff:* 5, *students:* 406

Medicine and Health Sciences (Health Sciences; Laboratory Techniques; Medicine; Nursing; Public Health; Surgery) *Dean*: Jamal Alimairi, *full-time staff:* 29, *part-time staff:* 30, *students:* 1,329

Centres

Adult Education and Extramural Studies (Adult Education; Preschool Education) *Director*: Awad Allkari Bakhet

Agriculture Irrigation, Animal Production and Crops Research (Agriculture; Cattle Breeding; Crop Production; Irrigation) *Director*: Ali Ahmed

Al-Faith Islamic Centre (Information Management; Islamic Studies) *Director*: Abdel Gadir Ali, *full-time staff:* 5, *part-time staff:* 10, *students:* 80

Education Development and Continuing Education (Continuing Education; Curriculum; Educational Sciences) *Director*: Ali Abdel Rahman Barri

Further Information: Also Teaching Hospitals

History: Founded 1990 as Faculties of Wadi Elneel University, acquired present status and title 1994.

Governing Bodies: University Council; Senate; Faculty Boards

Admission Requirements: Secondary school certificate or equivalent as required by the National Board of Administration

Main Language(s) of Instruction: Arabic, English

International Co-operation: University of Shanghai; University of Wales, Cardiff

Degrees and Diplomas: *Bachelor's Degree*: 8 Semesters; *Master's Degree*: Medicine and Surgery, 12 semesters; *Doctor of Philosophy*. Also Intermediate Diplomas; High Diplomas

Student Services: Social Counselling, Cultural Centre, Sports Facilities, Health Services, Canteen

Student Residential Facilities: Yes

Special Facilities: Movie Studio

Libraries: 6 Libraries and Internet

Publications: Journal of Shandi University, Scientific, Cultural, and Social Topics (bi-annually)

Academic Staff 2000			TOTAL
FULL-TIME			133
PART-TIME			77
TOTAL			**210**
STAFF WITH DOCTORATE	MEN	WOMEN	TOTAL
FULL-TIME	–	–	20
PART-TIME	–	30	30
TOTAL	–	–	**50**

Student Numbers 2000	TOTAL
All (Foreign Included)	**3,681**
FOREIGN ONLY	49

SINAR UNIVERSITY
Jameat Sinar
Sinar
Tel: +249(561) 785-614
Fax: +249(561) 730-697
Telex: 22115

Vice-Chancellor: Hassan Mohamed El-Hassan Biarem

Principal: Mohammed Awad Salih

Faculties
Agriculture
Arabic and Islamic Sciences (Arabic; Islamic Studies)
Education
Engineering
Medicine
Natural Resources and Environment (Environmental Studies; Natural Resources)

Centres
Da'awah
Extramural Studies

History: Founded 1977, acquired present status 1995.

*• SUDAN UNIVERSITY OF SCIENCE AND TECHNOLOGY
Jameat El-Sudan I'Leloom Wal Technologia (SUST)
PO Box 407, Khartoum
Tel: +249(11) 772-508
Fax: +249(11) 774-559
Cable: technology
EMail: sust@sudanet.net
Website: http://www.sustech.edu

Vice-Chancellor: Izzeldin Mohammed Osman (1994-2002)
Tel: +249(11) 775-292 EMail: izzeldin@acm.org

General Secretary: Ali Abdel-Rahman Ali
Tel: +249(11) 771-839

International Relations: Isam M. Abdulmajid
Tel: +249(11) 770-319

Colleges

Agricultural Studies *(Shambat)* (Agricultural Business; Agricultural Equipment; Agriculture; Agronomy; Food Technology; Horticulture; Rural Planning) *Dean*: Abd Elaziz Mackawi, *full-time staff*: 56, *part-time staff*: 34, *students*: 954

Business Studies (Accountancy; Banking; Business Administration; Business and Commerce; International Business) *Dean*: Ali Abdalla Adam, *full-time staff*: 51, *part-time staff*: 15, *students*: 2,304

Education (Art Education; Education; English; French; Mathematics; Technology Education) *Dean*: Ahmed Saad Masaod, *full-time staff*: 10, *part-time staff*: 4, *students*: 1,063

Engineering (Aeronautical and Aerospace Engineering; Architecture; Civil Engineering; Electrical Engineering; Electronic Engineering; Engineering; Mechanical Engineering; Petroleum and Gas Engineering; Surveying and Mapping; Textile Technology) *Dean*: Ahmed El Tayeb, *full-time staff*: 82, *part-time staff*: 25, *students*: 3,000

Fine and Applied Arts (Ceramic Art; Fine Arts; Graphic Design; Handicrafts; Industrial Design; Painting and Drawing; Printing and Printmaking; Sculpture; Textile Design) *Dean*: Ali Mohamed Osman, *full-time staff*: 25, *part-time staff*: 8, *students*: 313

Forestry (Ecology; Forest Biology; Forest Management; Forestry) *Dean*: Mahir Salih Solieman, *full-time staff*: 21, *part-time staff*: 14, *students*: 254

Medical Radiological Sciences (Radiology; Radiophysics) *Dean*: Bushra Hussein Ahmed, *full-time staff*: 30, *part-time staff*: 10, *students*: 458

Music and Drama *(HIMD)* (Music; Music Theory and Composition; Musical Instruments; Musicology; Theatre) *Dean*: Ahmed Abdela'al Ahmed, *full-time staff*: 48, *part-time staff*: 5, *students*: 304

Physical Education (Physical Education; Sports) *Dean*: Eldarouti Sharafeldin, *full-time staff*: 21, *students*: 194

Postgraduate Studies (Agriculture; Business Administration; Business and Commerce; Education; Engineering; Fine Arts; Forestry; Veterinary Science) *Dean*: Sabir Mohamed Salih, *full-time staff*: 65, *students*: 1,019

Science (Chemistry; Computer Science; Laboratory Techniques; Natural Sciences; Physics; Statistics) *Dean*: Hajou Ahmed Mohamed, *full-time staff*: 74, *part-time staff*: 33, *students*: 1,494

Technology and Human Development *(THD)* (Agriculture; Business Administration; Business and Commerce; Development Studies; Education; Engineering; Information Technology; Technology) *Dean*: Tagel Asfiya Alaagib, *full-time staff*: 125, *students*: 9,750

Veterinary Science and Animal Production (Animal Husbandry; Cattle Breeding; Veterinary Science) *Dean*: Osman Saad, *full-time staff*: 37, *part-time staff*: 6, *students*: 566

Institutes

Earth Sciences *(WAIESC, Wad El Magboul)* *Dean*: Abdulbagi Abdurahman Gorashi, *full-time staff*: 10, *part-time staff*: 18, *students*: 154

Centres

Women Development (Women's Studies) *Director*: Fatima Abdel Mahmoud

Research Centres

External Relations (International Relations) *Director*: Isam Mohamed Abdelmajid

Further Information: Also National Research Institute. English Language Unit; Arabic Language Unit; Arabic as foreign language

History: Founded 1950 as Khartoum Technical Institute. Became Khartoum Polytechnic 1975. Acquired present status and title 1990 with the incorporation of previously existing higher Technical Institutes and specialized Colleges.

Governing Bodies: University Council; Senate

Academic Year: September to June

Admission Requirements: Secondary school certificate or equivalent

Fees: According to student's family financial ability; foreign students, US Dollars 2000-3000

Main Language(s) of Instruction: Arabic, English

International Co-operation: Suez Canal University; University of Baghdad; University of Mosul; University of Technology Baghdad; University of Kufa; University of Basrah; Middle East Technical University Ankara; Uljanovsk State Technical University; University of Science and Technology, Sana'a

Degrees and Diplomas: *Diploma*: 2-3 yrs; *Bachelor's Degree*: (BSc; BA), 4-5 yrs; *Postgraduate Diploma*: 2 yrs; *Master's Degree*: a further 2 yrs; *Doctor of Philosophy*: (PhD), 3 yrs

Student Services: Academic Counselling, Social Counselling, Sports Facilities, Language Programmes, Health Services, Canteen

Student Residential Facilities: Yes

Libraries: Total, 66,000 vols

Publications: Journal of Science and Technology (biannually)

Press or Publishing House: Sudan University Printing Press and Distribution House

Academic Staff *1999*	TOTAL
FULL-TIME	700
PART-TIME	130
TOTAL	**830**

Staff with doctorate: Total: **203**

Student Numbers *1999*: All (Foreign Included): Men: c. 13,105 Women: c. 9,080 Total: c. 22,185
Foreign Only: Total: c. 470

*• UNIVERSITY OF GEZIRA

Jameat Algezira
PO Box 20, Wad Medani, Khartoum 2667
Tel: +249(511) 41355
Fax: +249(511) 40466
Telex: (0984) 50009 txowd sd

Vice-Chancellor: Ismail Hassan Hussein (2001-)
Tel: +249(511) 43174 Fax: +249(511) 772-062

Principal: E.K. Abu Salah

International Relations: I.M. Husayn

Faculties
Agricultural Sciences (Agriculture)

Animal Production (Animal Husbandry)

Communication Sciences (Communication Studies)

Economics and Rural Development (Economics; Rural Planning)

Education

Health and Environment Sciences (Environmental Engineering; Health Sciences)

Mathematics Science and Computer (Mathematics and Computer Science)

Medical Sciences (Health Sciences)

Pharmacy

Postgraduate

Science and Technology (Natural Sciences; Technology)

Textile Engineering (Textile Technology)

Centres

Agriculture and Natural Resources (Agriculture; Natural Resources)

Biological Technology (Biology; Technology)

Cereal Oil Manufacturing (Crop Production)

Demographic Studies (Demography and Population)

Development of Horticultural Exports (Horticulture)

Islamic Knowledge (Islamic Studies)

Neurological Medicine (Neurological Therapy)

Small Scale Industries and Technology (Small Business)

Sugar Research (Food Science)

Technological and Biological Sciences (Biological and Life Sciences; Technology)

Transfer

Water and Irrigation Management (Irrigation; Water Management)

History: Founded 1975. An autonomous State institution.

Governing Bodies: Council, comprising 29 members; Senate, 3 members

Academic Year: October to June (October-January; February-June)

Admission Requirements: Secondary school certificate

Main Language(s) of Instruction: English

Degrees and Diplomas: *Bachelor's Degree*: Agriculture (B.Sc (Agric.)); Economics (B.Sc (Econ.)); Technology (B.Sc (Tech.)), 5 yrs; Medicine and Surgery (M.B.N., B.Ch.), 6 yrs; *Master's Degree*: Philosophy (M.Phil); Science (M.Sc.); *Doctor of Philosophy*: (Ph.D.)

Student Residential Facilities: Yes

Libraries: c. 7550 vols

Academic Staff *1999:* Total: c. 150

Student Numbers *1999:* Total: c. 1,100

436

• UNIVERSITY OF HOLY QURAN AND ISLAMIC SCIENCES

Jameat El-Quraan El-Kareem Wa El-lloom El-Shamia
PO Box 1459, Omdurman
Tel: +249(15) 559-594
Fax: +249(15) 559-175
Telex: 78012

Vice-Chancellor: Ahmed Khalid Babiker (1991-)

Faculties

Arabic Language (Arabic)

Community Development *(Juba)* (Development Studies)

Da'wah and Media (Media Studies)

Education *(Malakal)*

Educational Sciences

Holy Qu'ran (Koran)

Islamic Law (Shari'a) and Law (Islamic Law)

Centres
Women's Studies

History: Founded 1990.

*• UNIVERSITY OF JUBA

Jameat Juba
PO Box 321, Khartoum Centre, Juba, Baher Elgebal 82
Tel: +249(11) 222-136   +249(11) 451-352
Fax: +249(11) 222-142
Telex: (0984) 22738 kupsd
Cable: jubasity juba
EMail: jucs@sudanet.net

Vice-Chancellor: Fathi Mohamed Ahmed Kaleel (2001-)
Tel: +249(11) 227-986

Principal: Hassan El-Tayeb Mohammed
Tel: +249(11) 222-123

International Relations: Hammed Elnil Bashier Garray
Tel: +249(11) 722-187

Faculties

Arts and Humanities

Business Administration

Education

Engineering

Law

Medicine

Social and Economic Studies (Accountancy; Arts and Humanities; Management; Political Science; Public Administration; Sociology)

Centres

Computer Studies (Computer Science)

Languages and Translation (Modern Languages; Translation and Interpretation)

Peace Studies (Peace and Disarmament)

History: Founded 1975. Accepted first students in 1977. An autonomous State institution.

Governing Bodies: University Council; Senate

Academic Year: March to December (March-July; August-December)

Admission Requirements: Secondary school certificate or foreign equivalent

Main Language(s) of Instruction: English

International Co-operation: Yarmouk University; Basra University; Al-Mustansiriyah University; University of Mosul

Degrees and Diplomas: *Bachelor's Degree*: Arts (BA); Science (BSc), 4 yrs; *Bachelor Honours Degree*: 5 yrs; *Master's Degree*: 1-2 yrs; *Doctor of Philosophy*: (PhD), 2-3 yrs. Also Diploma, 3 yrs.

Student Residential Facilities: Yes

Libraries: c. 50,000 vols

Publications: Juvarsity (monthly)

Press or Publishing House: Juba University Printing Unit

Academic Staff *1999*: Full-Time: c. 300 Part-Time: c. 100 Total: c. 400

Student Numbers *1999*: Total: c. 800

*• UNIVERSITY OF KHARTOUM

Jameat El-Khartoum
PO Box 321, Khartoum 80295
Tel: +249(11) 771-290
Fax: +249(11) 780-295
Telex: (0984) 22738 kup sd
EMail: info@uofk.edu
Website: http://www.sudan.net/uk

Vice-Chancellor: Abdel Malik Mohammed Abdel Rahman (2000-)

Secretary for Academic Affairs: Mahgoub Yahia
Tel: +249(11) 779-293

Faculties

Agriculture *(Shambat)* (Agricultural Economics; Agricultural Engineering; Agriculture; Biochemistry; Botany; Crop Production; Horticulture; Soil Science) *Dean*: Gaafer Mohammed Al-Hassan

Animal Husbandry (Animal Husbandry; Dairy; Meat and Poultry) *Dean*: Al-Fadil Ahmed Al-Zubier

Arts (Arabic; Archaeology; Arts and Humanities; Chinese; English; French; Geography; German; History; Information Sciences; International Relations; Islamic Studies; Library Science; Linguistics; Philosophy; Psychology; Russian) *Dean*: Majzoub Salim Bur

Dentistry (Dentistry; Orthodontics; Surgery) *Dean*: Ibrahim Ahmed Gandour

Economics and Social Studies (Econometrics; Economics; Political Science; Social Studies) *Dean*: Arbab Ismail Babikir

Education *(Omburman)* (Arabic; Biology; Chemistry; Curriculum; Education; Educational Psychology; Educational Technology; English; Family Studies; French; Geography; History; Mathematics; Pedagogy; Physics) *Dean*: Bashir Mohammed Osman Haj Al-Tom

Engineering and Architecture (Agricultural Engineering; Architecture; Chemical Engineering; Civil Engineering; Electrical Engineering; Mechanical Engineering; Mining Engineering;

Petroleum and Gas Engineering; Surveying and Mapping) *Dean*: Al-Nima Ibrahim Al-Nima

Forestry *(Shambat)* (Forest Management; Forestry) *Dean*: Hashim Ali Al-Ataa

Law (Commercial Law; International Law; Islamic Law; Law; Private Law; Public Law) *Dean*: Awad Abdallah Abu Bukr

Mathematics (Applied Mathematics; Computer Science; Mathematics; Statistics) *Dean*: Mohamed A. Moniem Ismail

Medicine (Anaesthesiology; Anatomy; Biochemistry; Community Health; Gynaecology and Obstetrics; Medicine; Microbiology; Orthopedics; Pathology; Physiology; Psychiatry and Mental Health; Surgery) *Dean*: Al Daw Mukhtar Ahmed Mukhtar

Pharmacy (Pharmacology; Pharmacy) *Dean*: Idris Babiker Al-Tayib

Public and Environmental Health (Epidemiology; Food Science; Health Sciences; Hygiene) *Dean*: Bashir Mohammed Al-Hassan

Science (Botany; Chemistry; Geology; Natural Sciences; Physics; Zoology) *Dean*: Osman Ibrahim Osman

Veterinary Science *(Shambat)* (Anatomy; Biochemistry; Gynaecology and Obstetrics; Medicine; Microbiology; Pathology; Pharmacology; Physiology; Surgery; Toxicology; Veterinary Science) *Dean*: Mohammed Taha Abdel Alla Shgadi

Colleges
Graduate *Dean*: Sidig Ahmed Ismail

Schools
Higher Nursing (Nursing) *Director*: Rugaia Abu Al-Gasim Abdel Rahim

Management Studies (Accountancy; Finance; Management) *Dean*: Ismail Al Khalipa Suliman

Institutes
African and Asian Studies (African Studies; Asian Studies; Folklore) *Director*: Madeni Mohammed Mohammed Ahmed

Building and Road Research (Building Technologies; Road Engineering) *Director*: Mohammed Ahmed Osman

Environmental Studies *Director*: Youssif Babikir Abu Gidari

Extramural Studies and Community Development (Distance Education) *Director*: Al Tayib Ahmed Al Mustafa Haiaty

Centres
Computer (Computer Science) *Director*: Hashim Al-Amin Mustafa

Further Information: Also Teaching Hospital

History: Founded 1951 as University College of Khartoum incorporating Gordon Memorial College, established 1902, and the Kitchener School of Medicine, established 1924. Became university 1956. An autonomous institution financed by the State.

Governing Bodies: University Council, comprising 29 members; Academic Senate, composed entirely of members of the academic staff

Academic Year: July to April (July-September; October-December; January-April)

Admission Requirements: Secondary school certificate

Main Language(s) of Instruction: English. Arabic in Departments of Islamic Law, of Islamic History, and of Arabic

Degrees and Diplomas: *Bachelor's Degree*: Law (Civil), 3 yrs; Accountancy; Arts (BA); Business Administration; Economics; Economics and Social Studies; Engineering; Law (Islamic); Political Science; Science (BSc); Social Anthropology; Social Studies; Statistics, 4 yrs; Architecture; Pharmacy (BPharm); Veterinary Science (BVSc), 5 yrs; Medicine (MB, BS), 6 yrs; *Bachelor Honours Degree*: Agriculture, 4 yrs; 5 yrs; *Postgraduate Diploma*; *Master's Degree*: all faculties; *Doctor of Philosophy*: all faculties

Student Residential Facilities: Yes

Special Facilities: Natural History Museum

Libraries: Main Library, c. 300,000 vols; Engineering and Architecture, c. 8500 vols; Medicine and Pharmacy, c. 9000 vols; Agriculture and Veterinary Science, c. 28,000 vols; Law, c. 5000 vols

Publications: Gazette (3 per annum); Research Committee Report (annually)

Press or Publishing House: University of Khartoum Press

Academic Staff *1999:* Total: c. 830

Student Numbers *1999:* Total: c. 17,000

UNIVERSITY OF WEST KORDOFAN

Jameat Gareb Kordofan

PO Box 16722 Khartoum, El-Foula, West Kordofan
Tel: +249(11) 785-614

Vice-Chancellor: Ibrahim Musa Tibin

Principal: Mohammed Farah

Faculties
Economics and Community Development (Economics)
Education
Islamic and Arabic Sciences (Arabic; Islamic Studies)
Natural Resources and Environmental Studies (Natural Resources)

History: Founded 1997.

• UPPER NILE UNIVERSITY

Jameat Al-Neel

PO Box 1660, Khartoum, Ali Elneel
Tel: +249(11) 483-856   +249(11) 222-174

Vice-Chancellor: Gashwa Atur Akul (1998-)

Faculties
Agriculture
Animal Production (Animal Husbandry)
Education
Engineering and Technical Studies (Engineering; Technology)
Forestry
Medicine and Health Studies (Health Sciences; Medicine)
Natural Resources and Environmental Studies (Environmental Studies; Natural Resources)

History: Founded 1991.

438

• UNIVERSITY OF ZALENGI

Jameat Zalengi

Zalengi, West Darfur 6
Tel: +249(713) 22013
Fax: +249(723) 22013
EMail: uzal@student.net

Vice-Chancellor: Mohammed Abaker Adam

Principal: Abdal Gadir Adam Ahmed

Faculties
Agriculture
Education
Lifelong Education

History: Founded 1994.

PRIVATE INSTITUTIONS

*• AHFAD UNIVERSITY FOR WOMEN

Jameat Al-Ahfad Llbanat

PO Box 167, Omdurman
Tel: +249(15) 579-112
Fax: +249(15) 553-363
Telex: (0984) 22271 medt
EMail: ahfad@sudanmail.net
Website: http://www.ahfad.org

Vice-Chancellor: Gasim Yousif Badri (1966-)
Fax: +249(15) 579-111

Vice-President: Awatif Mustafa Abdel Hail
Tel: +249(15) 560-050 Fax: +249(15) 564-401
EMail: awatifhalim@usa.net

Schools
Family Sciences (Family Studies; Food Science; Social and Community Services) *students:* 390
Organizational Management (Business Administration; Management) *full-time staff:* 17, *part-time staff:* 7, *students:* 1,757
Psychology and Pre-School Education (Child Care and Development; Preschool Education; Psychology) *students:* 1,551
Rural Education and Development (Education; Rural Planning) *students:* 268

History: Founded 1966. Acquired university status 1995.

Main Language(s) of Instruction: English

Degrees and Diplomas: *Bachelor's Degree*; *Master's Degree*: Gender Studies; Nutrition

*• INTERNATIONAL UNIVERSITY OF AFRICA

Jamitu Ifriqya Al-Alamiyyah

PO Box 2469, Khartoum
Tel: +249(11) 723-840
Fax: +249(11) 723-841

Vice-Chancellor: Abdelrahim Ali Muhammed Ibrahim (1998-2002) Tel: +249(11) 273-839

Registrar: Mahjub Mohammed Al Hussein
Tel: +249(11) 723-846

Faculties

Arabic Language *(For non-Arabic Speakers)* (Arabic)

Education and Humanities (Arabic; Arts and Humanities; Education; English; French; Natural Sciences; Social Sciences)

Islamic Law (Shari'a) and Islamic Studies (Islamic Law; Islamic Studies)

Pure and Applied Sciences (Biology; Chemistry; Geology; Mathematics; Natural Sciences; Physics)

Research and African Studies (Economics; Environmental Studies; Geography; Modern Languages; Political Science; Religion; Statistics)

Centres

Computer Science *(Iqra)*

Islamic African Studies (Curriculum; Education; Islamic Studies)

History: Founded 1977 as the Islamic African Centre. University Colleges affiliated to Omdurman Islamic University founded 1985. Acquired present status and title 1991. An independent international organization governed by its Constitution.

Governing Bodies: Board of Trustees

Academic Year: August to July (August-December; January-May; June-July)

Admission Requirements: Secondary school certificate or equivalent

Fees: (US Dollars): 1500 per annum

Main Language(s) of Instruction: Arabic

Degrees and Diplomas: *Bachelor's Degree*: Computer Science; Education; Law; Science, 4 yrs; *Master's Degree*: African Studies; Arabic Language; Education; Islamic Studies, a further 2 yrs; *Doctor of Philosophy*: (PhD), a further 3 yrs

Special Facilities: Audiovisual and T.V. Unit

Libraries: Main Library, 40,000 vols

Publications: Risalat Ifriqya, Africa Message, News magazine (monthly); Dirasat Ifriqiya, African Studies, Research Journal (biannually)

Press or Publishing House: Printing Press

Academic Staff *1999:* Total: **275**

STAFF WITH DOCTORATE	
FULL-TIME	30
PART-TIME	25
TOTAL	**55**

Student Numbers 1999	MEN	WOMEN	TOTAL
All (Foreign Included)	2,205	235	**2,440**
FOREIGN ONLY	–	–	1,995

KHARTOUM INTERNATIONAL INSTITUTE FOR ARABIC LANGUAGES
Mahad El-Khartoum Eldawally Lugha Elarabia
PO Box 26, Khartoum
Tel: +249(11) 223-721
Fax: +249(11) 223-722
Telex: 24065 lugha sd

Director: Abed Elraheem Ali

Arabic; Modern Languages

History: Founded 1974.

• OMDURMAN AHLIA UNIVERSITY
Jameat Omdurman Ahlia
PO Box 786, Omdurman, Khartoum
Tel: +249(11) 51489
Fax: +249(11) 57489
Telex: 22640 maltan sd

President: Mohammed Ahmed Khalifa
Registrar: Mohammed El-Hassan Ahmed

Faculties
Administrative Sciences (Administration)
Arabic Language (Arabic)

Departments
Administrative Sciences (Administration)
Arabic Language (Arabic)
Computer Studies (Computer Science)
English Language (English)
Environmental Studies
Management
Mathematics and Physics (Mathematics; Physics)

Centres
Interior Design
Library Science

History: Founded 1986.

OTHER INSTITUTIONS

PRIVATE INSTITUTIONS

AFRICA COLLEGE
Koliat Africa El-Jamia
PO Box 3493, Alreiad Street No.12, Khartoum
Tel: +249(11) 224-090

Dean: Hassan Suleiman (1991-)

Divisions
Accounting and Management
Home Economics and Social Development of Women

History: Founded 1976.

COLLEGE OF AVIATION SCIENCES
Koliat Uloom Altyaran
PO Box 714, Azhari Street Bahri, Khartoum-Bahari
Tel: +249(11) 613-163
Telex: 24212 Satco ASD

Dean: Osman Ahmed Eisa (1991-)
Secretary-General: Mohammed Alsafy Hassan Alzain

Programmes
Aviation Studies
Commerce (Business and Commerce)

History: Founded 1976.

COLLEGE OF TECHNICAL SCIENCES
Koliat Uloom Altgina
PO Box 30, Omdurman
Tel: +249(11) 555-769

Vice-Chancellor: Muttaz Mohammed Ahmed El-Birair
Registrar: Awad Alkarim Yousif

Programmes
Computer Engineering
Computer Science
Dentistry
Engineering and Architecture (Architecture; Engineering)
Medical Laboratory Science (Laboratory Techniques)
Medicine
Pharmacy
Science (Natural Sciences)

History: Founded 1995.

COMPUTERMAN COLLEGE FOR COMPUTER STUDIES
Koliat Elhasibat Elalia
PO Box 3173, Amarat 51, Khartoum
Tel: +249(11) 40296
Fax: +249(11) 451-664
Telex: 24288

Dean: Abu-Bakr Mustafa Mohamed Khair (1991-)

Programmes
Computer Engineering and Science

History: Founded 1991.

EAST NILE COLLEGE
Koliat Shark El-Neel
PO Box 1087, Omdurman
Tel: +249(11) 550-631

Dean: Al Tahir Mohamed Ali (1991-)
Secretary-General: Altigani Ahmed Abu Algasim

Programmes
Education
Engineering and Energy
Laboratory Technology

History: Founded 1991.

ELNASR TECHNICAL COLLEGE
Koliat Elnasr Elitagania
PO Box 744, Omdurman
Tel: +249(11) 54469

Dean: Mohamed Alrafia Mustafa (1990-)

Programmes
Architecture
Banking
Building (Building Technologies)
Commerce (Business and Commerce)

History: Founded 1990.

HIGH INSTITUTE FOR BANKING AND FINANCIAL STUDIES
El-Maahad El-Ali Lederasat El-Masrafia Walmalia
PO Box 1880, Jama'A Street, Khartoum, Khartoum
Tel: +249(11) 770-564
Fax: +249(11) 780-913

Director: Awatif Yousif (1998-) **Tel:** +249(11) 780-913
Secretary of Academic affairs: Mohamed. O.M Abdellah
Tel: +249(11) 788-942

Departments
Accounting (Accountancy)
Computer (Computer Science) Head: Abubaker Abdel Rahman
Law and Islamic Studies (Islamic Studies; Law) Head: Mohamed.S. Hussen
Management Studies (Management)
Research and Economics (Banking; Economics) Head: Isam Ellaythey

History: Founded 1963, upgraded into a higher Institute in 1993.
Governing Bodies: Board of Trustees and Board of Directors
Academic Year: August to May
Admission Requirements: Sudan School Certificate or equivalent
Fees: (Sudanese Dinar) : 100,000 per annum
Main Language(s) of Instruction: Arabic-English
Degrees and Diplomas: *Bachelor's Degree*: Banking, 4 yrs; *Postgraduate Diploma*: Banking, 3 yrs. Training Diplomas
Student Services: Academic Counselling, Foreign Student Adviser, Sports Facilities, Language Programmes, Canteen

Special Facilities: Computer Lab and Internet Lab

Publications: Banking and Financial Studies Journal, Academic Research Journal (2 per annum); Training Courses Program Publication, Time and contents of the year training program (1 per annum)

Academic Staff *1999/2000*	MEN	WOMEN	TOTAL
FULL-TIME	10	1	11
PART-TIME	40	3	43
TOTAL	**50**	**4**	**54**
STAFF WITH DOCTORATE			
FULL-TIME	6	1	7
PART-TIME	12	2	14
TOTAL	**18**	**3**	**21**

Student Numbers *1999/2000*	MEN	WOMEN	TOTAL
All (Foreign Included)	1,300	930	**2,230**
FOREIGN ONLY	–	–	2

Evening Students, 670

Note: Evening students are Bank staff studying for B.Sc or Diploma Degree

ISLAMIC INSTITUTION OF TRANSLATION
Mahad Elitergma Elislami
Central PO Box 44755, Khartoum

Director: Altigani Ismeel Elgizoli (1998-)

Programmes
Translation and Interpreting (Translation and Interpretation)

History: Founded 1994.

KHARTOUM COLLEGE FOR APPLIED STUDIES
Koliat Khartoum Al-Tatpigia
PO Box 3887, Khartoum
Tel: +249(11) 223-135

Dean: Abdalla Mohi Aldeen Algenaid (1990-)
Academic Secretary: Mohamed Kamal Albakri

Programmes
Architectural Drawing and Decoration
Management

History: Founded 1990.

KHARTOUM TECHNICAL COLLEGE
Koliat El-Khartoum Eltigania
PO Box 15027, Khartoum-Elamarrat

Dean: Mohammed Osman Abusag

Programmes
Commerce (Business and Commerce)
Engineering and Architecture (Architecture; Engineering)

PORT SUDAN ALHIA COLLEGE
Koliat Port Sudan Ahlia
Port Sudan
Tel: +249(11) 23899

Dean: Mustafa Baasher

Programmes
Computer Science
Medical Laboratory Sciences (Laboratory Techniques; Treatment Techniques)

History: Founded 1995.

SUDAN UNIVERSITY COLLEGE FOR GIRLS (SUC)
Koliat Sudan Alijamia
PO Box 1176, Building No.8 Block 17, Ryadh Town Khartoum
Tel: +249(11) 224-265
Fax: +249(11) 77844
Telex: 22657 vtco SD

Director: Fadwa Abd El-Rahman Ali Taha (1990-)

Programmes
Business Administration
Computer Science
Economics and Social Sciences (Economics; Social Sciences)
Languages and Translation (Modern Languages; Translation and Interpretation)
Mass Communication
Nutrition and Food Sciences

History: Founded 1990.

WAD MADANI AHLIA COLLEGE
Koliat Wad Madani Ahlia
PO Box 4, Wad Madani
Tel: +249(51) 42393

Dean: Isam El-Bushi (1992-)

Programmes
Business Administration
Computer Science
Home Economics

History: Founded 1992.

Swaziland

INSTITUTION TYPES AND CREDENTIALS

Types of higher education institutions:

University
College
Institute

School leaving and higher education credentials:

Cambridge Overseas School Certificate
General Certificate of Education 'O' Level
Certificate
Diploma
Bachelor's Degree
Master's Degree

STRUCTURE OF EDUCATION SYSTEM

Pre-higher education:

Structure of school system:

Primary
Type of school providing this education: Primary School
Length of programme in years: 7
Age level from: 6 to: 13
Certificate/diploma awarded: Swaziland Primary School Certificate

Junior Secondary
Type of school providing this education: Junior Secondary School
Length of programme in years: 3
Age level from: 13 to: 16
Certificate/diploma awarded: Junior Certificate

Second Cycle Secondary
Type of school providing this education: Senior Secondary School
Length of programme in years: 2
Age level from: 16 to: 18
Certificate/diploma awarded: Cambridge Overseas School Certificate/CGE 'O' Levels

School education:

Primary education lasts for seven years, leading to the Swaziland Primary Certificate. Secondary education is divided into a three-year cycle leading to the Junior Certificate and a two-year cycle leading to the Cambridge Overseas School Certificate or the General Certificate of Education 'O' Levels which give access to higher education.

Higher education:

Higher education is provided by the University of Swaziland established as a National Institution in 1982. The University is governed by the Council which consists of members appointed by the Chancellor from among academic members. The Senate is responsible for academic matters and consists of deans from each faculty. The government contributes about 60% of the recurrent budget of the university and study loans to about 80% of the Swazi students enrolled. Other institutions of higher education include teacher training Colleges, which are affiliated to the University, and specialized institutes.

Main laws/decrees governing higher education:

Decree: University of Swaziland Act (Act N° 2)   Year: 1983
Concerns: Establishment of the University

Academic year:

Classes from: August *to:* May
Long vacation from: 1 June *to:* 31 July

Languages of instruction:

English

Stages of studies:

Non-university level post-secondary studies (technical/vocational type):

The Swaziland College of Technology (SCOT) offers courses for those holding the Cambridge Overseas School Certificate in such fields as Electrical Engineering, Mechanical Engineering, Construction Studies, Hotel and Catering, and Teacher Training in technical fields. There is also a Management Centre and an Institute of Management and Public Administration, as well as a Nursing College and an Institute of Health Sciences.

University level studies:

University level first stage: Bachelor's Degree:
Courses leading to the Bachelor of Arts (BA) and Bachelor of Science (BSc) generally last for four years, divided into two two-year cycles. The normal entrance requirement is the Cambridge Overseas School Certificate with a pass in the first or second division, and with a credit in English language. A wide range of undergraduate Certificate and Diploma courses is also offered.

University level second stage: Master's Degree:
Courses lead to the award of a Master of Arts (MA), a Master of Science (MSc), or a Master of Education (MEd). The Master of Arts is usually conferred after one year's study beyond the Bachelor's Degree and the Master of Science after a minimum of two years' study beyond the Bachelor's Degree. In Education, the Master's Degree is awarded after a minimum of two years'

443

study beyond the Bachelor of Education Degree and at least two years' professional experience. A thesis is usually required for Master Degrees.

Teacher education:

Training of pre-primary and primary/basic school teachers
Primary school teachers are trained in three years at teacher training Colleges. They are awarded the Primary Teachers Diploma. There is also a four-year Bachelor of Education Degree in primary methods.

Training of secondary school teachers
A three-year course for holders of the Cambridge Overseas School Certificate leads to the Secondary Teachers Diploma. The University of Swaziland offers a Postgraduate Diploma in Education for in-service teachers. There is also a four- year Bachelor of Education in various subjects taught at secondary level.

Non-traditional studies:

Other forms of non-formal higher education
The extra-mural services of the University offer evening classes and short in-service training in Adult Education Skills. It also offers courses leading to a Certificate or Diploma in Adult Education and a Certificate in Accounting and Business Studies.

NATIONAL BODIES

Responsible authorities:

Ministry of Education
    Minister: John P. Carmichael
    PO Box 39
    Mbabane
    Tel: +268 404-5641
    EMail: amkhonza@realnet.co.sz
    WWW: http://www.swazi.com/government/ministries/min-edu.html

ADMISSIONS TO HIGHER EDUCATION

Admission to non university higher education studies

Name of secondary school credential required: Cambridge Overseas School Certificate

Admission to university-level studies

Name of secondary school credential required: Cambridge Overseas School Certificate
Minimum score/requirement: First or second division with credit in English.

Foreign students admission

Admission requirements: Foreign students seeking admission to the University of Swaziland as undergraduates should hold a minimum of six passes at GCE Ordinary ("O") level, including English (grade C or above) and at least five other relevant subjects.

Entry regulations: Students from certain countries need a visa.

Language requirements: A good knowledge of English is essential for all university courses.

Application procedures:

Application closing dates:

For university level studies: 1 April
For advanced/doctoral studies: 1 April

Recognition of studies and qualifications:

Studies pursued in foreign countries (bodies dealing with recognition of foreign credentials):
Ministry of Education
PO Box 39
Mbabane
Tel: +268 404-5641
WWW: http://www.swazi.com/government/ministries/min-edu.html

Multilateral agreements concerning recognition of foreign studies

Name(s) of agreement(s): Convention on the Recognition of Studies, Certificates, Diplomas, Degrees and Other Academic Qualifications in Higher Education in the African States
Year of signature: 1981

References to further information on foreign student admissions and recognition of studies

Title: Study Abroad 2000-2001
Publisher: UNESCO/IBE
Year of publication: 1999

Title: University of Swaziland Prospectus
Publisher: University of Swaziland

STUDENT LIFE

Main student services at national level

Dean of Student Affairs, University of Swaziland
Private Bag 4
Kwaluseni M201
Tel: +268 518-4011
Fax: +268 518-5276

Category of services provided: Social and welfare services

Student expenses and financial aid

Student costs:

Home students tuition fees: Minimum: 4,300 (Emalangeni)
Maximum: 8,300 (0)
Foreign students tuition fees: Minimum: 13,400 (Emalangeni)
Maximum: 20,400 (Emalangeni)

INTERNATIONAL COOPERATION AND EXCHANGES

Principal national bodies responsible for dealing with international cooperation and exchanges in higher education:

University of Swaziland
Private Bag 4
Kwaluseni M201
Tel: +268 518-4011
Fax: +268 518-5276
Telex: 2807 wd
EMail: postmaster@isdu.uniswa.sw

GRADING SYSTEM

Usual grading system in secondary school

Full Description: Individual subjects are marked as follows: 75-100% (1), 65-74% (2), 60-64% (3), 55-59% (4), 50-54% (5), 45-49% (6), 40-44% (7), 35-39% (8), 34-0% (9).
Highest on scale: 1
Lowest on scale: 9

Main grading system used by higher education institutions

Full Description: A (80-100%) excellent; B (70-79%) very good; C (60-69%) good; D (50-59%) pass; E (40-49%) fail, but student can take a supplementary examination; F (below 39%) complete fail.
Highest on scale: A
Pass/fail level: D
Lowest on scale: F

Other main grading systems

Bachelor degrees are classified: 1st class (B average) 2nd class first division (C average) 2nd class lower division (D average) pass (E, F average) fail

NOTES ON HIGHER EDUCATION SYSTEM

Data for academic year: 2000-2001
Source: International Association of Universities (IAU), updated from IBE website, 2000

INSTITUTIONS OF HIGHER EDUCATION

UNIVERSITIES

• UNIVERSITY OF SWAZILAND
Private Bag 4, Kwaluseni M201
Tel: +268 518-4011
Fax: +268 518-5276
EMail: uniswapgs@uniswa.sz
Website: http://www.uniswa.sz

Vice-Chancellor: Lydia P. Makhubu (1988-)
Tel: +268 518-5656 EMail: teresa@uniswac1.uniswa.sz

Registrar: Samuel S. Vilakati Tel: +268 518-4730
EMail: vilakati@isdu.uniswa.sz

International Relations: M. Kunene

Faculties
Agriculture (Agricultural Education; Agriculture; Crop Production; Economics; Home Economics; Management) *Dean*: G.N. Shongwe

Commerce (Accountancy; Business Administration; Business and Commerce) *Dean*: M.A. Khan

Education (Curriculum; Management; Primary Education) *Dean*: J.C.B. Bigala

Health Sciences (Health Sciences; Nursing; Occupational Health) *Dean*: M.D. Mathunjwa

Humanities (African Languages; Communication Studies; English; French; History; Religion; Religious Studies; Theology) *Dean*: B.A.B. Sinkhondze

Postgraduate Studies (Agriculture; Chemistry; Education) *Dean*: E.C.L. Kunene

Science (Biology; Chemistry; Electronic Engineering; Environmental Studies; Geography; Mathematics and Computer Science; Physics) *Dean*: V.S.B. Mtetwa

Social Sciences (Demography and Population; Economics; Law; Political Science; Sociology; Statistics) *Dean*: A.A. Al-Teraifi

Divisions
Extramural Services *Director*: A.M. Mkhwanazi
Health Sciences

Institutes
Distance Education (Accountancy; Business and Commerce; Law) *Director*: C.M. Magagula

Further Information: Also Luyengo and Mbabane Campuses

History: Founded 1982, the University was formerly University College of Swaziland, a constituent college of the University of Botswana ans Swaziland (founded 1976).

Governing Bodies: Council

Academic Year: August - April (August-December; January-April)

Admission Requirements: General Certificate of Education (GCE) O level with at least 6 passes (including English), obtained at no more than two sittings.

Fees: (Emalangeni): Tuition, undergraduate, 4300-4600 per annum; postgraduate, 6200-8300; foreign students, undergraduate, 13,400-13,600; Postgraduate, full time, 6200-8,300; foreign students, 19,000-20,400. Part time undergraduate, 900-3,300. Part time postgraduate, 3,300-4,300; foreign students, 9,400-10,100.

Main Language(s) of Instruction: English

Degrees and Diplomas: *Bachelor's Degree*: 4 yrs; *Master's Degree*: a further 2 yrs (or 3 yrs part-time)

Student Residential Facilities: For 1600 students

Libraries: c. 159,840 vols; c. 1500 periodicals

Publications: Uniswa Research Journal (biannually); Vice-Chancellor's Report; Prospectus; Science and Technology; Serialsin Swaziland University Libraries; Swaziland National Bibliography; Calendar; Uniswa Research Journal of Agriculture

Academic Staff *1999-2000:* Total: **252**

Student Numbers 1999-2000	MEN	WOMEN	TOTAL
All (Foreign Included)	1,724	1,701	**3,425**

NAZARENE TEACHER TRAINING COLLEGE
PO Box 14, Manzini
Tel: +268 505-4636
Fax: +268 505-5077

Principal: Z.M. Mavuso

Departments
Agriculture
Arts and Crafts (Crafts and Trades)
Education
English and Siswati (English)
Home Economics
Music and Physical Education (Music; Physical Education)
Science and Mathematics (Mathematics; Natural Sciences)
Social Studies

History: Founded 1933.

NGWANE TEACHER TRAINING COLLEGE
PO Box 474, Nhlangano
Tel: +268 207-8466
Fax: +268 207-8112

Principal: Peterson Dlamini

Departments
Agriculture
Arts and Crafts (Crafts and Trades)
Education
English and Siswati (English)
Home Economics

Music and Physical Education (Music; Physical Education)
Science and Mathematics (Mathematics; Natural Sciences)
Social Studies

History: Founded 1982.

WILLIAM PITCHER TRAINING COLLEGE
PO Box 87, Manzini
Tel: +268 505-2081
Fax: +268 505-4690

Principal: P. Magagula

Departments
Education
English and Religious Knowledge (English; Religious Studies)
English and Siswati (English)
History and Geography (Geography; History)
Science and Mathematics (Mathematics; Natural Sciences)

History: Founded 1962.

OTHER INSTITUTIONS

INSTITUTE OF DEVELOPMENT MANAGEMENT
PO Box 1534, Mbabane
Tel: +268 422-0734
Fax: +268 422-0733

Departments
Development Management (Management)

History: Founded 1979.

LUTHERAN FARMER TRAINING CENTRE
Private Bag, Piggs Peak
Tel: +268 437-1168

Departments
Farming (Agriculture)

MANANGA CENTRE FOR REGIONAL INTEGRATION AND MANAGEMENT DEVELOPMENT
PO Box 20, Mhlume
Tel: +268 416-3155
Fax: +268 416-3158
EMail: info@mananga.sz
Website: http://www.mananga.sz

Director: Ranga Taruvinga Tel: +268 416-3157

Departments
Agricultural Management, Training and Consultancy (Agricultural Management)

History: Founded 1972, acquired present status 1998.

MLALATINI DEVELOPMENT CENTRE
PO Box 547, Mbabane
Tel: +268 416-1171

Departments
Development Studies

History: Founded 1970.

NAZARENE NURSING COLLEGE
PO Box. 14, Manzini
Tel: +268 505-2211
Fax: +268 505-5292

Departments
Nursing

History: Founded 1968.

SWAZILAND COLLEGE OF TECHNOLOGY (SCOT)
PO Box 69, Mbabane H100
Tel: +268 404-2681 to +268 404-2683
Fax: +268 404-4521
EMail: scot@africaonline.co.sz

Principal: H. Sukati (1997-) Tel: +268 404-3684
Registrar: A.M Gule Tel: +268 404-8037

Faculties
Building and Civil Engineering (Building Technologies; Civil Engineering) *Dean*: C. Dube, *full-time staff:* 12, *students:* 104
Business Administration (Accountancy; Business Administration; Cooking and Catering; Hotel and Restaurant; Secretarial Studies) *Dean*: V. Nhlabatsi, *full-time staff:* 14, *students:* 108
Education and Technical Teaching (Business Education; Education; Technology Education; Vocational Education) *Dean*: T.P Sukati, *full-time staff:* 8, *students:* 79
Engineering and Science (Automotive Engineering; Computer Science; Electrical and Electronic Engineering; Engineering; Mechanical Engineering) *Dean*: M Maseko, *full-time staff:* 23, *students:* 181

History: Founded 1946, acquired present status and title 1975

Academic Year: August to June

Admission Requirements: Cambridge Overseas School Certificate (COSC) in approved subjects, such as English, Mathematics, Science, Accountancy

Fees: (Emalangeni): 4442 per annum

Main Language(s) of Instruction: English

Accrediting Agencies: AAT, City & Guilds, University of Swaziland

Degrees and Diplomas: *Diploma*: 3 yrs. City & Guilds

Student Services: Academic Counselling, Social Counselling, Sports Facilities, Health Services, Canteen

Student Residential Facilities: Yes

Special Facilities: Micro Teaching Studio

Libraries: Central Library, 17,458 vols

Publications: College Prospectus (annually)

Academic Staff 2000-2001	MEN	WOMEN	TOTAL
FULL-TIME	44	13	**57**

Student Numbers 2000-2001	MEN	WOMEN	TOTAL
All (Foreign Included)	356	116	**472**

Evening Students, 200

SWAZILAND INSTITUTE OF MANAGEMENT AND PUBLIC ADMINISTRATION (SIMPA)

PO Box 495, Mbabane 4100
Tel: +268 422-0740 +268 422-0745
Fax: +268 422- 0742
EMail: simpa@realnet.co.sz

Director: M. Khoza

Departments

Financial Management (Accountancy; Advertising and Publicity; Finance; Management; Marketing; Public Relations) *Head:* K Mmemma, *full-time staff: 4, part-time staff: 2*

Information Technology *Head:* Stephen Magongo, *full-time staff: 2*

Management (Communication Studies; Human Resources; Management) *Head:* Masilela Siboniso, *full-time staff: 5*

Public Administration

History: Founded 1965.

Academic Year: January to December

Main Language(s) of Instruction: English

Accrediting Agencies: ACCA London

Student Services: Sports Facilities, Health Services, Canteen

Student Residential Facilities: Yes

Special Facilities: Computer and Language laboratories

Libraries: Central Library 10,000 vols

Academic Staff 2000	MEN	WOMEN	TOTAL
FULL-TIME	10	5	15
PART-TIME	–	–	2
TOTAL	–	–	**17**

Student Numbers 2000	MEN	WOMEN	TOTAL
All (Foreign Included)	28	30	**58**

Evening Students, 25

Tanzania

INSTITUTION TYPES AND CREDENTIALS

Types of higher education institutions:

University
Institute
University College
Open University

School leaving and higher education credentials:

Advanced Certificate of Secondary Education
Diploma
Advanced Diploma
Bachelor Degree
Doctor
Master Degree
Postgraduate Diploma
Doctor of Philosophy

STRUCTURE OF EDUCATION SYSTEM

Pre-higher education:

Duration of compulsory education:

Age of entry: 7
Age of exit: 14

Structure of school system:

Basic First Stage
Type of school providing this education: Primary School (Lower Stage)
Length of programme in years: 4
Age level from: 7 to: 11

Basic Second Stage
Type of school providing this education: Primary School (Upper Stage)
Length of programme in years: 3
Age level from: 11 to: 14
Certificate/diploma awarded: Primary School Leaving Certificate

Lower Secondary
Type of school providing this education: Lower Secondary School
Length of programme in years: 4
Age level from: 14 to: 18
Certificate/diploma awarded: Certificate of Secondary Education (CSE)

Upper Secondary
Type of school providing this education: Upper Secondary School
Length of programme in years: 2
Age level from: 18 to: 20
Certificate/diploma awarded: Advanced Certificate of Secondary Education (ACSE)

School education:

Primary education lasts for seven years, divided into two stages of four and three years respectively. It culminates in the Primary School Leaving Certificate. Secondary school is divided into six Forms. Lower secondary school includes Forms I-IV and culminates in a national examination. Those who pass obtain the Certificate of Secondary Education (CSE). The curriculum is divided into four tracks: Agriculture, Commerce, Technical Skills, and Home Economics. The 1992 curriculum reform introduced into each stream three subjects: Social Studies, Computer Science and Unified Science. Unified Science is taught as an alternative to Biology, Chemistry and Physics, whereas Social Studies is offered as an alternative to Geography, History and Political Science. At the high school level, pupils study subject combinations of their choice, depending on their results in the examinations at the end of the first cycle of secondary education. Upper secondary school includes Forms V-VI and culminates in a national examination. Those who pass obtain the Advanced Certificate of Secondary Education (ACSE). Students must choose three principal subjects from the following: Languages, Arts and Social Sciences, Sciences and Mathematics, Commercial Subjects, and Military Science and Technology. The fourth subject is Political Education and is compulsory. Some secondary schools are technically oriented. The ACSE gives access to higher education. Students successfully completing the Certificate of Secondary Education may continue their studies at technical colleges which offer Certificate and Diploma level training.

Higher education:

Higher education is provided by nine universities and several training colleges and institutes. In addition there are several training centres designed primarily for Form VI-leavers. All higher education institutions are under the supervision of the Ministry of Science, Technology and Higher Education. The Universities are semi-autonomous and manage their own affairs under the Vice-Chancellor, who is appointed by the President of Tanzania. Their running costs are subsidized by the Government.

Academic year:

Classes from: September *to:* July

Languages of instruction:

English

452

Stages of studies:

Non-university level post-secondary studies (technical/vocational type):

In the last decade, the number of technical, vocational, and professional schools has increased substantially. They are the responsibility of the relevant Government Ministry under which they fall. The schools which award Certificates, Diplomas, Advanced Diplomas and Postgraduate Diplomas are categorized according to the type of programme offered. Diploma programmes, lasting two years, require Form VI and work experience. Certificates require two to three years' study. The Technician's Certificate requires two years of study. The Full Technician's Certificate requires three years of study. Advanced Diploma programmes, lasting three years, require Form VI and work experience. Postgraduate Diploma programmes require a Degree or Bachelor for admission and generally last one year.

University level studies:

University level first stage: *Undergraduate level*:

The first phase leads to a Bachelor's Degree. It usually lasts for three years, except for Pharmacy, Nursing, Veterinary Science and Engineering, which take four years, and Medicine, which takes five years. At the Open University courses generally last six years.

University level second stage: *Graduate level*:

A further one to three years' study leads to a Master's Degree. Postgraduate Diplomas require a Bachelor's Degree for admission and, generally, one year of study.

University level third stage: *Postgraduate level*:

A minimum of a further two years' original research and submission of a thesis leads to a PhD.

Teacher education:

Training of pre-primary and primary/basic school teachers

The Grade C Certificate entitles the holders to teach in the first two grades of primary education. The Grade B Certificate is obtained by promotion or by successfully completing a four-year course at a teacher training college after grade 7. The Grade A Certificate is obtained on successful completion of a two-year course at the end of Form IV and entitles the holder to teach in all seven grades of primary education.

Training of secondary school teachers

A two-year Diploma course at a College of National Education is required, after passing the ACSE, for teaching at lower secondary level. Teachers for upper secondary level should hold a Bachelor of Education or a Postgraduate Diploma in Education. Opportunities for in-service training have increased with the creation of village-based teacher training programmes.

Non-traditional studies:

Distance higher education

Distance education is offered by the Open University of Tanzania which opened in 1993 in Dar-es-Salaam. It provides courses in Law, Science, Arts, and Education leading to Bachelor Degrees.

Lifelong higher education
There are over 300 institutions offering specialist training at post-Form IV (or Form VI) level, leading to Certificates or Diplomas at semi-professional level in a wide variety of disciplines.

NATIONAL BODIES

Responsible authorities:

Ministry of Science, Technology and Higher Education
    Minister: Ng'wandu Pius
    PO Box 2645, Jamhuri Street
    Dar es Salaam
    Tel: +255(22) 211-2546   +255(22) 211-6331
    Fax: +255(22) 211-2805
    WWW: http://www.tanzania.go.tz/science.htm

Committee of Vice-Chancellors and Principals in Tanzania
    Chairman: Matthew Luhanga
    University of Dar es Salaam
    PO Box 33091
    Dar es Salaam

ADMISSIONS TO HIGHER EDUCATION

Admission to non university higher education studies

Name of secondary school credential required: Advanced Certificate of Secondary Education
For entry to: Diploma and Advanced Diplomas at postsecondary,vocational/technical/professional schools

Alternatives to credentials: Certificate of Secondary Education (11 years of primary and secondary school study) for Full Technician Certificate and Nurse Grade A Diploma.

Admission to university-level studies

Name of secondary school credential required: Advanced Certificate of Secondary Education
Minimum score/requirement: Passes in 5 approved subjects in Certificate of Secondary Education
For entry to: University studies.

Alternatives to credentials: Mature Age Entry Examination Scheme.

Foreign students admission

Admission requirements: Foreign students should have qualifications equivalent to the Advanced Certificate of Secondary Education or the East African General Certificate of Education (GCE) with 2 Advanced ("A") levels and 5 Ordinary ("O") levels.

Language requirements: Students must be fluent in English.

Application procedures:

Apply to: Ministry of Science, Technology and Higher Education
PO Box 2645, Jamhuri Street
Dar es Salaam
Tel: +255(22) 211-2546
Fax: +255(22) 211-2805
WWW: http://www.tanzania.go.tz/science.htm

Multilateral agreements concerning recognition of foreign studies

Name(s) of agreement(s): Convention on the Recognition of Studies, Certificates, Diplomas, Degrees and Other Academic Qualifications in Higher Education in the African States
Year of signature: 1981

STUDENT LIFE

Student expenses and financial aid

Student costs:

Home students tuition fees: Minimum: 900,000 (Tanzanian Shilling)
Maximum: 1,500,000 (Tanzanian Shilling)

Publications on student services and financial aid:

Title: Study Abroad, 2000-2001
Publisher: UNESCO
Year of publication: 1999

INTERNATIONAL COOPERATION AND EXCHANGES

Principal national bodies responsible for dealing with international cooperation and exchanges in higher education:

Ministry of Science, Technology and Higher Education
PO Box 2645, Jamhuri Street
Dar es Salaam
Tel: +255(22) 211-2546   +255(51) 211-6331
Fax: +255(22) 211-2805
WWW: http://www.tanzania.go.tz/science.htm

GRADING SYSTEM

Usual grading system in secondary school

Full Description: A-E principal passes; S subsidiary pass; F fail
Highest on scale: A

Pass/fail level: S

Lowest on scale: F

Main grading system used by higher education institutions

Full Description: Degrees are classified: 1st class Honours; 2nd class Honours (upper); 2nd class Honours (lower); pass

NOTES ON HIGHER EDUCATION SYSTEM

Data for academic year: 2000-2001

Source: International Association of Universities (IAU) updated from IBE website, 2001

INSTITUTIONS OF HIGHER EDUCATION

UNIVERSITIES AND UNIVERSITY COLLEGES

HUBERT KAIRUKI MEMORIAL UNIVERSITY (HKMU)
PO Box 65300, 322 Regent Estate, Dar es Salaam
Tel: +255(22) 270-0021/4
Fax: +255(22) 277-5591
EMail: info@hkmu.ac.tz
Website: http://www.angelfire.com

Vice-Chancellor: E. Mwaikambo

Faculties
Medicine (Anatomy; Behavioural Sciences; Biochemistry; Child Care and Development; Community Health; Dermatology; Epidemiology; Ethics; Gynaecology and Obstetrics; Medicine; Microbiology; Molecular Biology; Ophthalmology; Orthopedics; Paediatrics; Parasitology; Pathology; Pharmacology; Physiology; Psychiatry and Mental Health; Radiology; Sociology; Surgery) *Dean:* Paul Ndile
Nursing (Behavioural Sciences; Child Care and Development; Community Health; Ethics; Nursing; Psychiatry and Mental Health) *Dean:* P.P. Mella

History: Founded 1997.

Degrees and Diplomas: *Master Degree*

INTERNATIONAL MEDICAL AND TECHNOLOGICAL UNIVERSITY (IMTU)
PO Box 77594, Saruji Complex, New Bagamoyo Road, Dar es Salaam
Tel: +255(22) 264-7035
Fax: +255(22) 264-7038
EMail: imtu@afsat.com
Website: http://www.imtu.edu

Vice-Chancellor: H.D. Ballal

Deputy-Vice-Chancellor: V.S. Rakesh

Programmes
Engineering; Nursing; Pharmacy
Medicine (Anatomy; Forensic Medicine and Dentistry; Gynaecology and Obstetrics; Medicine; Ophthalmology; Paediatrics; Pathology; Pharmacology; Physiology; Surgery)

History: Founded 1995.

*• THE OPEN UNIVERSITY OF TANZANIA
Chuo Kikuu Huria Cha Tanzania (OUT)
PO Box 23409, Dar es Salaam
Tel: +255(51) 266-8445
Fax: +255(51) 266-8759
Telex: 24844 (Dar-es-Salaam)
EMail: avu@udsm.ac.tz; orvc@out.ac.tz

Vice-Chancellor: Geoffrey R.V. Mmari (1998-2004)
Tel: +255(51) 266-8455

Registrar: Egino.M. Chale Tel: +255(51) 266-8992

International Relations: Gaetan D. Msungu, Assistant to Vice-Chancellor Tel: +255(51) 266-8992

Faculties
Arts and Social Sciences (African Languages; Arts and Humanities; Business Administration; Business and Commerce; Economics; English; Geography; History; Linguistics; Literature; Philosophy; Religious Studies; Social Sciences) *Dean:* S.S. Kapalatu, *full-time staff:* 16, *part-time staff:* 58, *students:* 2,665
Education (Child Care and Development; Curriculum; Education; Educational Psychology; Philosophy of Education; Pre-school Education; Teacher Trainers Education) *Dean:* Edward Bagandanshwa, *full-time staff:* 11, *part-time staff:* 22, *students:* 1,779
Law *Dean:* M.C. Mukoyogo, *full-time staff:* 5, *part-time staff:* 17, *students:* 1,923
Science, Technology and Environmental Studies (Biology; Botany; Chemistry; Environmental Studies; Home Economics; Mathematics; Physics; Zoology) *Dean:* J.R. Mhoma, *full-time staff:* 7, *part-time staff:* 32, *students:* 813

Further Information: Also Regional Centres in: Arusha, Bukoba, Dar-Es-SAlaam, Dudoma, Dringa, Kibaha, Kigoma, Lindi, Mbeya, Moroguro, Moshi, Mtwara, Musoma, Mwanza, Ruwma, Stimyanga, Singuda, Sumbawanga, Tabora, Tanga, Zanzibar

History: Founded 1992.

Governing Bodies: University Council, comprising 22 members

Academic Year: January to November (January-March; March-June; June-August; August-November)

Admission Requirements: Advanced Certificate of secondary education examination, or equivalent, plus 3 credit of passes in Certificate of Secondary Education Examination

Fees: (Tanzanian Shilling): 120 per annum for Tanzanian students and US$ 1263 for foreign students

Main Language(s) of Instruction: English, Kiswahili

International Co-operation: University of Nairobi; Indira Ghandi National Open University; University of Abuja; Makerere University

Degrees and Diplomas: *Bachelor Degree:* Arts (BA); Arts in Education (BEd); Law (LLB); Science (BSc), 6 yrs

Student Services: Academic Counselling, Handicapped Facilities

Publications: Huria, Journal of the Open University of Tanzania (biannually)

Academic Staff 2000	MEN	WOMEN	TOTAL
FULL-TIME	50	13	63
PART-TIME	–	–	135
TOTAL	–	–	**198**
STAFF WITH DOCTORATE			
FULL-TIME	5	1	6
PART-TIME	–	61	61
TOTAL	**5**	**62**	**67**

Student Numbers 2000	MEN	WOMEN	TOTAL
All (Foreign Included)	5,849	889	**6,738**

• SOKOINE UNIVERSITY OF AGRICULTURE (SUA)

PO Box 3000, Chuo Kikuu, Morogoro 23
Tel: +255(23) 60-3511   +255(23) 56-4088
Fax: +255(23) 60-4651
Telex: 5508 univmo tz

Vice-Chancellor: A.B. Lwoga (1988-) Tel: +255(23) 56-4651 EMail: sua@hnettan.gn.apc.org

Registrar: H.O. Dihenga Tel: +255(23) 56-4653

International Relations: K.A. Msagati

Faculties

Agriculture (Agricultural Business; Agricultural Economics; Agricultural Education; Agricultural Engineering; Agriculture; Agronomy; Animal Husbandry; Crop Production; Food Science; Food Technology; Horticulture; Soil Science) *Dean:* N.A. Urio, *part-time staff:* 3, *students:* 115
Forestry and Nature Conservation (Ecology; Forestry) *Dean:* R.C. Ishengoma, *full-time staff:* 34, *students:* 120
Science (Natural Sciences) *Dean:* R.L.B Kurwijila, *full-time staff:* 9, *part-time staff:* 2
Veterinary Medicine (Veterinary Science) *Dean:* D.M. Kambarage, *full-time staff:* 42, *students:* 130

Institutes

Continuing Education *Director:* A. Isinika, *full-time staff:* 6
Development Studies *Director:* D.S. Kapinga, *full-time staff:* 9, *part-time staff:* 2
Research and Postgraduate Studies *Director:* W.S. Abeli, *full-time staff:* 2, *students:* 250

Centres

Computer (Computer Science) *Director:* R.R. Kazwala, *full-time staff:* 4, *part-time staff:* 4
Sustainable Rural Development (Rural Planning) *Director:* A.Z. Mattee

History: Founded 1984. Previously Faculty of Agriculture, Forestry and Veterinary Sciences of the University of Dar es Salaam. Also Main Campus (Morogoro), Mazimbu Campus (Morogoro), Olmotonyi (Arusha).

Governing Bodies: University Council, comprising 45 members

Academic Year: September-July (September-December; December-March; April-July)

Admission Requirements: Certificate of Secondary Education Examination, or East African Certificate of Education Ordinary ('O') level, or equivalent, with passes in 5 approved subjects obtained prior to sitting Advanced Certificate of Secondary Education examination, or East African Certificate of Education Advanced ('A') level, or equivalent. Two principal level passes at 'A' level with a total of not less than 4 points

Fees: (Shillings): 42,000 per annum

Main Language(s) of Instruction: English

International Co-operation: Agricultural University of Norway, As; Tuskegee University; University of East Anglia and 38 other universities worldwide

Degrees and Diplomas: *Bachelor Degree:* Agricultural Sciences, 3-4 yrs; *Master Degree:* Agricultural Sciences, a further 2 yrs; *Doctor of Philosophy:* Agricultural Sciences (PhD), 4-6 yrs

Student Services: Academic Counselling, Social Counselling, Employment Services, Nursery Care, Cultural Centre, Sports Facilities, Health Services, Canteen

Student Residential Facilities: For 1600 students

Special Facilities: Botanical Garden

Libraries: Central Library, 60,000 vols

Publications: Annual Report (annually); Academic Staff Organization; Convocation Newsletter; Research Newsletter; University Calendar; University Prospectus; SUASA Newsletter

Academic Staff *1999:* Total: c. 230

Student Numbers *1999:* All (Foreign Included): Men: c. 940 Women: c. 315 Total: c. 1,255

ST. AUGUSTINE UNIVERSITY OF TANZANIA (SAUT)

PO Box 307, Mwanza
Tel: +255(28) 255-2727
Fax: +255(28) 255-0167
EMail: saut@maf.org
Website: http://www.members.tripod.com/~saut

Vice Chancellor: Deogratias Rweyongeza
Tel: +255(28) 255-0560 EMail: saut@africaonline.co.tz

Faculties

Business Administration (Accountancy; Business Administration; Finance; Health Administration; Human Resources; Management; Marketing) *Dean (Acting):* Michael Nungu, *full-time staff:* 18, *part-time staff:* 4, *students:* 153
Humanities and Mass Communication (Arts and Humanities; Journalism; Mass Communication; Media Studies) *Dean (Acting):* Nkwabi Ngwanakilala, *full-time staff:* 13, *part-time staff:* 4, *students:* 118

History: Founded 1960. Acquired present status and title 1998.

Governing Bodies: Board of Trustees; University Council; Senate

Academic Year: August to May

Admission Requirements: Certificate of secondary education (CSEE). For undergraduate and advanced diploma, minimum 2

principal ('A') level passes in the advanced certificate of secondary education examination (ACSEE)

Fees: (Tanzania Shillings): Degree courses, 1,504,000; Advanced Diploma courses, 1,034,000; Certificate courses, 974,000

Main Language(s) of Instruction: English

Accrediting Agencies: The Higher Education Accreditation Council of Tanzania

Degrees and Diplomas: *Advanced Diploma*: Accountancy, Journalism, Materials Management; *Bachelor Degree*: Accountancy and Finance, Marketing, Human Resource Management, Materials Management; Print Media, Electronic Media, Public Relations, 3 yrs

Student Services: Academic Counselling, Social Counselling, Nursery Care, Sports Facilities, Health Services, Canteen

Student Residential Facilities: For 490 students

Special Facilities: SAUT Radio Station; Video Centre; Computer Centre. Photo Laboratory

Libraries: 15,000 volumes and 30 titles of periodicals

Academic Staff *1999-2000*	MEN	WOMEN	TOTAL
FULL-TIME	25	6	31
PART-TIME	7	1	8
TOTAL	**32**	**7**	**39**
STAFF WITH DOCTORATE			
FULL-TIME			3
PART-TIME			2
TOTAL			**5**

Student Numbers *1999-2000*	MEN	WOMEN	TOTAL
All (Foreign Included)	156	115	**271**
FOREIGN ONLY	9	8	17

TUMAINI UNIVERSITY (TU)

PO Box 2200, Moshi
Tel: +255(27) 275-291
Fax: +255(27) 275-3612
EMail: kcmc@eoltz.com

IRINGA UNIVERSITY COLLEGE
PO Box 200, Iringa
Tel: +255(61) 720-900
Fax: +255(61) 720-904
EMail: iuco@twiga.com

Faculties
Arts and Social Sciences (Arts and Humanities; Journalism; Social Sciences)
Business and Economics (Business Administration; Business and Commerce; Economics)
Law
Theology

History: Founded 1993. Acquired present status 1998.

KILIMANJARO CHRISTIAN MEDICAL COLLEGE
PO Box 2240, Moshi
Tel: +255(27) 275-4377
Fax: +255(27) 275-4381
EMail: kcmcadmin@kcmc.ac.tz
Website: http://www.kcmc.ac.tz

Faculties
Medicine
Nursing
Rehabilitation Sciences (Occupational Therapy; Rehabilitation and Therapy)

Institutes
Allied Health Science (Health Sciences)
Postgraduate Studies and Research (Medicine; Public Health; Urology)

History: Founded 1971.

MAKUMIRA UNIVERSITY COLLEGE
PO Box 55, Usa River, Arusha
Tel: +255(27) 254-8599
Fax: +255(811) 512-050
Website: http://www.makurima.ac.tz

UNIVERSITY OF BUKOBA (UOB)

PO Box 1725, Bukoba
Tel: +255(28) 222-0979
Fax: +255(28) 222-0979
EMail: uob@udsm.ac.tz

*• UNIVERSITY OF DAR ES SALAAM (UDSM)

PO Box 35091, Dar es Salaam
Tel: +255(22) 241-0500 +255(22) 241-0508
Fax: +255(22) 241-0078
Cable: University of Dar es salaam
EMail: cad@admin.ac.tz
Website: http://www.udsm.ac.tz

Vice-Chancellor: Matthew L. Luhanga (1991-)
Tel: +255(22) 241-0700 +255(22) 211-3654
EMail: vc@admin.udsm.ac.tz

Chief Administrative Officer: D.J. Mkude
Tel: +255(22) 241-0394 EMail: cado@admin.udsm.ac.tz

International Relations: P.N. Materu
Tel: +255(22) 241-0169 EMail: caco@admin.udsm.ac.tz

Faculties
Arts and Social Sciences (Administration; Agriculture; Anthropology; Arts and Humanities; Development Studies; Economics; Environmental Studies; Fine Arts; Geography; History; Industrial Management; International Relations; Literature; Performing Arts; Political Science; Public Administration; Regional Planning; Rural Studies; Social Sciences; Social Studies; Sociology; Statistics) *Dean:* Rwekaza S. Mukandala, *full-time staff:* 160, *students:* 1,612

459

Commerce and Management (Accountancy; Business and Commerce; Finance; Management; Marketing) *Dean*: E.S. Kaijage, *full-time staff: 41, students: 589*

Education (Adult Education; Curriculum; Education; Educational Administration; Educational Psychology; Educational Sciences; Physical Education; Sports) *Dean*: G.A. Malekela, *full-time staff: 44, students: 282*

Engineering (Chemical Engineering; Civil Engineering; Electrical Engineering; Engineering; Engineering Management; Mechanical Engineering) *Dean*: B.L.M. Mwamila, *full-time staff: 93, students: 912*

Law (Administrative Law; Civil Law; Criminal Law; International Law; Law) *Dean*: S.E. Mvungi, *full-time staff: 30, students: 545*

Science (Botany; Chemistry; Computer Science; Geology; Marine Biology; Mathematics; Microbiology; Natural Sciences; Physics; Zoology) *Dean*: R.T. Kivaisi, *full-time staff: 111, students: 589*

Institutes

Development Studies *Director*: H.M. Mlawa, *full-time staff: 23, students: 10*

Kiswahili Research (Native Language) *Director*: M. M Mulokozi, *full-time staff: 15*

Marine Science *(Zanzibar)* (Marine Science and Oceanography) *Director*: A.M. Dubi, *full-time staff: 17*

Production Innovation (Production Engineering) *Director*: O. Kaunde, *full-time staff: 15*

Resource Assessment (Agriculture; Demography and Population; Environmental Studies; Food Science; Natural Resources; Nutrition; Regional Planning; Water Management) *Director*: R.B.B. Mwalyosi, *full-time staff: 15*

History: Founded 1961 as University College, Dar es Salaam. Acquired present status and title 1970.

Governing Bodies: University Council

Academic Year: September to August (September-December; December-March; March-June; June-August)

Admission Requirements: Completion of form 6 at Tanzanian Schools in previous year. Candidates must also complete basic military training (National Service)

Fees: (Tanzanian Shillings): Tuition, 900,000 per annum

Main Language(s) of Instruction: English

Degrees and Diplomas: *Bachelor Degree*: Arts (BA); Commerce (Bcomm); Law (LLB); Science (BSc); Science in Computer Science (BScComp); Science in Electronics, Science and Communication (BScElectrSc & Comm), 3 yrs; Education (BEd); Pharmacy (BPharm); Science in Engineering (BSc(Eng)); Science in Nursing (BScNurs), 4 yrs; Lands and Architecture (BSc), 5-4 yrs; Arts in Education (BAEd); Science in Education (BScEd), a further 1 term; *Doctor*: Dentistry (DDS); Medicine (MD), 5 yrs; *Master Degree*: a further 2 yrs; *Doctor of Philosophy*: (PhD), 6 yrs

Student Services: Academic Counselling, Social Counselling, Employment Services, Foreign Student Adviser, Nursery Care, Cultural Centre, Sports Facilities, Language Programmes, Handicapped Facilities, Health Services, Canteen, Foreign Student Centre

Student Residential Facilities: Yes

460

Special Facilities: University Flower Nursery; Botanical Garden

Libraries: Main Library, c. 500,000 vols

Publications: Research Bulletin (biannually); Calendar; Annual Report

Press or Publishing House: DUP (1996) Ltd

Academic Staff *1999-2000:* Total: **564**

Staff with doctorate: Total: **481**

Student Numbers *1999-2000*	MEN	WOMEN	TOTAL
All (Foreign Included)	4,617	1,551	**6,168**

MUHIMBILI UNIVERSITY COLLEGE OF HEALTH SCIENCES
PO Box 65001, Dar es Salaam
Tel: +255(22) 215-0331
Fax: +255(51) 15196
Telex: muhmed41501tz
Cable: uniumed
EMail: principal@muchs.ac.tz

Principal: J.P. Mtabaji

Faculties

Dentistry *Dean*: B.S. Lembariti, *full-time staff: 17, students: 125*
Medicine *Dean*: F.S. Mhalu, *full-time staff: 119, students: 115*
Nursing *Dean*: Thecla W. Kohi, *full-time staff: 9, students: 25*
Pharmacy *Dean*: M.H.S. Chambuso, *full-time staff: 23, students: 85*

Institutes

Allied Health Sciences (Health Sciences; Paramedical Sciences) *Director*: S.S. Senya, *full-time staff: 23*

Development Studies *Director*: A.D. Kiwara, *full-time staff: 3, part-time staff: 3*

Primary Health Care and Continuing Health Education (Health Education) *Director*: F.D.E. Mtango, *full-time staff: 3*

Public Health *Director*: M.T. Leshabari, *full-time staff: 26*

Traditional Medicine (Medicine; Traditional Eastern Medicine) *Director*: R.L.A. Mahunah, *full-time staff: 10*

History: Founded 1991. Formerly Faculty of Medicine, University of Dar es Salaam.

UNIVERSITY COLLEGE OF LAND AND ARCHITECTURAL STUDIES
PO Box 35176, Dar es Salaam
Tel: +255(22) 275-004
Fax: +255(22) 754-48
Cable: ardhichuo
EMail: alfeo@uclas.ud.co.tz

Principal: A.M. Nikundine

Faculties

Architecture, Quantity Surveying and Urban and Rural Planning (Architecture) *Dean*: W.J. Kombe, *full-time staff: 39, students: 207*

Housing Studies and Building Research *Director*: J.O. Ngana, *full-time staff: 6*

Land Surveying, Land Management and Valuation and Environmental Engineering (Surveying and Mapping) *Head*: E. Mtalo, *full-time staff*: 38, *students*: 163

Centres
Continuing Education *Co-ordinator*: F.F. Halla, *full-time staff*: 3

History: Founded 1996. Acquired present status and title 1970.

Academic Staff *1999-2000*	MEN	WOMEN	TOTAL
FULL-TIME	15	1	16
PART-TIME	–	–	1
TOTAL	–	–	**17**

Staff with doctorate: Total: 1

Student Numbers *1999-2000*	MEN	WOMEN	TOTAL
All (Foreign Included)	129	25	**154**
FOREIGN ONLY	84	12	96

ZANZIBAR UNIVERSITY (ZU)
PO Box 2440, Zanzibar
Tel: +255(24) 223-2642
EMail: zanvarsity@zitec.org

OTHER INSTITUTIONS

CO-OPERATIVE COLLEGE OF MOSHI (CCOM)
PO Box 35176, Moshi
Tel: +255 (22) 215-0176
Fax: +255 (22) 150-178

Principal: S.A. Chambo

History: Founded 1963

COLLEGE OF AFRICAN WILDLIFE MANAGEMENT, MWEKA
PO Box 3031, Moshi
Tel: +255 (27) 320-255
Fax: +255 (27) 511-13

Principal: D.M. Gamassa Tel: +255(27) 783-887
EMail: dgamassa@twiga.com

Divisions
Wildlife Management (Teacher Training; Wildlife) *Director*: Wilfred Foya, *full-time staff*: 30, *students*: 154

History: Founded 1963

Governing Bodies: Drawing members from various African countries and International Conservation organizations

Academic Year: July to June

Fees: (US Dollars): 6000 per annum

Main Language(s) of Instruction: English

Degrees and Diplomas: *Diploma*: 2 yrs; *Advanced Diploma*: 1 yr; *Postgraduate Diploma*: 1 yr

Student Services: Academic Counselling, Social Counselling, Sports Facilities, Language Programmes, Health Services, Canteen

Student Residential Facilities: Yes

Special Facilities: Good Collection of Wildlife Specimens

Libraries: Central Library, c. 12,000 vols

Publications: News at Mweka (bi-annual)

COLLEGE OF BUSINESS EDUCATION
PO Box 1968, Dar es Salaam
Tel: +255(51) 31056

Principal: G.A.M. Chale

Departments
Business Administration

History: Founded 1965

COLLEGE OF EDUCATION ZANZIBAR (CEZ)
PO Box 1933, Zanzibar
Tel: +255(22) 275-004
Fax: +255(22) 754-48
EMail: alfeo@uclas.ud.co.tz

Education

COLLEGE OF NATIONAL EDUCATION
PO Box 533, Dar es Salaam

Principal: F.D. Ntemo

Departments
Education

DAR ES SALAAM INSTITUTE OF TECHNOLOGY (DIT)
PO Box 2958, Dar es Salaam
Tel: +255(22) 215-0174
Fax: +255(22) 215-2504
EMail: principaldit@intafrica.com

Principal: John W.A. Kondoro

Director, Finance and Administration: Mhina M. Setebe

Departments
Civil Engineering
Computer Engineering
Electrical Engineering
Electronics and Telecommunications Engineering (Electronic Engineering; Telecommunications Engineering)
General Studies
Laboratory Technology (Laboratory Techniques)
Mechanical Engineering

History: Founded 1957 as Dar es Salaam Technical Institute.

DAR ES SALAAM SCHOOL OF ACCOUNTANCY (DSA)

PO Box 9522, Dar es Salaam
Tel: +255(22) 285-1035
Fax: +255(22) 851-036

EASTERN AND SOUTHERN AFRICAN MANAGEMENT INSTITUTE

PO Box 3030, Arusha
Tel: +255(57) 8383
Fax: +255 (57) 8285
EMail: esami_arusha@marie.grn.org
Website: http://www.esamihq.org/

Director-General: Bonard Mwape

Programmes

Agriculture, Energy and Environment
Corporate Management and Entrepreneurship (Business Administration)
Finance and Banking (Banking; Finance)
Gender, Development and Entrepreneurship Management (Business Administration; Development Studies; Gender Studies)
Health Management (Health Administration)
Human Resource Management (Human Resources)
Information Technology
Policy Analysis and Public Sector (Political Science)
Transport and Infrastructure Development (Transport and Communications)

Schools

Business (Business Administration; Management; Public Relations; Secretarial Studies; Transport Management)

History: Founded 1974, acquired present status and title 1980.

INSTITUTE OF ACCOUNTANCY ARUSHA (IAA)

PO Box 2798, Arusha
Tel: +255(27) 250-1416
Fax: +255(27) 250-8421
EMail: iaa@habari.co.tz

INSTITUTE OF COMMUNITY DEVELOPMENT TENGERU (ICDT)

PO Box 1006, Tengeru, Arusha

INSTITUTE OF DEVELOPMENT MANAGEMENT

PO Box 1, Mzumbe, Morogoro
Tel: +255(56) 4380
Fax: +255(56) 4011

Principal: Moses M.D. Warioba

462

Departments

Development Management (Management)

History: Founded 1972

INSTITUTE OF FINANCE MANAGEMENT (IFM)

PO Box 3918, Shaaban Robert Street, Dar es Salaam
Tel: +255(51) 112-931 +255(51) 112-9314
Fax: +255(51) 112-935
Telex: 41969 IFM TZ
Cable: INSFINANCE
EMail: ifm@twiga.com

Principal: Harun Madoffe
Tel: +255(51) 114-817 +255(811) 322-505
EMail: principal@africaonline.co.tz
Director of Studies: Justine Mwandu Tel: +255(51) 123-468
EMail: ifm@twiga.com

Departments

Banking *Head*: Mtemi Naluyaga, *full-time staff:* 9, *students:* 58
Computer Science and Information Technology (Computer Science; Information Technology) *Head*: Elias Otaigo, *full-time staff:* 10, *part-time staff:* 5, *students:* 173
Executive Development and Consultancy *(Short Courses)* (Management)
Graduate Studies (Accountancy; Banking; Finance; Insurance; Taxation) *Head*: Paul Luchemba, *full-time staff:* 8, *part-time staff:* 4, *students:* 93
Insurance and Social Security Administration (Insurance; Public Administration) *Head*: Ignace Mowo, *full-time staff:* 7, *part-time staff:* 3, *students:* 43
Professional Accountancy (Accountancy) *Head*: Maximus Bishagazi, *full-time staff:* 14, *part-time staff:* 2, *students:* 371
Tax Management (Taxation) *Head*: Nicholaus Kessy, *full-time staff:* 9, *part-time staff:* 4, *students:* 72

Further Information: Global Distance Learning Centre (GDLC)

History: Founded 1972 by Act n°3 of Parliament. Offers courses at both undergraduate and postgradute levels, undertakes research and provides consultancy services in finance and related subjects. IFM has established, over the years, an international reputation for the quality of it courses. It has attracted students from Uganda, Ethiopia, Ghana, Kenya, Lesotho, Mozambique, Namibia, Sierra Leone, South Africa, Swaziland, Zambia and Zimbabwe

Governing Bodies: Council

Academic Year: October to September

Admission Requirements: Completion of form 6 ('A') level or equivalent with 2 principal level passes and at least 2 years of relevant working experience. 0r completion of form 4 ('O') level or equivalent with 5 credit passes including English and Mathematics plus at least 4 years of relevant working experience

Fees: (Tanzanian Shillings): Tuition, 1,044,200 (US$, 4824)

Main Language(s) of Instruction: English

International Co-operation: University of Strathclyde; University of Natal

Accrediting Agencies: Higher Learning Accreditation Council

Degrees and Diplomas: *Advanced Diploma*: Information Technology (ADIT); Accountancy (ADA); Banking (ADB); Computer Science (ADCS); Insurance (ADI); Social Security (ADSSA); Taxation (ADTM), 3 yrs; *Master Degree*: Finance (MScFin); *Postgraduate Diploma*: Finance (PGDFM); Taxation (PGDTM), 1 yr; Accountancy (PGDA), 1yr

Student Services: Academic Counselling, Social Counselling, Nursery Care, Health Services, Canteen

Student Residential Facilities: For 700 students

Special Facilities: Function Hall. Global Teleconference Centre. 2 Lecture Theatres

Libraries: Central Library, c. 15,000 vols

Publications: IFM newsletter, Provides institutional news (quarterly); The African Jounal of Finance and Management, Provides a scholarly forum for professionals and academics in these disciplines (bi-annual)

Academic Staff *1999-2000*	MEN	WOMEN	TOTAL
FULL-TIME	49	8	57
PART-TIME	–	–	18
TOTAL	–	–	**75**
STAFF WITH DOCTORATE			
FULL-TIME	2	1	3
PART-TIME	–	–	1
TOTAL	–	–	**4**

Student Numbers *1999-2000*	MEN	WOMEN	TOTAL
All (Foreign Included)	544	266	**810**
FOREIGN ONLY	10	6	16

Evening Students, 400

INSTITUTE OF RURAL DEVELOPMENT PLANNING (IRDP)
PO Box 138, Dodoma
Tel: +255(26) 230-2147

KIVUKONI ACADEMY OF SOCIAL SCIENCES
PO Box 9193, Dar es Salaam
Tel: +255(51) 820-019

Principal: John M.J. Magotti

Departments
Economics
Political Studies (Political Science)
Social Studies

History: Founded 1961

NATIONAL INSTITUTE OF TRANSPORT
PO Box 705, Dar es Salaam
Tel: +255(51) 48328

Departments
Transport Studies (Transport and Communications)

NATIONAL SOCIAL WELFARE TRAINING INSTITUTE
PO Box 3375, Dar es Salaam
Tel: +255(51) 74443

Principal: T.F. Ngalula

Departments
Social Welfare

History: Founded 1974

TANZANIA SCHOOL OF JOURNALISM (TSJ)
PO Box 4067, Dar es Salaam
Tel: +255(22) 270-0236
Fax: +255(22) 700-239
EMail: habari@tsj.tznet
Website: http://www.tznet.tsj.net/

Togo

INSTITUTION TYPES AND CREDENTIALS

Types of higher education institutions:

Université (University)
Ecole supérieure (Higher School)
Institut (Institute)

School leaving and higher education credentials:

Baccalauréat
Capacité en Droit
Diplôme de Technicien supérieur (DTS)
Diplôme universitaire de Technologie (DUT)
Diplôme universitaire d'Etudes générales (DUEG)
Diplôme universitaire d'Etudes littéraires (DUEL)
Diplôme universitaire d'Etudes scientifiques (DUES)
Diplôme d'Ingénieur de Travaux
Licence
Licence d'Enseignement
Certificat d'Aptitude au Professorat de l'Enseignement secondaire (CAPES)
Diplôme d'Ingénieur de Conception
Doctorat en Médecine
Maîtrise
Agrégation
Certificat d'Etudes spécialisées (CES)
Diplôme d'Etudes approfondies (DEA)
Diplôme d'Etudes supérieures (DES)
Doctorat d'Ingénieur
Doctorat de Spécialité de Troisième Cycle
Doctorat unique

STRUCTURE OF EDUCATION SYSTEM

Pre-higher education:

Duration of compulsory education:

Age of entry: 5
Age of exit: 15

Structure of school system:

Primary

Type of school providing this education: Ecole primaire or Enseignement du premier degré

Length of programme in years: 6

Age level from: 5 to: 11

Certificate/diploma awarded: Certificat de Fin d'Etudes de l'Enseignement du premier Degré (CEPD)

First Cycle Secondary

Type of school providing this education: Ecole secondaire du Premier Cycle or Enseignement du Second Degré

Length of programme in years: 4

Age level from: 11 to: 15

Certificate/diploma awarded: Brevet d'Etudes du Premier Cycle du Second Degré (BEPC)

Technical Secondary

Type of school providing this education: Enseignement Technique Cycle Court

Length of programme in years: 3

Age level from: 11 to: 14

Certificate/diploma awarded: Certificat d'Aptitude Professionnelle (CAP)

Second Cycle Secondary

Type of school providing this education: Ecole secondaire Deuxième Cycle ou Enseignement du Troisième Degré

Length of programme in years: 3

Age level from: 15 to: 18

Certificate/diploma awarded: Baccalauréat/Diplôme de Bachelier de l'Enseignement du Troisième Degré

Technical

Type of school providing this education: Ecole secondaire technique ou Enseignement Technique Cycle Long

Length of programme in years: 3

Age level from: 15 to: 18

Certificate/diploma awarded: Diplôme de Bachelier de l'Enseignement Technique

School education:

Primary school lasts for five years and leads to the Certificat de Fin d'Etudes de l'Enseignement du premier Degré. Pupils are streamed at the end of primary schooling for entry to the first cycle of secondary education. This cycle of lower secondary education lasts for four years (6ème, 5ème, 4ème, and 3ème) after which students take the examination for the Brevet d'Etudes du Premier Cycle du Second Degré. Students are then streamed again and oriented into vocational or training institutes or enter the university preparatory cycle at the Lycée. This second cycle lasts three years and is called 3ème degré (2ème, 1ère and terminale). The Baccalauréat (1ère partie) is taken on completion of the '1ère'. On completion of this cycle, pupils take the examinations for the Baccalauréat 2ème partie. The

Certificat de Fin d'Etudes secondaires, which represents class attendance in the last year of secondary school, is not equivalent to the Baccalauréat.

Higher education:

Higher education in Togo is provided by the Université du Bénin, recently renamed Université de Lomé, which includes several faculties, higher schools and institutes (including a recently founded National Institute of Educational Sciences) and several private schools and institutes. A second university, the Université de Kara, has been founded but is not yet operational. The university is French orientated and modelled on similar French institutions. In 1972, major reforms were implemented in the curriculum and structure of courses. Education and scientific research in Togo is the responsibility of the Ministry of National Education and Research.

Academic year:

Classes from: October *to:* June

Long vacation from: 1 July *to:* 30 September

Languages of instruction:

French

Stages of studies:

University level studies:

University level first stage: *Premier Cycle*:

The first cycle of two years' study leads, in the Science Faculty, to the Diplôme universitaire d'Etudes scientifiques (DUES), and, in the Arts Faculty, to the Diplôme universitaire d'Etudes littéraires (DUEL) or the Diplôme d'Etudes universitaires générales (DEUG).

University level second stage: *Deuxième Cycle*:

In Arts and Humanities, Science, Law, Economics and Management, a second stage corresponding to second-cycle studies leads, after one year, to the Licence. Students then have to obtain a Certificat de Maîtrise and submit a short thesis. In Science, the Maîtrise may be obtained without holding a Licence. The course takes one year from Licence (Humanities) or two years from DUES (Science). A Diplôme d'Ingénieur de conception is awarded in Agriculture and Engineering after five years' study.

University level third stage: *Troisième Cycle*:

The Diplôme d'Etudes supérieures spécialisées (DESS) and the Diplôme d'Etudes approfondies (DEA) represent completion of a further one or two years of academic studies beyond the Maîtrise. The Doctorat de Spécialité de Troisième Cycle requires one or two years' further study beyond the DES or DEA. It is now being replaced by the Doctorat unique, awarded two or three years after the DEA and the presentation of a major thesis. In Medicine, the professional qualification of Docteur en Médecine is awarded to candidates who have undertaken seven years' study. The Doctorat d'Ingénieur requires three years' study beyond the Diplôme d'Ingénieur.

Teacher education:

Training of pre-primary and primary/basic school teachers

Primary school teachers must hold the Baccalauréat and follow a one-year course at a teacher training institution called Ecole Normale d'Instituteurs (ENI). Studies lead to the Certificat de Fin d'Etudes Normales des Instituteurs (CFEN-ENI).

Training of secondary school teachers

Secondary school teachers are mostly trained at the University. At lower secondary level, teachers must hold a three-year degree or a DEUG plus one year. A one-year course is open to practising teachers. Teachers at the upper secondary level must hold a Licence d'Enseignement or a Maîtrise and a Diplôme de Formation pédagogique. Moreover, in public education, access to teaching positions normally requires the passing of a competitive examination (CAPES).

Training of higher education teachers

Teachers at this level must theoretically hold the Doctorat de troisième Cycle. However, owing to a shortage of Doctorats, many university lecturers are temporary lecturers (Vacataires). The Agrégation de l'Enseignement du second Degré and the Agrégation de l'Université are certificates of outstanding proficiency in teaching and are obtained by examination before a committee. The Agrégation is not in itself a degree and requires no specific course or research qualification.

NATIONAL BODIES

Responsible authorities:

Ministry of National Education and Research (Ministère de l'Education nationale et de la Recherche)
  Minister: Koffi Sama
  Secretary-General: Adji Otèth Ayassor
  BP 398 or BP 12195
  Lomé
  Tel: +228(21) 24-73; +228(22) 09-93
  Fax: +228(22) 07-83

Ministry of Technical Education and Professional Training and Crafts (Ministère de l'Enseignement technique et de la Formation professionnelle)
  Minister: Edoh K. Maurille Agbobli
  Secretary-General: Yawo Amouzouvi
  BP 398
  Lomé
  Tel: +228(21) 85-17
  Fax: +228(21) 89-34

ADMISSIONS TO HIGHER EDUCATION

Admission to university-level studies

Name of secondary school credential required: Capacité en Droit
For entry to: Only for registration in first year of Faculty of Law

Name of secondary school credential required: Baccalauréat
Minimum score/requirement: 10/20
For entry to: All institutions

Alternatives to credentials: Special entrance examination for those who do not hold the Baccalauréat or obtain between 10 and 12/20 in the Capacité en Droit examination

Entrance exams required: Every faculty organizes its own test every year

Numerus clausus/restrictions: No

Foreign students admission

Definition of foreign student: Students who do not have Togolese nationality

Quotas: Foreign student quotas are fixed each year for technical studies

Admission requirements: Foreign students must hold a Baccalauréat or an equivalent qualification. Students who do not hold the Baccalauréat must sit for an entrance examination for the faculties of Letters, Law, Science, Economics and Management.

Entry regulations: Foreign students must have a visa (except for students from CEDEAO countries) and a residence permit.

Health requirements: Students must have a health certificate.

Language requirements: Students must have a good knowledge of French. Courses are organized by the Village du Bénin to become proficient in French.

Application procedures:

Apply to: Université de Lomé
  B.P. 1515
  Lomé
  Tel: +228(21) 30-27
  Fax: +228(21) 87-84
  Telex: 5258 ubto
  EMail: ub-lomé@tgrefer.org
  WWW: http://www.ub.tg

Recognition of studies and qualifications:

Studies pursued in home country (System of recognition/accreditation): There is a university equivalence commission that examines the dossiers of foreign or Togolese students who wish to change courses

Studies pursued in foreign countries (bodies dealing with recognition of foreign credentials):
Commission nationale de Reconnaissance et d' Equivalence des Etudes, Diplômes, Grades et Titres
  Head: Ananivi Doh
  Secretary: Akouété Edan
  BP 1515
  Lomé
  Tel: +228(21) 51-13
  Fax: +228(21) 85-95
  WWW: http://www.ub.tg

  Deals with credential recognition for entry to: Profession
  Services provided and students dealt with: Meets every three months to study Diplomas for professional purposes

Multilateral agreements concerning recognition of foreign studies

Name(s) of agreement(s): CAMES

Convention of Arusha
Year of signature: 1981

Convention on the Recognition of Studies, Certificates, Diplomas, Degrees and Other Academic Qualifications in Higher Education in the African States
Year of signature: 1981

STUDENT LIFE

Main student services at national level

Centre national des Oeuvres universitaires (CNOU)
  B.P. 1515
  Lomé

  Category of services provided: Social and welfare services

Direction des Affaires académiques et de la Scolarité, Université de Lomé
  B.P. 1515
  Lomé
  Tel: +228(21) 30-27
  Fax: +228(21) 87-84
  WWW: http://www.ub.tg

  Category of services provided: Academic and career counselling services

Health/social provisions

Social security for home students: No

Social security for foreign students: No

Special student travel fares:

By road: No
By rail: No
By air: No

Student expenses and financial aid

Student costs:

Average living costs: 50,000 (CFA Franc)
Home students tuition fees: Minimum: 5,500 (CFA Franc)
Foreign students tuition fees: Minimum: 5,500 (CFA Franc)
Maximum: 200,000 (CFA Franc)

Bodies providing information on student financial aid:

Direction des Bourses et Stages
Lomé
398
Tel: +228(21) 49-91
Fax: +228(21) 57-98

Publications on student services and financial aid:

Title: Study Abroad 2000-2001
Publisher: UNESCO/IBE
Year of publication: 1999

INTERNATIONAL COOPERATION AND EXCHANGES

Principal national bodies responsible for dealing with international cooperation and exchanges in higher education:

Direction de l'Information des Relations Externes et de la Coopération Internationale
Director: Koffi Akibodé
BP 1515
Lomé
Tel: +228 25-01-50
Fax: +228 22-85-95
WWW: http://www.ub.tg

Direction des Affaires académiques et de la Scolarité
Director: Nicoué Gayibor
Principal Secretary: Messan Anani
BP 398
Lomé
Tel: +228 21-39-26
Fax: +228 22-07-83

Direction des Etudes et Programmes de l'Université de Lomé
Director: Ananivi Doh
B.P. 1515
Lomé
Tel: +228-25-08-37
Fax: +228-21-85-95
Telex: 5258 ubto

GRADING SYSTEM

Usual grading system in secondary school

Full Description: The grading system is as follows: 16-20: très bien (very good), 14-16: bien (good), 12-14: assez bien (quite good), 10-12: passable (average).
Highest on scale: 20
Pass/fail level: 10
Lowest on scale: 0

Main grading system used by higher education institutions

Full Description: Grading is usually on a scale of 0-20 (maximum): 16-20: très bien (very good), 14-16: bien (good), 12-14: assez bien (quite good), 10-12: passable (average).
Highest on scale: 20
Pass/fail level: 10
Lowest on scale: 0

Other main grading systems

Très bien; Bien; Assez bien; Passable; Refusé

NOTES ON HIGHER EDUCATION SYSTEM

Data for academic year: 2000-2001
Source: Université de Lomé, 2001

INSTITUTIONS OF HIGHER EDUCATION

UNIVERSITIES

*• UNIVERSITY OF LOME
Université de Lomé (UL)
BP 1515, Lomé, Préf.du Golfe
Tel: +228(21) 30-27
Fax: +228(21) 87-84
Telex: 5258 ubto
EMail: ub-lomé@tgrefer.org
Website: http://www.ub.tg

Recteur, Chancelier: Ampah Johnson (1999-)
Tel: +228(21) 52-41 Fax: +228(25) 52-41

Secrétaire général: Abalo Tabo Tel: +228(21) 53-61
Fax: +228(21) 85-95

International Relations: Koffi Akibode Tel: +228(25) 01-50
Fax: +228(22) 85-95 EMail: ub.lome@tg.refea.org

Faculties
Economics and Management *(FASEG)* (Accountancy; Computer Science; Economics; Management; Mathematics; Statistics)
Law *(FDD)* (Administrative Law; Constitutional Law; International Law; Law; Public Law)
Letters and Human Sciences *(FLESH)* (Anthropology; Arts and Humanities; English; Geography; German; History; Linguistics; Philosophy; Sociology; Spanish)
Medicine and Pharmacy *(FMMP)* (Medicine; Pharmacy)
Science *(FDS)* (Chemistry; Mathematics; Natural Sciences; Physics)

Higher Schools
Agriculture *(ESA)* (Agricultural Economics; Agricultural Engineering; Agriculture; Animal Husbandry; Rural Planning; Rural Studies)
Biological and Food Techniques (Biological and Life Sciences; Environmental Studies; Food Technology; Water Management; Water Science)
Engineering *(ENSI)* (Civil Engineering; Computer Engineering; Electrical Engineering; Engineering; Mechanical Engineering)
Medical Assistants *(EAM)* (Health Sciences)
Secretarial Studies *(ESSD)*

Institutes
Educational Sciences *(INSE)* (Education; Educational Sciences; Teacher Training)
Management Technology *(IUT)* (Management; Technology)

Centres
Computer *(CIC-CAFMICRO)* (Computer Engineering; Computer Science; Information Technology; Microelectronics; Systems Analysis)
Distance Learning Education *(CFAD)* (Educational Sciences; Law)

Research Units
Demography *(URD)* (Demography and Population)

History: Founded 1970 replacing former Centre d'Enseignement supérieur, established 1962 with sections in Dahomey and Togo under an agreement between the governments of the two countries and government of France. A State institution enjoying academic and financial autonomy.

Governing Bodies: Grand Conseil, comprising 13 members; Conseil de l'Université, comprising 21 members

Academic Year: October to July (October-February; March-July)

Admission Requirements: Secondary school certificate (baccalauréat) or equivalent

Fees: (Francs CFA): 5500; foreign students, 5500-200,000

Main Language(s) of Instruction: French

Degrees and Diplomas: *Capacité en Droit*: Law, 2 yrs; *Diplôme de Technicien supérieur (DTS)*: Laboratory Techniques, 3 yrs; *Diplôme universitaire de Technologie (DUT)*: Business Administration; Engineering, 3 yrs; *Diplôme universitaire d'Etudes générales (DUEG)*: 2 yrs; *Diplôme universitaire d'Etudes littéraires (DUEL)*: Arts and Humanities, 2 yrs; *Diplôme universitaire d'Etudes scientifiques (DUES)*: Science, 2 yrs; *Diplôme d'Ingénieur de Travaux*: 3 yrs; *Licence*: Arts and Humanities; Economics; Educational Sciences; Law; Science, 3 yrs; *Diplôme d'Ingénieur de Conception*: Agronomy; Civil Engineering; Electrical Engineering; Mechanical Engineering, 5 yrs; *Doctorat en Médecine*: 7 yrs; *Maîtrise*: 1 yr after Licence; *Certificat d'Etudes spécialisées (CES)*: Paediatrics; Surgery; *Diplôme d'Etudes approfondies (DEA)*: Science; *Doctorat d'Ingénieur*: 3 yrs; *Doctorat de Spécialité de Troisième Cycle*. Also Assistant médical, Paramedicine, 3 yrs.

Student Residential Facilities: For c. 2990 students

Libraries: Central Library, 70,000 vols; Specialized libraries

Publications: Actes des Journées Scientifiques; Annales de l'Université du Bénin; Annuaire de l'Université du Bénin (annually)

Press or Publishing House: Presses de l'Université du Bénin

Academic Staff *1999*: Full-Time: c. 390 Part-Time: c. 260 Total: c. 650

Student Numbers *1999*: All (Foreign Included): c. 13,125 Foreign Only: c. 480

OTHER INSTITUTIONS

AFRICAN SCHOOL OF ARCHITECTURE AND TOWN PLANNING
Ecole africaine des Métiers de l'Architecture et de l'Urbanisme (EAMAU)
BP 2067, 422, rue des Balises, Quartier Doumassesse, Lomé
Tel: +228(21) 62-53
Fax: +228(22) 06-52
EMail: eamau@cafe.tg
Website: http://www.eamau.tg.refer.org

Directeur général: N'Da N' Guessan Kouadio (1997-)
Tel: +228(25) 31-96 EMail: kouadio07@yahoo.com

International Relations: Gabriel Yabo Ogalama
Tel: +228(21) 70-79 EMail: gogalama@tg.refer.org

Architecture; Town Planning; Urban Management (Architecture; Town Planning; Urban Studies)

History: Founded 1975

ADVANCED TEACHERS' TRAINING SCHOOL ATAKPAMÉ
Ecole normale supérieure d'Atakpamé (ENS)
BP 7, Atakpamé, Ogou
Tel: +228(40) 00-61
Directeur: Adji Sardji Aritiba (2000-)
Directeur des Etudes: Koffi Séto Notokpe

Departments
Art and Science Education (Art Education; Science Education) *Head*: Tohonon Gbeasor, *full-time staff: 13, part-time staff: 15, students: 235*
English (Education; English; French; Linguistics) *Head*: Ms Degboe , *full-time staff: 2, part-time staff: 1, students: 29*

French (Civics; Education; French; Linguistics) Djabare , *full-time staff: 4, students: 32*
History and Geography (Civics; Education; Geography; History) *Head*: Nadjombé and Notokpe, *full-time staff: 2, part-time staff: 5, students: 37*
Mathematics (Chemistry; Education; Mathematics; Physics) *Head*: M. Sewonou, *full-time staff: 1, part-time staff: 3, students: 37*
Natural Sciences (Chemistry; Education; Natural Sciences; Physics) *Head*: M. Akpagnonité, *full-time staff: 3, students: 76*
Physics and Chemistry (Chemistry; Education; Mathematics; Physics) *Head*: M. Mensah, *full-time staff: 1, part-time staff: 6, students: 24*

History: Founded 1968, acquired present status and title 1983

Academic Year: September to June

Admission Requirements: Secondary school certificate (baccalauréat)

Fees: None (students are granted monthly allowances)

Main Language(s) of Instruction: French

Degrees and Diplomas: *Certificat d'Aptitude au Professorat de l'Enseignement secondaire (CAPES)*: English, French, History and Geography (CFENS); Mathematics, Natural Sciences, Physics and Chemistry (CFENS), 3 yrs

Student Services: Sports Facilities, Canteen

Student Residential Facilities: Yes

Libraries: Main Library and Department Libraries

Academic Staff *1999-2000*	MEN	WOMEN	TOTAL
FULL-TIME	12	1	13
PART-TIME	15	–	15
TOTAL	**27**	**1**	**28**
STAFF WITH DOCTORATE			
FULL-TIME			4
PART-TIME			15
TOTAL			**19**

Student Numbers *1999-2000*	MEN	WOMEN	TOTAL
All (Foreign Included)	196	39	**235**

473

Tunisia

INSTITUTION TYPES AND CREDENTIALS

Types of higher education institutions:

Université (University)
Institut supérieur (Higher Institute)
Ecole supérieure (Higher School)
Institut supérieur des Etudes technologiques (Higher technological Institute)

School leaving and higher education credentials:

Baccalauréat
Certificat d'Aptitude
Diplôme universitaire de Technologie (DUT)
Technicien supérieur
Certificat de Capacité
Diplôme d'Etudes universitaires de Premier Cycle (DEUPC)
Diplôme universitaire d'Etudes littéraires
Diplôme universitaire d'Etudes scientifiques
Diplôme
Licence
Diplôme d'Ingénieur
Maîtrise
Diplôme d'Architecte
Diplôme d'études supérieures spécialisées (DESS)
Diplôme de Recherches approfondies
Diplome d'Etudes approfondies (DEA)
Doctorat

STRUCTURE OF EDUCATION SYSTEM

Pre-higher education:

Duration of compulsory education:

Age of entry: 6
Age of exit: 16

Structure of school system:

Basic First Stage
Type of school providing this education: Enseignement de Base (Premier Cycle)
Length of programme in years: 6
Age level from: 6 to: 12

Basic Second Stage
Type of school providing this education: Enseignement de Base (Second Cycle)
Length of programme in years: 3
Age level from: 12 to: 15
Certificate/diploma awarded: Diplôme de Fin d'Etudes de l'Enseignement de Base

Secondary
Type of school providing this education: Ecole secondaire
Length of programme in years: 4
Age level from: 15 to: 19
Certificate/diploma awarded: Baccalauréat

School education:

Basic education lasts for nine years, divided into two cycles of six and three years respectively. It culminates in the Diplôme de Fin d'Etudes de l'Enseignement de Base. Secondary education lasts four years and is divided into two stages (two years of general education and two years of prespecialized education). It leads to the Baccalauréat in Arts, Mathematics, Experimental Sciences, Technology, Economy and Management. Vocational studies are available for those who have completed basic education. They lead to a Certificat d'Aptitude professionnelle (CAP). Students who have obtained 12 out of 20 at the CAP or students who have completed the first cycle of secondary education may apply to study for a Brevet de Technicien professionnel (BTP).

Higher education:

Higher education is mainly provided by universities and their numerous higher institutes and schools. There are now a total of eight universities, one of them being private. Institutions of higher education come under the responsibility of the Ministry of Higher Education or the Ministry most appropriate to their speciality. The Conseil supérieur de l'Education, set up in 1988, is presided over by the Prime Minister and composed of all ministers having an interest in education and higher education. It is called upon to give its opinion on all major matters including financial policy. The Comité national d'Evaluation, created in 1995, evaluates higher education and university research as well as project results. Twelve new institutions opened in the year 2000-2001.

Main laws/decrees governing higher education:

Decree: Loi n° 2000-67   Year: 2000
Concerns: Modifies Law n° 89-70 of 1989

Decree: Loi n° 2000-73   Year: 2000
Concerns: Private higher education

Decree: Arrêté du Ministère de l'Enseignement supérieur   Year: 1996
Concerns: Composition of the Comité national d'Evaluation

Decree: Décret n °95-470   Year: 1995
Concerns: Comité national d'évaluation

Decree: Loi n° 90-72   Year: 1990
Concerns: Higher agricultural education

Decree: Loi n° 89-70   Year: 1989
Concerns: Organization of Higher Education

Academic year:

Classes from: October *to:* June

Long vacation from: 1 July *to:* 30 September

Languages of instruction:

Arabic, French

Stages of studies:

Non-university level post-secondary studies (technical/vocational type):

Higher technical education is mainly offered in higher institutes of technological studies (Instituts supérieurs des Etudes technologiques) where studies last for two-and-a-half years. Entrance is on a competitive basis.Training is also offered in such fields as Agriculture, Nursing, Transport, Communications and Journalism. Studies come under the responsibility of the relevant ministries. A Brevet de Technicien supérieur is conferred after three years.

University level studies:

University level first stage: *Premier Cycle*:
The first cycle of university studies lasts for two years and leads to the Diplôme d'Etudes universitaires du 1er Cycle. In Engineering, studies start with two years in a preparatory institute, after which candidates must sit for a competitive examination. Engineering studies last for five years and lead to the Diplôme national d'Ingénieur.

University level second stage: *Deuxième Cycle*:
The second cycle lasts for a further two years and leads to the award of the Maîtrise or Licence. In Engineering, studies last for three years after the two preparatory years and lead to the Diplôme d'Ingénieur. The Ministry is introducing a Diplôme des Etudes supérieures technologiques. The Diplôme d' Etudes supérieures spécialisées (DESS) is conferred after one year's study following upon the Maîtrise. There is a reform of studies leading to the Maîtrise and in Engineering.

University level third stage: *Troisième Cycle*:
The third cycle leads to a Diplôme d'Etudes approfondies (DEA) after a further one or two years' study and to the Doctorat. The Doctorat de 3ème Cycle and the Doctorat d'Etat have been replaced by a single Doctorate. A Doctorate in Agricultural Sciences was introduced in 1993. In Medicine, the professional title of Docteur en Médecine is conferred after seven years.

Teacher education:

Training of pre-primary and primary/basic school teachers

Primary school teachers are trained in higher institutes (Instituts supérieurs de Formation des Maîtres) where they study for two years. They must hold the Baccalauréat.

Training of secondary school teachers

Secondary school teachers are usually university graduates in the arts and sciences. On-site training and formal retraining through continued education are also provided. A Doctorat en Sciences de l'Education, a Certificat d'Enseignement supérieur en Sciences de l'Education et en Pédagogie and a Maîtrise d'Education civique have been created for the teachers of the second cycle of basic education and secondary education.

Training of higher education teachers

The Maîtres-Assistants must hold the new Doctorate. Assistants must hold the Diplôme d'Etudes approfondies and have started work on their doctoral thesis. Maîtres de conférence must hold a university research degree. In some disciplines, there exists a Tunisian form of Agrégation which is awarded after taking a competitive examination.

Non-traditional studies:

Lifelong higher education

Tunisia now has an Institute of Education and Continued Education which caters for primary and secondary school teachers. Lifelong training is also offered in Agriculture. Students can then become Technical Assistants, Assistant Engineers and Works Engineers. Nine institutions offer this kind of training.

NATIONAL BODIES

Responsible authorities:

Ministry of Higher Education (Ministère de l'Enseignement supérieur)
Minister: Sadok Chaâbane
Secretary of State: Montacer Ouaîli
International Relations: Noomane Ghodbane
Avenue Ouled Haffouz
1030 Tunis
Tel: +216(71) 784-170
Fax: +216(71) 786-711
Telex: 1380 minsup tn
EMail: mes@mes.tn
WWW: http://www.mes.tn

ADMISSIONS TO HIGHER EDUCATION

Admission to non university higher education studies

Name of secondary school credential required: Baccalauréat

Admission to university-level studies

Name of secondary school credential required: Baccalauréat

Foreign students admission

Admission requirements: Foreign students must hold the Baccalauréat or an equivalent qualification. For some faculties, an entrance examination is also required. They are entitled to social and welfare services and to grants and scholarships.

Entry regulations: A visa is necessary

Language requirements: Students must have a good knowledge of French and in some cases of Arabic (Theology, Arts, Law and Economics). A preparatory course in Arabic is organized at the Institut Bourguiba des Langues vivantes.

Recognition of studies and qualifications:

Studies pursued in foreign countries (bodies dealing with recognition of foreign credentials): Commission nationale d'Equivalence et d'Agrément des Ecoles techniques, Ministère de l'Enseignement supérieur
    Rue Ouled Haffouz
    Tunis
    Tel: +216(71) 784-170
    Fax: +216(71) 786-711
    Telex: 1380 minsup tn
    EMail: mes@mes.tn
    WWW: http://www.mes.tn

Multilateral agreements concerning recognition of foreign studies

Name(s) of agreement(s): Convention on the Recognition of Studies, Diplomas and Degrees in Higher Education in the Arab States
Year of signature: 1978

References to further information on foreign student admissions and recognition of studies

Title: Guide du bachelier en langue française
Publisher: Office national des Oeuvres universitaires

STUDENT LIFE

Main student services at national level

Office national des Oeuvres universitaires (ONOU)

57 rue de Palestine

Tunis

Category of services provided: Social and welfare services

National student associations and unions

Union générale des Etudiants tunisiens

13 rue Essadikia

Tunis

Student expenses and financial aid

Student costs:

Average living costs: 4,000 (Tunisian Dinar)

Bodies providing information on student financial aid:

Direction de la Coopération internationale et des Relations extérieures, Ministère de l'Enseignement supérieur

Avenue Ouled Haffouz

1030 Tunis

Tel: +216(71) 786-300

Fax: +216(1) 791-424

Category of students: Students from all countries having a Secondary School Leaving Certificate (French or Arabic compulsory)

Office national du Tourisme tunisien

1, avenue Mohamed-V

Tunis

Tel: +216(71) 835-844

Fax: +216(71) 350-997

WWW: http://www.tourismtunisia.com

Category of students: Students from Francophone and Arab countries in the field of hotel management and tourism

Publications on student services and financial aid:

Title: Study Abroad 2000-2001

Publisher: UNESCO/IBE

Year of publication: 1999

GRADING SYSTEM

Usual grading system in secondary school

Full Description: 0-20; 16-20 très bien; 14-15 bien; 12-13 assez bien; 10-11 passable; 0-9 insuffisant.
Highest on scale: 20
Pass/fail level: 10
Lowest on scale: 0

Main grading system used by higher education institutions

Full Description: 0-20; 16-20 très bien; 14-15 bien; 12-13 assez bien; 10-11 passable; 0-9 insuffisant.
Très bien is rarely awarded.
Highest on scale: 20
Pass/fail level: 10-11
Lowest on scale: 0

NOTES ON HIGHER EDUCATION SYSTEM

Data for academic year: 2000-2001
Source: Ministère de l'Enseignement supérieur, Tunis, updated by the International Association of Universities (IAU) from IBE website, 2001

INSTITUTIONS OF HIGHER EDUCATION

UNIVERSITIES

PUBLIC INSTITUTIONS

EZZITOUNA UNIVERSITY TUNIS
Université Ezzitouna Tunis
21, rue Sidi Jelizi , Place Maâkel Ez-Zaïm, Montfleury, 1008 Tunis
Tel: +216(71) 575-514
Fax: +216(71) 576-151

Président: Mohamed Toumi Tel: +216(71) 575-870
Secrétaire général: Mohamed Dhelfani
International Relations: Khira Chibani

Institutes
Religious Studies (Islamic Law; Islamic Studies; Islamic Theology; Koran; Religious Education; Religious Studies) *Directeur*: Mouheddine Gadi

History: Founded 1987.

Academic Year: September to June

Admission Requirements: Secondary school certificate (baccalauréat)

Main Language(s) of Instruction: Arabic, French

International Co-operation: Institut Pontifical d'Etudes Arabes et Islamiques; Université Pontificale Grégorienne; United Arab Emirates University

Degrees and Diplomas: *Maîtrise*: Sciences religieuses, religion, 4 yrs; *Diplôme de Recherches approfondies*: 2 yrs; *Doctorat*: 4 yrs

Student Services: Academic Counselling, Social Counselling, Cultural Centre, Sports Facilities, Handicapped Facilities, Health Services, Foreign Student Centre

Libraries: Bibliothèque centrale de l'Université, c. 40,000 vols

Publications: Al Mickat (annually)

Academic Staff *1999*: Full-Time: c. 75 Part-Time: c. 10 Total: c. 85

Student Numbers *1999:* Total: c. 1,200

CENTRE FOR ISLAMIC STUDIES, KAIROUAN
CENTRE D'ETUDES ISLAMIQUES DE KAIROUAN
BP 209, Rue Beït el Hikma, 3100 Kairouan
Tel: +216(77) 232-669
Fax: +216(77) 234-844

Directeur: Mohamed Lazhar Bey

Programmes
Islamic Studies (Islamic Law; Islamic Studies; Islamic Theology; Koran)

History: Founded 1989.

HIGHER INSTITUTE OF ISLAMIC CIVILIZATION STUDIES, TUNIS
INSTITUT SUPÉRIEUR DE LA CIVILISATION ISLAMIQUE DE TUNIS
11, rue Jamaâ El Hawa, Place Maâkel Ez-Zaïm, Montfleury, 1088 Tunis
Tel: +216(71) 569-233
Fax: +216(71) 574-575

Directeur: Mehrez Hamdi Tel: +216(71) 569-237
Secrétaire général: Allala Maamouri

Programmes
Islamic Civilization Studies (Ancient Civilizations; Islamic Studies)

History: Founded 1987.

HIGHER INSTITUTE OF THEOLOGY, TUNIS
INSTITUT SUPÉRIEUR DE THÉOLOGIE DE TUNIS
4, avenue Abou Zakaria El Hafsi, Montfleury, 1008 Tunis
Tel: +216(71) 575-870
Fax: +216(71) 576-555

Directeur: Salem Bouyahya Tel: +216(71) 569-237
Secrétaire général: Rachid Zaafrane

Programmes
Islamic Theology (Islamic Studies; Islamic Theology; Koran; Theology)

History: Founded 1995.

LA MANOUBA UNIVERSITY, TUNIS
Université de La Manouba, Tunis
6, rue Sanaa, Cité Al Amal, 2010 La Manouba 2
Tel: +216(71) 562-700
Fax: +216(71) 562-700

Président: Moncef Hergli
Secrétaire général: Naceur Ouestli

Faculties
Letters (Arabic; English; French; Geography; History) *Dean*: Mohamed Drissa

History: Founded 2001 from Faculty of Letters of Université des Lettres, des Arts et des Sciences humaines (Tunis 1).

Main Language(s) of Instruction: Arabic, French

HIGHER INSTITUTE OF ACCOUNTANCY AND BUSINESS ADMINISTRATION
INSTITUT SUPÉRIEUR DE COMPTABILITÉ ET D'ADMINISTRATION DES ENTREPRISES
4, rue des Entrepreneurs, Zone industrielle, La Charguia-Aéroport, 2035 Tunis
Tel: +216(71) 941-348
Fax: +216(71) 701-270
Directeur: Samir Ghazouani Tel: +216(71) 940-480
EMail: samir.ghazouani@iscae.rnu.tn
Secrétaire général: Hédi Drine

Departments
Accountancy
Economics and Quantitative Methods (Economics; Management Systems)
Law (Administrative Law; Commercial Law; Law)
Management

History: Founded 1988 as Ecole supérieure de Comptabilité, acquired present title 1995.
Academic Year: September to July (September-January; February-July)
Academic Staff *1999:* Full-Time: c. 140 Part-Time: c. 40 Total: c. 180
Student Numbers *1999:* Total: c. 2,465

HIGHER INSTITUTE FOR THE ADVANCEMENT OF THE DISABLED
INSTITUT SUPÉRIEUR DE PROMOTION DES HANDICAPÉS
2, rue Jabran Khalil Jabran, La Manouba, 2010 Tunis
Tel: +216(71) 520-588
Fax: +216(71) 521-267
EMail: iph@iph.org.tn
Directrice: Sarra Jarraya (1999-) Tel: +216(71) 523-575
Secrétaire générale: Mounira Chaabouni

Programmes
Special Education Teacher Training (Education of the Handicapped; Psychology; Psychometrics; Social Psychology; Special Education; Teacher Trainers Education) *Director:* Tahar Midouni

History: Founded 1983, acquired present status and title 1990.

HIGHER INSTITUTE OF ARTS AND CRAFTS, TUNIS
INSTITUT SUPÉRIEUR DES ARTS ET MÉTIERS DE TUNIS
Ed Dendane, 2011 Tunis
Directeur: Raïf Malek (2000-)
Secrétaire général: Taïeb Ben Attia

Departments
Environmental Design (Architectural and Environmental Design; Design; Interior Design)
Graphic Design (Advertising and Publicity; Graphic Design)
Industrial Design (Crafts and Trades; Industrial Design; Packaging Technology)

History: Founded 2000.

Main Language(s) of Instruction: Arabic, French

HIGHER INSTITUTE OF DOCUMENTATION, TUNIS
INSTITUT SUPÉRIEUR DE DOCUMENTATION DE TUNIS
Campus universitaire, La Manouba, 2010 Tunis
Tel: +216(71) 601-550
Fax: +216(71) 600-200
Directeur: Khaled Miled
Secrétaire général: Belgacem Rajeh

Departments
Documentation (Archiving; Documentation Techniques; Library Science)

History: Founded 1981.

HIGHER INSTITUTE OF MULTIMEDIA ARTS, LA MANOUBA
INSTITUT SUPÉRIEUR DES ARTS DU MULTIMÉDIA DE LA MANOUBA
Campus universitaire, La Manouba, Tunis
Directeur: Moncef Gafsi
Secrétaire général: Rejeb Khouaja

Programmes
Multimedia Arts (Graphic Design; Multimedia)

History: Founded 2001.

HIGHER INSTITUTE OF PHYSICAL EDUCATION AND SPORTS, KSAR SAÏD
INSTITUT SUPÉRIEUR D'EDUCATION PHYSIQUE ET DES SPORTS DE KSAR SAÏD
ISEPS Ksar Saïd, La Manouba, 2010 Tunis
Tel: +216(71) 508-416
Fax: +216(71) 513-425
EMail: crd@issep-ks.rnu.tn
Website: http://www.mes.tn/issep/default.htm
Directeur: Kamel Benzarti Tel: +216(71) 513-298
Secrétaire général: Salem Boughattas

Departments
Biological Sciences (Biological and Life Sciences)
Educational Sciences and Pedagogy (Educational Sciences; Pedagogy)
Physical Education and Sports *(collective level)* (Physical Education; Sports)
Physical Education and Sports *(individual level)* (Physical Education; Sports)

History: Founded 1957 as Institut national d'Education physique et sportive, moved to Ksar Saïd 1959. Reorganized 1980 as Ecole normale supérieure de l'Education physique et du Sport. Acquired present status 1992 as Institut supérieur du Sport et de l'Education physique de Ksar Saïd, and present title 2001.
Governing Bodies: Conseil scientifique
Admission Requirements: Secondary school certificate (Baccalauréat) and entrance examination
Main Language(s) of Instruction: Arabic, French

HIGHER INSTITUTE OF THE PRESS AND INFORMATION
SCIENCES
INSTITUT SUPÉRIEUR DE PRESSE ET DES SCIENCES DE
L'INFORMATION
Campus universitaire, La Manouba, 2010 Tunis
Tel: +216(71) 600-980
Fax: +216(71) 600-465

Directeur: Mustapha Hassen (1995-) Tel: +216(71) 600-981

Departments
Communication Studies
Fundamental Training (Information Sciences; Journalism)
Newspaper and Audioviual Press (Journalism)

History: Founded 1967 within Faculty of Letters of University of
Tunis I, became autonomous institution 1973.

HIGHER SCHOOL OF COMMERCE, TUNIS
ECOLE SUPÉRIEURE DE COMMERCE DE TUNIS
4, rue des Entrepreneurs, Zone industrielle , La
Charguia-Aéroport, 2035 Tunis
Tel: +216(71) 710-751
Fax: +216(71) 940-424

Directeur: Mahmoud Zouaoui Tel: +216(71) 703-767

Secrétaire général: Habib Habouria

Departments
Banking
General Studies
Hospital Management (Health Administration)
International Trade (International Business)
Tourism Management (Tourism)

History: Founded 1987.
Academic Year: September to July (September-January;
February-July)
Academic Staff *1999:* Full-Time: c. 110 Part-Time: c. 30 Total: c.
140
Student Numbers *1999:* Total: c. 2,010

INSTITUTE OF THE NATIONAL MOVEMENT
INSTITUT DU MOUVEMENT NATIONAL
Campus Universitaire, La Manouba, 2010 Tunis
Tel: +216(71) 600-950
Fax: +216(71) 600-277

Directeur: Mohamed Lotfi Chaïebi

Secrétaire général: Mohamed Riadh Khammassi

Programmes
African Studies
Contemporary History (Contemporary History; History)

History: Founded 1990.

NATIONAL SCHOOL OF COMPUTER SCIENCE
ECOLE NATIONALE DES SCIENCES DE L'INFORMATIQUE
Campus universitaire, La Manouba, 2010 Tunis
Tel: +216(71) 706-267
Fax: +216(71) 706-297

Directeur: Abdelhamid Ben Youssef Tel: +216(71) 706-454

Secrétaire général: Naceur Mrabet

Programmes
Computer Science (Computer Engineering; Computer Net-
works; Computer Science; Software Engineering; Systems
Analysis)

History: Founded 1985.

NATIONAL SCHOOL OF VETERINARY MEDICINE, SIDI
THABET
ECOLE NATIONALE DE MÉDECINE VÉTÉRINAIRE DE SIDI
THABET
Sidi Thabet, 2020 Ariana
Tel: +216(71) 552-200
Fax: +216(71) 552-441

Directeur: Atef Malek

Departments
Animal Husbandry (Animal Husbandry; Zoology)
Clinical Sciences (Surgery; Veterinary Science; Zoology)
Fundamental Sciences (Animal Husbandry; Veterinary Sci-
ence; Zoology)

History: Founded 1974.

* UNIVERSITY OF THE CENTRE, SOUSSE
Université du Centre, Sousse
43 bis, avenue Mohamed El Karoui, 4002 Sousse
Tel: +216(73) 234-011
Fax: +216(73) 234-014

Président: Sadok El Korbi Tel: +216(73) 239-660

Secrétaire général: Béchir Bel Hadj Yahya
Tel: +216(73) 239-344

Faculties
Dentistry *(Monastir)* (Dental Technology; Dentistry) *Dean:*
Mongi Mejdoub
Economics and Management *(Mahdia)* (Economics; Manage-
ment) *Dean:* Ali Fraj
Law, Economics and Political Science (Commercial Law;
Economics; Finance; Fiscal Law; International Economics;
Law; Management; Political Science; Private Law; Public Law)
Dean: Mongi Tarchouna
Letters and Humanities (Arabic; Arts and Humanities; English;
French; Geography; History) *Dean:* Hédi Jatlaoui
Letters and Humanities *(Kairouan)* (Arabic; Arts and Human-
ities; English; French; Philosophy) *Dean:* Leïla Marzouki
Rammah
Medicine (Community Health; Gynaecology and Obstetrics;
Medicine; Nursing; Paediatrics; Surgery) *Dean:* Béchir Bel Hadj
Ali
Medicine *(Monastir)* (Community Health; Gynaecology and
Obstetrics; Medicine; Nursing; Paediatrics; Surgery) *Dean:*
Amor Ganouni
Pharmacy *(Monastir)* (Animal Husbandry; Biochemistry; Biol-
ogy; Botany; Cell Biology; Haematology; Immunology;

Microbiology; Parasitology; Pharmacology; Pharmacy; Physiology; Toxicology) *Dean*: Mohamed Kallel

Science *(Monastir)* (Analytical Chemistry; Applied Mathematics; Biological and Life Sciences; Chemistry; Computer Science; Earth Sciences; Electronic Engineering; Mathematics; Natural Sciences; Physics) *Dean*: Mongi Ben Amara

History: Founded 1986.

Governing Bodies: University Senate, comprising the President, the Secretary-General and the Deans and delegates of the University

Academic Year: September to July (September-February; February-July)

Admission Requirements: Secondary school certificate (baccalauréat)

Main Language(s) of Instruction: Arabic, French, English

International Co-operation: University Cadi Ayyad Marrakech; Université des Sciences sociales Toulouse I; Université Paul Sabatier Toulouse III; Université de Montpellier I; Université des Sciences humaines Strasbourg II

Degrees and Diplomas: *Technicien supérieur*: Horticulture; Marine Transport; Science, 2-3 yrs; *Diplôme d'Etudes universitaires de Premier Cycle (DEUPC)*: Arts and Humanities (DEUPC); Economics (DEUPC); Law (DEUPC); Management (DEUPC), 2 yrs; *Diplôme*: Pharmacy, 5 yrs; *Diplôme d'Ingénieur*: Engineering; Horticulture; *Maîtrise*: Accountancy; Arts and Humanities; Economics; Law; Management; Science, 4 yrs; *Diplôme d'études supérieures spécialisées (DESS)*: Medicine (DESS); Pharmacy (DESS); Science (DESS); *Diplome d'Etudes approfondies (DEA)*: Law (DEA); Pharmacy (DEA); Science (DEA); Engineering (DEA), 5-6 yrs; *Doctorat*: Pharmacy; Science; Dentistry, 6 yrs; Medicine, 7 yrs

Student Residential Facilities: Yes

Publications: Publications of the faculties

Academic Staff *1999*: Full-Time: c. 1,250 Part-Time: c. 450 Total: c. 1,700

Student Numbers *1999*: All (Foreign Included): c. 24,015 Foreign Only: c. 670

HIGHER INSTITUTE OF APPLIED LANGUAGES FOR BUSINESS AND TOURISM, MOKNINE
INSTITUT SUPÉRIEUR DES LANGUES APPLIQUÉES AUX AFFAIRES ET AU TOURISME DE MOKNINE
Avenue des Martyrs, Route de Jammel, 5050 Moknine
Tel: +216(73) 437-100

Directeur: Mansour Mhenni (2001-)

Secrétaire général: Mohamed Basine

Programmes

Applied Languages (Applied Linguistics; Arabic; Business and Commerce; English; French; German; Modern Languages; Spanish; Tourism)

History: Founded 2001.

HIGHER INSTITUTE OF APPLIED SCIENCE AND TECHNOLOGY, SOUSSE
INSTITUT SUPÉRIEUR DES SCIENCES APPLIQUÉES ET DE TECHNOLOGIES DE SOUSSE
Cité Taffala, Ibn Khaldoun, 4003 Sousse
Tel: +216(73) 332-657
Fax: +216(73) 333-659

Directeur: Younès Bouwezra (2001-) Tel: +216(73) 333-659 Fax: +216(73) 332-656

Secrétaire général: Najib Frigui

Programmes

Applied Science and Technology (Applied Chemistry; Applied Mathematics; Applied Physics; Technology)

History: Founded 2001.

HIGHER INSTITUTE OF BIOTECHNOLOGY, MONASTIR
INSTITUT SUPÉRIEUR DE BIOTECHNOLOGIE DE MONASTIR
Monastir

Directeur: Ahmed Noureddine Helal (2001-)

Secrétaire général: Abderrazak Hachana

Programmes
Biotechnology

History: Founded 2001.

HIGHER INSTITUTE OF COMPUTER SCIENCE AND COMMUNICATION TECHNOLOGY, HAMMAM SOUSSE
INSTITUT SUPÉRIEUR D'INFORMATIQUE ET DES TECHNIQUES DE COMMUNICATION DE HAMMAM SOUSSE
Rue du 1er juin 1955, 4089 Hammam-Sousse
Tel: +216(73) 364-410
Fax: +216(73) 364-411

Directeur: Rafik Brahem (2001-)

Secrétaire général: Chiheb Belkhiria

Programmes
Communication Technology (Communication Studies; Information Technology)
Computer Science

History: Founded 2001.

HIGHER INSTITUTE OF FINE ARTS, SOUSSE
INSTITUT SUPÉRIEUR DES BEAUX ARTS DE SOUSSE
Place de la Gare, 4000 Sousse
Tel: +216(73) 214-333
Fax: +216(73) 214-334

Directrice: Aziza Mrabet (2000-) Tel: +216(73) 214-334

Secrétaire général: Lotfi Chouri

Programmes
Computer-Aided Conception and Drawing (Painting and Drawing; Visual Arts)
Fine Arts (Fine Arts; Painting and Drawing; Sculpture)
Interior Design

History: Founded 2000.

Main Language(s) of Instruction: Arabic, French

HIGHER INSTITUTE OF MANAGEMENT, SOUSSE
INSTITUT SUPÉRIEUR DE GESTION DE SOUSSE
Rue Abed Aziz El Bahi, 4000 Sousse
Tel: +216(73) 332-976
Fax: +216(73) 332-978

Directeur: Faïçal Mansouri Tel: +216(73) 332-977

Secrétaire général: Salem Mahjoub

Departments
Economics
Law (Commercial Law; Law; Private Law; Public Law)
Management (Management; Management Systems)
Quantitative Methods (Management Systems)

History: Founded 1995.

Main Language(s) of Instruction: Arabic, French, English

HIGHER INSTITUTE OF MEDICAL TECHNOLOGY,
SOUSSE
INSTITUT SUPÉRIEUR DES TECHNIQUES MÉDICALES DE
SOUSSE
4000 Sousse
Tel: +216(73) 219-497
Fax: +216(73) 219-497

Directrice: Rafiaa Nouira (2001-)

Programmes
Medical Technology (Dental Technology; Medical Technology)

History: Founded 2001.

HIGHER INSTITUTE OF MUSIC, SOUSSE
INSTITUT SUPÉRIEUR DE MUSIQUE DE SOUSSE
Avenue Abou El Kacem Echebbi, 4000 Sousse
Tel: +216(73) 239-553
Fax: +216(73) 239-555

Directeur: Mohamed Zinelabidine (2000-)
Tel: +216(73) 239-554

Programmes
Music (Music; Music Theory and Composition; Musical Instruments; Musicology)

History: Founded 2000.

HIGHER INSTITUTE OF TRANSPORT MANAGEMENT,
SOUSSE
INSTITUT SUPÉRIEUR DU TRANSPORT ET DE LA
LOGISTIQUE DE SOUSSE
12, rue Abdallah Ibn Zoubeïr, 4029 Sousse

Directeur: Mustapha Belhareth (2001-)

Secrétaire général: Ali Chamsi

Programmes
Transport Management
Transports (Transport and Communications)

History: Founded 2001.

HIGHER SCHOOL OF HEALTH SCIENCES AND
TECHNIQUES, MONASTIR
ECOLE SUPÉRIEURE DES SCIENCES ET TECHNIQUES
DE LA SANTÉ DE MONASTIR
Rue Ibn Sina, 5000 Monastir
Tel: +216(73) 462-477
Fax: +216(73) 464-599

Directeur: Habib Hassine Tel: +216(73) 460-482

Secrétaire général: Lamjed Saâd

Departments
Anaesthesiology
Dental Prosthetics (Dental Technology)
Human Biology (Biology)
Natural Medicine (Medicine)
Obstetrics (Gynaecology and Obstetrics)
Radiology and Radiotherapy (Radiology)

History: Founded 1990.

Main Language(s) of Instruction: Arabic, French

HIGHER SCHOOL OF HORTICULTURE, CHOTT-MERIEM
ECOLE SUPÉRIEURE D'HORTICULTURE DE
CHOTT-MERIEM
4042 Chott-Meriem
Tel: +216(73) 348-546
Fax: +216(73) 348-691

Directeur: Mohamed Habib Ben Hamouda
Tel: +216(73) 348-544

Secrétaire général: Ridha Rouis

Departments
Biological Sciences (Animal Husbandry; Biochemistry; Biological and Life Sciences; Botany; Cattle Breeding; Chemistry; Food Technology; Plant and Crop Protection; Plant Pathology; Zoology)
Economics and Social Sciences (Agricultural Economics; Economics; Management; Mathematics; Rural Planning; Social Sciences; Statistics)
Horticulture (Crop Production; Fruit Production; Horticulture; Landscape Architecture; Plant and Crop Protection; Plant Pathology)
Plant Protection (Entomology; Parasitology; Plant and Crop Protection; Plant Pathology)
Soil, Water and Environment (Agricultural Engineering; Agronomy; Environmental Studies; Mechanics; Meteorology; Natural Resources; Physics; Soil Science; Water Science)

History: Founded 1983.

NATIONAL MERCHANT MARINE SCHOOL
ECOLE NATIONALE DE LA MARINE MARCHANDE
12, rue Abdallah Ibn Zoubeïr, 4000 Sousse
Tel: +216(73) 262-365
Fax: +216(73) 332-658

Directeur: Moncef Souguir Tel: +216(73) 226-211

Secrétaire général: Amara Hamdi

Programmes

Naval Technology (Marine Engineering; Marine Transport; Nautical Science; Naval Architecture)

History: Founded 1968.

Main Language(s) of Instruction: Arabic, French

NATIONAL SCHOOL OF ENGINEERING, MONASTIR
ECOLE NATIONALE D'INGÉNIEURS DE MONASTIR
Rue Ibn El Jazzar, 5019 Monastir
Tel: +216(73) 500-244
Fax: +216(73) 500-514
EMail: enim@rnrt.tn

Directeur: Sassi Ben Nasrallah Tel: +216(73) 500-405

Secrétaire général: Mohamed Fekri Kraïem

Departments

Electrical Engineering (Electrical Engineering; Electronic Engineering; Systems Analysis)
Energy Engineering (Energy Engineering; Environmental Engineering; Thermal Engineering)
Mechanical Engineering (Industrial Design; Industrial Engineering; Mechanical Engineering)
Textile Engineering (Chemical Engineering; Polymer and Plastics Technology; Textile Technology)

History: Founded 1987.

Main Language(s) of Instruction: Arabic, French

PREPARATORY INSTITUTE FOR ENGINEERING STUDIES,
MONASTIR
INSTITUT PRÉPARATOIRE AUX ETUDES D'INGÉNIEURS
DE MONASTIR
Route de Kairouan, 5000 Monastir
Tel: +216(73) 500-273
Fax: +216(73) 500-512

Directeur: Mohamed Ali Hamza Tel: +216(73) 500-277

Secrétaire général: Béchir Drira

Departments

Mathematics and Physics (Mathematics and Computer Science; Physics)
Physics and Chemistry (Chemistry; Mechanical Engineering; Mechanics; Physics)
Technology (Engineering; Natural Sciences; Technology)

History: Founded 1992.

Main Language(s) of Instruction: Arabic, French

PREPARATORY INSTITUTE FOR ENGINEERING STUDIES,
SOUSSE
INSTITUT PRÉPARATOIRE AUX ETUDES D'INGÉNIEURS
DE SOUSSE
Cité Ettafala, 4029 Sousse
Tel: +216(73) 332-659
Fax: +216(73) 332-658

Directeur: Younes Bouwazra Tel: +216(73) 332-656

Secrétaire général: Ali Ouselati

Departments

Engineering (Engineering; Technology)

• UNIVERSITY OF 7TH NOVEMBER IN CARTAGENA
Université du 7 novembre à Carthage
29 rue Asdrubal, 1002 Tunis
Tel: +216(1) 787-502
Fax: +216(1) 788-768

Président: Taïëb Hadhri (2001-) Tel: +216(71) 788-768

Secrétaire général: Mohamed Ameur Ismaïl

Faculties

Economics and Management *(Nabeul)* (Economics; International Economics; Management; Social Policy) *Dean*: Ezzeddine Zouari
Law, Political and Social Sciences *(Ariana)* (Commercial Law; Criminal Law; Law; Political Science; Public Administration; Public Law; Social Sciences) *Dean*: Kalthoum Mziou
Science *(Bizerte)* (Biology; Chemistry; Mathematics and Computer Science; Natural Sciences; Physics) *Dean*: Chaabane Chefi

Further Information: Branches in Mateur, Nabeul and La Marsa

History: Founded 1987, reorganized 1989 as Université de Droit, d'Economie et de Gestion (Tunis III), and acquired present title 2001.

Academic Year: September to June (September-January; February-June)

Admission Requirements: Secondary school certificate (baccalauréat)

Fees: (Dinars): c. 30-100 per annum

Main Language(s) of Instruction: French, Arabic, English

International Co-operation: University of Ottawa; Concordia University; University du Québec à Trois-Rivières; Bilkent University, Ankara; Istanbul University; Montreal School of Higher Commercial Studies (HEC); University of Sherbrooke; Laval University; Université de Bordeaux I; University of Social Sciences, Toulouse I; Université d'Aix-Marseilles II; University of Law and Health Sciences, Lille II; University of Limoges; University of Corsica, Corté; Université Paris VIII (Vincennes Saint-Denis); Université Paris X (Nanterre); Free University of Brussels; State University of Liège; University of Bologna; University of Rome Tor Vergata; University of Pisa; University of Nice-Sophia Antipolis; Université de Lyon II; Conservatoire national des Arts et Métiers de Paris (CNAM); Centre national de la Recherche scientifique (CNRS); Institut de Formation européen et de Coopération de Dunkerque; Atlanta Management Institute; Institut du Travail de Bruxelles; Institut catholique des hautes Etudes commerciales de Bruxelles; University of Constantine; Hassan II University Ain Chok, Casablanca

Degrees and Diplomas: *Diplôme d'Etudes universitaires de Premier Cycle (DEUPC)*: Accountancy (DEUPC); Administration (DEUPC); Commerce (DEUPC); Economics (DEUPC); Labour Studies (DEUPC); Law (DEUPC); Management (DEUPC); Social Studies (DEUPC), 2 yrs; *Diplôme*: Hotel Management; Tourism; *Maîtrise*: Accountancy; Administration; Economics; Labour Studies; Law; Management; Social Studies, 4 yrs; *Diplôme d'études supérieures spécialisées (DESS)*: Commerce (DESS); Economics (DESS), a year following Maitrîse; Management (DESS), a year following Maîtrise; *Diplome d'Etudes approfondies (DEA)*: Management (DEA), a further 1-2 years following Maîtrise; Accountancy (DEA); Economics (DEA); Labour Studies (DEA); Law (DEA), a further 1-2 years foolowing Maîtrise; *Doctorat*: Economics; Law; Management. Also Certificat d'Etudes Spécialisées (CES) awarded in Accountancy by the University of Law, Economics and Management (Tunis III)

Student Services: Social Counselling, Sports Facilities, Handicapped Facilities, Canteen

Student Residential Facilities: Yes

Libraries: University Library

Academic Staff *1999*: Full-Time: c. 865 Part-Time: c. 375 Total: c. 1,240

Student Numbers *1999*: All (Foreign Included): c. 29,775 Foreign Only: c. 260

CENTRE FOR LAW AND JUSTICE STUDIES
CENTRE D'ETUDES JURIDIQUES ET JUDICIAIRES
2, rue de l'Artisanat, Zone industrielle, La Charguia, 2035
Tunis
Tel: +216(71) 707-992
Fax: +216(71) 702-896

Directrice: Saida Jaouida Guiga

Programmes
Law and Justice Studies (Law)
Main Language(s) of Instruction: Arabic, French

HIGHER INSTITUTE OF EXECUTIVES FOR YOUTH
INSTITUT SUPÉRIEUR DES CADRES DE L'ENFANCE
26, avenue Taïeb Mhiri, 2016 Carthage
Tel: +216(71) 730-436
Fax: +216(71) 233-715
EMail: isce@email.ati.tn

Directeur: Tahar Abid Tel: +216(71) 720-044
Secrétaire général: Mohamed Raouf Fakhfakh

Programmes
Teacher Trainers Education (Arts and Humanities; Communication Studies; Environmental Studies; Health Education; Music Education; Native Language Education; Preschool Education; Primary Education; Statistics; Teacher Trainers Education; Teacher Training)

History: Founded 1989.

Main Language(s) of Instruction: Arabic, French

HIGHER INSTITUTE OF FINE ARTS, NABEUL
INSTITUT SUPÉRIEUR DES BEAUX ARTS DE NABEUL
Avenue Ali Belhaouane, 8000 Nabeul
Tel: +216(72) 232-210

Directeur: Hayet Tlili Tel: +216(72) 232-144
Secrétaire général: Bader Eddine Mechmech

Departments
Fine Arts

HIGHER INSTITUTE OF MODERN LANGUAGES, TUNIS
INSTITUT SUPÉRIEUR DES LANGUES VIVANTES DE
TUNIS
11, Rue Ibn Maja, Cité El Khadra, 1003 Tunis
Tel: +216(71) 773-813
Fax: +216(71) 770-134

Directeur: Mohamed Miled Tel: +216(71) 772-460
Secrétaire général: Mohamed Yakhlef

Departments
Arabic and Translation (Arabic; Translation and Interpretation)
English
French
Languages (Modern Languages)
Specialized English (English)

History: Founded 1968.

Main Language(s) of Instruction: Arabic, French

HIGHER INSTITUTE OF STATISTICS AND INFORMATION
ANALYSIS
INSTITUT SUPÉRIEUR DES STATISTIQUES ET
D'ANALYSE DE L'INFORMATION
Tunis

Programmes
Information Analysis (Information Sciences)
Statistics

History: Founded 2001.

HIGHER SCHOOL OF AGRICULTURE, LE KEF
ECOLE SUPÉRIEURE D'AGRICULTURE DU KEF
7119 Boulifa Le Kef
Tel: +216(78) 226-160
Fax: +216(78) 223-137

Directeur: Ahmed Marouani Tel: +216(78) 223-137
Secrétaire général: Mohamed Snoussi

Departments
Agriculture (Agricultural Engineering; Agriculture)

History: Founded 1981.

HIGHER SCHOOL OF AGRICULTURE, MATEUR
ECOLE SUPÉRIEURE D'AGRICULTURE DE MATEUR
7030 Mateur
Tel: +216(72) 465-565
Fax: +216(72) 468-088

Directeur: Hédi Abdouli

Secrétaire général: Tahar Mazlout

Departments
Agriculture (Agricultural Engineering; Agriculture)

History: Founded 1981.

HIGHER SCHOOL OF AGRICULTURE, MOGRANE
ECOLE SUPÉRIEURE D'AGRICULTURE DE MOGRANE
1121 Mograne-Zaghouan
Tel: +216(72) 660-283
Fax: +216(72) 660-563
EMail: mehouachi.tijani@iresa.agrinet.tn

Directeur: Abderrazak Souissi Tel: +216(72) 660-283

Secrétaire générale: Rhouma Ezbidi

Departments
Agriculture (Agricultural Engineering; Agriculture)

History: Founded 1981.

HIGHER SCHOOL OF COMMUNICATION, TUNIS
ECOLE SUPÉRIEURE DES COMMUNICATIONS DE TUNIS
Route de Raoued Km. 3,5, Cité El Gharella, 2083 Ariana
Tel: +216(71) 857-000
Fax: +216(71) 856-829

Directeur: Naceur Ammar
EMail: naceur.ammar@supcom.rnu.tn

Secrétaire général: Sadok Mabrouk

Departments
Communication Studies (Postal Services; Telecommunications Engineering; Telecommunications Services)

History: Founded 1974.

HIGHER SCHOOL OF FOOD INDUSTRIES, TUNIS
ECOLE SUPÉRIEURE DES INDUSTRIES ALIMENTAIRES DE TUNIS
58, avenue Alain Savary, Cité El Khadra, 1003 Tunis
Tel: +216(71) 797-236
Fax: +216(71) 799-680

Director: Abdelkader Chérif Tel: +216(71) 799-680

Secrétaire général: Rachid Ben Daameche

Faculties
Agro-Food Industry (Agronomy; Food Technology) *Director:* Abdelkader Chérif

History: Founded 1976.

488

HIGHER SCHOOL OF RURAL ENGINEERING, MEDJEZ EL BAB
ECOLE SUPÉRIEURE DES INGÉNIEURS DE L'EQUIPEMENT RURAL DE MEDJEZ EL BAB
Route du Kef Km. 5, 9070 Medjez El Bab
Tel: +216(78) 456-773
Fax: +216(78) 457-681

Directeur: Tijani El Mehouachi Tel: +216(78) 456-266

Secrétaire général: El Hechemi Abed El Melak

Schools
Agricultural Engineering (Agricultural Engineering; Agricultural Equipment) *Associate-Professor:* Abderrazah Souissi, *full-time staff:* 40, *part-time staff:* 23, *students:* 352
Rural Engineering (Regional Planning) *full-time staff:* 66

Departments
Civil Engineering
Fundamental Sciences (Computer Science; Mathematics; Physics)
Hydraulic Engineering
Mechanical Engineering

History: Founded 1976.

INSTITUTE OF BUSINESS MANAGEMENT, CARTAGENA
INSTITUT DES HAUTES ETUDES COMMERCIALES DE CARTHAGE
Carthage Présidence, 2016 Carthage
Tel: +216(71) 774-720
Fax: +216(71) 775-944

Directeur: Khalled Melouli Tel: +216(71) 703-103

Secrétaire général: Youssef Charfeddine

Departments
Accountancy
General Studies
Management Studies (Business and Commerce; Economics; Law; Management; Marketing; Mathematics)
Tourism

History: Founded 1942.

Academic Year: September to June (September-January; February-June)

Academic Staff *1999:* Full-Time: c. 120 Part-Time: c. 20 Total: c. 140

Student Numbers *1999:* Total: c. 2,350

INSTITUTE OF FORESTRY, TABARKA
INSTITUT SYLVO-PASTORAL DE TABARKA
8110 Tabarka
Tel: +216(78) 670-542
Fax: +216(78) 670-471

Directeur: Hamda Saoudi

Secrétaire générale: Aïssa Chaabani

Programmes
Forestry

History: Founded 1970.

NATIONAL AGRICULTURAL INSTITUTE, TUNIS
INSTITUT NATIONAL AGRONOMIQUE DE TUNIS
43, avenue Charles Nicolle , Cité Mahrajène, Le Belvédère,
1082 Tunis
Tel: +216(71) 287-110
Fax: +216(71) 799-391

Director: Mohamed Moncef El Harrabi (1998-)
Tel: +216(71) 840-270 EMail: harrabi.moncef@inat.agrinet.tn
Secrétaire général: Ammar Yakoubi

Programmes
Agronomy (Agriculture; Agronomy) *Head*: Moncef Harrabi,
full-time staff: 125, *part-time staff:* 80, *students:* 900

History: Founded 1970, acquired present status 1989.

NATIONAL AGRICULTURAL RESEARCH INSTITUTE OF
TUNISIA
INSTITUT NATIONAL DE LA RECHERCHE AGRONOMIQUE
DE TUNISIE
Rue Hédi Karray, 2049 Ariana
Tel: +216(71) 230-739
Fax: +216(71) 752-897

Directeur: Netij Ben Mchila (2001-) Tel: +216(71) 230-024

Institutes
Crop Production and Small Ruminants Research (Agricultural Economics; Agronomy; Animal Husbandry; Botany; Cattle Breeding; Crop Production; Laboratory Techniques; Plant Pathology; Zoology)

Further Information: Also 18 Research stations all over the country

History: Founded 1913, acquired present status and title 1964.
Main Language(s) of Instruction: Arabic, French

NATIONAL INSTITUTE OF APPLIED SCIENCE AND
TECHNOLOGY
INSTITUT NATIONAL DES SCIENCES APPLIQUÉES ET DE
TECHNOLOGIE
BP 676, Centre urbain nord, Cedex 1080 Tunis
Tel: +216(71) 703-627
Fax: +216(71) 704-329
EMail: webmaster@insat.rnu.tn
Website: http://www.mes.tn/insat/index.htm

Director: Mekki Ksouri (2000-) Tel: +216(71) 703-746
EMail: mekki.ksouri@isetr.rnu.tn
Secrétaire général: Brahim Toumi

Departments
Biological and Chemical Engineering (Applied Chemistry; Applied Mathematics; Applied Physics; Bioengineering; Biological and Life Sciences; Chemical Engineering; Natural Sciences; Technology)
Mathematics and Computer Engineering (Computer Engineering; Mathematics and Computer Science)
Physical and Measurement Engineering (Measurement and Precision Engineering; Physical Engineering)

History: Founded 1996.

Governing Bodies: Conseil d'administration; Conseil scientifique et pédagogique

Main Language(s) of Instruction: Arabic, French

NATIONAL INSTITUTE OF LABOUR AND SOCIAL STUDIES
INSTITUT NATIONAL DU TRAVAIL ET DES ETUDES
SOCIALES
44, rue de l'Artisanat, 2035 La Charguia
Tel: +216(71) 706-207
Fax: +216(71) 703-464
EMail: intes@intes.rnu.tn
Website: http://www.intes.rnu.tn

Directeur: Mustapha Nasraoui Tel: +216(71) 703-103
Secrétaire général: Hayet Ayadi

Departments
Labour Sciences (Labour and Industrial Relations)
Law (Labour Law; Law; Private Law; Public Law)
Social Studies (Economics; Social Studies; Statistics)

History: Founded 1993.
Academic Year: September to July (September-January; February-July)
Main Language(s) of Instruction: Arabic, French
Academic Staff *1999:* Full-Time: c. 110 Part-Time: c. 75 Total: c. 185
Student Numbers *1999:* Total: c. 1,560

NATIONAL RESEARCH INSTITUTE OF RURAL, WATER
AND FORESTRY ENGINEERING
INSTITUT NATIONAL DE RECHERCHES EN GÉNIE
RURAL, EAUX ET FORÊTS
BP 10, 2080 Ariana
Tel: +216(71) 718-055
Fax: +216(71) 717-952

Director: Mohamed Néjib Rejeb (1996-)
Tel: +216(71) 709-033 EMail: rejeb.nejib@iresa.agrinet.tn
Secrétaire générale: Khalifa Gharsallah

Departments
Regional Planning

Institutes
Rural, Water and Forestry Engineering (Agricultural Engineering; Agricultural Equipment; Forest Management; Forestry; Irrigation; Rural Planning; Soil Conservation; Water Management; Water Science) *Director*: Mohamed Nejib Rejeb, *full-time staff:* 301, *part-time staff:* 4

History: Founded 1996.

Main Language(s) of Instruction: Arabic, French

NATIONAL SCHOOL OF ARCHITECTURE AND TOWN
PLANNING, TUNIS
ECOLE NATIONALE D'ARCHITECTURE ET D'URBANISME
DE TUNIS
Rue El Kodes, 2016 Sidi Bou Saïd
Tel: +216(71) 729-798
Fax: +216(71) 729-179

Directeur: Mouldi Chaâbani (1995-)
Secrétaire général: Jalel Meftah

Departments
Architecture
Town Planning

History: Founded 1972.

POLYTECHNIC SCHOOL OF TUNISIA
ECOLE POLYTECHNIQUE DE TUNISIE
BP 743, Rue El Khawarezmi, 2078 La Marsa
Tel: +216(71) 774-611
Fax: +216(71) 748-843

Directeur: Jmaiel Ben Ibrahim (2001-)
Secrétaire général: Mohamed Zouali

Departments
Applied Mathematics and Computer Science (Applied Mathematics; Mathematics and Computer Science) *Director:* Riadh Robbana
Economics *Director:* Adel Dhif
Electricity (Electrical Engineering) *Director:* Abdelaziz Samet
Languages and Communication (Communication Studies; Modern Languages) *Director:* Bechir Bouaicha
Mechanics (Mechanical Engineering; Mechanics) *Director:* Lamia Guellouz

History: Founded 1991 as Branch of Université de Tunis El Manar, became Branch of Université du 7 novembre à Carthage 2001.

PREPARATORY INSTITUTE FOR ENGINEERING STUDIES, MATEUR
INSTITUT PRÉPARATOIRE AUX ETUDES D'INGÉNIEURS DE MATEUR
Route de Tabarka, 7030 Mateur
Tel: +216(72) 466-481
Fax: +216(72) 466-044

Directeur: Abdelhak Ben Younes Tel: +216(72) 448-544

Institutes
Engineering (Chemistry; Engineering; Mathematics; Physics; Technology) *Director:* Radhouane Tarhouni

History: Founded 1995 as Branch of Université Tunis El Manar, became Branch of Université du 7 Novembre à Carthage 2001.
Main Language(s) of Instruction: Arabic, French

PREPARATORY INSTITUTE FOR ENGINEERING STUDIES, NABEUL
INSTITUT PRÉPARATOIRE AUX ETUDES D'INGÉNIEURS DE NABEUL
Campus Universitaire Merazka, 8000 Nabeul
Tel: +216(72) 220-093
Fax: +216(72) 220-181
EMail: ipein@ipein.rnu.tn
Website: http://www.mes.tn/ipein/index.htm

Directeur: Abdelghani Ben Hadj Amor Tel: +216(72) 220-093
Secrétaire général: Med Moncef Belhadj Salem

Departments
Mathematics and Physics (Mathematics; Physics)
Physics and Chemistry (Chemistry; Physics)
Technology (Engineering; Technology)

Research Units
Physics and Chemistry (Chemistry; Materials Engineering; Optics; Physics; Thermal Engineering)

History: Founded 1986 as Branch of Université de Tunis El Manar, became Branch of Université du 7 Novembre à Carthage 2001.
Governing Bodies: Conseil scientifique
Accrediting Agencies: Ministère de l'Enseignement Supérieur

PREPARATORY INSTITUTE FOR SCIENTIFIC AND TECHNICAL STUDIES, LA MARSA
INSTITUT PRÉPARATOIRE AUX ETUDES SCIENTIFIQUES ET TECHNIQUES DE LA MARSA
BP 51, 2070 La Marsa
Tel: +216(71) 740-048
Fax: +216(71) 746-551

Directeur: Hassen Maaref Tel: +216(71) 741-836
Secrétaire générale: Nabiha Trabelsi

Departments
Science and Technology (Mathematics and Computer Science; Natural Sciences; Technology)

History: Founded 1992.

UNIVERSITY OF THE SOUTH IN SFAX
Université du Sud à Sfax (USS)
Route de l'Aérodrome Km. 0,5, 3029 Sfax
Tel: +216(74) 240-678
Fax: +216(74) 240-913
EMail: sodki.triki@uss.rnu.tn
Website: http://www.mes.tn/uss/index.htm

Président: Hamed Ben Dhia Tel: +216(74) 240-986
EMail: hamed.bendhia@uss.rnu.tn

Secrétaire général: Mohamed Mahfoudh
Tel: +216(74) 240-200 Fax: +216(74) 240-200

Faculties
Economics and Management (Accountancy; Business and Commerce; Business Computing; Economics; Finance; Human Resources; Management; Management Systems; Marketing) *Dean:* Abdelfettah Ghorbel, *full-time staff:* 300, *students:* 7,000
Law (Commercial Law; International Law; Law; Private Law; Public Law) *Dean:* Ahmed Omrane, *full-time staff:* 150, *students:* 5,000
Letters and Humanities (Arabic; Arts and Humanities; English; French; Geography; History; Philosophy; Sociology) *Dean:* Mohamed Ali Malouni, *full-time staff:* 260, *students:* 5,000
Medicine (Biology; Biophysics; Community Health; Embryology and Reproduction Biology; Gender Studies; Genetics;

Gynaecology and Obstetrics; Haematology; Histology; Medicine; Microbiology; Neurosciences; Paramedical Sciences; Sports Medicine; Urology) *Dean*: Abdelmagid Zahaf, *full-time staff*: 160, *students*: 1,457

Science (Biology; Computer Science; Earth Sciences; Mathematics; Natural Sciences; Physics) *Dean*: Mabrouk Montassar, *full-time staff*: 260, *students*: 5,000

Science *(Gabès)* (Biological and Life Sciences; Chemistry; Earth Sciences; Mathematics; Natural Sciences; Physics) *Dean*: Sahbi Alaya, *full-time staff*: 70, *part-time staff*: 453, *students*: 1,550

Science *(Gafsa)* (Biological and Life Sciences; Chemistry; Computer Science; Earth Sciences; Mathematics; Natural Sciences; Physical Therapy) *Dean*: El Aïd Belkhiri

Further Information: Branches in Gabès and Gafsa

History: Founded 1986.

Governing Bodies: Conseil de l'Université, comprising 42 members

Academic Year: September to July (September-January; February-July)

Admission Requirements: Secondary school certificate (baccalauréat)

Main Language(s) of Instruction: French, Arabic

International Co-operation: Links with Institutions in Mauritania, Morocco, Algeria, Libya, France, Belgium, Italy, Egypt, Saudi Arabia

Degrees and Diplomas: *Technicien supérieur*: Engineering; Health Sciences; Management; Technology, 2 yrs; *Diplôme d'Etudes universitaires de Premier Cycle (DEUPC)*: Arts and Humanities; Economics; Management; Science, 2 yrs; *Diplôme*: Arts; Physical Education, 2 yrs; *Diplôme d'Ingénieur*: 4-6 yrs; *Maîtrise*: Commerce; Arts and Humanities; Economics; Law; Music; Physical Education; Science, 4 yrs; *Diplôme d'études supérieures spécialisées (DESS)*: Medicine; *Diplôme d'Etudes approfondies (DEA)*: Economics; Engineering; Law, a further 2 yrs after Maîtrise; Science, a further 2 yrs following Maîtrise; *Doctorat*: Economics; Science; Medicine, 7 yrs. Thèse d'Université, 3 yrs

Libraries: Total, c. 215,500 vols

Academic Staff *2000-2001*: Total: c. 2,440

Student Numbers *2000-2001*: All (Foreign Included): c. 45,000 Foreign Only: c. 500

CENTRE FOR BIOTECHNOLOGY, SFAX
CENTRE DE BIOTECHNOLOGIE DE SFAX
BP 358, Route de Soukra Km. 4, 3038 Sfax
Tel: +216(74) 274-110
Fax: +216(74) 275-970
EMail: ellouz@cbs.rnrt.tn

Directeur: Radhouane Ellouz (1988-)

Units
Bioenergy (Biotechnology)
Cell Biology
Metabolites (Biotechnology; Cell Biology)

Sugar (Food Technology)
Vegetal Biotechnology (Biotechnology; Genetics; Microbiology)

History: Founded 1988.

Main Language(s) of Instruction: Arabic, French

Academic Staff: Total: c. 20

HIGHER INSTITUTE OF APPLIED STUDIES IN HUMANITIES, GAFSA
INSTITUT SUPÉRIEUR DES ETUDES APPLIQUÉES EN HUMANITÉS DE GAFSA
Cité Ecchabeb, 2133 Gafsa
Tel: +216(76) 224-328
Fax: +216(76) 224-328

Directeur: Ibrahim Jadla (2001-) Tel: +216(76) 211-051

Secrétaire général: Béchir Raddaoui

Programmes
Arts and Humanities

History: Founded 2001.

Main Language(s) of Instruction: Arabic, French

HIGHER INSTITUTE OF ARTS AND CRAFTS, GABÈS
INSTITUT SUPÉRIEUR DES ARTS ET MÉTIERS DE GABÈS
Avenue Abou Elkacem Echbbi, 6000 Gabès
Tel: +216(75) 273-522
Fax: +216(75) 273-499

Directeur: Ezzeddine Dekhil (2001-)

Secrétaire général: Mohamed Hfidhi

Programmes
Arts and Crafts (Crafts and Trades)

History: Founded 2001.

Main Language(s) of Instruction: Arabic, French

HIGHER INSTITUTE OF BUSINESS ADMINISTRATION, SFAX
INSTITUT SUPÉRIEUR D'ADMINISTRATION DES AFFAIRES DE SFAX
BP 1013, Route de Mharza Km. 1, 3018 Sfax
Tel: +216(74) 452-632
Fax: +216(74) 452-632

Directeur: Abdelwaheb Rebaï (2001-) Tel: +216(74) 452-640

Secrétaire général: Raouf Turki

Programmes
Business Administration (Administration; Business Administration; Management; Management Systems)

History: Founded 2001.

Main Language(s) of Instruction: Arabic, French

HIGHER INSTITUTE OF COMPUTER SCIENCE AND
MULTIMEDIA, SFAX
INSTITUT SUPÉRIEUR D'INFORMATIQUE ET DE
MULTIMÉDIA DE SFAX
Route El Mharza Km. 1,5, 3000 Sfax
Tel: +216(74) 452-632
Fax: +216(74) 452-632

Directeur: Abdelmajid Ben Hamadou (2001-)

Secrétaire général: Hamda Kamoun

Programmes
Computer Science
Multimedia Studies (Multimedia)

History: Founded 2001.

Main Language(s) of Instruction: Arabic, French

HIGHER INSTITUTE OF FINE ARTS, SFAX
INSTITUT SUPÉRIEUR DES BEAUX ARTS DE SFAX
34, avenue du 5 Août, 3002 Sfax
Tel: +216(74) 299-593
Fax: +216(74) 297-286

Directeur: Noureddine El Hani Tel: +216(74) 299-511

Secrétaire général: Noureddine El Hadj Hassine

Programmes
Design (Architectural and Environmental Design; Design; Fashion Design; Industrial Design; Interior Design; Textile Design)
Plastic Arts (Aesthetics; Art History; Ceramic Art; Engraving; Handicrafts; Painting and Drawing; Photography; Sculpture; Visual Arts; Weaving)

History: Founded 1995.

Main Language(s) of Instruction: Arabic, French

HIGHER INSTITUTE OF LANGUAGES, GABÈS
INSTITUT SUPÉRIEUR DES LANGUES DE GABÈS
6029 Gabès
Tel: +216(75) 274-244
Fax: +216(75) 274-522

Directeur: Noureddine Lammouchi (2000-)
Tel: +216(75) 274-344

Secrétaire général: Mohamed Zekri

Departments
English
French
Services and Communication Studies (Administration; Administrative Law; Arabic; Communication Studies; Geography; German; Italian; Labour Law; Secretarial Studies; Sociology; Tourism; Translation and Interpretation)

History: Founded 2000.

Main Language(s) of Instruction: Arabic, French

492

HIGHER INSTITUTE OF MANAGEMENT, GABÈS
INSTITUT SUPÉRIEUR DE GESTION DE GABÈS
Avenue Jilani Habib, 6002 Gabès
Tel: +216(75) 270-096
Fax: +216(75) 270-686

Directeur: Aleya Jilani (1998-) Tel: +216(75) 272-280

Secrétaire général: Sahbi Souaissa Tel: +216(75) 276-090

Departments
Economics
Finance
Management (Accountancy; Management)
Quantitative Methods (Management Systems)

History: Founded 1998.

Governing Bodies: Conseil scientifique

Main Language(s) of Instruction: Arabic, French

HIGHER INSTITUTE OF MUSIC, SFAX
INSTITUT SUPÉRIEUR DE MUSIQUE DE SFAX
BP 143, Rue du Maghreb arabe, 3049 Sfax
Tel: +216(74) 225-545
Fax: +216(74) 229-683

Directeur: Mourad Siala (1999-) Tel: +216(74) 220-610

Secrétaire général: Mohamed Triki

Programmes
Music (Music; Music Theory and Composition; Musical Instruments)
Musicology (Folklore; Musicology; Oriental Studies)

History: Founded 1999.

Admission Requirements: Secondary school certificate (Baccalauréat) and entrance examination

Main Language(s) of Instruction: Arabic, French

HIGHER INSTITUTE OF PHYSICAL EDUCATION AND
SPORTS, SFAX
INSTITUT SUPÉRIEUR DU SPORT ET DE L'EDUCATION
PHYSIQUE DE SFAX
BP 384, Route de l'Aérodrome Km. 3,5, 3023 Sfax
Tel: +216(74) 278-504
Fax: +216(74) 278-502

Directeur: Amor Draoui Tel: +216(74) 278-505

Secrétaire général: Noureddine Menif

Departments
Physical Education and Sports (Physical Education; Sports)

History: Founded 1989.

Main Language(s) of Instruction: Arabic, French

HIGHER SCHOOL OF COMMERCE, SFAX
ECOLE SUPÉRIEURE DE COMMERCE DE SFAX
Route de l'Aérodrome Km. 4,5, 3018 Sfax
Tel: +216(74) 279-620
Fax: +216(74) 278-630

Directeur: Abdelkader Chaâbane Tel: +216(74) 279-410

Secrétaire général: Abdelmajid Torjmène
Tel: +216(74) 278-870

Departments

Accountancy

Business and Commerce (Business and Commerce; Management)

Finance (Finance; Management Systems)

International Business (International Business; International Relations; Management)

History: Founded 1995.

Main Language(s) of Instruction: Arabic, French

HIGHER SCHOOL OF HEALTH SCIENCES AND
TECHNIQUES, SFAX
ECOLE SUPÉRIEURE DES SCIENCES ET TECHNIQUES
DE LA SANTÉ DE SFAX
Avenue Majida Boulila, 3003 Sfax
Tel: +216(74) 241-971
Fax: +216(74) 246-821

Directrice: Mongia Soussou Hachicha Tel: +216(75) 241-923

Secrétaire général: Abdelwaheb Mseddi
Tel: +216(74) 241-902

Departments

Health Sciences and Technology (Alternative Medicine; Anaesthesiology; Biology; Gynaecology and Obstetrics; Health Sciences; Medical Technology; Physical Therapy; Psychiatry and Mental Health; Radiology)

History: Founded 1989.

Main Language(s) of Instruction: Arabic, French

INSTITUTE OF ARID ZONE STUDIES, MÉDENINE
INSTITUT DES RÉGIONS ARIDES DE MÉDENINE
El Fjè, 4119 Médenine
Tel: +216(75) 633-121
Fax: +216(75) 633-006

Directeur: Houcine Khatelli Tel: +216(75) 633-122

Laboratories

Agronomy

Animal Husbandry (Animal Husbandry; Environmental Management)

Environmental Studies (Arid Land Studies; Environmental Studies)

Pastoral Ecology (Ecology; Environmental Management)

Rural Planning (Environmental Studies; Natural Resources; Rural Planning; Rural Studies)

History: Founded 1976.

Main Language(s) of Instruction: Arabic, French

NATIONAL SCHOOL OF ENGINEERING, GABÈS
ECOLE NATIONALE D'INGÉNIEURS DE GABÈS
Rue Omar Ibn El Khattab, 6029 Gabès
Tel: +216(75) 392-100
Fax: +216(75) 392-190
EMail: contact@enig.rnu.tn
Website: http://www.mes.tn/enig/index.htm

Directeur: Abdellatif El Gadri Tel: +216(75) 392-380

Secrétaire général: Malek Zammouri Tel: +216(75) 392-257

Departments

Automation and Electrical Engineering (Automation and Control Engineering; Electrical Engineering; Power Engineering)

Chemical Engineering (Analytical Chemistry; Applied Mathematics; Chemical Engineering; Computer Science; Industrial Chemistry; Thermal Engineering)

Civil Engineering (Applied Mathematics; Arabic; Architecture; Civil Engineering; Computer Science; Construction Engineering; Electronic Engineering; English; French; Geology; Materials Engineering; Road Engineering; Town Planning; Water Management)

Centres

Computer Science (Mathematics and Computer Science; Statistics)

History: Founded 1975.

Main Language(s) of Instruction: Arabic, French

NATIONAL SCHOOL OF ENGINEERING, SFAX
ECOLE NATIONALE D'INGÉNIEURS DE SFAX
Route de la Soukra Km. 4, 3038 Sfax
Tel: +216(74) 274-090
Fax: +216(74) 275-595

Directeur: Boubaker El Euch (1998-) Tel: +216(74) 274-409

Secrétaire général: Moncef Abida

Departments

Applied Mathematics and Computer Science (Applied Mathematics; Mathematics; Mathematics and Computer Science) *Director*: Fahti Ghribi

Biological Engineering (Bioengineering; Environmental Engineering) *Director*: Youssef Talel Gargouri

Electrical Engineering *Director*: Lofti Kammoun

Geological Engineering (Geological Engineering; Natural Resources) *Director*: Mohamed Jamel Rouis

Materials Engineering (Chemistry; Materials Engineering) *Director*: Mohieddine Fourati

Mechanical Engineering (Automation and Control Engineering; Industrial Engineering; Mechanical Engineering) *Director*: Chedli Bradai

History: Founded 1983.

Main Language(s) of Instruction: Arabic, French

PREPARATORY INSTITUTE FOR ENGINEERING STUDIES, GABÈS
INSTITUT PRÉPARATOIRE AUX ETUDES D'INGÉNIEURS DE GABÈS
Route de Médenine, 6029 Gabès
Tel: +216(75) 392-108
Fax: +216(75) 392-390

Directeur: Mohieddine Alaoui (1992-) Tel: +216(75) 392-404
Secrétaire général: Hassen Trabelsi

Departments
Chemistry (Biological and Life Sciences; Chemistry) *Director:* Farhat Habachi
Mathematics and Computer Science *Director:* Jilani Alaya
Physics and Technology (Physics; Technology) *Director:* Romdhane Ben Slama

History: Founded 1992.
Main Language(s) of Instruction: Arabic, French
Academic Staff *1999:* Total: c. 65
Student Numbers *1999:* Total: c. 775

PREPARATORY INSTITUTE FOR ENGINEERING STUDIES, SFAX
INSTITUT PRÉPARATOIRE AUX ETUDES D'INGÉNIEURS DE SFAX
Route Menzel Chaker Km. 0,5, 3018 Sfax
Tel: +216(74) 241-403
Fax: +216(74) 246-347

Directeur: Fethi Ladhar Tel: +216(74) 241-733
Secrétaire général: Ridha Triki

Departments
Biology *Director:* Fayçel Turki
Chemistry *Director:* Samir Djemel
Mathematics and Computer Science *Director:* Ameur Ch'hayder
Physics *Director:* Hassiba B. Halima Ketata

History: Founded 1992.
Main Language(s) of Instruction: Arabic, French
Academic Staff *1999:* Total: c. 80
Student Numbers *1999:* Total: c. 1,210

ZITOUNA INSTITUTE, SFAX
INSTITUT ZITOUNA DE SFAX
BP 1087, Route de l'Aérodrome Km. 1,5, 3029 Sfax
Tel: +216(74) 241-589
Fax: +216(74) 241-033

Directeur: Taïeb Jardak Tel: +216(74) 241-240

Programmes
Olive Research (Agricultural Economics; Agronomy; Arid Land Studies; Biology; Food Science; Harvest Technology; Physiology; Plant and Crop Protection; Rubber Technology; Technology; Vegetable Production)

History: Founded 1982.
Main Language(s) of Instruction: Arabic, French

494

UNIVERSITY OF TUNIS

Université de Tunis
92, avenue du 9 avril 1938, 1007 Tunis
Tel: +216(71) 567-322
Fax: +216(71) 560-633

Président: Abderraouf Mahbouli Tel: +216(71) 562-700
Secrétaire général: Lamied Massouadi

Faculties
Human and Social Sciences (Arabic; Arts and Humanities; Civics; English; French; Geography (Human); History; Philosophy; Psychology; Social Sciences; Sociology) *Dean:* Habib Dlala
Law, Economics and Management *(Jendouba)* (Economics; Law; Management) *Dean:* Chokri Mamoghli
Letters *(Jendouba)* (Arts and Humanities; Literature; Philosophy)

History: Founded 1960, incorporating Ez-Zitouna Islamic University, the Institut des hautes Etudes established in 1945, and other existing institutions of higher education. Reorganized as Université de Tunis from former Université des Lettres, des Arts et des Sciences humaines (Tunis I) 2001 when the Faculty of Letters became independent institution (Université de La Manouba).

Governing Bodies: Councils of the University and its constituent faculties and schools

Academic Year: October to June (October-February; February-June)

Admission Requirements: Secondary school certificate (baccalauréat) or foreign equivalent

Main Language(s) of Instruction: Arabic, French

Degrees and Diplomas: *Certificat d'Aptitude:* Journalism, 2 yrs; *Technicien supérieur:* Economics and Management, a further 2 yrs following Licence; *Certificat de Capacité:* Economics; Law, 2 yrs; *Diplôme universitaire d'Etudes littéraires:* 2 yrs; *Diplôme universitaire d'Etudes scientifiques:* 2 yrs; *Diplôme:* Commerce; Education, 4 yrs; Engineering, 4-6 yrs; *Licence:* Economics; Journalism; Law; Religious Sciences; Theology, 4 yrs; *Maîtrise:* Letters; Science, 4 yrs; *Diplôme d'Architecte:* Architecture and Town Planning, 7 yrs; *Diplome d'Etudes approfondies (DEA):* Science (DEA), a further 1-2 yrs following Maîtrise; *Doctorat:* Arabic Language and Literature; Medicine, 6 yrs; Letters; Science, a further 2-3 yrs following DEA

Student Services: Cultural Centre, Sports Facilities, Health Services

Libraries: Total, c. 186,000 vols

Publications: Cahiers de Tunisie (quarterly); Revue des Sciences sociales; Annales de l'Université de Tunis (in Arabic)

Academic Staff *1999:* Total: c. 850
Student Numbers *1999:* Total: c. 23,745

CENTRE FOR ECONOMIC AND SOCIAL STUDIES AND
RESEARCH
CENTRE D'ETUDES ET DE RECHERCHES
ÉCONOMIQUES ET SOCIALES
23, rue d'Espagne, 1000 Tunis
Tel: +216(71) 244-810
Fax: +216(71) 343-237

Directeur: Hachmi Labaïed

Programmes
Economics and Social Studies (Economics; Social Studies)

HIGHER INSTITUTE OF APPLIED STUDIES IN
HUMANITIES, TUNIS
INSTITUT SUPÉRIEUR DES ETUDES APPLIQUÉES EN
HUMANITÉS DE TUNIS
23, avenue Hédi Saidi, El Omrane, 1005 Tunis
Tel: +216(71) 899-006

Directeur: Jamel Ben Tahar (2000-)

Secrétaire général: Abdellah Belarbi

Programmes
Executive Manager Training (Arabic; Computer Science;
English; French; Modern Languages; Painting and Drawing;
Psychology; Sociology; Sports)
Executive Tourism Training (English; French; Leisure
Studies; Modern Languages; Painting and Drawing; Tourism)

History: Founded 2000.

Main Language(s) of Instruction: Arabic, French

HIGHER INSTITUTE OF CULTURAL SCIENCES AND
HERITAGE, TUNIS
INSTITUT SUPÉRIEUR DES SCIENCES CULTURELLES ET
MÉTIERS DU PATRIMOINE DE TUNIS
10, rue Kelibia, 1002 Tunis

Directeur: Habib Baklouti

Secrétaire général: Mohamed Salah Ben Miled

Programmes
Cultural Studies
Heritage (Cultural Studies; Heritage Preservation)

Main Language(s) of Instruction: Arabic, French

HIGHER INSTITUTE OF DRAMATIC ART
INSTITUT SUPÉRIEUR D'ART DRAMATIQUE
16, rue Mikhaïl Nouaima, El Omrane, 1005 Tunis
Tel: +216(71) 891-333
Fax: +216(71) 289-612

Directeur: Mohamed Messaoud Idriss (1995-)

Secrétaire général: Faouzi Mahmoud

Programmes
Dramatic Art (Acting; Performing Arts; Theatre)

History: Founded 1982.

HIGHER INSTITUTE OF EDUCATION AND FURTHER
EDUCATION
INSTITUT SUPÉRIEUR DE L'EDUCATION ET DE LA
FORMATION CONTINUE
43, rue de la Liberté, Le Bardo, 2000 Tunis
Tel: +216(71) 563-170
Fax: +216(71) 568-954

Directrice: Malika Trabelsi (1995-) Tel: +216(71) 564-727
EMail: malika.trabelsi@isefc.rnu.tn

Departments
Arabic Language and Letters (Arabic; Arts and Humanities)
Education
Foreign Languages (Modern Languages)
Human Sciences (Arts and Humanities)
Mathematics
Natural Sciences
Physics and Technology (Physics; Technology)

History: Founded 1982.

Main Language(s) of Instruction: Arabic, French

HIGHER INSTITUTE OF FINE ARTS, TUNIS
INSTITUT SUPÉRIEUR DES BEAUX ARTS DE TUNIS
Route de l'Armée nationale, El Omrane, 1005 Tunis
Tel: +216(71) 898-447
Fax: +216(71) 568-291

Directeur: Naceur Ben Cheikh Tel: +216(71) 898-441

Departments
Plastic Arts (Fine Arts)
Science and Technology of Arts (Fine Arts; Technology)

History: Founded 1995.

HIGHER INSTITUTE OF MANAGEMENT, TUNIS
INSTITUT SUPÉRIEUR DE GESTION DE TUNIS
41, rue de la Liberté, Cité Bouchoucha, Le Bardo, 2000 Tunis
Tel: +216(71) 560-378
Fax: +216(71) 568-767

Directeur: Abdelwahed Trabelsi (2001-)
Tel: +216(71) 560-313

Secrétaire général: Jellali Noureddine

Departments
Applied Computerized Management (Business Computing;
Management)
Finance and Accountancy (Accountancy; Finance)
Management, Human Resources and Law (Commercial Law;
Human Resources; Law; Management)
Marketing, International Business and Languages (English;
French; German; International Business; Marketing; Modern
Languages; Spanish)
Quantitative Methods and Economics (Economics; Manage-
ment Systems)

History: Founded 1969.

Academic Year: September to June (September-January;
February-June)

Academic Staff *1999*: Full-Time: c. 215 Part-Time: c. 80 Total: c. 295

Student Numbers *1999:* Total: c. 3,300

HIGHER INSTITUTE OF MUSIC, TUNIS
INSTITUT SUPÉRIEUR DE MUSIQUE DE TUNIS
20, avenue de Paris, 1000 Tunis
Tel: +216(71) 255-577
Fax: +216(71) 245-575

Directeur: Mustapha Aloulou (1982-) Tel: +216(71) 257-526
Secrétaire général: Mohamed Tlili

Programmes
Music (Music; Music Theory and Composition; Musical Instruments; Musicology)

History: Founded 1982.
Main Language(s) of Instruction: Arabic, French

HIGHER INSTITUTE OF PHYSICAL EDUCATION, LE KEF
INSTITUT SUPÉRIEUR D'EDUCATION PHYSIQUE DU KEF
Cité Eddir, 7100 Le Kef
Tel: +216(78) 202-873
Fax: +216(78) 201-679

Directeur: Mohamed El Hadj Yahmed (1998-)
Tel: +216(71) 201-679
Secrétaire général: Ahmed Rabhi

Institutes
Physical Education and Sports (Physical Education; Sports)
Director: Ahmed Rabhi, *full-time staff:* 34, *students:* 280

History: Founded 1990, acquired present status 1992.

HIGHER INSTITUTE FOR YOUTH AND CULTURE
INSTITUT SUPÉRIEUR DE L'ANIMATION POUR LA JEUNESSE ET LA CULTURE
Bir El Bey, 2055 Tunis
Tel: +216(71) 420-075
Fax: +216(71) 420-608

Directeur: Mohamed Taoufik Haouet (1995-)
Tel: +216(71) 420-090
Secrétaire général: Abdeljelil Bourgou

Departments
Animation Techniques (Leisure Studies)
General Training (Leisure Studies)

History: Founded 1968, merged with the Institut supérieur de l'Animation culturelle 1995. Acquired present status and title 1995.

HIGHER SCHOOL OF ECONOMICS AND COMMERCE, TUNIS
ECOLE SUPÉRIEURE DES SCIENCES ÉCONOMIQUES ET COMMERCIALES DE TUNIS
4, rue Abou Zakaria El Hafsi, Montfleury, 1008 Tunis
Tel: +216(71) 333-518
Fax: +216(71) 333-518

Directeur: Chokri Mamoghli Tel: +216(71) 334-190
Secrétaire général: Fethi Ben Echeikh

Programmes
Economics and Commerce (Business and Commerce; Economics)

HIGHER SCHOOL OF SCIENCE AND TECHNOLOGY, TUNIS
ECOLE SUPÉRIEURE DES SCIENCES ET TECHNIQUES DE TUNIS
5, avenue Taha Hussein, Montfleury, 1008 Tunis
Tel: +216(71) 496-066
Fax: +216(71) 391-166

Directeur: Slaheddine Gherissi Tel: +216(71) 392-591
EMail: slah.gherissi@esstt.rnu.tn

Departments
Civil Engineering *Head:* Mohamed Ali Komiha
Electrical Engineering *Head:* Abdelkader Chaari
Mathematics and Computer Science *Head:* Jounaidi Abdeljaoued
Mechanical Engineering *Head:* Mohamed Tmar
Physics and Chemistry (Chemistry; Physics) *Head:* Mohamed Daoud

History: Founded 1973, acquired present status and title 1994.

HIGHER TEACHER TRAINING SCHOOL, TUNIS
ECOLE NORMALE SUPÉRIEURE DE TUNIS
8, place aux Chevaux, El Gorjani, Montfleury, 1008 Tunis
Tel: +216(71) 562-305
Fax: +216(71) 562-998

Directeur: Samir Marzouki
EMail: samir.marzouki@ens.rnu.tn
Secrétaire générale: Hmaida El Hedfi

Departments
Letters and Human Sciences (Arabic; Arts and Humanities; English; French; Geography; History; Mathematics; Physics; Psychology; Social Sciences)

Main Language(s) of Instruction: Arabic, French

NATIONAL INSTITUTE OF HERITAGE
INSTITUT NATIONAL DU PATRIMOINE
4, place du Kaser, Bab Menara, 1008 Tunis
Tel: +216(71) 561-693
Fax: +216(71) 562-452

Directeur: Boubaker Ben Fredj Tel: +216(71) 561-622
Secrétaire général: Béchir El Aloui

Programmes
Heritage Studies (Heritage Preservation; Museum Management; Museum Studies; Restoration of Works of Art)

History: Founded 1957.

PREPARATORY INSTITUTE FOR ENGINEERING STUDIES, TUNIS
INSTITUT PRÉPARATOIRE AUX ETUDES D'INGÉNIEURS DE TUNIS
2, rue Jawaher El Nahrou, Montfleury, 1008 Tunis
Tel: +216(71) 336-641
Fax: +216(71) 337-323

Directeur: Mohamed Abedelmanaf Ben Abdrabou
Tel: +216(71) 336-653

Secrétaire général: Mohamed Sakly

Programmes
Engineering (Engineering; Technology)

History: Founded 1995.

* UNIVERSITY OF TUNIS EL MANAR
Université de Tunis El Manar
BP 94, El Romana, 1068 Tunis
Tel: +216(71) 873-366
Fax: +216(71) 872-055
EMail: unitumanar@tun2.rnu.tn

Président: Youssef Alouane (2001-) Tel: +216(71) 871-567

Secrétaire général: Ismaïl Khelil
EMail: ismail.khelil@tun2.rnu.tn

Faculties
Economics and Management (Economics; Management; Management Systems) *Dean:* Messaoud Boudhiaf
Law and Political Science (Criminal Law; Political Science; Private Law; Public Law) *Dean:* Mohamed Ridha Ben Hammed
Mathematics, Physics and Natural Sciences (Applied Mathematics; Biological and Life Sciences; Biotechnology; Chemistry; Computer Science; Earth Sciences; Electronic Engineering; Environmental Engineering; Mathematics; Natural Sciences; Physics) *Dean:* Chedli Touibi, *full-time staff:* 391, *students:* 8,137
Medicine (Acupuncture; Cardiology; Education of the Handicapped; Genetics; Gerontology; Neurological Therapy; Rehabilitation and Therapy; Social and Preventive Medicine; Sports Medicine; Toxicology) *Dean:* Rachid Mechmech, *full-time staff:* 811, *students:* 1,994

History: Founded 1988 incorporating existing faculties.

Academic Year: September to June

Main Language(s) of Instruction: French, Arabic, English

International Co-operation: University of Cadi Ayadh, Marrakech; University of Ottawa; Laval University; University of Oran; Université de Nice-Sophia Antipolis; Université de Toulouse-le-Mirail II; Université Bordeaux I; Université Bordeaux II; Politecnico di Torino; Università degli Studi di Ferrara; University of Amsterdam; Princeton University; United Arab Emirates University

Degrees and Diplomas: *Diplôme universitaire de Technologie (DUT):* Civil Engineering (DUT); Electrical Maintenance (DUT), 2 yrs; *Technicien supérieur:* Agricultural Engineering; Agriculture; Engineering (DTS); Food Technology; Forestry; Health Sciences; Telecommunications, 2 yrs; *Diplôme universitaire*

d'Etudes scientifiques: Science (DUES), 2 yrs; *Diplôme:* Agronomy; Computer Engineering; Technology; Veterinary Medicine; *Diplôme d'Ingénieur:* Agricultural Engineering; Agriculture; Agronomy; Computer Engineering; Engineering; Food Technology; Geology, 4 yrs; *Maîtrise:* Art; Engineering; Physical Education; Science; Technology, 4 yrs; *Diplôme d'Architecte:* Architecture and Town Planning; *Diplome d'Etudes approfondies (DEA):* Computer Engineering (DEA); Engineering (DEA); Mathematics (DEA); Natural Sciences (DEA); Physics (DEA); Technology (DEA), a further 2 yrs following Maîtrise; *Doctorat:* Biology; Chemistry; Computer Science; Geology; Mathematics; Medicine; Physics; Town Planning; Veterinary Medicine; Engineering, 6 yrs

Academic Staff *1999:* Total: c. 2,735

Student Numbers *1999:* Total: c. 22,530

BOURGUIBA INSTITUTE OF MODERN LANGUAGES
INSTITUT BOURGUIBA DES LANGUES VIVANTES
47, avenue de la Liberté, 1002 Tunis
Tel: +216(71) 835-885
Fax: +216(71) 833-684
Website: http://www.mes.tn/iblv/index.html

Directeur: Abed El Majid El Bedoui Tel: +216(71) 833-393

Secrétaire général: Béchir El Manaï

Departments
Arabic and Translation (Arabic; Translation and Interpretation)
English
French
Modern Languages (German; Hebrew; Italian; Modern Languages; Spanish; Turkish)

History: Founded 1964.

Main Language(s) of Instruction: Arabic, French

'EL KHAWARIZMI' COMPUTER CENTRE
CENTRE DE CALCUL 'EL KHAWARIZMI'
Campus Universitaire, 1060 Tunis
Tel: +216(71) 873-756
Fax: +216(71) 871-032
EMail: cck@cck.rnu.tn
Website: http://www.cck.rnu.tn

Directrice: Henda Hadjami Ben Ghezala
Tel: +216(71) 873-740

Programmes
Computer Science (Computer Science; Mathematics and Computer Science; Statistics)

History: Founded 1976.

Main Language(s) of Instruction: Arabic, French

HIGHER INSTITUTE OF COMPUTER SCIENCE, EL MANAR
INSTITUT SUPÉRIEUR D'INFORMATIQUE D'EL MANAR
2, rue Abou Raihan El Bayrouni, 2080 Ariana
Tel: +216(71) 706-317
Fax: +216(71) 706-164

Directeur: Samir Ben Ahmed (2001-)

Secrétaire général: Salah Kamoun

Programmes

Computer Science (Computer Networks; Mathematics and Computer Science; Statistics)

History: Founded 2001.

HIGHER INSTITUTE OF HUMANITIES, TUNIS
INSTITUT SUPÉRIEUR DES SCIENCES HUMAINES DE TUNIS
26, avenue Darghouth Bacha, 1007 Tunis
Tel: +216(71) 563-170
Fax: +216(71) 571-911

Directeur: Mohamed Mahjoub **Tel:** +216(71) 569-499

Secrétaire général: Ali Fetehi

Departments

Arabic
English
French
Psychology
Social Sciences

Main Language(s) of Instruction: Arabic, French

HIGHER INSTITUTE OF MEDICAL TECHNOLOGY
INSTITUT SUPÉRIEUR DES TECHNOLOGIES MÉDICALES
9, rue Zouheir Safi, 1006 Tunis
Tel: +216(71) 563-710
Fax: +216(71) 563-710

Directrice: Fatma Slim (2001-)

Secrétaire général: Mehdi Badreddine

Programmes

Medical Technology

History: Founded 2001.

HIGHER SCHOOL OF HEALTH SCIENCES AND TECHNOLOGY, TUNIS
ECOLE SUPÉRIEURE DES SCIENCES ET TECHNIQUES DE LA SANTÉ DE TUNIS
BP 176, Bab Souika, 1006 Tunis
Tel: +216(71) 562-455
Fax: +216(71) 570-062

Directeur: Mohamed Habib Jaâfoura

Secrétaire général: Chedly Beji

Programmes

Health Sciences and Technology (Dental Technology; Dentistry; Health Sciences; Medical Technology; Medicine; Surgery)

History: Founded 1990.

NATIONAL RESEARCH INSTITUTE OF SCIENCE AND TECHNOLOGY
INSTITUT NATIONAL DE RECHERCHE SCIENTIFIQUE ET TECHNIQUE
BP 95, Bordj Cedria, 2050 Hammam Lif
Tel: +216(71) 430-215
Fax: +216(71) 430-934

Directeur: Mohamed Nabli

Programmes

Science and Technology (Natural Sciences; Technology)

NATIONAL SCHOOL OF ENGINEERING, TUNIS
ECOLE NATIONALE D'INGÉNIEURS DE TUNIS
BP 37, Le Belvédère, Campus Universitaire, 1060 Tunis
Tel: +216(71) 874-700
Fax: +216(71) 872-729
Telex: 15051
EMail: enit.info@enit.rnu.tn

Directeur: Khalifa Maâlel (1998-) **Tel:** +216(71) 872-880
EMail: khalifa.maalel@enit.rnu.tn

Secrétaire général: Tahar Friâa

Departments

Civil Engineering (Civil Engineering; Construction Engineering; Environmental Engineering; Hydraulic Engineering)
Electical Engineering (Computer Engineering; Electrical Engineering; Telecommunications Engineering)
Industrial Engineering
Mechanical Engineering

History: Founded 1969.

NATIONAL UNIVERSITY CENTRE FOR SCIENTIFIC AND TECHNICAL DOCUMENTATION
CENTRE NATIONAL UNIVERSITAIRE DE DOCUMENTATION SCIENTIFIQUE ET TECHNIQUE
BP 85, 1, avenue de France, 1002 Tunis
Tel: +216(71) 336-708
Fax: +216(71) 354-216

Directrice: Fatma Chammam-Ben Abdallah

Programmes

Scientific and Technical Documentation (Documentation Techniques; Information Technology; Library Science)

Main Language(s) of Instruction: Arabic, French

PASTEUR INSTITUTE
INSTITUT PASTEUR
13, place Pasteur, 1002 Tunis
Tel: +216(71) 843-755
Fax: +216(71) 791-833
Telex: 14391 PASTU TN

Directeur: Koussaoi Edalaji **Tel:** +216(71) 845-452

Secrétaire général: Souad Hajjem

Programmes

Biological Research (Biological and Life Sciences; Biology; Immunology; Microbiology; Pharmacology)

History: Founded 1893.

PREPARATORY INSTITUTE FOR ENGINEERING STUDIES, EL MANAR
INSTITUT PRÉPARATOIRE AUX ETUDES D'INGÉNIEURS D'EL MANAR
BP 37, Le Belvédère, Campus universitaire, 1002 Tunis
Tel: +216(71) 872-330
Fax: +216(71) 872-729

Directeur: Mohamed Abaad (2001-)
Secrétaire général: Abderraouf Chaouch

Programmes
Engineering (Engineering; Technology)

History: Founded 2001.

SCHOOL OF CIVIL AVIATION AND METEOROLOGY, BORJ EL AMRI
ECOLE DE L'AVIATION CIVILE ET DE LA MÉTÉOROLOGIE DE BORJ EL AMRI
1142, Aérodrome de Borj El Amri, Route de Medjez El Bab, 9070 Borj El Amri
Tel: +216(71) 540-837

Directeur: Mohamed Touil

Programmes
Civil Aviation and Meteorology (Air Transport; Meteorology)

VETERINARY RESEARCH INSTITUTE, TUNIS
INSTITUT DE RECHERCHE VÉTÉRINAIRE DE TUNIS
Rue Jabal El Akdah Errabta, 1006 Tunis
Tel: +216(71) 562-602
Fax: +216(71) 569-692

Directeur: Malek Ezzrelli Tel: +216(71) 564-321

Research Institutes
Veterinary Science (Animal Husbandry; Biotechnology; Veterinary Science)

PRIVATE INSTITUTIONS

FREE UNIVERSITY OF TUNIS
Université libre de Tunis (ULT)
30, avenue Khéreddine Pacha, 1002 Tunis
Tel: +216(71) 890-391
Fax: +216(71) 782-260
EMail: intac.ult@planet.tn
Website: http://www.ult.ens.tn

Président: Mohamed Boussaïri Bouebdelli
Tel: +216(71) 890-393

Faculties
Arts (Architecture; Arts and Humanities; Graphic Arts; Interior Design; Journalism; Painting and Drawing; Sculpture)

Humanities (Arts and Humanities; English; French; Geography; German; History; Italian; Linguistics; Philosophy; Psychology; Sociology; Spanish; Translation and Interpretation)
Law and Political Science (Commercial Law; Law)
Management (Economics; Hotel Management; Management; Tourism)
Science and Applied Science (Biochemistry; Biology; Chemistry; Civil Engineering; Computer Science; Electrical Engineering; Mathematics; Mechanical Engineering; Natural Sciences; Notary Studies; Physics; Statistics)

Higher Schools
Agriculture and Food Science *(ESAA)* (Agriculture; Food Science)
Buildings and Public Works *(ESBTP)* (Building Technologies; Civil Engineering; Construction Engineering)
Climatic and Energy Engineering *(ESEGC)* (Energy Engineering; Meteorology)
Computer Science *(ESI)*
Electronics and Automation *(ESEA)* (Automation and Control Engineering; Electronic Engineering)
Mechanics and Electricity *(ESME)* (Electrical Engineering; Mechanics)

Centres
Continuing Education *(CUFOC)*
Training and Correspondence Education *(International, CIFEC)*

History: Founded 1992 from a merge of Ecole d'Electronique et d'Automatisme and Institut des Technologies avancées et des Etudes commerciales. A private Institution.

Governing Bodies: Conseil d'Administration; Conseil scientifique; Conseil des Etudes et de la Vie universitaire; Conseil de Parrainage

Admission Requirements: Secondary school certificate (Baccalauréat) or equivalent, and entrance examination

Main Language(s) of Instruction: Arabic, French

International Co-operation: Université de Paris I Panthéon Sorbonne; Université du Québec à Montréal; Université Laval; Université de Montréal; Université d'Ottawa; Université de Sherbrooke; Institut national polytechnique de Toulouse; Institut des Etudes politiques d'Aix en Provence

Degrees and Diplomas: *Certificat d'Aptitude*: French; *Diplôme universitaire de Technologie (DUT)*: (DUT), 2 yrs; *Certificat de Capacité*; *Diplôme d'Etudes universitaires de Premier Cycle (DEUPC)*: Business Computing (DEUPC); Economics (DEUPC); Graphic Communication (DEUPC); Management (DEUPC); Plastic Arts (DEUPC), 2 yrs; *Diplôme*: Journalism, 4 yrs; *Diplôme d'Ingénieur*: Civil Engineering; Computer Engineering; Electrical Engineering; Mechanical Engineering, 4 yrs; *Maîtrise*: Arts and Humanities; Business Computing; Commercial Law; Economics; Graphic Communication; International Tourism and Hotel Management; Management; Modern Languages; Plastic Arts, 4 yrs; *Diplôme d'Architecte*: Architecture; Interior Design, 4 yrs; *Diplôme d'études supérieures spécialisées (DESS)*: (DESS), a further yr following Maîtrise; *Diplome d'Etudes approfondies (DEA)*: (DEA), a further 1-2 yrs following Maîtrise

Student Services: Academic Counselling, Foreign Student Adviser, Cultural Centre, Sports Facilities, Language Programmes, Health Services, Canteen, Foreign Student Centre

Student Residential Facilities: Yes

Special Facilities: Studies and Research Centre, Computer Laboratories, Language Laboratories

Libraries: Central Library (2 centres)

OTHER INSTITUTIONS

PUBLIC INSTITUTIONS

HIGHER INSTITUTE OF TECHNOLOGICAL STUDIES, CHARGUIA
Institut supérieur des Etudes technologiques de Charguia (ISET Charguia)
Rue des Entrepreneurs, Charguia II, 2035 Tunis
Tel: +216(71) 704-405

Directeur: Habib Zenguer

Secrétaire général: Ahmed Ktari

Programmes
Engineering
Technology

Main Language(s) of Instruction: Arabic, French

HIGHER INSTITUTE OF TECHNOLOGICAL STUDIES, GABÈS
Institut supérieur des Etudes technologiques de Gabès (ISET Gabès)
Cité El Manara, 6029 Gabès
Tel: +216(75) 282-053
Fax: +216(75) 280-041

Directeur: Mohamed Abderrazak Jdaï **Tel:** +216(75) 280-651

Secrétaire général: Jamel Amari

Programmes
Engineering
Technology

History: Founded 1995.

Main Language(s) of Instruction: Arabic, French

HIGHER INSTITUTE OF TECHNOLOGICAL STUDIES, GAFSA
Institut supérieur des Etudes technologiques de Gafsa (ISET Gafsa)
Campus universitaire 2, Sidi Hmid Zarrou, 2119 Gafsa
Tel: +216(76) 211-081
Fax: +216(76) 211-080

Directeur: Jalel Kdhiri **Tel:** +216(76) 211-040

Secrétaire général: Mohamed Gedouara
Tel: +216(76) 211-041

Programmes
Engineering (Engineering; Industrial Engineering; Mining Engineering)

History: Founded 1995.

Main Language(s) of Instruction: Arabic, French

Student Numbers *1999:* Total: c. 765

HIGHER INSTITUTE OF TECHNOLOGICAL STUDIES, DJERBA
Institut supérieur des Etudes technologiques de Djerba (ISET Djerba)
Route Houmet Essouk Km. 2, 4116 Midoun Djerba
Tel: +216(75) 603-109
Fax: +216(75) 603-111

Directeur: Mohamed Elkouni Ben Gaïed
Tel: +216(75) 603-110

Secrétaire général: Béchir Mahdhaoui

Programmes
Engineering
Technology

Main Language(s) of Instruction: Arabic, French

HIGHER INSTITUTE OF TECHNOLOGICAL STUDIES, KAIROUAN
Institut supérieur des Etudes technologiques de Kairouan (ISET Kairouan)
Avenue Assad Ibn El Fourat, 3100 Kairouan
Tel: +216(77) 228-456
Fax: +216(77) 228-503

Directeur: Mohamed Nabil Mzoughi

Programmes
Engineering
Technology

Main Language(s) of Instruction: Arabic, French

HIGHER INSTITUTE OF TECHNOLOGICAL STUDIES, KSAR HELLAL
Institut supérieur des Etudes technologiques de Ksar Hellal (ISET Ksar Hellal)
Rue Hadj Ali Soua, 5070 Ksar Hellal
Tel: +216(73) 475-907
Fax: +216(73) 475-163

Directeur: Faouzi Sakli **Tel:** +216(73) 475-900

Secrétaire général: Mustapha Khouja

Programmes
Textile Technology

History: Founded 1995.
Main Language(s) of Instruction: Arabic, French

HIGHER INSTITUTE OF TECHNOLOGICAL STUDIES, MAHDIA
Institut supérieur des Etudes technologiques de Mahdia (ISET Mahdia)
Avenue Mourouj, Hiboum, 5111 Mahdia
Tel: +216(73) 672-399
Fax: +216(73) 219-497
Directeur: Hamadi Ben Naceur (2001-)
Secrétaire général: Ridha Nasr

Programmes
Engineering
Technology

History: Founded 2001.
Main Language(s) of Instruction: Arabic, French

HIGHER INSTITUTE OF TECHNOLOGICAL STUDIES, NABEUL
Institut supérieur des Etudes technologiques de Nabeul (ISET Nabeul)
Campus Universitaire Mrezgua, 8000 Nabeul
Tel: +216(72) 220-051
Fax: +216(72) 220-033
Directeur: Mohamed Kerkeni Tel: +216(72) 220-035
Secrétaire général: Souayeh Kheder

Programmes
Civil Engineering
Electrical Engineering
Maintenance Technology

History: Founded 1995.
Main Language(s) of Instruction: Arabic, French

HIGHER INSTITUTE OF TECHNOLOGICAL STUDIES, RADÈS
Institut supérieur des Etudes technologiques de Radès (ISET Radès)
Rue El Kods, 2080 Radès
Tel: +216(71) 460-100
Fax: +216(71) 442-322
Directeur: Naceur Hadj Braïek Tel: +216(71) 461-610
Secrétaire général: Ahmed Ktari

Programmes
Engineering
Technology

History: Founded 1992.
Main Language(s) of Instruction: Arabic, French

HIGHER INSTITUTE OF TECHNOLOGICAL STUDIES, SFAX
Institut supérieur des Etudes technologiques de Sfax (ISET Sfax)
BP 88a, Route de Medhia Km. 2,5, El Bosten, 3002 Sfax
Tel: +216(74) 237-425
Fax: +216(74) 237-386
Directeur: Slimène Gabsi Tel: +216(74) 237-493
Secrétaire général: Abdellatif Yengui Tel: +216(74) 237-495

Programmes
Engineering
Technology

History: Founded 1992.
Main Language(s) of Instruction: Arabic, French

HIGHER INSTITUTE OF TECHNOLOGICAL STUDIES, SOUSSE
Institut supérieur des Etudes technologiques de Sousse (ISET Sousse)
Cité Erriadh, 4032 Sousse
Tel: +216(73) 307-960
Fax: +216(73) 307-963
Directeur: Abdelwaheb Dogui Tel: +216(73) 307-961
Secrétaire général: Abdessattar Ben Dhia

Programmes
Engineering
Technology

History: Founded 1992.
Main Language(s) of Instruction: Arabic, French

HIGHER INSTITUTE OF TECHNOLOGICAL STUDIES IN COMMUNICATION, TUNIS
Institut supérieur des Etudes technologiques en Communications de Tunis (ISET'COM)
Route de Raoued Km. 3,5, Cité El Ghazala, 2083 Ariana
Tel: +216(71) 857-000
Fax: +216(71) 857-555
EMail: couriel@isetcom.rnu.tn
Website: http://www.isetcom.mincom.tn
Directeur: Lofti Ammar Tel: +216(71) 857-788
Secrétaire général: Abdelhamid Meddeb

Departments
Postal Services
Telecommunications Services (Telecommunications Engineering; Telecommunications Services)

History: Founded 1998.
Main Language(s) of Instruction: Arabic, French

Uganda

INSTITUTION TYPES AND CREDENTIALS

Types of higher education institutions:

University
Polytechnic
Technical College
Teachers' College

School leaving and higher education credentials:

Uganda Advanced Certificate of Education
Grade III Teachers' Certificate
Grade IV Teachers' Certificate
Ordinary Diploma in Electrical Engineering
Ordinary Technician's Diploma
Grade V Teachers' Certificate
Higher Diploma in Electrical Engineering
Higher Technician's Diploma
Certificate
Diploma
Bachelor's Degree
Postgraduate Diploma
Master's Degree
Doctor's Degree

STRUCTURE OF EDUCATION SYSTEM

Pre-higher education:

Structure of school system:

Primary
Type of school providing this education: Primary School
Length of programme in years: 7
Age level from: 6 to: 13

Lower Secondary
Type of school providing this education: Lower Secondary School
Length of programme in years: 4

Age level from: 13 to: 17
Certificate/diploma awarded: Uganda Certificate of Education

Technical Secondary
Type of school providing this education: Technical Secondary School
Length of programme in years: 3
Age level from: 13 to: 16
Certificate/diploma awarded: Uganda Junior Technical Certificate

Upper Secondary
Type of school providing this education: Upper Secondary School
Length of programme in years: 2
Age level from: 17 to: 19
Certificate/diploma awarded: Uganda Advanced Certificate of Education

School education:

Primary education lasts for seven years, leading to the Primary School Leaving Certificate. Secondary education is divided into two cycles: lower secondary and upper secondary. Lower secondary education lasts for four years. At the end of Form 4 pupils sit for the examinations for the Uganda Certificate of Education. Upper secondary education lasts for two years and leads to the Uganda Advanced Certificate of Education at the end of Form 6. Technical secondary schools offer three-year full-time courses to pupils who successfully pass the Primary School Leaving Examination. Students sit for the Uganda Junior Technical Certificate at the end of the course. Qualifying students who do very well can enter the technical institutes. Agriculture is compulsory in all secondary schools.

Higher education:

Higher education is provided by universities, both public and private, a polytechnic, teachers' colleges and technical colleges. The key body which is responsible for planning university education is the University Council in consultation with the appropriate government agencies such as the Ministry of Education. The University Council acts as the main governing body and has a joint membership of both academic staff and representatives of society. It is assisted by a Senate which is responsible for all academic concerns.

Academic year:

Classes from: October *to:* July

Languages of instruction:

English

Stages of studies:

Non-university level post-secondary studies (technical/vocational type):

Higher technical and vocational education is provided by technical colleges which offer two-year courses leading to the Ordinary Technician's Diploma to holders of the Uganda Advanced Certificate of Education with at least one principal pass in Physics and a subsidiary pass in Mathematics or vice versa. A further two years lead to the Higher Technician's Diploma. A full-time three-year course at

503

the Uganda Polytechnic leads to the Ordinary Diploma in Electrical Engineering. Requirements for entry are at least two principal passes in Mathematics, Chemistry or Physics and one subsidiary pass in any of them. The Higher Diploma in Electrical Engineering is conferred at the end of a two-year full-time course. Students must hold an Ordinary Diploma pass with grade passes 1-2 and 3-6. They must also have completed one year's practical work experience.

University level studies:

University level first stage: Certificate, Diploma, Bachelor's Degree:
Certificates are awarded after six months in Librarianship and after one year in Theology. Diplomas are conferred in Music, Dance and Drama after two years and an entrance examination. The Bachelor's Degree is conferred after studies lasting between three (Arts, Science, Law), four (Engineering, Agriculture, Forestry, Agricultural Engineering) and five years (Medicine, Pharmacy, Engineering).

University level second stage: Diploma, Master's Degree:
In Education, a Diploma is conferred after one year's postgraduate education or two years after the Post-Higher School Certificate. The Master's Degree is conditional upon the student's being resident in the University and is awarded after eighteen months' study following upon the Bachelor's Degree in Fine Arts, Arts, Science, Agriculture, Education and Surgery. Candidates must submit a thesis and, in some cases, must do course work as well. In Medicine, three years' research work and courses are required. An advanced professional qualification, the Diploma, is awarded in Education and Medicine (Paediatrics, Public Health and Obstetrics) one year after the Bachelor's Degree.

University level third stage: Doctor's Degree:
The Doctor's Degree is conferred in all faculties except Law and Technology after a minimum of three years' research subsequent to the Master's Degree. Candidates must submit a thesis. In Medicine, the Doctor's Degree is a professional title (Doctor of Medicine, MD) awarded at least one year after the Bachelor's Degree upon submission of a thesis.

Teacher education:

Training of pre-primary and primary/basic school teachers
Primary school teachers are trained at Grade III primary teachers colleges. For lower primary school, candidates who have completed four years of secondary education follow a two-year course leading to the Grade III Teachers Certificate. Upper primary school teachers who hold the Uganda Certificate of Education follow a one-year course leading to the Grade IV Teachers Certificate.

Training of secondary school teachers
Secondary school teachers are trained at the National Teachers' Colleges, the University and the Institute of Teacher Education, Kyambogo. Courses last two years. There is also a three-year upgrading course for grade IV teachers leading to the Grade V Teachers Certificate. To teach in Form 6, teachers must hold a Bachelor of Education Degree.

Non-traditional studies:

Distance higher education
Distance education is offered by the Centre for Continuing Education of Makerere University. It

provides university type instruction in various parts of the country by correspondence and via the press, radio and television.

Lifelong higher education
The Centre for Continuing Education of Makerere University organizes a one-year full-time course for adults leading to a certificate and a special course which prepares mature students for higher studies.

NATIONAL BODIES

Responsible authorities:

Ministry of Education and Sports
    Minister: Makubuya Kiddu
    PO Box 7063
    Kampala
    Tel: +256(41) 257-200
    Fax: +256(41) 230-437
    WWW: http://www.education.go.ug

Role of governing body: Oversees teacher training, technical and commercial education. Plans university education in conjunction with the university councils

ADMISSIONS TO HIGHER EDUCATION

Admission to non university higher education studies

Name of secondary school credential required: Uganda Advanced Certificate of Education
Minimum score/requirement: One principal pass in Physics and a subsidiary pass in Maths or vice versa.
For entry to: Technical Colleges

Name of secondary school credential required: Uganda Advanced Certificate of Education
Minimum score/requirement: Two principal passes in Maths, Physics or Chemistry and one subsidiary pass in any of them.
For entry to: Uganda Polytechnic

Admission to university-level studies

Name of secondary school credential required: Uganda Advanced Certificate of Education
Minimum score/requirement: Six passes in approved subjects at Uganda Certificate of Education and two at Advanced Certificate level.

Foreign students admission

Admission requirements: Foreign students wishing to study in Ugandan universities should possess the Ugandan Advanced Level Certificate or an equivalent qualification.

Entry regulations: They should obtain a visa from the Ugandan Embassy in their country and must be proficient in English.

Health requirements: Health Certificate.

Recognition of studies and qualifications:

Studies pursued in foreign countries (bodies dealing with recognition of foreign credentials):
National Curriculum Development Centre
    Director: Peter Muyanda-Mutebi
    PO Box 7002
    Kampala
    Tel: +256(41) 285-885
    Telex: 62039 IDAMOE UGA

References to further information on foreign student admissions and recognition of studies

Title: Makerere University Calendar
Publisher: Makerere University

Title: Prospectus
Publisher: Uganda Martyrs University

Title: Study Abroad 2000-2001
Publisher: UNESCO/IBE
Year of publication: 1999

STUDENT LIFE

Student expenses and financial aid

Student costs:

    Home students tuition fees: Minimum: 1,000,000 (Uganda Shilling)
    Maximum: 3,800,000 (Uganda Shilling)
    Foreign students tuition fees: Minimum: 1,700 (US Dollar)
    Maximum: 3,500 (US Dollar)

Bodies providing information on student financial aid:

Central Scholarships Committee, Ministry of Education and Sports
    PO Box 7063, Crested Towers
    Kampala
    Tel: +256(41) 234-451
    Fax: +256(41) 345-994
    Deals with: Grants

GRADING SYSTEM

Usual grading system in secondary school

Full Description: A-F; 1-9; 1-2 very good (distinction); 3-6 credit pass; 7-8 pass grade; 9 fail.

Highest on scale: A 1

Pass/fail level: 7-8

Lowest on scale: F 9

Main grading system used by higher education institutions

Full Description: Bachelor's degree: class I top honours; class II(i) honours upper; class II(ii) honours lower; pass general pass; fail

NOTES ON HIGHER EDUCATION SYSTEM

Data for academic year: 2000-2001

Source: International Association of Universities (IAU)

INSTITUTIONS OF HIGHER EDUCATION

UNIVERSITIES

PUBLIC INSTITUTIONS

*• MAKERERE UNIVERSITY (MAK)

PO Box 7062, Kampala
Tel: +256(41) 532-631   +256(41) 542-803
Fax: +256(41) 541-068   +256(41) 531-288
Telex: 61351
Cable: makunika
EMail: postmaster@mak.ac.ug
Website: http://www.makerere.ac.ug

Vice-Chancellor: John P.M. Ssebuwufu (1993-)
EMail: vc@mak.ac.ug

University Secretary: Sam Byanagwa
Tel: +256(41) 533-332 EMail: us@mak.ac.ug

Academic Registrar: Sebastian M. Ngobi
Tel: +256(41) 532-752 Fax: +256(41) 533-640
EMail: acadreg@mak.ac.ug

Faculties

Agriculture (Agricultural Economics; Agricultural Engineering; Agriculture; Animal Husbandry; Crop Production; Food Science; Food Technology; Soil Science; Technology) *Dean:* E.N. Sabiiti, *full-time staff:* 93, *students:* 696

Arts (Art History; Arts and Humanities; Dance; English; Geography; History; Literature; Mass Communication; Modern Languages; Music; Philosophy; Printing and Printmaking; Religious Studies; Sculpture; Theatre) *Dean:* O. Ndoleriire, *full-time staff:* 104, *students:* 4,135

Education (Education; Natural Sciences; Technology Education) *Dean:* C. J. Sekamwa, *full-time staff:* 57, *students:* 2,346

Forestry and Nature Conservation (Ecology; Forest Biology; Forest Management; Forestry) *Dean:* J.R.S Kaboggoza, *full-time staff:* 23

Law *Dean:* J. Oloka-Onyango, *full-time staff:* 33, *students:* 971

Medicine *Dean:* N.K. Sewankambo, *full-time staff:* 149, *students:* 722

Science (Botany; Chemistry; Geology; Mathematics; Natural Sciences; Physics; Zoology) *Dean:* L.S. Luboobi, *full-time staff:* 130, *students:* 966

Social Sciences (Educational Psychology; Human Rights; Political Science; Public Administration; Social Sciences; Social Work; Sociology; Women's Studies) *Dean:* Joy Kwesiga, *full-time staff:* 89, *students:* 1,667

Technology (Civil Engineering; Electrical Engineering; Mathematics and Computer Science; Mechanical Engineering; Surveying and Mapping; Technology) *Dean:* B. Kiggundu, *full-time staff:* 81, *students:* 737

Veterinary Medicine (Embryology and Reproduction Biology; Microbiology; Parasitology; Pathology; Physiology; Public Health; Social and Preventive Medicine; Surgery; Veterinary Science) *Dean:* E.R. Katunguka, *full-time staff:* 76, *students:* 211

Schools

Industrial and Fine Arts *(Margaret Trowell School)* (Fine Arts) *Director:* P.K. Kwesiga, *full-time staff:* 27, *students:* 221

Library and Information Science *(EASLIS)* (Information Sciences; Library Science) *Director:* S.A.H. Abidi, *full-time staff:* 7, *students:* 271

Institutes

Adult and Continuing Education (Communication Studies; Distance Education) *Director:* A.N. Sentongo, *full-time staff:* 24, *students:* 204

Agricultural Research *(MUARIK, Kabanyolo)* (Agriculture) *Director:* M.A. Bekunda

Computer Science *Director:* J.N. Mulira

Economics *Director:* J. Dumba Ssentamu, *full-time staff:* 12

Environment and Natural Resources (Environmental Studies; Natural Resources; Surveying and Mapping; Town Planning) *Director (Acting):* P. Kasoma

Psychology *Director:* J. Nambi

Social Research (Social Studies) *Director:* B. Nakanyike Musisi, *full-time staff:* 11

Statistics and Applied Economics (Demography and Population; Economics; Rural Planning; Statistics) *Director:* M. Mugisha, *full-time staff:* 41, *students:* 374

Centres

Human Rights and Peace *(HURIPEC)* (Human Rights; Peace and Disarmament) *Director (Acting):* S.B. Tindifa

Regional Quality of Health Care (Health Administration)

Research Institutes

Makerere University Agricultural Research Institute Kabanyolo *(MAURIK)* (Agriculture)

Further Information: Also Teaching Hospital

History: Founded 1922 as Makerere College and became Makerere University College 1949. Acquired present status 1970 and title 1975.

Governing Bodies: Council, comprising 37 members; Senate, comprising 99 members

Academic Year: October to September (October-February; March-July;July-September)

Admission Requirements: Uganda Certificate of Education (UCE) or equivalent with at least 6 passes in approved subjects, and 2 passes in approved subjects at the same sitting of Uganda Advanced Certificate of Education (UACE) or equivalent

Main Language(s) of Instruction: English

Degrees and Diplomas: *Bachelor's Degree:* 3-5 yrs; *Postgraduate Diploma:* 1 yr; *Master's Degree:* a further 1-3 yrs; *Doctor's Degree:* (PhD), at least 2 yrs

Student Services: Academic Counselling, Social Counselling, Sports Facilities, Language Programmes, Health Services, Canteen

Student Residential Facilities: For 4780 students

Special Facilities: Art Gallery (Margaret Trowell School of Industrial and Fine Arts). Botany and Zoology Biodiversity Data Bank

Libraries: Main Library, c. 550,000 vols

Publications: Annual Report (annually); Handbook 31; University Calendar

Press or Publishing House: Makerere University Printerly

Academic Staff *1999*	TOTAL
FULL-TIME	988
PART-TIME	200
TOTAL	**1,188**

Student Numbers *1999:* Total: **22,000**

• MBARARA UNIVERSITY OF SCIENCE AND TECHNOLOGY (MUST)

PO Box 1410, Kabale Road, Mbarara
Tel: +256(485) 20-785
Fax: +256(485) 20-782
Telex: 21373
Cable: must uga
EMail: mustmed@infocom.co.ug; must@uga.healthnet.org

Vice-Chancellor: Frederick I.B. Kayanja (1988-)
Tel: +256(485) 20-783

Registrar: S.B. Bazirake EMail: vcmust@infocom.co.ug

International Relations: S.B. Bazirake

Faculties

Development Studies (Computer Science; Development Studies) *Dean:* Pamela Mbabazi, *full-time staff:* 11, *part-time staff:* 2, *students:* 75
Medicine *Dean:* E.K. Mutakooha, *full-time staff:* 78, *part-time staff:* 3, *students:* 279
Science Education (Biology; Chemistry; Mathematics; Physics; Science Education) *Dean:* J. Barranga, *full-time staff:* 17, *students:* 135

Institutes

Tropical Forest Conservation (Forestry) *Director:* Richard Malenky, *full-time staff:* 4

History: Founded 1989.

Governing Bodies: Council

Academic Year: October to August (October-December; January-March; April-August)

Admission Requirements: Uganda Certificate of Education or equivalent, or at least 2 principal passes of the Uganda Advanced Certificate of Education or its equivalent

Fees: (Uganda Shillings): 1m.-2.12m. per annum; foreign students, US$,1700-3500

Main Language(s) of Instruction: English

International Co-operation: University of Nottingham; University of Hull

Degrees and Diplomas: *Bachelor's Degree:* Applied Sciences; Development Studies; Science Education, 3 yrs; Medicine, 5 yrs; *Master's Degree:* Science, 2 yrs; Development Studies, a further 2 yrs; Medicine, a further 3 yrs

Student Services: Sports Facilities, Health Services, Canteen

Student Residential Facilities: For 450 students

Libraries: Total, 15,000 vols

Publications: Mbarara Medical School Journal (annually)

Academic Staff *2000*	TOTAL
FULL-TIME	94
PART-TIME	4
TOTAL	**98**

Staff with doctorate: Total: **11**

Student Numbers *2000*	MEN	WOMEN	TOTAL
All (Foreign Included)	378	157	**535**
FOREIGN ONLY	–	–	9

PRIVATE INSTITUTIONS

BUGEMA UNIVERSITY

PO Box 6529, Luwero, Kampala
Tel: +256(41) 542-455
Fax: +256(41) 345-597

Vice-Chancellor: Moses L. Golola-Kajubi

Registrar: José D. Dial

Schools

Business (Business and Commerce)
Humanities and Social Sciences (Arts and Humanities; Social Sciences)
Theology and Religion (Religion; Theology)

History: A private institution.

Admission Requirements: Uganda Certificate of Education or equivalent

Main Language(s) of Instruction: English

Degrees and Diplomas: *Bachelor's Degree:* 3 yrs

ISLAMIC UNIVERSITY IN UGANDA

PO Box 2555, Mbale
Tel: +256(45) 33-502
Fax: +256(45) 34-452 +256(45) 34-461
Telex: 66176isluniv ug
EMail: iuiu@infocom.co.ug
Website: http://www.iuiu.ac.ug

Rector: Mahdi Adamu (1994-)

University Secretary: Ahmad K. Sengendo

Faculties

Arts and Social Sciences (Arts and Humanities; Economics; English; French; Geography; History; Literature; Modern Languages; Political Science; Social Sciences) *Dean:* Tigiti Sengo, *full-time staff:* 25, *part-time staff:* 6

Education (Curriculum; Education; Educational Administration; Educational Psychology; Educational Sciences) *Dean*: Victoria Mukibi, *full-time staff: 7, part-time staff: 8*
Islamic Heritage (Arabic; Islamic Law; Islamic Studies; Sociology) *Dean (Acting)*: Abodulqadir Bolande, *full-time staff: 22, part-time staff: 5*
Management Studies (Management; Public Administration) *Dean*: Haroonah Nsubuga, *full-time staff: 6, part-time staff: 4*
Science (Botany; Chemistry; Computer Science; Mathematics; Natural Sciences; Physics; Zoology) *Dean*: Mustafa A. Allam, *full-time staff: 12, part-time staff: 19*

Programmes

Remedial Studies (Arabic; Biology; Chemistry; Economics; English; History; Islamic Studies; Physics) *Head*: Ibrahim Ngozi, *students: 87*

Centres

Postgraduate Studies *(CPS)* (Islamic Studies; Management; Natural Sciences; Social Sciences) *Director*: Muhammad Jagaba, *students: 47*

History: Founded 1988, acquired present status and title 1990.

Governing Bodies: Organization of Islamic Conference

Academic Year: October to June (October-December; January-March; April-June)

Admission Requirements: Uganda Certificate of Education, or equivalent, with 2 passes at Advanced ('A') Level

Fees: (US Dollars): 600 per annum; postgraduate degrees, 900

Main Language(s) of Instruction: English, Arabic (for Faculty of Islamic Heritage)

International Co-operation: International Islamic University (Petaling Jaya)

Degrees and Diplomas: *Bachelor's Degree*: Arabic Language; Business Studies; Education; Islamic Studies; Public Administration; Science, 3 yrs; *Postgraduate Diploma*: Education, a further yr

Student Services: Academic Counselling, Social Counselling, Sports Facilities, Health Services

Student Residential Facilities: For 662 students

Publications: Islamic University Journal (annually)

Academic Staff 2000			TOTAL
FULL-TIME			77
PART-TIME			54
TOTAL			**131**
STAFF WITH DOCTORATE	MEN	WOMEN	TOTAL
FULL-TIME	–	–	18
PART-TIME	–	12	12
TOTAL	–	–	**30**
Student Numbers 2000	MEN	WOMEN	TOTAL
All (Foreign Included)	811	324	**1,135**

NDEJJE CHRISTIAN UNIVERSITY
PO Box 7088, Gulu Road, Kampala, Central Province
Tel: +256(41) 610-058
Fax: +256(41) 245-597
Vice-Chancellor: Livingstone Walusimbi (1997-2002)

Registrar: Joyce Nkalubo
International Relations: David Mpagi

Schools

Business Administration and Computer Science (Accountancy; Finance; Management; Marketing)
Education

History: Founded 1992 by the Luwero/Namirembe Dioceses of the Anglican Church of Uganda. Acquired present status 1995.

Governing Bodies: University Council

Academic Year: October to August (October-January;February-May; May-August)

Admission Requirements: Uganda Certificate of Education or equivalent

Main Language(s) of Instruction: English

Degrees and Diplomas: *Diploma*: 1-2 yrs; *Bachelor's Degree*: 2-3 yrs

Student Residential Facilities: For c. 300 students

Libraries: Main Library, c. 40,000 vols

NKUMBA UNIVERSITY
PO Box 237, Entebbe Road, Entebbe
Tel: +256(41) 320-134
Fax: +256(41) 321-448
Vice-Chancellor: William Senteza Kajubi (1994-)
Registrar: David Kasasa

Schools

Business Administration (Business Administration; Computer Science; Economics; Statistics)
Commercial, Industrial Art and Design (Business Education; Computer Education; Computer Engineering; Painting and Drawing; Printing and Printmaking; Textile Technology)
Hotel Management, Catering and Tourism (Cooking and Catering; Hotel Management; Tourism)
Management and Education (Accountancy; Business Education; Secretarial Studies)

History: Founded 1951, acquired present status and title 1994.

Governing Bodies: Board of Trustees; University Council

Academic Year: January to December (January-April; May-August; September-December)

Admission Requirements: Uganda Certificate of Education or equivalent

Main Language(s) of Instruction: English

Degrees and Diplomas: *Diploma*: 2 yrs; *Bachelor's Degree*: 3 yrs

Libraries: Nkumba University Library, c. 2000 vols

Publications: Nkumba University Business Journal (annually)

Academic Staff *1999:* Total: c. 55

Student Numbers *1999:* Total: c. 710

UGANDA CHRISTIAN UNIVERSITY

PO Box 4, Bishop Tucker Campus, Mukono
Tel: +256(41) 290-231
Fax: +256(41) 290-139
EMail: ucu@africaonline.co.ug

Vice-Chancellor: Stephen Noll
Academic Registrar: Alex Kagume Mugisha
University Secretary: Gordon Kahangi

Business Administration; Education; Law; Social Studies

History: Founded 1997.
Student Services: Academic Counselling, Social Counselling, Employment Services, Sports Facilities, Health Services, Canteen, Foreign Student Centre

UGANDA MARTYRS UNIVERSITY (UMU)

PO Box 5498, Kampala
Tel: +256(481) 21-894
Fax: +256(481) 21-898
EMail: umu@umu.ac.ug
Website: http://www.fiuc.org/umu

Vice-Chancellor: Michel Lejeune (1992-)
Tel: +256(481) 21-897 EMail: vcumu@afsat.com
Registrar: Bernard Onyango Tel: +256(481) 21-894
International Relations: Michel Lejeune

Faculties
Agriculture
Building Design, Technology and Architecture (Architectural and Environmental Design; Architecture; Technology)
Business Administration and Management *(Nkozi)* (Accountancy; Business Administration; Commercial Law; Computer Science; Economics; Finance; Management; Marketing; Mathematics) *Dean*: Peter Opio, *full-time staff: 6, part-time staff: 1, students:* 167
Science *(Nkozi)* (Natural Sciences) *Dean*: Marie-Esther Haflett, *full-time staff: 3, part-time staff: 3, students:* 37

Institutes
Ethics and Development Studies *(Nkozi)* (African Studies; Development Studies; Ethics) *Director*: Deirdre Carabine, *full-time staff: 7, part-time staff: 1, students:* 85

Centres
African Research and Documentation *(ARDC/CARD)* (African Studies; Peace and Disarmament) *Director*: Peter Kanyandago, *full-time staff: 3*
Extramural Studies *(Nkozi)* (Computer Science; Distance Education; Farm Management; Finance; Human Resources; Management) *Director*: Martin O'Reilly, *full-time staff: 3*
Good Governance and Civil Society *(International)* (Government; Sociology) *Director*: Michael Mawa, *full-time staff: 9, part-time staff: 1*

History: Founded 1991, first academic year 1993, and officially opened 1994. A private Institution under the supervision of the Catholic Church in Uganda.
Governing Bodies: Governing Council; Senate; Advisory Board
Academic Year: October to June (October-January; February-June)
Admission Requirements: Uganda Advanced Certificate of Education or equivalent
Fees: (Uganda Shillings): 3m. per annum; postgraduate, 3.8m.
Main Language(s) of Instruction: English
Degrees and Diplomas: *Bachelor's Degree*: Building Design and Technology; Business Administration and Management; Computer; Economics; Ethics and Development Studies; Mathematics; Statistics, 3 yrs; *Master's Degree*: Finance and Banking, a further yr; Ethics and Development Studies; Hospital Management, a further yr
Student Services: Academic Counselling, Nursery Care, Sports Facilities, Health Services, Canteen
Student Residential Facilities: For 240 students
Libraries: University Library, c. 20,000 vols
Publications: UMU Studies in Contemporary Africa (biannually)
Press or Publishing House: UMU Press.

Academic Staff *1999-2000*	MEN	WOMEN	TOTAL
FULL-TIME	14	6	20
PART-TIME	–	5	5
TOTAL	**14**	**11**	**25**
STAFF WITH DOCTORATE			
FULL-TIME	3	2	**5**

Student Numbers *1999-2000*	MEN	WOMEN	TOTAL
All (Foreign Included)	94	140	**234**
FOREIGN ONLY	16	30	46

Distance Students, 350

OTHER INSTITUTIONS

PUBLIC INSTITUTIONS

INSTITUTE OF TEACHER EDUCATION, KYAMBOGO

PO Box 1, Kampala
Tel: +246(41) 285-001
Teacher Education (Teacher Training)

Zambia

INSTITUTION TYPES AND CREDENTIALS

Types of higher education institutions:

University
Technical and Vocational College
Institute

School leaving and higher education credentials:

General Certificate of Education
Zambian School Certificate
Certificate
Diploma
Bachelor's degree
Master's degree
Doctorate

STRUCTURE OF EDUCATION SYSTEM

Pre-higher education:

Duration of compulsory education:

    Age of entry: 7
    Age of exit: 14

Structure of school system:

    First Cycle Primary
    Type of school providing this education: Lower Primary School
    Length of programme in years: 4
    Age level from: 7 to: 11

    Second Cycle Primary
    Type of school providing this education: Upper Primary School
    Length of programme in years: 3
    Age level from: 11 to: 14
    Certificate/diploma awarded: Primary School Certificate

    Junior Secondary
    Type of school providing this education: Junior Secondary School
    Length of programme in years: 2

Age level from: 14 to: 16
Certificate/diploma awarded: Junior Secondary School Certificate

Senior Secondary
Type of school providing this education: Senior Secondary School
Length of programme in years: 3
Age level from: 16 to: 19
Certificate/diploma awarded: General Certificate of Education or Zambian School Certificate

School education:

Primary education lasts for seven years, divided into two parts, and leading to the Primary School Certificate. The secondary school system is also divided into two parts: Junior Secondary consisting of Grades 8 and 9, and Senior Secondary consisting of Grades 10-12. To proceed from Grade 9 to 10, one has to sit for an examination, the Junior Secondary School Certificate. At the end of senior secondary education, students sit for the Zambian School Certificate or the General Certificate of Education "O" Level.

Higher education:

Higher education is provided by two universities under the Ministry of Education, and various specialized institutions (colleges and institutes) controlled by the Ministry of Science, Technology and Vocational Training. The highest administrative body of the constituent universities is the Council on which serve members of the Government, students, teaching staff, graduates and representatives of outside bodies. The highest academic body is the Senate.

Main laws/decrees governing higher education:

Decree: The University of Zambia Act   Year: 1987
Concerns: University

Decree: Technical Education and Vocational Training Act   Year: 1973
Concerns: Technical Education and Vocational Training

Academic year:

Classes from: February *to:* December

Languages of instruction:

English

Stages of studies:

Non-university level post-secondary studies (technical/vocational type):

At this level, a Craft Certificate is offered in two years, plus one year of industrial practice. A Technician Diploma is offered in two years and four months. Certificates and Diplomas in non-Technical subjects require two years of study. Diplomas underwritten by the University of Zambia also require two years.

University level studies:

University level first stage: *Bachelor's Degree*:

The first stage consists of university level degrees taking from four to seven years. Degree courses are the following: BA, BSc, BSc Education, BA Library Studies, BA Education, Bachelor of Social Work, Bachelor of Law, BSc in Nursing, Bachelor of Accounting, Bachelor of Business Administration, four years; Bachelor of Mineral Science, Bachelor of Agriculture, Bachelor of Engineering, Bachelor of Architecture, BSc in Building, five years; Bachelor of Veterinary Medicine, six years; Bachelor of Medicine, seven years. Undergraduate Certificates and Diplomas are the following: Certificate in Law, Certificate in Adult Education, one year; Diploma in Adult Education, two years; Diploma in Social Work and Technology Diploma, three years.

University level second stage: *Master's Degree*:

This stage consists of courses leading to a qualification at Masters' level. Studies generally last for two years. The following Master's courses are offered: Law (15 months); Business Administration (18 months); Agronomy, Education, Engineering, Economics, Educational Psychology, Political Science, Sociology, Public Administration, Veterinary Medicine, MSc (all two years); Medicine (four years).

University level third stage: *Doctorate*:

This stage leads to PhD qualifications which are offered in a limited number of specializations. The course takes up to four years to complete.

Teacher education:

Training of pre-primary and primary/basic school teachers

The training of teachers at this level takes place in primary school teacher training colleges. After completion of the course, students are awarded certificates. The duration of the course is two years.

Training of secondary school teachers

The training of teachers at this level takes place in teachers' colleges and at the University of Zambia. Colleges award Certificates and Diplomas after three and four years respectively. Those trained at University level are awarded degrees after four or five years.

Non-traditional studies:

Distance higher education

This type of education is offered by technical and vocational colleges and the University of Zambia. Entrance requirements are lower than for those who enter a full-time course. The duration of studies is also much longer since students do not take all the courses for a given year at one time.

NATIONAL BODIES

Responsible authorities:

Ministry of Education
    Minister: Godfrey Miyanda
    PO Box 50093
    Lusaka
    Tel: +260(1) 227-636 +260(1) 227-639

Fax: +260(1) 222-396
Telex: 42621

Ministry of Science, Technology and Vocational Training
Minister: Valentine Kayope
PO Box 50464
Lusaka
Tel: +260(1) 229-673 +260(1) 252-053
Fax: +260(1) 252-951
Telex: 40406

Role of governing body: Coordinates Technical Training Institutions

ADMISSIONS TO HIGHER EDUCATION

Admission to university-level studies

Name of secondary school credential required: General Certificate of Education
Minimum score/requirement: Pass in at least 5 subjects at GCE 'O' level
For entry to: University admission

Name of secondary school credential required: Zambian School Certificate
Minimum score/requirement: Passes at credit level in five approved subjects.
For entry to: University

Alternatives to credentials: A two-year Diploma from a college which has a special relationship with the University.

Numerus clausus/restrictions: Dependent upon the number of places available.

Other admission requirements: Students not entering university directly from school are required to sit for a mature age examination.

Foreign students admission

Entry regulations: Foreign students have to obtain a visa and have full financial support.

Health requirements: The applicant has to undergo a medical examination, and is admitted only if declared fit by a Medical Doctor.

Language requirements: Foreign students must be proficient in English.

Application procedures:

Apply to individual institution for entry to: All Higher Education Institutions.

Recognition of studies and qualifications:

Studies pursued in home country (System of recognition/accreditation): Credentials are recognized by the State and the Professional Bodies

Studies pursued in foreign countries (bodies dealing with recognition of foreign credentials): Ministry of Science, Technology and Vocational Training

PO Box 50464
Lusaka
Tel: +260(1) 229-673 +260(1) 252-053
Fax: +260(1) 252-951
Telex: 40406

Deals with credential recognition for entry to: University

Other information sources on recognition of foreign studies: Universities

Special provisions for recognition:

For access to non-university post-secondary studies: They should be equivalent to local qualifications

For access to university level studies: They should be equivalent to national entry requirements

For access to advanced studies and research: First degree or equivalent

For the exercise of a profession: This is left to individual professions and the Ministries under which a given profession falls. The Law Assocation of Zambia has its own rules and regulations for Law credentials.

Multilateral agreements concerning recognition of foreign studies

Name(s) of agreement(s): Convention on the Recognition of Studies, Certificates, Diplomas, Degrees and Other Academic Qualifications in Higher Education in the African States
Year of signature: 1981

References to further information on foreign student admissions and recognition of studies

Title: Handbooks and Calendars produced by individual institutions

Title: Study Abroad 2000-2001
Publisher: UNESCO/IBE
Year of publication: 1999

STUDENT LIFE

National student associations and unions

National Student Union
PO Box 32379
Great East Road
Lusaka
10101
Tel: +260(1) 293-058
Fax: +260(1) 253-952

Health/social provisions

Social security for home students: No

516

Special student travel fares:

By road: No
By rail: No
By air: No
Available to foreign students: No

Student expenses and financial aid

Student costs:

Home students tuition fees: Maximum: 2,500,000 (Zambian Kwacha)

INTERNATIONAL COOPERATION AND EXCHANGES

Principal national bodies responsible for dealing with international cooperation and exchanges in higher education:

Directorate of Manpower Development Training
PO Box 50340
Independence Avenue
Lusaka
Tel: +260(1) 252-704

GRADING SYSTEM

Usual grading system in secondary school

Full Description: The grading system is expressed in points which are also represented in percentages. The Zambian School Certificate is graded 1-9, 9 being a fail.
Highest on scale: 1
Pass/fail level: 7-8
Lowest on scale: 9

Main grading system used by higher education institutions

Full Description: Letters grading system are represented by A,B,C,D,and E: A+=90, A=80, B+=75, B=65, C+=55, C=45, D=35 and below
Highest on scale: A+
Pass/fail level: C
Lowest on scale: E

NOTES ON HIGHER EDUCATION SYSTEM

Data for academic year: 2000-2001
Source: University of Zambia, Lusaka, updated by the International Association of Universities (IAU) from IBE website, 2000

INSTITUTIONS OF HIGHER EDUCATION

UNIVERSITIES

PUBLIC INSTITUTIONS

• COPPERBELT UNIVERSITY
PO Box 21692, Jambo Drive, Riverside, Kitwe
Tel: +260(2) 212-066
Fax: +260(2) 212-469
Telex: (0902) 53270 cbu za
Cable: cbu kitwe
EMail: vcsearch@zamnet.zm
Website: http://www.cbu.edu.zm

Vice-Chancellor (Acting): J. Lungu (1993-)
Tel: +260(2) 228-797 Fax: +260(2) 228-319
EMail: lunguj@cbu.ac.zm

Registrar: K.K. Kapika Tel: +260(2) 223-015
Fax: +260(2) 222-469 EMail: kkk@cbu.ac.zm

International Relations: G.W. Silavwe Tel: +260(2) 220-552

Schools
Architecture and Land Economy, Civil Engineering (Agricultural Economics; Architecture; Building Technologies; Civil Engineering; Regional Planning; Town Planning) *Dean*: Mitulo Silengo, *full-time staff: 44, part-time staff: 7, students: 400*
Business (Accountancy; Business Administration; Business and Commerce; Industrial and Production Economics) *Dean*: F.P. Tailoka, *full-time staff: 22, part-time staff: 4, students: 601*
Forestry and Wood Science (Ecology; Forestry; Wildlife; Wood Technology) *Dean*: Felix Njobvu, *full-time staff: 8, part-time staff: 1, students: 94*
Technology (Chemical Engineering; Computer Science; Electrical and Electronic Engineering; Technology) *Dean*: Felix Kanungwe, *full-time staff: 56, part-time staff: 23, students: 600*

Departments
Built Environment Research (Building Technologies; Town Planning) *Head*: Binwell N. Dioma, *full-time staff: 1*
Business Research *(ICARES)* (Business Administration; Business and Commerce) *Head*: P. Malanda, *full-time staff: 2*
Technical Research *(ICARES)* (Electrical Engineering; Metallurgical Engineering; Mining Engineering; Surveying and Mapping; Technology) *Head*: Mulemwa Akombelwa, *full-time staff: 2*

Institutes
Applied Research and Extension Studies *Director*: Thomas Kweku Taylor, *full-time staff: 3, part-time staff: 44, students: 274*
Environmental Management *Director*: Kakoma Maseka, *full-time staff: 4*

Centres
Lifelong Education *(ICARES)* (Accountancy; Business and Commerce; Human Resources; Marketing) *Director*: Emmanuel Chunda, *full-time staff: 1, part-time staff: 44, students: 274*

History: Founded 1987. Previously University of Zambia at Ndola, a Constituent Institution of the University of Zambia.

Governing Bodies: Council; Senate

Academic Year: March to December (March-May; June-August; August-December)

Admission Requirements: Zambian School Certificate with passes at credit level in 5 approved subjects, or General Certificate of Education (GCE) with passes in 5 approved subjects at Ordinary ('O') level

Fees: (Kwacha): 2.5m. per annum

Main Language(s) of Instruction: English

International Co-operation: University of Newcastle; Aberdeen University, Jomo Kenyatta University of Science and Technology

Degrees and Diplomas: *Bachelor's degree*: 4 yrs; *Master's degree*: Business Administration (MBA), a further 1 1/2 yrs

Student Services: Academic Counselling, Social Counselling, Employment Services, Nursery Care, Sports Facilities, Health Services, Canteen

Student Residential Facilities: For 1800 students

Libraries: University Library, c. 24,575 vols

Publications: Journal of Business (2)

Academic Staff *1999*: Full-Time: c. 125 Part-Time: c. 25 Total: c. 150

Student Numbers *1999*: All (Foreign Included): Men: c. 1,450 Women: c. 250 Total: c. 1,700
Foreign Only: Total: c. 20

*• UNIVERSITY OF ZAMBIA
PO Box 32379, Lusaka
Tel: +260(1) 251-593   +260(1) 293-058
Fax: +260(1) 253-952
Telex: 44370 za
Cable: unza lusaka
EMail: registrar@unza.gn.ape.org; registrar@unza.zm
Website: http://www.unza.zm/

Vice-Chancellor (Acting): Mutale W. Chanda (1997-)
Tel: +260(1) 250-871 Fax: +260(1) 250-871
EMail: vc@admin.unza.zm; vc@unza.zm

Registrar: Susan M. Kapena
EMail: registrar@admin.unza.zm

Schools
Agricultural Sciences (Agricultural Economics; Agricultural Education; Agriculture; Animal Husbandry; Crop Production; Education; Soil Science) *Dean*: F.A. Mwape

Education (Adult Education; Science Education; Special Education) *Dean*: I.W. Chikalanga
Engineering (Agricultural Engineering; Civil Engineering; Electrical Engineering; Electronic Engineering; Engineering; Mechanical Engineering; Mining Engineering; Surveying and Mapping) *Dean*: S.B. Kanyanga
Humanities and Social Sciences (Arts and Humanities; Development Studies; Economics; History; Humanities and Social Science Education; Literature; Mass Communication; Modern Languages; Philosophy; Political Science; Psychology; Social Sciences) *Dean*: J.D. Chileshe
Law *Dean*: F. Ng'andu
Medicine (Anatomy; Community Health; Gynaecology and Obstetrics; Medicine; Microbiology; Nursing; Paediatrics; Pathology; Physiology; Psychiatry and Mental Health; Surgery) *Dean*: L. Munkonge
Mines (Metallurgical Engineering; Mineralogy; Mining Engineering) *Dean*: R. Krishna
Natural Sciences (Biochemistry; Biology; Chemistry; Computer Science; Geography; Mathematics; Natural Sciences; Physics) *Dean*: D. Theo
Veterinary Science (Biomedicine; Veterinary Science) *Dean*: K.L. Samui

Institutes
Economic and Social Research (Economics; Social Sciences) *Director*: O. Saasa

Centres
Computer (Computer Science)
Creative Arts (Fine Arts) *Director*: M. Mapopa
Distance Education *Director*: R.C.M. Siaciwena
Research and Postgraduate Studies

History: Founded 1965.

Governing Bodies: Council; Senate

Academic Year: February to December (February-June; July-December)

Admission Requirements: Certificate with passes at credit level in 5 approved subjects, or General Certificate of Education (GCE) with passes in 5 approved subjects at Ordinary ('O') level

Fees: (Kwacha): 2m.-3m. per annum.

Main Language(s) of Instruction: English

International Co-operation: University of Birmingham; University of Leeds; University of East Anglia; University of Stirling; University of Newcastle; University of Glasgow; University of Ghent; Royal Institute of Technology, Stockholm; Technical University of Delft; Technical University of Eindhoven; Technical University of Twente; University College of Swansea

Degrees and Diplomas: *Bachelor's degree*: Arts (BA); Arts in Library Science (BALS); Arts with Education (BAEd); Laws (LLB); Mass Communication (BMassComm); Science (BSc); Science in Human Biology (BScHB); Science in Nursing (BScN); Science with Education (BScEd); Social Work (BSW), 4 yrs; Agricultural Science (BAgSc); Engineering (BEng); Mineral Sciences (BMinSc), 5 yrs; Veterinary Medicine (BVetMed), 6 yrs; Medicine and Surgery (MB ChB), 7 yrs; *Master's degree*: Arts (MA); Education (MEd); Engineering (MEng); Laws (LLM); Medicine (MMEd); Mineral Sciences (MMinSc); Public Administration (MPA); Science (MSc); Veterinary Medicine (MVM), a further 2-4 yrs; *Doctorate*: (PhD), up to a further 4 yrs. Also undergraduate and postgraduate Certificates and Diplomas

Student Residential Facilities: Yes

Special Facilities: UNZA Nursery (for plants/horticulture)

Libraries: Main Library, c. 251,750 vols; Medical Library; Veterinary Medicine Library

Academic Staff 2000: Full-Time: c. 430 Part-Time: c. 60 Total: c. 490

Staff with Doctorate: Total: c. 230

Student Numbers 2000: All (Foreign Included): Men: c. 2,667 Women: c. 797 Total: c. 3,464

Distance Students, c. 490

COPPERBELT SECONDARY TEACHERS' COLLEGE
PO Box 20382, Kitwe
Tel: +260 711-202

Principal: A.K. Sikazwe

Colleges
Teacher Training (Home Economics Education; Mathematics Education; Science Education; Teacher Training)

GEORGE BENSON CHRISTIAN COLLEGE
Namwianga
Tel: +260(32) 324-304

Principal: F. Chona

LUANSHYA TECHNICAL AND VOCATIONAL TEACHERS' COLLEGE
PO Box 90199, Luanshya
Tel: +260(2) 512-244

Principal: G.D. Zulu

Colleges
Teacher Training (Vocational Education)

History: Founded 1976.

NKRUMAH SECONDARY TEACHERS' COLLEGE
PO Box 80404, Kabwe
Tel: +260 221-525

Principal: S.B. Mpundu

Teacher Training (Teacher Training; Technology Education; Vocational Education)

History: Founded 1967.

OTHER INSTITUTIONS

PUBLIC INSTITUTIONS

EVELYN HONE-COLLEGE OF APPLIED ARTS AND COMMERCE
PO Box 30029, Lusaka
Tel: +260(1) 211-752
EMail: ehcbs@zamnet.zm

Principal: Edrick A.Y. Mwambazi (1995-)
Tel: +260(1) 225-127 Fax: +260(1) 225-127

Registrar: Aaron P. Chitsulo Tel: +260(1) 222-387

Departments
Academic and Applied Sciences (Natural Sciences)
Business Studies (Business and Commerce)
Comunication Skills (Communication Studies)
Education
Media Studies
Paramedical Studies (Paramedical Sciences)
Secretarial Studies

History: Founded 1963.

NATIONAL INSTITUTE OF PUBLIC ADMINISTRATION
PO Box 31990, Lusaka
Tel: +260(1) 228-802
Fax: +260(1) 227-113

Principal: M.C. Bwalya (1998-) Tel: +260(1) 222-480
Registrar: R. Mwambu Tel: +260(1) 228-802, Ext 102

Divisions
Accountancy and Financial Management Training (Accountancy; Business Education; Management)
Burma Road Campus
Legal Training (Law)
Management and Administration Training (Business Education; Management)
Research, Consultancy and Development (Development Studies; Educational and Student Counselling) *Head*: T.D.C. Syamunyangwa

History: Founded 1963. A semi-autonomous institution.

NATURAL RESOURCES DEVELOPMENT CENTRE
PO Box 310099, Lusaka
Agricultural Education; Agricultural Engineering; Agriculture; Fishery; Natural Resources; Nutrition; Water Science

History: Founded 1965

NORTHERN TECHNICAL COLLEGE
PO Box 250093, Chela Road, Ndola
Tel: +260(2) 680-141
Fax: +260(2) 680-423

Head: Godfrey Mwango Kapambwe (1995-)
Tel: +260(2) 680-739

Automotive Engineering; Business and Commerce; Communication Studies; Electrical Engineering; Mechanical Engineering; Technology

History: Founded 1961.

Zimbabwe

INSTITUTION TYPES AND CREDENTIALS

Types of higher education institutions:

University
Polytechnic
Technical College
Teacher Training College

School leaving and higher education credentials:

Cambridge School Certificate (CSC)
General Certificate of Education 'O' Level
Cambridge Higher School Certificate (HSC)
General Certificate of Education 'A' Level
National Certificate
Diploma
Bachelor Degree
Bachelor Honours Degree
Master Degree
Graduate Certificate
Master of Philosophy
Doctorate

STRUCTURE OF EDUCATION SYSTEM

Pre-higher education:

Duration of compulsory education:

    Age of entry: 5
    Age of exit: 12

Structure of school system:

    Primary
    Type of school providing this education: Primary School
    Length of programme in years: 7
    Age level from: 5 to: 12
    Certificate/diploma awarded: Grade 7 Certificate Examinations

Lower Secondary
Type of school providing this education: Secondary School (Forms I to IV)
Length of programme in years: 4
Age level from: 12 to: 16
Certificate/diploma awarded: Cambridge School Certificate (CSC)/CGE 'O' Level

Upper Secondary
Type of school providing this education: Secondary School (Forms V and VI)
Length of programme in years: 2
Age level from: 16 to: 18
Certificate/diploma awarded: Cambridge Higher School Certificate (HSC)/CGE 'A' Level

School education:

The school system is organized in a 7-4-2 pattern covering primary, lower secondary and upper secondary education. Secondary school lasts from Form I to Form VI: a student usually studies eight subjects at the end of which he takes the Cambridge School Certificate (CSC) or General Certificate of Education 'O' Level (which ended in August 1999 in Zimbabwe). From Form V to VI, students study only three subjects. At the end, they take the Cambridge Higher School Certificate (HSC) or CGE 'A' Level Certificate.

Higher education:

Zimbabwe has five State universities, three university colleges, four private universities with the Great Zimbabwe University which has just been granted its charter, teacher training colleges and technical colleges, including two polytechnics. After CGE 'O' or 'A' levels, students can train and be awarded Diplomas in Teaching, Agriculture, Nursing and several technical courses. With good 'A' level passes, a student can enrol at University for undergraduate studies.

Academic year:

Classes from: August *to:* June

Languages of instruction:

English

Stages of studies:

Non-university level post-secondary studies (technical/vocational type):

The following Diplomas and Certificates (National Certificate) are offered after 'O' or 'A' level Certificates: Library and Information Science; Teaching; Nursing, Agriculture, Business Studies, etc. Studies leading to these qualifications last between two and three years. These studies are offered in: Agricultural Colleges, Nursing Schools attached to Hospitals, Polytechnics and Teacher Training Colleges. Students with good grades at the Diploma level may apply to the University for undergraduate studies.

University level studies:

University level first stage: *Undergraduate studies*:
On completion of undergraduate studies, students obtain Bachelor Degrees in Arts, Science,

Commerce, Engineering, Education, Social Studies, Agriculture, Veterinary Science and Medicine. Studies vary in length from three years for the Bachelor of Arts Degree to five years for the Bachelor of Medicine and Bachelor of Surgery Degrees.

University level second stage: *Graduate studies*:
This stage comprises two types of Degrees. The Master Degree by coursework and dissertation; and the Master of Philosophy by research. The length of study varies from one to three years.

University level third stage: *Doctorate*:
The third stage requires a minimum of three years specialization and research and the presentation of a thesis. It leads to the Degree of Doctor of Philosophy, (PhD), which is conferred by all faculties.

University level fourth stage:
A Higher Doctorate is awarded in Law (LLD), Humanities (DLitt) and Science (DSc) after submission of published work and after at least eight years' study following upon the first Degree.

Teacher education:

Training of pre-primary and primary/basic school teachers
Students intending to train as primary school teachers must have a full 'O' or 'A' level Certificate with good grades including English Language. The training offered in teacher training colleges lasts for three years. Studies include theoretical and practical courses. Most of the training colleges are now affiliated with the University of Zimbabwe Faculty of Education. Students, on completion of their studies, obtain a University of Zimbabwe Diploma in Education. Good grades in Mathematics and Science are required.

Training of secondary school teachers
Secondary School Teachers are trained at two levels. The first level is open to students who have full 'O' and 'A' level Certificates. Training is held in two different types of Colleges, those for primary school teachers and those for secondary school teachers. Studies consist of compulsory courses in Education after which students specialize in the subjects they will teach. The second level of training is for students who have completed a Bachelor Degree and a one-year Postgraduate Certificate in Education at the University of Zimbabwe, Faculty of Education. These teachers will also teach subjects which they studied for the Bachelor's Degree.

Training of higher education teachers
Higher education teachers are those who teach Undergraduate and Postgraduate programmes at university. Most hold Master and Doctoral Degrees. Normally the University selects students with First Class passes at the Bachelor Degree level for advanced training at the Master and Doctoral levels at any good University . When students finish their studies they return to the University to teach.

Non-traditional studies:

Higher education training in industry
Training in industry covers many kinds of skills and qualifications. There are private Colleges which train individuals in Banking, Personnel and Manpower Training, Motor Mechanics, Insurance etc...

NATIONAL BODIES

Responsible authorities:

Ministry of Higher Education and Technology
   Minister: Herbert Murerwa
   PO Box UA 275
   Old Mutual Centre, Union Avenue
   Harare
   Tel: +263(4) 707-137
   Fax: +263(4) 707-137
   Cable: education

   Role of governing body: Financing, Development and Co-ordination of Higher Education in Zimbabwe

National Council for Higher Education
   Chairman: Christopher Chetsanga
   Executive Secretary: Felicity Joyce Mkushi
   International Relations: Felicity Joyce Mkushi
   PO Box UA 94
   Union Avenue
   Harare
   Tel: +263(4) 796-441
   Fax: +263(4) 728-730
   EMail: mkushij@mhet.gov.zw

   Role of governing body: facilitates the establishment of universities and university colleges, accreditation and standardization of programmes.

Zimbabwe Universities' Vice-Chancellors' Association
   Chairperson: Phinias Makhurane
   PO Box AC 939
   Ascot
   Bulawayo
   Tel: +263(9) 282-843
   Fax: +263(9) 286-803

ADMISSIONS TO HIGHER EDUCATION

Admission to non university higher education studies

Name of secondary school credential required: General Certificate of Education 'O' Level

Name of secondary school credential required: Cambridge School Certificate (CSC)
Minimum score/requirement: passes in 5 subjects
For entry to: Polytechnic etc..

Admission to university-level studies

Name of secondary school credential required: Cambridge Higher School Certificate (HSC)
Minimum score/requirement: Two or three subjects with C or better

Name of secondary school credential required: General Certificate of Education 'A' Level
Minimum score/requirement: Two or three subjects with C or better

Alternatives to credentials: Holders of Diplomas in Education, Nursing, Agriculture, Business studies can enter undergraduate studies. Provisions for special and mature student entry with approval from the University of Zimbabwe Senate.

Other admission requirements: Experience relevant to the subject is also used as an entry criterion for students who do not hold Advanced ("A") levels.

Foreign students admission

Admission requirements: Foreign students must have qualifications equivalent to the CGE with 5 Ordinary ('O') level passes plus 2 Advanced ('A') level. Some provision is made for special and mature students entry with approval from the University Senate. Admission is directed to the Admission Office of each University.

Entry regulations: Student permits are normally provided on arrival in Zimbabwe with proof of acceptance to the University

Language requirements: English

Application procedures:

Apply to individual institution for entry to: Universities

Apply to: Admissions Office

Recognition of studies and qualifications:

Studies pursued in foreign countries (bodies dealing with recognition of foreign credentials):
National Council for Higher Education
    Chairman: Christopher Chetsanga
    Executive Secretary: Joyce Mkushi
    PO Box UA 94 Union Ave
    Harare
    Tel: +263(4) 796-441
    Fax: +263(4) 728-730
    EMail: mkushij@mhet.gov.zw

    Deals with credential recognition for entry to: University and Profession
    Services provided and students dealt with: Holders of Diplomas and Degrees

References to further information on foreign student admissions and recognition of studies

Title: Prospectus (Annual publication)
Author: Students Enquiries Office
Publisher: University of Zimbabwe

Title: Study Abroad 2000-2001
Author: UNESCO/IBE
Year of publication: 1999

STUDENT LIFE

Student expenses and financial aid

Student costs:

Home students tuition fees: Minimum: 1,500 (Zimbabwean Dollar)
Maximum: 2,400 (Zimbabwean Dollar)
Foreign students tuition fees: Minimum: 1,450 (US Dollar)
Maximum: 8,000 (US Dollar)

GRADING SYSTEM

Usual grading system in secondary school
Full Description: A-F for Ordinary ("O") Level and Advanced ("A") Level.
Highest on scale: A
Pass/fail level: E for"A" Level and D for "O" Level.
Lowest on scale: F

Main grading system used by higher education institutions
Full Description: 80%+ =1 (First Division); 70%-79%=2.1 (Upper Second Division); 60%-69% =2.2 (Lower Second Division); 50%-59%= 3(Third Division); Below 50%= Fail. (used by University of Zimbabwe for undergraduate and masters degrees by coursework)
Highest on scale: 80%+= 1 (First Division)
Pass/fail level: 50%= 3 (Third Division)
Lowest on scale: below 50%

Other main grading systems
80%+= Distinction; 70%-79%= Merit; 50%-69%= Pass; Below 50%= Fail.(used by University of Zimbabwe for all certificates and diplomas).

NOTES ON HIGHER EDUCATION SYSTEM

Data for academic year: 2000-2001
Source: National Council for Higher Education, Harare, 2001

526

INSTITUTIONS OF HIGHER EDUCATION

UNIVERSITIES

PUBLIC INSTITUTIONS

BINDURA UNIVERSITY OF SCIENCE EDUCATION (BUSE)
Private Bag 1020, Bindura, Mashonaland Central
Tel: +263(71) 75-32 +263(71) 75-36
Fax: +263(71) 75-34
Website: http://www.buse.ac.zw

Vice-Chancellor: C.E.M. Chikombah (2000-2005)
Tel: +263(71) 75-31 Fax: +263(71) 75-52
EMail: chikombah@mailhost.buse.ac.zw

Registrar: Elliot Dzaramba
EMail: dzaramba@mailhost.buse.ac.zw

Faculties
Environmental Science (Environmental Studies)
Science Education (Biology; Chemistry; Geography; Mathematics; Physics; Science Education) *full-time staff:* 155, *students:* 400

History: Founded in 1995 as University of Zimbabwe college, acquired present title and status 2000

Academic Year: August to July

Admission Requirements: General Certificate of Education with at least 2 ('A') level passes

Main Language(s) of Instruction: English

Degrees and Diplomas: *Bachelor Degree*: Science Education (BScEd)

Student Residential Facilities: For 398 students

Libraries: Central Library, 6900 vols, 94 current periodicals, access to internet

Publications: University Prospectus (annually)

Academic Staff *1999*	MEN	WOMEN	TOTAL
FULL-TIME	29	8	**37**

Student Numbers *1999*	MEN	WOMEN	TOTAL
All (Foreign Included)	70	364	**434**

MIDLANDS STATE UNIVERSITY (MSU)
Private Bag 9055, Gweru
Tel: +263(54) 604-50
Fax: +263(54) 607-53

Vice-Chancellor: N. Bhebe (1999-2004)
Tel: +263(54) 645-73 EMail: nbhebe@zarnet.ac.zw

Registrar (Acting): G.T. Gurira Tel: +263(54) 604-09
Fax: +263(54) 603-11

Faculties
Arts and Social Sciences (Arts and Humanities; Social Sciences)
Commerce (Business and Commerce)
Education
Natural Resources Management and Agriculture (Agriculture; Natural Resources)
Science (Natural Sciences)

History: Founded 1999

• NATIONAL UNIVERSITY OF SCIENCE AND TECHNOLOGY, BULAWAYO (NUST)
PO Box 346, Bulawayo
Tel: +263(9) 74-626   +263(9) 76-833
Fax: +263(9) 79-804   +263(9) 79-671
EMail: mkariwo@esanet.zw
Website: http://www.nust.ac.zw/

Vice-Chancellor: P.M. Makhurane (2001-)
Tel: +263(9) 284-814 Fax: +263(9) 289-651
EMail: pmmakhurane@nust.ac.zw

Registrar: M.T. Kariwo

Faculties
Applied Sciences (Biochemistry; Biology; Chemistry; Computer Science; Mathematics; Physics) *Dean*: T.S. Dlodlo
Architecture and Quantity Surveying (Architecture and Planning; Surveying and Mapping)
Art, Social Studies and Education (Education; Fine Arts; Social Studies)
Commerce (Accountancy; Banking; Business and Commerce; Finance; Insurance; Management) *Dean*: T. Nkomo
Communication and Information Sciences (Communication Studies; Information Sciences)
Environmental Sciences (Environmental Studies)
Industrial Technology (Chemical Engineering; Civil Engineering; Electronic Engineering; Industrial Engineering; Textile Technology; Water Science) *Dean*: L. Sihwa
Sports Science (Sports)

Centres
Research and Development

History: Founded 1991, following the establishment in 1988 of a Commission of Inquiry into the establishment of a second University in Zimbabwe. A State Institution.

Governing Bodies: University Council; Senate

Academic Year: August to May (August-December; January-May)

Admission Requirements: General Certificate of Education (GCE) with either passes at Ordinary ('O') level and 2 at Advanced ('A') level, or passes in 4 subjects at 'O' and minimum 3 passes at 'A' level. A pass in English Language at 'O' level and general paper at 'A' level or equivalent compulsory. Details of approved subjects shown in General Information and Registration Handbook

Main Language(s) of Instruction: English

International Co-operation: California Polytechnic University; Virginia Polytechnic Institute and University

Degrees and Diplomas: *Bachelor Honours Degree*: Applied Sciences; Commerce, 4 yrs; Engineering, 5 yrs

Student Services: Academic Counselling, Social Counselling, Employment Services, Nursery Care, Health Services, Foreign Student Centre

Libraries: Central Library, 12,500 vols

Publications: NUST Newsletter (bimonthly); NUST Yearbook (annually)

Academic Staff *1999*: Full-Time: c. 100 Part-Time: c. 90 Total: c. 190

Student Numbers *1999*: All (Foreign Included): c. 1,820 Foreign Only: c. 5

• UNIVERSITY OF ZIMBABWE

PO Box MP 167, Mount Pleasant, Harare
Tel: +263(4) 303-211
Fax: +263(4) 333-407
EMail: ghill@vc.uz.zw; postmaster@zimbix.uz.zw
Website: http://www.uz.ac.zw

Vice-Chancellor: F.W.G. Hill (1997-2002)
Tel: +263(4) 333-493 Fax: +263(4) 334-018

Registrar: W. Mukondiwa Tel: +263(4) 308-941
EMail: wililpaul@icon.co.zw

International Relations: Margaret S. Murandu
Tel: +263(4) 333-676

Faculties

Agriculture *Dean*: O.A. Chivinge, *full-time staff*: 69, *students*: 469

Arts (Arts and Humanities) *Dean*: S. Pwiti, *full-time staff*: 130, *students*: 1,689

Commerce (Business and Commerce) *Dean*: T. Mutaviri, *full-time staff*: 34, *students*: 1,362

Education *Dean*: M.P.N. Peresuh, *full-time staff*: 91, *students*: 1,162

Engineering *Dean*: E. Wright, *full-time staff*: 63, *students*: 806

Law *full-time staff*: 28, *students*: 358

Medicine *Dean*: J. Mufunda, *full-time staff*: 169, *students*: 1,419

Science (Natural Sciences) *full-time staff*: 151, *students*: 1,132

Social Studies *full-time staff*: 95, *students*: 1,761

Veterinary Science *Dean*: S. Mukaratirwa, *full-time staff*: 32, *students*: 153

Colleges

Distance Education *Dean*: F.W.G. Hill

Teacher Education (Teacher Training) *Dean*: J.E.N. Bourdillan

Institutes

Development Studies *Director*: P. Chimanikire, *full-time staff*: 20

Environmental Studies *Director*: B.M. Campbell, *full-time staff*: 2

Family Science, Food and Nutrition (Family Studies; Food Science; Nutrition) *full-time staff*: 10, *part-time staff*: 7, *students*: 119

Water and Sanitation (Sanitary Engineering; Water Science) *Director*: P. Taylor, *full-time staff*: 8

Centres

Computer (Computer Science) *Director*: G. Hapanyengwi, *full-time staff*: 1

Development Technology (Technology) *Director*: T. Rukuni, *full-time staff*: 5

Human Resources *Director*: C.M. Nherera, *full-time staff*: 2

University Teaching and Learning (Higher Education Teacher Training; Pedagogy) *Director*: C.T. Nziramasanga, *full-time staff*: 2

History: Founded 1955 as University College of Rhodesia in Nyasaland. Acquired present title 1980 and present status 1982.

Governing Bodies: Council

Academic Year: March to November (March-June; August-November)

Admission Requirements: General Certificate of Education (GCE) or equivalent at Advanced ('A') level

Fees: (Zimbabwe Dollars): 15,000 per annum

Main Language(s) of Instruction: English

International Co-operation: California State University; Michigan State University

Degrees and Diplomas: *Bachelor Degree*: 3-5 yrs; *Master Degree*: a further 1-2 yrs; *Master of Philosophy*: 2-6 yrs; *Doctorate*: (PhD), 3-8 yrs. Also Certificates and Diplomas, 2 yrs

Student Services: Academic Counselling, Social Counselling, Sports Facilities, Handicapped Facilities, Health Services, Canteen, Foreign Student Centre

Student Residential Facilities: For 4002 students

Special Facilities: Audiovisual Teaching Unit. Drug and Toxicology Information Service. University Lake Kariba Research Station

Libraries: 450,000 vols

Publications: Zimbabwe Journal of Education Research; The Central African journal of Medicine (CAJM); Journal of Applied Social Sciences in Africa (JASSA) Zimbazia

Press or Publishing House: University of Zimbabwe Publications

Academic Staff *1999-2000*	MEN	WOMEN	TOTAL
FULL-TIME	658	331	**989**

Student Numbers *1999-2000*	MEN	WOMEN	TOTAL
All (Foreign Included)	7,130	3,156	**10,286**

ZIMBABWE OPEN UNIVERSITY (ZOU)

PO Box MP 1119, Mount Pleasant, Harare
Tel: +263(4) 333-457
Fax: +263(4) 30-351 +263(4) 307-136

Vice-Chancellor: Peter K. Dzvimbo (1999-2004)
Tel: +263(4) 333-452 Fax: +263(4) 303-151
EMail: kdzvimbo@icon.co.zw

Registrar: M. Mhasvi Tel: +263(4) 307-145

Programmes

Distance Education (Accountancy; Agricultural Management; Business Administration; Communication Studies; Educational Administration; Educational Sciences; English; Environmental Studies; Geography; Labour and Industrial Relations; Mathematics; Media Studies; Nursing; Physical Education; Psychology; Special Education; Sports; Statistics)

History: Founded 1996 as University College of Distance Education, acquired present status and title 1999.

PRIVATE INSTITUTIONS

AFRICA UNIVERSITY (AU)
PO Box 1320, Mutare
Tel: +263(20) 60-026
Fax: +263(20) 61-785
EMail: africa@africau.uz.zw

Vice-Chancellor: R. Murapa (1992-) Tel: +263(20) 60-075
EMail: vc@syscom.co.zw

Registrar: F. Chikange EMail: aureg@syscom.co.zw

Faculties

Agriculture and Natural Resources (Agriculture; Natural Resources)
Content Studies (African Studies; English; History; Music)
Theology

History: Founded 1992. A private Institution related to the United Methodist Church.

Governing Bodies: Board of Directors

Academic Year: August to May (August-December; January-May)

Admission Requirements: General Certificate of Education (GCE) with passes at Advanced ('A') level in relevant subjects and passes in 5 subjects at Ordinary ('O') level

Main Language(s) of Instruction: English

Degrees and Diplomas: *Bachelor Degree*: Agriculture (BAgr); Divinity (BD), 4 yrs; *Master Degree*: Management and Administration (MMan MAdmin), a further 2 yrs

Student Residential Facilities: For 160 students

Libraries: Africa University Library, c. 8000 vols

Academic Staff: Total: c. 20

Student Numbers: Total: c. 100

CATHOLIC UNIVERSITY IN ZIMBABWE (CUZ)
PO Box CY 3442, Causeway, Harare
Tel: +263(4) 705-368
Fax: +263(4) 706-911
EMail: cocuz@mango.zw

Rector: S. Nondo (1999-) Tel: +263(4) 570-169
Fax: +263(4) 573-973

Administrative Officer: A. Mukeredzi Tel: +263(4) 570-570

• SOLUSI UNIVERSITY
Private Bag T5399, Bulawayo
Tel: +263(83) 226 +263(83) 228
Fax: +263(83) 229
EMail: solusi@esanet.zw

Vice-Chancellor: Norman Maphosa (1992-)
Tel: +263(83) 267 EMail: vchancellor@solusi.ac.zw

Registrar: Richard Sithole Tel: +263(83) 383

Faculties

Arts and Sciences (Arts and Humanities; Natural Sciences) *Dean*: Tommy Nkungula, *full-time staff:* 21, *part-time staff:* 14, *students:* 235
Business (Business and Commerce) *Dean*: Ropafadzo Maphango, *full-time staff:* 10, *students:* 443
Theology and Religious Studies (Religious Studies; Theology) *Dean*: Zacchaeus Mathema, *full-time staff:* 5, *part-time staff:* 4, *students:* 66

Departments

Accountancy *Head*: Davison Mwanahiba, *full-time staff:* 2, *part-time staff:* 4, *students:* 190
Computer Management and Information Systems (Computer Engineering; Information Management; Systems Analysis) *Head (Acting)*: Nation Madikiza, *full-time staff:* 4, *students:* 95
Education *Head*: Eunice Mgeni, *full-time staff:* 5, *part-time staff:* 3, *students:* 38
English *Head*: Betty Mkwinda-Nyasulu, *full-time staff:* 3, *part-time staff:* 5, *students:* 68
Family and Consumer Sciences (Consumer Studies; Family Studies; Nutrition; Textile Technology) *Head*: Lloyd Makamure, *full-time staff:* 4, *part-time staff:* 2, *students:* 62
Fine Arts (Fine Arts; Music) *Head*: Lesley Hall, *full-time staff:* 1
History *Head*: Meshack Zimunya, *full-time staff:* 3, *part-time staff:* 1, *students:* 18
Management (Business Administration; Economics; Finance; Management) *Head*: Daniel Bwonda, *full-time staff:* 4, *part-time staff:* 2, *students:* 157
Mathematics and Natural Sciences (Agriculture; Biology; Chemistry; Electronic Engineering; Mathematics; Natural Sciences; Physics) *Head*: Gertahun Merga, *full-time staff:* 5, *part-time staff:* 1, *students:* 18

Centres

Research Information and Publications (Documentation Techniques; Publishing and Book Trade) *full-time staff:* 1

History: Founded 1894, acquired present status and title 1994

529

Governing Bodies: University Council

Academic Year: August to May (August-December; January-May)

Admission Requirements: General Certificate of Education passes at Ordinary ('O') level and a pass in English language at ('A') level

Fees: (Zimbabwe Dollars): 46,960 per semester

Main Language(s) of Instruction: English

Accrediting Agencies: Nattional Council for Higher Education

Degrees and Diplomas: *Bachelor Degree*: 3 yrs; *Master Degree*: 2 yrs (full-time), 4 yrs (part-time); *Graduate Certificate*: Education, 1 yr

Student Services: Nursery Care, Sports Facilities, Health Services, Canteen

Student Residential Facilities: For 600 students

Special Facilities: Solusi Museum

Libraries: Solusi Library, 43 356 vols

Publications: Solusi Echo (3 per annum); Solusi University News; Solusi University of Research (biannually)

Academic Staff *1999-2000*	MEN	WOMEN	TOTAL
FULL-TIME	24	14	38
PART-TIME	–	–	8
TOTAL	–	–	**46**
STAFF WITH DOCTORATE			
FULL-TIME	9	2	11
PART-TIME	–	–	3
TOTAL	–	–	**14**
Student Numbers *1999-2000*	MEN	WOMEN	TOTAL
All (Foreign Included)	372	375	**747**
FOREIGN ONLY	84	55	139

OTHER INSTITUTIONS

PUBLIC INSTITUTIONS

BULAWAYO POLYTECHNIC (BYO POLY)
PO Box 1392 , CNR Park Road/12th Avenue, Bulawayo, Matabele Land
Tel: +263(9) 631-81
Fax: +263(9) 711-65

Principal: A. Mwadiwa (1997-) Tel: +263(9) 778-53
EMail: mwadiwa@hotmail.com

Vice-Principal: H.M. Talukder EMail: talukder@mweb.co.zw

International Relations: M. Vimbai Tel: +263(9) 631-83

Institutes
Adult and Continuing Education (Adult Education; Continuing Education) *Director*: P.C. Moyo, *full-time staff: 207, part-time staff: 207, students: 6,652*
Applied Arts and Design (Design; Fine Arts; Graphic Arts) *Director*: C. Craven, *full-time staff: 8, part-time staff: 8, students: 149*
Business Administration and Secretarial Studies (Accountancy; Business Administration; Management; Marketing;

Secretarial Studies) *Director*: B. J Ndlovu, *full-time staff: 42, part-time staff: 42, students: 2,984*
Engineering (Automotive Engineering; Civil Engineering; Construction Engineering; Electrical Engineering; Engineering; Mechanical Engineering) *Director*: Edmond Jaya, *full-time staff: 115, part-time staff: 55, students: 3,450*
Hospitality and Tourism (Cooking and Catering; Hotel Management; Tourism) *Director*: Margaret Nyamuda, *full-time staff: 20, part-time staff: 5, students: 362*
Science and Technology (Applied Chemistry; Food Science; Health Sciences; Laboratory Techniques; Metallurgical Engineering; Natural Sciences; Polymer and Plastics Technology; Rubber Technology; Technology) *Director*: Andrew Sibanda, *full-time staff: 35, part-time staff: 20, students: 565*

History: Founded 1961. Acquired present status and title 2000.

GWERU TEACHERS COLLEGE (GTC)
Private Bag 9055, Gweru
Principal: Chipamaunga Tel: +263(54) 607-53

Teacher Training

HARARE POLYTECHNIC
Causeway, PO Box 8074, Harare
Tel: +263(4) 705-951
Fax: +263(4) 720-955

Principal: C. Chivanda (1988-) Tel: +263(4) 794-880
Deputy Principal and Director: Stephen T. Raza Tel: +263(4) 753-029
International Relations: B.A. Mapondera, Registrar

Departments
Adult and Continuing Education (Clothing and Sewing)
Business and Secretarial Studies (Business Administration; Secretarial Studies)
Electrical Engineering (Electrical and Electronic Engineering) *Head*: Irene Olga Mbwanda, *full-time staff: 32, part-time staff: 11, students: 309*
Engineering and Construction (Architecture; Architecture and Planning; Civil Engineering; Construction Engineering; Interior Design; Landscape Architecture; Painting and Drawing; Regional Planning; Surveying and Mapping; Urban Studies; Wood Technology) *Head (Acting)*: Joseph Ruzive, *full-time staff: 30, part-time staff: 18, students: 421*
Graphic and Design (Design; Graphic Arts)
Mass Communication
Printing and Printmaking (Graphic Design; Packaging Technology; Photography; Printing and Printmaking) *Head*: Samson Moyo, *full-time staff: 17, part-time staff: 12, students: 287*
Science and Technology (Natural Sciences; Technology) *Head*: Eldah Matikiti, *full-time staff: 14, part-time staff: 11, students: 309*

History: Founded 1927.

Governing Bodies: Advisory Council

Main Language(s) of Instruction: English

Accrediting Agencies: Higher Education Examination Council